A

TREATISE

OF

MUSICK,

𝔖𝔭𝔢𝔠𝔲𝔩𝔞𝔱𝔦𝔳𝔢, 𝔓𝔯𝔞𝔠𝔱𝔦𝔠𝔞𝔩, and 𝔥𝔦𝔰𝔱𝔬𝔯𝔦𝔠𝔞𝔩.

By ALEXANDER MALCOLM.

Hail Sacred Art! *deſcended from above,*
To crown our mortal Joys: Of thee we learn,
How happy Souls communicate their Raptures;
For thou'rt the Language of the Bleſt in Heaven:
— Divum hominumq; voluptas.

EDINBURGH,
Printed for the AUTHOR. MDCCXXI.

A

TREATISE

OF

MUSICK,

Speculative, Practical, and Historical.

By ALEXANDER MALCOLM.

Hail Sacred Art! *descended from above,*
To crown our mortal Joys : Of thee we learn,
How happy Souls communicate their Raptures ;
For thou'rt the Language of the Blest in Heaven:
—— Divum hominumq; voluptas.

EDINBURGH,

Printed for the AUTHOR. MDCCXXI.

Alexander Malcolm:

A Treatise of Musick:
Speculative, Practical and Historical

First published by the author in 1721.

Republished Travis & Emery 2008.

Published by
Travis & Emery Music Bookshop
17 Cecil Court, London, WC2N 4EZ, United Kingdom.
(+44) 20 7240 2129
neworders@travis-and-emery.com

Hardback: ISBN10: 1-904331-55-6   ISBN13: 978-1904331-55-1
Paperback: ISBN10: 1-904331-56-4   ISBN13: 978-1904331-56-8

TO

The most Illustrious

DIRECTORS

OF THE

Royal Academy of Musick,

VIZ.

The most Noble, *Thomas*, Duke of
Newcastle, Governour,

Lord *Bingley*, Deputy-Governour,

Duke of *Portland*,	Brigadier-Gen. *Dor-mer*,
Duke of *Queensberry*,	
Earl of *Burlington*,	*Bryan Fairfax* Esq;
Earl of *Stairs*,	Colonel *O Hara*,
Earl of *Wadeck*,	*George Harrison* Esq;
Lord *Chetwind*,	Brigadier-Gener. *Hunter*,
Lord *Stanhope*,	
James Bruce Esq;	*William Poultney* Esq;
Colonel *Blathwayt*,	Sir *John Vanbrugh*,
Thomas Coke of *Norfolk* Esq;	Major-General *Wade*,
	Fran. Whitworth Esq;
Conyers Darcey Esq;	

My Lords and Gentlemen,

NOTHING will be
a sufficient Apology
for the Presumption
of an Address of this sort,
from

from one, so much a Stranger as I am, if the Treatise, it presents you, deserves not a favourable Regard. As you are the best Judges of the Work, as well as the greatest Patrons and Encouragers of the Science, I have taken the liberty to send it abroad, under the Sanction of your Names: A Liberty! which I would not have allow'd myself to use, if I were not conscious that I have done all I could to deserve publick Approbation, in explaining the fundamental Grounds and Principles, which are so little known or studied, even by some celebrated Practisers of the Art.

Art. How I have succeed-
ed, I leave to you to determine. Nor shall I be much
concern'd at others Censure,
if you think me not unpro-
fitable.

May your Academy long
flourish, with continual new
Improvement, and never
want a Body of such gene-
rous Patriots to direct and
adorn it. Be my Praise, at
distance, to love and admire
it. I am,

My Lords and Gentlemen,

Your most Obedient,

And most Devoted,

Humble Servant,

Alexander Malcolm.

AN
ODE
ON THE
Power of MUSICK,
Inscrib'd to
Mr. MALCOLM,
AS A
Monument of Friendſhip,
By Mr. MITCHELL.

I.

WHEN *Nature* yet in *Embrio* lay,
    Ere Things began to be,
  The ALMIGHTY from eternal Day
    Spoke loud his deep Decree:
The Voice was tuneful as his Love,
  At which Creation ſprung,
And all th' *Angelick* Hoſts above
  The Morning Anthem ſung.

II. At

II.

At *Musick*'s sweet prevailing Call,
  Thro' boundless Realms of Space,
The Atoms danc'd, obsequious all,
And, to compose this wondrous Ball,
  In Order took their Place.
How did the Piles of Matter part,
And huddled Nature from her Slumber start?
  When, from the Mass immensely steep,
  The Voice bid Order sudden leap,
    To usher in a World.
What heavenly Melody and Love
Began in ev'ry Sphere to move?
When Elements, that jarr'd before,
Were all aside distinctly hurl'd,
  And *Chaos* reign'd no more.

III.

Musick the mighty Parent was,
  Empower'd by GOD, the sovereign Cause.
Musick first spirited the lifeless Waste,
Sever'd the sullen, bulky Mass,
And active Motion call'd from lazy Rest.
Summon'd by *Musick*, *Form* uprear'd her Head,
  From Depths, where Life it self lay dead,
While sudden Rays of everliving Light
  Broke from the Abyss of ancient Night,
Reveal'd the new-born Earth around and its fair
    Influence spread.
  GOD saw that all the Work was good;
The Work, the Effect of Harmony, its won-
    drous Offsprings stood.

IV. *Musick*

IV.

Musick, the best of Arts divine,
Maintains the Tune it first began,
And makes ev'n Opposites combine
   To be of Use to Man.
Discords with tuneful Concords move
   Thro' all the spacious Frame ;
Below is breath'd the Sound of Love,
While mystick Dances shine *Above*,
And *Musick*'s Power to nether Worlds proclaim.
  What various Globes in proper Spheres,
  Perform their great Creator's Will ?
  While never silent never still,
   Melodiously they run,
  Unhurt by Chance, or Length of Years,
   Around the central Sun.

V.

  The little perfect World, call'd Man,
  In whom the *Diapason* ends,
  In his Contexture, shews a Plan
  Of Harmony, that makes Amends,
By God-like Beauty that adorns his Race,
  For all the Spots on Nature's Face.
  He boasts a pure, a tuneful Soul,
  That rivals the celestial Throng,
  And can ev'n savage Beasts controul
   With his inchanting Song.
Tho' diff'rent Passions struggle in his Mind,
Where Love and Hatred, Hope and Fear are
   joyn'd.
  All, by a sacred Guidance, tend
   To one harmonious End.

VI. Its

VI.

Its great Original to prove,
And ſhew it bleſs'd us from above,
In creeping Winds, thro' Air it ſweetly flotes,
And works ſtrange Miracles by Notes.
Our beating Pulſes bear each bidden Part,
And ev'ry Paſſion of the maſter'd Heart
Is touch'd with Sympathy, and ſpeaks the Won-
ders of the Art.
Now Love, in ſoft and whiſpering Strains,
Thrills gently thro' the Veins,
And binds the Soul in ſilken Chains.
Then Rage and Fury fire the Blood,
And hurried Spirits, riſing high, ferment the
boiling Flood ;
Silent, anon, we ſink, reſign'd in Grief :
But ere our yielding Paſſions quite ſubſide,
Some ſwelling Note calls back the ebbing
Tide,
And lifts us to Relief.
With Sounds we love, we joy, and we deſpair,
The ſolid Subſtance hug, or graſp deluſive Air.

VII.

In various Ways the Heart-ſtrings ſhake,
And different Things they ſpeak.
For, when the meaning Maſters ſtrike the
Lyre,
Or *Hautboys* briskly move,
Our Souls, like Lightning, blaze with quick
Deſire,
Or melt away in Love.
But when the martial *Trumpet*, ſwelling high,
Rolls

Rolls its fhrill Clangor thro' the ecchoing
    Sky;
If, anfwering hoarfe, the fullen *Drum's* big
    Beat
Does, in dead Notes, the lively Call repeat;
Bravely at once we break o'er Nature's Bounds,
Snatch at grim Death, and look, unmov'd,
    on Wounds.
Slumb'ring, our Souls lean o'er the trembling
    Lute ;
Softly we mourn with the complaining *Flute* ;
    With the *Violin* laugh at our Foes,
By Turns with the *Organ* we bear on the Sky,
    Whilft, exulting in Triumph on *Æther* we
    fly,
Or, falling, grone upon the *Harp,* beneath a
    Load of Woes.
    Each Inftrument has magick Power
      To enliven or deftroy,
    To fink the Heart, and, in one Hour,
      Entrance our Souls with Joy.
At ev'ry Touch, we lofe our ravifh'd Thoughts,
And Life, it felf, in quivering clings, hangs o'er
    the varied Notes.

VIII.

How does the ftarting *Treble* raife
    The Mind to rapt'rous Heights ;
It leaves all Nature in Amaze,
    And drowns us with Delights.
But, when the manly, the majeftick, *Bafs*
    Appears with awful Grace,

What

What folemn Thoughts are in the Mind in-
      fus'd ?
    And how the Spirit's rous'd?
In flow-plac'd Triumph, we are led around,
And all the Scene with haughty Pomp is
      crown'd;
   Till friendly *Tenor* gently flows,
     Like fweet, meandring Streams,
   And makes an Union, as it goes,
     Betwixt the Two Extremes.
The blended Parts in *That* agree,
As Waters mingle in the Sea,
And yield a Compound of delightful Melody.

IX.

Strange is the Force of modulated Sound
That, like a Torrent, fweeps o'er ev'ry Mound!
   It tunes the Heart at ev'ry Turn;
With ev'ry Moment gives new Paffions Birth;
   Sometimes we take Delight to mourn;
    Sometimes enhance our Mirth.
  It fooths deep Sorrow in the Breaft;
  It lul's our waking Cares to Reft,
  Fate's clouded Brow ferenes with Eafe,
    And makes ev'n Madnefs pleafe.
As much as Man can meaner Arts controul,
  It manages his mafter'd Soul,
  The moft invet'rate Spleen difarms,
   And, like *Aurelia*, charms:
Aurelia ! dear diftinguifh'd Fair !
In whom the Graces center'd are !
Whofe Notes engage the Ear and Mind,

                          As

As Violets breath'd on by the gentle Wind;
Whofe Beauty, *Mufick* in Difguife !
Attracts the gazing Eyes,
'Thrills thro' the Soul, like *Haywood*'s melting
Lines,
And, as it certain Conqueft makes, the favage
Soul refines.

X.

Mufick religious Thoughts infpires,
And kindles bright poetick Fires;
Fires! fuch as great *Hillarius* raife
'Triumphant in their Blaze !
Amidft the *vulgar verfifying* Throng,
His Genius, with Diftinction, fhow,
And o'er our *popular Metre* lift his Song
High, as the Heav'ns are arch'd o'er Orbs below.
As if the Man was pure Intelligence,
Mufick tranfports him o'er the Heights of
Senfe,
'Thro' Chinks of Clay the Rays above lets in,
And makes Mortality divine.
Tho' Reafon's Bounds it ne'er defies,
Its Charms elude the Ken
Of heavy, grofs-ear'd Men,
Like Myfteries conceal'd from vulgar Eyes.
Others may *that* Diftraction call,
Which *Mufick* raifes in the Breaft,
To *me* 'tis Extafy and Triumph all,
The Foretaftes of the Raptures of the Bleft.
Who knows not this, when *Handel* plays,
And *Senefino* fings?

Our

Our Souls learn Rapture from their Lays,
While rival'd Angels fhow Amaze,
    And drop their golden Wings.

XI.

Still, God of Life, entrance my Soul
With fuch Enthufiaftick Joys;
And, when grim Death, with dire Con-
    troul,
My Pleafures in this lower Orb deftroys,
Grant this Requeft whatever you deny,
    For Love I bear to Melody,
    That, round my Bed, a facred Choir
    Of skilful Mafters tune their Voice,
And, without Pain of agonizing Strife,
    In Confort with the *Lute* confpire,
    To untie the Bands of Life;
    That, dying with the dying Sounds
    My Soul, well tun'd, may raife
And break o'er all the common Bounds
Of Minds, that grovel here below the Skies.

XII.

When Living die, and dead Men live,
And Order is again to *Chaos* hurl'd,
    Thou, *Melody*, fhalt ftill furvive,
    And triumph o'er the Ruins of the World.
A dreadful Trumpet never heard before,
    By Angels never blown, till then,
    Thro' all the Regions of the Air fhall rore
    That Time is now no more:
    But lo! a different Scene!
    Eternity appears.

Like

Like Space unbounded and untold by Years.
High in the Seat of Happiness divine
   Shall Saints and Angels in full *Chorus*
      joyn.
    In various Ways,
    Seraphick Lays
The unceasing Jubile shall crown,
And, whilst Heav'n ecchoes with his Praise,
The ALMIGHTY's self shall hear, and look,
    delighted, down.

XIII.

Who would not wish to have the Skill
Of tuning Instruments at Will?
Ye Pow'rs, who guide my Actions, tell
Why I, in whom the Seeds of *Musick*
    dwell,
Who most its Pow'r and Excellence admire
   Whose very Breast, it self's, a *Lyre*,
   Was never taught the heav'nly Art
    Of modulating Sounds,
And can no more, in Consort, bear a Part
Than the wild *Roe*, that o'er the Mountains
    bounds?
   Could I live o'er my Youth again,
   (But ah! the Wish how idly vain!)
   Instead of poor deluding Rhime,
   Which like a *Syren* murders Time,
   Instead of dull, scholastick Terms,
   Which made me stare and fancy Charms;
   With *Gordon*'s brave Ambition fir'd,
   Beyond the tow'ring *Alps*, untir'd,
       To

To tune my Voice to his sweet Notes, I'd
    roam ;
Or search the Magazines of Sound,
Where *Musick*'s Treasures ly profound,
   With *M——* here at Home.
M——, the dear, deserving Man,
    Who taught in Nature's Laws,
   To spread his Country's Glory can
Practise the Beauties of the Art, and shew its
    Grounds and Cause.
       *   *   *

TABLE

TABLE

OF

CONTENTS.

CHAP.

xviii

I N-

INTRODUCTION.

I Have no secret Hiſtory to entertain my *Reader* with, or rather to be impertinent with, concerning the Occaſion of my ſtudying, writing, or publiſhing any Thing upon this Subject: If the Thing is well done, no matter how it came to paſs. And tho' it be ſomewhat unfaſhionable, I muſt own it, I have no Apology to make: My Lord *Shaftsbury*, indeed, aſſures me, that the Generality of Readers are not a little raiſed by the Submiſſion of a confeſſing Author, and very ready on theſe Terms to give him Abſolution, and receive him into their good Grace and Favour; whatever may be in it, I have Nothing of this Kind wherewith to bribe their Friendſhip; being neither conſcious of *Lazineſs*, *Precipitancy*, or any other *wilful Vice*, in the Management of this Work, that ſhould give me great Uneaſineſs about it; if there be a Fault, it lies ſomewhere elſe; for, to be plain, I have taken all the Pains I could.

I

I have always thought it as impertinent for an Author to offer any Performance to the World, with a flat Pretence of suspecting it, as it is ridiculous to commend himself in a conceited and saucy Manner; there is certainly something just and reasonable, that lies betwixt these Extremes; perhaps the best Medium is to say Nothing at all; but if one may speak, I think he may with a very good Grace say, he has designed well and done his best; the Respect due to Mankind requires it, and as I can sincerely profess this, I shall have no Anxiety about the Treatment my Book may meet with. The *Criticks* therefore may take their full Liberty : I can lose Nothing at their Hands, who examine Things with a true Respect to the real Service of Mankind; if they approve, I shall rejoyce, if not, I shall be the better for their judicious Correction: And for those who may judge rashly thro' Pride or Ignorance, I shall only pity them.

Bur there is one common Place of Criticism I would beg Leave to consider a little. Some People, as soon as they hear of a new Book upon a known Subject, ask what Discovery the Author has made, or what he can say, which they don't know or cannot find elsewhere ? I might desire these curious Gentlemen to read and see; but that they may better understand my Pretences, and where to lay their Censures, let them consider, there are Two Kinds of Discoveries in Sciences; one is that of new *Theorems* and *Propositions*, the other is of the proper
Re-

Relation aad *Connection* of the Things already found, and the eafy Way of reprefenting them to the Underftanding of others; the firft affords the Materials, and the other the Form of thefe intellectual Structures which we call Sciences: How ufelefs the firft is without the other, needs no Proof; and what an Odds there may be in the Way of explaining and difpofing the Parts of any Subject, we have a Thoufand Demon-ftrations in the numerous Writings upon every Subject. An Author, who has made a Science more intelligible, by a proper and diftinct Ex-plication of every fingle Part, and a juft and na-tural Method in the Connection of the Whole; tho' he has faid Nothing, as to the Matter, which was not before difcovered, is a real Be-nefactor to Mankind : And if he has gathered together in one *Syftem*, what, for want of know-ing or not attending to their true Order and De-pendence, or whatever other Reafon, lay fcat-tered in feveral Treatifes, and perhaps added many ufeful Reflections and Obfervations; will not this Author, do ye think, be acquitted of the Charge of *Plagiarifm*, before every reafo-nable Judge ; and be reckoned juftly more than a mere Collector, and to have done fomething new and ufeful? If you appeal to a very wife and learned A N C I E N T, the Queftion is clearly determined. — *Etiamfi omnia a veteribus.in-venta funt, tamen erit hoc femper novum, ufus & difpofitio inventorum ab aliis.* S E N E C A *Ep.* 64. How far this Character of a new Author will be found in the following T R E A T I S E, de-

pends

pends upon the Ability and Equity of my Judges, and I leave it upon their Honour.

BUT you must have Patience to hear another Thing, which Justice demands of me in this Place. It is, to inform you, that the 13 *Ch.* of the following Book was communicated to me by a Friend, whose Modesty forbids me to name. The speculative Part, and what else there is, besides the Subject of that *Chapter*, were more particularly my Study: But I found, there would certainly be a Blank in the Work, if at least the more general Principles of Composition were not explained; and whatever Pains I had taken to understand the Writers on this Branch, yet for want of sufficient Practice in it, I durst not trust my own Judgment to extract out of them such a Compend as would answer my Design; which I hope you will find very happily supplied, in what my Friend's Genius and Generosity has afforded: And if I can judge any Thing about it, you have here not a mere Compend of what any Body else has done, but the first Principles of *harmonick Composition* explained in a Manner peculiarly his own.

AFTER so long a personal Conference, you'll perhaps expect I should say something, in this *Introduction,* to my Subject; but this, I believe, will be universally agreeable, the Experience of some Thousand Years giving it sufficient Recommendation; and for any Thing else I have little to say in this Place: The Contents you have in the preceeding Table, and I shall only make this short Transition to the Book it self.

THE

Of the *original* and various *Significations* of the Word *Musick*, you'll have an Account in the Beginning of *Chap.* 14. For, an historical Account of the *ancient Musick* being one Part of my Design, I could not begin it better, than with the various Use of the Name among the *Ancients*. It shall be enough therefore to tell you here, that I take it in the common Sense, for that Science which considers and explains those Properties and Relations of Sounds, that make them capable of exciting the agreeable Sensations, which the Experience of all Mankind assures us to be a natural Effect of certain Applications of them to the Ear. And for the same Reason I forbear to speak, in this Place, any Thing particularly of the *Antiquity*, *Excellency*, and various *Uses* and *Ends* of *Musick*, which I shall at large consider in the forementioned *Chapter*, according to the Sentiments and Experience of the *Ancients*, and how far the Experience of our Times agrees with that.

Corrigenda.

xxiv

p. 319. l. 26. Tune or *r.* human. l. 30 *dele* in.
p. 341. l. 11. a *r.* or. p. 356. l. 27. g𝕩, e♭. *r.*
a♭, d𝕩. p. 435. l. 7. the *r.* in the. p. 452. l. 29.
dele other. p. 458. l. 22. are *r.* is. l. 23. leaſt *r.*
beſt. p. 550. l. 10. Objects *r.* Subjects.

*Pray excuſe a few ſmaller Eſcapes which the
Senſe will eaſily correct.*

Addenda.

PAge 408. l. 8. after Bar, *add,* or of any particular Note. p. 411. l. 1. after Crotchets, *add,*
in the Triples ⁶⁄₄ ¹²⁄₄ ⁹⁄₄. p. 413. *add at the End;* and
if ♭ or 𝕩 is annexed to theſe Figures, it ſignifies
leſſer or *greater,* ſo 3𝕩 is *3d g,* and 6♭ is *6th* l. p.
415. l. 21. *after* Example, *add* Plate 4. *and* mind,
that all the Examples of Plates 4, 5, 6. *belong
to the* 13 Chap. p. 485. l. 11. *after* Memory, *add,*
we have a very old and remarkable Proof of this
Virtue of Muſick.

N. B. In the Table of Examples *Page* 258. the different Characters of
Letters are neglected; but the Numbers of each Example will diſcover
what they ought to be, in Conformity to *Fig.* 5. *Plate* 1. from whence they
are taken.

N. B. See *Page* 50. at *Line* 7. and conſequently, *&c.* A wrong Con-
cluſion has here eſcaped me, *viz.* that ſince the Chord paſſes the Point O,
therefore it is accelerated. I own the only Thing that follows from its
paſſing that Point is, that the Chord in every Point *d.* (of a ſingle Vibration) has more Force than would retain it there: And the true Reaſon of
Acceleration, is this, *viz.* in the outmoſt Point *D.* it has juſt as much
Force as is equal to what would keep it there: This Force is ſuppoſed not to
be deſtroyed, but at the next Point *d.* to receive an Addition of as much
as would keep it in that Point, and ſo on through every Point till it paſs
the ſtraight Line, and that it loſes its Force by the ſame Degrees; from
whence follows the Law of Acceleration mentioned.

N. B. See *Plate* 6. *Example* 35. the 2d, 3d, 4th, 5th, and 6th Notes of
the Baſs ought to be each a Degree lower.

A
TREATISE
OF
MUSICK.

CHAP. I.

Containing an Account of the *Object* and
End of MUSICK, and the Nature of
the Science, in the *Definition* and *Di-*
vision of it.

§ 1. *Of* SOUND: *The Cause of it; and the va-*
rious Affections of it concerned in Musick.

MUSICK is a Science of *Sounds,*
whose *End* is *Pleasure. Sound*
is the *Object* in general; or, to
speak with the *Philosophers*, it
is the *material Object*. But it
is not the Business of *Musick*,
taken in a strict and proper Sense, to consider
every Phenomenon and Property of Sound; that
belongs to a more universal Philosophy: Yet,
that we may understand what it is in Sounds
upon

upon which the *Formality of Mufick* depends,
i. e. whereby it is diftinguifhed from other Sciences, of which *Sound* may alfo be the Object:
Or, What it is in Sounds that makes the particular and proper Object of *Mufick*, whereby it
obtains its End ; we muft a little confider the
Nature of Sound.

Sound is a Word that ftands for every Perception that comes by the *Ear* immediately.
And for the Nature of the Thing, it is now
generally agreed upon among Philofophers, and
alfo confirmed by Experience, to be the Effect
of the mutual Collifion, and confequent tremulous Motion in Bodies communicated to the
circumambient Fluid of *Air,* and propagated
thro' it to the Organs of Hearing.

A Treatife that were defigned for explaining
the Nature of *Sound* univerfally, in all its
known and remarkable *Phænomena,* fhould, no
doubt, examine very particularly every Thing
that belongs to the Caufe of it ; *Firft,* The
Nature of that Kind of Motion in Bodies (excited by their mutual Percuffion) which is communicated to the Air ; *then,* how the Air receives and propagates that Motion to certain
Diftances : And, *laftly,* How that Motion is
received by the Ear, explaining the feveral
Parts of that Organ, and their Offices, that are
employed in *Hearing.* But as the Nature and
Defign of what I propofe and have *effayed* in
this Treatife, does not require fo large an Account of Sounds, I muft be content only to confider fuch *Phænomena* as belong properly to
Mufick,

Mufick, or ferve for the better Underftanding of it. In order to which I fhall a little further enlarge the preceding general Account of the Caufe of *Sound*. And,

Firft, That *Motion* is neceffary in the Production of *Sound*, is a Conclufion drawn from all our Experience. *Again, that Motion* exifts, firft among the fmall and infenfible Parts of fuch Bodies as are *Sonorous*, or capable of *Sound*; excited in them by mutual Collifion and Percuffion one againft another, which produces that tremulous Motion fo obfervable in Bodies, efpecially that have a free and clear Sound, as Bells, and the Strings of mufical Inftruments; *then*, this Motion is communicated to, or produces a like Motion in the Air, or fuch Parts of it as are apt to receive and propagate it: For no Motion of Bodies at Diftance can affect our Senfes, (or move the Parts of our Bodies) without the Mediation of other Bodies, which receive thefe Motions from the Sonorous Body, and communicate them immediately to the Organs of Senfe; and no other than a Fluid can reafonably be fuppofed. But we know this alfo by Experience; for a Bell in the exhaufted Receiver of an Airpump can fcarcely be heard, which was loud enough before the Air was drawn out. In the *laft Place*, This Motion muft be communicated to thofe Parts of the Ear that are the proper and immediate Inftruments of Hearing. The Mechanifm of this noble Organ has ftill great Difficulties, which all the Induftry of the moft capable and curious Enquirers has not furmounted:

There

There are Queftions ftill unfolved about the Ufe of fome Parts, and perhaps other neceffary Parts never yet difcovered: But the moft important Queftion among the Learned is about the laft and immediate Inftrument of Hearing, or that Part which laft receives the fonorous Motion, and finifhes what is neceffary on the Part of the Organ. Confult thefe with the Philofophers and Anatomifts ; I fhall only tell you the common Opinion, in fuch general Terms as my Defign permits, *thus :* Next to the external vifible Cavity or Paffage into the Ear, there is a Cavity, of another Form, feparate from the former by a thin Membrane, or Skin, which is called the Tympan or Drum of the Ear, from the Refemblance it has to that Inftrument : Within the Cavity of this Drum there is always Air, like that external Air which is the Medium of Sound. Now, the external Air makes its Impreffion firft on the Membrane of the Drum, and this communicates the Motion to the internal Air, by which it is again communicated to other Parts, till it reaches at laft to the auditory Nerve, and there the Senfation is finifhed, as far as Matter and Motion are concerned ; and then the *Mind*, by the Laws of its Union with the Body, has that Idea we call *Sound.* It is a curious Remark, that there are certain Parts fitted for the bending and unbending of the Drum of the Ear, in order, very probably, to the perceiving Sounds that are raifed at greater or leffer Diftances, or whofe Motions have different Degrees of Force, like what we are more

fenfible

fenfible of in the Eye, which by proper Mufcles (which are Inftruments of Motion) we can move outwards or inwards, and change the very Figure of, that we may better perceive very diftant or near Objects. But I have gone far enough in this.

LEST what I have faid of the Caufe of Sound be too general, particularly with refpect to the Motion of the fonorous Body, which I call the original Caufe, let us go a little farther with it. That Motion in any Body, which is the immediate Caufe of its founding, may be owing to two different Caufes ; one is, the mutual Percuffion betwixt it and another Body, which is the Cafe of Drums, Bells, and the Strings of mufical Inftruments, &c. Another Caufe is, the beating or dafhing of the fonorous Body and the Air immediately againft one another, as in all Kind of Wind-inftruments, Flutes, Trumpets, Hautboys, &c. Now in all thefe Cafes, the Motion which is the Confequence of the mutual Percuffion betwixt the whole Bodies, and is the immediate Caufe of the fonorous Motion which the Air conveys to our Ears, is an invifible tremulous or undulating Motion in the fmall and infenfible Parts of the Body. To explain this ;

ALL vifible Bodies are fuppofed to be compofed of a Number of fmall and infenfible Parts, which are of the fame Nature in every Body, being perfectly hard and incompreffible : Of thefe infinitely little Bodies are compofed others that are fomething greater, but ftill infenfible, and thefe are different, according to the different Figures

and

and Union of their component Parts: Thefe are
again fuppofed to conftitute other Bodies greater,
(which have greater Differences than the laft)
whofe different Combinations do, in the laft
Place, conftitute thofe grofs Bodies that are vifible and touchable. The firft and fmalleft Parts
are abfolutely hard ; the others are compref-
fible, and are united in fuch a Manner, that being, by a fufficient external Impulfe, compreffed,
they reftore themfelves to their natural, or ordinary, State : This Compreffion therefore happening upon the Shock or Impulfe made by one
Body upon another, thefe fmall Parts or Particles, by their reftitutive Power (which we alfo
call elaftick Faculty) move to and again with
a very great Velocity or Swiftnefs, in a tremulous and undulating Manner, fomething like the
vifible Motions of groffer Springs, as the
Chord of a mufical Inftrument ; and this is what
we may call the *Sonorous Motion* which is propagated to the Ear. But obferve that it is the
infenfible Motion of thefe Particles next to the
fmalleft, which is fuppofed to be the immediate
Caufe of Sound ; and of thefe, only thofe next
the Surface can communicate with the Air;
their Motion is performed in very fmall Spaces,
and with extreme Velocity ; the Motion of the
Whole, or of the greater Parts being no further
concerned than as they contribute to the other.

And this is the Hypothefis upon which Monfieur
Perrault of the Royal Society in *France*, explains
the Nature and *Phænomena* of Sound, in his curious
Treatife upon that Subject, *Effais de Phyfique*;
Tom.

Tom. **II.** *Du Bruit.* How this Theory is supported I shall briefly shew, while I consider a few Applications of it.

O F those hard Bodies that sound by Percussion of others, let us consider a Bell: Strike it with any other hard body, and while it sounds we can discern a sensible Tremor in the Surface, which spreads more sensibly over the Whole, as the Shock is greater. This Motion is not only in the Parts next the Surface, but in all the Parts thro' the whole Solidity, because we can perceive it also in the inner Surface of the Bell, which must be by Communication with those Parts that are immediately touched by the striking Body. And this is proven by the ceasing of the Sound when the Bell is touched in any other Part; for this shews the easy and actual Communication of the Motion. Now this is plainly a Motion of the several small and insensible Parts changing their Situations with respect to one another, which being so many, and so closely united, we cannot perceive their Motions separately and distinctly, but only that Trembling which we reckon to be the Effect of the Confusion of an infinite Number of little Particles so closely joyned and moving in infinitely small Spaces. Thus far any Body will easily go with the Hypothesis: But Monsieur *Perrault* carries it farther, and affirms, That that visible Motion of the Parts is no otherwise the Cause of the Sound, than as it causes the invisible Motion of the yet smaller Parts, (which he calls *Particles,* to distinguish them from the other which he
calls

calls *Parts*, the leaft of all being with him *Cor-pufcles*.) And this he endeavours to prove by other Examples, as of Chords and Wind-inftruments. Let us confider them.

TAKE a Chord or String of a Mufical Inftrument, ftretched to a fufficient Degree for Sounding; when it is fixt at both Ends, we make it found by drawing the Chord from its ftraight Pofition, and then letting it go; (which has the fame Effect as what we properly call Percuffion) the Parts by this drawing, whereby the Whole is lengthned, being put out of their natural State, or that which they had in the ftraight Line, do by their E-lafticity reftore themfelves, which caufes that vibratory Motion of the Whole, whereby it moves to and again beyond the ftraight Line, in Vibrations gradually fmaller, till the Motion ceafe, and the Chord recover its former Pofition. Now the fhorter the Chord is, and the more it is ftretched in the ftraight Line, the quicker thefe Vibrations are: But however quick they are, Monfieur *Perrault* denies them to be the immediate Caufe of the Sound; becaufe, fays he, in a very long Chord, and not very fmall, ftretched only fo far as that it may give a diftinct Sound, we can perceive with our Eye, befides the Vibrations of the whole Chord, a more confufed Tremor of the Parts, which is more difcernible towards the Middle of the Chord, where the Parts vibrate in greater Spaces in the Motion of the Whole; this laft Motion of the *Parts* which is caufed by the firft Vibrations of the Whole, does again occafion a
Motion

Motion in the leffer Parts or *Particles*, which
is the immediate Caufe of the Sound. And
this he endeavours to confirm by this Experiment, *viz.* Take a long Chord (he fays he made
it with one of 30 Foot) and make it found; then
wait till the Sound quite ceafe, and then alfo
the vifible Undulations of the whole Chord will
ceafe: If immediately upon this ceafing of the
Sound, you approach the Chord very foftly with
the Nail of your Finger, you'll perceive a tremulous Motion in it, which is the remaining
fmall Vibrations of the whole Chord, and of
the *Parts* caufed by the Vibrations of the
Whole. Now thefe Vibrations of the *Parts*
are not the immediate Caufe of Sound; elfe how
comes it that while they are yet in Motion they
raife no Sound? The Anfwer perhaps is this,
That the Motion is become too weak to make
the Sound to be heard at any great Diftance,
which might be heard were the Tympan of the
Ear as near as the Nail of the Finger, by which
we perceive the Motion. But to carry off this,
Mr. *Perrault* fays, That as foon as this fmall Motion is perceived, we fhall hear it found; which
is not occafioned by renewing or augmenting
the greater Vibrations, becaufe the Finger is
not fuppofed to ftrike againft the Chord, but
this againft the Finger, which ought rather to
ftop that Motion; the Caufe of this renewed
Sound therefore is propably, That this weak
Motion of the *Parts*, which is not fufficient to
move the *Particles* (whofe Motion is the Firft
that ceafes) receives fome Affiftance from the
dafhing

dashing against the Nail, whereby they are en-
abled to give the *Particles* that Motion which
is neceffary for producing the Sound. But left
it fhould ftill be thought, that this Encounter
with the Nail may as well be fuppofed to increafe the Motion of the Parts to a Degree fit
for founding, as to make them capable of moving
the *Particles*; we may confider, That the Particles being at Reft in the *Parts*, and having each a
common Motion with the whole *Part*, may very
eafily be fuppofed to receive a proper and particular Motion by that Shock; in the fame Manner that Bodies which are relatively at Reft in
a Ship, will be fhaked and moved by the Shock
of the Ship againft any Body that can any thing
confiderably oppofe its Motion. Now for as
fimple as this Experiment appears to be, I am
afraid it cannot be fo eafily made as to give
perfect Satisfaction, becaufe we can hardly touch
a String with our Nail but it will found.

But Mr. *Perrault* finishes the Proof of his Hypothefis by the Phenomena of Wind-inftruments.
Take, for example, a *Flute*; we make it found
by blowing into a long, broad, and thin Canal,
which conveys the Air thrown out of the Lungs,
till 'tis dafhed againft that thin folid Part which
we call the Tongue, or Wind-cutter, that is
oppofite to the lower Orifice of the forefaid Canal; by which Means the *Particles* of that
Tongue are compreffed, and by their reftitutive
Motion they communicate to the Air a Sonorous
Motion, which being immediately thrown a-
gainft the inner concave Surface of the Flute,
and

and moving its *Particles*, the Motion communicated to the Air, by all these *Particles* both of the Tongue and inner Surface, makes up the whole Sound of the Flute.

Now to prove that only the very small *Particles* of the inner Surface and Edge of the Tongue are concerned in the Sound of the Flute, we must consider, That Flutes of different Matter, as Metal, Wood, or Bone, being of the same Length and Bore, have none, or very little sensible Difference in their Sound; nor is this sensibly altered by the different Thickness of the Flute betwixt the outer and inner Surface; nor in the last place, is the Sound any way changed by touching the Flute, even tho' it be hard pressed, as it always happens in Bells and other hard Bodies that sound by mutual Percussion. All this Mr. *Perrault* accounts for by his Hypothesis, thus: He tells us, That as the *Corpuscles* are the same in all Bodies, the *Particles* which they immediately constitute, have very small Differences in their Nature and Form; and that the specifick Differences of visible Bodies, depend on the Differences of the *Parts* made up of these *Particles*, and the various Connections of these Parts, which make them capable of different Modifications of Motion. Now, hard Bodies that sound by mutual Percussion one against another, owe their sounding to the Vibrations of all their *Parts*, and by these to the insensible Motions of their *Particles*; but according to the Differences of the Parts and their Connections, which
make

make them, either Silver, or Brafs, or Wood,
&c. fo are the Differences of their Sounds. But
in Wind-inftruments (for example, Flutes) as
there are no fuch remarkable Differences anfwering to their Matter, their Sound can only be
owing to the infenfible Motion of the Particles
of the Surface; for thefe being very little different in all Bodies, if we fuppofe the Sound is
owing to their Motions only, it can have none,
or very fmall Differences: And becaufe we find
this true in Fact, it makes the Hypothefis extremely probable. I have never indeed feen Flutes
of any Matter but Wood, except of the fmall
Kind we call Flageolets, of which I have feen
Ivoryo nes, whofe Sound has no remarkable Difference from a wooden one; and therefore I
muft leave fo much of this Proof upon Monfieur
Perrault's Credit. As to the other Part, which
is no lefs confiderable, That no Compreffion of
the Flute can fenfibly change its Sound, 'tis certain, and every Body can eafily try it. To
which we may add, That Flutes of different
Matter are founded with equal Eafe, which
could not well be if their *Parts* were to be
moved; for in different Bodies thefe are differently moveable. But I muft make an End of this
Part, in which I think it is made plain enough,
That the Motion of a Body which caufes a
founding Motion in the Air, is not any Motion which we can poffibly give to the whole
Body, wherein all the Parts are moved in one
common Direction and Velocity; but it is the
Motion of the feveral fmall and undiftinguifhable
Parts,

Parts, which being compreffed by an external
Force, do, by their elaftick Power, reftore themfelves, each by a Motion particular and proper
to it felf. But whether you'll diftinguifh *Parts*
and *Particles* as Mr. *Perrault* does, I leave to
your felves, my Defign not requiring any accurate Determination of this Matter. And now to
come nearer to our Subject, I fhall next confider
the Differences and Affections of Sounds that are
any way concerned in *Mufick*.

SOUNDS are as various, or have as many
Differences, as the infinite Variety of Things
that concur in their Production; which may be
reduced to thefe general Heads : 1*ft*, The
Quantity, Conftitution, and Figure of the fonorous Body ; with the Manner of Percuffion, and
the confequent Velocity of the Vibrations of the
Parts of the Body and the Air ; alfo their E-
quality and Uniformity, or Inequality and Irre-
gularnefs. 2*dly*, The Conftitution and State of
the fluid Medium through which the Motion is
propagated. 3*dly*, The Difpofition of the Ear
that receives that Motion. And, 4*thly*, The
Diftance of the Ear from the fonorous Body. To
which we may add, *laftly*, the Confideration of
the Obftacles that interpofe betwixt the fonorous
Body and the Ear ; with other adjacent Bodies
that, receiving an Impreffion from the Fluid fo
moved, react upon it, and give new Modifica-
tion to the Motion, and confequently to the
Sound. Upon all thefe do our different Perceptions of Sound depend.

THE

THE Variety and Differences of Sounds, owing to the various Degrees and Combinations of the Conditions mentioned, are innumerable; but to our prefent Defign we are to confider the following Diftinctions.

I. *SOUNDS*, come under a fpecifick Diftinction, according to the Kinds of Bodies from which they proceed: Thus, Metal is eafily diftinguifhed from other Bodies by the Sound; and among Metals there is great difference of Sounds, as is difcernible, for Example, Betwixt Gold, Silver, and Brafs. And for the Purpofe in hand, a moft notable Difference is that of ftringed and Wind-inftruments of Mufick, of which there are alfo Subdivifions: Thefe Differences depend, as has been faid, upon the different Conftitutions of thefe Bodies; but they are not ftrictly within the Confideration of *Mufick*, not the *Mathematical* Part of it at leaft, tho' they may be brought into the *Practical*; of which afterwards.

II. EXPERIENCE teaches us, That fome Sounds can be heard, by the fame Ear, at greater Diftances than others; and when we are at the fame Diftance from two Sounds, I mean from the fonorous Body or the Place where the Sound firft rifes, we can determine (for we learn it by Experience and Obfervation) which of the Two will be heard fartheft: By this Comparifon we have the Idea of a Difference whofe oppofite Terms are called *LOUD* and *LOW*, (or *ftrong* and *weak*.) This Difference depends both upon the Nature of different Bodies, and upon

upon other accidental Circumstances, such as their *Figure* ; or the different Force in the Percussion ; and frequently upon the Nature of the circumjacent Bodies, that contribute to the strengthning of the Sound, that is a Conjunction of several Sounds so united as to appear only as one Sound : But as the Union of several Sounds gives Occasion to another Distinction, it shall be considered again, and we have only to observe here that it is always the Cause of *Loudness* ; yet this Difference belongs not strictly to the Theory of Musick, tho' it is brought into the Practice, as that in the First Article.

III. THERE is an Affection or Property of Sound, whereby it is distinguished into ACUTE, *sharp* or *high*; and GRAVE, *flat* or *low.* The Idea of this Difference you'll get by comparing several Sounds or Notes of a musical Instrument, or of a human Voice singing. *Observe* the Term, *Low,* is sometimes oppos'd to *Loud,* and sometimes to *acute,* which yet are very different Things: *Loudness* is very well measured by the Distance or Sphere of Audibility, which makes the Notion of it very clear. *Acuteness* is so far different, that a Voice or Sound may ascend or rise in Degree of *Acuteness,* and yet lose nothing of its *Loudness,* which can easily be demonstrated upon any Instrument, or even in the Voice; and particularly if we compare the Voice of a Boy and a Man.

THIS Relation of *Acuteness* and *Gravity* is one of the principal Things concerned in Musick, the Nature of which shall be particularly con-

confidered afterwards; and I fhall here obferve
that it depends altogether upon the Nature of
the fonorous Body it felf, and the particular Figure and Quantity of it; and in fome Cafes upon the Part of the Body where it is ftruck. So
that, for Example, the Sounds of two Bells of
different Metals, and the fame Shape and Dimenfions, being ftruck in the fame Place, will
differ as to *Acutenefs* and *Gravity*; and two
Bells of the fame Metal will differ in *Acutenefs*,
if they differ in Shape or in Magnitude, or be
ftruck in different Parts: So in Chords, all o-
ther Things being equal, if they differ either in
Matter, or Dimenfions, or the Degree of Tenfion, as being ftretched by different Weights,
they will alfo differ in *Acutenefs*.

But we muft carefully *remark*, That *Acutenefs* and *Gravity*, alfo *Loudnefs* and *Lownefs*
are but relative Things; fo that we cannot call
any Sound *acute* or *loud*, but with refpect to
another which is *grave* or *low* in reference to
the former; and therefore the fame Sound may
be *acute* or *grave*, alfo *loud* or *low* in different
Refpects. *Again*, Thefe Relations are to be
found not only between the Sounds of different
Bodies, but alfo between different Sounds of the
fame Body; for different Force in the Percuffion will caufe a *louder* or *lower* Sound, and
ftriking the Body in different Parts will make
an *acuter* or *graver* Sound, as we have
remarkably demonftrated in a Bell, which as
the Stroke is greater gives a greater or *louder*
Sound, and being ftruck nearer the open End,
gives

gives the *graver* Sound. How thefe Degrees
are meafured, we fhall learn again, only *mind*
that thefe Degrees of *Acutenefs* and *Gravity*
are alfo called different and diftinguifhable *Tones*
or *Tunes* of a Voice or Sound; fo we fay one
Sound is in *Tune* with another when they are in
the fame Degree : *Acute* and *Grave* being but
Relations, we apply the Name of *Tune* to them
both, to exprefs fomething that's conftant and
abfolute which is the Ground of the Relation ;
in like manner as we apply the Name *Magnitude* both to the Things we call *Great* and *Little*,
which are but relative Idea's: Each of them have a
certain Magnitude, but only one of them is great
and the other little when they are compared; fo
of Two Sounds each has a certain *Tune*, but only
one is *acute* and the other *grave* in Comparifon.

IV. There is a Diftinction of *Sounds*, whereby they are denominated *long* or *fhort* ; which
relates to the *Duration*, or continued, and fenfibly uninterrupted Exiftence of the *Sound*. This
is a Thing of very great Importance in *Mufick*;
but to know how far, and in what refpect it
belongs to it, we muft diftinguifh betwixt the
natural and *artificial Duration* of Sound. I call
that the *natural Duration* or *Continuity* of
Sound, which is lefs or more in different Bodies,
owing to their different Conftitutions, whereby
one retains the Motion once received longer
than another does ; and confequently the Sound
continues longer (tho' gradually weaker) after
the external Impulfe ceafes ; fo Bells of different Metals, all other Things being equal and
alike

alike, have differentContinuity ofSound after the
Stroke : And the fame is very remarkable in
Strings of different Matter : There is too a Difference in the fame Bell or String, according to
the Force of the Percuffion.   This Continuity
is fometimes owing to the fudden Reflection
of the Sound from the Surface of neighbouring
Bodies; which is not fo properly the fame Sound
continued, as a new Sound fucceeding the Firſt
fo quickly as to appear to be only its Continuation : But this Duration of Sound does not
properly belong to Mufick, wherefore let us
confider the other.   The *artificial* Continuity
of Sound is, that which depends upon the continued Impulfe of the efficient Caufe upon the
fonorous Body for a longer or ſhorter Time.
Such are the Notes of a Voice,or anyWind-inftru-
ment, which are longer or ſhorter as we continue to blow into them; or, the Notes of a Violin and all ftring'd Inftruments that are ftruck
with a Bow, whofe Notes are made longer or
ſhorter by Strokes of different lengths or Quicknefs of Motion;for a long Stroke, if it is quickly drawn, may make a ſhorter Note than a ſhort
Stroke drawn flowly.   Now this kind of Continuity is properly the Succeffion of feveralSounds,
or the Effect of feveral diftinct Strokes,or repeated
Impulfes, upon the fonorous Body, fo quick that
we judge it to be one continued Sound, efpecially if it is continued in one Degree of Strength
and Loudnefs; but it muſt alfo be continued in
one Degree of *Tune*, elfe it cannot be called
one Note in Mufick. And this leads me naturally

ly to confider the very old and notable Diftinction of a twofold Motion of Sound,
thus.

S o u n d may move thro' various Degrees of
Acuteness in a continual Flux, fo as not to reft
on any Degree for any affignable, or at leaft fenfible Time ; which the Ancients called the *continuous Motion* of Sound, proper only to Speaking and Converfation. Or, *2do.* it may pafs
from Degree to Degree, and make a fenfible
Stand at every Pitch, fo as every Degree fhall
be diftinct; this they called the *difcrete* or *dif-
continued Motion* of Sound, proper only to Mufick
or Singing. But that there may be no Obfcurity
here, *confider*, That as the Idea's of *Motion* and
Diftance are infeparably connected, fo they belong in a proper Senfe to *Bodies* and *Space* ;
and whatever other Thing they are applied to,
it is in a figurative and metaphorical Senfe, as
here to Sounds; yet the Application is very intelligible, as I fhall explain it. *Voice* or *Sound*
is confidered as one individual Being, all other
Differences being neglected except that of *A-
cutenefs* and *Gravity*, which is not confidered
as conftituting different Sounds, but different
States of the fame Sound ; which is eafy to conceive : And fo the feveral *Degrees* or Pitches
of *Tune*, are confidered as feveral Places in
which a Voice may exift.   And when we hear
a Sound fucceffively exifting in different Degrees
of *Tune*, we conceive the Voice to have moved
from the one Place to the other ; and then 'tis
eafy to conceive a Kind of Diftance between the
two

two Degrees or Places ; for as Bodies are said
to be distant, between which other Bodies may
be placed, so two Sounds are said to be at Distance, with respect to *Tune*, between which
other Degrees may be conceived, that shall be
acute with respect to the one, and *grave* with
respect to the other. But when the Voice continues in one Pitch, tho' there may be many
Interruptions and sensible Rests whereby the
Sound doth end and begin again, yet there is
no Motion in that Case, the Voice being all
the Time in one Place. Now this Motion, in
a simple and proper Sense, is nothing else but
the successive Existence of several Sounds differing in *Tune*. When the successive Degrees are
so near, that like the Colours of a Rainbow, they
are as it were lost in one another, so that in any
sensible Distance there is an indefinite Number
of Degrees, such kind of Succession is of no use
in *Musick* ; but when it is such that the Ear is
Judge of every single Difference, and can compare several Differences, and apply some known
Measure to them, there the Object of Musick
does exist ; or when there is a Succession of several
Sounds distinct by sensible Rests, tho' all in the same
Tune, such a Succession belongs also to Musick.

F R O M this twofold Motion explain'd,
we see a twofold *Continuity* of Sound,
both subject to certain and determinate Measures
of *Duration* ; the one is that arising from the
continuous Motion mentioned, which has nothing to do in *Musick* ; the other is the Continuity or uninterrupted Existence of Sound in
one

one Degree of *Tune*. The Differences of Sounds in this refpect, or the various Meafures of *long* and *fhort*, or, (which is the fame, at leaft a Confequence) *fwift* and *flow*, in the fucceffive Degrees of Sound, while it moves in the fecond Manner, make a principal and neceffary Ingredient in *Mufick*; whofe Effect is not inferior to any other Thing concerned in the Practice; and is what deferves to be very particularly confidered, tho' indeed it is not brought under fo regular and determinate Rules as the Differences of *Tune*.

V. S o u n d s are either *fimple* or *compound*; but there is a twofold Simplicity and Compofition to be confidered here; the Firft is the fame with what we explain'd in the laft Article, and relates to the Number of fucceffive Vibrations of the Parts of the fonorous Body, and of the Air, which come fo faft upon the Ear that we judge them all to be one continued Sound, tho' it is really a Compofition of feveral Sounds of fhorter Duration. And our judging it to be *one*, is very well compared to the Judgment we make of that apparent Circle of Fire, caufed by putting the fired End of a Stick into a very quick circular Motion; for fuppofe the End of the Stick in any Point of that Circle which it actually defcribes, the Idea we receive of it there continues till the Impreffion is renewed by the fudden Return; and this being true of every Point, we muft have the Idea of a Circle of Fire; the only Difference is, that the End of the Stick has actually exifted in every Point of the Circle,

whereas

whereas the Sound has had Interruptions, tho'
infenfible to us because of their quick Succeffion;
but the Things we compare are, the Succeffion
of the Sounds making a fenfible Continuity with
refpect to Time, and the Succeffion of the End
of the Stick in every Point of the Circle after a
whole Revolution; for 'tis by this we judge it
to be a Circle, making a Continuity with refpect
to Space. The Author of the *Elucidationes
Phyficæ* upon *D' Cartes* Mufick, illuftrates it in
this Manner, fays he, As ftanding Corns are
bended by one Blaft of Wind, and before they
can recover themfelves the Wind has repeated
the Blaft, fo that the Corn's ftanding in the fame
inclined Pofition for a certain Time, feems to
be the Effect of one fingle Action of the Wind,
which is truly owing to feveral diftinct Operations; in like Manner the fmall Branches (*capil-
lamenta*) of the auditory Nerve, refembling fo
many Stalks of Corn, being moved by one Vibration of the Air, and this repeated before the
Nerve can recover its Situation, gives Occafion to
the Mind to judge the whole Effect to be one Sound.
The Nature of this kind of *Compofition* being
fo far explain'd, we are next to confider what
Simplicity in this Senfe is; and I think it muft
be the Effect of one fingle Vibration, or as
many Vibrations as are neceffary to raife in us
the Idea of Sound; but perhaps it may be a
Queftion, Whether we ever have, or if we can
raife fuch an Idea of Sound: There may be alfo another Queftion, Whether any Idea of Sound
can exift in the Mind for an indivifible Space
of

of Time ; the Reason of this Question is, That if every Sound exists for a finite Time, it can be divided into Parts of a shorter Duration, and then there is no such Thing as an absolute Simplicity of this Kind, unless we take the Notion of it from the Action of the external Cause of Sound, *viz.* the Number of Vibrations necessary to make Sound actually exist, without considering how long it exists ; but as it is not probable that we can ever actually produce this, *i. e.* put a Body in a sounding Motion, and stop it precisely when there are as many Vibrations finished as are absolutely necessary to make Sound, we must reckon the Simplicity of Sound, considered in this Manner, and with respect to Practice, a relative Thing; that being only simple to us which is the most simple, either with respect to the Duration or the Cause, that we ever hear: But whether we consider it in the repeated Action of the Cause or the consequent Duration, which is the Subject of the last Article, there is still another Simplicity and Composition of Sounds very different from that, and of great Importance in Musick, which I shall next explain.

A *simple Sound* is the Product of one Voice or individual Body, as the Sound of one Flute or one Man's Voice. A *compound Sound* consists of the Sounds of several distinct Voices or Bodies all united in the same individual Time and Measure of Duration, *i. e.* all striking the Ear together, whatever their other Differences may be. But we must here distinguish a *natural*

and

and *artificial Compofition;* to underftand this, remember, That the Air being put into Motion by
any Body, communicates that Motion to other
Bodies; the *naturalCompofition* of Sounds is therefore, that which proceeds from the manifold Reflexions of the Firft Sound, or that of the Body
which firft communicates founding Motion to
the Air, as the Flute or Violin in one's Hand ;
thefe Reflexions, being many, according to the
Circumftances of the Place, or the Number,
Nature, and Situations of the circumjacent Bodies, make Sounds more or lefs *compound.*
This is a Thing we know by common Experience ; we can have a hundred Proofs of it e-
very Day by finging, or founding any mufical
Inftrument in different Places, either in the
Fields or within Doors; but thefe Reflexions
muft be fuch as returning very fuddenly don't
produce what we call an *Eccho,* and have only
this Effect, to increafe the Sound, and make
an agreeable Refonance ; but ftill in the fame
Tune with the original Note ; or, if it be a
Compofition of different Degrees of Tune, they
are fuch as mix and unite, fo that the Whole
agrees with that Note. But this Compofition
is not under Rules of Art ; for tho' we learn by
Experience how to difpofe thefe Circumftances
that they may produce the defired Effect, yet
we neither know the Number or different Tunes
of the Sounds that enter into this Compofition;
and therefore they come not under the Mufician's Direction in what is hereafter called the
Compofition of Mufick ; his Care being only a-
                                              bout

bout the *artificial Compofition*, or that Mixture
of feveral Sounds, which being made by Art,
are feparable and diftinguifhable one from another.   So the diftinct Sounds of feveral Voices
or Inftruments, or feveral Notes of the fame Inftrument, are called *fimple Sounds*, in Diftinction
from the artificial*Compofition*, in which to anfwer
the End of Mufick, the *Simples* muft have fuch
an Agreement in all Relations, but principally
and above all in *Acutenefs* and *Gravity*, that
the Ear may receive the Mixture with Pleafure.

   VI. THERE remains another Diftinction of
Sounds neceffary to be confidered, whereby they
are faid to be *fmooth* and *evenly*, or *rough*
and *harfh*; alfo *clear* or *blunt*, *hoarfe* and *obtufe* ,
the Idea's of thefe Differences muft be fought
from Obfervations ; as to the Caufe of them,
they depend upon the Difpofition and State of the
fonorous Body, or the Circumftances of the
Place.   *Smooth* and *rough* Sounds depend upon
the Body principally ; We have a notable Example of a *rough* and *harfh* Sound in Strings
that are unevenly and not of the fame Conftitution and Dimenfion throughout; and for this
Reafon that their Sounds are very grating, they
are called falfe Strings. I will let you in few Words
hear how Monfieur *Perrault* accounts for this.
He affirms that there is no fuch Thing as a fimple
Sound, and that the Sound of the fame Bell or
Chord is a Compound of the Sounds of the feveral Parts of it ; fo that where the Parts are
homogeneous, and the Dimenfions or Figure u-
niform, there is always fuch a perfect Union
                                                      and

and Mixture of all thefe Sounds that makes
one uniform, fmooth and evenly Sound ; and
the contrary produces Harfhnefs ; for the
Likenefs of Parts and Figure makes an Uniformity of Vibrations, whereby a great Number of
fimilar and coincident Motions confpire to for-
tify and improve each other mutually, and u-
nite for the more effectual Production of the
fame Effect. He proves his Hypothefis by the
Phenomena of a Bell, which differs in *Tone* according to the Part you ftrike, and yet ftrike it
any where there is a Motion over all the Parts ;
he confiders therefore the Bell as compofed of an
infinite Number of Rings, which according to
their different Dimenfions have different *Tones*;
as Chords of different Lengths have (*cæteris paribus*) and when it is ftruck, the Vibrations of
the Parts immediately ftruck fpecify the *Tone*,
being fupported by a fufficient Number of confonant Tones in other Parts : And to confirm
this, he relates a very remarkable Thing; He
fays, He happen'd in a Place where a Bell founded a *Fifth* acuter than the Tone it ufed to
give in other Places ; which in all Probability,
fays he, was owing to the accidental Difpofition
of the Place, that was furnifhed with fuch an
Adjuftment for reflecting that particular Tone
with Force, and fo unfit for reflecting others,
that it abfolutely prevailed and determined the
Concord and total Sound to the *Tone* of that
Fifth. If we confider the Sound of a Violin,
and all ftring'd Inftruments, we have a plain
Demonftration that every Note is the Effect of
feve-

feveral more fimple Sounds ; for there is not
only the Sound refulting from the Motion of
the String, but alfo that of the Motion of the
Parts of the Inftrument ; that this has a very
confiderable Effect in the total Sound is certain, becaufe we are very fenfible of the tremulous Motion of the Parts of the Violin, and
efpecially becaufe the fame String upon different
Violins founds very differently, which can be
for no other Reafon but the different Conftitution of the Parts of thefe Inftruments, which
being moved by Communication with the String
increafe the Sound, and make it more or lefs
agreeable, according to their different Natures :
But *Perrault* affirms the fame of every String
in it felf without confidering the Inftrument ;
he fays, Every Part of the String has its particular Vibrations different from the grofs and
fenfible Vibrations of the Whole, and thefe are
the Caufes of different Motions (and Sounds)
in the *Particles*; which being mix'd and unite,
as was faid of the Sounds that compofe the
total Sound of a Bell, make an uniform and
evenly Compofition, wherein not only one
Tone prevails, but the Mixture is fmooth and
agreeable; but when the Parts are unevenly and
irregularly conftitute, the Sound is harfh and
the String from that called falfe. And therefore
fuch a String, or other Body having the like
Fault, has no certain and diftinct *Tone*, being
a Compofition of feveral *Tones* that don't u-
nite and mix fo as to have one Predominant
that fpecifies the *total Tone.*

AGAIN

AGAIN for *clear* or *hoarfe* Sounds, they depend upon Circumftances that are accidental to the fonorous Body; fo a Man's Voice, or the Sound of an Inftrument will be hollow and hoarfe, if it is raifed within an empty Hogfhead, which is clear and bright out of it; the Reafon is very plainly the Mixture of other and different Sounds raifed by Reflexion, that corrupt and change the Species of the primitive and direct Sound.

Now that Sounds may be fit for obtaining the End of *Mufick* they ought to be *fmooth* and *clear*; efpecially the Firft, becaufe if they have not one certain and difcernible *Tone*, capable of being compared to others, and ftanding to them in a certain Relation of *Acutenefs*, whofe Differences the Ear may be able to judge of and meafure, they cannot poffibly anfwer the End of *Mufick*, and therefore, are no Part of the Object of it.

BUT there are alfo Sounds which have a certain *Tone*, yet being exceffive either in Acutenefs or Gravity, bear not that juft Proportion to the Capacity of the Organs of Hearing, as to afford agreeable Senfations. Upon the Whole then we fhall call that *harmonick* or *mufical Sound*, which being *clear* and *evenly* is agreeable to the *Ear*, and gives a certain and difcernible *Tune* (hence alfo called *tunable Sound*) which is the Subject of the whole Theory of Harmony.

THUS we have confidered the Properties and Affections of Sound that are any way neceffary

ceffary to the Subject in hand ; and of all
the Things mentioned, the Relation of *Acutenefs* and *Gravity,* or the *Tune* of Sounds, is the
principal Ingredient in *Mufick*; the Diftinctnefs
and Determinatenefs of which Relation gives
found the Denomination of *harmonical* or
mufical: Next to which are the various Meafures
of *Duration.* There is nothing in Sounds without thefe that can make *Mufick*; a juft *Theory*
whereof abftracts from all other Things, to confider the Relations of Sounds in the Meafures
of *Tune* and *Duration* ; tho' indeed in the
Practice other Differences are confidered (of
which fomething more may be faid afterwards) but they are fo little, compared to the
other Two, and under fo very general and uncertain *Theory*, that I don't find they have e-
ver been brought into the Definition of *Mufick.*

---

§ 2. *Containing the* Definition *and* Divifion *of*
Mufick.

WE may from what is already faid affirm,
That *Mufick* has for its Object, in general, *Sound*; and particularly, *Sounds* confidered
in their Relations of *Tune* and *Duration,* as
under that *Formality* they are capable of affording agreeable Senfations. I fhall therefore define MUSICK, *A* SCIENCE *that teaches how*
SOUNDS, *under certain Meafures of* TUNE
and

and TIME, *may be produced; and so ordered
or disposed, as in* CONSONANCE (i. e. *joynt
sounding*) *or* SUCCESSION, *or both, they may
raise agreeable Sensations.*

PLEASURE, I have said, is the immediate
End of *Musick*; I suppose it therefore as a *Principle*, That the Objects proposed are capable,
being duly applied, to affect the Mind agreeably;
nor is it a precarious Principle ; Experience
proves, and we know by the infallible Testimony of our Senses, that some *simple* Sounds
succeed others upon the Ear with a positive
Pleasure, others disagreeably ; according to certain Relations of Tune and Time ; and some
compound Sounds are agreeable, others offensive
to the Ear ; and that there are Degrees and
Variety in this Pleasure, according to the various Measures of these Relations. For what
Pretences are made of the Application of *Musick* to some other Purposes than mere Pleasure
or Recreation, as these are obtain'd chiefly by
Means of that Pleasure, they cannot be called
the immediate End of it.

FROM the *Definition* given, we have the
Science divided into these two general Parts.
First, The *Knowledge* of the MATERIA MUSICA, or, how to produce Sounds, in such relations of *Tune* and *Time* as shall be agreable
in *Consonance* or *Succession*, or both. I don't
mean the actual producing of these Sounds by
an Instrument or Voice, which is merely the
mechanical or *effective* Part ; But the Knowledge of the various Relations of *Tune* and *Time*,
which

which are the effential Principles out of which
the Pleafure fought arifes, and upon which it depends. This is the pure *fpeculative* Part of
Mufick. Second, How thefe Principles are to
be applied; or, how Sounds, in the Relations
that belong to *Mufick* (as thefe are determined
in the Firft Part) may be ordered, and varioufly put together in *Succeffion* and *Confonance* fo
as to anfwer the End; which Part we rightly
call The Art of Composition; and it is
properly the *practical* Part of *Mufick.*

Some have added a Third Part, *viz.* The *Knowledge* of Instruments; but as this depends
altogether upon the Firft, and is only an Application or Expreffion of it, it could never be brought
regularly into the Definition; and fo can be no
Part of the Divifion of the Science; yet may it
deferve to be treated of, as a Confequent or
Dependent of it, and neceffary to be underftood for the *effective* Part. As this has no
Share in my Defign, I fhall detain you but
while I fay, in a few Words, what I think fuch
a Treatife fhould contain. And 1*mo,* There
fhould be a *Theory* of *Inftruments,* giving an
Account of their Frame and Conftruction, particularly, how, fuppofing them completely provided of all their *Apparatus,* each contains in it
the *Principles* of *Mufick i. e.* how the feveral
Degrees of *Tune* pertaining to *Mufick* are to
be found upon the *Inftruments.* The *Second Part*
fhould contain the Practice of Inftruments, in fuch
Directions as might be helpful for the dextrous and
nice handling of them, or the elegant Performance

of

of *Musick*: And here might be annex'd Rules for the right Use of the *Voice*. But after all, I believe these Things will be more successfully done by a living Instructor, I mean a skilful and experienced Master, with the Use of his Voice or Instrument; tho' I doubt not such might help us too by Rules; but I have done with this.

You must next *observe* with me, That as the *Art* of common *Writing* is altogether distinct from the Sciences to which it is subservient by preserving what would otherwise be lost, and communicating Thoughts at Distance; so there is an *Art* of *Writing* proper to *Musick*, which teaches how, by a fit and convenient Way of representing all the Degrees and Measures of Sound, sufficient for directing in the *executive Part* one who understands how to use his Voice or Instrument: The *Artist* when he has invented a Composition answering the Principles and End of Musick, may preserve it for his own Use, or communicate it to another present or absent. To this I have very justly given a Place in the following Work, as it is a Thing of a general Concern to *Musick*, tho' no Part of the Science, and merely a Handmaid to the Practice ; and particularly as the Knowledge of it is necessary for carrying on my Design. I now return to the Division above made, which I shall follow in explaining this Science.

THE First general Branch of this Subject, which is the *contemplative* Part, divides naturally into these. *First*, the Knowledge of the Relations and Measures of *Tune*. And *Secondly*, of
Time.

Time. The Firſt is properly what the Ancients called HARMONICA, or the Doctrine of *Harmony* in Sounds ; becauſe it contains an Explication of the Grounds, with the various Meaſures and Degrees of the Agreement (*Harmony*) of Sounds in reſpect of their *Tune.* The other they called *Rythmica,* becauſe it treats of the Numbers of Sounds or Notes with reſpect to *Time,* containing an Explication of the Meaſures of *long* and *ſhort,* or *ſwift* and *ſlow* in the Succeſſion of Sounds.

The Second general Branch, which is the PRACTICAL Part, as naturally divides into Two Parts anſwering to the Parts of the Firſt: That which anſwers to the *Harmonica,* the Ancients called *Melopœia* ; becauſe it contains the Rules of making Songs with reſpect to *Tune* and *Harmony* of Sounds; tho' indeed we have no Ground to believe that the Ancients had any Thing like Compoſition in Parts. That which anſwers to the *Rythmica,* they called *Rythmopœia,* containing the Rules concerning the Application of the *Numbers* and *Time.* I ſhall proceed according to this natural Diviſion, and ſo the *Theory* is to be firſt handled.

CHAP.

CHAP. II.

Of Tune, *or the Relation of* Acuteness *and* Gravity *in Sounds*; particularly, *of the* Cause *and* Measure *of the Differences of* Tune.

§ 1. *Containing some necessary* Definitions *and* Explications, *and the particular* Method *of treating this Branch of the Science concerning* Tune *or* Harmony.

FIRST, The Subject to be here explained is, That Property of Sounds which I have called their *Tune*; whereby they come under the Relation of *acute* and *grave* to one another : For as I have already observed, there is no such Thing as *Acuteness* and *Gravity* in an absolute Sense, these being only the Names given to the Terms of the Relation ; but when we consider the Ground of the Relation which is the *Tune* of the Sound, we may justly affirm this to be some thing absolute ; every Sound having its own proper and peculiar *Tune*, which must be under some determinate Measure in the Nature of the Thing, (but the Denominations of *acute* and *grave* respect always another Sound.) Therefore as to *Tune*, we must remark that the only Difference can possibly be betwixt one *Tune* and another,

is

is in their Degrees, which are naturally infinite; *that is*, we conceive there is something positive in the Cause of Sound which is capable of less and more, and contains in it the Measure of the Degrees of *Tune*; and because we don't suppose a least or greatest Quantity of this, therefore we say the Degrees depending on these Measures are infinite: But commonly when we speak of these Degrees, we call them several Degrees of *Acutenefs* and *Gravity*, without supposing these Terms to express any fixt and determinate Thing; but it implies some supposed Degree of *Tune*, as a Term to which we tacitely compare several otherDegrees; thus we suppose any one given or determinate Measure of *Tune*, then we suppose a Sound to move on either Side, and acquire on the one greater Measures of *Tune*, and on the other lesser, *i. e.* on the one Side to become gradually more *acute*, and on the other more *grave* than the given *Tune*, and this *in infinitum*: Why I ascribe the greater Measure to *Acutenefs* will appear, when we see upon what that Measure depends. Now tho' these Degrees are infinite, yet with respect to us they are limited, and we take some middle Degree, within the ordinary Compass of the human Voice, which we make the Term of Comparison when we say of a Sound that it is very *acute* or very *grave*, or, as we commonly speak, very *high* or very *low*.

II. If Two or more Sounds are compared in the Relation we now treat of, they are either

ther *equal* or *unequal* in the Degree of *Tune*:
Such as are *equal* are called *Unisons* with regard
to each other, as having one *Tune* ; the *unequal*, being at Distance one from another (as I have
already explain'd that Word) constitute what
we call an *Interval* in *Musick*, which is properly the Difference of *Tune* betwixt Two
Sounds. Upon this Equality or Difference does
the whole Effect depend ; and in respect of this
we have these Relations again divided into,

 I I I. *Concord* and *Discord*.   *Concord* is
the Denomination of all these Relations that
are always and of themselves agreeable, whether
applied in *Succession* or *Consonance* (by which
Word I always mean a mere sounding together;)
that is, If two simple Sounds are in such a Relation, or have such a Difference of *Tune*, that
being sounded together they make a Mixture
or *compound* Sound which the Ear receives with
Pleasure, that is called *Concord*; and whatever Two
Sounds make an agreeable Compound; they will
always follow other agreeably. *Discord* is the
Denomination of all the Relations or Differences
of *Tune* that have a contrary Effect.

 I V. *Concords* are the essential Principles
of Musick ; but their particular Distinctions,
Degrees and Names, we must expect in another Place. *Discords* have a more general and
very remarkable Distinction, which is proper to
be explained here; they are either *concinnous*
or *inconcinnous Intervals* ; the *concinnous* are
such as are apt or fit for *Musick*, next to and
in

in Combination with *Concords*; and are neither
very agreeable nor very difagreeable in themfelves;
they are fuch Relations as have a good Effect
in *Mufick* only as, by their Oppofition, they
heighten and illuftrate the more effential Principles of the Pleafure we feek for ; or by their
Mixture and Combination with them, they produce a Variety neceffary to our being better
pleafed; and therefore are ftill called *Difcord*,
as the Bitternefs of fome Things may help to
fet off the Sweetnefs of others, and yet ftill be
bitter : And therefore in the Definition of *Concord* I have faid *always and of themfelves a-
greeable*, becaufe the *concinnous* could have no
good Effect without thefe, which might fubfift
without the other, tho' lefs perfectly.   The other
Degrees of *Difcord* that are never chofen in
Mufick come under the Name of *inconcinnous*
and have a greater Harfhnefs in them, tho' even
the greateft Difcord is not without its Ufe.
Again the *concinnous* come under a Diftinction
with refpect to their Ufe, fome of them being
admitted only in *Succeffion*, and others only in
Confonance ; but enough of this here.

V.   N o w to apply the Second and Third
Article obferve, *Unifons* cannot poffibly have
any Variety, for there muft be Difference
where there is Variety, therefore *Unifonance* flow-
ing from a Relation of Equality which is invariable, there can be no Species or Diftinction
in it; all *Unifons* are *Concord*, and in the Firft
and moft perfect Degree ; but an *Interval* depending upon a Difference of *Tune* or a Relation

lation of Inequality; admits of Variety, and so the
Terms of every *Interval,* according to the particular Relation or Difference, make either *Concord* or *Difcord.* Some indeed have reftrained
the Word *Concord* to *Intervals,* making it include a Difference of *Tune* ; but it is precarious ;
for as the Word *Concord* fignifies an Agreement
of Sounds, 'tis certainly applicable to *Unifons* in
the Firft Degree.

OBSERVE, the Words *Concord* ard *Harmony* are of the fame Senfe ; yet they are arbitrarily made different Terms of Art; *Concord*
fignifies the agreeable Effect of two Sounds in
Confonance; *Harmony* is applied to the Agreement of any greater Number of Sounds in
Confonance. Again *Harmony* always fignifies *Confonance,* but *Concord* is applied fometimes alfo
to *Succeffion,* yet never but when the Terms
can ftand agreeably in *Confonance* : The Effect of an agreeable *Succeffion* of feveral
Sounds being particularly called *Melody.*

VI. INTERVALS differ in *Magnitude* ; and
in this there is an infinite Variety, according
to the poffible Degrees of *Tune* ; for there is
no Difference fo great or little but a greater or
lefs is further imaginable : But if we confider
it with regard to what's practicable, there are
Limits, which are the leaft and greateft *Intervals* our Ears are Judges of, and can be actually
produced by Voice or Inftruments ; befides
which there is yet a further Limitation from
what's ufeful for attaining the Ends of *Mufick.*

VII.

VII. I<small>NTERVALS</small> are diftinguifhed into *fimple* and *compound* ; a *fimple Interval* is without Parts or Divifion ; a *compound* confifts of feveral leffer *Intervals*. Now 'tis plain this Diftinction has a Regard to Practice only, becaufe there is no fuch Thing as a leaft *Interval*: Befides, by a *fimple Interval* is not meant here the leaft practifed, but fuch as, tho' it were equal to Two or more leffer which are in Ufe, yet, when we would make a Sound move fo far up or down, we always pafs immediately from its one Term to the other ; what is meant then by a *compound Interval* will be very plain, it is fuch whofe Terms are, in Practice, taken either in immediate Succeffion, or we make the Sound to rife and fall from the one to the other by touching fome intermediate Degrees, fo that the Whole is a Compofition of all the *Intervals* from one Extreme to the other. What I call a *fimple Interval* the Ancients called a *Diaftem* ; and they called the *compound* a *Syftem* : Each of thefe has Differences ; even of the *fimple* there are fome greater and leffer, and they are always *Difcord*; but of the *compound* or *Syftem*, fome are *Concord*, fome *Difcord*. But again,

VIII. S<small>YSTEMS</small> of the fame Magnitude (and confequently of the fame Degree of *Concord* and *Difcord*)may differ in refpect of their Compofition, as containing and being actually divided into more or fewer *Intervals*. And when that Number is equal, yet the Parts may differ in Magnitude. *Laftly*, when they confift of the very
fame

fame Parts or leffer Intervals, there may be a Difference of the Order and Pofition of them betwixt the Extremes.

IX. A moft remarkable Diftinction of *Syftems* is into *concinnous* and *inconcinnous*. How thefe Words are applied to fimple Intervals we have already feen ; but to *Syftems* they are applied in a twofold Manner, thus, In every *Syftem* that is concinnoufly divided, the Parts confidered as fimple Intervals muft be *concinnous* in the Senfe of Article *Third* ; but not only fo, they muft be placed in a certain Order betwixt the Extremes, that the Succeffion of Sounds from one Extreme to the other, may be agreeable, and have a good Effect in Practice. An *inconcinnous Syftem* therefore is that where the fimple Intervals are *inconcinnous*, or ill difpofed betwixt the Extremes.

X. A *Syftem* is either *particular*, or *univerfal*, containing within it every particular Syftem that belongs to *Mufick*, and is called, THE SCALE OF MUSICK, which may be defined, *A Series of Sounds rifing or falling towards* ACUTENESS *or* GRAVITY *from any given Sound, to the greateft Diftance that is fit and practicable, thro' fuch intermediate Degrees, as make the Succeffion moft agreeable and perfect, and in which we have all the concording Intervals moft concinnoufly divided.*

THE right Compofition of fuch a *Syftem* is of the greateft Importance in *Mufick*, becaufe it will contain the whole Principles ; and fo the

Task

Task of this Part may be concluded in this, *viz.* To explain the Nature, Conſtitution and Office of the *Scale of Muſick* ; for in doing this, the whole fundamental Grounds and Principles of *Muſick* will be explain'd ; which I ſhall go through in this Order. 1*mo.* I ſhall explain upon what the *Tune* of a Sound depends, or at leaſt ſomething which is inſeparably connected with it; and how from this the *relative Degrees of Tune*, or the *Intervals* and *Differences* are determined and meaſured. 2*do.* I ſhall conſider the Nature of *Concord* and *Diſcord*, to explain, or at leaſt ſhow you what has been or may be ſaid to explain the Grounds of their different Effects. 3*tio* and 4*to.* I ſhall more particularly conſider the Variety of *Concords*, with all their mutual Relations : In order to which I ſhall deliver as ſuccinctly as I can the *harmonical Arithmetick.* teaching how muſical Intervals are compounded and reſolved, in order particularly to find their Differences and mutual Relations, Connections with, and Dependencies one on another. 5*to.* I ſhall explain what may be called *The geometrical* Part of the Theory, or, how to expreſs the *Degrees* and *Intervals* of *harmonick Sound* by the Sections and Diviſions of right Lines. 6*to.* I ſhall explain the *Compoſition* and *Degrees* of *Harmony* as that Term is already diſtinguiſhed from *Concord.* 7*mo.* I ſhall conſider the *concinnous Diſcords* that belong to *Muſick*; and explain their Number and Uſe; how with the *Concords* they make up the *univerſal Syſtem*, or conſtitute what we call *The Scale*

Scale of Mufick, whofe Nature and Office I
fhall very particularly explain ; wherein there
will be feveral Things handled that are fundamental to the right underftanding of the *pratti-
cal Part*; particularly, *8vo.* The Nature of
Modes and *Keys in Mufick* (fee the Words
explain'd in their proper Place:) And *9no.* The
Confequences with refpect to Practice, that follow from having a Scale of fix'd and determinate Sounds upon Inftruments ; and how the
Defects arifing from this are corrected.

§ 2. *Of the* Caufe *and* Meafure *of* Tune ; *or
upon what the Tune of a Sound depends ; and
how the relative Degrees or Differences of
Tune are determined and meafured.*

IT was firft found by Experience, That
many Sounds differing in *Tune*, tho' the
Meafures of the Differences were not yet known,
raifed agreeable Senfations, when applied either
in *Confonance* or *Succeffion* ; and that there
were Degrees in this Pleafure. But while the
Meafures of thefe Differences were not known,
the Ear muft have been the only Director;
which tho' the infallible Judge of what's agreeable to its felf ; yet perhaps not the beft Provi-
for: *Reafon* is a fuperior Faculty, and can make
ufe of former Experiences of Pleafure to contrive and invent new ones ; for, by examining
the Grounds and Caufes of Pleafure in one Inftance,

ſtance, we may conclude with great Probability, what Pleaſure will ariſe from other Cauſes that have a Relation and Likeneſs to the
former; and tho' we may be miſtaken, yet it
is plain, that *Reaſon*, by making all the probable Concluſions it can, to be again examined by the Judgment of Senſe, will more readily diſcover the agreeable and diſagreeable,
than if we were left to make Experiments at
Random, without obſerving any Order or Connection, *i. e.* to find Things by Chance. And
particularly in the preſent Caſe, by diſcovering
the Cauſe of the Difference of *Tune*, or ſomething at leaſt that is inſeparably connected with
it, we have found a certain Way of meaſuring
all their relative Degrees; of making diſtinct
Compariſons of the Intervals of Sound; and in
a Word, we have by this Means found a perfect Art of raiſing the Pleaſure, of which this
Relation of Sounds is capable, founded on a
rational and well ordered *Theory*, which
Senſe and Experience confirms. For unleſs we
could fix theſe Degrees of *Tune*, *i. e.* meaſure them, or rather their Relations, by
certain and determinate Quantities, they could
never be expreſt upon Inſtruments: If the Ear
were ſufficient for this as to *Concords*, I may
ſay, at leaſt, that we ſhould never otherwiſe
have had ſo perfect an Art as we now have;
becauſe, as I hope to make it appear, the Improvement is owing to the Knowledge of the
Numbers that expreſs theſe Relations: Without which, again, how could we know what
Pro-

Progreſs were made in diſcovering the Relations of *Tune* capable to pleaſe; for in all Probability it was with this, as much more of our
Knowledge, the firſt Diſcovery was by Accident, without any deliberate Enquiry, which
Men could never think of till ſomething accidental as to them made a Firſt Diſcovery ; nor
could we at this Day be reaſonably ſure that
ſome ſuch Accident ſhall not diſcover to us a new
Concord, unleſs we ſatisfied our ſelves by what
we know of the Cauſe of *Acuteneſs* and *Gravity*, and the mutual Relations of *concording
Intervals*, which I am now to explain.

ACCORDING to the Method I have propoſed
in this *Eſſay*, you muſt expect in another Place,
an Account of the Firſt Enquirers into the Meaſures of *Acuteneſs* and *Gravity* ; and here I go
on to explain it as our own Experience and Reaſon confirms to us.

THIS Affection of Sounds depends, as I
have already ſaid, altogether upon the ſonorous
Body ; which differs in *Tune.* 1mo. According
to the ſpecifick Differences of the Matter ;
thus the Sound of a Piece of Gold is much *graver* than that of a Piece of Silver of the ſame Shape
and Dimenſions; and in this Caſe the *Tones* are
proportional to the ſpecifick Gravities, (*cæteris
paribus*) *i. e.* the Weights of Two Pieces of the
ſame Shape and Dimenſion. Or, 2do. According to the different Quantities of the ſame ſpecifick Matter in Bodies of the ſame Figure; thus
a ſolid Sphere of Braſs one Foot Daimeter will
ſound *acuter* than one of the ſame Braſs Two
Foot

Foot Diameter; and here the *Tones* are proportional to the Quantities of Matter, or the
abſolute Weights.

B u t neither of theſe Experiments can reaſonably ſatisfy the preſent Enquiry. There appears indeed no Reaſon to doubt that the ſame
Ratio's of Weights (*cæteris paribus*) will always
produce Sounds with the ſame Difference of
Tone, *i. e.* conſtitute the ſame *Interval*; yet we
don't ſee in theſe Experiments, the immediate Ground or Cauſe of the Differences of
Tone ; for tho' we find them connected with
the Weights, yet it is far from being obvious
how theſe influence the other ; ſo that we cannot refer the Degrees of *Tone* to theſe Quantities as the immediate Cauſe ; for which Reaſon we ſhould never find, in this Method of
determining theſe Degrees, any Explication of the
Grounds of *Concord* and *Harmony* ; which can
only be found in the Relations of the Motions
that are the Cauſe of Sound ; in theſe Motions
therefore muſt we ſeek the true Meaſures of
Tune ; and this we ſhall find in the Vibrations
of Chords : For tho' we know that the Sound
is owing to the vibratory Motion of the Parts of
any Body, yet the Meaſures of theſe Motions
are tolerably plain, only in the Caſe of
Chords.

I t has been already explained; that Sounds
are produced in Chords by their vibratory Motions; and tho' according to what has been explained in the preceeding *Chapter*, theſe ſenſible Vibrations of the whole Chord are not the immediate

ate Cauſe of the Sound, yet they influence theſe inſenſible Motions that immediately produce it; and, for any Reaſon we have to doubt of it, are always proportional to them; and *therefore* we may meaſure Sounds as juſtly in theſe, as we could do in the other if they fell under our Meaſures. But even theſe ſenſible Vibrations of the whole Chord cannot be immediately meaſured, they are too ſmall and quick for that; and therefore we muſt ſeek another Way of meaſuring them, by finding what Proportion they have with ſome other Thing: And this can be done by the different *Tenſions*, or *Groſſneſs*, or *Lengths* of *Chords* that are in all other reſpects, except any one of theſe mentioned, equal and alike; the Chords in all Caſes being ſuppoſed evenly and of equal Dimenſions throughout: And of all Kind of Chords Metal or Wireſtrings are beſt to make the following. Experiments with.

Now, in *general*, we know by Experience that in two Chords, all Things being equal and alike except the *Tenſion* or the *Thickneſs* or the *Length*, the *Tones* are different; there muſt therefore be a Difference in the Vibrations, owing to theſe different Tenſions,&c. which Difference can only be in the Velocity of the Courſes and Recourſes of the Chords, thro' the Spaces in which they move to and again beyond the ſtraight Line : We are therefore to examine the Proportion between that Velocity and the Things mentioned on which it depends. And *mind* that to prevent ſaying ſo oft *cæteris paribus*,

bus, you are always to suppose it when I speak of Two Chords of different *Tensions, Lengths,* or *Grossness.*

P R O P O S I T I O N **I.** *If the elastick Chord* A B. (*Plate* 1. *Fig.*1.)*be drawn by any Point* o, *in the Direction of the Line* o D, *every Vibration it makes will be in a lesser Space as* o d, *till it be at perfect Rest in its natural Position* A o B; *and the elastick or restituent Force at each Point* d *of the Line* o D (i. e. *at the Beginning of each Vibration*) *will be in a simple direct Proportion of the Lines* o D, o d, o d.

D E M O N S T R A T I O N. That the Vibrations become gradually less till the Chord be at Rest, is plain ; and that this must proceed from the Decrease of the elastick Force is as plain; *lastly* that this Force decreases in the Proportion mentioned, is proven by this Experiment made upon a Wire-string, *viz.* that being stretched lengthwise by any Weight, if several Weights are applied successively to the Point o, drawing the Chord in the same Direction as o D, they bend it so that the Distances o D, o d, to which the several Weights draw it, are in simple direct Proportion of these Weights : But Action and Reaction are equal and contrary, *therefore* the Resistance which the Chord by its Elasticity makes to the Weight, is equal to the Gravity or drawing Force of that Weight, *i. e.* the restituent Forces in the Points D, d, are as the Lines o D, o d; now it is the same Case whether the Chord be stretcht by Weight or any other Force; for when we suppose it
stretcht

ftretcht to D, or d, the elaftick Force is the fame Thing, and in the fame Proportion at thefe Points, whatever the bending Force is ; therefore the Propofition is true.

COROLLARY. The Vibrations of the fame Chord are all performed in equal Time; *becaufe* in the Beginning of each Vibration, the reftituent or moving Force, is as the Space to be gone thro' ; for it is as the half Space o D, but Halfs are as the Wholes.

SCHOLIUM. In the preceeding Experiment (which is Dr. *Gravefande*'s) the Vibrations are taken very fmall, *that is*, at the greateft bending the Line o D is not above a Quarter of an Inch, the Chord being Two Foot and a Half long. And if the Propofition be but phyfically true with refpect to the very fmall Vibrations, it will fufficiently anfwer our Purpofe; for indeed Chords while they found vibrate in very fmall Spaces.

BUT *again*, as to the *Corollary*, which is the principal Thing we have ufe for, it will perhaps be objected, that I have only confidered the Motion of the Point o or D, without proving that the elaftick Force in the reft of the Points are alfo proportional to the Diftances; but as the whole bending Force is immediately applied to one Point, (tho' thereby it acts upon them all) the reftitutive Force may be referred all to the fame Point ; or, we may confider the whole *Area* ABD, which is the Effect of the bending, as the Space to be run thro' by the whole Body or Chord A B D, and thefe *Areas* are as the

Lines

Lines o D, o d, *viz.* The Altitudes of different Figures having the fame common Bafe A B, and a fimilar Curve A D B, and A d B; for ftrictly fpeaking the Chord is a Curve in its Vibrations; and if we take A D, and D B for ftraight Lines, as they are very nearly, and without any fenfible Variation in fuch fmall Vibrations as we now fuppofe, then it will be more plain that thefe *Areas* are as the Lines o D, o d; and becaufe in this Way we confider the Action upon, and Reaction of all the Points of the Chord, *therefore* the Objection is removed.

B u т there remains one Thing more, *viz.* That the Conclufion is drawn from the Forces or Velocities in the feveral Points D, d, as if they were uniform thro' all the Space; whereas in the Nature of the Thing they are accelerated from D to o, and in the fame Proportion retarded on the other Side of o : The *Anfwer* to this is plainly, that fince the Acceleration is of the fame Nature in all the Vibrations, it muft be the fame Cafe with refpect to the Time, as if the Motion were uniform.

N o w from the Confideration of this Acceleration, there is another *Demonftration* drawn of the preceeding *Corollary* ; and that I may fhow it, let me *firft* prove that there muft be an Acceleration, and *then* explain the Nature of it. *Firft.* Suppofe any one Vibration from D to o, in that the Point D muft move into d, d, fuccetfively, before it come to O ; and if there were no Acceleration, but that the Point D, in
every

every Pofition of the Chord, as A d B, had no
more elaftick Force than is equal to a Force that
could keep it in that Pofition; 'tis plain it could
never pafs the Point o; *becaufe* thefe Forces are
as the Diftances, and therefore it is nothing in
the Point o; but it actually paffes that Point,
and *confequently* the Motion is accelerated; and
the Law of the Acceleration is this, In every
Point of the fame Vibration, the Point D is
accelerated by a Force equal to what would be
fufficient to retain it in that Pofition; but thefe
Points being as the Diftances o d, o d, the Motion of the Point D agrees with that of a Body
moving in a *Cycloid*, whofe Vibrations the
Mathematicians demonftrate to be of equal Duration (*vid.* KEIL's *Introductio ad veram phyfi-
cam*) and therefore the Times of the Vibrations
of the Chord are alfo equal(*vid.* GRAVESANDE's
mathematical Elements of Phyficks. Book I.
Chap. 26.)

BEFORE we proceed farther, I fhall apply
this Propofition to a very remarkable *Phænomenon*; that Experience and our Reafonings
may mutually fupport one another. It is a very
obvious Remark, That the Sound of any Body
arifing from one individual Stroke, tho' it grows
gradually weaker, yet continues in the fame
Tone: We fhall be more fenfible of this by making the Experiment on Bodies that have a
great Refonance, as the larger Kind of Bells
and long Wire-ftrings.

NOW fince the *Tone* of a Sound depends
upon the Nature of thefe Vibrations, whofe
Dif-

Differences we can conceive no otherwise than as having different Velocities; and since we have proven that the small Vibrations of the same Chord are all performed in equal Time ; and *lastly*, since it is true in Fact that the *Tone* of a Sound which continues for some Time after the Stroke, is from first to last the same ; it follows, I think, that the *Tone* is necessarily connected with a certain Quantity of Time in making every single Vibration ; *or*, that a certain Number of Vibrations, accomplished in a given Time, constitutes a certain and determinate *Tone* ; for this being supposed we have a good Reason of that *Phænomenon* of the Unity of *Tone* mentioned: And this mutually confirms the Truth of the *Proposition*, that the Vibrations are all made in equal Time ; for this Unity of *Tone* supposes an Unity in that on which the *Tone* depends, or with which our Perception of it is connected ; and this cannot be supposed any other Thing than the Equality of the Vibrations, in the Time of their Courses and Recourses : For the absolute Velocity, or elastick Force, in the Beginning of each Vibration is unequal, being proportional to the Power that could retain it in that Position.

AGAIN, if we could absolutely determine how many Vibrations any Chord, of a given *Length, Thickness* and *Tension*, makes in a given Time, this we might call a *fix'd Sound* or rather a *fix'd Tone*, to which all others might be compared, and their Numbers be also determined

mined; but this is a mere Curiofity, which neither promotes the Knowledge or Practice of
Mufick ; it being enough to determine nd
meafure the *Intervals* in the Proportions and
relative Degrees of *Tone*, as in the following *Propofitions*.

P ROPOSITION II. *Let there be Two ela-*
ftick Chords A *and* C (*Plate* 1. *Fig*. 2.) *diffe-*
ring only in Tenfion, i. e. *Let them be ftretcht*
Length-wife by different Weights which are
the Meafures of the Tenfion ; *the Time of a*
Vibration in the one is to that of the other in-
verfely as the fquare Root of the Tenfions *or*
Weights that ftretch them. For Example, if
the Weights are as 4 : 9. *the Times are*
as 3 : 2.

D EMONSTRATION. If Two Chords C and
A (*Plate* 1. *Fig*. 2.) differ only in *Tenfion*,
they will be bended to the fame Diftance O D
by Weights (fimilarly applied to the Points o)
which are directly proportional to their *Ten-*
fions ; this is found by Experiment (*vid*. Gravefande's *Elements*.) *Again*, thefe Two Chords
bended equally, may be compared to Two
Pendulums vibrating in the fame or like *Cycloid*
with different accelerating Forces ; in which Cafe,
the Mathematicians know, it is demonftrated,
that the Times are inverfely as the fquare Roots
of the *Tenfions*, which are as the accelerating,
i. e. the bending Forces, when they are drawn
to equal Diftances ; but the Propofition is true
whether the Diftances O D be equal or not ;

be-

becaufe all the Vibrations of the fame Chord
are of equal Duration by *Prop.* 1.

Coʀᴏʟʟᴀʀʏ. *The Numbers of the Vibrations accompliſhed in the ſame Time are directly as the ſquare Roots of their Tenſions. For
Example, If the Tenſions are as 9 to 4. the
Numbers of Vibrations in the ſame Time will
be as 3 to 2.*

Pʀᴏᴘᴏꜱɪᴛɪᴏɴ III. *The Numbers of Vibrations made in the ſame Time by Two Chords,
A and B (Plate 1. Fig. 3.) that differ only in
Thickneſs, are inverſely as the ſquare Roots of
the Weights of the Chords, i. e. as the Diameter,
of their Baſes inverſely.*

Dᴇᴍᴏɴꜱᴛʀᴀᴛɪᴏɴ. We know by com-
mon Experience that the *thicker* and *groſſer*
any Chord is, being bended by the fame
Weight, it gives the more *grave* Sound ; fo
that the *Tone* is as the *Thickneſs* in general :
But for the particular Proportion, we have this
Experiment, viz. Take Two Chords B and C
(*Plate* 1. *Fig.* 3.) differing only in *Thickneſs*;
let the Weights they are ftretched with be as
the Weights of the Chords themſelves, *i. e.* as
the Squares of their Diameters ; their Sounds
are *uniſon*, therefore the Number of Vibrations
in each will be equal in the fameTime: And confequently if the thick *Chord* B be compared to a-
nother of equal Length A(in the fame *Figure*)
ftretched with the fame Weight, but whoſe
Thickneſs is only equal to that of the
fmaller Chord C laft compared to it ; the
Numbers of Vibrations of B and A will be
as

as the fquare Roots of the Weights of the
Chords inverfely: That is, inverfely   as   the
Diameters of their Bafes, or the Bores thro'
which the Wire is drawn.

P R O P O S I T I O N IV. *If Two Chords* A
and B, *in Plate* 1. *Fig.* 2. *differ only in their*
Lengths, *the Time of a Vibration of the one*
is to that of the other as the Lengths *directly*;
andconfequently as theNumber of Vibrations in
the fame Time inverfely. For Example,Let the
one be Three Foot and the other Two,the Firft
will make Two Vibrations and the other Three
in the fame Time.

D E M O N. "Tis Matter of common Obfervation, that if you take any Number of Chords
differing only in *Length,* their Sounds will be
gradually *acuter* as   the   Chords are *fhorter*;
and for the Proportion of the *Lengths* and
Vibrations, it will be plain from what has been
already faid ; for the fame *Tone* is conftitute
by the fame Number of Vibrations in a given
Time ; and we know by *Experience* that if
Two Chords C and B (*Plate* 1. *Fig.* 2.)
differing only in *Length,* are tended by Weights
which are as the Squares of their *Lengths,*
their Sounds are *unifon* ; therefore they make
an equal Number of Vibrations in the fame
Time.   But *again*, by *Propofition* 2. the
N mber of Vibrations of the longeft of
thefe Two Chords C, is to the Number in the
fame Time, of an equal and like Chord A
(in the fame *Figure*) lefs tended, as the fquare
Roots of the Tenfions directly ; therefore if
                                                    A is

A is tended equally with the ſhorter Chord
B (whoſe Vibrations are equal to thoſe of the
longer Chord D that's moſt tended)'tis plain the
Number of Vibrations of theſe two muſt be
as their Lengths, becauſe theſe Lengths are
directly as the ſquare Roots of the unequal Tenſions.

Observe, that if we ſuppoſe this Proportion
of the Time and Lengths to be otherwiſe demonſtrated, then what is here advanced as an
Experiment will follow as a Conſequence from
this *Propoſition* and the Second. But I think
this Way of demonſtrating the *Propoſition*
very plain and ſatisfying. You may alſo ſee
from what Conſiderations Dr. *Graveſande* concludes it. Or we may prove it independently
of the Second *Propoſition*, after the Manner
of the Firſt by the following

Experiment. *Viz.* If the ſame or equal Weight
is ſimilarly applied to ſimilar Points O o, of Two
elaſtick Chords A and B (*Plate* 1. *Fig.* 2.) that
differ only in Lengths; the Points O, o will
be drawn to the Diſtances O D, o d, that ſhall
be as the Lengths of the Chords A, B; ſo
that the Figures ſhall be ſimilar, and the whole
Areas proportional to the Lengths of the
Chords.

Now the bending Forces in D and d are
equal and equally applied, therefore the re-
ſtituent Forces are equal; the Times conſequently are as the Spaces, *i. e.* as the Areas or
the Chords A, B, and this holds whatever the
Difference of o d and O D is, ſince all the Vibrations

rations of the fame Chord are made in equal
Time ; and therefore, *laftly*, the Numbers of
Vibrations in a given Time are as thefe Lengths
inverfely.

OBSERVE. From this Demonftration and
the Experiment ufed in the former Demonftration, we fee the Truth of *Propofition* 2. in ano-
her View.

GENERAL *Corollary* to the preceeding *Propofitions. The Numbers of Vibrations made
in the fame Time by any Two Chords of the
fame Matter, differing in Length, Thicknefs and
Tenfion, are in the compound Ratio of the
Diameters and Lengths inverfely, and the fquare
Roots of the Tenfions directly.*

Now let us fum up and apply what has been
explained, and, *firft*, We have concluded that
the Differences of *Tone* or the *Intervals* of
harmonick Sound are necessarily connected
with the Velocity of the Vibrations in their
Courfes and Recourfes, *i. e.* the Number of Vibrations made in equal Time by the Parts of the fonorous Body : And becaufe thefe Numbers cannot be. meafured in themfelves immediately,
we have found how to do it in Chords, by
the Proportions betwixt them and the different *Tenfions* or *Thicknefs* or *Lengths*; we have
not fought any abfolute and determinate Number of Vibrations in any Chord, but only the
Ratio or Proportion betwixt the Numbers accomplifhed in the fame Time, by feveral Chords
differing in *Tenfion* or *Thicknefs* or *Length*, or
in all thefe; *therefore* we have difcovered the
true

true and juſt Meaſures of the relative Degrees
of *Tone*, not only in *Chords*, but in all other
Bodies ; for if it is reaſonable to conclude, from
the Likeneſs of Cauſes and Effects, that the
ſame *Tone* is conſtitute in every Body, by the ſame
Number of Vibrations in the ſame Time, it follows, that whatever Numbers expreſs the *Ratio*
of any Two Degrees in one kind of Body, they
expreſs the *Ratio* of theſe Two Degrees univerſally : But this would hold without that
Suppoſition, becauſe we can find Two Chords,
whoſe *Tones* ſhall be *uniſon* reſpectively to any
other Two Sounds ; and therefore all the Concluſions we can make from the various
Compoſitions and Diviſions of theſe *Ratio*'s will
be true of all Sounds, whatever Differences there
be in the Cauſe.

IT follows *again*, that in the Application of
Numbers to the different *Tones* of Sound,
whereby we expreſs the Relations of one Degree to another, the *grave* is to the *acute* as
the leſſer Number to the greater, becauſe the
graver depends upon the leaſt Number of Vibrations : But if we apply theſe Numbers to the Times
of the Vibrations, then, the *grave* is repreſented
by the greater Number, and the *acute* by the leſſer.

IF we expreſs the ſame *Tones* by the Quantity of the different *Tenſions* of Chords that are
otherwiſe equal and like, then the *Ratio* will
be different, becauſe the *Tenſions* are as the
Squares of the Vibrations, and the *grave* will be
to the *acute* as the leſſer to the greater : But
the Reaſon why we ought not to uſe theſe
Num-

Numbers is, that tho' different *Tenfions* make different *Tones*, yet we can only examine the Grounds of *Concord* and *Difcord*, in the *Ratio*'s of the Vibrations, which are immediately the Caufe of Sound ; and this is a more accurate Way, becaufe thefe reprefent fomething that's common in all Sounds; and befides, being always lefler Numbers (*viz.* the fquare Roots of the other) are more convenient for the eafy Comparifon of *Intervals*. As to the *Diameters* or *Lengths* of different Chords, becaufe they are in a fimple Proportion of the Numbers of Vibrations, therefore the fame Numbers reprefent either them or the Vibrations, but inverfely ; fo that the *graver* Tone is reprefented by the *longer* or *groffer* Chord : And becaufe *Experiments* are more eafily made with Chords differing only in Lengths; and alfo becaufe thefe Proportions are more eafily conceived, and more fenfibly reprefented by right Lines; *therefore* we alfo reprefent the Degrees of *Tone* by thefe Lengths, tho' in examining the Grounds of *Concord* we muft confider the Vibrations, which are expreft by the fame Numbers.

T H I S brings to Mind a Queftion which *Vincenzo Galilei* makes in his Dialogues upon *Mufick* ; he asks, Whether the expreffing of the Interval which we call an *Oɛtave* by the *Ratio* of 1:2. be reafonably grounded upon this, That if a Chord is divided into Two equal Parts, the *Tone* of the Half is an *Oɛtave* to that of the Whole? The Reafons of his Doubt he propofes thus,

thus, says he, There are Three Ways we can make the Sound of a Chord *acuter, viz.* by *shortning* it, by a *greater Tension,* and by making it *smaller, cæteris paribus.* By *shortning* it the *Ratio* of an *Octave* is 1 : 2. By *Tension* it is 1 : 4. and by lessening the *Thickness* it is also 1 : 4. He means in the last Case, when the Tones are measured by the Weights of the Chord. Now he would know why it is not as well 1 : 4. as 1 : 2. which is the ordinary Expression : I think this Difficulty we have sufficiently answered above ; for these Weights are not the immediate Cause of the Sound; it is true we may say that the *acute* Term of the *Octave* is to the *grave* as 4. to 1. meaning only that the *acute* is produced by Four Times the Weight which determines the other ; and if *Intervals* are compared together by *Ratio*'s taken this Way, we can compound and resolve them, and find their mutual Connections and Relations of Quantity, as truly as by the other Expressions ; but the Operations are not so easy, because they are greater Numbers :   *And* then, if the Sounds are produced any other Way than by Chords of different *Tensions* or *Thickness,* the *Tones* are to one another as these Numbers in a very remote Sense ; for they express nothing in the Cause of these Sounds themselves, but only tell us, that Two Chords being made *unisons* to these Sounds, their *Tensions* or *Thickness* are as these Numbers: But, all Sounds being produced by Motion, when we express the *Tones* by the Numbers of Vibrations in the same Time, we represent something
that's

that's proper to every Sound; this therefore is the only Thing that can be confidered in examining the Grounds of *Concord* and *Difcord*: And becaufe the fame Numbers exprefs the Vibrations and Lengths of Chords, we apply them fometimes alfo to thefe Lengths, for Reafons already faid.

WE have alfo gained this further Definition of *Acutenefs* and *Gravity, viz.* That *Acutenefs* is a relative Property of Sound, which with refpect to fome other is the Effect of a greater Number of Vibrations accomplifhed in the fame Time, or of Vibrations of a fhorter Duration; and *Gravity* is the Effect of a leffer Number of Vibrations, or of Vibrations of a fhorter Duration. And by confidering that the Vibrations proceeding from one individual Stroke are gradually in leffer Spaces till the Motion ceafe, and that the Sound is always louder in the Beginning, and gradually weaker, therefore we may define *Loudnefs* the Effect of a greater abfolute Velocity of Motion or a greater Vibration made in the fame Time; and *Lownefs* is the Effect of a leffer.

BEFORE I end this *Chapter*, let us confider a Conclufion which *Kircher* makes, in his *Mufurgia univerfalis.* Having proven in his own Way, the Equidiurnity of the Vibrations of the fame Chord, he draws this Conclufion, That the Sound of a Chord grows gradually more *grave* as it ceafes (tho' he owns the Difference is not fenfible) becaufe the abfolute Velocity of Motion becomes lefs, *i. e.* That Velocity where-

by

by the Chord makes a Vibration of a certain Space in a certain Time. By this Argument he makes the Degrees and Differences of *Tune* proportional to the abfolute Velocity : But if this is a good Hypothefis, I think it will follow, contrary to Experience, that two Chords of unequal Length (*cæteris paribus*) muft give an equal *Tune* ; for to demonftrate the reciprocal Proportion of the Lengths and the Number of Vibrations, he fuppofes the *Tenfion* or elaftick Force, which is the immediate Caufe of the abfolute Velocity, to be equal when the Chords are drawn out to proportional Diftance ; for by this Equality the fhorter Chord finifhes its Vibrations in fhorter Time, in Proportion as the Spaces are lefler, which are as the Lengths. *Again*, the Elafticity of the Chord diminifhes gradually, fo that in any affignable Time there is at leaft an indefinite Number of Degrees ; and fince the Elafticity has fuch a gradual Decreafe, it feems odd that the Differences of *Tune*, if they have a Dependence on the abfolute Velocity, fhould not be fenfible. But in the other Hypothefis, where I fuppofe the Degrees of *Tune* are connected with and proportional to the Duration of a fingle Vibration, and confequently to the Number of Vibrations in a given Time, there can no abfurd Confequence follow. I am indeed aware of a Difficulty that may be ftarted, which is this, That the Duration of a fingle Vibration is a Thing the Mind has nothing whereby to judge of,

of, whereas it can eafily judge of the Difference
of abfolute Velocity by the different Percuffions
upon the Ear; and the Defenders of this
Hypothefis may further alledge, that the
Vibrations that produce Sound are the fmall
and almoft infenfible Vibrations of the Body;
fo far infenfible at leaft that we can only difcern
a Tremor, but no diftinct Vibrations; and we
cannot, fay they, be furprized if the Differences
of *Tune* are infenfible. But I fuppofe the Degrees
of *Tune* of the firft Vibrations are predominant,
and determine the particular *Tune* of the Sound;
and then it is no lefs unaccountable how
Two Chords drawn out to fimilar Figures, as in
Prop. 4. fhould not give the fame *Tune*, and
indeed it feems impoffible to be otherwife in
this Hypothefis, which yet is contrary to Experience; and for the Difficulty propofed in the other
Hypothefis it is at leaft but a Difficulty and no
Contradiction, efpecially if we fuppofe it depends
immediately on a certain Number of Vibrations
in a given Time, which is the Confequence
of a fhorter Duration of every fingle Vibration;
and this again, I own, fuppofes there can be
no Sound heard till a certain Number of Vibrations are accomplifhed, the contrary whereof I
believe will be difficult to prove. I fhall therefore leave it to the *Philofophers*, becaufe I think
the chief Demand of this particular Part is
fufficiently anfwered, which was to know how
to take the juft Meafures of the relative Degrees
of Tune, and their Intervals or Differences.
You'll remember too, what Reafon I have
already,

already alledged for expreffing the Degrees of *Tune* by the Numbers of Vibrations accomplifh-ed in the fame Time ; for whether the Caufe of our perceiving a different *Tone* lies here or not, the only Way we have of accounting for the *Concord* and *Difcord* of different *Tones,* is the Confideration of thefe Proportions, and whatever may be required in a more univerfal Enquiry into the Nature and *Phænomena* of Sound, this will be fufficient to fuch a Theory, as by the Help of Experience and Obfervation, may guide us to the true Knowledge of the Science of Mufick.

BESIDES, in this Account of the Caufe of the Differences of *Tune*, I follow the Opinion not only of the Ancients but of our more modern Philofophers; Dr. *Holder*'s whole Theory of the natural Grounds and Principles of *Harmony,* is founded on this Suppofition; take his own Words, *Chap.* 2. " The Firft and great " Principle upon which the Nature of *harmo-* " *nical* Sounds is to be found out and difco- " vered is this: That the *Tune* of a Note (to fpeak " in our vulgar Phrafe) is conftituted by the " Meafure and Proportion of Vibrations of the " fonorous Body ; I mean, of the Velocity of " thefe Vibrations in their Recourfes, for the " frequenter thefe Vibrations are, the more *a-* " *cute* is the Tune ; the flower and fewer they " are in the fame Space of Time, by fo much " the more *grave* is the Tune. So that any " given Note of a Tune is made by one cer- " tain Meafure of Velocity of Vibrations, *viz.*
" fuch

" fuch a certain Number of Courfes and Re-
" courfes, *e. g.* of a Chord or String in fuch *a*
" certain Space of Time, doth conftitute fuch
" a determinate Tune.

D O C T O R *Wallis* in the *Appendix* to his
Edition of *Ptolomey*'s Books of *Harmony*, owns
this to be a very reafonable Suppofition ; yet
he fays he would not pofitively affirm, that
the Degrees of *Acutenefs* anfwer the Number
of Vibrations as their only true Caufe, becaufe
he doubted whether it had been fufficiently confirm'd by Experience. Now that Sound depends
upon the Vibrations of Bodies, I think, needs
no further Proof than what we have; but
whether the different Numbers of Vibrations
in a given Time, is the true Caufe, on the
Part of the Object, of our perceiving a Difference of Tune, is a Thing I don't conceive
how we can prove by Experiments ; and to
the prefent Purpofe 'tis enough that it is a
reafonable Hypothefis ; and let this be the
only true Caufe or not, we find by Experience and Reafon both, that the Differences
of *Tune* are infeparably connected with the
Number of Vibrations; and therefore thefe, or
the Lengths of Chords to which they are proportional, may be taken for the true Meafure
of different *Tunes*. The Doctor owns that the
Degrees of *Acutenefs* are reciprocally as the
Lengths of Chords, and thinks it fufficiently
plain from Experience ; fince we find that the
fhorter Chord (*cæteris paribus*) gives the more
acute Sound, *i. e.* that the *Acutenefs* increafeth

as

as the Length diminisheth; and therefore the *Ratios* of these Lengths are just Measures of the Intervals of *Tune*, whatever be the immediate Cause of the Differences, or whatever Proportion be betwixt the Lengths of the Chords and their Vibrations. So far he owns we are upon a good Foundation as to the arithmetical Part of this Science; but then in *Philosophy* we ought to come as near the immediate Cause of Things as possibly we can; and where we cannot have a positive Certainty, we must take the most reasonable Supposition; and of that we judge by its containing no obvious Contradiction; and then by its Use in explaining the Phenomena of nature; how well the present Hypothesis has explained the sensible Unity of *Tune* in a given Sound we have already heard, and the Success of it in the Things that follow will further confirm it.

I shall end this Part with observing, that as the Lengths of Chords determine the Measure of the Velocity of their Vibrations, and this determines the Measure of their *Gravity* and *Acuteness*, so 'tis thus that *Harmony* is brought under Mathematical Calculation; the True object of the Mathematical Part of *Musick* being the Quantity of the Intervals of Sounds; which are capable of various Additions, Substractions, &c. as other Quantities are; tho' performed in a Manner suitable to the Nature of the Thing.

C H A P.

C H A P. III.

Of the Nature of CONCORD *and* DISCORD
as contained in the Caufes thereof.

§ I. *Wherein the* Reafons *and* Characte-
rifticks *of the feveral Differences of* Concords
and Difcords *are enquired into.*

WE have already confidered the Reafon of the Differences of *Tune*, and
the Meafures of thefe Differences, or
of the *Intervals* of Sound arifing from them :
We now enquire into the Grounds and Reafons of their different Effects. When Two
Sounds are heard in immediate Succeffion, the
Mind not only perceives Two fimple Ideas,
but by a proper Activity of its own, comparing
thefe Ideas, forms another of their Difference
of *Tune*, from which arife to us various Degrees of Pleafure or Offence ; thefe are the Effects we are now to confider the Reafons
of.

But it will be fit in the Firft Place to know
what is mean'd by the Queftion, or what we
propofe and expect to find ; in order to this
obferve, That there is a great Difference betwixt knowing what it is that pleafes us, and
why we are pleafed with fuch a Thing : Pleafure

sure and Pain are simple Ideas we can never make plainer than Experience makes them, for they are to be got no other Way; and for that Question, Why certain Things please and others not, as I take it, it signifies this, *viz.* How do these Things raise in us agreeable or disagreeable Ideas? Or, What Connection is there betwixt these Ideas and Things? When we consider the World as the Product of infinite Wisdom, we can say, that nothing happens without a sufficient Reason, I mean, that whatever is, its being rather than not being is more agreeable to the infinite Perfection of GOD, who knew from Eternity the whole Extent of Possibility, and in his *perfect Wisdom* chose to call to a real Existence such Beings, and make such a World, as should answer the best and wisest End. The Actions of the SUPREME BEING flow from *eternal Reasons* known and comprehensible only to his *infinite Wisdom;* and here lies the ultimate Reason and Cause of every Thing. To know how *perfect Wisdom* and *Omnipotence* exerted it self in the Production of the World; to find the *original Reason* and Grounds of the Relations and Connection which we see among Things, is altogether out of the Power of any created Intelligence; but not to carry our Contemplation beyond what the present Subject requires, I think the Reason of that Connection which we find by Experience betwixt our agreeable and disagreeable Ideas, and what we call the Objects of Sense, our *Philosophy* will never reach; and for any

Thing

Thing we shall ever find (at least in our mortal State) I believe it will remain a Question whether that Connection flows from any Necessity in the Nature of Things, or be altogether an arbitrary Disposition; for to solve this, would require to know Things perfectly, and understand their whole Nature ; which belongs only to that GLORIOUS BEING on whom all others depend. We shall therefore, as to this Question, be content to say, in the *general*, that 'tis the Rule of our Constitution, whereby upon the Application of certain Objects to the Organ of Sense, considered in their present Circumstances, an agreeable or disagreeable Idea shall be raised in the Mind. We have a conscious Perception of the Existence of other Things besides our selves, by the irresistible Impressions they make upon us ; if the Effect is Pleasure we pursue it farther ; if it is Pain we far less doubt of the Reality : And so in our Enquiries into Nature, we must be satisfied to examine Observations already made, or make new ones, that from Nature's constant and uniform Operations we may learn her Laws. Things are connected in a regular Order ; and when we can discover the *Law* or *Rule* of that Order, then we may be said to have discovered the *secondary Reason* of Things; for Example, tho' we are forced to resolve the Cause of *Gravitation* into the arbitrary Will of GOD ; yet having once discovered this Rule in Nature, that all the Bodies within the Atmosphere of the Earth have a Tendency downward

ward perpendicularly as to a common Centre within the Earth, and will move towards it in a Right Line, if no other Body interpofes; upon this Principle we can give a good Reafon why Timber floats in Water, and why Smoke afcends. I call it a *fecondary Reafon*, becaufe is is founded on a Principle of which we can give no other Reafon but that we find it conftantly fo. Accordingly in Matters of Senfe we have found all we can expect, when we know with what Conditions of the Object and Organs of Senfe our Pleafure is connected; fo in the *Harmony* of Sounds we know by Experience what Proportions and Relations of *Tune* afford Pleafure, what not; and we have alfo found how to exprefs the Differences of *Tune* by the Proportion of Numbers; and if we could find any Thing in the Relation of thefe Numbers, or the Things they immediately reprefent, with which *Concord* and its various Degrees are connected; by this Means we fhould know where Nature has fet the Limits of *Concord* and *Difcord*; we fhould with Certainty determine what Proportions conftitute *Concord*, and the Order of Perfection in the various Degrees of it; and all other Relations would be left to the Clafs of *Difcords*. And this I think is all we can propofe in this Matter; fo that we don't enquire why we are pleafed, but what it is that pleafes us; we don't enquire why, for Example, the *Ratio* of 1 : 2 conftitutes *Concord*, and 6 : 7 *Difcord*, *i. e.* upon what *original Grounds* agreeable or difagreeable Idea's are connected with thefe Relations; and the

pro-

proper Influence of the one upon the other ; but what common Property they agree in that make *Concord* ; and what Variation of it makes the Differences of *Concord;* by which we may alfo know the Marks of *Difcord* : In *fhort*, I would find, if poffible, the diftinguifhing Cha-racter of *Concord* and *Difcord* ; or, to what Condition of the Object thefe different Effects are annexed, that we may have all the Certain-ty we can, that there are no other *Concords* than what we know already; or if there are we may know how to find them; and have all poffible Affiftance, both from Experience and Reafon, for improving the moft innocent and ravifhing of all our fenfual Entertainments; and as far as we are baffled in this Search, we muft fit down content with our bare experi-mental Knowledge, and make the beft Ufe of it we can. Now to the Queftion.

BY EXPERIENCE we know, that thefe *Ratios* of the Lengths of Chords, are all *Concord*, tho' in various Degrees, *viz.* $2:1$, $3:2$, $4:3$, $5:4$, $6:5$, $5:3$, $8:5$, *that is*, Take any Chord for a Fundamental, which fhall be reprefented by 1. and thefe Sections of it are *Concord* with the Whole, *viz.* $\frac{1}{2}$, $\frac{2}{3}$, $\frac{3}{4}$, $\frac{4}{5}$, $\frac{5}{6}$, $\frac{3}{5}$, $\frac{5}{8}$, for, as 2 to 1, fo is 1 to $\frac{1}{2}$, and fo of the reft. The firft Five you fee, are found in the natural Order of Numbers 1, 2, 3, 4, 5, 6; but if you go on with the fame Series, thus, $7:6$, $8:7$, we find no more Agreement; and for thefe Two $3:5$, and $5:8$, they depend upon the others, as we fhall fee. There are alfo other *Intervals* that are

Con-

Concord befides thefe, yet none lefs than 2 : 1, (the *Octave*) or whofe *acute* Term is greater than $\frac{1}{2}$; nor any greater than *Octave*, or whofe *acute* Term is lefs than $\frac{1}{2}$, but what are compofed of the *Octave* and fome leffer *Concord*, which is all the Judgment of Experience.

I fuppofe it agreed to that the vibratory Motion of a Chord is the Caufe, or at leaft proportional to the Motion which is the immediate Caufe of its Sound; we have heard already that the Vibrations are quicker, *i. e.* the Courfes and Recourfes are more frequent, in a given Time, as the Chord is fhorter; I have obferved alfo that *acute* and *grave* are but Relations, tho' there muft be fomething abfolute in the Caufe of Sound, capable of lefs and more, to be the Ground of this Relation which flows only from the comparing of that lefs and more ; and whether this be the abfolute Velocity of Motion, or the Frequency of Vibrations, I have alfo confidered, and do here affume the laft as more probable. We have alfo proven that the Lengths of Chords are reciprocally as the Numbers of Vibrations in the fame Time; and therefore their *Ratios* are the true Meafures of the *Intervals* of Sound. But I fhall apply the *Ratios* immediately to the Numbers of Vibrations, and examine the Marks of *Concord* and *Difcord* upon this Hypothefis.

Now then, the univerfal Character whereby *Concord* and *Difcord* are diftinguifhed, is to be fought in the Numbers which contain and exprefs the *Intervals* of Sound: But not in thefe Num-

bers abſtractly; we muſt conſider them as expreſſing the very Cauſe and Difference of Sound with
reſpect to *Tune, viz.* the Number of Vibrations
in the ſame Time: I ſhall therefore paſs all theſe
Conſiderations of Numbers in which nothing
has been found to the preſent Purpoſe.

UNISONS are in the Firſt Degree of *Concord,*
or have the moſt perfect Likeneſs and Agreement
in *Tune* ; for having the ſame Meaſure of
Tune they affect the Ear as one ſimple Sound ;
yet I don't ſay they produce always the beſt
Effect in *Muſick* ; for the Mind is delighted
with Variety ; and here I conſider ſimply the
Agreement of Sounds and the Effect of this
in each *Concord* ſingly by it ſelf. *Uniſonance*
therefore being the moſt perfect Agreement
of Sounds, there muſt be ſomething in this,
neceſſary to that Agreement, which is to be
found leſs or more in every *Concord.* The
Equality of *Tune* (expreſt by a *Ratio* of Equality
in Numbers) makes certainly the moſt perfect
Agreement of Sound ; but yet 'tis not true that
the nearer any Two Sounds come to an Equality of *Tune* they have the more Agreement,
therefore 'tis not in the Equality or Inequality
of the Numbers ſimply that we are to ſeek this
ſecondary Reaſon of the Agreement or Diſagree-
ment of Sounds, but in ſome other Relation of
them, or rather of the Things they expreſs.

IF we conſider the Numbers of Vibrations made in any given Time, by Two
Chords of equal *Tune,* they are equal upon
the Hypotheſis laid down ; and ſo the
Vi-

Vibrations of the Two Chords coincide or begin together as frequently as poffible with refpect to both Chords, *viz.* at the leaft Number poffible of the Vibrations of each; for they coincide at every Vibration: And in this Frequency of Coincidence or united Mixture of the Motions of the Two Chords, and of the Undulations of the Air caufed thereby, not in the Equality or Inequality of the Number of Vibrations, muft we feek the Difference of *Concord* and *Difcord*; and therefore the nearer the Vibrations of Two Strings accomplifhed in the fame Time, come to the leaft Number poffible, they feem to approach the nearer to the Condition, and confequently to the A-greement of *Unifons.* Thus far we reafon with Probability, but let us fee how Experience approves of this Rule.

If we take the natural Series 1, 2, 3, 4, 5, 6, and compare every Number to the next, as expreffing the Vibrations (in the fame Time) of Two Chords, whofe Lengths are reciprocally as thefe Numbers; we find the Rule holds exactly; for 1 : 2. is beft than 2 : 3, *&c.* and the Agreement diminifhes gradually; fo that after 6 the *Confonance* is unfufferable, becaufe the Coincidences are too rare; but there are other *Ratio*'s that are agreeable befides what are found in that continued Order, whereof I have already mentioned thefe Two, *viz.* 3 : 5, and 5 : 8 which with the preceeding Five are all the *concording* Intervals within, or lefs than *Octave* 1 : 2. *i. e.* whofe acute Term is greater

than

than ⅘, the Fundamental being 1. Now to judge of these by the Rule laid down, 3 : 5 will be pre-ferr'd to 4 : 5, because being equal in the Number of Vibrations of the *acuter* Term, there is an Advantage on the Side of the Fundamental in the *Ratio* 3 : 5, where the Coincidence is made at every Third Vibration of the Fundamental, and 5*th* of the *acute* Term : Again as to the *Ratio* 5 : 8 'tis less perfect than 5 : 6, because tho' the Vibrations of the fundamental Term of each that go to one Coincidence are equal, yet in the *Ratio* 5 : 6 the Coincidence is at every 6 of the *acute* Term, and only at every 8 in the other Case. Thus does our Rule determine the Preference of the *Concords* already mentioned ; nor doth the Ear con-tradict it ; so that these *Concords* stand in the Order of the following Table, where I annex the Names that these Intervals have in Pra-ctice, and which I shall hereafter assume till we come to the proper Place for explaining the Original and Reason of them.

	Vibrations.		
	acute,		*grave,*
Unison.	1	:	1
Octave.	2	:	1
Fifth.	3	:	2
Fourth.	4	:	3
Sixth greater.	5	:	3
Third greater.	5	:	4
Third lesser.	6	:	5
Sixth lesser.	8	:	5
	grave,		*acute.*
	Lengths,		N o w

Now you muſt *obſerve* that this Frequency
of Coincidence does not reſpect any abſolute
Space of Time; for 'tis ſtill an *Octave*, for Example, whatever the Lengths of the Chords are,
if they be to one another as 1 : 2; and yet 'tis
certain that a longer Chord, *cæteris paribus*,
takes longer Time to every Vibration :   It
has a Reſpect to the Number of Vibrations of
both Chords accompliſhed in the ſame Time:
It does not reſpect the Vibrations of the *Fundamental* only, for then 1 : 2 and 1 : 3 would be
equal in *Concord*, and ſo would theſe 4 : 7 and
4 : 5 which they are not nor can be; for where
the *Ratios* differ there muſt the Agreement differ
from the very Nature of the Thing, becauſe it
depends altogether on theſe *Ratios* ; ſo that
equal Agreement muſt proceed from an **equal**
(*i. e.* from the ſame) *Ratio* ; nor can it reſpect the *acuter* Term only, elſe 3 : 5 and 4 : 5
would be equal; therefore neceſſarily a Conſide-
ration muſt be made of the Number of Vibrations of both Chords accompliſhed in equal
Time.   And if from the known *Concords*
within an *Octave*, we would make a *general Rule*, it is this, *viz.* that when the
Coincidences are moſt frequent with reſpect
to both Chords (*i. e.* with reſpect to the
Numbers of Vibrations of each that go to
every Coincidence) there is the neareſt Approach to the Condition of *Uniſons :* So that
when in Two Caſes we compare the ſimilar
Terms (*i. e.* the Number of Vibrations of the
Fundamental of the one to that of the other,
and

and the *acute* Term of the one to the *acute*
Term of the other) if both fimilar Terms
of the one are lefs than thefe of the other,
that one is preferable; and any one of the
fimilar Terms equal and the other unequal,
that which has the leaft is the preferable *Interval*, as we find by the Judgment of the
Ear in all the *Concords* of the preceeding Table.

No w if this be the true Rule of Nature, and an univerfal Character for judging
of the comparative Perfection of Intervals, with
refpect to the Agreement of their Extremes in
Tune; then it will be approven by Experience,
and anfwer every Cafe : But it is not fo, for
by this Rule 4 : 7 or 5 : 7, both *Difcords*, are
preferable to 5 : 8 a *Concord*, tho' indeed in a low
Degree; and 1 : 3, an *Octave* and *Fifth* compounded, will be preferable to 1 : 4 a double
Octave, contrary to Experience. But fuppofe
the Rule were good as to fuch Cafes where both
fimilar Terms of the one Cafe compared are
lefs than thefe of the other, or the one fimilar
Term equal and the other not; yet there are
other Cafes to which this Character will not
extend, *viz.* when there is an Advantage (as
to the Smalnefs of the Number of Vibrations
to one Coincidence) on the Part of the *Fundamental* in one Cafe, and on the Part of the
acute Term in the other; which Advantage
may be either equal or unequal, as here 5 : 6
and 4 : 7; the Advantages are equal, the Coincidence in the Firft being made fooner, by Two
Vibrations of the *Fundamental*, than in the
Second

Second, which again makes its Coincidences
fooner by ½ Vibrations of the *acute* Term. If we
were to draw a Rule from this Comparifon, where
the Ear prefers 5 : 6 a 3d leffer, to 4 : 7 a
Difcord, then we fhould always prefer that one,
of Two Cafes whofe mutual Advantages are
equal, which coincides at the leaft Number of
Vibrations of the *acute* Term. But Experience
contradicts this Rule, for 3 : 8, an *Octave* and 4th
compounded, is better than 4 : 7 ; fo that we
have nothing to judge by here but the Ear. If,
laftly, the mutual Advantages are unequal, we find
generally that which has the greateft Advantage
in whatever Term is preferable, tho' 'tis uncertain in many Cafes. Upon the Whole I
conclude that there is fomething befides the
Frequency of Coincidence to be confidered in
judging of the comparative Perfection of *Intervals*; which lies probably in the Relation of
the Two Terms of the Interval, *i. e.* of their
Vibrations to every Coincidence ; fo that it is
not altogether leffer Numbers, but this joined with
fomething elfe in the Form of the *Ratio,* which
how to exprefs fo as to make a complete Rule,
no Body, that I know, has yet found.

As to the *Concord*s of the preceeding *Table*
fome have taken this Method of comparing
them : They find the relative Number of Coincidences that each of them makes in a given
Time, thus, Find the leaft common Dividend
to all the Numbers that exprefs the Vibrations
of the Fundamental to one Coincidence ; take
this for a Number of Vibrations made in any
Time by a common *fundamental* Chord ; if
it

it is divided feverally by the Numbers whofe
common Dividend it is, *viz*. the Terms of
the feveral *Ratios* that exprefs the Vibrations of
the Fundamental to one Coincidence; the Quotes
are the relative Numbers of Coincidences made
in the fame Time by the feveral Concords;
thus, the common Dividend mentioned is 60,
and it is plain while the common Fundamental
makes 60 Vibrations, there are 60 Coincidences
of it with the *acute Octave*, and 30 Coincidences
with the *5th*, and fo on as in the *Table* annexed.

	Ratios		Coin.
8*ve*,	2 : 1		60
5th,	3 : 2		30
4th,	4 : 3		20
6th gr.	5 : 3		20
3d gr.	5 : 4		15
3d lefs.	6 : 5		12
6th lefs.	8 : 5		12

THE Preference in this
Method is according to
greater Number of Co-
incidences,   and where
that is equal the Prefe-
rence is to that *Interval*
whofe *acuteft* Term has
fewer Vibrations to one
Coincidence. And fo the
Order here is the fame as formerly determined;
but we are left to the fame Difficulties and Uncertainty as before; for this Rule refers all to the
Confideration of the Vibrations of the Fundamental to one Coincidence; and therefore of
Two Cafes that whofe leffer Term is leaft will
be preferable, whatever Difference there be of
the other Term, which is contrary to Experience.

Merfennus, in his *Book* I. of *Harmony*, *Art.*
1. of *Harmonick* Numbers, has a Propofition
which promifes an univerfal Character, for
diftinguifhing the Perfection of Intervals as to
the

the Agreement of their Extremes in *Tune :* The
Subftance of the whole *Art.* I fhall give you
briefly in the feveral *Propofitions* of it, becaufe
it may help to explain or confirm what I have
delivered; and then I fhall examine that particular
Propofition which refpects the Thing directly
before us; he tells us, That, 1*mo.* Every Sound
has as many Degrees of *Acutenefs* as it confifts
of Motions of the Air, *i.e.* as oft as the Tympan
of the Ear is ftruck by the Air in Motion. 'Tis
plain he means that the Degree of Acutenefs
depends on the Number of Vibrations of the
Air, and confequently of the fonorous Body,
accomplifhed in a given Time, agreeable to
what I have faid of it above, elfe I do not underftand the Senfe of the Propofition. 2*do.*
The Perception of *Concord* is nothing but the
comparing of Two or more different Motions,
which in the fame Time affect the auditory Nerve.
3*tio.* We cannot make a certain Judgment
of any *Confonance* until the Air be as oft ftruck
in the fame Time, by Two Chords, or other
Inftruments, as there are Unites in each Number, expreffing the *Ratio* of that *Concord :* For
Example, We cannot perceive a 5*th*, till 2 Vibrations of the one Chord, and 3 of the other are accomplifhed together, which Chords are in Length
as 3 to 2. 4*to.* The greater Agreement and
Pleafure of *Confonance* arifes from the more
frequent Union (or Coincidence) of Vibrations.
But, *obferve*, this is faid without determining
what this Frequency has refpect to; and
how incomplete a Rule it is, I think we have
already

already feen.   5_to._ That Number of Motions (or Vibrations) is the Caufe that the _arithmeti-cal_ Divifion of _Confonancies_ (or Intervals) has more agreeable Effects than the _harmonical_; but this cannot be undreftood till afterwards.   Now follows the _Propofition_ which is the 4_th_ in _Merfennus,_ but placed laft here, becaufe 'tis what I am particularly to examine.   6_to._ The more fimple   and _agreeable Confonancies_ are generated before the more _compound_ and _harfh._ Example. Let 1, 2, 3, be the Lengths of Three Chords, 1 : 2. is an _Octave,_   2 : 3 a 5_th_; and it is plain 1 : 3 is an _Octave_ and 5_th compounded,_ or a _Twelfth._   But the Vibrations of Chords are reciprocally   as   their Lengths,   therefore the Chord 2 vibrates once   while the   Chord 1 vibrates twice, and then exifts an _Octave;_ but the 12_th_ does not yet exift, becaufe the Chord 3 has not vibrated once,   nor the Chord 1 vibrat-ed thrice (which is neceffary to a 12_th;_) again for generating a 5_th,_ the Chord 2 muft vibrate thrice, and the   Chord 3 twice, which cannot be unlefs the Chord   1 in the fame Time vibrate 6 Times, and then the 12_th_ will be twice pro-duced, and the _Octave_ thrice,   as is manifeft; for the Chord 2 unites its Vibrations fooner with the Chord 1 than with the Chord 3, and they are fooner confonant than the Chord 1 or 2 with 3.   Whence many of the Myfteries of Harmony, _viz._ concerning the Preference of Concords and their Succeffion may be deduced, by the fagacious Practifer. Thus far _Merfennus;_ and _Kircher_ repeats his very Words.

But

But when we examine this Propofition by other Examples, it will not anfwer; and we are as far as ever from the univerfal Charadter fought. Take this Example, 2 : 3 : 6, the very fame Intervals with *Merfennus*'s Example, only here the *Octave* is betwixt the Two greateft Numbers, which was formerly betwixt the Two leffer; now here the Chord 2 unites every Third Vibration with every Second Vibration of the Chord 3, and then the 5*th* exifts; but alfo at every Third Vibration of the fame Chord 2 there is a Coincidence of every fingle Vibration of the Chord 6 (becaufe as 2 to 6 fo 1 to 3) and then doth the 12*th* exift, and alfo the *Octave*, becaufe at every fecond Vibration of the Chord 3, and every fingle Vibration of the Chord 6, there is an *Octave*; fo that in 3 Chords whofe Lengths are as 2 : 3 : 6, containing the *Octave* : 5*th* : 12*th*, all the Three are generated in the fame Time, *viz.* while the Chord 2 makes Three Vibrations; for when the Chord 3 has made Two, precifely then the 5*th* exifts; at the fame Time alfo the Chord 6 has made 1 Vibration, and then doth the 12*th* firft exift : But while the Chord 3 vibrates twice (*i. e.* while the Chord 2 vibrates thrice) the Chord 6 vibrates once, and not till then doth the *Octave* exift. From this Example 'tis plain the *Propofition* is not true in the Senfe in which *Merfennus* explains it, or at leaft, that I can underftand it in : It is true that taking the Series 1, 2, 3, 4, 5, 6, 8, and comparing every Three of them immediately next other in the Manner

of

of the preceeding Example, the Preference will be determined the same way as has been already done, *viz.* *Octave : 5th : 4th : 6th,* greater; 3*d* greater, 3*d* lesser, 6*th* lesser: But yet it will not hold of the very same Concords taken another way, as is made sufficiently plain in the last Example. Take this other, 6: 4: 3, containing a 5*th,* 4*th,* and *Octave* ; while the Chord 4 makes 3 Vibrations, the Chord 3 makes 4 Vibrations; and then there is a 4*th*: Also while the Chord 4 makes 3 Vibrations, the Chord 6 makes 2 Vibrations, and then there is a 5*th*: So that we have here a 5*th* and 4*th* generated in the same Time; tho' if you take the same *Concords* in another Order, thus, 2 :3 :4 ; then the Rule will hold. Take lastly this Example : Suppose Three Chords *a : b : c,* where *a :b,* is as 4 : 7, and *b : c* as 5 : 6, while *b* vibrates 4 Times, *a* vibrates 7 *Times,* and then that *Discord* 4 :7 exists; but the 3*d* lesser, 5 : 6, is not generated till *b* has vibrated 6 Times, so that the *Discord* 4: 7 is generated before the *Concord* 5 : 6. It will be so also if you take them thus; suppose *a : b* as 8 : 5, and *a : c* as 7 : 4, here the *Discord* exists whenever *a* has made 4 Vibrations, and the *Concord* not till *a* has made 5 Vibrations. Now if this were a just Rule, it would certainly answer in all Positions of the Intervals with respect to one another, which it does not; or there must be a certain Order wherein we ought to take them; but no one Rule with respect to the Order will make this Character answer to Experience in every Case.

Now

Now after all our Enquiry for an universal Character, whereby the Degrees of *Concord* may be determined, we are left to our Experience, and the Judgment of the Ear. We find indeed that where the radical Numbers which express any Interval are great, it is always grofs *Difcord*; and that all the *Concords* we know are expreft by fmall Numbers : And of all the *Concords* within an *Octave*, thefe are beft which are contained in fmalleft Numbers ; fo that we may eafily conclude that the frequent Coincidences of Vibrations is a neceffary Condition in the Production of *Harmony* ; but ftill we have no certain general Rules that afford an univerfal Character for judging of the Agreement of any Two Sounds, and of the Degree of their Approach to the Perfection of *Unifons*; which was the Thing we wanted in all this Enquiry : However, as to the Ufe of what we have already done, I think I may fay, that in a Philofophical Enquiry, all our Pains is not loft, if we can fecure our felves from falfe and incomplete Notions, and taking fuch for juft and true ; not that I fay 'tis a wrong Notion of the Degrees of *Concord*, to think they depend upon the more and lefs frequent uniting the Vibrations, and the Ear's being confequently more or lefs uniformly moved; for that this Mixture and Union of Motions is the true Principle, or at leaft a chief Ingredient of *Concord*, is fufficiently plain from Experience ; but I fpeak thus, becaufe there feems to be fomething in the Proportion of the Two Motions that we have not

yet

yet found, which ought to be known, in order
to our having an univerfal Rule, that will infallibly determine the Degrees of *Concord*, agreeable
to Senfe and Experience. And if any Body can
be fatisfied with the general Reafon and Principle of *Concord* and *Difcord* already found, they
may take this *Definition*, *viz. That* Concord
*is the Refult of a frequent Union and Coinci-
dence of the Vibrations of Two fonorous Bodies,
and confequently of the undulating Motions of
the Air, which being caufed by thefe Vibrations, are like and proportional to them; which
Coincidence the more frequent it is with refpect to the Number of Vibrations of both Bodies performed in the fame Time,* cæteris paribus, *the more perfect is that* Concord, *till the
Rarity of the Coincidence in refpect of one or
both the Motions become* Difcord.

I can find no better or more particular Account of this Matter among our modern Enquirers ; you have already heard *Merfennus*, and
I fhall give you Dr. *Holder*'s Definition in his
own Words, who has written chiefly on this One
Point, as the Title of his Book bears : Says he,
" *Confonancy* (the fame I call *Concord*) is the
" Paffage of feveral tunable Sounds through the
" Medium, frequently mixing and uniting in
" their undulated Motions caufed by the well
" proportioned commenfurate Vibrations of the
" fonorous Bodies, and confequently arriving
" fmooth and fweet and pleafant to the Ear.
" On the contrary, *Diffonancy* is from difpropor-
" tionate Motions of Sounds, not mixing, but
" jarring

" jarring and clashing as they pass, and arriving
" to the Ear harsh and grating and offen-
" five.' If the Dr. means by our Pleasure's being a Consequence of the frequent Mixture of
Motions, any other Thing than that we find
these Things so connected, I do not conceive
it; but however he understood this, he has applied his *Definition* to the Preference of *Concord* no further than these Five, 1 : 2, 2 : 3,
3 : 4, 5 : 4, 5 : 6. Yet after all I hope we shall,
in what follows, find other Considerations
to satisfie us, that we have discovered all the
true natural Principles of musical Pleasure, with
respect to the *Harmony* of the different Tunes
of Sound ; and I should have done with this
Part, but that there are some remarkable Phenomena, depending on the Things already explained, which are worth our Observation.

----

§ 2. *Explaining some remarkable Appearances
relating to this Subject, upon the preceeding
Grounds of* Concord.

I. IF a Sound is raised with any confiderable *Intenseness*, either by the human
Voice, or from any sonorous Body; and if there
is another sonorous Body near, whose *Tune* is
unison or *octave* above that Sound, this
Body will also sound its proper Note *unison* or
octave to the given Note, tho' nothing visibly
has touched it. The Experiment can be made
most sensibly with the Strings of a musical In-
                                          stru-

ftrument; for if a Sound is raifed *unifon* or *oEtave* below the Tune of any open String of the Inftrument, it will give its Sound diftinctly. And we might make a pleafant Experiment with a ftrong Voice finging near a well tuned Harpfichord. We find the fame *Phænomenon* by raifing Sound near a Bell, or any large Plate of fuch Metal as has a clear and free Sound, or a large chryftal drinking Glafs. Now our *Philofophers* make Ufe of the Hypothefis already laid down to explain this furprizing Appearance; they tell us, That, for Example, when one String is ftruck, and the Air put in Motion, every other String within the Reach of that Motion receives fome Impreffion from it; but each String can move only with a certain determinate Velocity of Recourfes in vibrating, becaufe all the Vibrations from the greateft to the leaft are equidiurnal ; again, all *Unifons* proceed from equal or equidiurnal Vibrations, and other *Concords* from other Proportions, which as they are the Caufe of a more perfect Mixture and Agreement of Motion, *that is*, of the undulated Air, fo much better is that *Concord* and nearer to *Unifon* : Now the *unifon* String keeping an exact equal Courfe with the founded String, becaufe it has the fame Meafure of Vibrations, has its Motion continued and improven till it become fenfible and give a diftinct Sound; and other concording Strings have their Motions propagated in different Degrees, according to the Commenfuratenefs of their Vibrations with thefe of the founded String ; the

OEtave

Octave moſt ſenſibly, then the 5th; but after
this the croſſing of the Motions hinders any
ſuch Effect : And they illuſtrate it to us in this
Manner ; ſuppoſe a Pendulum ſet a moving, the
Motion may be continued and augmented, by
making frequent light Impulſes, as by blowing
upon it, when the Vibration is juſt finiſhed and
the Pendulum ready to return; but if it is
touched before that, or by any croſs Motion,
and this done frequently, the Motion will be
ſo interrupted as to ceaſe altogether; ſo of Two
uniſon Strings, if the one is forcibly ſtruck it
communicates Motion by the Air, to the o-
ther ; and being equidiurnal in their Vibrations, they finiſh them preciſely together ; and
the Motion of that other is improven by the
frequent Impulſes received from the Vibrations
of the Firſt, becauſe they are given preciſely
when that other Chord has finiſhed its Vibrations,
and is ready to *return*; but if the Two Chords
are unequal in Duration, there will be a croſſing
of Motions leſs or more, according to the Proportion of that Inequality ; and in ſome Caſes
the Motion of the untouched String is ſo checked as never to be ſenſible, or at leaſt to give
any Sound; and in Fact we know, that in no
Caſe is this *Phænomenon* to be found but the
Uniſon, Octave and *Fifth*; moſt ſenſibly in the
Firſt, and gradually leſs in the other Two,
which are alſo limited to this Condition, that
the *graver* will make the *acuter* Sound, but not
contrarily. And as this is a tolerable Explication of the Matter, it confirms in a great Degree the
                                        Truth

Truth of the Equidiurnity of the Vibrations of the same Chord, and the Proportion of the Lengths and Duration of the Vibrations ; for we know that the Sound of the untouched Chord is weaker than that of the other, and its Vibrations confequently lefs ; now if they were not equidiurnal, and if the Proportion mentioned were not alfo true, we fhould not have fo good a Reafon of the *Phænomenon*, which joyned with the fenfible Identity of the *Tune*, is fufficient without other Demonftrations to make it highly probable that the Vibrations are all performed in equal Time, and that the Duration of a fingle Vibration of the one is to that of the other directly, or the Number of Vibrations in a given Time reciprocally as the Lengths of the Chords (*cæteris paribus.*)

II. I cannot omit to mention in this Place, how the Gentlemen of the Academy of Sciences in *France* apply this Hypothefis of *harmonick Motion*, for explaining the ftrange Recovery of one who has been bitten by the *Tarantula*, the Effect of which is a Lethargy and Stupifying of the Senfes; I fhall not here repeat the whole Story, but in fhort, the Recovery is by Means of *Mufick*; 'tis. not every Kind that will recover the fame Perfon, nor the fame Kind every Perfon; but having tried a great many various Meafures and Combinations of *Tune* and *Time*, they hit at random on the Cure, which excites Motion in the Patient by Degrees, till he is recovered. To account for this, thefe *Philofophers* tell us, that there is a certain Aptnefs

in

in thefe particular Motions, to give Motion to
the Nerves of that Perfon (for they fuppofe
the Difeafe lies all there) in their prefent Circumftances, as one String communicates Motion
to another, which neither a greater nor leffer,
nor any other Combination can do; being excited to Motion the Senfes return gradually.

III. THERE are other Inftances of this wonderful
Power, and, if I may call it fo, fympathetick
Virtue in fonorous Motions; I have felt a very
fenfible tremulous Motion in fome Parts of my
Body when near a bafs Violin, upon the founding of certain Notes ftrongly ftruck, tho' the Sound
of a Cannon would not produce fuch an Effect.
And from all our Obfervations we are affured that
it is not a great or ftrong Motion in the Parts of
one Body that is capable to produce Motion by
this Kind of Communication in the Parts of
another, but it depends on a certain inexpref-
fible Likenefs and Congruity of Motions; whereof take this one Example more, which is not
lefs furprifing than the reft: If a Man raifes his
Voice *unifon* to the Tune of a drinking Glafs,
and continue to blow for fome time in it with
a very intenfe or ftrong Voice, he fhall not only
make the Glafs found, but at laft break it;
whereas a Motion much ftronger, if it is out of
Tune to the Glafs, will never make it found and
far lefs break it (I have known perfons to whom
this Experiment fucceeded.) The Reafon of this
feems very probably to be, that when the Glafs
founds, its Parts are put into a vibratory or
tremulous Motion, which being continued long
by

by a ftrong Voice, their Cohefion is quite broken;
but fuppofe another Voice much ftronger, yet
if 'tis out of Tune, there will be fuch a croffing
of Motions that prevents both the Sound of
the Glafs and the breaking of it. It is a noted
Experiment, that by preffing one's Finger upon
the Brim of a Glafs, and fo moving it quickly
round, it will found; and to demonftrate that
this is not effected without a very fwift Motion
of the infenfible Parts of the Glafs, we need
but fill fome Liquor into it, and then repeating
the Experiment, we fhall have the Liquor put
gradually into a greater Motion, till the Glafs
found very diftinctly, and continuing it with a
brisk Motion, the Liquor will be put into a
very Ferment. The Confideration of this may
perhaps make the Explication of the laft Cafe
more reafonable.

IV. D O C T O R *Holder*, to confirm his
general Reafon of *Confonancy* alledges fome Experiments that happened to himfelf, particularly,
" fays he, " Being in an arched founding Room
" near a fhrill Bell of a Houfe-clock, when the A-
" larm ftruck I whiftled to it, which I did with
" Eafe in the fame Tune with the Bell; but
" endeavouring to whiftle a Note higher or lower,
" the Sound of the Bell and its crofs Motions
" were fo predominant, that my Breath and
" Lips were checked, fo that I could not
" whiftle at all, nor make any Sound of it in
" that difcording Tune. After I founded a
" fhrill whiftling Pipe, which was out of Tune
" to the Bell, and their Motions fo clafhed
                                         that

" that they feemed to found like fwitching one
" another in the Air." To confirm this of the
Doctor's, there is a common Experiment, that
if Two Sounds, fuppofe the Notes of a
mufical Inftrument, are brought to unifon
Octave or 5*th*, and then one of them raifed
or depreffed a very little, there will be a
Clafhing of the Two Sounds, like a Beating,
as if they ftrove together; and this will continue
till they are reftored to exact *Concord,* or carried
a little further from it, for then alfo this Beating
will ceafe, tho' the *Difcord* will perhaps increafe. Now if we confider that *Concords* are
fuch a Mixture and Agreement of Sounds that
the compound feems not to partake more of
the one Simple than of the other, but they are
fo evenly united that the one does not prevail
over the other fo as to be more obfervable;
We fee that this ftriving, in which we find an
alternate prevailing of either Sound, ought naturally to happen when they are neareft to their
moft perfect Agreement, but when they are
farther removed, the one has gained too much
upon the other not to make that one moft
obfervable. All thefe Things ferve to fhow
us how neceffary an Ingredient in the Caufe
of *Concord* the Union and Conicidence of the
Motions is, and I fhall beg a little more of your
Patience to confider the following Illuftration.

I т is not an unpleafant Entertainment to con-
template the beautiful Uniformity of Nature in
her feveral Productions ; the Refemblance difcovered among Things, if it don't let us farther
                                                    into

into the Knowledge of the Effence and original
Reafon of them, it does at leaft increafe our
Knowledge of the common Laws of Nature;
and we are helped to explain and illuftrate one
Thing by another. To the Matter in Hand,
we may compare *Sight* and *Hearing*, and to
manage the Comparifon to greateft Advantage,
let us confider, *Senfation* is the fame Thing
with refpect to the Mind that perceives, whatever be the Inftrument of Senfe, *i. e.* without
diftinguifhing the external Senfe (as *Philofophers* fpeak) the internal is the fame, which
is properly *Senfation*, as this implies a certain
Mode of the Mind caufed by the Admittance
(or, with Mr. *Lock*, the actual Entrance) of an
Idea into the Underftanding by the Senfes ;
which is a Definition plainly unconfin'd to one
or other of the Five Ways whereby Ideas enter, when the Mind is faid to perceive by the
Senfes ; hence we have good Reafon to think,
that it is not improper to compare one Senfe
with another, as Seeing and Hearing ; for tho'
their Objects are different, and the Means whereby they make their Impreffion on the Mind be
fuited to them, by which Senfations very diftinct
are produced ; yet they may be equally agreeable in their Kind, and have fome common Principle in both Cafes neceffary to that Agreeable-
nefs. We believe that Nature works by the
moft fimple and uniform Ways; accordingly we
find by Experience that fimple Ideas have a much
eafier Accefs than compound ; and the more
Difficulty the lefs Pleafure ; yet the more eafy

are

are not always the moſt agreeable ; for as we
have no Pleaſure in what falls confuſedly on the
Senſes, and wearies the Mind with the manifold and perplex'd Relations of its Parts; neither does that afford much Pleaſure that is too
eaſily perceived, at leaſt we are ſoon cloyed with
it ; but a middle betwixt theſe Extremes is beſt.
Again, we know that Variety entertains, both
of ſimple Ideas and theſe variouſly connected
and joyned together . And becauſe the Mind is
beſt pleaſed with Order, Uniformity, and the diſtinct Relation of its Ideas, the compound Idea
ought to have its Parts uniform and regularly
connected, and their Relations ſo diſtinct that
the Mind may perceive them without Perplexity : In ſhort, when the Cauſe is moſt uniform, and involves not too great Multiplicity in
the Senſation, the Idea will be entertained with
the more Pleaſure; hence it is that a very intricate Figure, perplex'd with many Lines, and
theſe not very regular, nor their *Ratios* diſtinct, does not pleaſe the Eye ſo well as a Figure
of fewer Lines and in a more diſtinct Relation.

  But the Compariſon muſt run between the
Eye and Ear in Perceptions that have ſomething common : *Motion* is the Object of Sight
very properly ; and tho' it be not ſo of Hearing
immediately ; yet Sound being the immediate
Product of Motion, we may conclude that if
the Eye is gratify'd with the Uniformity of
Motion, for the ſame Reaſon (whatever it be
in its ſelf) will the Ear be with Uniformity in
                                        Sounds ,

Sounds, which ow themſelves to Motion, and
are in a Manner nothing elſe but Motion for-
cing on us a Perception of its Exiſtence by o-
ther Organs than the Eye, and therefore makes
that different Idea we call *Sound.* In *Seeing* the
Thing is plain ; for if Two Motions are at
once in our View, where the Senſe attends to
nothing but the Motion, then, as the Relation
of the Velocities is more diſtinct, we compare
the Motions, and view them with the greater
Pleaſure ; but were the Relation leſs ſenſible,
there could but little Pleaſure ariſe from theſe
Ideas : Thus, were it obvious that the one Motion were to the other as 2 : 1 or 3 : 2 uniformly and conſtantly, we could look on them with
Delight ; but were the *Ratio* leſs perceiveable
as 13 : 7; or the one being uniform Motion,
and the other irregularly accelerate ; the Mind
would weary in the Compariſon, and perhaps
never reach it, therefore find no Pleaſure : I
do not ſay that in many Caſes, which might be
viewed with Satisfaction, we could be determi-
nately ſure what were the *Ratio* of Velocity ;
but from Experience we know, that the more
commenſurable the Extremes are to one another,
it is the more agreeable, becauſe diſtinct ;
therefore it is certain we perceive the one
more than the other: And in many Caſes there
would be a Pain in viewing ſuch Objects, the
Irregularity of the Motion creating a Giddineſs
in the Brain, while we endeavour to entertain
both the Motions ; and by Experience we
                                    know

know, that to follow very quick Motions with the Eye, especially if circular, this is constantly the Effect. It is the same Way in Hearing, some simple Sounds are painful and harsh, because the Quickness of the Vibrations bears no Proportion to the Organs of Sense, which is necessary to all agreeable Sensation. But we have a particular Example that comes nearer the Purpose.

Let us view the Motion of Two Pendulums; if they are of equal Length, and let fall from equal Height they describe equal Arches; their Motions continue equal Time, and their Vibrations begin always together: The Motions of these Two Pendulums are like and equal, so that if we suppose the Eye to follow the one, and describe an equal Arch with it (which would be if the visual Ray in every Point of the Arch were perpendicular to the pendulum Chord) then that one would always eclipse the other, and the Eye perceive but one Motion; and suppose the Eye at a considerable Distance, it would not perceive Two different Motions, tho' it self moved not; consequently there could be no jarring of these Ideas: This is exactly the Case of Two Chords every way the same, and equally impelled to Motion; for their Vibrations give the Parts of the Air alike and equal Motion, so that the Ear is always struck equally and at the same Time, hence we perceive but one simple Sound; and with respect to the Effect it is no more a compound Idea than Two Bottles of Water from the same Fountain make

a

a compound Liquor, which only increase the Quantity; as the foresaid Unisons only fill the Ear with a greater Sound increasing the Intenseness.

I<small>F</small> in the same Case we suppose the Eye so situated as to see distinctly the Motion of both Pendulums; or suppose the Pendulums fall from different Heights, then this Variety would afford a greater Pleasure; for the Mind perceives a Difference, but a very distinct Relation; because we see the Vibrations begin always at the same Time; and this explains the greater Pleasure we have in *Unisons* which proceed from Chords differing in some Circumstances, as if the one were more intense or of a different Species; in which we perceive the Unity of Acuteness, but these other different Circumstances make them perceiveably distinct simple Sounds, which heightens the Pleasure. If we carry this Comparison further, we'll find, that if Two Pendulums of unequal Length be let fall together from similar Points of their Arch, they begin not every Vibration together, but they will coincide more or less frequently, according to a certain Proportion of their Lengths, which is always reciprocally subduplicate; and tho' this is quite another Proportion than that of simple Chords which are in reciprocal simple Proportion of their Number of Vibrations to every Coincidence, yet the Illustration drawn from this Comparison stands good, because we consider only the *Ratios* of the Number of Vibrations to each Coincidence in both Cases; and in this we find it true in general, that the

more

more frequently the Vibrations coincide, the Profpect is the more agreeable; but it is alfo according
to the Number of Vibrations of both Pendulums in the fame Time, in fo much that the
fameNumbers which make lefs or more Concord
in Sound, will alfo give a greater or lefs pleafant
Profpect, if the Pendulums are fo proportioned,
according to the known Laws of their Motion;
and if the Pendulums feldom or never coincide, or
begin their Vibrations together, there will be
fuch a thwarting of the Images as cannot
mifs to offend the Sight.

C H A P. IV.

Containing the Harmonical Arithmetick.

HERE I propofe to explain as much
of the *Theory* of Numbers as is neceffary to be known, for making and underftanding the Comparifons of *mufical Intervals,* which are expreft by Numbers; in order to our
finding their mutual Relations, Compofitions and
Refolutions But I muft premife TwoThings. *Firft;*
That I fuppofe the Reader acquainted with the
more general and common Properties and Operations of Numbers; fo that I fhall but barely propofe
what of thefe I have Ufe for, without any Demonftration, and demonftrate Things that are
lefs

lefs common. *Second.* That I confine my felf
to the principal and more neceffary Things;
leaving a Thoufand Speculations that may be
made, as lefs ufeful to my Defign, and alfo becaufe thefe will be eafily underftood when you
meet with them, if the fundamental Things
here explained be well underftood.

§ 1. *Definitions.*

I. THERE is a twofold *Comparifon* of
Numbers, in both of which we diftinguifh an *Antecedent* or Number compared, and
Confequent or Number to which the other is
compared. By the *Firft* we find how much
they differ, or by how many Units the *Antecedent* exceeds or comes fhort of the *Confequent;*
which Difference is called the *arithmetical
Ratio* (or *Exponent* of the *arithmetical Relation* or *Habitude*) of thefe Two Numbers:
So if 5 and 7 are compared, their *arithmetical
Ratio* is 2; and all Numbers that have the
fame Difference, whatever they are themfelves, are in the fame *arithmetical Habitude* to one another. By the *Second* Comparifon we find how oft or how many Times the
Antecedent contains (if greateft) or is contained
(if leaft) in the other; and this Number is called the *geometrical Ratio* (or *Exponent* of the
geometrical Relation) of the Numbers compared;

red; fo compare 12 to 4, the *Ratio* is 3, fignifying that 12 contains 4, or that 4 is contained in 12, thrice.

THE *geometrical Ratio* thus conceived is always the *Quote* of the greater divided by the leffer : But *obferve* when the leffer is *antecedent* to the greater, the Senfe of the Comparifon is alfo this, *viz.* To find what Part or Parts of the greater that leffer is equal to ; and according to this Senfe the *geometrical Ratio* of Two Numbers is made univerfally the *Quote* of the *Antecedent* divided by the *Confequent,* and is expreft by fetting the *Antecedent* over the *Confequent* Fraction-wife ; fo that if the *Antecedent* is greateft, the *Ratio* is an improper Fraction, equal to fome whole or mix'd Number, and fignifies that the *Antecedent* contains the *Confequent* as many Times, and Parts of a Time, as that *Quote* contains Units and Parts of an Unit. *Example.* The *Ratio* of 12 to 4 is $\frac{12}{4}$ equal to 3 (for 12 contains 4 thrice.) The *Ratio* of 18 to 7 is $\frac{18}{7}$ equal to $2\frac{4}{7}$, fignifying that 18 contains 7 Two Times and $\frac{4}{7}$ Parts of a Time, *i. e.* $\frac{4}{7}$ Parts of 7 ; which is plainly this, that 18 contains 2 Times 7, and 4 over. But if the *Antecedent* is leaft, the *Ratio* is a proper Fraction, fignifying that the *Antecedent* is fuch a Part of the *Confequent;* fo the *Ratio* of 7 to 9 is $\frac{7}{9}$, *i. e.* that 7 is $\frac{7}{9}$ Parts of 9.

IN what follows I fhall take the *geometrical Ratio* of Numbers both ways, as it happens to be moft convenient.

II.

II. A N Equality of *Ratios* conſtitutes *Proportion*, which is *arithmetical* or *geometrical* as the *Ratio* is. A *Ratio* exiſts betwixt Two Terms, but *Proportion* requires at leaſt Three; ſo theſe 1, 2, 3, are in *arithmetical Proportion*, or theſe, 2, 5, 8, becauſe there is the ſame Difference betwixt the Numbers compared, which are 1 to 2, and 2 to 3, or 2 to 5, and 5 to 8. *Again* theſe are in *geometrical Proportion*, 2, 4, 8, or 9, 3, 1, becauſe as 2 is a Haſf of 4, ſo is 4 of 8, alſo as 9 is triple of 3 ſo is 3 of 1.

OBSERVE, 1*mo.* In all *Proportion*, as there are at leaſt Two Couple of Terms, ſo the Compariſon muſt run alike in both, *i. e.* if it is ſrom the leſſer to the greater, or contrary, in the one Couple, it muſt be ſo in the other alſo; *thus* in 2, 6, 9 the Proportion runs, as 2 to 6 ſo is 6 to 9, or as 9 to 6 ſo 6 to 2.

2*do.* IF three proportional Numbers are right diſpoſed, it will always be, as the 1*ſt* to the 2*d*, ſo the 2*d* to 3*d*, as above; but 4 Numbers are in Proportion when the 1*ſt* is to the 2*d* as the 3*d* to the 4*th*, without conſidering the *Ratio* of the 2*d* and 3*d*; as here 2 : 4 : 3 : 6; for in a proper Senſe *Proportion* is the Equality of the *Ratios* of Two or more Couples of Numbers, whether they have any common Term or not; and ſo, ſtrictly, there muſt be Four Terms to make *Proportion*, tho' there need be but Three different Numbers.

III. From the laſt Thing explained we have a Diſtinction of *continued* and *interrupted Pro-*

portion Continued *Proportion* is when in a Series
of Numbers there is the same *Ratio* of every
Term to the next, as of the 1*st* to the 2*d*; as
here 1 : 2 : 3 : 4 : 5, which is *arithmetical*
and 1, 2, 4, 8, 16, which is *geometrical.*
Interrupted is when betwixt any Two Terms
of the Series there is a different *Ratio* from
that of the rest; as 2 : 5 : 6 : 9, *arithmetical,*
where 2 is to 5 as 6 : 9 (*i. e.* differing by 3,)
but not so 5 and 6, or 2, 4, 3, 6; *geometrical,*
where 2 is to 4 as 3 to 6 (*i. e.* a *Half,*) but not
so 4 to 3; and *observe* that of 4 Terms, if there
is any Interruption of the *Ratio* it must be betwixt
the 2*d* and 3*d*, else these 4 are not *proportional.*

IV. Out of these Two *Proportions* arises a
Third Kind, which we call *harmonical Pro-*
portion, thus constituted; of Three Numbers, if
the 1*st* be to the 3*d* in *geometrical Proportion,*
as the Difference of the 1*st* and 2*d* to the
Difference of the 2*d* and 3*d*, these Three Numbers are in *harmonical Proportion. Example.*
2 : 3 : 6 are *harmonical*, because 2 : 6 ::
1 : 3 are *geometrical.* And Four Numbers are
harmonical, when the 1*st* is to the 4*th*, as the
Difference of the 1*st* and 2*d* to the Difference
of the 3*d* and 4*th*, as here 24 : 16 : 12 : 9
are *harmonical*, because 24 : 9 :: 8 : 3 are
geometrical.

AGAIN, of 4 or more Numbers, if every Three
immediate Terms are *harmonical*, the Whole
is a Series of *continual harmonical Proportionals*
as 30 : 20 : 15 : 12 : 10. or if every 4 immediately next are *harmonical*, 'tis also a *continued*
Series

Series, but of another Species, as 3, 4, 6, 9 18, 36.

How this came by the Name of *harmonical Proportion* fhall be fhewn afterwards ; and here I fhall explain the fundamental Properties of this Kind, having firft propofed as much of the Doctrine of *arithmetical* and *geometrical Proportion* as is neceffary for the Explanation of the other.

§ 2. *Of* Arithmetical *and* Geometrical Proportion.

THEOREM I. If any Number is given as the Firft of a Series of Proportionals, and alfo the common *Ratio*, the Series may be continued thus : 1*mo.* In *arithmetical Proportion* by adding the *Ratio* (or common Difference) to the 1*ft* Term given, and then to the Sum ; and fo on to every fucceeding Sum ; thefe feveral Sums are the Terms fought in an *increafing Series,* which may be continued *in infinitum.* But to make a *decreafing Series,* fubftract the *Ratio* from the Firft Term, and from every fucceeding Remainder ; the feveral Remainders are the Terms fought. But 'tis plain this Series has Limits, and cannot defcend *in infinitum. Example.* Given 3 for the 1*ft* Term of an increafing Series, and 2 the *arithmetical Ratio,* or common Difference ; the Series is 3, 5, 7, 9, &c. Or, given 8 the 1*ft* Term, and

and 3 the common Difference in a decreasing
Series, it is 8, 5, 2, and can go no further in
positive Numbers. 2*do.* In *geometrical Proportion*, by multiplying the given Term into the
Ratio (which I take here for the Quote of
the greater Term divided by the lesser) and
that Product again by the *Ratio,* and so on
every succeeding Product by the *Ratio*; the
several Products make the Series sought increasing, but for a decreasing Series divide. *Example.* Given 2 the 1*st* Term, and 3 the *Ratio*
for an increasing Series it is 2 : 6 : 18, 54, 162
&c. Or, given 24 the 1*st* Term and the *Ratio* 2,
the decreasing Series is 24 : 12 : 6 : 3. 1½, &c. It
is plain a *geometrical Series* may increase or
decrease *in infinitum* in positive Numbers.

THEOREM II. If Three Numbers are in
arithmetical or *geometrical Proportion,* the
Sum of the Extremes in the first, and the *Product* in the second Case, is equal to double the
middle Term in the 1*st,* and to the Square of
the middle Term in the second Case. *Example.*
3 : 7 : 11 *arithmetical,* the Sum of the Extremes 3 and 11 is equal to twice 7, *viz.* 14.
And in these, 4 : 6 : 9 *geometrical,* the *Product*
of 4 and 9, *viz.* 36, is equal to the Square of
6, or 6 Times 6.

COROLLARY. Hence the Rule for finding
a Mean proportional, either *arithmetical* or
geometrical, betwixt Two given Numbers is
very obvious, *viz.* Half the Sum of the Two
given Numbers is an *arithmetical* Mean, and
the Square Root of their Product is a *geomtrical*
Mean. THEOR.

THEOREM III. If Four Numbers are in *Proportion arithmetical* or *geometrical*, whether *continued* or *interrupted*, the Sum of the Extremes in the firſt Caſe, and *Product* in the 2*d*, is equal to the Sum of the middle Terms in the 1*ſt* and the Product in the 2*d* Caſe. *Example*. In theſe, 2 : 3 : 4 : 5 *arithmetical*, the Sum of 2 and 5 is equal to the Sum of 3 and 4; and theſe *geometrical* 2 : 5 : 4 : 10. the *Product* of 2 and 10 is equal to that of 5 and 4, *viz*. 20.

COROLLARY. If Four Numbers repreſented thus, *a* : *b* :: *c* : *d*, are *proportional* either *arithmetically* or *geometrically*, comparing *a* to *b* and *c* to *d* ; they will alſo be *proportional* taken *inverſely*, thus, *d* : *c* :: *b* : *a*, or *alternately* thus, *a* : *c* :: *b* : *d*, or *inverſely* and *alternately* thus, *d* : *b* :: *c* : *a*. The *reaſon* is obvious, becauſe in all theſe Forms the Extremes and the middle Terms are the ſame, whoſe Sums, if they are *arithmetical*, or *Products* if *geometrical*, being equal, is a Sign of their Proportionality by this *Theorem*.

THEOREM IV. In a Series of *continued Proportionals*, *arithmetical* or *geometrical*, the Two Extremes with the middle Term, or the Extremes with any Two middle Terms at equal Diſtance from them, are alſo *proportional*. *Example*. 2, 3, 4, 5, 6, 7, 8 *arithmetical*, here 2, 5, 8, are *arithmetically proportional*, alſo 2, 4, 6, 8, or 2 : 3 : 7 : 8. *Again* in this *geometrical* Series, 2 : 4 : 8 : 16 : 32 :

64 : 128, thefe are *geometrically proportional*
2 : 16, 128, or 2 : 8, 32 : 128.

THEOREM V. If Two Numbers in any
geometrical Ratio are added to, or fubftracted
from other Two in the fame *Ratio* (the lefs
with the lefs and greater with the greater) the
Sums or *Differences* are in the fame *Ratio. Example.* 6 : 3 :: 10 : 5 are *proportional*, the common *Ratio* being 2, and 6 added to 10 makes
16, as 3 to 5 makes 8, and 16 to 8 are in
the fame *Ratio* as 6 to 3 or 10 to 5; and again
16 being to 8 as 6 to 3, their Differences 10
and 5 are in the fame *Ratio.*

THE Reverfe of this *Propofition* is true, *viz.*
That if to or from any Two Numbers be added
or fubftracted other Two, then, if the Sums or
Differences are in the fame *geometrical Ratio*
of the Firft Two, the Numbers added or fubftracted are in the fame *Ratio.*

COROLLARY. If any Two given Numbers
are equally multiplied or divided, *i. e.* multiplied or divided by the fame Number, the
Two *Products* or *Quotes* are in the fame *Ratio*
with the given Numbers, *i. e.* are proportional
with them. *Example.* 3 and 5 multiplied each
by 7 produce 21 and 35, and thefe are proportional 3 : 5, 21 : 35. *Again* 24 and 16, divided each by 8 *quote* 3 and 2 and thefe are proportional 24 : 16, 3 : 2.

IT follows alfo that if every Term of any
continued Series is equally multiplied or divided
it is ftill a *continued* Series in the fame *Ratio.*

THEOREM.

THEOREM VI. If Two Numbers in any *arithmetical Ratio* be added to other Two in the same *Ratio* (the lefs to the lefs and greater to the greater) the *Sums* are in a doub e *Ratio*, *i. e.* their *Difference* is double that of the refpective Parts added; fo, if to thefe 3 : 5, you add thefe 7 : 9 the Sums are 10, 14 whofe Difference 4 is double the Difference of 3 : 5 or 7 : 9. And if to this Sum you add other Two in the fame *Ratio*, the Difference of the laft Sum will be triple the Difference of the Firft Two, and fo on.

OBSERVE. If Two Numbers in any *arithmetical Ratio* are fubftracted from other Two in the fame *Ratio* (the lefs from the lefs, *&c.*) the *arithmetical Ratio* of the Remainders is o, fo from 7 : 9 take 3 : 5 the Remainders are 4, 4.

COROLLARY. If Two Numbers in any *arithmetical Ratio* be both multiplied by the fameNumber, the *Difference* of the *Products* fhall contain the Firft *Difference*, as oft as the Multiplier contains Unity; fo 3, 5 multiplied by 4 produce 12, 20, whofe Difference 8 is equal to 4 Times 2 (the Difference of 3 and 5) and fo if any *continued arithmetical* Series has each Term multiplied by the fame Number, the Products will make a *continued* Series with a Difference containing the former Difference as oft as the Multiplier contains Unity. But if divided, the Difference of the Quotes will be fuch a Part of the Firft Difference as the Divifor denominates.

THEOREM.

THEOREM VII. If Two Numbers in any *Ratio arithmetical* or *geometrical*, be added to, or multiplied by other Two in any other *Ratio* of the same Kind (the lesser by the lesser, and the greater by the greater) the *Sums* in the one Case and *Products* in the other are in a *Ratio* which is the Sum or Product of the *Ratios* of the Numbers added, or multiplied : An *Example* will explain it, Let 2 : 4 and 3 : 9 be added in the Manner mentioned, the Sums are 5, 13, whose *arithmetical Ratio* or Difference is 8 the Sum of 2 and 6 the Differences of the Numbers given; or if they are multiplied, *viz.* 2 by 3, and 4 by 9, the Products 6 and 36 are in the *geometrical Ratio* of 6, equal to the Product of 2 and 3 the *Ratios* of the given Numbers.

THEOREM VIII. If any Two Numbers are multiplied by same Number, and the Products taken for the Extremes of a Series, they will admit of as many middle Terms as the Multiplier contains Units less one ; and the whole Series will be in the *arithmetical Ratio* of the First Numbers ; so let 3 and 7 be multiplied by 4 the Products are 12 and 28 (in the same *geometrical Ratio* as 3 and 7 by *Corollary* to *Theorem* 5*th*) and their *arithmetical Ratio* or Difference 16, is 4 Times as great as that of 3 and 7, which is 4 (by *Corol.* to *Theor.* 6.) and therefore they are capable of 3 such middle Terms as that the common Difference of the whole Series shall be 4; the Series is 12 : 16,

20 : 24 : 28. *Corollary.* Hence we have a So-
lution to this *Problem.*

PROBLEM I. To find an *arithmetical
Series,* of a given Number of Terms, whofe
Extremes fhall be in the *geometrical Ratio,* and
the intermediate Terms in the *arithmetical
Ratio* of Two given Numbers; the *Rule* is;
Multiply the given Numbers by the Number of
Terms lefs 1, and then fill up the middle
Terms by the given *Ratio. Example.* Let 3
to 5 be given for the *Ratio* of the Extremes,
and 10 for the Number of Terms; I multiply
3 and 5 by 9, which produces 27 and 45, and
the Series is 27, 29, 31, 33, 35, 37, 39, 41,
43, 45.

LET us now compare the *arithmetical* and
geometrical Proportions together.

THEOREM IX. If there is a Series of Numbers in continued *arithmetical Proportion,*
then the *geometrical Ratios* of each Term to
the next muft necefsarily differ; and from the
leaft Extreme to the greateft, thefe *Ratios* ftill
increafe ; but from the greateft they decreafe,
comparing always the lefler to the greater; but
contrarily if we compare the greater to the lefler,
Example. In this *arithmetical Series* 1, 2, 3,
4, 5, 6. the *geometrical Ratios* are $\frac{1}{2}$, $\frac{2}{3}$, $\frac{3}{4}$, $\frac{4}{5}$, $\frac{5}{6}$,
increafing from $\frac{1}{2}$, and confequently decreafing
from $\frac{5}{6}$. *Again,* if we take a *continued geometrical Series,* the *arithmetical Ratios* or Diffe-
rencesincre afe from the leaft Extreme to the
greateft, and contrarily from the greateft to the
leaft. *Example.* 1, 2, 4, 8, 16, the *arithmetical
Ratios* are 1, 2, 4 8. COROL-

COROLLARY. It is plain, that if an *arithmetical Mean* is put betwixt Two Numbers, the *geometrical Ratios* betwixt that middle Term and the Extremes are unequal ; and that of the leſſer Extreme to the middle Term is leſs than that of the ſame middle Term to the other Extreme. *Example.* 2, 4, 6 the two *geometrical Ratios* are $\frac{2}{4}$ and $\frac{4}{6}$ comparing the leſſer Number to the greater ; but it is contrary if we compare the greater to the leſſer.

---

§ 3. *Of* Harmonical Proportion.

THEOREM X. If Three or Four Numbers in *harmonical Proportion* are multiplied or divided by any the ſame Number, the *Products* or *Quotes* will alſo be in *harmonical Proportion* ; becauſe as the Products or Quotes made of the Extremes are in the ſame *Ratio* of the Extremes, ſo the Differences of the Products of the intermediate Terms, tho' they are greater or leſſer than the Differences of theſe Terms, yet they are proportionally ſo, being equally multiplied or divided. *Example.* If 6, 8, 12, which are *harmonical*, be divided by 2, the Quotes are 3, 4, 6, which are alſo *harmonical* ; and reciprocally, ſince 3, 4, 6, are *harmonical*, their Products by 2, *viz.* 6, 8, 12 are *harmonical*.

THEOREM.

Theorem XI. If double the *Product* of any Two Numbers be divided by their *Sum*, the *Quote* is an *harmonical Mean* betwixt them. *Example*. Let 3 and 6 be given for the Extremes to find an *harmonical Mean*, their Product is 18, which doubled is 36; this divided by 9 (the *Sum* of 3 and 6) quotes 4, and these Three are in *harmonical Proportion, viz.* 3 : 4 : 6.

To them that have the least Knowledge of *Algebra*, the following *Demonstration* will be plain; suppose any Two Numbers *a* and *b*, and *a* the greater, let the *harmonical Mean* sought be *x*; from the Definition of *harmonical* Proportion, we have this true in *geometrical* Proportion, *viz.* $a : b :: a\text{-}x : x\text{-}b$. And by *Theorem* 3d, $ax\text{-}ab = ab\text{-}xb$: Then, $ax + bx = 2ab$; and lastly, $x = \frac{2ab}{a+b}$ *W. W. D.*

Theorem XII. Take any Two Numbers in Order, and call the one the First Term, and the other the Second; if you multiply them together, and divide the Product by the Number that remains, after the Second is subtracted from double the First, the Quote is a Third in *harmonical* Proportion, to be taken in the same Order. *Example*, Take 3 : 4 their Product is 12, which being divided by 2 (the Remainder after 4 is taken from 6 the double of the First) the Quote is 6, the Third *harmonical* Term sought: Or reversely, take 6, 4, their Product is 24, which divided by 8 (the Difference of 4 and 12) quotes 3, the Third Term sought.

De-

DEMONSTRATION. Take a and b known Numbers, and a the greatest; let x be the Third Term sought, less than b; then, since these are *harmonical, viz. a, b, x*, these are *geometrical, viz. a : x :: a-b : b-x* (by *Definition* 4. § 1. of this *Chapter*) then, taking the Products of the Extremes and Means, we have $ab-ax=ax-xb$; and $ab=2ax-xb$. And lastly $x=\frac{ab}{2a-b}$ *W. W. D.* The *Demonstration* proceeds the same way when a is supposed less than b, and x greater.

OBSERVE. When a is greater than b, then x can always be found because in the Divisor $(2a-b)$ $2a$ is necessarily greater than b. But if a is less than b, it may happen that $2a$ shall be equal to or less than b, and in that Case x is impossible. *Example*. Take 3 and 6, if a $3d$ greater than 6 be required it cannot be found; for $2a$, *viz.* twice 3, or 6, is equal to b or 6; and so the Divisor is 0; or if $2a$ be greater than b, as here 3, 5, where twice 3 or 6 is greater than 5, then it is more impossible.

HENCE again *observe*, that from any given Number a Series of *continued harmonical Proportionals* (of the 1*st* Species, *i. e.* where every 3 immediate Terms are *harmonical*) may be found decreasing *in infinitum* but not increasing.

LASTLY, *observe* this remarkable Difference of the Three Kinds of Proportionals, *viz.* That from any given Number we can raise by *Theorem* 1. a *continued arithmetical Series* increasing *in infinitum*; but not decreasing. The *harmonical* is decreasable but not increasable *in infinitum* by

by the prefent *Obferve*; the *geometrical* is both
(by *Theorem* 1.)

THEOREM XIII. Take any Three Numbers
in Order, multiply the 1*ft* into the 3*d*, and
divide the Product by the Number that remains
after the middle or 2*d* is fubftracted from double
the 1*ft*; and that Quote fhall be a 4*th* Term
in *harmonical Proportion* to the Three given.
Example. Take thefe Three, 9, 12, 16, a 4*th*
will be found by the Rule to be 24.

DEMONSTRATION. Let any Three given
Numbers be *a*, *b*, *c*, and *a* lefs than *b*, let the
Number fought be *x* greater than *c*, then by *Defi-
nition 4th*, it is $a : x :: b-a : x-c$, and $ax-ac=bx-ax$, laftly $x=\frac{ac}{2a-b}$. The Demonftration is the fame
when *a* is greater than *b*, and *x* lefs then *c*.
Obferve here alfo that if *b* is equal to or greater
than 2*a*, then there can be no 4*th* found, fo
that *x* is impoffible. But this can only happen
when the Terms increafe, *i. e.* when *a* is lefs
than *b*, and *c* lefs than *x*. See this *Example*, 1, 2,
3, to which a 4*th* harmonical is impoffible.

THEOREM XIV. Take any Series of *continued
arithmetical Proportionals*, and out of thefe may
be made a Series of *continued harmonical Proportionals* of the firft Species, where every Two
Terms fhall be in a reciprocal *geometrical* Proportion of the correfpondent Terms of the *arithmetical*
Series. The *Rule* is, Take the Two firft Couplets
of the arithmetick Series, fet them down in a
reverfe Order, (as in the Operation below)
multiply each of the 1*ft* Couple by the greater
of the 2*d*, and the leffer of the one by the
leffer

leffer of the other; and fet down the Products;
then, take the next Couplet, and multiply each
of the laft Products by the greater of this Couplet,
and alfo the leaft of thefe Products by the leaft
of this Couplet, and fet down thefe new Products: Repeat this Operation with every Couplet,
and the laft Line of Products is the Series fought.
The following *Example* and Operation will
make it plain.

Arithmetical Series.

$$2 : 3 : 4 : 5 : 6, \ \&c.$$
$$3 : 2$$
$$\ \ 4 : 3$$
$$12 : 8 : 6$$
$$\ \ \ \ \ \ 5 : 4$$
$$60 : 40 : 0 : 24$$
$$\ \ \ \ \ \ 6 : 5$$
$$360 : 240 : 180 : 144 : 120, \ \&c.$$

Harmonical Series.

NOTE, After
this Operation
is finifhed, the
Series found
may be redu-
ced by equal
Divifion, if pof-
fible ; fo the
Series found in
this *Example*,
is reduced to
this, 30, 20, 15,
12, 10.

T H E *Demonftration* of this Rule is eafily made,
1*mo.* If we take any Three Numbers in *arithmetical Proportion*, and multiply them according
to the Rule, 'tis manifeft the Products will be
harmonical; for the Two Extremes of the Three
arithmetical being multiplied by the fame middle
Term, their Products (which are the Extremes
of the Three *harmonical*) are in the fame *geometrical Ratio* ; and then the Two Extremes
being multiplied together, and the Product made
the middle Term, it muft be an *harmonical
Mean,*

Mean, becaufe the *arithmetical Ratio* of the Two Couplets being equal, and the 1*ft* Couplet being multiplied by the greater Extreme, and the other by the leffer Extreme, the Differences of the Products are increafed in Proportion of thefe Multipliers (*viz.* the Extremes) *confequently* the Three Products are in *harmonical Proportion*, according to the *Theorem.* But the fame being true of every Three Terms immediately next in the *arithmetical* Series thus multiplied; and it being alfo true by *Theorem* 10. that the Terms of any *harmonical* Series being equally multiplied the Products are alfo *harmonical*, and in the fame *geometrical Ratio*, it will be evident that working according to the Rule we muft have an *harmonical Series*.

T HE *Reverfe* of this *Theorem* is alfo true, *viz.* that if you take a Series of continued *Harmonicals* of the 1*ft* Species, and multiply them in the Manner prefcribed in the Rule, there will come out a Series of *Arithmeticals*, whofe every Two Terms fhall be reciprocally in the *geometrical Ratio* of their correfpondent *Harmonicals. Example.* Take 3, 4, 6, the Products according to the Rule are 24 : 18 : 12; or by Reduction 4 : 3 : 2, which are *arithmetical*; fee the Operation. The *Reafon* is plain, for the

3 : 4 : 6

4 : 3

6 : 4

24 : 18 : 12

Difference of the Two Couplets 4 : 3 and 6 : 4 being *geometrically* as the Extremes 3 : 6, when the 1*ft* Couplet is multiplied by the greater Extreme, and the other by the leaft, the Dif-

Differences of the Products muſt be equal; every Thing elſe is plain.

COROLLARY. From the *Demonſtration* of this *Theorem* it follows, that taking any Series of whatever Nature, another may be made out of it, whoſe every Two Terms ſhall be reſpectively in a reciprocal *geometrical Proportion* of their Correſpondents in the given Series.

THEOREM XV. In a Series of *continued Harmonicals* of the 1ſt Species, any Term with any Two at equal Diſtance from it are in *harmonical Proportion. Example.* 10, 12, 15, 20, 30, 60; becauſe every Three immediate Terms are *harmonical,* therefore theſe are ſo, 10, 15, 30; and theſe, 12, 20, 60. The Reaſon is eaſily deduced from the laſt. But of *Harmonicals* of the 2d Species, (See *Definition* 4.) it will not always hold that any Two with any other Two at equal Diſtance are alſo *harmonical;* an *Example* will demonſtrate this: See here 3, 4, 6, 9, 18, 36, tho' every Four next other are *harmonical,* yet theſe are not ſo, 3 : 6 : 9 : 36.

THEOREM XVI. If there are Four Numbers diſpoſed in Order, whereof one Extreme and the Two middle Terms are in *arithmetical Proportion,* and the ſame middle Terms with the other Extreme are in *harmonical Proportion,* the Four are in *geometrical Proportion,* as here, 2 : 3 : 4 : 6, which are *geometrical,* and whereof 2 : 3 : 4 are *arithmetical,* and 3, 4, 6 *harmonical.*

DEM-

Demonstration. This *Theorem* contains 4 Cafes. 1*mo.* If the Firft Three Terms are *arithmetical* increafing, and the laft Three *harmonical*, the Four together are *geometrical. Demonftration.* Let $a : b : c : d$ be Three Numbers, whereof a, b, c are *arithmetical* increafing from a, and b, c, d *harmonical*; then are a, b, c, d, *geometrical*; for fince out of the *Harmonicals* we have this *geometrical Proportion,* viz. $b : d :: c$-$b : d$-c and alfo b-a=c-b (fince a, b, c are *arithmetical*) therefore $b : d : b$-$a : d$-c ; and confequently (by *Theor.* 5.) $b : d :: a : c$, or $a : b :: c : d$. *W. W. D. Example.* 2, 3, 4, 6. 2*do.* If the Firft Three are *harmonical* decreafing, and the laft Three *arithmetical*, the Four are *geometrical* ; this is but the Reverfe of the laft Cafe, and needs no other Proof. 3*tio.* If the Firft Three are *arithmetical* decreafing, and the other Three *harmonical*, the Four are *geometrical*, fuppofe a, b, c are *arithmetical* decreafing, and b, c, d, *harmonical*, then a, b, c, d, are *geometrical*, for out of the *Harmonicals* we have this *geometrical Proportion*, viz. $b : d :: b$-c (=a-b) : c-d, therefore $b : d :: a : c$, and $a : b :: c : d$. *Example.* 8 : 6 :: 4 : 3. 4*to.* If the firft Three are *harmonical* increafing, and the other Three *arithmetical*, the Four are *geometrical* ; this is the Reverfe of the laft.

Observe. It muft hold reciprocally that if Four Numbers are *geometrical*, and the firft Three *arithmetical* or *harmonical*, the other Three muft be contrarily *harmonical* or *arithmetical*; for to the fame Three Numbers there can be but

one

one individual Fourth *geometrical*, and to the Two laſt of them but one individual Third *arithmetical* or *harmonical*, therefore the *Obſerve* is true.

THEOREM XVII. If betwixt any Two Numbers you put an *arithmetical* Mean, and alſo an *harmonical* one, the Four will be in *geometrical Proportion*. *Example*. Betwixt 2 and 6 an *arithmetical Mean* is 4, and an *harmonical* one is 3, and the Four are 2 : 3 : : 4 : 6 *geometrical*; the *Demonſtration* you'll find here : Let a and b be Two given Numbers, an *arithmetical Mean* by *Theor.* 2. is $\frac{a+b}{2}$ and an *harmonical Mean* by *Theor.* 11. $\frac{2ab}{a+b}$, and theſe · Four are *geometrical* $a : \frac{a+b}{2} :: \frac{2ab}{a+b} : b$, which is proven by the equal Products of the Extremes and Means.

---

§ 4: *The* Arithmetick *of* Ratios geometrical, *or of the Compoſition and Reſolution of* Ratios.

BY the preceeding *Definitions*, the Exponent of the *geometrical Relation* of Two Numbers is a proper Fraction, when we compare the leſſer to the greater, ſignifying that the leſſer is ſuch a Part or Parts of the greater ; ſo the *Ratio* of 2 to 3 is $\frac{2}{3}$, ſignifying that 2 is Two thirds of 3. Or, if we compare the greater to the leſſer, it is an improper Fraction, which being reduced to its equivalent Whole

or

or mix'd Number, expresses how many Times and Parts of a Time the greater contains the lesser ; so the *Ratio* of 13 to 5 is $\frac{13}{5}$ or $2\frac{3}{5}$, for 13 is equal to 2 Times 5, and 3 over : Or being kept in the fractional Form signifies that the greater is equal to so many Times such a Part of the lesser as that lesser denominates ; and this Difference of comparing the greater as *Antecedent* to the lesser, or the lesser to the greater, constitutes Two different Species of *Ratios*.

ONE Number is said to be composed of others, when it is equal to the Sum of these others ; the *Compound* therefore must be greater than any of these of which it is composed ; and this is the proper Sense of Composition of Numbers, so 9 is composed of 4 and 5, or 6 and 3, &c. also $\frac{2}{3}$ is composed of, or equal to the Sum of $\frac{1}{2}$ and $\frac{1}{6}$. But tho' *Ratios* are Fractions proper or improper, as they express what Part or Parts, or how many Times such a Part of one Number another Number is equal to ; yet in the *Arithmetick* proposed they are taken in a Notion very different from that of mere Numbers ; for if we take the *Exponents* of Two Relations as Numbers, and add them together, the Sum is a Number compounded of the Numbers added, but it is not a *Ratio* or the Exponent of a Relation compounded of the other Two *Ratios* ; so that *Composition* and *Resolution* of *Ratios* is not adding and subtracting them as Numbers. What it is see in the following *Definition*, wherein I take the *Ratio* or *Exponent* of the *Relation* of Two

Num-

Numbers to be the Quote of the *Antecedent* divided by the *Confequent*.

DEFINITION. One *Ratio* is faid to be compounded of others, when it is equal to the *Ratio* betwixt the continual Product of the *Antecedents* of thefe others, and the continual Product of their *Confequents* multiplied as Numbers (*i. e.* by the Rules of common *Arithmetick*) or *thus*, one *Ratio* is compounded of others, when, as a Number, it is equal to the continual Product of thefe others confidered alfo as Numbers. *Example.* The *Ratio* of 1 to 2 is compounded of the *Ratios* of 2 to 3, and 3 to 4, becaufe $\frac{1}{2}$ is equal to $\frac{2}{3}$ multiplied by $\frac{3}{4}$, alfo 40 to 147 is in the compound *Ratio* of thefe, *viz.* 2 : 3, 5 : 7 and 4 : 7.

THEOREM XVIII. Take any Series whatever, the *Ratio* of the Firft Term to the laft confidered as a Number, is equal to the continual Product of all the intermediate *Ratios* multiplied as Numbers, taking every Term in Order from the Firft as an *Antecedent* to the next. For *Example*. In this Series 3, 4, 5, 6, the *Ratio* of 3 and 6 is $\frac{1}{2}$, equal to the continual Product of thefe $\frac{3}{4}$, $\frac{4}{5}$, $\frac{5}{6}$, for when all the *Numerators* are multiplied together, and all the *Denominators*, it is plain the Products are as 3 to 6, becaufe all the other Multipliers are common to both Products ; and it muft be true in every Series for the fame Reafon.

COROLLARY. If the Series is in *continued geometrical Proportion*, the *Ratio* of the Extremes is equal to the common *Ratio* taken and

mul-

multiplied into it felf, as a Number, as oft as there are Terms in the Series lefs one.

Problem II. To find a Series of Numbers which fhall be to one another (comparing them in Order each to the next) in any given *Ratios*, taken in any Order affigned. Rule. Multiply both Terms of the 1*ft* *Ratio* by the *Antecedent* of the 2*d*, and the *Confequent* of this by the *Confequent* of the 1*ft* ; and thus you have the 1*ft* Two *Ratios* reduced to Three Terms, which multiply by the *Antecedent* of the 3*d Ratio*, and the *Confequent* of this by the laft of thefe Three, and you have the 1*ft* Three *Ratios* reduced to 4 Terms : Go on thus, multiplying the laft Series by the *Antecedent* of the next *Ratio*, and the *Confequent* of this by the laft Term of that laft Series. The Juftnefs of the Rule appears from this, That the Terms of each *Ratio* are equally multiplied. *Example.* The *Ratios* of 2 : 3, of 4 : 5 and 6 : 7 are reduced to this Series 48 : 72 : 90 : 105. See the Operation.

2 : 3
   4 : 5
_____
8. 12. 15
     6 : 7
_____
48 : 72 : 90 : 105

Observe. From the Operation of this Rule it is plain, that the Extremes of the Series found are, *the One* equal to the continual Product of all the *Antecedents*, and *the other* to the continual Product of all the *Confequents* of the given *Ratios* ; fo that thefe Extremes are in the *compound Ratio* of the given Ones ; which is otherwife

wife plain from the laft *Propofition,* fince all the intermediate Terms of this Series are in the *Ratios* given refpectively. And it follows alfo, that where any Number of *Ratios* are reduced to a Series, tho' the Number of the Series will differ according to the different Orders, yet becaufe the intermediate *Ratios* are the fame in every Order, the Extremes muft ftill be in the fame *Ratio.*

THEOREM XIX. Every *Ratio* is compofed of an indefinite Number of other *Ratios;* for, by *Corol.* to *Theor.* 5. if any Two Numbers are equally multiplied, the Products are in the fame *geometrical Ratio,* and by *Corol.* to *Theor.* 6. their Difference contains the Firft Difference, as oft as the Multiplier contains Unity; therefore it is plain that thefe Products are the Extremes of a Series, which can have as many middle Terms as their Difference has Units lefs one; and confequently by taking the Multiplier greater you make the Difference of the Products greater, which admitting ftill a greater Number of middle Terms, reduces the *Ratio* given into more intermediate Ones: So take the *Ratio* of 2 : 3, multiply both Terms by 4, the Products are 8 : 12, and the Series is 8 : 9 : 10 : 11 : 12, but multiply by 7, the Series is 14 : 15 : 16 : 17 : 18 : 19 : 20 : 21.

OBSERVE. We may fill up the middle Terms very differently, fo as to make many different Series betwixt the fame Extremes: And hereby we learn how to take a View of all the

mean *Ratios*, of which any other is compofed.

THEOREM XX. The *geometrical Ratio* of
any Two Numbers taken as a proper Fraction,
(*i. e.* making the leffer Number the *Antecedent*)
is lefs than that of any other Two Numbers
which are themfelves refpectively greater, and
yet have the fame *arithmetical Ratio* or Difference. *Example.* The *Ratio* 2 : 3 taken as a
Fraction is $\frac{2}{3}$ lefs than that of 3 : 4, *viz.* $\frac{3}{4}$, or
than 5 : 6, *viz.* $\frac{5}{6}$.

DEMONSTRATION. Let a and $a+b$ reprefent any Two Numbers, let $a+c$ and $a+c+b$
reprefent other Two which are refpectively
greater than the firft Two, but have the fame
Difference b; take them Fraction-wife thus,
$\frac{a}{a+b}$ and $\frac{a+c}{a+c+b}$, if we reduce them to one common Denominator, the new Numerators will
be found $aa+ac+ab$, and $aa+ac+ab+bc$,
which is greater than the other by bc; therefore
the Firft Fraction, to which the Numerator
$aa+ac+ab$ correfponds, is leaft.

PROBLEM III. To reduce any Number of
Ratios to one common *Antecedent* or *Confe-*
quent. RULE. Multiply all their *Antecedents*
continually into one another, that Product is
the common *Antecedent* fought: Then multiply each *Confequent* into all the *Antecedents*
(except its own) continually, and the laft Product is the *Confequent* correfpondent to the
Confequent that was now multiplied. Or, multiply all the *Confequents* for a common *Confe-*
quent, and each *Antecedent* into all the *Confe-*
quents (except its own) for a new *Antecedent*. So
these

thele *Ratios*, 2 : 3, 3 : 4, 4 : 5 reduced to one *Antecedent*, are 24 : 36, 24 : 32, 24 : 30, which in one Series are 24 : 36 : 32 : 30.

The *Reason* of the Rule is plain from this, that the Terms of each *Ratio* are equally multiplied.

ADDITION of *RATIOS.*

PROBLEM IV. To add one or more *Ratios* together, or to find the Compound of these *Ratios*. RULE. Multiply all the *Antecedents* continually into one another, and all the *Consequents*; the Two Products contain the *Ratio* sought; which is plainly this; Take the *Ratios* Fraction-wise, (the *Antecedent* of each, whether 'tis greater or lesser than the *Consequent*, being the Numerator, and the *Consequent* the Denominator) and as fractional Numbers multiply them continually into another, the last Product is the *Exponent* of the *Relation* sought. *Example:* Add the *Ratios* of 2 : 3, 5 : 7 and 8 : 9, the *Sum* or *compound Ratio* sought is 80 : 189. The *Reason* of the *Rule* is plain from the *Definition* of a compound *Ratio* in § 4. of this *Chapter.*

OBSERVE 1*mo.* To understand in what Sense this Operation is called *Addition* of *Ratios*, we must consider that to compound Two or more *Ratios* is in effect this, *viz.* to find the Extremes of a Series whose intermediate Terms are respectively in the *Ratios* given; so to compound or add the *Ratios*, 2 : 3 and 4 : 5,

is

is to find the Extremes of Three Numbers,
whereof the 1*st* shall be to the 2*d* as 2 to 3,
and the 2*d* to the 3*d* as 4 to 5. Such a Series
may in any Case be found by *Probl.* 2. and
in this *Example* it is 8 : 12 : 15, for 8 is to 12
as 2 to 3, and 12 : 15 as 4 : 5, and 8 : 15 is
the *compound Ratio* sought, which is called the
Sum of the given *Ratios*, because it is the Effect
of taking to the *Consequent* of the 1*st Ratio*,
considered now as an *Antecedent*, a new *Consequent* in the 2*d Ratio* ; and so of more *Ratios*
added.

2*do.* There is no Difference, as to this *Rule*,
whether all the *Ratios* to be added are of one
Species or not, *i. e.* whether all the *Antecedents*
are greater than their *Consequents*, or all less, or
some greater some less. For in this Rank 3 :
4 : 5 : 2 the *Ratio* of 3 to 2 is compounded of
the intermediate *Ratios* 3 : 4, 4 : 5, and 5 : 2 :
tho' the last is of a different Species from the
other Two; what Difference there is in the
Application to *musical Intervals* shall be explained
in its Place.

SUBSTRACTION of *RATIOS:*

P̲r̲o̲b̲l̲e̲m̲ **V.** To substract one *Ratio* from
another. R̲u̲l̲e̲. Multiply the *Antecedent* of
the Substrahend into the *Consequent* of the Substractor, that Product is *Antecedent* of the
Remainder sought ; then multiply the *Antecedent*
of the Substractor into the *Consequent* of the
Substrahend, and that Product is the *Consequent*
of

of the Remainder fought; which is plainly
this; Take the Two *Ratios* Fraction-wife, and
divide the one by the other according to the
Rules of Fractions. *Example.* To fubftract
the *Ratio* of 2 : 3 from that of 3 : 5; the Re-
mainder is 9 : 10, for $\frac{3}{5}$ divided by $\frac{2}{3}$ quotes
$\frac{9}{10}$.

THE *Reafon* of this Rule is plain; for, as
the Senfe of Subftraction is oppofite to Addition,
fo muft the Operation be; and to fubftract one
Ratio from another fignifies the finding a *Ratio*,
which being added (in the fenfe of *Probl.* 4.)
to the Subftracter, or *Ratio* to be fubftracted, the
Compound or Sum fhall be equal to the Sub-
ftrahend; and therefore, as Addition is done by
multiplying the *Ratios* as Fractions, fo muft Subftraction be done by dividing them as Fractions;
and fo in this Series 6 : 9 : 10, the *Ratio* 6 :
10 (or 3 : 5) is compofed of 6 : 9 (or 2 : 3)
and 9 : 10; which Compofition is done by
multiplying $\frac{9}{10}$ into $\frac{2}{3}$ whofe Product is $\frac{18}{30}$ or $\frac{3}{5}$:
So to fubftract 6 : 9 or 2 : 3 from 6 : 10 or 3 :
5, it muft be done by a reverfe Operation divid-
ing $\frac{3}{5}$ by $\frac{2}{3}$ whofe Quotient is $\frac{9}{10}$.

OBSERVE. As in Addition, the *Ratios* added
may be of the fame or different Species, fo
it may be in Subftraction; but it is to be obferved here that the Two given *Ratios* to be fubftracted, being confidered as Fractions, and both
proper Fractions, then, the leaft being fubftracted from the greater, the Remainder is a *Ratio* of a different Species, as in this Series, 5 :
2 : 7, for take $\frac{2}{7}$ from $\frac{5}{7}$ the Remainder is $\frac{3}{7}$: But take
the

the greater from the leſſer, and the Remainder
is of the ſame Species ; ſo $\frac{5}{7}$ from $\frac{7}{7}$ there remains $\frac{5}{7}$, as in this Series 2 : 5 : 7. *Again* ſuppoſe both the given *Ratios* are improper Fractions (*i. e.* the *Antecedents* greater than the
Conſequents) if the leaſt is ſubſtracted from the
greater, the Remainder is of the ſame Species;
but the greater from the leſſer and the Remainder is of a different Species. *Example.* $\frac{7}{5}$ from
$\frac{7}{2}$ remains $\frac{5}{2}$, as in this Series 7 : 5 : 2. But $\frac{7}{2}$ from
$\frac{7}{5}$ remains $\frac{2}{5}$, as here 7 : 2 : 5 ; theſe Obſervati-
ons are all plain from the *Rule.*

MULTIPLICATION of *RATIOS.*

PROBLEM VI. To multiply any *Ratio* by
a Number. This Problem has Two *Caſes.*

CASE I. To multiply any *Ratio* by a whole
Number. RULE. Take the given *Ratio* as oft
as the Multiplier contains Unity, and add them
all by *Probl. 4th. Example.* 2 : 3 multiplied by
4, produces 16 : 81 ; or thus, Take the *Ratio*
as a Fraction, and raiſe it to ſuch a Power as
the Multiplier expones, that is, to the Square if
'tis 2, to the *Cube* if 3, and ſo on.

FOR the Reaſon of the *Rule* conſider, That
as the multiplying any Number ſignifies the
adding it to it ſelf, or taking it ſo many Times
as the Multiplier contains Unity, ſo to multiply
any *Ratio* ſignifies the adding or compounding
it with it ſelf, ſo many Times as the Multiplier
contains Unity, *i. e.* to find a new *Ratio* that
ſhall be equal to the given one ſo oft compounded

ed, thus, to multiply the *Ratio* of 2 : 3 by the Number 4 fignifies the finding a *Ratio* equal to the *compound Ratio* of 2 : 3 taken 4 Times, which is 16 : 81; for 2 : 3, 2 : 3, 2 : 3, 2 : 3, being added by *Probl.* 4. amount to 16 : 81, and to fill up the Series apply *Probl.* 2.

Observe. The Product is always a *Ratio* of the fame Species with the given *Ratio*; as is plain from the *Rule.* And if you'll complete the Series by *Probl.* 2. *i. e.* turn the given *Ratio* fo oft taken as the Multiplier exprefles into a Series, it will be a *continued geometrical* one. Thus, 2, 3 multiplied by 4, produces 16, 81, and the Series is 16 : 24 : 36 : 54 : 81; and this Series fhows clearly the Import of this Multiplication, that it is the finding the Extremes of a Series, whofe intermediate Terms have a common *Ratio* equal to the given *Ratio*, and which contains that *Ratio* as oft repeated as the Multiplier contains 1.

Case II. To multiply any *Ratio* by a Fraction, *that is*, to take any Part of a given *Ratio.* Rule. Multiply it by the Numerator of the Fraction, according to the laft *Cafe*, and divide that Product which is alfo a *Ratio* by the Denominator, after the Method of *Cafe* 1. of the following *Probl.* the Quote is the *Ratio* fought. *Example.* To multiply the *Ratio* 8 : 27, by $\frac{2}{3}$. *Firft*, I multiply 8 : 27 by 2, the Product is 64 : 729, and this divided by 3, according to the next *Probl.* quotes the *Ratio* 4 : 9, fo that the *Ratio* 4 : 9 is $\frac{2}{3}$ Parts of the *Ratio* 8 : 27.

THE

THE *Reason* of the Operation is this, since $\frac{2}{3}$ Parts of 1 (*i. e.* of once the *Ratio* to be multiplied) is equal to $\frac{1}{3}$ Part of 2 (or of twice the *Ratio* to be multiplied) therefore having taken that *Ratio* twice, I muft take a Third of that Product, to have the true Product fought : And fo of other *Cafes.* The Senfe of this *Cafe* will appear plain in this Series 8:12:18:27 which is in *continued geometrical Proportion,* the common *Ratio* being that of 2 : 3 ; confequently 8 : 27 : contains 2 : 3 Three Times; or 2 : 3 multiplied by 3 produces 8 : 27 : Alfo 8 : 18 (equal to 4 : 9) contains 2 : 3 twice, and confequently is equal to $\frac{2}{3}$ Parts of 8 : 27.

OBSERVE. It produces the fame Thing to divide the given *Ratio* by the Denominator of the given Fraction, and multiply the Quote (which is a *Ratio*) by the Numerator ; becaufe, for Example, 2 Times $\frac{1}{3}$ of a Thing is equal to $\frac{1}{3}$ of twice that Thing.

COROLLARY. To multiply a *Ratio* by a mix'd Number, we muft multiply it feparately, *Firft*, By the integral Part (by *Cafe* 1.) and then by the fractional Part (by *Cafe* 2.) and fum thefe Products (by *Probl.* 4.) or reduce the mix'd Number to an improper Fraction, and apply the *Rule* of the laft *Cafe*. *Example.* To multiply 4 : 9 by $1\frac{1}{2}$ or $\frac{3}{2}$, the Product is 8 : 27, for in this Series 8 : 12 : 18 : 27, it is plain 6 : 27 is 3 Times 2 : 3. And this is $\frac{1}{2}$ of 4 : 9 (equal to 8 : 18) confequently 8 : 27 is equal to 3 Halfs or 1 and $\frac{1}{2}$ of 4 : 9.

D I-

DIVISION of *RATIOS.*

PROBLEM VII. To divide any *Ratio* by a Number. This *Probl.* has Three *Cafes.*

CASE I. To divide any *Ratio* by a whole Number, *that is,* to find fuch a *Ratio* as being multiplied (or compounded into it felf) as oft as the Divifor contains Unity, fhall produce the given *Ratio,* RULE. Out of the *Ratio,* taken as a Fraction, extract fuch a Root as the Divifor is the Index of, *i. e.* the fquare Root if the Divifor is 2, the cube Root if the Divifor is 3, *&c.* and that Root is the *Exponent* of the *Relation* fought. *Example.* To divide the *Ratio* of 9 : 16 by 2, the fquare Root of $\frac{9}{16}$ is $\frac{3}{4}$ which is the *Ratio* fought.

THE *Reafon* of this *Rule* is obvious, from its being oppofite to the like Cafe in Multiplication ; and is plain in this Series, 9 : 12 : 16, which is in the *continued Ratio* of 3 : 4. and fince the multiplying 3 : 4 by 2, to produce 9 : 16, is performed by multiplying $\frac{3}{4}$ by $\frac{3}{4}$, or fquaring $\frac{3}{4}$, the Divifion of 9 : 16 by 2 to find 3 : 4, can be done no other ways than by extracting the fquare Root of $\frac{9}{16}$, which is $\frac{3}{4}$; and fo of other Cafes; which will be all very plain to them who underftand any Thing of the Nature of Powers and Roots. Or folve the *Probl.* thus ; Find the firft of as many *geometrical Means* betwixt the Terms of the given *Ratio* as the Divifor contains of Units lefs one, that compared with the lefser Term of the given *Ratio* contains

tains the *Ratio* fought; thus 9 : 12 is the Anfwer of the preceeding *Example.*

CASE II. To divide a *Ratio* by a Fraction, *that is,* to find a *Ratio* of which fuch a Part or Parts as the given Fraction expreffes fhall be equal to the given *Ratio.* RULE. Multiply it by the Denominator (by *Probl.* 6. 1 *Cafe*) and divide the Product by the Numerator (by *Cafe* 1 of this *Probl.*) the Quote is the *Ratio* fought. Or divide the *Ratio* by the Numerator, and multiply the Quote by the Denominator. *Example.* To divide 4 : 9 by $\frac{2}{3}$ or to find $\frac{2}{3}$ Parts of 4 : 9, I take the *Cube* of $\frac{4}{9}$, it is $\frac{64}{729}$, whofe fquare Root is $\frac{8}{17}$ the *Ratio* fought. The *Reafon* of the Operation is contained in this, that it is oppofite to *Cafe* 2. of Multiplication. And becaufe 8 : 27 multiplied by $\frac{2}{3}$, produces 4 : 9, fo 4 : 9 divided by $\frac{2}{3}$ ought to quote 8 : 27.

COROLLARY. To divide a *Ratio* by a mix'd Number ; reduce the mix'd Number to an improper Fraction, and divide as in the laft *Cafe.*

CASE III. To divide one *Ratio* by another, both being of one Species; *that is,* to find how oft the one is contained in the other ; or how oft the one ought to be added to it felf to make a *Ratio* equal to the other. RULE. Subftract the Divifor from the Dividend (by *Probl.* 5.) and the fame Divifor again from the laft Remainder ; and fo on continually, till the Remainder be a *Ratio* of Equality ; and then the Number of Subftractions is the

Number

§ 4. *of* MUSICK. **131**

Number fought; or, till the Species of the *Ratio* change, and then the Number of Subftra-ctions lefs one is the Number of Times the whole Divifor is found in the Dividend, and the laft Remainder except one is what the Dividend contains over fo many Times the Divifor. *Ex-ample.* To divide the *Ratio* 16 : 81 by 2 : 3, I fubftract 2 : 3 from 16 : 81, the Remainder is 48 : 162 equal to 8 : 27; from this I fubftract 2 : 3, the 2d Remainder is 24 : 54, equal to 4 : 9; from this I fubftract 2 : 3, the 3d Remain-der is 12 : 18 or 2 : 3; from this I fubftract 2 : 3, the 4th Remainder is 6 : 6 or 1 : 1, a *Ratio* of Equality; therefore the Quote fought is the Number 4, fignifying that the *Ratio* 2 : 3 taken 4 Times, is equal to 16 : 54; as you fee it all in this Series 16 : 24 : 36 : 54 : 81. *Ex-ample* 2. To divide 12 : 81 by 2 : 3, proceed in the fame Manner as before, and you'll find the Remainders to be 2 : 9, 1 : 3, 1 : 2, 3 : 4, 9 : 8, and becaufe the laft changes the Species, I juftly conclude that the *Ratio* 12 : 81 does not con-tain 2 : 3 five Times, but it contains it 4 Times and 3 : 4 over; for 2 : 3 multiplied by 4 produces 16 : 81, which added to 3 : 4 makes exactly 12 : 81, as in this Series 16 : 24 : 36 : 54 : 81 : 108 whofe Extremes 16 : 108, (equal to 12 : 81) is in a *Ratio* compounded of 16 : 81 and 81 : 108 (equal to 3. 4.)

OBSERVE. The Two *Ratios* given muft be of one Species ; becaufe the Senfe of it is, to find how oft the Divifor muft be added to it felf to make a *Ratio* equal to the Dividend;

and

and in multiplying, any *Ratio* by a whole Number, that *Ratio* and the Product are always of one Species, as was observed in *Probl.* 6. therefore 'tis plain that the *Ratio* of the Dividend, taken as a Fraction, must be lesser than the Divisor so taken, the *Antecedent* being least, *i. e.* these Fractions being proper, and contrarily if they are improper; the *Reason* is plain, because in an increasing Series, *i. e.* where all the *Antecedents* are lesser than their *Consequents*, the *Ratio* of the First to the least Extreme is less than the *Ratio* of any Two of the intermediate Terms, and yet, according to the Nature of *Ratios*, contains them all in it; but in a decreasing Series, *i. e.* where all the *Antecedents* are greater than the *Consequents*, the 1*st* to the least, or the greatest *Antecedent* to the least *Consequent*, is in a greater *Ratio* than any of the intermediate, and also contains them all: So in this Series 2 : 3 : 4 : 5, the *Ratio* 2 : 5 contains all the intermediate *Ratios*, and yet $\frac{2}{5}$ is less than $\frac{2}{3}$ or $\frac{3}{4}$ or $\frac{4}{5}$; but take the Series reversely, then $\frac{5}{2}$ is greater than $\frac{5}{4}$ or $\frac{4}{3}$ or $\frac{3}{2}$.

§5. *Containing an Application of the preceeding Theory of Proportion to the* INTERVALS
of Sound.

IT has been already ſhewn that the Degrees
of *Tune* are proportional to the Numbers of
Vibrations of the ſonorous Body in a given
Time, or their Velocity of Courſes and Recourſes ; which being proportional, in Chords, to
their Lengths (*cæteris paribus*) we have the juſt
Meaſures of the relative Degrees of *Tune* in the
Ratios of theſe Lengths; the *grave* Sound being to the *acute* as the greater Length to the
leſſer.

THE Differences of *Tune* make *Diſtance* or
Intervals in *Muſick,* which are greater and leſſer as theſe Differences are; whoſe Quantity is
the true Object of the mathematical Part of
Muſick. Now theſe *Intervals* are meaſured,
not in the ſimple Differences, or *arithmetick
Ratios* of the Numbers expreſſing the Lengths
or Vibrations of Chords, but in their *geometrical
Ratios* ; ſo that the ſame Difference of *Tune,*
i. e. the ſame *Interval* depends upon the ſame
geometrical Ratio ; and different Quantities or
Intervals ariſe from a Difference of the *geometrical Ratios* of the Numbers expreſſing the Extremes, as has been already ſhewn ; *that is,*
equal

equal *geometrical Ratios* betwixt whatever Numbers, conftitute equal *Intervals,*but unequal *Ratios* make unequal *Intervals.*

But now *obferve,* that in comparing the Quantity of *Intervals,* the *Ratios* expreffing them muft be all of one Species ; otherwife this Abfurdity will follow, that the fame Two Sounds will make different *Intervals* ; for *Example,* Suppofe Two Chords in Length, as 4 and 5, 'tis certainly the fame *Interval* of Sound, whether you compare 4 to 5, or 5 to 4, yet the *Ratios* of 4 : 5 and 5 : 4 taken as Numbers, and expreft Fraction-wife would differ in Quantity, and therefore different *Ratios* cannot without this Qualification make in every Cafe different *Intervals.*

In what Manner the Inequality of *Intervals* are meafured, fhall be explained immediately and here take this general Character from the Things explained, to know which of Two or more *Intervals* propofed are greateft. *If all the* Ratios *are taken as proper Fractions, the leaft Fraction is the greateft Interval.* But to fee the Reafon of this, take it thus; The *Ratios* that exprefs feveral *Intervals* being all of one Species, reduce them (by *Probl.* 3. of this *Chap.*) to one common *Antecedent,* which being leffer than the *Confequents,* that *Ratio* which has the greateft Confequent is the greateft *Interval.* The Reafon is obvious, for the longeft Chord gives the *graveft* Sound, and therefore muft be at greateft Diftance from the common *acute* Sound. Or contrarily, reduce them to one common Confequent greater than the Antecedents,

dents, and the leſſer Antecedent expreſſes the *acuter* Sound, and conſequently makes with that common fundamental or *graveſt* Sound, the greater *Interval.*

I⊤ follows that if any Series of Numbers are in *continual arithmetical Proportion,* comparing each Term to the next, they expreſs a Series of *Intervals* differing in Quantity from firſt to laſt; the greateſt *Interval* being betwixt the Two leaſt Numbers, and ſo gradually to the greateſt, as here 1 : 2 : 3 : 4. 1 : 2 is a grea⁻ter *Interval* than 2 : 3, as this is greater than 3 : 4. The Reaſon why it muſt hold ſo in eve-ry Caſe is contained in *Theor.* 20. where it was demonſtrated that the *geometrical Ratio* of any Two Numbers taken as a proper Fraction (*i. e.* making the leſſer the Antecedent) is leſs than that of any other Two Numbers, which are themſelves reſpectively greater, and yet have the ſame *arithmetical Ratio* or Difference : And by what has been explained we ſee that the leſſer proper Fraction makes the greater *Interval.*

T H U S we can judge which of any *Intervals* propoſed is greateſt, and which leaſt, in gene-ral; but how to meaſure their ſeveral Differences or Inequalities is another Queſtion ; that whoſe Extremes make the leaſt Fraction is the great-eſt *Interval,* and ſo, in general, the Quantities of ſeveral *Intervals* are reciprocally as theſe Fracti-ons; but this is not always in a ſimple Propor-tion. For *Example,* The Interval 1 : 2, is to the Interval 1 : 4 exactly as $\frac{1}{2}$ to $\frac{1}{4}$ (or as 1 to 2) the Quantity of the laſt being double the other.

But

But 2 : 3 to 4 : 9 is not as $\frac{2}{3}$ to $\frac{1}{3}$, but as 1 to 2, as fhall be explained. Sounds themfelves are expreffed by Numbers, and their Intervals are reprefented by the *Ratios* of thefe Numbers, fo thefe *Intervals* are compared together by comparing thefe *Ratios*, not as Numbers, but as *Ratios*; and I fuppofe every given *Interval* is expreffed by expreffing diftinctly the Two Extremes, *i. e.* their relative Numbers.

I fhall now explain the *Compofition* and *Refolution* of *Intervals*, which is the Application of the preceeding *Arithmetick* of *Ratios*; and this I fhall do, *Firft* in general, without Regard to the Difference of *Concord* and *Difcord*, which fhall imploy the reft of this *Chapter*; and in the next make Application to the various *Relations* and *Compofitions* of *Concords*; and after that of *Difcords* in their Place.

IN what Senfe *Ratios* are faid to be added and fubftracted, *&c.* has been explained, but in the *Compofition* of *Intervals* we have a more proper Application of the true Senfe of adding and fubftracting, *&c.* The Notions of Addition and Subftraction, *&c.* belong to Quantity; concerning which it is an *Axiom*, that the Sum or what is the Refult of Addition, muft be a Quantity greater than any of the Quantities added, becaufe it is equal to them all : And in fubftracting we take a leffer Quantity from a greater, and the Remainder is lefs than that greater, which is equal to the Sum of the Thing taken away and the Remainder. A mere Relation cannot properly be called

Quan-

Quantity, and therefore the *geometrical Ratio*
of Numbers can be no otherwise called Quantity than as by taking the *Antecedent* and *Confequent* Fraction-wife, they exprefs what Part
or how many Times fuch a Part of the *Confequent* the *Antecedent* is equal to ; and then
the greater Fraction is always the greater *Ratio.*
But the *Compofition* of *Ratios* is a Thing of a
quite different Senfe from the *Compofition* of
mere Numbers or Quantity ; for in Quantities,
Two or more added make a Total greater
than any of them that are added; but in the
Compofition of *Ratios*, the *Compound* confidered as a Number in the Senfe abovementioned,
may be lefs than any of the component Parts.
Now we apply the Idea of Diftance to
the Difference of Sound in *Acutenefs* and
Gravity in a very plain and intelligible Manner,
fo that we have one univerfal Character to determine the greater or leffer of any Intervals
propofed ; according to which Notion of Greatnefs and Littlenefs all Intervals are added and
fubftracted, *&c.* and the Sum is the true and
proper Compound of feveral leffer Quantities;
and in Subftraction we actually take a leffer
Quantity from a greater ; but the Intervals
themfelves being expreffed by the *geometrical
Ratio* of Numbers applied to the Lengths of
Chords (or their proportional Vibrations) the
Addition and Subftraction, *&c.* of the Quantities
of *Intervals* is performed by Application of
the preceeding *Arithmetick* of *Ratios.*

NOTE.

NOTE. In the following *Problems* I conftantly apply the Numbers to the Lengths of Chords,
and fo the leffer of Two Numbers that exprefs
any *Interval* I call the *acute* Term and the
other the *grave*.

ADDITION of *INTERVALS.*

PROBLEM VIII. To add Two or more *Intervals* together. RULE. Mutiply all the *acute*
Terms continually, the Product is the *acute*
Term fought ; and the Product of the *grave*
Terms continually multiplied, is the *grave* Term
fought; *that is,* Take the *Ratios* as proper
Fractions; and add them by *Probl.* 4. *Example.* Add a *5th* 2 : 3 and, a *4th* 3 : 4, and a
3*d g.* 4 : 5, the Sum is 24 : 60 equal to 2 : 5,
a 3*d g.* above an *Octave.*

OBSERVE. This is a plain Application of
the RULE for adding of *Ratios,* and to make
it better underftood, fuppofe any given Sound
reprefented by *a,* and another Sound, *acuter*
or *graver* in any *Ratio,* reprefented by *b* ; if
again we take a Third Sound ftill *acuter* or
graver than *b,* and call it *c,* then the Sound
of *c* being at greater Diftance from *a,* towards
Acutenefs or *Gravity,* than *b* is, the *Interval*
betwixt *a* and *c* is equal to the other Two
betwixt *a b* and *b c.* And fo let any Number
of *Intervals* be propofed to be added, we are
to conceive fome Sound *a* as one Extreme of
the *Interval* fought ; to this we take another
Sound *b acuter* or *graver* in any given *Ratio*; then
a Third Sound *c acuter* or *graver* than *b* in
an-

another given *Ratio*, and a 4*th* Sound *d acuter* or *graver* than *c*, and fo on ; every Sound always exceeding another in *Acutenefs* or *Gravity*, and all of them taken the fame way, *i. e.* all *acuter*, or all *graver* than the preceeding, and confequently than the firft Sound *a* ; and then the firft and laft are at a Diftance equal to the Sum of the intermediate Diftances. For *Example*, If 5 Sounds are reprefented by *a, b, c, d, e* exceeding each other by certain *Ratios* of *Acutenefs* or *Gravity* from *a* to *e*, the *Interval a : e* is equal to the Sum of the *Intervals a : b, b : c, c : d, d : e.*

Now that the Rule for finding the true Diftance of *a : e* is juft, you'll eafily perceive by confidering that Intervals are reprefented by *Ratios* ; therefore feveral *Intervals* are added by compounding the *Ratios* that exprefs them; for if the given *Intervals* or *Ratios* are reduced, by *Probl.* 2. to a Series continually increafing or decreafing, wherein every Number being *antecedent* to the next, they fhall contain in Order the *Ratios* given, *i. e.* exprefs the given *Intervals*, 'tis plain the *Ratio* of the Extremes of this Series fhall be compofed of all the intermediate (which are the given) *Ratios*, and therefore be the Sum of them according to the true Senfe in which *Intervals* are added, as it has been explained ; fo in the preceeding *Example*, in which we have added a 5*th* 2 : 3, a 4*th* 3 : 4 and a 3*d g.* 4 : 5, the Compound of thefe *Ratios* is 24 : 60 or 2 : 5 ; for take them in the Order propofed they

are

are contained in this· fimple Series, 2 : 3 : 4 :
5, which reprefents a Series of Sounds gradually
exceeding each other in *Gravity* from 2 to 5
by the intermediate Degrees or *Ratios* propofed ; fo that 2 : 5 being the true Sum of
thefe *Intervals*, and the true *Compound* of the
given *Ratios*, fhews the *Rule* to be juft.

AGAIN take Notice, that tho' in the *Compofition* of *Ratios* it is the fame Thing whether
they are all of one Species or not, yet in their
Application to *Intervals* they muft be of one
Kind. I have already fhewn what Abfurdity
would follow if it were otherwife, but you may
fee more of it here; fuppofe Three Sounds reprefented by 4 : 5 : 3, tho' 4 : 3 is the true *Compound* of thefe *Ratios* 4 : 5 and 5 ꞉ 3, yet it
cannot exprefs the Sum of the *Intervals* reprefented by thefe ; if 4 reprefent one
Extreme and 5 the middle Sound (*gracer* than
the former) 3 cannot poffibly reprefent another
Sound at a greater Diftance towards Gravity,
becaufe 'tis *acuter* than 5, and therefore inftead of adding to the Diftance from 4, it
diminifhes it; but it is the fame *Interval* (tho'
in fome Senfe not the fame *Ratio*) whether
the leffer or greater is *antecedent* ; and the Sum
of thefe Two *Intervals* cannot be reprefented
but by the Extremes of a Series continually
increafing or decreafing from the leaft or
greateft of the Numbers propofed, becaufe they
cannot otherwife reprefent a Series of Sounds
continually rifing or falling, the *Ratio* of the
Extremes of which Kind of Series can only be
                                        cal-

called the Sum of the intermediate Diftances
or ntervalof Sound; and fo the preceeding Example muft be taken thus, 3 : 4 : 5, where 3 :
5 is not only the *compound Ratio* of 3 : 4 and
4 : 5, but expreffes the true Sum of the *Intervals* reprefented by thefe *Ratios*.

It is plain then from this Explication, that
in Addition of *Intervals* the Sum is a greater
Quantity than any of the Parts added, as it
ought to be, according to the juft Notion of
the Quantity of *Intervals* ; but it would be
otherwife and abfurd if the *Ratios* expreffing
Intervals were not taken all one way ; fo in the
preceeding Example tho' 4 : 3 is the Compound
of 4 : 5 and 5 : 3, yet confidered as a Fracti-
on $\frac{1}{4}$ it is greater than $\frac{1}{5}$, and confequently a
leffer *Interval*, by the Character already efta-
blifhed.

PROBLEM IX. To add Two or more
Intervals, and find all the intermediate Terms ;
a certain Order of their Succeffion being affigned,
from the *graveft* or the *acuteft* Extreme.
RULE. If the given *Intervals* are to proceed in Order from the *acuteft* Term, make
the leffer Numbers *Antecedents*; if from the
graveft, make the greater *Antecedents*, and
then apply the Rule of *Probl.* 2.

EXAMPLE. To find a Series of Sounds, that
from the *acuteft* to the *graveft* fhall be in Order (comparing the 1*ft* to the 2*d*, and the 2*d*
to the 3*d*, and fo on) a 3*d g* : 4*th* : 3*d l* : 5*th*.
Working by the *Rule* I find this Series 120 : 150 :
200

200 .240: 360, or reduced to lower Terms by Division they are 12 : 15 : 20 : 24 : 36. See the Operation here. But if the same *Intervals* are to proceed in that Order from the *gravest* Extremes, the Series is 90 : 72 : 54 : 45 : 30.

4 : 5 - - - - - 3d gr.

   3 : 4 - - - - 4th.

12 : 15 : 20

     5 : 6 - - 3d less.

60 : 75 : 100 : 120

     2 : 3 - 5th.

120 : 150 : 200 : 240 : 360

Observe. In adding several *Intervals* in a continued Series, the Sum or *Ratio* of the Extremes must always be the same, whatever Order they are taken in ; because in any Order the *Ratio* of the Extremes is the true Compound of all the intermediate *Ratios*; or the *Ratios* added, which being individually the same, only in a different Order, the Sum must be the same ; but then according to the different Orders the Series of Numbers will be different, so if we add a *4th* 3 : 4, *3d gr.* 4 : 5 and a *3d less.* 5 : 6, they can be taken in Six different Orders, which are contained in these Six different Series, which contain all the different Orders both from *Gravity* and *Acuteness*.

3 : 4 : 5 : 6

4 : 5 : 6 : 8

5 : 6 : 8 : 10

16 : 8 : 10 : 20

12 : 15 : 20 : 24

15 : 20 : 24 : 30

SUB-

SUBSTRACTION of *INTERVALS.*

PROBLEM X. To fubftract a leffer *Interval* from a greater. RULE. Multiply the *acute* Terms of each of the given Intervals by the *grave* Term of the other, and the Two Products are in the *Ratio* of the Difference fought, *that is,* take the *Ratios* given as proper Fractions, and fubftract them by *Probl* 5.

EXAMPLE. Subftract a *5th* 2 : 3 from an *Octave* 1 : 2, the Remainder or Difference is a *4th* 3 : 4. See the *Intervals* in this Series (made by reducing both the *Intervals* given to a common Fundamental by *Probl.* 3) 6 : 4 : 3 the Extremes 6 : 3 are *Octave*, the intermediate *Ratios* are 6 : 4 a *5th*, and 4 : 3 a *4th*, therefore any one of them taken from *Octave* leaves the other.

THE *Reafon* and Senfe of the Rule is obvious; for as Subftraction is oppofite to Addition, fo muft the Operation be; and this is a plain Application of the Subftraction of *Ratios*, with the fame Limitation as in Addition, *viz.* that the *Ratios* muft be taken both one way, fo that we take always a leffer Quantity from a greater, and the Remainder is lefs than that greater, according to the true Character whereby the greater and lefs *Intervals* are diftinguifhed.

OBSERVE. The Difference of any Two *Intervals* expreffes the mutual Relation betwixt any Two of their fimilar Terms, *i. e.* Suppofe any Two *Intervals* reduced to a common *acute*

of

or *grave* Term, their Difference is the *Interval* contained betwixt the other Two Terms; and the *Ratio* expreſſing it is called the mutual Relation of the Two given *Intervals* ; ſo the Difference or mutual Relation of an *Octave* and 5*th* is a 4*th*

MULTIPLICATION of *INTERVALS.*

BECAUSE it is the ſame *Interval* whether the greater or leſſer Number be *Antecedent* of the *Ratio,* and in all Multiplication the Multiplier muſt be an abſolute Number, therefore Multiplication of *Intervals* is an Application of *Probl.* 6. without any Variation or Limitation. I need therefore only make Examples, and refer to that *Problem* for the *Rule.*

PROBLEM XI. *Caſe* 1. To multiply an *Interval* by a whole Number. *Example.* To multiply a 5*th* 2 : 3 by 4. the Product is 16 : 81 the 4*th* Power of 2 and 3 ; and the Series of intermediate Terms being filled up is 16 : 24 : 36 : 54 : 81, expreſſing 4 *Intervals* in the continued *Ratio* of 2 : 3.

CASE II. To multiply an *Interval* by a Fraction. *Example.* Multiply the *Interval* 8 : 27 by $\frac{2}{3}$, the Product, *i. e.* $\frac{2}{3}$ Parts of the given *Interval* is 4 : 9, for $\frac{4}{9}$ is the Square of the cube Root of $\frac{8}{27}$. See this Series, 8 : 12 : 18 : 27, in the *continued Ratio* of 2 : 3, where 8 : 18 (or 4 : 9) is plainly 2 Thirds of 8 : 27.

NOTE. If theſe Two Caſes are joyned we can multiply any *Interval* by any mixt Number: Or we may turn the mixt Number to an improper Fraction, and apply the 2*d Caſe.* Co-

CoROLLARY. From the Nature of Multiplication it is plain, that we have in these Cases a *Rule* for finding an *Interval*, which shall be to any given one, as any given Number to any other ; for 'tis plain if we take these given Numbers in form of a Fraction, and by that Fraction multiply the given *Interval*, we shall have the *Interval* sought, which is to that given as the Numerator to the Denominator ; so in the preceeding *Example*, the *Interval* 4 : 9 is to 8 : 27 as 2 to 3. But *observe*, if the Root to be extracted cannot be found, then the *Problem*, strictly speaking, is impossible, and we can express the *Interval* sought only by irrational Numbers. *Example.* To multiply a 4th 3 : 4 by ⅓, *i.e.* to take ⅓ Parts of it, it can only be expressed by the *Ratio* of the Cube Root of 9 to the Cube Root of 16, or the Square of the Cube Root of 3, to the Square of the Cube Root of 4. And the best we can do with such Cases, if they are to be reduced to Practice, is to bring the Extraction of the Root as near the Truth as may serve our Purpose without a very gross Error.

But if 'tis proposed to find Two *Intervals* that are as Two given Numbers, this can easily be done by multiplying any *Interval*, taken at Pleasure, by the Two given Numbers severally ; 'tis plain the Products are in the *Ratio* of these Numbers.

DIVI-

DIVISION of *INTERVALS*.

HERE alfo there is nothing but the Application of *Probl.* 7. to which I refer for the *Rules*, and only make *Examples*.

PROBLEM XII. *Cafe* 1. To divide an *Interval* by a whole Number, *i. e.* to find fuch an *aliquot* Part of that *Interval* as the given Number denominates.

Example. Divide the *Interval* 4 : 9 by 2, *that is*, find the Half of it ; the Anfwer is a 5*th* 2.: 5, for Two 5*hts* make 4 : 9, as in this *Series*, 4 : 6 : 9.

CASE II. To divide an *Interval* by a Fraction, *that is*, to find an *Interval* that fhall be to the given one, as the Denominator of the Fraction to the Numerator.

Example. Divide the *Interval* 1 : 4 by $\frac{2}{3}$, the Quote is 1 : 8, which is to 1 : 4, as 3 to 2. See this Series, 1, 2, 4, 8.

NOTE. To divide by a mixt Number, we can turn it to an improper Fraction, and do as in *Cafe* 3.

OBSERVE. As Multiplication and Divifion are directly oppofite, fo we have by Divifion as well as by Multiplication, a *Rule* to find an *Interval*, which fhall be to a given one, as any given Number to another : Thus, if the *Interval* fought muft be greater than the given one, make the leaft of the given Numbers the Numerator, and the other the Denominator of a Fraction, by which divide the given *Interval* ; but

but if the fought *Interval* muft be leffer than
the given, make the greater Number the Numerator ; which is all directly oppofite to the
Rule of Multiplication : And, as I have already
obferved in Multiplication, if the Roots to be
extracted by the Rule cannot be found, then
there is no *Interval* that is accurately to the given one as the Two given Numbers.

CASE III. To divide one *Interval* by another, *that is*, to find how oft the leffer is contain'd in the greater. *Rule*. Subftract (by
Probl. 10.) the leffer from the greater, and
the fame Divifor from the laft Remainder
continually till the Remainder be a *Ratio*
of Equality, or change the Species; the
Number of Subftractions, if you come to a
Ratio of Equality, is the Number of Times
the whole Divifor is to be found in the Dividend : But if the Species change, the Number
of Subftractions preceeding that in which the
Remainder changed, is the Number fought: But
then, there is a Remainder which belongs alfo
to the Quote, and it is the Remainder of the
Operation preceeding that which changed ; fo
that the Dividend contains the Divifor fo oft as
that Number of Subftractions denotes and contains that Remainder over, which is properly
the Remainder of the Divifion.

EXAMPLE I. To find how oft the *Interval* 64 : 125 contains 4 : 5. By the *Rule* I find
ThreeTimes.

EXAMPLE II. To find how oft an 8*ve* 1 : 2
contains a 3d *g*. 4 : 5. you'll find Three Times,
and

and this *Interval* over, *viz.*125 : 128. For,*Firſt,*
I ſubſtract 4 : 5 from 1 : 2,   the firſt Remainder is 5 : 8 ; from this I ſubſtract 4 : 5, the 2*d*
Remainder is 25 : 32 ; from this I ſubſtract 4 :
5, the 3*d* Remainder is 125 : 128 ; from this I
ſubſtract 4 : 5, the 4*th* Remainder is 625 : 512,
which is of a different Species, the Antecedent
being here greateſt, which in the other *Ratio*
is leaſt ; therefore the Quote is 3, and the *Ra-*
tio or *Interval* 125 : 128 over.   See the Proof
in this Series, 64 : 80 : 100 : 125 : 128. which
is in the continued *Ratio* of 4 : 5.   64 : 125
is equal to Three times 4 : 5, and 64 : 128 is
equal to 1 : 2.

Thus far only I proceeded with the Anſwer
in *Caſe* 3. of *Probl.* 7. for dividing of one *Ratio*
by another. Now I add, that if we would
make the Quote complete and perfect, ſo that
it may accurately ſhew how many Times and
Parts of a Time the Dividend contains the Diviſor, (if 'tis poſſible) then proceed thus, *viz.*
Take the Remainder preceeding that which
changed, by it divide the given Diviſor, until
you come to a *Ratio* of Equality,   or till the
Species change, and then take the Remainder
(preceeding that which changed of this Diviſion)
and by it divide the laſt Diviſor ; and ſo on
continually till you find a Diviſion that ends in
a *Ratio* of Equality ; then take the given Dividend and Diviſor, and the Remainders of each
Diviſion, and place them all in order from Left
to Right, as in the following Example. Now,
each of theſe *Ratios* having been divided by the
next

next towards the right Hand, they have all
been Dividends except the leaft (or that next
the right) therefore over each I write the Quote
or whole Number of Times the next leffer was
found in it; then numbring thefe Dividends
and Quotes from the Right, I fet the firft Quote
under the firft Dividend, and multiplying the
firft Quote by the fecond, and to that Product
adding 1, I fet the Sum under the 2*d* Dividend:
Again, I multiply that laft Sum by the 3*d* Quote,
and to the Product add the Quote fet under the
firft Dividend; and this Sum I fet under the 3*d*
Dividend; again, I multiply the laft Sum by the
4*th* Quote, and to the Product add the Number
fet under the 2*d* Dividend, and I fet this Sum
under the 4*th* Dividend; and fo on continually,
multiplying the Number fet under every Dividend by the Quote fet over the next Dividend
(on the Left), to the Product I add the Number fet under the laft Dividend (on the Right):
When all this is done, the Numbers that ftand
under each Dividend, exprefs how oft the
laft Divifor (which is the firft Number on the
Right of the Series of Dividends) is contained in
each of thefe Dividends; and confequently
thefe Dividends are to one another as the Number fet under them: Therefore, in the *laft*
Place, if the Numbers under the given Dividend and Divifor are divided, the greater of
them by the leffer, the Quote fignifies how oft
the *Interval* given to be divided contains the
other given one.

EXAMPLE.

EXAMPLE. Divide the *Interval* 1 : 2048 by
1 : 16. According to the *Rule* I fubftract 1 : 16
from 1 : 2048, and have two Subftractions, with
a Remainder 1 : 8 (for the 4*th* Subftraction
changes the Species) then I fubftract 1 : 8 from
1 : 16, and after one Subftraction there remains
1 : 2 (the 2*d* Subftraction changing.) Again I fubftract 1 : 2 from 1 : 8, and after Three Subftractions there remains a *Ratio* of Equality. Now
place thefe according to the Rule, as in the following Scheme, and divide 11 by 4, the Quote
fhews, that the

	2	1	3	
1: 2048,	1: 16,	1: 8,	1: 2	1 : 2048, contains
	11	4	3	

given Dividend
1 : 2048, contains
the Divifor 1 :
16, 2 and $\frac{3}{4}$

Parts of a Time, *i. e.* that it contains 1 : 16
twice ; and moreover. 3 4*th* Parts of 1 : 16,
which you may view all in this *Series* 1 : 2 : 4 :
8 : 16 : 32 : 64· 128 : 256 : 512 : 1024 : 2048,
in the *continual Ratio* of 1 : 2 ; in which we
fee 1 : 16 contained two Times, as in thefe
three Terms 1 : 16 : 256, then remains 256 :
2048, equal to 1 : 8. which you fee is equal to
3 4*th* Parts of 1 : 16, *viz.* three Times 1 : 2,
which is a 4*th* of 1 : 16, as you fee in the *Series.*

FOR a more general *Demonftration*, fuppofe any *Quantity*, *Number* or *Interval*, reprefented by *a* and a leffer by *b*; let a contain *b*
Two Times (which Two is fet over *a*) and
c the Remainder. Again let *b* contain *c* Three
times (which Three is fet over *b*) and *d* the
Re-

Remainder. Then let *c* contain *d* Five times (which Five is set over *c*) and *e* the Remainder. *Lastly*, Let *d* contain *e* Four times (set over *d*) and no Remainder (*i. e.* a *Ratio* of Equality.) Now because *d* contains *e* Four times, I set 4 under *d*,

	2	3	5	4	
	a:	*b*:	*c*:	*d*: *e*	
	155:	67:	21:	4	

then *c* containing *d* Five times, and *d* containing *e* Four times, therefore *c* must contain *e* as many times as the Product of Five into Four, *viz.* Twenty times; but because *c* is equal to Five times *d* and to *e* over, and *e* is contained in the Remainder, *viz.* it self once, therefore *e* is contained in *c* Twenty one times. Again *b* contains *c* Three times and *d* over, and *c* contains *e* Twenty one times precisely, therefore *b* must contain *e* as oft as the Sum of Three times 21, *viz.* 63 and 4 which is 67; then *a* contains *b* Two times and *c* over, also *b* contains *e* Sixty seven times, therefore *a* contains *e* as oft as the Sum of Two times Sixty seven, *viz.* 134 and 21, which is 155. The other Inferences are plain, *viz.* 1*mo.* That each of those Intervals *a*: *b*: *c*, &c. are to one another, as the Numbers set under them ; for these are the Numbers of Times they contain a common Measure *e*. And consequently, 2*do.* If any of these Numbers be divided by another, the Quote will shew how oft the *Interval* under which the Dividend stands, contains the other.

COROLLARY. Thus we have found a Way to discover the *Ratio* betwixt any Two *Intervals,*

vals, if they are commenfurable; fo in the preceeding *Example*, the *Interval* 1 : 2048 is to
1 : 16, as the Number 11 to 4. But *obferve*, if
the *Divifions* never came to a *Ratio* of Equality, the given *Intervals* are not commenfurable,
or as Number to Number; yet we may come
near the Truth in Numbers, by carrying on the
Divifion a confiderable Length.

C H A P. V.

*Containing a more particular Confidera-
tion of the* Nature, Variety *and* Compofition *of* CONCORDS, *in Application of the preceeding* Theory.

WE have already diftinguifhed and defined *fimple* and *compound Intervals*,
which we fhall now particularly apply
to that Species of *Intervals* which is called
CONCORD.

DEFINITION. A *fimple* CONCORD is fuch,
whofe Extremes are at a Diftance lefs than
the Sum of any Two other *Concords*. A com-
pound CONCORD is equal to Two or more
Concords. This in general is agreeable to the
common Notion of *fimple* and *compound*; but
the *Definition* is alfo taken another Way a-
mong the Writers on *Mufick*; thus an *Octave*

I :

1 : 2, and all the leſſer *Concords* (which have been already mentioned) are called *ſimple* and *original* Concords; and all greater than an *Octave* are called *compound* Concords, becauſe all *Concords* above an *Octave* are compoſed of, or equal to the Sum of one or more *Octaves,* and ſome ſingle *Concord* leſs than an *Octave*; and are ordinarily in Practice called by the Name of that *ſimple Concord*; of which afterwards.

---

§ 1. *Of the* original Concords, *their Riſe and Dependence on each other,* &c.

SEe theſe *original Concords* again in the following *Table,* where I have placed them in Order, according to their Quantity.

Table of ſimple Concords.

5 : 6 a 3d *l.*	LET us now firſt examine
4 : 5 a 3d *g.*	the *Compoſition* and *Relations*
3 : 4 a 4th.	of theſe *original Concords* a-
2 : 3 a 5th.	mong themſelves.
5 : 8 a 6th *l.*	IF we apply the preceeding
3 : 5 a 6th *g*	Rules of the Addition and Sub-
1 : 2 a 8ve.	ſtraction of *Intervals* to theſe
	Concords, we ſhall find them

divided into *ſimple* and *compound,* according to the

the firſt and more general Notion, in the Manner expreſſed in the following *Table*.

Simple.	Compound.			Proof in Numb.
5 : 6. a 3d *l.*	5th.	3d *g.* & 3d *l.*		4. 5. 6.
	6th *l.*	4th,	3d *l.*	5. 6. 8.
4 : 5. a 3d *g*	5th *g.*	4th,	3d *g.*	3. 4. 5.
		5th,	4th. or	2. 3. 4.
3 : 4. a 4th.		5th *g.*	3d *l.* or	3. 5. 6.
	8ve.	6th *l.*	3d *g.* or	4. 5. 8.
		3d *g.*	3d *l.*4th.	4. 5. 6. 8.

(composed of)

The 3d *l.* 3d *g.* and 4*th*, are equal to the Sum of no other *Concords*; for the 3d *l.* is it ſelf the leaſt *Interval* of all *Concords*. The 3d *g.* is the next, which is equal to the 3d *l.* and a Remainder which is *Diſcord.* The 4*th* is equal to either of the 3*ds* and a *Diſcord* Remainder ; and theſe Three are therefore the leaſt Principles of *Concord,* into which all other *Intervals* are diviſible : For the Compoſition of the 5*th*, 6*th* and 8*ve*, you ſee it proven in the Numbers annexed; and that they can be compounded of no other *Concords*, you'll prove by applying the Rules of Addition and Subſtraction.

As to the Proofs in Numbers which are annex'd, they demonſtrate the Thing, taking the component Parts in one particular Order ; but it is alſo true in whatever Order they are taken, as is proven in *Probl.* 2. *Chap.* 4. Or ſee all the Variety in this Table ; in the laſt Column of which you ſee the Names of all the component Parts ſet down in the ſeveral Orders of
which

which they are capable, either from the *acuteſt* Term or the *graveſt.*

TABLE of the various Orders of the har-monical Parts of the greater Concords.

5th, 2 : 3
$\begin{cases} 4 \ . \ 5 \ . \ 6 & \text{3d g. 3d l.} \\ 10 \ . \ 12 \ . \ 15 & \text{3d l. 3d g.} \end{cases}$

6th, l. 5 : 8
$\begin{cases} 5 \ . \ 6 \ . \ 8 & \text{3d l. 4th.} \\ 15 \ . \ 20 \ . \ 24 & \text{4th. 3d l.} \end{cases}$

6th, g. 3 : 5
$\begin{cases} 3 \ . \ 4 \ . \ 5 & \text{4th, 3d g.} \\ 12 \ . \ 15 \ . \ 20 & \text{3d g. 4th.} \end{cases}$

8ve 1 : 2
$\begin{cases} \begin{cases} 2 \ . \ 3 \ . \ 4 & \text{5th, 4th.} \\ 3 \ . \ 4 \ . \ 6 & \text{4th, 5th.} \end{cases} \\ \begin{cases} 3 \ . \ 5 \ . \ 6 & \text{6th g. 3d l.} \\ 5 \ . \ 6 \ . \ 10 & \text{3d l. 6th g.} \end{cases} \\ \begin{cases} 4 \ . \ 5 \ . \ 8 & \text{3d g. 6th l.} \\ 5 \ . \ 8 \ . \ 10 & \text{6th l. 3d g.} \end{cases} \\ \begin{cases} 3 \ . \ 4 \ . \ 5 \ . \ 6 & \text{4th, 3d g. 3d l.} \\ 4 \ . \ 5 \ . \ 6 \ . \ 8 & \text{3d g. 3d l. 4th.} \\ 5 \ . \ 6 \ . \ 8 \ . \ 10 & \text{3d l. 4th. 3d g.} \\ 10 . 12 . 15 . 20 & \text{3d l. 3d g. 4th.} \\ 12 . 15 . 20 . 24 & \text{3d g. 4th. 3d l.} \\ 15 . 20 . 24 . 30 & \text{4th, 3d l. 3d g.} \end{cases} \end{cases}$

Here you may obſerve, that the Varieties of the Compoſition of Octave by Three Parts, viz. 3d g. 3d l. 4th, include the other Three Ways by Two Parts ; and alſo all the Varieties of the Compoſition of the 5th and 6th.

W 1

WE have already, by Addition of the various *Concords* within an *Octave*, found and proven that the *5th*, *6ths* and *8ve*, are equal to the Sum of lesser *Concords*, as in the preceeding *Table* : Now we shall consider, by what Laws of Proportion these *Intervals* are resolvable back into their component Parts ; or, how to put such middle Numbers betwixt the Extremes of these *Intervals*, that the intermediate *Ratios* shall make *harmonical Intervals* ; by which we shall have a nearer View of the Dependence of these *original Concords* upon one another.

OF the Seven *original Concords* we examine their *Composition* among themselves, *i. e.* what lesser ones the greater are equal to ; therefore the *Octave* being the greatest, its *Resolutions* must include the *Resolutions* of all the rest.

PROPOSITION I. If betwixt the Extremes of an *Octave* we place an *arithmetical Mean* (by *Corol.* to *Theor.* 2. *Chap.* 4.) it shall resolve it into Two *Ratios*, which are the *Concords* of *5th* and *4th* ; and the *5th* shall be next the lesser Extreme : So betwixt 1 and 2 an *arithmetical Mean* is 1½ ; or because 1 and 2 can have no middle Term in whole Numbers ; therefore if we multiply them by 2, the Products 2 and 4 being in the same *Ratio*, can receive one *arithmetical Mean* (by *Theor.* 8th) which Mean is 3, and the Series 2 : 3 : 4, *viz.* a *5th* and a *4th.*

PROPOSITION II. If betwixt the Extremes of an *Octave* we take an *harmonical Mean*, by *Theor.* 11th, the intermediate *Ratios* shall be

a

a 4*th* and a 5*th*, and the 4*th* next the leſſer
Extreme ; ſo betwixt 1 : 2 an *harmonical Mean*
is 1⅓ ; or multiplying all by 3, to bring them to
wɭ oɭ Numbers, the Series is 3, 4, 6, which
is *harmonical.*

  COROLLARY. 'Tis plain, that if betwixt the
Extremes of the *Octave* we put Two *Means*,
one *arithmetical* and one *harmonical*, the Four
Numbers ſhall be in *geometrical Proportion*, as
here, 6, 8, 9, 12. The *Reaſon* is, that the
4*th* and 5*th* are the Complements of each other
to an *Octave* ; and therefore a 4*th* to the lower
Extreme leaves a 5*th* to the upper, and contrarily : And in this Diviſion of the *Octave*, we
have the Three Kinds of *Proportion*, ARITH-
METICAL, HARMONICAL *and* GEOME-
TRICAL, mixt, for 6 : 9 : 12. *viz.* the 5*th*, 4*th*,
and 8*ve*, are *arithmetical* ; 6 : 8 : 12, the 4*th*,
5*th*, and 8*ve*, are *harmonical*; and 6 : 8 : 9 : 12,
geometrical.

  OBSERVE. The 5*th* and 4*th* are the Reſult of
the immediate and moſt ſimple Diviſion of the
Octave into Two Parts : The 4*th* is not reſol-
vable into other *Concords*, ſince the only leſſer
Concords are the 3*d g.* and 3*d l.* and either of theſe
taken from a 4*th*, leaves a *Diſcord*; and therefore 'tis in vain to ſeek any *mean* Terms that
will reſolve it into *Concords*. 'Tis natural therefore next to enquire into the *Reſolutions* of the
5*th*, which by a remarkable Uniformity, we
find reducible into its conſtituent leſſer *Concords*
by the ſame Laws of Proportion.

PRO-

Proposition III. An *arithmetical Mean* put betwixt the Extremes of a 5*th*, refolves it into a 3*d g*. and a 3*d l*. with the 3*d g*. next the leffer Extreme, as here, 2 : 2 ½ : 3. which multiplied by 3 are reduced to thefe whole Numbers 4 : 5 : 6.

Proposition IV. An *harmonical Mean* put betwixt the Extremes of a 5*th*, refolves it into a 3*d g*. and 3*d l*. with the 3*d l*. next the leffer Extreme ; as 2 : 2⅖ : 3, which multiplied by 5 are reduced to thefe, 10 : 12 : 15.

Corollary. The fame Thing follows here as from the two firft Propofitions, *viz.* That taking both an *arithmetical* and *harmonical Mean* betwixt the Extremes of a 5*th*, the Four Numbers are in *geometrical Proportion*, as in thefe, 20, 24, 25, 30.

Now out of the various Mixtures of thefe fimple Divifions of the 8*ve* and 5*th*, we can bring not only all the *Refolutions* of the 6*th*, and the other *Refolutions* of the 8*ve*, but all the Varieties with refpect to the Order in which the Parts can be taken, as follows, *viz.*

1*mo.* If with the *arithmetical* Divifion of the *Octave*, we mix the *arithmetical* Divifion of the 5*th*, *i. e.* if we put an *arithmetical Mean* betwixt the Extremes of the *Octave*, and then another *arithmetical Mean* betwixt the leffer Extreme and the laft *mean* Term found, and reduce all the 4 to whole Numbers, then we have this Series 4, 5, 6, 8, in which we have the *Octave* refolved into its three conftituent *Concords*, 3*d* greater, 3*d* leffer, and 4*th* ; and

within

within that Series the 5*th* refolved into its two
conftituent *Concords*, 3*d* greater, and 3*d* leffer : And if we confider the Extremes of the
Octave with the leaft of the two middle Terms
5, then thefe 4, 5, 8 fhew us the *Octave* refolved into a 3*d g.* and a 6*th l. Laftly.* It
fhews us the 6*th l.* refolved into a 3*d l.* and
a 4*th, viz.* 5, 6, 8.

2*do.* I f we mix the *harmonical* Divifion of
Octave, with the *arithmetical* Divifion of
the 5*th, i. e.* if we put an *harmonical Mean*
betwixt the Extremes of *Octave*, and then an
arithmetical Mean betwixt the greateft Extreme and middle Term laft found, as in this
Series, 3, 4, 5, 6, then we have the *Refolution* of the *Octave* into a 6*th g.* and 3*d l.* as
in thefe 3, 5, 6 ; alfo the 6*th g. refolved* into
a 4*th* and 3*d g.* in thefe, 3, 4, 5; and taking
the whole Series, we have a 2*d* Order of the
Three Parts of the *Octave*.

W e have feen all the *harmonical* Parts of
the *Octave* and 5*th*, and both the 6*ths* ; and as
to the Variety of Order in which thefe may be
placed betwixt the Extremes, it may all be
found by other Mixtures of the Parts of the
Octave, and 5*th* or 6*th* ; as you'll eafily find by
comparing the 6 Orders of the *Compofition* of
Octave by 3 *Concords*, in the preceeding *Table*.

O r, you may find them all in one Series, if
you'll divide the *Octave* thus, *viz.* Put both an
arithmetical and *harmonical Mean* betwixt its
Extremes, and you'll have a 4*th* and 5*th* to each
of the Extremes ; both of which 5*ths* divide
arith-

arithmetically and alfo *harmonically*, and at every Divifion reduce all to a Series of whole Numbers; and 'tis plain you'll have a Series of 8 Terms, among which you'll have Examples of the 7 *original Concords* with their *Compofitions*, and all the different Orders in which their Parts can be taken. Or, you may make the Series by taking the 7 *Concords*, and reducing them to a common *Fundamental*, by *Problem* 3. the Series is 360 : 300 : 288 : 270 : 240 : 225 : 216 : 180. See *Plate* 1. *Fig.* 4. wherein I have connected the Numbers fo as all the *Compofition* may be eafily traced.

THERE is this remarkable in that Series, that you have all the *Concords* in a Series, both afcending toward *Acutenefs* from a common *Fundamental*, or greateft Number 360, and defcending towards *Gravity*, from a common *acute* Term 180. and for that Reafon the Series has this Property, that taking the Two Extremes, and any other Two at equal Diftance, thefe 4 are in *geometrical Proportion*.

Nota. IF betwixt the Extremes of any *Interval* you take Two middle Terms, which fhall be to the Extremes in the *Ratios* of any Two component Parts of that *Interval*, *i. e.* if the two middle Terms divide the *Interval* into the fame Parts only in a different Order, the Four Numbers are always *geometrical*.

Now, from the Things laft explained, we fhall make fome more *particular Obfervations* concerning

concerning the *Dependence* of the *original Con-cords* one upon another.

T H E *Octave* is not only the greateſt Interval of the Seven *original Concords,* but the firſt in Degree of Perfection; the Agreement of whoſe Extremes is greateſt, and in that reſpect moſt like to *Uniſons* : As it is the greateſt *Interval,* ſo all the leſſer are contained in it; but the Thing moſt remarkable is, the Manner how theſe leſſer *Concords* are found in the *Octave,* which ſhews their mutual Dependences; by tak-ing both an *harmonical* and *arithmetical Mean* betwixt the Extremes of the *Octave,* and then both an *arithmetical* and *harmonical Mean* be-twixt each Extreme, and the moſt diſtant of the Two Means laſt found, *viz.* betwixt the leſſer Extreme, and the firſt *arithmetical Mean,* alſo betwixt the greater Extreme and the firſt *harmonical Mean* we have all the leſſer *Con-cords* : Thus if betwixt 360 and 180 the Ex-tremes of *Octave,* we take an *arithmetical Mean,* it is 270, and an *harmonical Mean* is 240; then betwixt 360, the greateſt Extreme, and 240, the *harmonical Mean,* take an *arith-metical Mean,* it is 300, and an *harmonical Mean* is 288; again, betwixt 188 the leſſer Extreme of the *Octave,* and 270 the firſt *arith-metical Mean,* take an *arithmetical Mean,* it is 225, and an *harmonical* it is 216, and the whole Numbers make this Series, 360 : 300 : 288 : 270 : 240 : 216 : 180.

O B S E R V E. The immediate Diviſion of the *Octave* reſolves it into a 4*th* and 5*th*; the a-
rithmetical

rithmetical Division puts the 5*th* next the leffer Extreme, as here 2, 3, 4, and the *harmonical* puts it next the greater Extreme, as
here 3 : 4 : 6 ; and you may fee both in thefe
four Numbers 6, 8, 9, 12. *Again* the immediate Division of the 5*th* produces the Two
3*ds* ; the *arithmetical* Division puts the leffer
3*d*, and the *harmonical* the greater 3*d* next the
leffer Extreme ; as in thefe 4, 5, 6, and 10,
12, 15 ; or fee both in one Series, 20, 24, 25,
30. The two 6*ths* are therefore found by Divifion of the *Octave*, tho' not by any immediate
Division. The fame is true alfo of the two 3*ds*;
fo that all the other *fimple Concords* are found
by Division of the *Octave*. The 5*th* and 4*th*
arife immediately and directly out of it, and the
3*ds* and 6*ths* proceed from an accidental Divifion of the *Octave* ; for the 3*ds* arife immediately out of the 5*th*, which having one Extreme common with the *Octave*, the mean
Term which divides it directly, divides the
Octave in a Manner accidentally.

N o w, if we confider how perfectly the Extremes of an *Octave* agree, that when they are
founded together, 'tis impoffible to perceive two
different Sounds ; fo great is their Likenefs, and
the Mixture fo evenly, that it is impoffible to
conceive a greater Agreement ; we fee plainly
there is no Reafon to expect that there fhould
be any other *Concord* within the Order of Nature that comes nearer, or fo near to the Perfection of *Unifons* : And if we confider again,
how thefe Seven *original Concords* gradually
decreafe

decrease from the *Octave* to the lesser *6th*, which has but a small Degree of *Concord*; and with that Confideration joyn this of the mutual Dependence of these Seven *Concords* upon one another, and especially how they all rise out of the Division of the *Octave*, according to a most simple Law, *viz.* The taking an *arithmetical* and *harmonical Mean* betwixt its Extremes which gives the Two *Concords* next in Perfection to the *Octave*, whereof the *5th* is best; and the same Law being applied to this, discovers all the rest of the *Concords*; for out of the *5th* arise immediately the two *3ds*, whose Complements to *Octave* are the two *6ths*; and for that Reason these *6ths* and *3ds* are said to rise accidentally out of the *Octave*; (and afterwards we shall see how by the same Law, some other principal *Intervals* belonging to the System of *Musick* are found.) Upon all these Confiderations we may be fatisfied, that we have discovered the true natural System of *Concords* within the *Octave*; and that we have no reasonable Ground to believe there are any more, nor even a Poffibility of it, according to the prefent State and Order of Things.

Now as to the Order of their Perfection, we have already stated them according to the Ear thus, *Octave, 5th, 4th, 6th gr. 3d gr. 3d leff. 6th leff.* In which Order we find this Law, That the best *Concords* are expreft by least Numbers. Yet, as I obferved, this is not an univerfal Character; and we are only certain of this from Experience, that the frequent Coincidence of Vibrations,

brations, is a neceffary Part of the Caufe of *Harmony*; Senfe and Obfervation muft fupply the reft, in determining the Preference of *Concords*; and fo we take thefe 7 *original Concords* in the Order mentioned; and upon what Confiderations they are otherways ranked by practical *Muficians*, fhall be explain'd in its proper Place.

YET before I go further, let us notice this one Thing concerning the Difference of the *arithmetical* and *harmonical* Divifion. An *arithmetical* or *harmonical Mean* put betwixt the Extremes of any *Interval*, divides it into two unequal Parts; the *arithmetical* puts the greateft *Interval* next the leffer Extreme, the *harmonical* contrarily, as in thefe, 2 : 3 : 4, and 3 : 4 : 6, where the *Octave* is divided into its conftituent 5*th* and 4*th*; or the Refolutions of the 5*th*, as here 4 : 5 : 6, and 10 : 12 : 15. Now let us apply thefe Numbers either to the Lengths of Chords or their Vibrations, and we find this Difference, that applied to the Vibrations, the *arithmetical* Divifion puts the beft *Concord* next the *fundamental*, or *grave Extreme*, and the *harmonical* puts it next the *acute* Extreme; but contrarily in both when applied to the Lengths of Chords. As thefe two Divifions refolve the *Octave* or 5*th* into the fame Parts, they are in that refpect equal; but if we fuppofe the Extremes of the *Octave* or 5*th*, with their *arithmetical* or *harmonical Means*, to be founded all together, there will be a confiderable Difference; and that Divifion which

which puts the beft *Concord* loweft is beft,
which is the *arithmetical* if the Numbers are
applied to the Vibrations, but the *harmonical*
if applied to the Lengths of Chords. The obferving this fhall be enough here; I fhall more
fully explain it when I treat of *compound Sounds,*
under the Name of *Harmony.* This however
we find true, That *geometrical Proportion* affords no *fimple Concords* (how it comes among
the *compound* fhall be feen prefently) and it
has no Place in the Relation and Dependence
of the *original Concords,* but fo far as a Mixture of the *arithmetical* and *harmonical* produces it, as in thefe, 6, 8, 9, 12. And here I fhall
obferve, That the *harmonical* Proportion received that Denomination from its being
found among the Numbers, applied to the
Length of Chords, that exprefs the chief *Concords* in *Mufick, viz.* the *Octave,* 5th, and 4th,
as here, 3, 4, 6. But this Proportion does not
always conftitute *Concords,* nor can poffibly do,
becaufe betwixt the Extremes of any *Interval*
we can put an *harmonical Mean,* yet every *Interval* is not refolvable into Parts that are *Concords ;* therefore this Definition has been rejećt-
ed, particularly by *Kepler ;* and for this he in-
ftitutes another Definition of *harmonical Proportion, viz.* When betwixt the Extremes of
any *Ratio* or *Interval,* one or more middle
Terms are taken, which are all *Concord* among
themfelves, and each with the Extremes, then
that is an *harmonical* Divifion of fuch an *Interval ;* fo that *Octave,* 6th and 5th are capable
of

of being *harmonically* divided in this Senfe; all the Variety whereof you fee in a Table at the Beginning of this Chapter: And thefe middle Terms will be in fome Cafes *arithmetical* Means, as 1 : 2 : 3 ; in fome *geometrical*, as 1, 2, 4; in fome *harmonical* (in the firft Senfe) as 3 : 4 : 6 ; and in others they will depend on no certain *Proportion*, as 5, 6, 8.

HITHERTO we have confidered the *Refolution* and *Compofition* of *Intervals*, as they are expreft by *Ratios* of Numbers ; but there are other Ways of deducing the Relation and Dependence of the *Concords*, not from the Divifion or Refolution of a *Ratio*, but the Divifion of a fimple Number, or rather of a Line expreft by that Number, which may be call'd the *geometrical* Part of this *Theory*. But it will be better if I firft confider and explain the remaining *Concords* belonging to the *Syftem* of *Mufick*, which are particularly called *compound Concords*.

§ 2. *Of*

§ 2. *Of* Compound Concords; *and of the* Harmonick Series; *with several Observations relating to both simple and compound Concords.*

HITHERTO we have taken it upon Experience, That there are no *concording Intervals* greater than *Octave,* but what are composed of the 7 *original Concords* within an *Octave;* the *Reason* of which is deduced from the Perfection of the *Octave.* We have seen already how all the other *simple* and *original Concords* are contained in, and depend upon the *Octave,* and derive their Sweetness from it, as they arise more or less directly out of it: We have observed, that it has in all Respects the greatest Perfection of any *Interval,* and comes nearest to *Unisons;* and tho' there seems to be something still wanting, to make a general Character, by which we may judge of the Approach of any *Interval* to the perfect Agreement of *Unisons,* yet 'tis plain the *Octave* 1 : 2 comes nearest to it; for 'tis contained not only in the least of all Numbers, but that Proportion is of the most perfect Kind, *viz. Multiple;* and of all such it is the most simple, which makes the greatest Degree of Commensurateness or Agreement in the Motions of the Air that produce these Sounds. Let me add this
other

other Remark, That if Wind-inftruments are
overblown, the Sound will rife firft to an *Octave*,
and to no other *Concord* ; why it fhould not as
well rife to a *4th*, *&c.* is owing probably to
the Perfection of *Octave*, and its being next to
Unifon. Again, take into the Confideration
that furprifing *Phænomenon* of Sound being raifed from a Body which is touched by nothing
but the Air, moved by the fonorous Motion of
another Body; particularly that if the Tune of
the untouched Body be *Octave* above the
given Sound, it will be moft diftinctly heard ;
and fcarcely will any other but the *Octave* be
heard.

FROM this fimple and perfect Form of the
Octave, arifes this remarkable Property of it,
that it may be doubled, tripled, *&c.* and ftill be
Concord, *i. e.* the Sum of Two or more
Octaves are *Concord*, tho' the more *compound*
will be gradually lefs agreeable ; but it is not fo
with any other *Concord* lefs than *Octave*, the
Double, *&c.* of thefe being all *Difcords* ; and
as continued *geometrical Proportion* conftitutes
a Series of equal *Intervals*, fo we fee that fuch
a Series has no Place in *Mufick* but among
Octaves, the Continuation of other *Concords* producing *Difcord*. Thefe Things remarkably confirm to us the Perfection of the *Octave* : There
is fuch a Likenefs and Agreement betwixt its
Extremes, that it feems to make a Demonftration *a priori*, that whatever Sound is *Concord* to one Extreme of the *Octave*, will be fo
to the other alfo ; and in Experience it is fo.
We

We have feen already, that whatever Sound
betwixt the Extremes of an *Octave*, is *Concord*
to the one, is in another Degree *Concord* to
the other alfo ; for we found that the *Octave*
is refolvable into *Concords*. *Again*, if we add
any other *fimple Concord* to an *Octave*, we find
by Experience that it agrees to both its Extremes; to the neareft Extreme it is a *fimple
Concord*, and to the fartheft it is a *compound Concord :* Now, take this for a Principle, That
whatever agrees to one Extreme of *Octave*, a-
grees alfo to the other, and we eafily conclude,
That there cannot be any *concording Interval*
greater than an *Octave*, but the *Compounds* of
an *Octave* and fome leffer *Concord* : For if we
fuppofe the Extremes of any *Interval* greater
than an *Octave* to be *Concord*, 'tis plain we can
put in a middle Term, which fhall be *Octave*
to one Extreme of that *Interval*, confequently
the other Extreme fhall be alfo *Concord* with
this middle Term, and be diftant from it
by an *Interval* lefs than an *Octave*; and therefore if we add a *Difcord* to one Extreme of an
Octave, it will be alfo *Difcord* to the other ;
the fame will apply alfo to the *Compounds* of
Two or more *Octaves*; but the Agreement
will ftill be lefs as the Compofition is greater.

I cannot but mention here how *D' Cartes*
concludes this Principle to be true; he obferves, what I have done, *That the Sound of
a Whiftle or Organ-pipe will rife to an*
Octave, *if 'tis forcibly blown; which proceeds,*
says

says he, *from this, That it differs leaft from*
Unifon.   *Hence again,* says he, *I judge that no*
Sound is heard, but its acute Octave *feems*
fome way to eccho or refound in the Ear ; for
which Reafon it is that with the groffer Chords
(or thofe which give the graver Sound) of fome
ftringed Inftruments (he mentions the *Teftudo*)
others are joyned an Octave *acuter, which are*
always touched together, whereby the graver
Sound is improven, fo as to be more diftinctly
heard.   From this he concludes it plain, *That*
no Sound which is Concord *to one Extreme of an*
Octave, *can be* Difcord *to the other.*   From
all this we fee how the *Octave* comprehends the
whole *Syftem* of *Concords,* (excepting the *Uni-*
fon) becaufe they are all contained in it, or
compofed of it and thefe that are cotained in it.

THE Author already mentioned of the *E-*
lucidationes Phyficæ upon *D' Cartes's Compend*
of *Mufick,* advances an *Hypothefis* to explain
how this happens, which *D' Cartes* affirms,
viz. That the *Fundamental* never founds but
the *acute Octave* feems to do fo too.   He fuppofes that the Air contains in it feveral Parts of
different Conftitution, capable, like different
Chords, of different Meafures of Vibrations,
which may be the Reafon, fays he, that the
human Voice or Inftruments, and chiefly thefe
of Metal never found, but fome other *acuter*
Sounds are heard to refound in the Air.

IN the Beginning of this *Chapter* I obferved
two different Senfes in which *Concords* were
called *fimple* and *compound :* The *Octave* and
all

all within it are called *fimple* and *original Concords*; and all greater than an *Octave*, are *compound*, becaufe all fuch are compofed of an *Octave*, and fome lefler *Concord.* Now, the 5*th*, 6*ths* and *Octave* are alfo compofed of the 3*ds* and 4*ths* which are the moft *fimple Concords*; but then all the 7 *Concords* within an *Octave* have different Effects in *Mufick*, whereas the *compound Concords* above an *Octave* have all in Practice the fame Name and Effect with thefe fimple ones, lefs than an *Octave*, of which with the *Octave* they are compofed; fo a 5*th* and an *Octave* added make 1 : 3, and is called a *compound* 5*th*. Now as there are 7 *original Concords*, fo thefe 7 added to *Octave*, make 7 *compound Concords*; and added to two *Octaves*, make other 7 more compound, and fo on. We have feen already, in *Prob.* 8. how to add *Intervals*, and according to that *Rule* I have made the following *Table* of *Concords*, which I place in Order, according to the Quantity of the *Interval*, beginning with the leaft. I fuppofe 1 to be a common *fundamental* Chord, and exprefs the *acute* Term of each *Concord* by that Fraction or Part of the *Fundamental* that makes fuch *Concord* with it, and have reduced each to its radical Form, *i. e.* to the loweft Number; fo an *Octave* and 5*th* added, is in the *Ratio* 2 : 6, equal by Reduction to 1 : 3; and others.

Follows the general Table of CONCORDS,

Octaves

	Simple Concords	Compounds above one Octave	Compounds above two Octaves	
Octaves	1: 2:	1: 4:	1: 8:	$\frac{1}{16}$ &c.
6th g.	: $\frac{3}{5}$	: $\frac{3}{10}$	: $\frac{3}{20}$	&c.
6th l.	$\frac{5}{8}$:	$\frac{5}{16}$:	$\frac{5}{32}$:	
5th	: $\frac{2}{3}$	: $\frac{1}{3}$	: $\frac{1}{6}$	
4th	$\frac{3}{4}$:	$\frac{3}{8}$:	$\frac{3}{16}$:	
3d g.	: $\frac{4}{5}$	: $\frac{2}{5}$	: $\frac{1}{5}$	
3d l.	$\frac{5}{6}$:	$\frac{5}{12}$:	$\frac{5}{24}$:	

These *Compounds* are ordinarily called by the Name of the *simple Concord* of which they are compofed, tho' they have alfo other Names, of which in another Place.

If this Table were continued infinitely, 'tis plain we fhould have all the poffible *harmonical Ratios*, and in their radical Forms; 'tis alfo certain, that there fhould be no other Numbers found in it than thefe, 1, 3, 5, and their Multiples by 2, *i. e.* their Products by 2, which are 2, 6, 10, and the Products of thefe by 2, *viz.* 4, 12, 20, and fo on *in infinitum*, multiplying the laft Three Products by 2. The *Reafon* of which is, that in this Series 1, 2, 3, 4, 5, 6, 8, we have no other Numbers but 1, 3, 5, and their Products by 2; and we have here alfo all the Numbers that belong to the *fimple original Concords*; and if we confider how the *Compounds* are raifed by adding an *Octave* continually, we fee plainly that

no

no new Number can be produced, but the Product of these that belong to the *simple Concords*
multiplied by 2 continually. All which Numbers make up this Series, *viz.* 1, 2, 3, 4, 5,
6, 8, 10, 12, 16, 20, 24, 32, 40, 48, 64,
80, *&c.* which is continued after the Number 5,
by multiplying the last Three by 2, and their
Products *in infinitum* by 2; whereby 'tis plain,
we shall have all the Multiples of these original
Numbers 1, 3, 5, arising from the continual
Multiplication of them by 2. And this I call the
HARMONICAL SERIES, because it contains
all the possible *Ratios* that make *Concord*,
either *simple* or *compound* : And not only so,
but every Number of it is *Concord* with every
other, which I shall easily prove: That it contains all possible *Concords* is plain from the Way
of raising it, since it has no other Numbers than
what belong to the preceeding general *Table* of
Concords; and that every Number is *Concord*
with every other is thus proven : After the Number 5 every Three Terms of the Series are the
Doubles of the last Three ; but the Numbers 1,
2, 3, 4, 5, are *Concord* each with another, and
consequently each of these must be *Concord*
with every other Number in the Series, since all
the rest are but Multiples of these; for whatever
Concord any lesser Number of these 5 makes
with another of them that is greater, it will with
the Double of that greater make an *Octave* more,
and with the Double of the last another *Octave*
more, and so on : Thus, 2 to 3, is a 5*th*, and
2 to 6 is a 5*th* and 8*ve* ; but, comparing any
greater

greater Number of thefe Five with a leffer, whatever *Concord* that is, it will with the Double of
that leffer be an *8ve* lefs, providing that Double
be ftill lefs than the Number compared to it, (fo
5 to 2 is a *3d g.* and *8ve*, and 5 to 4 is only a
3d g.)But if 'tis greater, then it will be the Complement of the firft *Concord* to *8ve*, *i.e.* the Difference of it and *8ve*, (fo 5 to 6 is a *3d l.* the
Complement of a *6th g.* 5 : 3 to an *8ve*) and
taking another Double it will be an *8ve* more
than the laft, and fo on. Now the Thing being true of thefe Five Numbers compared together, and with all the other Numbers in the Series, it muft hold true of all thefe others compared together, becaufe they are only Multiples
of the firft. The Ufe of this *harmonick Series*
you'll find in the next *Chapter.* I fhall end this
with fome further Obfervations relating to the
harmonical Numbers, and the whole *Syftem* of
Concords both *fimple* and *compound.*

IN the preceeding *Chapter* I have endeavou-
red to difcover fome Character, in the Proportion of *mufical Intervals*, whereby their various
Perfections may be ftated, tho' not with all the
Succefs to be wifhed ; fo that we are in a great
Meafure left to Senfe and Experience. We have
feen that the principal and chief *Concords*, are
contain'd within the firft and leaft of the natural Series of Numbers; the *Octave*, *5th*, *4th*,
and *3ds*, in the natural Progreffion 1, 2, 3, 4, 5,
6; and the Two *6ths* arife out of the Divifion
of the *Octave*, and are contain'd in thefe Numbers 3, 5, 8. Confidering what a neceffary Condition

dition of *Concord*, frequent Union and Coincidence of Motion is, we have concluded, that the smaller Numbers any Proportion consists of, *cæteris paribus*, the more perfect is the *Interval* expressed by such a Proportion of Numbers. But then I observed, that besides this Smalness of the Numbers on which the Coincidence depends, there is something still a Secret in the Proportion or Relation of the Numbers that represent the Extremes of an *Interval*, that we ought to know for making a general Character, whereby the Degrees of *Concord* may be determined; so 4 : 7 is *Discord*, and yet 5 : 6 is *Concord*, and 5 : 8. Now again we see in this *Table* of *Concords*, that the Smalness of the Numbers does not absolutely determine the Preference, else 1 : 3 an *Octave* and 5*th*, would be better than 1 : 4 a double *Octave*, which it is not, and so would all the other *compound* 5*ths* *in infinitum.* Again, the *compound* 3*d* 1 : 5 would be better than either the *compound Octave* 1 : 8, or the *compound* 5*th* 1 : 6, which is all contrary to Experience; and this demonstrates, that there must be something else in it than barely the Smalness of the Numbers. *D' Cartes* observes here, that the 3*d* 1 : 6, compos'd of Two *Octaves*, is better than either the *simple* 3*d*, 4 : 5, or the first *Compound* 2 : 5; and gives this Reason, *viz.* that 1 : 5 is a multiple Proportion, which the others are not; and o_,t of multiple Proportion, he says, the best *Concor*^d*s* proceed, because it is the most simple Form, and easily perceived : By the same Reason all
the

the *compound* 5*ths* are better than the *simple*
5*th*; and *D' Cartes* himfelf makes the firft
compound 5*th* 1 : 3 the moft perfect, becaufe it
is Multiple, and in fmaller Numbers than the
fimple 5*th.* But we muft obferve, that every
multiple Proportion will not conftitute *Concord,*
fo 1 : 9 is grofs *Difcord,* being equal to Three
Octaves, and this *Difcord* 8 : 9. Now confider either the Numbers or their multiple Proportion, and this of 1 : 9 fhould be better
than 3 : 8, or than 3 : 16; yet it is otherwife,
for thefe are *compound* 4*ths,* which are *Concord;*
we muft therefore refer this to fome other thing,
in the Relation of the Numbers, that we cannot exprefs.

OBSERVE next how *D' Cartes* ftates thefe
Concords; he puts them in this Order, *Octave,*
5*th,* 3*d* g. 4*th,* 6*th* g. 3*d* l. 6*th* l. and gives
this Reafon, *viz.* That the Perfection of any
Concord is not to be taken from its *fimple* Form
only, but from a joynt Confideration of all its
Compounds; becaufe, fays he, it can never be
heard alone fo fimply, but there will be heard
the Refonance of its *Compound;* as in the *Unifon,* or a fingle given Sound, the Refonance of
the *acute Octave* is contained; and therefore he
places the 3*d* g. before the 4*th,* becaufe being
contain'd in leffer Numbers, it is more perfect.
But we muft obferve again, that as *Concord*
does not depend altogether upon multiple Proportion, neither does it upon the Smalnefs of
the Numbers; for then *D' Cartes* fhould have
put the 5*th* before the *Octaves,* becaufe all its
                                              Com-

Componuds are contained in leſſer Numbers than the *Octaves.* We ſee then how difficult it is to deduce the Perfection of the *Concords* from the Numbers that expreſs them.

L E T us conſider this other Remark of *D' Cartes,* he obſerves that only the Numbers 2, 3, 5, are ſtrictly *muſical* Numbers, all the other Numbers of the Table being only *Compounds* or Multiples of theſe Three, which belong in the firſt Place to the *Octave, 5th,* and 3*d* g. which he calls *Concords* properly, and *per ſe,* as he calls all others *accidental,* for Reaſons I ſhall ſhow you immediately.

N o w, tho' the *compound 5ths* are contain'd in leſſer Numbers than the *Octaves,* perhaps the Preference of the *Octaves* is due to the radical Number 2, which belongs originally and in the firſt Place to that *Concord;* whereas the *compound 5ths* depend on the Number 3 which is more complex : But we ſhall leave this Way of Reaſoning as uncertain and chimerical ; yet this we have very remarkable, that the firſt ſix of the natural Series of Numbers,*viz.*1, 2, 3, 4, 5, 6, are *Concords* comparing every one with every other, which is true of no other Series of Numbers, except the Equimultiples of theſe 6, which, in reſpect of *Concord,* are the ſame with theſe. Again, if each of theſe Numbers be multiplied by it ſelf, and by each of the reſt, and theſe Products be diſpoſed in a Series, each Number of that Series with the next conſtitutes ſome *Interval* that belongs to the Syſtem of *Muſick,* tho' they are not at all *Concord,* as
will

will appear afterwards : That Series is 1. 2. 3.
4. 5. 6. 8. 9. 10. 12. 15. 16. 18. 20. 24.
25. 30. 36.   It would be of no great Ufe to repete what wonderful Properties fome Authors
have found in the Number 6, particularly *Kir-*
cher, who tells us, that it is the only Number
that is abfolutely *harmonical,* and clearly reprefents the *divine Idea* in the Creation, about
which he imploys a great deal of Writing.
But thefe are fine imaginary Difcoveries, that I
fhall leave every one to fatisfy himfelf about,
by confulting their Authors or Propagators.

A N O T H E R Thing remarkable in this *Syftem*
of *Concords* is, that the greateft Number of Vibrations of the *Fundamental* cannot be above
5, or, there is no *Concord* where the *Funda-*
mental makes more than 5 Vibrations to one
Coincidence with the *acute* Term : For fince it
is fo in the *fimple Concords,* it cannot be otherwife in the *Compounds,* the *Octave* being ¦,
which by the *Rule* of Addition can never alter
the lefler Number of any *fimple Concord* to which
it is added.   It is *again* to be *remarked,* that
this Progrefs of the *Concords* may be carried on
to greater Degrees of Compofition *in infinitum;*
but the more *compound* ftill the lefs agreeable,
if you'll except the Two Cafes abovementioned
of the *5th* 1 : 3 , and *3d* 1 : 5 ; fo a fingle *O-*
ctave is better than a double *Octave,* and this
better than the Sum of 3 *Octaves,* &c. and fo of
5ths and other *Concords.* And *mind,* tho' a
compound Octave is the Sum of 2 or more *O-*
ctaves, yet by a *compound 5th* or other *Con-*
                                                    cord,

cord, is not meant the Sum of Two or more *5ths*, but the Sum of an *Octave* and *5th*, or of Two *Octaves* and a *5th*, &c. Now, tho' this Compofition of *Concords* may be carried on infinitely, yet 3 or 4 *Octaves* is the greateft Length we go in ordinary Practice; the old Scales of *Mufick* were carried no further than 2, or at moft 3 *Octaves*, which is fully the Compafs of any ordinary Voice: And tho' the *Octave* is the moft perfect *Concord*, yet after the Third *Octave* the Agreement diminifhes very faft; nor do we go even fo far at one Movement, as from the one Extreme to the other of a triple or double *Octave*, and feldom beyond a fingle *Octave*; yet a Piece of Mufick may be carried agreeably thro' all the intermediate Sounds, within the Extremes of 3 or 4 *Octaves*; which will afford all the Variety of Pleafure the *Harmony* of Sounds is capable to afford, or at leaft we to receive: For we can hardly raife Sounds beyond that Compafs, either by Voice or Inftruments, that fhall not offend the *Ear*. *Chords* are fitteft for raifing a great Variety of Degrees of Sound; and if we fuppofe any *Chord* ½ Foot long, which is but a fmall Length to give a good Sound, the Fourth *Octave* below muft be Eight Foot, which is fo long, that to give a clear Sound, it muft have a good Degree of Tenfion; and this will require a very great Tenfion in the ½ Foot *Chord*: Now if we go beyond the Fourth *Octave*, either the *acute* Term will be too fhort, or the *grave* Term too long; and if in this the Length be fupplied by the Greil-
nefs

nefs of the *Chord*, or in the other the Shortnefs
be exchanged with the Smalnefs, yet the Sound
will by that means become fo blunt in the one,
or fo flender in the other, as to be ufelefs.

D' Cartes fuppofes we can go no further than
Three *Octaves*, but he muft mean only, that
the Extremes of any greater *Interval* heard
without any of the intermediate Terms, have
little *Concord* to our Ears; but it will not follow,
that a Piece of *Mufick* may not go thro' a greater Compafs, efpecially with many Parts.

C H A P. VI.

Of the Geometrical *Part of* Mufick; *or, how to divide right Lines, fo as their Sections or Parts one with another, or with the Whole, fhall contain any given Interval of Sound.*

THE *Degrees* of Sound with refpect to
Tune, are juftly expreft by the Lengths
of Chords or right Lines; and the Proportions which we have hitherto explained being found, firft by Experiments upon Chords,
and

and again confirmed by Reafoning; the Divifion of a right Line into fuch Parts as fhall conftitute one with another, or with the Whole, a-
ny *Interval* of Sound is a very eafy Matter:
For in the preceeding Parts we have all along
fuppofed the Numbers to reprefent the Lengths
of *Chords*; and therefore they may again be
eafily applied to them, which I fhall explain in
a few *Problems.*

---

§ 1. *Of the more general Divifion of* Chords.

Problem
I.   To affign fuch a Part of any
right Line, as fhall confti-
tute any *Concord* (or other *Interval*) with
the Whole.

Rule. Divide the given Line into as many
Parts, as the greateft Number of the *Interval*
has *Units*; and of thefe take as many as the
leffer Number; this with the Whole contains the
Interval fought. *Example.* To find fuch a Part
of the Line *A B*, as fhall be a 5*th* to the
Whole. The 5*th* is 2 : 3, therefore I divide the
Line into Three Parts, whereof 2, *viz. A C*,
is the Part fought; that is, Two Lines, whofe
Lengths are as *A B* to *A C*, *cæteris paribus*,
make a 5*th*.

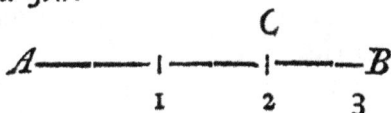

$$A \text{———} | \text{———} | \text{———} B$$
$$1 \qquad 2 \qquad 3$$

Corol-

COROLLARY. Let it be propofed to find
Two or more different Sections of the Line *A*
B. that fhall be to the Whole in any given Proportion. 'Tis plain, we muft take the given
Ratios, and reduce them to one *Fundamental*
(if they are not fo) by *Probl*. 3. *Chap*. 4.
and then divide the Line into as may Parts as
that *Fundamental* has *Units* ; fo, to find the
Sections of the Line *A*. *B*. that fhall be *Octave*,
5*th* and 3*d g*. I take the *Ratios* 1 : 2, 2 : 3,
and 4 : 5, and reduce them to One *Fundamental*, the Series is 30 : 24, 20 : 15. the *Fundamental* is 30, and the Sections fought are 24
the 3*d g*. 20 the 5*th*, and 15 the *Octave*.

PROBLEM II. To find feveral Sections of
a Line, that from the leaft gradually to the
Whole, fhall contain a given Series of *Intervals*,
in a given Order, *i. e.* fo as the leaft Section to
the next greater fhall contain a certain *Interval*,
from that to the next fhall be another; and fo
on. *Rule*. Reduce all the *Ratios* to a continued Series, by *Probl*. 2. *Chap*. 4. Then divide the Line into as many Parts as the greateft
Extreme of that Series ; and number the Parts
from the one End to the other, and you have
the Sections fought, at the Points of Divifion
anfwering the feveral Numbers of the Series.
Example. To find feveral Sections of the Line
A B, fo that the leaft to the next greater
fhall contain a 3*d g*. that to the next greater a
5*th*, and that to the Whole an *Octave*. The
Three *Ratios* 4 : 5, 2 : 3, 1 : 2, reduced to
One Series, make 8 : 10 : 15 : 30. So the Line
A

A B being divided into Thirty equal Parts, we have the Sections fought at the Points *C D* and *E*, fo as *A C* to *A D* is a 3d g. *A D* to *A E* a 5th, and *A E* to *A B* Octave.

```
         8  10   15                    30
A——·———————·—·—·———·————————————B
         C  D    E
```

PROBLEM III. To divide a Line into Two Parts, which fhall be any given *Interval. Rule.* Add together the Numbers that contain the *Ratio* of that *Interval*, and divide the Line into as many Parts as that Sum ; the Point of Divifion anfwering to any of the given Numbers is the Point which feparates on either Hand the Parts fought. *Example.* To divide the Line *A B* into Two Parts which fhall contain betwixt them a 4*th*, I add 3 and 4, and divide the Line into 7 Parts, and the Point 4 or *C* gives the Thing fought, for *A C* is 4, and *C B* is 3. *A*——·——·——·——·——·——·——*B*.

NOTA. The Difference of this and the laft *Problem* is, that there we found feveral Sections of the Line which were not confidered as altogether precifely equal to the Whole ; but here the Point fought muft be fuch as their Sum fhall be exactly equal to the Whole.

COROLLARY. If it is propofed to divide a Line into more than Two Parts, which fhall be to one another as any given *Intervals* from the leaft to the greateft; we muft take the given *Ratios*, and reduce them to one continued Series, as in the laft *Probl.* and add them all together; then divide the Line into as many Parts as that Sum.

Ex-

Example. To divide the Line *AB* into 4 Parts, which fhall contain among them, from the leaft to the greateft, a 3*d g.* 4*th* and 5*th*, I take the *Ratios* 4 : 5, 3 : 4 and 2 : 3, which reduced to one Series, it is 12 : 15 : 20 : 30, whofe Sum is 77 ; let the Line be divided into 77 Parts; and if you firft take off 12, then 15, then 20, and laftly 30 Parts, you have the Parts fought equal to the Whole.

THE preceeding *Problems* are of a more general Nature, I fhall now particularly treat of the *harmonical* Divifion of Chords.

---

§ 2. Of *the* harmonical *Divifion of* Chords.

I Explained already Two different Senfes in which any *Interval* is faid to be *harmonically* divided ; the *Firft,* When the Two Extremes with their Differences from the middle Term are in *geometrical Proportion* ; the 2*d,* when an *Interval* is fo divided, as the Extremes and all the middle Terms are *Concord* each with another. *Now,* we are to confider, not the *harmonical* Divifion of an *Interval* or *Ratio,* but the Divifion of a fingle Number or Line, into fuch Sections or Parts as, compared together and with the Whole, fhall be *harmonical* in either of the Two Senfes mentioned, *i. e.* either with refpect to the Proportion of their Quantity, which is the firft Senfe, or of their
Qua-

Quality or *Tune*, which is the second Sense of
harmonical Division.

PROBLEM IV. To find Two Sections of a
Line which with the whole shall be in *harmonical* Proportion of their Quantity.   To answer
this Demand, we may take any Three Numbers
in *harmonical* Proportion, as 3,4,6, and divide the
whole Line into as many Parts as the greatest
of these Three Numbers (as here into 6), and at
the Points of Division answering the other two
Numbers (as at 3 and 4) you have the Sections
sought.   And an infinite Number of *Examples*
of this Kind may be found, because betwixt any
Two Numbers given, we can put an *harmonical
Mean*, by *Theor.* 11. *Chap.* 4.

NOTE. The *harmonical* Sections of this *Problem* added together, will ever be greater than
the Whole, as is plain from the Nature of that
Kind; and this is therefore not so properly a
Division of the Line as finding several Sections,
or the Quotes of several distinct Divisions.

These Sections with the Whole, will also constitute an *harmonical* Series of the 2*d* Kind, but
not in every Case; for *Example*, 2, 4, 6, is *harmonical* in both Senses ; also 2 : 3 : 6; but 21,
24, 28 is *harmonical* only in the First Sense because there is no *Concord* amongst them but
betwixt 21, 28, (equal to 3 : 4.)

To know how many Ways a Line may be
divided *harmonically* in both Senses, shall be pre-
sently explained.

PROBLEM V. To find Two Sections of a
Line, that together and with the Whole shall be

har-

harmonical in the Second Senſe ; *that is,* in re-
ſpeﾄ of Quality or *Tune.* *Rule.* Take any
Three Numbers that are *Concord* each with a-
nother, and divide the Line by the greateſt, the
Points of Diviſion anſwering the other Two
give the Seﾄions ſought : Take, for Example,
the Numbers 2, 3, 8, or 2, 5, 8, and apply them
according to the *Rule.*

I obſerved in the former *Problem,* That the
Two Seﾄions together are always greater than
the whole Line ; but here they may be either
greater, as in this *Example,* 2, 3, 4, or leſs, as
in this *Example,* 1, 2, 5, or equal, as here, 2,
3, 5, which laſt is moſt properly Diviſion of
the Line, for here we find the true conſtituent
Parts of the Line : They may alſo be *harmonical* in the firſt Senſe, as 2 : 3 : 6, or otherwiſe as
2 : 3 : 4.

Now, to know all the Variety of Combinations of Three Numbers that will ſolve this
Problem, we muſt conſider the preceeding *general Table* of *Concords, Pag.* 172. and the *harmc-
nical Series* made out of it, which contains the
Numbers of the *Table* and no other. I have
ſhewn that all the Numbers of the *Table* of
Concords, are *Concords* one with another, as well
as thoſe that are particularly conneﾄed : We
have alſo ſeen that, tho' the *Table* were carried
on *in infinitum,* the leſſer Number of every *Ratio* is one of theſe, 1. 2. 3. 4. 5; and the greater
Number of each *Ratio* one of theſe, 2. 3. 5. or
their Produﾄs by 2. *in infinitum.* 'Tis plain
therefore, that if we ſuppoſe this *Table* of *Concords*

cords carried on *in infinitum*, we can find in it infinite Combinations of Three Numbers that shall be all *Concord*. For *Example*, Take any Two that have no common Divisor, as 2 : 3, you'll find an Infinity of other Numbers greater to joyn with these ; for we may take any of the Multiples *in infinitum* of either of these Two Numbers themselves, or the Number 5, or its Multiples : But if we suppose the Table of *Concords* limited (as with respect to Practice it is) so will the Variety of Numbers sought be: Suppose it limited to Three *Octaves*, then the *harmonical Series* goes no farther than the Number 64, as here, 1. 2. 3. 4. 5. 6. 8. 10. 12. 16. 20. 24. 32. 40. 48. 64, &c. and as many Combinations of Three Numbers as we can find in that Series, which have not a common Divisor, so many Ways may the *Problem* be solved. But besides these we must consider again, that as many of the preceeding Combinations as are *arithmetically* proportional (such as 2. 3. 4, and 2. 5. 8) there are so many Combinations of correspondent *Harmonicals* (in the first Sense) which will solve this *Problem*. These joyned to the preceeding, will exhaust all the Variety with which this *Problem* can be solved, supposing 3 *Octaves* to be the greatest *Concord*. *Again*, we are to take Notice, that of that Variety there are some, of which the Two lesser Numbers will be exactly equal to the greatest, as 1. 2. 3. tho' the greater Numbers are otherwise.

I shall

I shall now in Two distinct *Problems* show you, *First*, The Variety of Ways that a Line may be cut, so as the *Sections* compared together and with the Whole shall be *harmonical* in both the Senses explained; and *2do.* How many Ways it may be divided into Two Parts equal to the Whole, and be *harmonical* in the Second Sense; for these can never be *harmonical* in the First Sense, as shall be also shewn.

PROBLEM **VI.** To find how many Ways 'tis possible to take Two Sections of a Line, that with the Whole shall constitute Three Terms *harmonical* both in Quantity and Quality.

FROM the *harmonical Series* we can easily find an Answer to this Demand : In order to which consider, *First*, That every Three Numbers in *harmonical Proportion* (of Quantity) have other Three in *arithmetical Proportion* corresponding to them, which contain the same *Intervals* or *geometrical Ratios*, tho' in a different Order ; and reciprocally every *arithmetical Series* has a correspondent *Harmonical*, as has been explained in *Theor.* 14. *Chap.* 4. Let us *next* consider, That there can no Three Numbers in *arithmetical Proportion* be taken, which shall be all *Concord* one with another, unless they be found in the *harmonical Series* : Therefore it is impossible that any Three Numbers which are in *harmonical Proportion* (of Quantity) can be all *Concord* unless their correspondent *Arithmeticals* be contain'd in the *harmonical* Series. Hence 'tis plain, that as many Combinations of Three Numbers in *arithmetical Proportion* as

can

can be found in that Series, ſo many Combinations of Three Numbers in *harmonical Proportion* are to be found, which ſhall be *Concord*
each with another; and ſo many Ways only
can a Line be divided *harmonically* in both
Senſes.

A n d in all that Series 'tis impoſſible to find
any other Combination of Numbers in *arithmetical Proportion*, than thoſe in the following
Table; with which I have joyned their *correſpondent Harmonicals.*

Arithmet.			*Harmon.*		
1	2	3	2	3	6
2	3	4	3	4	6
3	4	5	12	15	20
4	5	6	10	12	15
1	3	5	3	5	15
2	5	8	5	8	20

N o w, to ſhow
that there are
no other Com-
binations to be
found in the
Series to an-
ſwer the pre-
ſent Purpoſe,
obſerve, the Three *arithmetical* Terms muſt be
in radical Numbers, elſe tho' it may be a different *arithmetical Series*, yet it cannot contain
different *Concords*, ſo 4 : 6 : 8 is a different
Series from 2 : 3 : 4, yet the *geometrical Ratios*,
or the *Concords* that the Numbers of the one
Series contain, being the ſame with theſe in the
other, the correſpondent *harmonical* Series gives
the ſame Diviſion of the Line.	Now by a ſhort
and eaſy Induction, I ſhall ſhow the Truth of
what's advanced : Look on the *harmonical Series*, and you ſee, 1*mo.* That if we take the
Number 1, to make an *arithmetical Series* of
Three

Three Terms, it can only be join'd with 2 : 3.
or 3 : 5, for if you make 4 the middle
Term, the other Extreme muſt be 7, which is
not in the Series ; or if you make 5 the Middle,
the other Extreme is 9, which is not in the Series : Now all after 5 are even Numbers, ſo that
if you take any of theſe for the middle Term,
the other Extreme in *arithmetical Proportion*
with them, muſt be an odd Number greater
than 5, and no ſuch is to be found in the Series : Therefore there can be no other Combination in which 1 is the leſſer Extreme, but
theſe in the *Table.*

2*do.* Take Two for the leaſt Extreme, and
the other Two Terms can only be 3 : 4, or 5 :
8; for there is no other odd Number to take
as a middle Term, but 3 or 5; and if we take
4 or any even Number, the other Extreme muſt
be an even Number, and theſe Three will neceſſarily reduce to ſome of the Forms wherein
1 is concerned, becauſe every even Number is
diviſible by 2, and 2 divided by 2 quotes 1.
3*tio.* Take 3 for the leſſer Extreme, the other
Two Terms can only be 4, 5; for if 5 is the
middle Term, the other Extreme muſt be 7,
which is not in the Series: But there are no o-
ther Numbers in the Series to be made middle
Terms, 3 being the leſſer Extreme, except even
Numbers ; and 3 being an odd Number, the o-
ther Extreme muſt be an odd Number too, but
no ſuch is to be found in the *Series* greater than
5. 4*to.* The Number 4 can only joyn with 5,
6, for all the reſt are even Numbers, and where
the

the Three Terms are all even Numbers, they are reducible. *5to.* There can be no Combination where 5 is the leaft Extreme, becaufe all greater Numbers in the *Series* are even; for where one Extreme is odd, the other muft be odd too, the middle Term being even. *Laftly.* All the Numbers above 5 being even, are reducible to fome of the former Cafes : *Therefore* we have found all the poffible Ways any Line can be divided, that the Sections compared together and with the Whole, may be *harmonical* both in Quantity and Quality, as thefe are explain'd.

PROBLEM VII. To divide a Line into Two Parts, equal to the Whole, fo as the Parts among themfelves, and each with the Whole fhall be *Concord*; and to difcover all the poffible Ways that this can be done. For the firft Part of the *Problem*, 'tis plain, that if we take Three Numbers which are all *Concord* among themfelves, and whereof the Two leaft are equal to the greateft, then divide the given Line into as many Parts as that greateft Number contains *Units*, the Point of Divifion anfwering any of the leffer Numbers folves the *Problem* : So if we divide a Line *A B* into Three Parts, one Third *A C*, and Two Thirds *C B*, or *A D* and *D B* are the Parts fought, for all thefe are *Concord* 1 : 2, 2 : 3, 1 : 3. $A—\frac{1}{c}—\frac{2}{b}—{}^{3}B$.

I fhall next fhew how many different Ways this *Problem* can be folved ; and I affirm, that there can be but Seven Solutions contained in

the

the following *Table*, in which I have diſtinguiſhed the Parts and the Whole.

THAT theſe are *har-*
monical Sections is plain,
becauſe there are no other
Numbers here but what
belong to the *harmonical*
Series; and 'tis remarkable
too, that there are no o-
ther here but what belong
to the *ſimple Concords*.
But then to prove, that
there can be no other *har-*
monical Sections, conſider

Parts.		Whole.
1 ✠ 1 =	2
1 ✠ 2 =	3
1 ✠ 3 =	4
1 ✠ 4 =	5
1 ✠ 5 =	6
2 ✠ 3 =	5
3 ✠ 5 =	8

that no other Number can poſſibly be any radical Term of a *Concord*, beſides theſe of the preceeding *harmonical Series*. Indeed we may
take any *Ratio* in many different Numbers, but
every *Ratio* can have but one radical Form,
and only theſe Numbers are *harmonical* ; ſo 5 :
15 is a *compound 5th*, yet 15 is no *harmonical*
Number, becauſe 5 : 15 is reducible to 1 : 3;
alſo 7 : 14 is an *Octave*, yet neither 7 nor 14
are *harmonical*, ſince they are reducible to 1 : 2.
Now ſince all the poſſible *harmonical Ratios*,
in their radical Forms, are contained in the *Se-*
ries, 'tis plain, that all the poſſible *harmonical*
Sections of any Line or Number are to be found,
by adding every Number of the *Series* to it ſelf,
or every Two together, and taking theſe Numbers for the Two Parts, and their Sum for the
whole Line. Now let us conſider how many
of ſuch Additions will produce *harmonical Se-*
ctions,

ctions, and what will not : It is certain, that if
the Sum of any Two Numbers of the Series be
a Number which is not contain'd in it, then
the Division of a Line in Two Parts, which are
in Proportion as these Two Numbers, can never be *harmonical* ; for *Example* the Sum
of 3 and 4 is 7, which is not an *harmonical Section*, because 7 is no *harmonical* Number, or is not the radical Number of any *harmonical Ratio*. Again 'tis certain, That if any Two Numbers, with their
Sum, are to be found all in the Series, these
Numbers constitute an *harmonical Section*. But
observe, if the Numbers taken for the Parts are
reducible, they must be brought to their radical
Form ; for the *Concords* made of such Parts as
are reducible, must necessarily be the same with
these made of their radical Numbers ; so if we
take 4 and 6 their Sum is 10, and 4 : 6 are
harmonical Parts of 10 ; but then the Case is
not different from 2. 3. 5. *Next,* We see that
all the Numbers in that Series after the Number 5, are Compounds of the preceeding Numbers, by the continual multiplying of them by 2 ;
therefore we can take no Two Numbers in that
Series greater than 5, (for Parts) but what are
reducible to 5, and some Number less, or both
less ; and if we take 5 or any odd Number less,
and a Number greater than 5, they can never
be harmonical Parts, because their Sum will be
an odd Number, and all the Numbers in the Series
greater than 5, are even Numbers ; therefore
that Sum is not in the Series ; and if we take

an

an even Number lefs than 5, and a Number greater, the Sum is even and reducible; therefore
all the Numbers that can poffibly make the Two
Parts of different *harmonical* Sections, are thefe,
1. 2. 3. 4. 5; and if we add every Two of
thefe together, we find no other different
harmonical Sections but thefe of the preceeding Table, becaufe their Sum is either
odd or reducible; and when the Parts are
equal, 'tis plain there can be but one fuch
Section, which is 1 : 1 : 2, becaufe all other
equal Sections are reducible to this.

---

§ 3. *Containing further Reflections upon the Division of* CHORDS.

WE have feen, in the laft *Table*, that the
harmonical Divifions of a Line depend
upon the Numbers 2. 3. 4. 5. 6. 7. 8; and if
we reflect upon what has been already obferved
of thefe 1. 2. 3. 4. 5. 6. *viz.* That they are *Concord*, comparing every one with every other,
we draw this Conclufion, That if a Line is divided into 2 or 3, 4, 5 or 6 Parts, every Section
or Number of fuch Parts with the Whole, or
one with another, is *Concord*; becaufe they are
all to one another as thefe Numbers 1. 2. 3. 4.
5. 6. I fhall add now, that, taking in the Number 8, it will ftill be true of the Series, 1. 2. 3.

4. 5. 6. 8. that every Number with every other is *Concord* ; and here we have the whole *original Concords.* And as to the Conclusion last drawn, it will hold of the Parts of a Line divided into 8 Parts, except the Number 7, which is *Concord* with none of the rest. So that we have here a Method of exhibiting in one Line all the *simple* and *original Concords, viz.* by dividing it into 8 equal Parts, and of these, taking , 1. 2. 3. 4. 5. 6. and comparing them together, and with the whole 8.

BUT if it be required to show how a Line may be divided in the most simple Manner to exhibite all these *Concords;* here it is : Divide the Line *A B* into Two equal Parts at *C;* then divide the Part *C B* into Two equal Parts at *D;* and again the Part *C D* into Two equal Parts at *E.* 'Tis plain that *A C* or *C B,* are each a Half of *A B;* and *C D* or *B D* are each equal to a 4*th* Part of the Line *A B;* and *C E* or *E D* are *A*————————⌐—⌐—⌐——*B,* each an 8*th* Part of *A B;* therefore *A E* is equal to Five 8*th* Parts of *A B;* and *A D* is Six 8*th* Parts, or Three 4*th* Parts of it ; and *A E* is therefore Five 6*th* Parts of *A D.* Again, since *A D* is Three 4*th* Parts of *A B,* and *A C* is a Half, or Two 4*ths* of *A B,* therefore *A C* is Two 3*d* Parts of *A D ; then,* because *A E* is Five 8*th* Parts of *A B,* and *A C* Four 8*ths* (or a Half) therefore *A C* is Four 5*ths* of *A E.* *Lastly,* *E B* is Three 8*ths* of *A B.* *Consequently A C* to *A B* is an *Octave;* *A C* to *A D* a 5*th;* *A D* to *A B,* a 4*th; A C*

to

to *A E* a 3*d g. A E* to *A D* a 3*d l. A E* to *E B* a 6*th g. A E* to *A B* a 6*th l.* which is all agreeable to what has been already explained ; for *A C* and *A B* containing the *Octave*, we have *A D* an *arithmetical Mean*, which therefore gives us the 5*th*,with the *acute* Term *A C*, and a 4*th* with the lower Term *A B* of the *Octave*. Again, *A E* is an *arithmetical Mean* betwixt the Extremes of the 5th *A C* and *A D*, and gives us all the reft of the *Concords*.

IT will be worth our Pains to confider what *D' Cartes* obferves upon this Divifion of a Line : But in order to the underftanding what he fays here, I muft give you a fhort Account of fome general Premifles he lays down in the Beginning of his Work. Says he, ' Every Senfe is capable
' of fome Pleafure, to which is required a cer-
' tain Proportion of the Object to the Organ :
' Which Object muft fall regularly, and not very
' difficultly on the Senfes, that we may be able
' to perceive every Part diftinctly : Hence,
' thefe Objects are moft eafily perceived, whofe
' Difference of Parts is leaft, *i. e.* in which there
' is leaft Difference to be obferved ; and there-
' fore the Proportion of the Parts ought to be
' *arithmetical* not *geometrical* ; becaufe there
' are fewer Things to be noticed in the *arith-*
' *metical Proportion*, fince the Differences are
' every where equal, and fo does not weary the
' Mind fo much in apprehending diftinctly e-
' very Thing that is in it. He gives us this
' Example : Says he, ,The Proportion of thefe
'   ' Lines

' Lines ▦ is eafier diftinguifhed by the
' Eye, than the Proportion of thefe ▦
' becaufe in the firft we have nothing to notice
' but that the common Difference of the Lines
' is 1.' He makes not the Application of this
exprefly to the Ear, by confidering the Number
of Strokes or Impulfes made upon it at thefame
Time, by Motions of various Velocities; and
what Similitude that has to perceiving the Difference of Parts by the Eye: He certainly
thought the Application plain; and takes it alfo
for granted, That one Sound is to another in
*Tune,*as the Lengths of Two Chords,*cæteris paribus.* From thefe Premiffes he proceeds to
find the *Concords* in the Divifion of a Line, and
obferves, That if it be divided into 2, 3, 4, 5,
or 6 equal Parts, all the Sections are *Concord*;
the firft and beft *Concord Octave* proceeds from
dividing the Line by the firft of all Numbers 2, and the next beft by the next Number 3, and fo on to the Number 6. But
then, fays he, we can proceed no further,
becaufe the Weaknefs of our Senfes cannot eafily diftinguifh greater Differences of Sounds: But
he forgot the *6th* leffer, which requires a Divifion by 8, tho' he elfewhere owns it as *Concord.*
We fhall next confider what he fays upon the
preceeding Divifion of the Line *A B,* from
which he propofes to fhow how all the other
Concords are contained in the *Octave,* and proceed from the Divifion of it, that their Nature
may be more diftinctly known. Take it in his
own

own Words, as near as I can tranflate them.
" *Firft* then, from the Thing premifed it is
" certain,this Divifion ought to be *arithmetical,*
" or into equal Parts, and what that is which
" ought to be divided is plain in the Chord *A B,*
" which is diftant from *A C* by the Part *C B;*
" but the Sound of *A B,* is diftant from the
" Sound of *A C* by an *Octave* ; therefore the
" Part *C B* fhall be the Space or *Interval* of an
" *Octave :* This is it therefore which ought to
" be divided into Two equal Parts to have the
" whole *Octave* divided, which is done in the
" Point *D* ; and that we may know what *Con-*
" *cord* is generated properly and by it felf (*pro-*
" *prie & per fe,* as he calls it) by this Divifion,
" we muft confider, that the Line *A B,* which
" is the *lower* or *graver* Term of the *Octave,*
" is divided in *D,* not in order to it felf (*non*
" *in ordine ad feipfum,* I fuppofe he means not
" in order to a Comparifon of *A D* with *A B*)
" for then it would be divided in *C,* as is al-
" ready done (for *A C* compared to *A B* makes
" the *Octave*) neither do we now divide the
" *Unifon* (*viz. A B*) but the *Octave,* (*viz.* the
" *Interval* of 8*ve,*which is *C B,*as he faid alrea-
" dy) which confifts of Two Terms ; therefore
" while the *graver* Term is divided,that's done
" in order to the *acuter* Term, not in order to
" it felf. Hence the *Concord* which is properly
" generated by that Divifion, is betwixt
" the Terms *A C* and *A D,* which is a 5*th,*
" not betwixt *A D, A B,* which is a 4*th ;* for
" the Part *D B* is only a Remainder, and
　　　　　　　　　　　　　" generates

" generates a *Concord* by Accident, becaufe
" that whatever Sound is *Concord* with one
" Term of *Octave*, ought alfo to be *Concord*
" with the other." In the fame Manner he
argues, that the 3*d g.* proceeds *properly*, *& per
fe* out of the Divifion of the 5*th*, at the Point
E, whereby we have *A E* a 3*d g.* to the *acute*
Term of the 5*th*, *viz.* to *A C* (for *AC* to *A D*
is 5*th*) and all the reft of the *Concords* are accidental; and thus alfo he makes the *tonus major* (of which afterwards) to proceed directly
from the 3*d g.* and the *tonus minor* and *Semitones* to be all accidental : And to fhow that
this is not an imaginary Thing, when he fays,
the 5*th* and 3*d g.* proceed *properly* from the Divifion of *Octave*, and the reft by Accident, he
fays, He found it by Experience in ftringed Inftruments, that if one String is ftruck, the Motion of it fhakes all the Strings that are *acuter*
by any Species of 5*th* or 3*d g.* but not thefe that
are 4*th* or other *Concord* ; which can only proceed, fays he, from the Perfection of thefe *Concords*, or the Imperfection of the other, *viz.*
that the firft are *Concords per fe*, and the others
per accidens, becaufe they flow neceffarily from
them. *D' Cartes* feems to think it a Demonftration *a priori* from his Premiffes, that if there
is fuch a Thing as *Concord* among Sounds, it
muft proceed from the *arithmetical* Divifion of
a Line into 2. 3, *&c.* Parts, and that the more
fimple produce the better *Concords*. 'Tis true,
that Men muft have known by Experience,
that there was fuch a Thing as *Concord* before
                                                    they

they reafoned about it ; but whether the general Reflection which he makes upon Nature, be
fufficient to conclude that fuch Divifion muft
infallibly produce fuch *Concords*, I don't fo
clearly fee; yet I muft own his Reafoning is
very ingenious, excepting the fubtil Diftinction
of *Concords per fe & per accidens*, which I
don't very well underftand; but let every one
take them as they can.

C H A P. VII.

Of H A R M O N Y, *explaining the Nature
and Variety of it, as it depends upon the
various Combinations of* concording
Sounds.

IN *Chap.* II. § 1. I fhewed you the Diftinction that is made betwixt the Word *Concord*, which is the Agreement of Two
Sounds confidered either in *Confonance* or *Succeffion*, and *Harmony*, which is the Agreement
of more, confidered always in *Confonance*, and
requires at leaft Three Sounds. In order to produce a perfect *Harmony*, there muft be no *Dif-*
                                                    cord

cord found between any Two of the simple Sounds; but each must be in some Degree of *Concord* to all the rest. Hence *Harmony* is very well defined, *The Sum of* CONCORDS arising from the Combination of Two or more *Concords, i. e.* of Three or more simple Sounds striking the Ear all together; and different Compositions of *Concords* make different *Harmony.*

To understand the Nature, and determine the Number and Preference of *Harmonies,* we must consider, that in every *compound* Sound, where there are more than Two *Simples,* we have Three Things observable, 1*st.* The *primary Relation* of every *simple* Sound to the *Fundamental* (or *gravest*) whereby they make different Degrees of *Concord* with it. 2*dly.* The *mutual Relations* of the *acuter* Sounds each with another, whereby they mix either *Concord* or *Discord* into the *Compound.* 3*dly.* The *secondary Relation* of the Whole, whereby all the Terms unite their Vibrations, or coincide more or less frequently.

THE Two first of these depend upon one another, and upon them depends the last. Let us suppose Four Sounds *A. B. C. D.* whereof *A* is the *gravest, B* next *acuter,* then *C,* and *D* the *acutest; A* is called the *Fundamental,* and the Relations of *B, C,* and *D,* to *A,* are *primary Relations :* So if *B* is a 3*d* g. above *A,* that *primary Relation* is 4 to 5 : and if *C* is 5*th* to *A,* that *primary Relation* is 2 to 3 ; and if *D* is 8*ve* to *A,* that is 1 to 2. *Again,* to find the *mutual Relations* of all the *acute* Terms

B C,

B, C, D, we muſt take their *primary Relations* to the *Fundamental,* and ſubſtract each leſſer from each greater, by the Rule of *Subſtraction* of *Intervals;* ſo in the preceeding *Example, B* to *C* is 5 to 6, a 3*d l. B* to *D* is 5 to 8, a 6*th l.* and *C* to *D* 3 to 4, a 4*th.* Or, if we take all the *primary Relations,* and reduce them to one common *Fundamental,* by *Probl.* 3. *Chap.* 4. we ſhall ſee all the *mutual Relations* in one Series ; ſo the preceeding *Example* is 30. 24. 20. 15.

A G A I N, having the *mutual Relations* of each Sound to the next in any Series, we may find the *primary Relations,* by *Addition* of *Intervals;* and then by theſe all the reſt of the *mutual Relations;* or reduce the given Relations to a continued Series by *Probl.* 2. *Chap.* 4. and then all will appear at once. *Laſtly,* to find the *ſecondary Relation* of the Whole, find the leaſt common Dividend to all the leſſer Terms or Numbers of the *primary Relations, i. e.* the leaſt Number that will be divided by each of them exactly without a Remainder; that is the Thing ſought, and ſhows that all the ſimple Sounds coincide after every ſo many Vibrations of the *Fundamental* as that Number found expreſſes : So in the preceeding *Example,* the leſſer Terms of the Three *primary Relations* are 4. 2. 1. whoſe leaſt common Dividend is 4, therefore at every Fourth Vibration of the *Fundamental* the Whole will coincide ; and this is what I call the *ſecondary Relation* of the Whole. I ſhall firſt ſhow how in every Caſe you may
find

find this leaft Dividend, and then explain how it expreffes the Coincidence of the Whole.

PROBLEM. To find the leaft common Dividend to any given Numbers. *Rule.* 1mo. If each greater of the given Numbers is a Multiple of each leffer, then the greateft of them is the Thing fought; as in the preceeding *Example.* 2do. If 'tis not fo, but fome of them are commenfurable together, others not; take the greateft of all that are commenfurable, and, paffing their *aliquot* Parts, multiply them together, and with the reft of the Numbers continually, the laft Product is the Number fought. *Example.* 2. 3. 4. 6. 8. Here 2. 4. 8, are commenfurable, and 8 their leaft Dividend; alfo 3. 6 commenfurable and 6 their leaft Dividend : Then 8. 6. multiplied together produce 48, the Number fought. Take another *Example.* 2. 3. 5. 4. Here 2 . 4 are commenfurable and all the reft incommenfurable, therefore I multiply 3. 4. 5. continually, the Product is 60 the Number fought. 3tio. If all the Numbers are incommenfurable, multiply them all continually, and the laft Product is the Anfwer. *Example.* 2. 3. 5. 7. the Product is 210. The Reafon of this *Rule* is obvious from the Nature of *Multiplication* and *Divifion.*

Now I fhall fhow that the leaft common Dividend to the leffer Terms of any Number of *primary Relations,* expreffes the Vibrations of the *Fundamental* to every Coincidence. Thus, of the Numbers that exprefs the *Ratio* of any *Interval,* the leffer is the Length of the *acuter* Chord,

Chord, and the greater the Length of the *graver* : Or reciprocally, the leffer is the Number
of Vibrations of the longer, and the greater the
Vibrations of the fhorter Chord, that are performed in the fame Time; *confequently* the leffer Numbers of all the *primary Relations* of any
compound Sound, are the Numbers of the Vibrations of the common *Fundamental* which go to
each Coincidence thereof with the feveral *a-
cute* Terms ; but 'tis plain if the *Fundamental*
coincide with any *acute* Term after every 3 (for
Example) of its own Vibrations, it will alfo coincide with it after every 6 or 9, or other Multiple, or Number of Vibrations which is divifible by 3, and fo of any other Number; confequently the leaft Number which can be exactly divided by every one of the Numbers of
Vibrations of the *Fundamental*, which go to a
Coincidence with the feveral *acute* Terms, muft
be the Vibrations of that *Fundamental* at which
every total Coincidence is performed. For *Example*, fuppofe a common *Fundamental* coincide with any *acute* Term after 2 of its own Vibrations, and with another at 3; then whatever the *mutual Relation* of thefe Two *acute*
Terms is, it is plain they cannot both together
coincide with that *Fundamental*, till Six Vibrations of it be finifhed ; and at that Number precifely they muft ; for the *Fundamental* coinciding with the one at 2, and with the other
at 3, muft coincide with each of them at Six ;
and no fooner can they all coincide, becaufe
6 is the leaft Multiple to both 2 and 3 : Or thus,
the

the *Fundamental* coinciding with the one after 2, muft coincide with that one alfo after 4. 6. 8. *&c.* ftill adding 2 more; and coinciding with the other after 3. muft coincide with it alfo after 6. 9. 12. *&c.* ftill adding 3 more; fo that they cannot all coincide till after 6. becaufe that is the leaft Number which is common to both the preceeding Series of Coincidences. Next for the Application of this to *Harmony.*

H A R M O N Y is a *compound* Sound confifting (as we take it here) of Three or more *fimple* Sounds; the proper Ingredients of it are *Concords*; and therefore all *Difcords* in the *primary Relations* efpecially, and alfo in the *mutual Relations* of the feveral *acute* Terms are abfolutely forbidden.

'T I s true that *Difcords* are ufed in *Mufick,* but not for themfelves fimply; they are ufed as Means to make the *Concords* appear more agreeable by the Oppofition; but more of this in another Place.

N o w any Number of *Concords* being propofed to ftand in *primary Relation* with a common *Fundamental;* we difcover whether or no they conftitute a perfect *Harmony,* by finding their *mutual Relations. Example.* Suppofe thefe *primary Intervals,* which are *Concords, viz.* 3*d g.* 5*th,* 8*ve,* their *mutual Relations* are all *Concord,* and therefore can ftand in *Harmony;* for the 3*d g.* and 5*th,* are to one another as 5 : 6 a 3*d. l.* The 3*d g.* and *Octave* as 5 : 8, a 6*th l.* the 5*th* and *Octave* are as 3 : 4, a
4th

4th; as appears in this Series to which the given Relations are reduced, *viz.* 30 : 24 : 20 : 15. *Again*, take *4th*, *5th*, and *Octave*, they cannot stand together, becaufe betwixt the *4th* and *5th* is a *Difcord*, the *Ratio* being 8 : 9. Or fuppofing any Number of Sounds, which are *Concord* each to the next, from the loweft to the higheft; to know if they can ftand in *Harmony* we muft find their *primary Relations*, and all the other *mutual Relations*, which muft be all *Concord*; fo let any Number of Sounds be as 4 : 5 : 6 : 8 they can ftand in *Harmony*, becaufe each to each is *Concord*; but thefe cannot 4. 6. 9, becaufe 4 : 9 is *Difcord*.

WE have confidered the neceffary Conditions for making *Harmony*, from which it will be eafy to enumerate or give a general Table of all the poffible Variety; but let us firft examine how the Preference of *Harmonies* is to be determined; and here comes in the Confideration of the *fecondary Relations*. Now upon all the Three Things mentioned, *viz.* the *primary*, *fecondary*, and *mutual Relations*, does the Perfection of *Harmonies* depend; fo that Regard muft be had to them all in making a right Judgment : It is not the beft *primary Relation* that makes beft *Harmony*; for then a *4th* and *5th* muft be better than a *4th* and *6th*; yet the firft Two cannot ftand together, becaufe of the *Difcord* in their *mutual Relation* : Nor does the beft *fecondary Relation* carry it; for then alfo would a *4th* and *5th*, whofe *fecondary Relation* with a common *Fundamental*

damental is 6, be better than 3*d l.* and 5*th,* whose *secondary Relation* is 10; but here also the Preference is due to the better *mutual Relation* of the 3*d l.* and 5*th,* which is a 3*d g.* and a 4*th* and *Octave* would be equal to a 6*th g.* and *Octave,* the *secondary Relation* of both being 3, which cannot possibly be, the Ingredients being different. As to the *mutual Relations,* they depend altogether upon the *primary,* yet not so as that the best *primary Relation* shall always produce the best *mutual Relation;* for 'tis contrary when two Terms are joyned to a *Fundamental;* so a 5*th* and *Octave* contain betwixt them a 4*th;* and a 4*th* and *Octave* contain a 5*th.* But the *primary Relations* are by far more considerable, and, with the *secondary,* afford us the following Rule for determining the Preference of *Harmony,* in which that must always be taken for a necessary Condition, that there be no *Discord* among any of the Terms; therefore this is the Rule, that comparing Two *Harmonies* (which have an equal Number of Terms) that which has both the best *primary* and *secondary Relation,* is most perfect; but in Two Cases, where the Advantage is in the *primary Relations* of the one, and in the *secondary* of the other, we have no certain Rule; the *primary Relations* are the principal and most considerable Things; but how the Advantage here ought to be proportioned to the Disadvantage in the *secondary,* or contrarily, in order to judge of the comparative Perfection, is a Thing we know not how to determine;

and

and therefore a well tuned Ear muſt be the laſt
Reſort in theſe Caſes.

Let us next take a View of the poſſible
Combinations of *Concords* that conſtitute *Harmony*; in order to which conſider, That as we
diſtinguiſhed *Concords* into *ſimple* and *compound*,
ſo is *Harmony* diſtinguiſhable : That is *ſimple
Harmony*, where there is no *Concord* to the
Fundamental above an *Octave*, and it is *compound*, which to the *ſimple Harmony* of one
Octave, adds that of another *Octave*. The Ingredients of *ſimple Harmony* are the 7 *ſimple o-
riginal Concords*, of which there can be but 18
different Combinations that are *Harmony*,
which I have placed in the following *Table*.

T A B L E of Harmonies.

		2dry Rel.		2dry Rel.	
5th	8ve	2	3d g. 5th	4	3d g. 5th, 8ve
4th	8ve	3	3d l. 5th	10	3d l. 5th, 8ve
6th g.	8ve	3	4th, 6th g.	3	4th, 6th g. 8ve
3d g.	8ve	4	3d g. 6th g.	12	3d g. 6th g. 8ve
3d l.	8ve	5	3d l. 6th l.	5	3d l. 6th l. 8ve
6th l.	8ve	5	4th, 6th l.	15	4th, 6th l. 8ve.

If we reflect on what has been explained of
theſe *original Concords*, we ſee plainly that
here are all the poſſible Combinations that make
Harmony; for the *Octave* is compoſed of a
5th and 4th, or a 6th and 3d, which have a Variety of greater and leſſer : Out of theſe are
the

the firſt Six Harmonies compoſed ; then the 5*th* being compoſed of 3*d g.* and 3*d. l.* and the 6*th* of 4*th* and 3*d,* from theſe proceed the next Six of the Table ; then an *Octave* joyned to each of theſe Six, make the laſt Six.

Now the firſt 12 Combinations have each 2 Terms added to the *Fundamental,* and their Perfection is according to the Order of the Table : Of the firſt 6 each has an *Octave ;* and their Preference is according to the Perfection of the other leſſer *Concord* joyned to that *Octave,* as that has been already determined ; and with this alſo agrees the Perfection of their *ſecondary Relations.* For the next 6, the Preference is given to the Two Combinations with the 5*th,* whereof that which hath the 3*d g.* is beſt ; then to the Two Combinations with the 6*th g.* of which that which has the 4*th* is beſt : Then follows the Combinations with the 6*th l.* where the 3*d l.* is preferred to the 4*th,* for the great Advantage of the *ſecondary Relation,* which does more than balance the Advantage of the 4*th* above the 3*d l.* So that in theſe Six we have not followed the Order of the *ſecondary Relations,* nor altogether the Order of the *primary,* as in the laſt Caſe. Then come in the laſt Place the Six Combinations ariſing from the Diviſion of the *Octave,* into 3 *Concords,* which I have placed laſt, not becauſe they are leaſt perfect, but becauſe they are moſt *complex,* and are the Mixtures of the other 12 one with another ; and for their Perfection, they are plainly preferable to the immediately pre-

preceeding Six, becaufe they have the very fame. Ingredients, and an *Octave* more, which does not alter the *fecondary Relation*, and fo are equal to them in that Refpect ; but as they have an *Octave*, they are much preferable ; and being compared with the firft Six, they have the fame Ingredients, with the Addition of one *Concord* more, which does indeed alter the *fecondary Relations*, and make the Compofition more fenfible, but ye adds an agreeable Sweetnefs, for which in fome Refpect they are preferable.

For *compound Harmony*, I fhall leave you to find the Variety for your felves out of the Combinations of the *fimple Harmonies* of feveral *Octaves*. And *obferve*, That we may have *Harmony* when none of the *primary Intervals* are within an *Octave*, as if to a *Fundamental* be joyned a 5*th* above *Octave*, and a double *Octave*. Of fuch *Harmonies* the *fecondary Relations* are ever equal to thofe of the *fimple Harmonies*, whofe *primary Intervals* have the fame Denomination ; and in Practice they are reckoned the fame, tho' feldom are any fuch ufed.

I have brought all the Combinations of *Concords* into the Table of *Harmony* which anfwer to that general Character,*viz.*That there muft be no Difcord among any of the Terms; yet thefe few Things muft be obferved. 1*mo.* That in Practice *Difcords* are in fome Circumftances admitted, not for themfelves, fimply confidered, but to prepare the Mind for a greater Relifh of the fucceeding more perfect *Harmony*. 2*do.* That tho' the 4*th*, taken by it felf, is *Concord*,

and

and in the next Degree to the 5*th* ; yet in Practice 'tis reckoned a *Difcord* when it ftands next to the *Fundamental* ; and therefore thefe Combinations of the preceeding Table, where it poffeffes that Place, are not to be admitted as *Harmonics* ; but 'tis admitted in every other Part of the *Harmony*, fo that the 4*th* is *Concord* or *Difcord*, according to the Situation ; for Example, if betwixt the Extremes of an *Octave* is placed an *arithmetical Mean*, we have it divided into a 4*th* and a 5*th* 2. 3. 4. which Numbers, if we apply to the Vibrations of Chords, then the 5*th* is next the *Fundamental*, and the *fecondary Relation* is in this Cafe, 2. But take an *harmonical* Mean, as here 3. 4. 6. and the 4*th* is next the *Fundamental*, and the *fecondary Relation* is 3. Now in thefe Two Cafes, the component Parts being the fame, *viz.* a 4*th*, 5*th*, 8*ve*, differing only in the Pofition of the 4*th* and 5*th*, which occafions the Difference of the *fecondary Relation*, the different Effects can only be laid on the different Pofitions of the 4*th* and 5*th* ; which Effect can only be meafured by the *fecondary Relation* ; and by Experience we find that the beft *fecondary Relation* makes the beft Compofition, fo 2. 3. 4. is better than 3 : 4. : 6 : And thus in all Cafes, where the fame *Interval* is divided into the fame Parts differently fituated, the Preference will anfwer to the *fecondary Relation*, the leffer making the beft Compofition, which plainly depends upon the primary Relation ; but the 4*th* next the *Fundamental* is not on'y worfe than the

5*th*

5*th*, but is reckoned *Difcord* in that Pofition ; and therefore all the other Combinations of the Table are preferr'd to it, or rather it is quite rejected ; the Reafon affigned for this is, that the *graver* Sounds are the moft powerful, and raife our Attention moft; fo that the 4*th* being next the *Fundamental*, its Imperfection compared with the *Octave* and 5*th* is made more remarkable, and confequently it muft be lefs agreeable than when it is heard alone ; whereas when it ftands next the *acute* Term of the *Octave*, that Imperfection is drowned by its being between the 5*th* and *Octave*, both in *primary* Relation to the *Fundamental*. But this does not hold in the 6*th* and 3*d*, becaufe they differ not in their Perfection fo much as the 5*th* and 4*th*. But we fhall hear *D' Cartes* reafoning upon this. Says he, *Hæc infæliciffima*, &c. *The* 4th *is the moft unhappy of all the* Concords, *and never admitted in Songs, but by Accident* (he means not next the *Fundamental*, but as it falls accidentally among the mutual Relations) *not that it is more imperfect than the* 3d *or* 6th, *but becaufe it is too near the* 5th, *and lofes its Sweetnefs by this Neighbourhood ; for underftanding which we muft notice, That a* 5th *is never heard, but the acuter* 4th *feems fome way to refound, which is a Confequent of what was faid before, that the* Fundamental *never founds but the* acuter Octave *feems to do fo too.*

LET the Lines A C *and* D B *be a* 5th, *and the Line* E F, *an* acuter Octave *to* A C, *it will be a* 4th *to* D B ; *and if it refound to the* Fundamental

damental, *then, when the* 5th *is founded with*
the Fundamental, *this*
Resonance is a 4th a-
bove the 5th *that always follows it, which is*
the Reason it is not admitted next the Bass ; *for*
since all the rest of the Concords *in* Musick *are*
only useful for varying of the 5th, *certainly the*
4th *which does not so is useless, which is plain*
from this, That if we put it next the Bass, *the*
acuter 5th *will resound, and there the Ear will*
observe it out of its Place, therefore the 4th
would be very displeasing, as if we had the Sha-
dow for the Substance, an Image for the real
Thing. Elsewhere he says it serves in Composition where the same Reason occurs not,
which hinders its standing next the Bass. It is
well observed, that the rest of the *simple Con-*
cords serve only for varying the *5th* ; Variety
is certainly the Life of all sensual Pleasure, without which the more exquisite but cloy the soon-
er; and in *Musick*, were there no more *Con-*
cords but *Octave* and 5th, it would prove a very
poor Fund of Pleasure ; but we have more, and
agreeable to *D' Cartes*'s Notion, we may say,
They are all designed to vary the 5th, for they
all proceed from it, as we saw in the Divisions
of the upper and lower 5th of the *Octave* in
Chap. 5. and that all the Variety in *Musick*
proceeds from these 3ds and 6ths arising from
the Division of the 5th directly. or accidentally,
as we shall see more particularly afterwards :
Mean time observe, that as the 4th rises naturally from the Division of the *Octave*, so it
serves

serves to vary it, and accordingly is admitted in Compofition in every Part but next the *Fundamental* or *Bafs*; for the 5*th* being more perfect and capable of Variety (which the 4*th* is not, fince no leffer *Concord* agrees to both its Extremes) by Means of the 3*ds*, ought to ftand next the *Fundamental*. Now if the 4*th* muft not ftand with the *Fundamental*, then this 4*th*, with the *Octave*, muft not be reckoned among *fimple Harmonies*. To prove that the 4*th* confidered by it felf is a *Concord*, *Kircher* makes a very odd Argument. Says he, A 4*th* added to a 5*th* makes an *Octave*, which is Concord; but *nothing gives what it has not*, therefore the 4*th* is a Concord: But by the fame Argument you may prove that any *Interval* lefs than *Octave* is a *Concord*.

I have obferved of the Series 1. 2. 3. 4. 5. 6, 8. that they are *Concords* each with other. They contain all the *original Concords*, and the chief of the *compound*; and they ftand in fuch Order that Seven Sounds in the Proportions and Order of this Series joyned in one *Harmony* is the moft complete and perfect that can be heard: For here we have the chief and principal of all the *Harmonies* of the preceeding Table, as you'll fee by comparing thefe Numbers with that *Table*; fo that in this fhort and fimple Series we have the whole effential Principles and Ingredients of *Mufick*; and all at once the moft agreeable Effect that Sounds in *Confonance* can have.

LET

LET us now confider how thefe Sounds may be raifed ; this will be eafily found from the Things already explained; but we muft firft obferve, that there will be a great Difference betwixt applying thefe Numbers to the Lengths of Chords, and to their Vibrations : If they are applied to the *Chords,* then 'tis eafy to find Seven Chords which fhall be as thefe Seven Numbers; but 8 being the longeft Chord, the lefs perfect *Concords* ftand in *primary Relation* to the *Fundamental ;* and the fecondary Relation is 15 : But if we have Seven Sounds whofe Vibrations are as thefe Numbers, then 1 is the Vibration of the *Fundamental,* and fo on in Order to 8 the Vibration of the *acuteft* performed in the fame Time : And thus the beft *Concords* ftand in *primary* Relation to the *Fundamental,* and 1 is the *fecondary* Relation : . Therefore to afford this moft perfect *Harmony,* we muft find Seven Sounds which from the loweft to the higheft fhall be as 1 : 2 : 3 : 4 : 5 : 6 : 8, the leaft Number reprefenting the *graveft* Sound. Now, to do this, let us mind that the Lengths of Chords are in fimple reciprocal Proportion of their Vibrations accomplifhed in the fame Time, out of which I fhall draw the Two following *Problems,* whereof the firft fhall folve the Queftion in hand.

PROBLEM I. To find the Lengths of feveral Chords, whofe Vibrations performed in the fame Time, fhall be as a given Rank of Numbers. *Rule.* Take the given Series, and out of it find another reciprocal to it, by *Theor.* 14.

Chap.

Chap. 4. which, according to the Demonstration there given, and what I have premised here, is the Series of Lengths sought, so the preceeding Series 1. 2. 3. 4. 5. 6. 8. being given as a Series of Vibrations performed in the same Time, the Lengths of Seven Chords, to which that Series of Vibrations agrees, are 120, 60. 40. 30. 24. 20. 15. And these Seven Chords being in every other Respect equal and alike, and all founded together, shall produce the *Harmony* required.

PROBLEM II. The Lengths of several Chords being given, to find the Number of Vibrations of each performed in the same Time. This is done the same Way as the former : And so if the Series 1. 2. 3. 4. 5. 6. 8. *&c.* be the Length of Seven Chords, their Vibrations sought are 120. 60. 40. 30. 24. 20. 15.

NOTE. From what has been explained in *Theor.* 14. *Chap.* 4. we see that if one of these, *viz.* the Lengths of several Chords, or their Vibrations accomplished in the same Time, make a *continued arithmetical* or *harmonical* Series, the other will be reciprocally an *harmonical* or *arithmetical* Series, so the preceeding Series 1. 2. 3. 4. 5. 6. being *continuedly arithmetical*, its correspondent Series 120. 60. 40. 30. 24. 20. is *continuedly harmonical* ; but the Number 8 in the first Series interrupts the *arithmetical Proportion*, and so is the *harmonical Proportion* interrupted by its Correspondent 15. But as in the first, 2. 4. 6. 8. are *continuedly arithmetical*, so are these correspondent to them in the other

harmo-

harmonical, viz. 60 : 30 : 20 : 15. Alſo it will hold univerſally, that taking any Numbers out of the one Series in *continued arithmetical* or *harmonical Proportion*, their Correſpondents in the other will be reciprocally *harmonical* or *a-rithmetical.*

C H A P.   VIII.

Of concinnous Intervals, *and the* Scale of Muſick.

§ 1. *Of the Neceſſity and Uſe of* concinnous Diſ-cords, *and of their Original and Dependence on the* Concords.

WE have, in the preceeding *Chapters,* conſidered the firſt and moſt eſſenti-al Principles [as far as concerns the firſt Part of the Definition] of *Muſick, viz.* theſe Relations of Sound in *Acuteneſs* and *Gra-vity* whoſe Extremes are *Concord ;* for without theſe there can be no *Muſick :* The indefinite Number of other *Ratios* being all *Diſcord,* be-long not eſſentially to *Muſick,* becauſe of them-ſelves felves they produce no Pleafure ; yet fome of them are admitted into the *Syftem* as neceffary to the better being of it, both with refpect to *Confonance* and *Succeffion*, but moft remarkably in this ; and fuch are called *concinnous Intervals*, as being apt or fit for the Improvement of *Mufick*:All other*Difcords* are called *inconcinnous.* To explain what thefe *concinnous Intervals* are, their Number, Nature and Office, fhall employ this *Chapter*.

IN order to which, I fhall firft offer the following Confiderations, to prove that fome other than the *harmonical Intervals* of Sound (*i. e.* fuch whofe Extremes are *Concord*) are neceffary for the Improvement or better Being of *Mufick*.

WE know by Experience how much the Mind of Man is delighted with Variety : It can ftand no Difpute, whether we confider intellectual or fenfible Pleafures ; every one will be confcious of it to himfelf: If you ask the Reafon, I can only anfwer, That we are made fo : And if we apply this Rule to *Mufick*, then it is plain the more Variety there is in it, it will be the more entertaining, unlefs it proceed to an Excefs ; for fo limited are our Capacities, that too much or too little are equally fatal to our Pleafures. Let us then confider what muft be the Effect of having no other but *harmonical Intervals* in the *Syftem* of *Mufick*, and,

Firft, With refpect to a fingle Voice, if that fhould move always from one Degree of *Tune* to another, fo as every Note or Sound to the

next

next were in the *Ratio* of some *Concord*, the Variety which we happily know to be the Life of *Musick* would soon be exhausted. For to move by no other than *harmonical Intervals*, would not only want Variety, and so weary us with a tedious Repetition of the same Things; but the very Perfection of such Relations of Sounds would cloy the Ear, in the same Manner as sweet and luscious Things do the Taste, which are therefore artfully seasoned with the Mixture of sowr and bitter: And so in *Musick* the Perfection of the *harmonical Intervals* are set off, and as 'twere seasoned with other Kinds of *Intervals* that are never agreeable by themselves, but only in order to make the Agreement of the other more various and remarkable. *D' Cartes* has a Notion here that's worth our considering. He observes, that an *acute* Sound requires a greater Force to produce it either in the Motion of the vocal Organs of an Animal, or in striking a String; which we know by Experience, says he, in Strings, for the more they are stretched they become the *acuter*, and require the greater Force to move them: And hence he concludes, that *acute* Sounds, or the Motion of the Air that produce them immediately, strike the Ear with more Force : From which Observations he thinks may be drawn the true and primary Reason why *Degrees* (which are *Intervals* less than any *Concord*) were invented; which Reason he judges to be this, Lest if the Voice did always proceed by *harmonical* Distances, there should be too great Disproportion

tion or Inequality in the *Intenseness* of it (by
which *Intenseness* he plainly means that Force
with which it is produced, and with which also it strikes the Ear) which would weary both
Singer and Hearer. For *Example*. Let *A* and
B be at the Distance of a greater 3*d*, if one
would ascend from *A* to *B*, then because
B being acuter strikes the Ear with more
Force than *A* ; lest that Disproportion should
prove uneasy, another Sound *C* is put between
them, by which as by a Step we may ascend
more easily, and with less unequal Force in raising the Voice. Hence it appears, says he, that
the *Degrees* are nothing but a certain *Medium*
contrived to be put betwixt the Extremes of
the *Concords*, for moderating their Inequality,
but of themselves they have not Sweetness e-
nough to satisfy the Ear, and are of Use only
with regard to the *Concords* ; so that when the
Voice has moved one Degree, the Ear is not yet
satisfied till we come to another, which therefore must be *Concord* with the first Sound. Thus
far *D' Cartes* reasons on this Matter; the Substance of what he says being plainly this, *viz.*
That by a fit Division of the *concording Intervals* into lesser Ones, the Voice will pass smooth-
ly from one Note to another, and the Hearer
be prepared for a more exquisite Relish of the
perfecter *Intervals*, whose Extremes are the
proper Points in which the Ear finds the expected Rest and Pleasure. Yet moving by *harmonical* Distances is also necessary, but not so
frequently: The Thing therefore required as
to

to this Part is, fuch *Intervals* lefs than any *harmonical* one, which fhall divide thefe, in order that the Movement of a Sound from their one Extreme to another, by thefe *Degrees*, may be fmooth and agreeable ; and by the Variety improve the more effential Principles of *Mufick* to a Capacity of affording greater Pleafure, and all together make a more perfect *Syftem.*

2*dly.* Let us confider *Mufick* in *Parts, i. e.* when Two or more Voices joyn in *Confonance;* the *general Rule* is, That the fucceffive Sounds of each be fo ordered, that the feveral Voices fhall always be *Concord.* Now there ought to be a Variety in the Choice of thefe *fucceffive Concords,* and alfo in the Method of their Succeffions ; but all this depends upon the Movements of the fingle *Parts.* And if thefe could move in an agreeable Manner only by *harmonical* Diftances, there are but a few different Ways in which they could remove from *Concord* to *Concord;* and hereby we fhould lofe very much of the Ravifhment of Sounds in *Confonance.* As to this Part then, the Thing demanded is, a Variety of Ways, whereby each fingle Voice of more in *Confonance* may move agreeably in their *fucceffive* Sounds, fo as to pafs from *Concord* to *Concord,* and meet at every Note in the fame or a different *Concord* from what they ftood at in the laft Note. In what Cafes and for what Reafons *Difcords* are allowed, the *Rules* of *Compofition* muft teach : But joyn thefe Two Confiderations, and you fee manifeftly how imperfect *Mufick* would be without

out any other *Intervals* than *Concords* ; tho' these are the principal and moſt eſſential, and the others we now enquire into but ſubſervient to them, for varying and illuſtrating the Pleaſure that ariſes immediately out of the *harmonical Kind.*

B u t, *laſtly*, conſider, that tho' the *Melody* of a ſingle Voice is very agreeable, yet no *Conſonance* of *Parts* can have a good Effect ſeparately from the other ; therefore the Degrees which anſwer the firſt Demand, muſt ſerve the other too, elſe, however perfect the *Syſtem* be as to the firſt Caſe, it will be ſtill imperfect as to the laſt.

W h e n a *Queſtion* is about the Agreeableneſs of any Thing to the Senſes, the laſt Appeal muſt be to Experience, the only infallible Judge in theſe Caſes ; and ſo in *Muſick* the Ear muſt inform us of what is good and bad ; and nothing ought to be received without its Approbation. We have ſeen to what Purpoſes other *Intervals* than the *harmonical* are neceſſary ; now we ſhall ſee what they are ; and agreeable to what has been ſaid, we ſhall make *Experience* the Judge, which approves of thoſe, and thoſe only, with their *Dependents* (beſides the *harmonical Intervals*) as Parts of the true *natural Syſtem* of *Muſick, viz.* whoſe *Ratios* are 8 : 9. called a *greater Tone*, 9 : 10 called a *leſſer Tone*, and 15 : 16 called a *Semitone* : And theſe are the leſſer *Intervals*, particularly called *Degrees*, by which a Sound can move upwards or downwards ſucceſſively, from one Extreme

treme of any *harmonical Interval* to another, and produce true *Melody*; and by Means whereof also several Voices are capable of the necessary Variety in passing from *Concord* to *Concord*. By the *Dependents* of these Degrees, I mean their Compounds with *Octave*, (which are understood to be the same Thing in Practice, as we observed in another Place of *compound Concords*) and their *Complements* to an *Octave* (or Differences from it) *viz.* 9 : 16, 5 : 9, 8 : 15, which are also a Part of the *System*, tho' more imperfect, but of these afterwards: As to the *Semitone*, 'tis so called, not that it is geometrically the Half of either of these which we call *Tones* (for 'tis greater) but because it comes near to it ; and 'tis called the *greater Semitone*, being greater than what it wants of a *Tone*.

NOTE, Hitherto we have used the Words, *Tone* and *Tune* indifferently, to signify a certain Quality of a single Sound ; but here *Tone* is a certain *Interval*, and shall hereafter be constantly so used, and the Word *Tune* always applied to the other.

OUR next Work shall be to explain the *Original* of these *Degrees*, and their different Perfections; and then shew how they answer the Purposes for which they were required ; and, in doing this, I shall make such Reflections upon the Connection and Dependence of the several Parts of the *System*, that we may be confirmed both by Sense and Reason in the true *Principles* of *Musick*.

As

As to the *Original* of thefe *Degrees,* they arife out of the *fimple Concords,* and are equal to their Differences, which we take by *Probl.* 10. *Chap.* 4. Thus 8 : 9 is the Difference of a 5*th* and 4*th.* 9 : 10 is the *Difference* of a 3*d l.* and 4*th,* or of 5*th* and 6*th g.* 15 : 16, the *Difference* of 3*d g.* and 4*th,* or of 5*th* and 6*th l.*

We fhall prefently fee the Reafon why no other *Degrees* than fuch as are the Differences of *Concords* could be admitted; but there are other Differences among the *fimple Concords,* befides thefe (which you may obferve do all arife from a Comparifon of the 5*th* with the other *Concords*) yet none elfe could anfwer the Defign, which I fhall fhew immediately, and give you in the mean Time a *Table* of all thefe Differences of *fimple Concords,* which are not *Concords* themfelves.

Differences of			*Ratios.*
3*d l.* and	3*d g.*	=	24 : 25
	4*th*	=	9 : 10
	6*th g.*	=	18 : 25
3*d g.* and	4*th*	=	15 : 16
	6*th l.*	=	25 : 32
4*th* and 5*th*		=	8 : 9
5*th* and	6*th l.*	=	15 : 16
	6*th g.*	=	9 : 10
6*th l.* and	6*th g.*	=	24 : 25

I fhall now explain how thefe *Degrees* contribute to the Improvement of the *Syftem* of *Mufick* : In doing which I fhall ſhall endeavour to give the Reaſon why theſe only are proper and natural to that End.

Degrees were required both for improving the *Melody* of a ſingle· Voice conſidered by it ſelf ; and that ſeveral Voices, while they move melodiouſly each by it ſelf, might alſo joyn together in an agreeable Variety of *Harmony* ; and therefore I obſerved, that the *Degrees* required muſt anſwer both theſe Ends, if poſſible; accordingly, Nature has bounteouſly afforded us theſe neceſſary Materials of our Pleaſure, and made the preceeding *Degrees* anſwer all our Wiſh, as I ſhall now explain.

I ſhall firſt conſider it with reſpect to the *Conſonance* of Two or more Voices. *Suppoſe* Two Voices *A* and *B*, containing between them any *Concord*; they can change into another *Concord* only Two Ways. 1*mo.* If the one Voice as *A* keeps its Place, and the other *B* moves upward or downward (*i..e.* becomes either *acuter* or *graver* than it was before.) Now if the Movement of *B* can only be agreeable by *harmonical Intervals*, they can change only in theſe Caſes, *viz.* if the firſt *Concord* be *Octave*, then by *B*'s moving nearer the Pitch of *A*, either by the Diſtance of a 6*th*, 5*th*, 4*th* or 3*d*, the Two Voices will *concord* in a 3*d*, 4*th*, 5*th* or 6*th*, which is plain from the Compoſition of an Octave : And conſequently by *B*'s moving farther from *A*, the Voices can again change from any of theſe leſſer *Concords* to an *Octave*. Or ſuppoſe them at firſt at a 6*th*, by *B*'s moving either a 4*th* or 3*d*, they will meet in a 3*d* or

4*th*,

4th, or being at a *4th* or *3d*, they may meet in a *6th*, becaufe a *6th* is compofed of *4th* and *3d*. And *laftly*, being at a *5th*, they may meet in a *3d*, and contrarily. But by the Ufe of thefe *Degrees* the Variety is increafed; for now fuppofe *A* and *B* diftant by any *fimple Concord*, if *B* moves up or down one of thefe *Degrees* 8 : 9, or 9 : 10, or 15 : 16, there fhall always be a Change into fome other *Concord*, becaufe thefe *Degrees* are the very Differences of *Concords*. Then, 2*do*. If we fuppofe both the Voices to move, they may move either the fame Way (*i. e.* both become *acuter* or *graver* than they were) or move contrary to one another; and in both Cafes they may increafe their firft Diftance, or contract it, fo as to meet in a different *Concord*; but then if the Movements be by *harmonical Intervals*, the Variety will be far lefs here than in the firft Suppofition ; but this is abundantly fupplied by the Ufe of the *Degrees*. You muft *obferve* again, that befides the Want of Variety in moft of the Changes that can be made, from *Concord* to *Concord*, by the fingle Voices moving in *harmonical Diftances*, there will be too great a Difproportion or Inequality of the *Concord* you pafs from, and that you meet in, which muft have an ill Effect : For by Experience we are taught, that *Nature* is beft pleafed, where the Variety and Changes of our Pleafure (arifing from the fame *Objects*) are gradual and by fmooth Steps ; and therefore moving from one Extreme to another is to be feldom practis'd ; for this Reafon alfo
the

the *Degrees* are of neceſſary Uſe for making
the Paſſage of the *Concords* eaſy and ſmooth,
which generally ought to be from one *Concord*
into the next, which is confiſtent with the Motion of one or both Voices. But let me make
this laſt Remark, which we have alſo confirmed from Experience, *viz.* That of Two
Sounds in *Conſonance*, 'tis required not only
that every Note they make together be *Concord* (I have ſaid already that there are ſome
Exceptions to this Rule) but that, as much as
poſſible, the preſent Note of the one Voice be
Concord to the immediately preceeding Note of
the other; which can be done by no Means ſo
well as by ſuch *Degrees* as are the Differences
of *Concords* (where theſe happen to be *Diſcord*, *Muſicians* call it particularly *Relation*
in *harmonical.*) And indeed upon this Principle
it can eaſily be ſhewn, that 'tis impoſſible there
can be any other *Degrees* admitted, than what
are equal to the Differences of *ſimple Concords :*
If only one Voice move, the Thing is plain ; it
both move, let us ſuppoſe *A B* at any *Concord*,
and to move into another, and there let the
Two new Notes be expreſſed by *a b.* Then
ſince *a B* muſt be *Concord*, it follows, that the
Diſtance of *a* and *A* is equal to the Difference
of the Two *Concords A B*, and *a B* ; the ſame
Way 'tis proven that *b B* is the Difference of
the *Concords A B*, and *b A.*

'T is a very obvious Queſtion here, why the
ſucceſſive Notes of Two different Voices may
not as well admit of *Diſcords*, as theſe of the
ſame

same Voice; to which the Answer seems plainly to be this, that in the same Voice, the *Degrees*, which are the only *Discords* admitted, are regulated by the *harmonical Intervals* to which they are but subservient; and the *Melody* is conducted altogether with respect to these; for the *Degrees* of themselves without their Subserviency to the *Concords* could make no *Musick*, as shall be further explained afterwards: But in the other Case, the successive Motions can be brought under no such Regulation, and therefore must be *harmonical* as much as possible, lest it diminish the Pleasure of the succeeding *Concord*; besides, consider the *Discords* that are most ready to occur here, are greater than the *Degrees*, and would be intolerable in any Case.

BUT now, supposing that only these *Discords* belong to the *System* of *Musick*, which are the Differences of *Concords*, you'll ask why the other Differences marked in the preceeding *Table* are excluded, *viz.* 24 : 25 the Difference of the Two 3*ds*, or the Two 6*ths*; 18 : 25 the Difference of the 3*d l.* and 6*th g.* 25 : 32 the Difference of 3*d g.* and 6*th l.* To satisfie this, we are to consider, *First*, that the Passage of several Voices from *Concord* to *Concord* does not need them, there being a sufficient Variety from the other Differences; but chiefly the Reason seems to be, that they don't answer the Demands of a single Voice, which I shall explain in the next §, and desire you here only to observe ferve that they arife out of the *imperfect Con-cords, viz.* 3*ds* and 6*ths.*

---

§ 2. *Of the Ufe of* Degrees *in the Conftruction of the* Scale of Mufick.

WE have already obferved, that the *Concords* are the effential Principles of *Mufick* as they afford Pleafure immediately and of themfelves : Other Relations belong to *Mufick* only as they are fubfervient to thefe.   We have alfo explained what that Subferviency required is, *viz.* That by a fit Divifion of the *harmonical Intervals* a fingle Voice may pafs fmoothly from one Extreme to another, whereby the Pleafure of thefe perfect Relations may be heightned, and we may have a Variety neceffary to our more agreeable Entertainment: It follows, that to anfwer this End, the *Intervals* fought, or fome of them at leaft, muft be lefs than any *harmonical* one, *i. e.* lefs than a 3*d l.* 5 ; 6 ; and that they ought all to be lefs, will prefently appear from the Nature of the Thing.   For the *Degrees* fought we have already affigned thefe, *viz.* 8 : 9 called a *greater Tone,* 9 : 10 called a *leffer Tone,* and 15 : 16 called a *greater Semitone* : Now that every *harmonical Interval* is compofed of, and confequently refolvable into a certain Number of thefe *Degrees,* will appear from the following
Table,

Table, wherein I give you the Number and Kinds of thefe *Degrees* that each *Concord* is e-qual to, which you can prove by the *Addition* of *Intervals, Chap.* 4. Or you'll find it more ea-fily afterwards, when you fee them all ftand in order in the *Scale* ; we fhall afterwards confider in what Order thefe *Degrees* ought to be taken in the Divifion of any *Interval.*

TABLE of the component Parts of Concords.				
3d *l.*		1 *tg,* & 1 *ſ*		
3d *g.*		1 *tg,*	1 *tl,*	
4th	contains	1 *tg,*	1 *tl,*	1 *ſ*
5th		2 *tg,*	1 *tl,*	1 *ſ*
6th *l.*		2 *tg,*	1 *tl,*	2 *ſ*
6th *g.*		2 *tg,*	2 *tl,*	1 *ſ*
8ve		3 *tg,*	2 *tl,*	2 *ſ*

NOTE, That as in this *Table,* fo afterwards I fhall for Bre-vity mark a greater *Tone* thus *t g,* a *leſſer* thus *t l,* a *Semitone* thus *ſ.*

BUT now, *obſerve,* that fince we can con-ceive a Variety of other *Intervals* that will di-vide the *Concords* befides thefe, we are there-fore to confider for what Reafon they are pre-ferable to any other : To do this, I fhall firft fhew you, that no other but fuch as are equal to the Differences of *Concords* are fit for the Purpofe, and then for what Reafon only thefe Three are chofen.

FOR the *Firſt,* confider, that every greater *Concord* contains all the leſſer within it, in fuch a Manner, that betwixt the Extremes of any greater *Concord,* as many middle Terms may

be

be placed as there are leſſer *Concords*; which middle Terms ſhall be to any one Extreme of that greater *Concord* in the *Ratio* of theſe leſſer *Concords*; ſo betwixt the Extremes of the 8*ve* may be placed 6 Terms, which ſhall make all the leſſer *Concords* with any one of the Extremes, as in this Series,

$$1 : \frac{5}{6} \cdot \frac{4}{5} \cdot \frac{3}{4} \cdot \frac{2}{3} \cdot \frac{5}{8} \cdot \frac{3}{5} \cdot \frac{1}{2}$$

where comparing each Term with 1, you have all the *ſimple Concords* in their gradual Order, 3*d l.* 3*d g.* 4*th,* 5*th,* 6*th l.* 6*th g.* 8*ve*; and the mutual Relations of the Terms immediately next other in the Series are plainly the Differences of the *Concords* which theſe Terms make with the Extreme. Now it is natural and reaſonable that if we would paſs by *Degrees* from one Extreme to another of any greater *harmonical Interval,* in the moſt agreeable Manner, we ought to chooſe ſuch middle Terms as have an *harmonical Relation* to the Extremes of that greater, rather than ſuch as are *Diſcord*; for the *ſimple Concords* being different in Perfection, vary the Pleaſure in this Progreſſion very agreeably ; but we could not bear to hear a great many Sounds ſucceeding one another, among which there were no *Concord,* or where only the laſt is *concord* to the Firſt : And therefore it is plain that the *Degrees* required ought to be equal to the Differences of *Concords,* as you ſee evidently they muſt be where the middle Terms are *Concord*
with

with one or both the Extremes. But of all the
difcord Differences of *Concords*, only thefe are
agreeable, *viz.* 8 : 9, 9 : 10, 15 : 16 ; the o-
ther Three are rejected, *viz.* 24 : 25, 18 : 25,
25 : 32 ; the Reafon of which feems to be, that
the Two laft are too great, and the firft too
fmall ; but particularly 25 : 32 is an *Interval*
greater than a *4th*, as 18 : 25 is greater than a
3*d g.* and therefore would make fuch a dif-
proportioned and unequal Mixture with the o-
ther *Degrees*, that would be infufferable. Then
for 24 : 25 it is too fmall, and would alfo make
too much Inequality among the *Degrees*. But
at laft we fhall take Experience for the infallible
Proof that we have chofen the only proper *Degrees :* Our Reafon in Cafes like this can go no
further than the making fuch Obfervations upon
the Dependence and Connection of Things,
that from the Order and Analogy of *Nature*
we may draw a probable Conclufion that we
have difcovered the true natural Rule.   And of
this Kind we fhall immediately have further Demonftrations that the only true *natural Degrees*
are thefe already affign'd.

WE come now to confider the Order in which
the *Degrees* ought to be taken, in this Divifion
of the *harmonical Intervals,*for conftituting the
Scale of *Mufick* ; for tho' we have the true *Degrees*, yet it is not every Order and Progreffion
of them that will produce true *Melody*. For
Example, Tho' the greater *Tone* 8 : 9 be a true
Degree, yet there could be no *Mufick* made of
any Number of fuch *Degrees*, becaufe no Number

ber of them is equal to any *Concord*; the fame
is true of the other Two *Degrees*; which you
may prove by adding Two or Three, *&c.* of
any one Kind of them together, till you find the
Sum exceed an *Octave*, which it will do in 6
greater *Tones*, or 7 *leſſer Tones*, or 11
Semitones; and compare the Sum of 2, 3, 4,
&c. of them, till you come to that Number,
you'll find them equal to no *Concord*. Therefore there is a Neceſſity that theſe *Degrees* be
mixt together to make right *Muſick*; and 'tis
plain they muſt be ſo mixt, that there ought
never to be Two of one Kind next other. But
this we ſhall have alſo confirmed in examining
the Order they ought to be taken in.

The *Octave* containing in it all the other
ſimple Concords, and the *Degrees* being the Differences of theſe *Concords*, 'tis plain that the
Diviſion of the *Octave* will comprehend the
Diviſions of all the reſt : Let us therefore joyn
all the *ſimple Concords* to a common *Fundamental*, and we have this Series.

$$ 1 \cdot \frac{5}{6} \cdot \frac{4}{5} \cdot \frac{3}{4} \cdot \frac{2}{3} \cdot \frac{5}{8} \cdot \frac{3}{5} \cdot \frac{1}{2} $$

Fund. 3d *l.* 3d *g.* 4th, 5th 6th *l.* 6th *g.* 8ve.

Now if we ſhould aſcend to an *Octave* by
theſe Steps, 'tis evident we have all the poſſible *harmonical Relations* to the *Fundamental*;
and if we examine what *Degrees* are in this A-
ſcent

ſcent, or the mutual Relations of each Term to
the next, they are theſe.

$$\frac{5}{6} \cdot \frac{24}{25} \cdot \frac{15}{16} \cdot \frac{8}{9} \cdot \frac{15}{16} \cdot \frac{24}{25} \cdot \frac{5}{6}$$

But this we know is far from being a *melodious* Aſcent; there is too great Inequality among
theſe *Degrees*; the firſt and laſt are each a 3*d
l.* which ought alſo to be divided; it is e-
qual to a *t g.* and *ſ.* and ſo inſtead of $\frac{5}{6}$ we ſhall
have theſe Two Degrees 8 : 9 and 15 : 16. But
when this is done, yet the Diviſion of the O-
ctave will not be perfect; for we have too many *Degrees*, and an Exceſs is as much a Fault
as a Defect : So many ſmall *Degrees* would neither be eaſily raiſed, nor heard with Pleaſure :
The Two 3*ds* and Two 6*ths* have ſo ſmall a
Difference, 24 : 25, that the Diviſion of the O-
ctave does not require nor admit them both together, the Progreſs being ſmoother where we
have but one of the 3*ds* and one of the 6*th.*
If this Degree 24 : 25 be expelled, then will
9 : 10 have Place in the Series,which is not only
a better Relation of it ſelf, as it conſiſts of leſſer
Numbers, but it has a nearer Affinity with the
other Two 8 : 9 and 15 : 16, all theſe Three
proceeding from the 5*th,* as I have already
noted.

Now then if we take only one of the 3*ds*
and one 6*th* in the Diviſion of the 8*ve* we have
theſe Two different Series,

THE

Fund.	3d l.	4th,	5th,	6th l.	8ve
I .	$\frac{5}{6}$.	$\frac{3}{4}$.	$\frac{2}{3}$.	$\frac{5}{8}$.	$\frac{1}{2}$
I .	$\frac{4}{5}$.	$\frac{3}{4}$.	$\frac{2}{3}$.	$\frac{3}{5}$.	$\frac{1}{2}$
Fund.	3d g.	4th,	5th,	6th g.	8ve

THE 3d l. and 6th l. are taken together, as the 3d g. and 6th g. becaufe their Relation is the Concord of a 4th ; whereas the 3d l. and 6th g. alfo the 3d g. and 6th l. are one to the other a grofs *Difcord* ; and 'tis better how many *Concords* are among the middle Terms ; but if in fome particular Cafes of Practice this Order is changed, 'tis done for the fake of fome other Advantage to the *Melody*, of which I have an Occafion to fpeak afterwards. But the 3ds next each Extreme are yet undivided, which ought to be done to complete the Divifion of the *Octave.*

IN the firft of the preceeding Series we have the 3d l. next the *Fundamental,* and the 3d g. next the other Extreme: In the Second we have the 3d g. next the *Fundamental,* and the 3d l. next the *acute* Extreme. Now it is plain what *Degrees* will divide thefe 3ds, becaufe we fee them divided in the Divifions already made ; for in the firft Series, betwixt the 3d l. and the 5th we have a 3d g. (which is their Difference) divided into thefe *Degrees,* and in this Order afcending, *viz.* t l. and t g. and betwixt the 4th and 6th l. we have a 3d l. (which is their Dif-

Difference) divided into *t g.* and */.* We have the same *Intervals* divided in the other Series betwixt the 3*d g.* and 5*th*, and betwixt the 4*th* and 6*th g.* but the Order of the *Degrees* here is reverse of what it is in the other Series : And the Queſtion now is, what is the moſt natural Order for the Diviſion of theſe 3*ds* that ly next the Extremes in the *Octaves* ? It may at firſt ſeem that we have got a fair and natural Hint from theſe Places mentioned, and that the 3*ds* ought to be ordered the ſame Way towards the Extremes of each Series, as they are in theſe Places of it. In the 3*ds* next the *Fundamental* I have followed that Order, but not for that Reaſon ; and in the upper 3*ds* I have taken the contrary Order, which ſee in the Two following Series, where I have marked the *Degrees* from every Term to the next ; and you ſee I have divided

with a 3*d l.* - $1 : \dfrac{8}{9} . \dfrac{5}{6} . \dfrac{3}{4} . \dfrac{2}{3} . \dfrac{5}{8} . \dfrac{5}{9} . \dfrac{1}{2}$

$\qquad\qquad\quad tg. \quad ſ. \quad tl. \quad tg. \quad ſ. \quad tg. \quad tl.$

with a 3*d g.* - $1 : \dfrac{8}{9} . \dfrac{4}{5} . \dfrac{3}{4} . \dfrac{2}{3} . \dfrac{3}{5} . \dfrac{8}{15} . \dfrac{1}{2}$

$\qquad\qquad\quad tg. \quad tl. \quad ſ. \quad tg. \quad tl. \quad tg. \quad ſ.$

the 3*d g.* (.which is in the upper Place of the one and lower of the other Series) in this Order aſcending, *viz. t g.* and *t l.* And the 3*d l.* (which is alſo in the upper Place of the one

$\qquad\qquad\qquad\qquad\qquad\qquad\qquad$ and

and lower of the other) in this Order afcending, *viz. t g.* and *f.* The Reafon of this
Choice I fhall thus account for. *Firft*, As to
the 3*d* next the *Fundamental*, I place the *t g.*
loweft, becaufe it is the *Degree* which a natural Voice can moft eafily raife, being the moft
perfect of the Three, and we find it fo by Experience; and if you confider, that it is the Difference of a 4*th* and 5*th*, which two *Concords*
the Ear is perfectly Judge of, by practifing thefe
one learns very eafily how to raife a *t g.* with
Exactnefs : But for the *t l.* (the other Part of
the 3*d g.*) it is not fo eafily learned, for the
Difference betwixt the Two Tones being but
fmall, one cannot be fure of it, but will readily
fall into the more perfect. It is true, that in
rifing from any *Fundamental* to a 3*d g.* we take
a *t l.* at the fecond Step; but then I believe,
our taking it exactly here, is owing to the Idea
of the *Fundamental*, to which the Ear feeks
the *harmonical* Relation of 3*d g.* where it refts
with Pleafure; and whenever a Reafon like this
occurs, the Voice will eafily take a *t l.* even
at the firft Step; for *Example*, Suppofe Two
Voices concording in a *6th g.* if one of them
keeps its *Tune*, and the other moves to meet
it in a 5*th*, then muft that Movement be a *t l.*
which is the Difference of *6th g.* and 5*th* : As
to the Parts of the 3*d l. obferve*, that the *t g.*
and *f.* being remarkably different, there would
be no Hazard of taking the one for the other;
therefore as to that, any of them might ftand
next the *Fundamental*, yet the *t g.* being a
more

more perfect Relation, it is easier taken, and makes a more agreeable Ascent, tho' I know that in some Circumstances the *f.* is placed next the *Fundamental* (as I shall mark in its proper Place.) *Now* for the *Degrees* of the upper Third, the *t g.* is set in the lowest Place in both the Series ; the Effect of which is, that the middle Term proceeding from that Order, is in an *harmonical* Relation to more, and the more principal of the other Terms in the Series. *Kepler* upon *harmonical Proportions* places the *t g.* next both the Extremes in the *Octave*, and gives this Reason for it, lest the second and seventh Term of the one Series differ from these in the other (for it seems he would have them differ as little as possible, *viz.* only in the *3ds* and *6ths*) and this he concludes with a Kind of Triumph against the Authorities of *Ptolomy*, *Galileus* and *Zarline*, whom he mentions as contrary to him in this Point. But indeed I cannot see the Sufficiency of this Reason, there is nothing in it drawn from the Nature of the Thing :   And as to *3d* in the upper Place, the Order in which I've placed its *Degrees*, is approven by Experience, and is I think the constant Practice.

Thus we have the *Octave* completely divided into all its *concinnous Degrees*, and in it the Division of all the lesser *Concords*, with the most natural and agreeable Order in which these *Degrees* can follow, in moving from any given Sound through any *harmonical Interval.* There are only these Three different

De-

Degrees, viz. *t g.* 8 . 9, *t l.* 5 : 6, and *f.*
15 : 16. And how many of each Kind every
harmonical Interval contains, is to be feen in the
preceeding Series, which eafily confirms and
proves the *Table* of *Degrees* given a little a-
bove, where you fee alfo the•natural Order,
viz. in afcending, it is *t g. t l. f. t g. t l. t g.
f.* —— Or this, *t g. f. t l. t g. f. t g. t l.* according as you chofe the 3*d l.* or 3*d g.* to afcend by; and in defcending we take that Order
juft reverfe, by taking the fame individual middle
Terms.

Now the Syftem of *Octave* containing all the
original Concords, and the *compound Concords*
being the Sum of *Octave* and fome leffer *Concord,* therefore 'tis plain, that if we would
have a Series of *Degrees* to reach beyond an
Octave, we ought to continue them in the fame
Order thro' a fecond *Octave* as in the firft, and
fo on thro a third and fourth *Octave,* &c. and
fuch a Series is called *The Scale of Mufick,*
which as I have already defin'd, expreffes a Series of Sounds, rifing or falling towards *Acutenefs* or *Gravity,* from any given Pitch of
Tune, to the greateft Diftance that is fit or
practicable, thro' fuch intermediate *Degrees* as
makes the Succeffion moft agreeable and perfect; and in which we have all the *harmonical
Intervals* moft *concinnoufly* divided. And of
this we have Two different Species according
as the 3*d l.* or 3*d g.* and 6*th l.* or 6*th g.* are taken in, which cannot both ftand together in
relation to one *Fundamental,* and make an *harmonical*

monical Scale. But if either of these Ways we ascend from a *Fundamental* or given Sound to an *Octave,* the Succession is very *melodious,* tho' they make different Species of *Melody.* It is true, that every Note to the next is *Discord,* but each of them is *Concord* with the *Fundamental,* except the 2*d* and 7*th,* and many of them among themselves, which is the Ground of that Agreeableness in the Succession ; for we must reflect upon what I have elsewhere observed, that the *graver* Sounds are the more powerful, and are capable of exciting Motion and Sound in Bodies whose *Tune* is *acuter* in a Relation of *Concord,* particularly 8*ve* and 5*th,* which an *acute* Sound will not effect with respect to a *grave.* And this accounts for that *Maxim* in Practice, That all *Musick* is counted *upwards* ; the Meaning is, that in the Conduct of a successive Series of Sounds, the lower or *graver* Notes influence and regulate the *acuter,* in such a Manner that all these are chosen with respect to some *fundamental* Note which is called the *Key* ; but of this only in general here, in another Place it shall be more particularly considered.

WE have exprest the several Terms of the *Scale* by the proportional *Sections* of a Line represented by 1, which is the *Fundamental* of the Series ; but if we would express it in whole Numbers, it is to be done by the Rules of *Ch.* 4. by which we have the Two following Series, in each of which the greatest Number
expresses

expresses the longest *Chord,* and the other Num=
bers the rest in Order.

540 : 480 : 432 : 405 : 360 : 324 : 288 : 270
   tg.   *tl.*   *f.*   *tg.*   *tl.*   *tg.*   *f.*

216 : 192 : 180 : 162 : 144 : 135 : 120 : 108
   tg.   *f.*   *tl.*   *tg.*   *f.*   *tg.*   *tl.*

THE first Series proceeds by a 3*d g.* and the
other by a 3*d l.* and if any Number of Chords
are in these Proportions of Length, *cæteris paribus,* they will express the true *Degrees* and *Intervals* of the *System* of *Musick,* as 'tis contain'd
in an 8*ve concinnously* divided in the Two dif=
ferent Species mentioned.

§ 3. *Containing further Reflections upon the
Constitution of the* Scale *of* Musick ; *and explaining the Names of* 8ve, 5th, &c. *which
have been hitherto used without knowing all
their Meaning ; shewing also the proper
Office of the* Scale.

WE considered in *Chapter* 5. the Division
of the *Concords,* in order only to find
what *Intervals* they were immmediately divisible into: We find that either an *harmonical* or
arithmetical Mean divides the 8*ve* into a ri

and 4*th*, with this Difference, that the *harmo-nical* puts the 5*th*, and the *arithmetical* the 4*th* next the *Fundamental* : And from this the Invention of the *t g* (which is the Difference of 4*th* and 5*th*) was very obvious. Thefe Divifions of the 8*ve* we fuppofe indeed made only for difcovering the immediate *harmonical* Parts of it; but taking in both thefe middle Terms, then we fee the 8*ve* refolved into thefe Three Parts, and in this Order, *viz.* a 4*th*, a *t g* and a 4*th*, as in thefe Numbers 6 : 8 : 9 : 12. where 6 and 12 are 8*ve* ; 8 is an *harmonical* Mean, and 9 an *arithmetical* Mean ; 6 : 8 is a 4*th* ; 8 : 9 a *t g.* and 9 : 12 a 4*th* ; that thefe Two middle Terms are at a Diftance proper for making *Melody*, and confequently that their Relation 8 : 9 is a *concinnous Interval*, we have infallible Affurance of from Experience.

B u t I propofed to make fome Obfervations on the Connection and Dependence of the feveral Parts of the *Syftem* of *Mufick*; and *Firft*, we are to remark, that this *Degree* 8 : 9 proceeds from the Two *Concords* that are of the next perfect Form to 8*ve*, *viz.* 4*th* and 5*th*, which are the *harmonical* Parts of it; and ftands fo in the middle betwixt the upper and lower 4*th*, that added to either of them it makes up the 5*th*, and fo joyns the *harmonical* and *arithmetical* Divifion of 8*ve* in one Series : and this *t g* being the Difference of Two *Concords* of which the Ear is perfectly Judge, we very eafily learn to raife it ; and in Fact we know it is the *Degree* which a natural Voice can with moft Eafe

and

and Certainty raife from a *Fundamental* or given Sound. *Again*, we found that the fame
Law of an *harmonical* and *arithmetical Mean*
refolved the 5th into 3d *l.* and 3d *g.* By the
harmonical the 3d *g.* being next the greater
Number, as here 10 : 12 : 15, and by the *arithmetical* the 3d *l.* loweft, as here 4 : 5 : 6; and
applying this to the upper and lower 5th proceeding from the immediate Divifion of the 8*ve*,
we have 4 more middle Terms within the 8*ve*,
whereof the lower Two are 3*ds* to the *Fundamental* and 6*ths* to the other Extreme, and the
upper Two are 6*ths* to the *Fundamental*, and
3*ds* to the other Extreme, as you fee in the
preceeding Series : And this produces Two new
Degrees, *viz.* 24 : 25. the Difference of 3d *l.* and
3d *g.* or of 6*th l.* and 6*th g.* and 15 : 16, the
Difference of 3d *g.* and 4*th*, or of 5*th* and 6*th l.*
but this *Degree* 24 : 25 is too fmall, and upon
that Account rejected, as I have already faid.
Now we are to find why this *Degree* 24 : 25 is
inconcinnous, and 15 : 16 *concinnous*, from fome
fettled Conftitution and Rule in Nature, which
we fhall have from this Obfervation, *viz.* That
if we apply the fame Law which refolved the
8*ve* and 5*th* into their *harmonical* Parts, to the
3d *g.* we have it divided into a *t g.* and a *t l.* as
in this *arithmetical* Series 8 : 9 : 10 ; or this
harmonical, 36 : 40 : 45 ; and if we confider this
Analogy, it feems to determine thefe Two Degrees of *t g.* 8 : 9 and *t l.* 9 : 10, to be the true
concinnous Parts of 3d *g.* and thereby excludes
24 : 25, and confequently the Two 3*ds* and
Two

two *6ths* from ftanding both together in one *Scale*. And *now*, fince the *5th* does not admit of both thefe middle Terms together which proceed from its *harmonical* and *arithmetical* Divifion, it feems to be but the following of Nature, if we apply the fame Kind of Divifion to the upper and lower *5th* of the *8ve*; the Effect of which is, that as by the *harmonical* Divifion of the lower *5th* we have a *3d g.* next the *Fundamental*; fo by the *harmonical* Divifion of the upper *5th* we have a *6th g.* to the *Fundamental*; and by the *arithmetical* Divifions we have contrarily the *3d l.* and *6th l.* next the *Fundamental*, as you fee in the preceeding Series : And this is a Kind of natural Proof that the *3d l.* and *6th l.* alfo the *3d g.* and *6th g.* belong to one Series ; and here we have the Difcovery of the *t l.* which lies narally betwixt the *3d l.* and *4th*, or betwixt the *5th* and *6th g.* But tho' the Two *3ds* and Two *6ths* cannot ftand together, yet there muft none of them be loft, and therefore they conftitute Two different *Scales*. But the Divifion of the *8ve* is not finifhed, for the *3ds* that ly next the Extremes are undivided; as to the *3d g.* we fee how naturally 'tis refolved into a *t g.* and *t l.* which is another Way of difcovering thefe *Degrees* ; and 'tis worth remarking, that the fame general *Rule* which by a gradual Application refolved the *8ve* immediately into a *5th* and *4th.* and then the *5th* immediately into *3d g.* and *3d l.* (by which Divifions the Two *6ths* were alfo found indirectly) being applied to the *3d g.* produces immediately the Two principal

cipal *concinnous Intervals* ; and for the Original
of the *f.* 15 : 16. we fee 'tis the Difference of 3*d g.*
and 4*th,* and rifes not from the immediate Divifion of any other *Interval,* but falls here by
Accident, upon the Application of the preceeding general *Rule* to the 8*ve* and 5*th.* But we
have yet the 3*d l.* which is next the Extremes
to confider ; of what *concinnous* Parts it confifts
was eafy to fee betwixt the 3*d g.* and 5*th. viz.*
a *f.* and *t g*; but next the Extremes of the 8*ve*
they muft be in this Order afcending, *viz. t g.*
and *f.* Of the Reafon of this I have faid e-
nough already: And now the Divifion of the
Octave being completed, we have the whole
original Concords concinnoufly divided, and
thefe *Intervals* added to the *Syftem, viz.* 8 : 9,
9 : 10, and 15 : 16. which have all this in common, that they are the Differences of the 5*th*
and fome other *Concords.*

Of the particular Names of Intervals, *as* 8ve,
5th, &c.

W E have confidered the *concinnous* Divifion
of every *harmonical Interval,* and we find the
8*ve* contains 7 *Degrees* ; the 6*th,* whether leffer or greater; has 5 ; the 5*th* has 4; the 4*th*
has 3 ; the 3*d,* leffer or greater, has 2 : And if
we number the Terms or Sounds contained within the Extremes (including both) of each *harmonical Interval,* there will be one more than
there are of *Degrees, viz.* in the 8*ve* there are
8. in

8. in the *6th* 6. in the *5th* 5. in the *4th* 4. and in the *3d* 3. And now at laſt we underſtand from whence the Names of *8ve, 6th, 5th,* &c. come; the Relations to which theſe Names are annexed are ſo called, becauſe in the *natural Scale* of *Muſick* the Terms that are in theſe Relations to the *Fundamental* are the *Third, Fourth, &c.* in order from that *Fundamental* incluſively. Or thus, becauſe theſe *harmonical Intervals* being *concinnouſly* divided, contain betwixt their Extremes (including both) ſo many Terms or Notes as the Names *8ve, 6th, &c.* bear. For the ſame Reaſon alſo, the *Tone* or *ſ.* (whichever of them ſtands next the *Fundamental*) is called a *2d,* particularly the *Tone* (whoſe Difference of greater and leſſer is not ſtrictly regarded in common Practice) is called the *2d g.* and *ſ.* the *2d l.* Alſo that Term which is betwixt the *6th* and *8ve,* is called the *7th,* which is alſo the greater 8 : 15, or the leſſer 5 : 9. Concerning this *Interval* we muſt here remark, that as it ſtands in *primary Relation* to the *Fundamental* in the Diviſion of the *8ve,* it does in this reſpect belong to the *Syſtem* of *Muſick:* But it is alſo uſed as a *Degree* without Diviſion, *that is,* in Practice we move ſometimes the Diſtance of a *7th* at once; but it is in ſuch Circumſtances as removes the Offence that ſo great a *Diſcord* would of it ſelf create; of which we ſhall hear more in the next *Chapter*; and here *obſerve,* that it is the Difference of *8ve* and the *Degrees* of *Tone* and *Semitone.*

As

As to the Order in which the *Degrees* of this
Scale follow, we have this to remark, that if either Series, (*viz.* that with the 3*d l.* or with
the 3*d g.*) be continued *in infinitum*, the Two
Semitones that fall naturally in the Divifion of
the 8*ve*, are always afunder 2 *Tones* and 3 *Tones*
alternately, *i. e.* after a *Semitone* come 2 *Tones*,
then a *Semitone*, and then 3 *Tones* ; and of the
Two *Tones* one is a greater and the other a
leffer ; of the Three, one is leffer in the
middle betwixt Two greater. If you continue
either Series to a double *Octave*, and mark the
Degrees, all this will be evident. *Obferve* alfo,
that this is the *Scale* which the *Ancients* called
the D I A T O N I C K *Scale*, becaufe it proceeds by
thefe *Degrees* called *Tones* (whereof there are
Five in an 8*ve*) and *Semitones* (whereof there
are Two in an *Octave*) But we call it alfo the
N A T U R A L *Scale*, becaufe its *Degrees* and their
Order are the moft agreeable and *concinnous*,
and preferable, by the Approbation both of Senfe
and Reafon, to all other Divifions that have e-
ver been inftituted. What thefe other are, you
fhall know when I explain the *ancient Theory*
of *Mufick*; but I fhall always call this, *The Scale
of Mufick*, without Diftinction, as 'tis the only
true *natural Syftem*.

W E have already obferved, that if the *Scale*
of *Mufick* is to be carried beyond an *Octave*, it
muft be by the fame *Degrees*, and in the fame
Order thro' every fucceffive *Octave* as thro' the
firft. How to continue the Series of Numbers
by a continual Addition, is fufficiently explain'd

al-

already; and for the Names there are Two
Ways, either to compound the Names of the
fimple Interval with the *Octave* thus, *viz. tg.*
or *f.* or 3*d*, &c. above an *Octave*, or above Two
Octaves, &c. or name them by the Number
of *Degrees* from the *Fundamental*, as 9*th*, 10*th*,
&c. but the firft Way is more intelligible, as
it gives a more diftinct and fimple Idea of the
Diftance, juft as we conceive a certain Quantity
of Time more eafily, by calling it, for *Example*, 9 Weeks, than 63 Days. But that you
may readily know how far any Note is removed from the *Fundamental*, if you know how
far it is above any Number of *Octaves.* See the
following *Table*, wherein the firft Line contains the Names of the Notes within one O-
ctave ; the fecond Line the Names (with refpect to the firft *Fundamental*) of thefe Terms
that are as far above one *Octave*, as thefe ftanding over them in the firft are above the *Fundamental* ; and the Third Line the Names of
thefe above Two *Octaves.*

Fund. 1	2d	3d	4th	5th	6th	7th	8th
	9th	10th	11th	12th	13th	14th	15th
	16th	17th	18th	19th	20th	21ft	22d

And this *Table* may be continued as far as you
pleafe ; or if you take the Columns of Figures
downward, then each Column gives the Names
of the Notes or Terms that are equally removed from the *Fundamental*, from the firft O-
ctave,

Octave, the second *Octave*, &c. Thus the first
Column on the left shews the Names of such
as are a 2*d* above the *Fundamental*, above the
first *Octave*, &c. if we consider what is practical then the *Scale* is limited to Three or
Four *Octaves*, otherwise 'tis infinite. Again
observe, that let the *Scale* be continued to any
Extent, every *Octave* is but a Repetition of the
first; and therefore an *Octave* is said to be a
perfect *Scale* or *System*, which comprehends
Eight Notes with the Extremes; but the Eighth
being so like the first, that in Practice it has
the same Name, and is the same Way *fundamental* to the *Degrees* of a second *Octave*, and
so on from one *Octave* to another, gave Occasion
to say there are but seven different Notes in the
Scale of *Musick*; or that all *Musick* is comprehended in seven Notes ; because if we take o-
ther seven Notes higher, they are but Repetitions
of the first seven in *Octave*, and have the same
Names.

Of the Office of the SCALE.

The *Constitution* of the *Scale* being already
explained, the Office and Use of it shall be next
treated of, which you have exprest in general
in the preceeding Definition of it ; but that you
may have a distinct and clear Notion, I shall
be a little more particular. The Design then
of the *Scale* of *Musick* is to show how a Voice
may rise or fall, less than any *harmonical Interval*, and thereby move from the one Extreme

treme of any of these to the other, in the most
agreeable Succession of Sounds : It is a *System*
which ought to exhibit tous the whole *Principles*
of *Musick*, which are either *Concords* or *concinnous Intervals :* The *Concords* or *harmonical Intervals* are the *essential Principles,* the other
are subservient to them, for making their Application more various.   Accordingly we have
in this *Scale* the whole *Concords,* with all their
concinnous Degrees, placed in such Order   as
makes the most perfect Succession of Sounds
from any given *Fundamental,* which I suppose
represented in the preceeding Series by 1 ; so
that the true Order of *Degrees* thro' any *harmonical Interval* is, that in which they ly from
1 upwards, to the *acute* Term of the given *Con-
cord,* as to $\frac{1}{2}$ for the *Octave,* $\frac{2}{3}$ for the *5th,* &c.
or downwards from these Terms to the *Fun-
damental* 1. The Divisions of the *Octave,* 5*th*
and 4*th* are different, according to the Difference
of the 3*ds,* and these *Intervals* are to be found
in *primary Relation* to the *Fundamental,* in
both the preceeding *Scales;* but the 3*dl.* and
6*th l.* belong to the one, and 3*dg.* and 9*th g.*
to the other *Scale.*

   THIS *Scale* not only shews us, by what *Degrees* a Voice can move agreeably, but gives us
also this *general Rule,* that Two *Degrees* of
one Kind ought never to follow other immediately in a progressive Motion upwards or downwards ; and that no more than Three *Tones*
(whereof the middle is a lesser *Tone,* and the
other Two greater *Tones*) can follow other,
                                        but

but a *ſ.* or ſome *harmonical Interval* muſt come next; and every *Song* or *Compoſition* within this *Rule* is particularly called *diatonick Muſick,* from the *Scale* whence this *Rule* ariſes; and from the Effect we may alſo call it the only *natural Muſick:* If in ſome Inſtances there are Exceptions from this *Rule,* as I ſhall hereafter have more particular Occaſion to obſerve, 'tis but for Variety, and very ſeldom practis'd: But this *general Rule* may be obſerved, and yet no good *Melody* follow; and therefore ſome more particular *Rules* muſt be ſought from the *Art of Compoſition.* While we are only upon the *Theory,* you can expect but *Theory* and *general Notions,* yet I ſhall have. Occaſion afterwards to be more particular on the Limitations, which are neceſſary for the Conduct of the true *muſical Intervals* in making good *Melody,* as theſe Limitations are contained in the Nature of the *Scale* of *Muſick.* But don't miſtake the Deſign of this *Scale* of *Degrees,* as if a Voice ought never to move up or down by any ·other immediate Diſtances, but by *Degrees;* for tho' that is the moſt frequent Movement, yet to move by *harmonical Diſtances* at once is not excluded, and 'tis abſolutely neceſſary: For the Agreeableneſs of it, you may conſider the *Degrees* were invented only for Variety, that we might not always move up and down by *harmonical Intervals,* which of themſelves are the moſt perfect, the others deriving their Agreeableneſs from their Subſerviency to them. *Obſerve,* theſe *Tones* and *Semitones* are the *Diaſtems*

or

or *simple Intervals* of the *natural* or *diatonick
Scale.* In *Ch.* 2. § 1. I have defined a *Dia-
stem,* such an Interval as in Practice is never divided, tho' there may be of these some greater
some lesser. To understand the Definition perfectly, take now an *Example* in the *diatonick
Scale:* A *Semitone* is less than a *Tone,* and both
are *Diastems;* we may raise a *Tone* by *Degrees,*
first raising a *Semitone,* and then such a Distance
as a *Tone* exceeds a *Semitone,* which we may
call another *Semitone, i. e.* from *a* to *b* a *Semitone,* and then from *b* to *c* the Remainder of a
Tone which is supposed betwixt *a c.* But this is
never done if we would preserve the Character
of *diatonick Musick,* because in that *Scale* Two
Semitones are not to be found together; and if
we rise to the Distance of a *Tone,* it must be
done at once; all greater *Intervals* are divisible
in Practice of this Kind of *Melody;* but in other
Kinds practis'd by the *Ancients,* we find that
the *Tone* was a *System,* and some greater *Intervals* were practis'd as *Diastems,* which shall
be explain'd in another Place.

W E shall still want something toward a complete and finished Notion of the Use and Office
of the *Scale* of *Musick,* till we understand distinctly what a *Song* truly and naturally *concinnous* is, and particularly what that is which we
call the *Key* of a *Song;* and the true Notion of
these we shall easily deduce from the Things already explain'd concerning the Principles of
Musick; but I find it convenient first to dispatch
some remaining Considerations of the *Intervals*
of

of *Mufick*, particularly as they regard the
Scale.

_____

§ 4. *Of the accidental* Difcords *in the* Syftem
of Mufick.

WE have confidered thefe *Intervals* and
Relations of *Tune* that are the imme-
diate Principles of *Mufick*, and which are directly applied in the Practice ; I mean thefe *Inter-*
vals or Relations of *Tune*, which, to make true
Melody, ought to be betwixt every Note or
Sound and the immediately next ; thefe we
have confidered under the Diftinction of *Con-*
cords and *concinnous Intervals.* But there are o-
ther *difcord* Relations that happen unavoidably
in *Mufick*, in a kind of accidental and indirect
Manner; thus, in the Succeffion of feveral *Notes*
there are to be confidered not only the Relations of thefe that fucceed other immediately, but alfo of thefe betwixt which other
Notes intervene. *Now* the immediate Succeffion may be conducted fo as to produce good
Melody, yet among the diftant Notes there may
be very grofs *Difcords*, that would not be tole-
rated in immediate *Succeffion*, and far lefs in
Confonance. But particularly let us confider
how fuch *Difcords* are actually contained in the
Scale of *Mufick:* Let us take any one Species,
fuppofe

suppose that with the 3*d g.* as here, in which I mark the Degrees betwixt each Term, and the next.

Names	Fund. 2dg. 3dg. 4th,5th,6th g. 7th g. 8ve
Ratios.	$I : \frac{8}{9} : \frac{4}{5} : \frac{3}{4} : \frac{2}{3} : \frac{3}{5} : \frac{8}{15} : \frac{1}{2}$
Degr.	*tg* : *tl* : *f* : *tg* : *tl* : *tg* : *f.*

N o w tho' the Progression is *melodious,* as the Terms refer to one common *Fundamental,* yet there are several *Discords* among the mutual *Relations* of the Terms, for *Example,* from 4*th* to 7*th g.* is 32 : 45, also from 2*d g.* to 6*th g.* is 27 : 40, and from 2*d g.* to 4*th* is 27 : 32, all *Discords.* And if we continue the Series to another *Octave,* then 'tis plain we shall find all the *Discords,* less than *Octave,* that can possibly be in such a *Scale,* by comparing every Term, from 1 in order upwards, to every other, that's distant from it within an *Octave* ; and tho' there be Difference of the Two *Scales* of Ascent, the one using the 3*d l.* and 6*th l.* and the other the 3*d g.* and 6*th g.* yet all the Relations that can possibly happen in the one, will also happen in the other, as I shall immediately show you.

L e t us therefore take any one of these Series, as that with the 3*d g.* and 6*th g.* and continue it to a double *Octave,* and then examine the Relations of each Term to each. In order to this, I shall anticipate a little upon that

Part where I am to explain the *Art of writing Musick*; and here suppose several Sounds in the Order of the preceeding *Scala* to be represented by so many Letters; and because every *Octave* is but the Repetition of the 1*st*, so that from every Term to the 8*th inclusive*, is always a just *Octave* in the Relation of 1 : 2; therefore to represent such a Scale by Letters, we need but 7 different ones, A, B, C, D, E, F, G, which will answer the first 7 Terms of the *Octave*, and the 8*th* will be represented by the first Letter; and so in order again to another *Octave*. And that all Things may be as distinct as possible, we shall make every 7 Letters in order from the Beginning of a different Character; but for a Reason that will appear afterwards, instead of beginning with *A*, I shall begin with *C*, and proceed in this Order,

C : D : E : F : G : A : B : *c : d : e : f : g : a : b* :: *cc*.

where C represents the *Fundamental* and lowest Note of the *Scale*; and the rest are in order *acuter*. And now when any *Interval* is expressed by Two Letters, it will be easy to know in which *Octave* (*i. e.* whether in the first or second in order from the *Fundamental*) each Extreme is; for if they be both one Kind of Character, then they are both in one *Octave*, as *C-F*; otherwise they are in different *Octaves*, as *A - f*. And it will be easily known whether the *Interval* be equal to, or greater or less than an *Octave*; for from any Letter to the like Letter

is

is an *Octave*, or Two *Octaves*, as *c-c* is an
Octave, or *C-cc* Two *Octaves*, consequently
A-b is known at Sight to be greater than an
Octave, even as far as *b* is above *a*; and *B-
D* to be less. *Again*, by this Means we easily
know whether the Example is taken ascending or descending, so 'tis plain, that from *D* to
a is ascending, or from *d* to *g*; but from *f* to
d is descending, or from *d* to *E*: The Order of
the several Letters, and their different Characters determine all these Things with great
Ease.

ACCORDING to this Supposition, then, I have
express'd the *Scale* by these Letters, in a
Table calculated for the Purpose of this *Section,*
(See *Plate* 1. *Fig.* 5.) In the first Column on
the left you have the Names of the *Intervals,*
as they proceed in Order from a common *Fundamental*; in the 2*d* you have the Progression
of *Degrees* from every Term to the next; in the
3*d* you have the several Terms expressed by
Letters; in the 4*th* Column you have the Numbers that express the Relations of every Term
to the *Fundamental C* (which is 1) as far as
Two *Octaves,* taken in the natural Order of
the *concinnous* Parts of the *Octave,* as above
divided and explained, these being supposed to
be fixed Relations; then in the other Columns
you have expressed the Relations of every Term,
in order upwards from *C,* to all these above
them, as far as an *Octave;* reduced to a common *Fundamental* 1, which is the first Number
in every Column, and signifies that the Letter

or Note againſt which it ſtands, is ſuppoſed to
be a common *Relative* to the 7 Terms that
ſtand next above it, *i. e.* That the other Numbers of that Column compared to 1, expreſs the
Relations which the Notes, or Letters againſt
which they ſtand, bear to that againſt which
the 1 of that Column ſtands, according to the
fixt Relations ſuppoſed in the Fourth Column
of Numbers. The 11th Column is the ſame
with the 1ſt; and if we would carry on that
Table *in infinitum*, it would be but a Repetition of the preceeding 7 Columns of Numbers;
which ſhews us that Two *Octaves* was ſufficient to diſcover all the ſimple *Diſcords* that
could poſſibly be in the *Scale.* I have carried
theſe Columns no further than one *Octave*, except the firſt, becauſe all above are but an 8*ve*, and
ſome leſſer compounded; and therefore we needed
only to find all the ſimple *Diſcords* leſs than an
8*ve*: But the 1ſt Column is carried to Two 8*ves*,
becauſe the reſt are made out of it; for theſe
other expreſs the mutual Relations of each
Term of the 1ſt Column to all above it within
an *Octave*, reduced to a common *Fundamental* 1.

I'll next ſhow you that there are no other
Relations in the other Series, which aſcends
by a 3*d l.* and 6*th l.* than what are here. The
two Species differ only in the 7*ths*, 6*ths* and 3*ds*,
and if you'll look but a little back, you'll ſee the
true Relation of the Terms of that other Series
to the *Fundamental*, which if you compare
with that Column in this Table, which begins
againſt *E*, you'll find them the ſame in every
Term

Term but one ; for here the 2*d* Term is 15 :
16 which there is 8 : 9 ; but if you compare
the Column which begins againſt *A*, you'll find
that agree with the *Scale* we are ſpeaking of in
every Term but the 4*th*, which is here 20 : 27,
and there 3 : 4, the one wants the true 2*d*, and
the other the true 4*th* ; but both theſe are in
the firſt Column which begins at *C* ; therefore
'tis plain that if theſe Columns are continued, we
muſt find in them all the Relations that can
poſſibly be in that Scale ; which a little Examination will ſoon diſcover.

Now beſides the *harmonical Intervals* and
Degrees already explained, we have in this Table the following *diſcord* Relations, which proceed from the Differences of the *Degrees*, and
the particular Order in which they follow other

Exa.		*Ratios*
D	*F* =	27 : 32
F	*B* =	32 : 45
A	*D* =	20 : 27
D	*A* =	27 : 40
B	*F* =	45 : 64
F	*D* =	16 : 27
D	*C* =	9 : 16

in the Scale ; for we
may conceive a great
Variety of other *Diſ-*
cords from different
Combinations of theſe
Degrees, but the Spe-
culation would be of
no Uſe ; 'tis enough
to conſider what are
inavoidable in the Or-
der of the *Scale* of
Muſick, which are theſe mentioned. *Again*,
from the Table we find plainly that from any
Note or Letter of the *Scale*, to the 2*d*, 3*d*, 4*th*,
5*th*, &c. *incluſive*, either above or below, is not
always the ſame *Interval* ; becauſe tho' there is
an

an equal Number of *Degrees* in every such Case,
yet there is not always an equal Number of the
same *Degrees* ; so, from *C* to *F*, there are three
Degrees, whereof 1 is a *t g*. 1 is *t l*. and 1 a *s*.
but from *F* to *B* there are Three *Degrees*,
whereof 2 are *t g*. and 1 is a *t l*.

We have already settled the Definitions of
a 3*d*, 4*th*, &c. as they are *harmonical Intervals*,
they are either to be taken from the true *Ratios* of their Extremes ; or, respecting the *Scale*
of *Musick*, from the Number and particular
Kinds of *Degrees* ; yet we may make a general
Definition that will serve any Part of the *Scale*,
and call that *Interval*, which is from any Letter of the *Scale* to the 2*d*, 3*d*, 4*th*, &c. *inclusive*,
a 2*d*, a 3*d*, a 4*th*, &c. But then we must make
a Distinction, according as they are *harmonical* or not ; under which Distinction the *Octaves*
will not come, because every Eight Letter
inclusive is not only the same, but is a true
Octave in the *Ratio* of 1 : 2 ; which is plain
from this, That every *Octave* in order from the
Fundamental or lowest Note of the *Scale*,
is divided the same Way, into the same
Number of the same Kind of *Degrees*, and
in the same Order : And for other *Intervals*
less than an *Octave*, we have Three of each
Kind, differing in Quantity ; which Differences
arise from the Three different *Degrees*, as I
have expressed them in the following *Table*,
wherein the greatest stands uppermost, and so in
Order.

2*ds*:

2ds.	3ds.	4ths.	5ths.	6ths.	7ths.
8 : 9	4 : 5	32 : 45	2 : 3	16 : 27	8 : 15
9 : 10	5 : 6	20 : 27	27 : 40	3 : 5	5 : 9
15 : 16	27 : 32	3 : 4	45 : 64	5 : 8	9 : 16

T H E Three *2ds* or *Degrees* are all *concinnous* *Intervals*; of the *3ds* one is *Discord*, viz. 27 : 32, and therefore called a *false* *3d*; the other Two are particularly known by the Names of *3dg.* and *3dl.* of the *4ths* and *5ths* Two are *Discords*, and called *false* *4ths* and *5ths*; and therefore when we speak of a *4th* or *5th*, without calling it *false*, 'tis understood to be of the true *harmonical* Kind ; of the *6ths* one is *false*, and the other Two which are *harmonical*, are called *6thg.* and *6thl.* the *7ths* are neither *harmonical* nor *concinnous* *Intervals*, yet of Use in *Musick*, as I have already mentioned ; the Two greater are particularly known by the Name of greater or lesser *7th*, tho' some I know make the least 9 : 16 the *7th* lesser; I mean they make that *Ratio* a Term in the Division of the *Octave* by *3d l.* and *6th l.* but I shall have Occasion to consider this more particularly in another Place. *Now*, as to the Composition of the *Octave* out of the *Intervals* of this last *Table*, we have this to remark, that if we compare the *2ds* with the *7ths*, or the *3ds* with the *6ths*, or *4ths* with *5ths*, the greater of the one added to the lesser of the other, or the Middle of the one added to the Middle of
the

the other, is exactly equal to *Octave* ; and generally add the greatest of any Species of *Intervals* (for *Example* 5*ths*) to the lesser of any other (as 3*ds*) and the least of that to the greater of this; also the Middle of the one to the Middle of the other, the Three *Sums* or *Intervals* proceeding from that Addition are equal.

We shall next consider what the Errors of these *false Intervals* are. The Variety, as to the Quantity, of *Intervals* that have the same Number of *Degrees* in the *Scale*, arises, as I have already said, from the Differences of the Three *Degrees* ; and therefore the Differences among *Intervals* of the same Species and Denomination, *i. e.* the Excesses or Defects of the *false* from the *true*, are no other than the Differences of these *Degrees*, viz. 80 : 81, the Difference of a *tg.* and *tl.* which is particularly called a *Comma* among *Musicians* ; 24 : 25, the Difference of a *tl.* and *s.* which is sometimes called a lesser *Semitone*, because it is less than 15 : 16 ; then 128 : 135, the Difference of a *tg.* and *s.* which is a greater Difference than the last, and is also called a lesser *Semitone*, and is a Middle betwixt 15 : 16, and 24 : 25. Betwixt which of the greater *Intervals* these Differences do particularly exist, will be easily found, by looking into the former *Table*, and applying *Problem* 10. of *Chap.* 4. that is, multiplying the Two *Ratios* compared cross-ways, the greater Number of the one by the lesser of the other, the Products contain the *Ratio* or Dif-

Difference fought. *Observe* also, that the greateft of the 4*ths,* viz. 32 : 45 is particularly called a *Tritone,* for 'tis equal to 2 *t g.* and 1 *t l.*
and its Complement to an *Octave,* viz. 45 : 64,
which is the leaft of the 5*ths,* is particularly
called a leffer 5*th* or *Semidiapente* (the Original of the laft Name you'll hear afterwards.)
Thefe Two are the *falfe* 4*th* and 5*th,* which
are ufed as *Difcords* in the Bufinefs of *Harmony,* and they are the Two *Intervals* which divide the *Octave* into Two Parts neareft to E-
quality, for their Difference is only this very
fmall *Interval* 2025 : 2048. And becaufe in
common Practice the Difference of *t g.* and *t l.*
is neglected, tho' it has its Influence, as we
fhall hear of, therefore thefe *Intervals* are only
called *falfe,* which exceed or come fhort by a
Semitone ; and upon this Suppofition therefore
there is no *falfe* 3*d* or 6*th,* nor any *falfe* 4*th*
or 5*th,* except the *Tritone* and *Semidiapente*
mentioned, which with the 7*ths* and 2*ds* are
all the *Difcords* reckoned in the *Syftem ;* however when we would know the Nature of Things
accurately, we muft neglect no Differences.

T H E Diftinctions already made of the *Intervals* of the *Scale* of *Mufick,* regard their Contents as to the Number and Kind of *Degrees ;*
but in the *Scale* we find *Intervals* of the fame
Extent, differing in the Order of their *Degrees.*
We fhall eafily find the whole Variety, by examining the *Scales* of *Mufick ;* for the Variety is
increafed by the Two different *Series* or *Scales*
above explained, there being fome in the one
that

that are not to be found in the other. I shall
leave it to your selves to examine and find out
the Examples, and only mention here the *O-*
Etaves, whereof there are in this respect seven
different Species in each *Scale*, proceeding from
the seven different Letters; for it is plain at
sight, that the Order of *Degrees* from each of
these Letters upward to an *Octave* is different;
and that there can be no more Variety if the
Scale were continued *in infinitum*, because from
the same Letter taken in any Part of the *Scale*,
there is always the same Order. What Use
has been made of this Distinction of *Intervals*,
and particularly *Octaves*, falls to be considered
in another Place; I shall only observe here,
that tho' all this Variety happens actually within the Compass of Two *Octaves*, yet if you
ask, what is the most natural and agreeable Order. in the Division of the *Octave*, it is that
which belongs to the *Octave* from *C* in the preceeding *Scale*; or change the 3*d*, 6*th* and 7*th*
from greater to lesser, and that makes another
concinnous Order; the *Degrees* of each as they
follow other, you have already set down. Now
if you begin and carry on the *Series* in any of
these Two Orders to a double *Octave*, none of
the accidental *Discords* will give any Offence
to the Ear, because their Extremes are not
heard in immediate Succession; and the *Discord*
is rendred altogether insensible by the immediate
Notes; especially by the *harmonious* Relation
of each Term to the common *Fundamental*,
and the manifold *Concords* that are to be found
among

among the feveral middle 'Terms. For the Pofitions of the *Degrees*, which occafion thefe
Difcords, if we confider them with refpect .to
the *Fundamental C*, they are truly *concinnous*,
but with refpect to the loweft of Two Notes,
betwixt which they make the *Difcord*, they
follow   *inconcinnoufly* from it, becaufe they
were not defigned to follow it as a *Fundamen-*
tal, and fo are not to be referred to it : Therefore in all the *Scale*, only *C* can be made *funda-*
mental, becaufe from none of the other Six Letters do the *Degrees* follow in a right *concinnous*
Order, unlefs, as I faid before, we neglect the Difference of *t g.* and *t l.* and then the *Octave* from
A will be a right *concinnous* Series, proceeding by
a 3*d l.* when it proceeds by a 3*dg.* from *C*, and
contrarily ; and hereby we fhall have both the
Species in one Series ; otherwife there are Three
Terms that are variable, which are the 3*d*, 6*th*
and 7*th* from the *Fundamental*, i. e. *E, A, B*,
when the *Fundamental* is called *C* ; and this
muft be carefully minded when we fpeak of the
Scale of *Mufick*.   How unavoidable thefe Kinds
of *Difcords* are among the Notes of the *Scale*,
we have feen ; but, as I have already obferved,
there are other Succeffions that are *melodious*,
befides a conftant Succeffion of *Degrees* ;   for
thefe are mixt in Practice with *harmonical In-*
tervals :   And here alfo the immediate Succeffion many be *melodious*, tho' there be many *Dif-*
cords among the diftant Notes, whofe Harfhnefs is rendred altogether infenfible from their
Situation, efpecially becaufe of the *harmonical*
Relation

Relation of the feveral Notes to fome *funda-mental* or principal Note, which is called the *Key*, w th a particular Refpect to which the reft of t..e Notes are chofen.

⚜ ✿ ⚜ ✿ ⚜ ✿ ⚜ ✿ ⚜ ✿ ⚜ ✿ ⚜ ✿ ⚜ ✿ ⚜ ✿ ⚜ ✿

C H A P.   IX.

Of the Mode *or* Key *in* Mufick *; and a further Account of the true End and Office of the* Scale *of* Mufick.

---

§ 1. *Of the* Mode *cr* Key.

WE have already divided the Application of the *Tune* of *Sounds* into thefe Two, *Melody* and *Harmony*. When feveral fimple Sounds fucceed other agreeably in the Ear, that Effect is called *Melody*; the proper Materials of which are the *Degrees* and *harmonious Intervals* above explained. But 'tis not every Succeffion of thefe that can produce this Pleafure; Nature has marked out certain Limits for a general Rule, and left the Application to the Fancy and Imagination; but always under the Direction of the Ear. The other chief Ingredient in *Mufick* is the *Duration*, or Difference of Notes with refpect to their nnin-

terrup-

terrupted Continuance in one *Tune*, and the Quickness or Slowness of their Succession ; taking in both these, a *melodious Song* may be brought under this general Definition, *viz. A Collection of Sounds or Notes (however produced) differing in* Tune *by the* Degrees *or* harmonious Intervals *of the* Scale *of* Musick, *which succeeding other in the Ear, after equal or unequal* Duration *in their respective* Tunes, *affect the Mind with Pleasure.* But the Design of this *Chapter* is only to consider the Nature and general Limits of a Song, with respect to *Tune*, which is properly the *Melody* of it; and observe, That by a Song I mean every single Piece of *Musick*, whether contrived for a Voice or Instrument.

A *Song* may be compared not absurdly to an Oration; for as in this there is a *Subject, viz.* some *Person* or *Thing* the Discourse is referred to, that ought always to be kept in View, thro' the Whole, so that nothing unnatural or foreign to the *Subject* may be brought in ; in like Manner, in every regular and truly *melodious Song*, there is one Note which regulates all the rest ; the Song begins, and at least ends in this, which is as it were the principal Matter, or *musical Subject* that demands a special Regard to it in all the other Notes of the Song. And as in an Oration, there may be several distinct Parts, which refer to different Subjects, yet so as they must all have an evident Connection with the principal Subject which regulates and influences the Whole; so in *Melody*, there may

be

be feveral fubprincipal Subjects, to which the different Parts of that Song may belong, but thefe are themfelves under the Influence of the principal Subject, and muft have a fenfible Connection with it. This principal Note is called the *Key* of the Song, or the *principal Key* with refpect to thefe others which are the *fubprincipal Keys.* But a Song may be fo fhort, and fimply contrived, that all its Notes refer only to one *Key.*

THAT we may underftand this Matter diftinctly, let us reflect on fome Things already explained: We have feen how the *Octave* contains in it the whole Principles of *Mufick,* both with refpect to *Confonance* (or *Harmony*) as it contains all the original *Concords,* and the *harmonical* Divifion of fuch greater, as are equal to the Sum of leffer *Concords* ; and with refpect to *Succeffion* (or *Melody*) as in the *concinnous* Divifion of the *Octave,* we have all the *Degrees* fubfervient to the *harmonical Intervals,* and the Order in which they ought to be taken to make the moft agreeable Succeffion of Sounds, rifing or falling gradually from any given Sound, *i. e.* any Note of a given and determined Pitch of *Tune;* for the *Scale* fuppofes no Pitch, and only affigns the juft Relations of Sound which make true *mufical Intervals :* But as the 3*ds* and 6*ths* are each diftinguifhed into greater and leffer, from this arife Two different Species in the Divifion of the *Octave.* We have alfo obferved, That if either *Scale* (*viz.* That which proceeds by the 3*d l.* or by the 3*d g.*)

is

is continued to a double *Octave*, there fhall be
in that Cafe 7 different Orders of the *Degrees*
of an 8*ve*, proceeding from the 7 different Letters
with which the Terms of the *Scale* are marked;
none of which Orders but the firft, *viz.* from
C is the natural Order ; and tho' in raifing the
Series from *C* to the double *Octave*, we actually
go through the Degrees in each of thefe Orders,
yet *C* only being the *Fundamental*, to which all
the Notes of the Series are referred, there is nothing offenfive in thefe different Orders, which
are but accidental ; fo that in every *Octave* concinnoufly divided, there are 7 different *Intervals*
relative to the *Fundamental*, whofe acute
Terms are the effential Notes of the *Octave*, and
they are thefe, *viz.* the 2*d g.* 3*d g.* 4*th*, 5*th*, 6*th g.*
7*th g.* 8*ve*, or 2*d g.* 3*d l.* 4*th*, 5*th*, 6*th l.* 7*th*
l. 8*ve.*

Now, let us fuppofe any given Sound, *i. e.*
a Sound of any determinate Pitch of *Tune*, it
may be made the *Key* of a *Song*, by applying
to it the Seven effential or natural Notes that a-
rife from the *concinnous* Divifion of the 8*ve*, as
I have juft now fet them down, and repeating
the 8*ve* above or below as oft as you pleafe.
The given Sound is applied as the principal Note
or *Key* of the *Song*, by making frequent *Clofes*
or *Cadences* upon it ; and in the Courfe or
Progrefs of the *Melody*, none other than thefe
Seven natural Notes can be brought in, while
the *Song* continues in that *Key*, becaufe every
other Note is foreign to that *Fundamental* or
Key.

To

To underſtand all this more diſtinctly, let us
conſider, That by a *Cloſe* or *Cadence* is meant a
terminating or bringing the *Melody* to a Period
or Reſt, after which it begins and ſets out a-
new, which is like the finiſhing of ſome diſtinct
Purpoſe in an Oration ; but you muſt get a perfect Notion of this from Experience. Let us ſuppoſe a Song begun in any Note, and carried on
upwards or downwards by *Degrees* and *harmonical Diſtances,* ſo as never to touch any
Notes but what are referable to that firſt Note
as a *Fundamental, i. e.* are the true Notes of
the *natural Scale* proceeding from that *Fundamental* ; and let the *Melody* be conducted ſo
through theſe natural Notes, as to cloſe and
terminate in that *Fundamental,* or any of its
8ves above or below ; that Note is called the
Key of the *Melody,* becauſe it governs and regulates all the reſt, putting this general Limitation upon them, that they muſt be to it in the
Relation of the Seven eſſential and natural Notes
of an *8ve,* as abovementioned ; and when any
other Note is brought in, then 'tis ſaid to go out
of that *Key :* And by this Way of ſpeaking of
a Song's continuing in or going out of a *Key,*
we may obſerve, that the whole *8ve,* with all
its natural and *concinnous* Notes, belong to the
Idea of a *Key,* tho' the *Fundamental,* being
the principal Note which regulates the reſt, is in
a peculiar Senſe called the *Key,* and gives Denomination to it in a Syſtem of fixt Sounds, and
in the Method of marking Sounds by Letters,
as we ſhall hear of more particularly afterwards.
And

And in this Application of the Word *Key* to one *fundamental* Note, another Note is said to be out of the *Key*, when it has not the Relation to that Fundamental of any of the natural Notes that belong to the *concinnous* Division of the 8*ve*. And here too we must add a necessary Caution with respect to the Two different Divisions of the 8*ve*, *viz.* That a Note may belong to the same *Key*, *i. e.* have a just musical Relation to the same *Fundamental* in one Kind of Division, and be out of the *Key* with respect to the other : For *Example*, If the Melody has used the 3*d g.* to any *Fundamental*, it requires also the 6*th g.* and therefore if the 6*th l.* is brought in, the *Melody* is out of the first *Key*.

Now a Song may be carried thro' several *Keys*, *i e.* it may begin in one *Key*, and be led out of that to another, by introducing some Note that is foreign to the first, and so on to another : But a regular Piece must not only return to the first *Key*, these other Keys must also have a particular Connection and Relation with the first, which is the principal Key. The Rule which determines the Connection of *Keys*, you'll find distinctly explained in *Chap.* 13. for we may not change at random from one *Key* to another ; I shall only observe here, that these other *Keys* must be some of the Seven natural Notes of the *principal Key*, yet not any of them ; for which see the *Chapter* referred to.

But that you may conceive all this yet more clearly, we shall make *Examples*. Suppose the following *Scale* of Notes exprest by Letters, where-

wherein I mark the Degrees thus, *viz.* a *t g.* with a *Colon* (:) a *t l.* with a *Semicolon* (;) *Semitone* with a Point (.) And here I mark the Series that proceeds with the 3*d g*, &c.

$$C:D;E.F:G;A:B.c:d;e.f:g;a:b.c$$

The first Note represents any given Sound, and the rest are fixt according to their Relations to it, exprest by the Degrees: Let the first Note of the Song, which is also the designed *Key*, be taken *Unison* to *C.* (which represents any given Sound) all the rest of the Notes, while it keeps within one *Key*, must be in such Relation to the first, as if placed according to their Distances from it in a direct Series, they shall be *unison* each with some Note of the preceeding *Scale*: The *Example* is of a *Key* with the 3*d g*, &c. which is easily applied to the other Species. Let us now suppose the Conduct of the *Melody* such, that after a Cadence in *C* the Song shall make the next Cadence in a 3*d g*. above, *viz.* in *E*, and this is a new *Key* into which the *Melody* goes.

We have observed in the preceeding *Chap.* that the Order of Degrees from each of the Letters of the *diatonick Scale*, is different; and therefore while the Relation of these Notes are supposed fixt, 'tis plain none of the Notes of that *Scale* except *C* can be made a *Key*, because the Seven Notes within the 8*ve* are not in the true Relation of the essential and natural Notes of an 8*ve* concinnously divided;

and

and therefore the *natural Scale* (*i.e.* the Order from *C*) muſt be applied anew from every new *Key*; as in the preceeding *Example*, the 2d *Key* is *E*, which in that *Scale* has a 3d *l*. at *G*, but it has not all its Seven Notes in juſt Relation to the *Fundamental*, the firſt Degree being a *f*. which ought to be *t g*; and therefore if the *Melody* in that *Key* be ſo managed as to have Uſe for all the Seven natural Notes, they cannot be all found in the Series that proceeds *concinnouſly* from *C*, but requires the Application of the *natural Scale* to that new Pitch, *i. e.* requires that we make a Series of *concinnous* Degrees from that new *Fundamental*; which we may expreſs either by calling it *C*, and applying the ſame Names to the whole 8*ve*, above or below it, as to the former *Key*, or retaining ſtill the Names *E F*, &c. to an 8*ve*, but ſuppoſing their Relations changed.

  A Song may be ſo ordered, that it ſhall not require all the Seven natural Notes of the *Key*; and if the *Melody* be ſo contrived in the *ſub-principal Keys* of the *Song*, that it ſhall uſe none of the eſſential Notes of theſe *Keys*, but ſuch as coincide with theſe of the *principal Key*, then is the whole of that *Song* more ſtrictly limited to the *principal Key:* So that in a good Senſe it may be ſaid never to go out of it ; but then there will be leſs Variety under ſuch Limitations: And if a Song may be ſuppoſed to go through ſeveral *Keys*, the principal being always perfect as from *C*, and the Subprincipals taken with ſuch Imperfections as they unavoidably have, when

we

we are confined to one individual Series of determinate Sounds, the *Musick* may be said also in this Case never to depart from the *principal Key*; but 'tis plain, that the using such *Intervals* with respect to the *subprincipal Keys*, will make the *Melody* imperfect, and also occasion Errors of worse Consequence in the *Harmony* of Parts so conducted.

'T I S Time now to consider the *Distinctions* of *Keys*. We have seen that to constitute any Note or given Sound a *Key* or *fundamental* Note, it must have these Seven essential or natural Notes added to it, *viz.* 2d g. 3d g. or 3d l. 4th, 5th, 6th g. or 6th l. 7th g. or 7th l. 8ve out of which, or their 8ves, all the Notes of the *Song* must be taken while it keeps within that *Key, i. e.* within the Property of that *Fundamental*; 'tis plain therefore, that there are but Two different Species of *Keys*, according as we joyn the greater or lesser 3d, which are always accompanied with the 6th and 7th of the same Species, *viz.* the 3d g. with the 6th g. and 7th g; and the 3d l. with the 6th l. and 7th l; and this Distinction is marked with the Names of A SHARP KEY, which is that with the 3d g, &c. and A FLAT KEY with the 3d l, &c. Now from this it is plain, that however many different Closes may be in any Song, there can be but Two *Keys*, if we consider the essential Difference of *Keys*; for every *Key* is either *sharp* or *flat*, and all *sharp Keys* are of the same Nature, as to the *Melody*, and so are all *fla Keys* for *Example*, Let the *principal Key* o

a

a Song be *C* (with a 3*d g.*) in which the final
C ofe is made,   let   other Clofes be made   in
E (the 3*d* of the *principal Key*) with a 3*d g.*
and in *A* (the 6*th* of the *principal Key*) with
a 3*d l.* yet in all this there are but Two different *Keys, fharp* and *flat* : But *obferve*, in om-
mon Practice the *Keys* are faid to be different
when nothing is confidered, but the different
Tune or Pitch of the Note in which the different Clofes are made; and in this Senfe the
fame Song is faid to be in different Keys, according as it is begun in different Notes or Degrees of *Tune*.   But that we may fpeak accurately, and have Names anfwering to the real
Differences of Things, which I think neceffary
to prevent Confufion, I would propofe the
Word *Mode*, to exprefs the *melodious Conftitution* of the *Octave*, as it confifts of Seven effential or natural Notes, befides the *Fundamental*;
and becaufe there are Two Species, let us call
that with a 3*dg.* the *greater Mode*, and that
with a 3*d l.* the *leffer Mode* :   And the Word
Key may be applied to every Note of a Song,
in which a *Cadence* is made; fo that all thefe
(comprehending the whole *Octave* from each)
may be called different *Keys*, in refpect of their
different *Degrees* of *Tunes*, but with refpect
to the effential Difference in the Conftitution
of the *Octaves*,   on   which the   *Melody*
depends, there are only Two different *Modes*,
the greater and the leffer. Thus the Latin Writers ufe the Word *Modus*, to fignify the particular *Mode* or Way of conftituting the *Octave*;
and

and hence they alſo called it *Conſtitutio*; but of this in its own Place.

'Tis plain then, that a *Mode* (or *Key* in this Senſe) is not any ſingle Note or Sound, and cannot be denominated by it, for it ſignifies the particular Order or Manner of the *concinnous Degrees* of an 8*ve*, the *fundamental* Note of which may in another Senſe be called the *Key*, as it ſignifies that principal Note which regulates the reſt, and to which they refer : And even when the Word *Key*, applied to different Notes, ſignifies no more than their different Degrees of *Tune*, theſe Notes are always conſidered as *Fundamentals* of an 8*ve concinnouſly* divided, tho' the Mode of the Diviſion is not conſidered when we call them different *Keys* ; ſo that the whole 8*ve* comes within the *Idea* of a Key in this Senſe alſo : Therefore to diſtinguiſh properly betwixt *Mode* and *Key*, and to know the real Difference, take this Definition, *viz.* an 8*ve* with all its natural and *concinnous* Degrees is called a *Mode*, with reſpect to the Conſtitution or the Manner and Way of dividing it; and with reſpect to the Place of it in the *Scale* of *Muſick*, *i. e.* the *Degree* or Pitch of *Tune*, it is called a *Key*, tho' this Name is peculiarly applied to the *Fundamental*. Hence it is plain, that the ſame *Mode* may be with different *Keys*, that's to ſay, an *Octave* of Sounds may be raiſed in the ſame Order and Kind of *Degrees*, which makes the ſame *Mode*, and yet be begun higher or lower, *i. e.* taken at different *Degrees* of *Tune*, with reſpect to the Whole, which makes different

Keys.

Keys. It follows alſo from theſe Definitions, that the ſame *Key* may be with different *Modes,* that is, the Extremes of Two *Octaves* may be in the ſame *Degree* of *Tune,* and the Diviſion of them different. The Manner of dividing the *Octave,* and the *Degree* of *Tune* at which it is begun, are ſo diſtinct, that I think there is Reaſon to give them different Names; yet I know, that common Practice applies the Word *Key* to both ; ſo the ſame *Fundamental* conſtitutes Two different *Keys,* according to the Diviſion of the *Octave;* and therefore a Note is ſaid to be out of the *Key,* with reſpect to the ſame *Fundamental* in one Diviſion, which is not ſo in a-nother, as I have explained more particularly a little above ; and the ſame Song is ſaid to be in different *Keys,* when there is no other Diffe-rence, but that of being begun at different Notes. Now, if the Word *Key* muſt be uſed both Ways, to keep up a common Practice, we ought at leaſt to prevent the Ambiguity, which may be done by applying the Words *ſharp* and *flat.* For *Example.* Let the ſame *Song* be taken up at different Notes, which we call *C* and *A,* it may in that reſpect be ſaid to be in different *Keys,* but the Denomination of the *Key* is from the Cloſe; and Two Songs clo-ſing in the ſame Note, as *C,* may be ſaid to be in different *Keys,* according as they have a grea-ter or leſſer 3*d* ; and to diſtinguiſh them, we ſay the one is in the *ſharp Key C,* and the other in the *flat Key C;* and therefore, when *ſharp* or *flat* is added to the Letter or Name by which any

funda-

fundamental Note is marked, it expresses both the *Mode* and *Key*, as I have distinguished them above; but without these Words it expresses nothing but what I have called the *Key* in Distinction from *Mode*. But of the Denominations of *Keys* in the *Scale* of *Musick*, we shall hear particularly in *Chap.* 11.

Observe next, that of the natural Notes of every *Mode* or *Octave*, Three go under the Name of the *essential Notes*, in a peculiar Manner, *viz.* the *Fundamental*, the 3*d*, and 5*th*, their *Octaves* being reckoned the same, and marked with the same Letters in the *Scale*; the rest are particularly called *Dependents*. But again, the *Fundamental* is also called the *final*, because the Song commonly begins and always ends there: The 5*th* is called the *Dominante*, because it is the next principal Note to the *final*, and most frequently repeted in the Song; and if 'tis brought in as a new *Key*, it has the most perfect Connection with the *principal Key*: The 3*d* is called the *Mediante*, because it stands betwixt the *Final* and *Dominante* as to its Use. But the 3*d* and 5*th* of any *Mode* or *Key* deserve the Name of *essential Notes*, more peculiarly with respect to their Use in *Harmony*, because the *Harmony* of a 3*d*, 5*th* and 8*ve*, is the most perfect of all others; so that a 3*d* and a 5*th*, applied in *Consonance* to any *Fundamental*, gives it the Denomination of the *Key*; for chiefly by Means of these the Cadence in the *Key* is performed. The *Bass* being the governing Part with respect to the *Harmony*, ought finally to

clofe

clofe in the *Key*; and the Relation or *Harmony* of the Parts at the final Clofe, ought to be fo perfect, that the Mind may find entire Satisfaction in it, and have nothing farther to expect. Let us fuppofe Four Voices, making together the *Harmony* of thefe Four Notes *G* -- *c* -- *e* -- *g*, where *G* is the *Fundamental*, *c* a *4th*, *e* a *6th g*. and *g* an *8ve*; fo that *c* - *e* is a *3dg*. and *e* − *g* a *3d l*. and *c* − *g* a *5th*. The Ear would not reft in this Clofe, becaufe there is a Tendency in it to fomething more perfect; for the true *Key* in thefe Four is *c*, to which the *3d* and *5th* is applied; the *Bafs* clofing in *G* puts the *5th* out of its proper Place, for it ought to ftand next the *Fundamental*; nor can the *3d* be feparate from the *5th*, which can ftand with no other. Now the Thing required is, to reftore the *5th* to its due Place, and this is done, by removing the *4th* to the upper Place of the *Harmony*; fo in the preceeding *Example*, fuppofe the *Bafs* moves from *G* to *c*, and the reft move accordingly till the Four make thefe *c* -- *e* -- *g* -- *cc*, in which *c* -- *e* is *3dg*. *c* − *g* a *5th*; then we have a perfect Clofe, and the *Mufick* is got into the true and principal *Key*, which is *c*.

WE have one Thing more to obferve as to the *7th*, which is natural to every *Mode*; in the *greater Modes* or *fharp Keys* 'tis always the *7th g*. but *flat Keys* ufe both the *7th g*. and *7th l*. in different Circumftances: The *7th l*. moft naturally accompanies the *3d l*. and *6th l*. which conftitute a *flat Key*, and belongs to it

necef-

neceffarily, when we confider the *concinnous* Divifion of the *Octave*, and the moft agreeable Succeffion of *Degrees*; and it is ufed in every Place, except it is fometimes toward a Clofe, efpecially when we afcend to the *Key*, for then the 7*th g.* being within a *f.* of the *Key*, makes a fmooth and eafy Paffage into it, and will fome-times alfo occafion the 6*th g.* to be brought in. Again, 'tis by Means of this 7*th g.* that the Tranfition from one *Key* to another is chiefly performed; for when the *Melody* is to be tranf-ferred to a new *Key*, the 7*th g.* of it (whether 'tis a *fharp* or *flat Key*) is commonly introdu-ced: But you fhall have more of this in *Chap.* 13.

I have faid, that the 7*th* is ufed in *Melody* as a fingle *Degree*, but in fuch Circumftances as removes the Harfhnefs of fo great a *Difcord*, as particularly in quick Movements; and we may here confider, that a 7*th* being the Comple-ment of a true *Degree* to *Octave*, partakes of the Nature of a *Degree* fo far, that to move up-ward by a *Degree*, or downwards by its Cor-refpondent 7*th*, and contrarily downwards by a *Degree*, or upwards by a 7*th*, brings us into the fame Note; and from this Connection of it with the true *Degrees*, 'tis frequently ufeful.

§ 2. *Of the Office of the* Scale *of* Mufick.

NOw from what has been explained, we ve-ry eafily fee the true and proper *Office* of the *Scale of Mufick*, which, ftrictly fpeaking, is all comprehended in an *Octave*, what is above or

below

below being but a Repetition. The *Scale* supposes no determinate Pitch of *Tune,* but that
being affigned to the *Fundamental,* it marks
out the *Tune* of the Reft with relation to it.
We learn here how to pafs by *Degrees* moft
melodioufly, from any given Note to any *harmonical* Diftance. The *Scale* fhews us, what
Notes can be naturally joyned to any *Fundamental,* and thereby teaches us the juft and natural
Limitations of *Melody.* It exhibites to us all
the *Intervals* and Relations that are effential
and neceffary in *Mufick,* and contains virtually
all the. Variety of Orders, in which thefe Relations can be taken fucceffively; if a Song is
confined to one *Key,* the Thing is plain, if 'tis
carried thro' feveral *Keys,* it may feem to require feveral diftinct Series; yet the *Mufick* in
every Part being truly *diatonick,* 'tis but the
fame natural *Scale* (with its Two different Species) applied to different *fundamental* Notes.
And this brings us to confider the Effect of
having a Series of Sounds fixt to the Relations
of the *Scale* : If we fuppofe this, it will eafily
appear how infufficient fuch a *Scale* is for all
the agreeable Variety of *Melody*: But then,
this Imperfection is not any Defect in the natural *Syftem,* but follows accidentally, upon its being confined to this Condition : For this is
not the *Nature* and *Office* of the *Scale of Mufick,* that fuppofing its Relations all expreffed
in a Series of determinate Sounds, that individual Series fhould contain all the Variety of
Notes, that can *melodioufly* fucceed other ; unlefs

lefs you'll fuppofe every Song ought to be limited to one *Key*; but otherwife one individual *diatonick* Series of fixt Sounds is not fufficient. Let us fuppofe the *Scale* of *Mufick* thus defin'd, *viz.* a Series of Sounds, whofe Relations to one another are fuch, that in one individual Series, determined in thefe Relations, all the Notes may be found that can be taken fucceffively to make true *Melody*; fuch a *Syftem* would indeed be of great Ufe, and be juftly reckoned a *perfect Syftem*; but if the Nature of Things will not admit of fuch a Series, then 'tis but a *Chimera*; and yet it is true, that the natural *Scale* is a *juft* and *perfect Syftem*, when we confider its proper Office as I have expreft it above, and as we fhall underftand further from the next *Chapter*, in which I fhall confider more particularly the *Defect* of *Inftruments* having fixt and determinate Sounds, and the Remedy applied to it; and comparing this with the Capacity of the *human Voice*, we fhall plainly underftand, in what different Senfes the *Scale* of *Mufick* explained, ought to be called a *perfect* or *imperfect Syftem*.

CHAP.

CHAP. X.

Concerning the Scale *of* Mufick *limited to fixed Sounds, explaining the* Defects *of* Inftruments, *and the Remedies thereof; wherein is taught the true* Ufe *and* Original *of the Notes we commonly call* fharp *and* flat.

§ 1. *Of the* Defects *of* Inftruments, *and of the Remedy thereof in general, by the Means of what we call* Sharps *and* Flats.

THE Ufe of the *Scale* of *Mufick* has been largely explain'd, and the general Limitations of *Melody* contained in it. Why the *Scale* exhibited in the preceeding *Chapters* is called the *natural*, and the *diatonick Scale*, has been alfo faid, and how *Mufick* compofed under the Limitations of that *Scale* is called *diatonick Mufick*.

LET us now conceive a Series of Sounds determined and fixt in the Order and Proportions of that *Scale*, and named by the fame Letters. Suppofe, for *Example*, an *Organ* or *Harpfichord*, the loweft or graveft Note being taken at any Pitch of *Tune*; it is plain, 1mo. That we can proceed from any Note only by one particular Order of

of *Degrees*; for we have fhewn before, that from
every Letter of the *Scale* to its *Octave*, is contain'd a different Order of the *Tones* and *Semitones*. 2*do.* We cannot for that Reafon find a-
ny *Interval* required from any Note or Letter
upward or downward; for the *Intervals* from
every Letter to all the reft are alfo limited; and
therefore, 3*tio.* A *Song* (which is truly *diatonick*) may be fo contrived, that beginning
at a particular Letter or Note of the Inftrument,
all the *Intervals* of the *Song*, that is, all the o-
ther Notes, according to the juft Diftances and
Relations defigned by the Compofer, fhall be
found exactly upon that Inftrument, or in that
fixt Series; yet fhould we begin the Song at any
other Note, we could not proceed. This will
be plain from *Examples*, in order to which,
view the *Scale* expreffed by Letters, in which
I make a *Colon* (:) betwixt Two Letters, the
Sign of a greater *Tone* 8 : 9, a *Semicolon* (;)
the Sign of a leffer *Tone* 9 : 10, and a *Point*
(.) the Sign of a *Semitone* 15 : 16. And thefe
Letters I fuppofe reprefent the feveral Notes of
an Inftrument, tuned according to the Relations
marked by thefe *Tones* and *Semitones*——

$$C : D ; E . F : G ; A : B . c : d ; e . f : g ; a : b . cc$$

Here we have the *diatonick* Series with the
3*d* and 6*th* greater, proceeding from *C*; and
therefore, if only this Series is expreffed, fome
Songs compofed with a *flat Melody*, i. e. whofe
Key has a leffer 3*d*, &c. could not be performed

on

on this Inftrument, becaufe none of the *Octaves*
of this Series has all the natural *Intervals* of
the *diatonick* Series, with a 3*d* leffer, as they
have been fhewn in *Chap.* 8. For *Example*, the
Octave proceeding from *E* has a 3*d l.* but inftead of a *t g.* next the *Fundamental*, it has a
Semitone. Again, the *Octave A* has a 3*d l.*
but it has a *falfe* 4*th* from *A* to *d*, being Two
greater *Tones* and a *Semitone* in the *Ratio* of
20 : 27. Let us then fuppofe, that a Note is
put betwixt *c* and *d*, making a true 4*th* with
A, to make the *Octave A* a true *diatonick* Series. By this Means we can perform upon this
Inftrument moft Songs, that are fo fimple as to
be limited within one *Key*, I mean that make
Clofes or *Cadences* only in one Note; for every
Piece of *diatonick Melody* being regulated by
the *Intervals* of that *Scale*, and every *Key* or
Mode being either the *greater* or *leffer* (i. e. having either a 3*d* greater or leffer, with the o-
ther *Intervals* that properly accompany them,
which have been already fhewn) 'tis plain,
that beginning at *A* or *E* on this Inftrument,
we can find the true Notes of any fuch fimple
Song, as was fuppofed; unlefs the *Melody* in the
flat Key is fo contrived, as to ufe the *6th* and
7*th* greater, as I have faid it may do in fome
Circumftances, for then there will be ftill a Defect, even as to fuch fimple Songs.

    B u t there are many other confiderable Rea-
fons why this Inftrument is yet very imperfect.
And 1*mo.* Confider what has been already faid
concerning the Variety of *Keys* or *Clofes*, which
                                                may

may be in *one Piece of Melody*; and then we
fhall find that this fixt Series will be very
infufficient for a Song contrived with fuch Variety ; for *Example*, a Song whofe principal
Key is *C* with its 3*d g.* may modulate or change
into *F* ; but on this Inftrument *F* has a falfe
4*th* at *B*, and if a true 4*th* is required in the
Song, 'tis not here ; or if it modulate into *D*,
then we have a falfe 3*d* at *F*, and a falfe 5*th* at
A, which are altogether inconfiftent with right
Melody ; 'tis true that the Errors in this laft
Cafe are only the Difference of a greater and
lefler *Tone*, as you'll find by confidering how
many, and what Kind of *Degrees* the true 3*d*
and 5*th* contains ; or by confidering their Proportions in Numbers, in the Tables of *Chap.* 8.
And this Difference is in the common Account
neglected, tho' it has an Influence, of which I
fhall fpeak afterwards ; but where the Error is
the Difference of a *Tone* and *Semitone*, it is fo
grofs, that it can in no Cafe be neglected; as
the falfe 4*th* betwixt *F* and *B*; or when a *Se-*
mitone occurs where the *Melody* requires a
Tone ; for *Example*, if from the *Key C* there
is a Change into *E*, to which a *t g.* is required,
we have in the Inftrument only a *Semitone*. And,
to fay it all in few Words, 1*mo.* The *harmoni-*
cal and *concinnous Intervals* of which all true
Melody confifts, may be fo contrived, or taken
in *Succeffion*, that there is no Letter or Note of
this Inftrument at which we can begin, and find
all the reft of the Notes in true Proportion,
which yet is not the Fault of the *Scale*, that not

being the Office of it. *2do.* When the same
Song is to be performed by an Inftrument and
a Voice, or by Two Inftruments in *Unifon*, it
may be required, for accommodating the one
to the other, either to alter the Pitch of the
Tuning, fo as the whole Notes may be equally
lower or *higher*; or, becaufe this is in fome
Cafes inconvenient, and in others impoffible, as
when any Wind-inftrument, as *Organ* or *Flute*,
is to accompany a Voice, and the Note at
which the Song is begun on the Inftrument is
too high or low for the Voice to carry it thro'
in; in fuch Cafes the only Remedy is to begin
at another Note, from which, perhaps, you cannot proceed and find all the true Notes of the
Song, for the Reafons fet forth above; or let it
be yet further illuftrated by this *Example.* A
Song is contrived to proceed thus, *Firft*, upward
a *t g.* then a *t l.* then a *Sem.* &c. fuch a Progrefs is *melodious*, but is not to be found from
any Note of the preceeding *Scale*, except *c*; and
therefore we can begin only there, unlefs the Inftrument has other Notes than in the Order of
the *diatonick Scale.*

We fee then plainly the Defect of *Inftru-*
ments, whofe Notes are fixt; and if this is cu-
rable, 'tis as plain that it can only be effected
by inferting other Notes and Degrees betwixt
thefe of the *diatonick Series:* How far this is,
or may be obtained, fhall be our next Enquiry;
and the firft Thing I fhall do, is, to demonftrate
that there cannot poffibly be a perfect *Scale*
fixed upon Inftruments, *i. e.* fuch as from any
Note

Note upward or downward, fhall contain any *harmonical* or *concinnous Interval* required in their exact Proportions.

Since the Inequality of the *Degrees* into which the *natural Scale* is divided, is the Reafon that Inftruments having fixt Sounds are imperfect; for hence it is that all *Intervals* of an equal Number of Degrees, or whofe Extremes comprehend an equal Number of Letters, are not equal; fo from *C* to *E* has Two Degrees, and *E* to *G* has as many ; but the Degrees, which are the component Parts of thefe *Intervals*, differ, and fo muft the whole *Intervals:* Therefore it is manifeft, that if there can be a *perfect Scale* (as above defined) fixt upon Inftruments, it muft be fuch as fhall proceed from a given Sound by equal Degrees falling in with all the Divifions or Terms of the *natural Scale*, in order to preferve all its *harmonious Intervals*, which would otherwife be loft, and then it could be no *mufical Scale.*

If fuch a Series can be found, it will be abfolutely perfect, becaufe its Divifions falling in with thefe of the *natural Scale*, each *Degree* and *Interval* of this will contain a certain Number of that new *Degree* ; and therefore we fhould have, from any given Note of this *Scale*, any other Note upward or downward, which fhall be to the given Note in any *Ratio* of the *diatonick Scale* ; and confequently any Piece of *Melody* might begin and proceed from any Note of this Scale indifferently : But fuch a Divifion is impoffible, which I fhall demonftrate thus.

thus. 1*mo*. If any Series of Sounds is expreſſed
by a Series of Numbers, which contain betwixt
them the true *Ratios* or *Intervals* of theſe
Sounds, then if the Sounds exceed each other
by equal Degrees or Differences of *Tune*, that
Series of Numbers is in *continued geometrical
Proportion*, which is clear from what has been
explained concerning the Expreſſion of the *Intervals* of Sound by Numbers. 2*do*. Since it is
required that the new Degree ſought, fall in
with the Diviſions of the *natural Scale*, 'tis evident that this new Degree muſt be an exact
Meaſure to every *Interval* of that *Scale*; *that
is*, This Degree muſt be ſuch, that each of
theſe *Intervals* may be exactly divided by it, or
contain a certain preciſe Number of it without
a Remainder ; and if no ſuch Degree or common Meaſure to the *Intervals* of the *natural
Scale* can be found, then we can have no ſnch
perfect Scale as is propoſed.   But that ſuch a
Degree is impoſſible is eaſily proven ; *conſider* it
muſt meaſure or divide every *diatonick Interval*,
and therefore to prove the Impoſſibility of it
for any one *Interval* is ſufficient ; take for Example the *Tone* 8 : 9, it is required to divide
this *Interval* by putting in ſo many *geometrical*
Means betwixt 8 and 9 as ſhall make the Whole
a continued Series, with theſe Qualifications, *viz*.
That the common *Ratio*, (which is to be the
firſt and common Degree of the new *Scale*) may
be a Meaſure to all the other *diatonick Intervals :* But chiefly, 2*do*. 'Tis required that it
be a rational Quantity, expreſſible in rational or
known

known Numbers. Now fuppofe one *Mean*, it is the fquare Root of 72 (*viz.* of 8 multiplied by 9) which, not being a fquare Number, has no fquare Root in rational Numbers; and *univerfally*, let *n* reprefent any Number of *Means*, the firft and leaft of them, is by an *univerfal Theorem* (as the *Mathematicians* know) thus expreft $\overline{8^n \times 9}\ ^{\frac{1}{n+1}}$, equal to this $\overline{8^n}\ ^{\frac{1}{n+1}} \times 9\ ^{\frac{1}{n+1}}$: But fuppofe *n* to be any Number you pleafe, fince 9 is a figurate Number of no Kind but a Square, therefore this *Mean* will in every Cafe be *furd* or irrational, and confequently the *Tone* 8 : 9 cannot be divided in the Manner propofed; and fo neither can the *diatonick Scale*.

Again, if the Divifion cannot be made in rational Numbers, we can never have a *mufical Scale*; for fuppofe that by fome *geometrical* Method we put in a certain Number of Lines, *mean Proportionals* betwixt 8 and 9, yet none of thefe could be Concord with any Term or Note of the *diatonick Scale*; becaufe the Coincidence of Vibrations makes *Concord*, but Chords that are not as Number to Number, can never coincide in their Vibrations, fince the Number of Vibrations to every Coincidence are reciprocally as the Lengths, which not being as Number to Number, they could not make a *mufical Scale*. In the laft Place, Let us fuppofe the *Interval* 8 : 9 divided by any Number of fuch *geometrical Means*, and fuppofe (tho' abfurd) that they make *Concord* with the rational Terms of the *Scale*, yet it is certain we could never find a common Meafure to the whole *Scale*;

for

for every Term of a *geometrical* Series multiplied by the common *Ratio*, produces the next
Term; but the *Ratio* here is a furd Quantity,
viz. $\overline{8^a \times 9} \rfloor \frac{1}{n+1} : 8$, and therefore, tho' it were
multiplied *in infinitum* with any rational Num-
ber, could never produce any Thing but a Surd;
and confequently never fall in with the Terms
of the *natural Scale :* Therefore, fuch a perfect
Series or *Scale* of fixt Sounds is impoffible.

Tho' the Defects of Inftruments cannot be
perfectly removed, yet they are in a good Meafure cured, as we fhall prefently fee; in order to
which let me premife, that the nearer the *Scale*
in fixt Sounds, comes to an Equality of the Degrees or Differences of every Note to the next,
providing always that the natural *Intervals* be
preferved, the nearer it is to abfolute Perfection;
and the Defects that ftill remain after any Divifion, are lefs fenfible as that Divifion is greater, and the Degrees thereby made fmaller and
more in Number; but by making too many we
render the Inftrument impracticable; the Art is
to make no more than that the Defects may be
infenfible, or very nearly fo, and the Inftrument
at the fame Time fit for Service.

I know that fome Writers fpeak of the Divifion of the *Octave* into 16, 18, 20, 24, 26, 31,
and other Numbers of Degrees, which, with
the Extremes, make 17, 19, 21, 25, 27, and
32 Notes within the Compafs of an *Octave;*
but 'tis eafily imagined how hard and difficult
a Thing it muft be to perform upon fuch an Inftrument; fuppofe a *Spinet*, with 21 or 32
Keys

Keys within the Compaſs of an *Octave*; what an Embaraſſment and Confuſion muſt this occaſion eſpecially to a Learner. Indeed if the Matter could not be tolerably rectified another Way, we ſhould be obliged patiently to wreſtle with ſo hard an Exerciſe : But 'tis well that we are not put to ſuch a difficult Choice, either to give up our Hopes of ſo agreeable Entertainment as *muſical Inſtruments* afford, or reſolve to acquire it at a very painful Rate ; no, we have it eaſier, and a *Scale* proceeding by 12 Degrees, *that is*, 13 Notes including the Extremes, to an *Octave*, makes our Inſtruments ſo perfect that we have no great Reaſon to complain. This therefore is the preſent *Syſtem* for Inſtruments, *viz.* betwixt the Extremes of every *Tone* of the *natural Scale* is put a Note, which divides it into Two unequal Parts called *Semitones*; and the whole may be called the *ſemitonick Scale*, containing 12 *Semitones* betwixt 13 Notes within the Compaſs of an *Octave* : And to preſerve the *diatonick* Series diſtinct, theſe inſerted Notes take the Name of the *natural* Note next below, with this Mark ✳ called a *Sharp*, as *C*✳ or *C ſharp*, to ſignify that it is a *Semitone* above *C* (*natural* ;) or they take the Name of the *natural* Note next above, with this Mark ♭, called a *Flat*, as *D*♭ or *D flat*, to ſignifie a *Semitone* below *D* (*natural*;) and tho' it be indifferent upon the main which Name is uſed in any Caſe, yet, for good Reaſons, ſometimes the one Way is uſed, and ſometimes the other, as I ſhall have Occaſion to explain : But that I

may

may proceed here upon a fixt Rule, I denomi-
nate them from the Note below, excepting that
betwixt *A* and *B,* which I always mark ♭, fimply without any other Letter ; underftand the
fame of any other Character of thefe Letters ;
as always when I name any Letters for Examples, I fay the fame of all the other Characters
of thefe Letters, *i. e.* of all the Notes through
the whole *Scale* that bear thefe Names; and
thus the whole *Octave* is to be expreffed, *viz.*
C. C✳. D. D✳ E. F. F✳ G. G✳ A. ♭. *B. C*—

THE *Keys* of a Spinet reprefent this verydiftinct-
ly to us; the foremoft Range of continued *Keys*
is in the Order of the *diatonick Scale,* and the
other *Keys* fet backward are the *artificial* Notes.

WHY we don't rather ufe 12 different
Letters; will appear afterwards. The Two *natural Semitones* of the *diatonick Scale* being betwixt *E F* and *A B* fhew that the new Notes
fall betwixt the other natural ones as they are fet
down. Thefe new Notes are called *accidental*
or *fictitious,* becaufe they retain the Name of
their *Principals* in the *natural Syftem :* And
this Name does alfo very well exprefs their Defign and Ufe; which is not to introduce or ferve
any new Species of *Melody* diftinct from the
diatonick Kind; but, as I have faid in the Beginning of this Chapter, to ferve the Modulation from one *Key* to another in the Courfe of
any Piece, or the Tranfpofition of the Whole
to a different Pitch, for accommodating Inftruments to a Voice, that beginning at a convenient Note, the Inftrument may accompany the
Voice

Voice in *Unison.* How far the **Luxury,** if I may so call it, of the prefent *Mufick* is carried, fo as to change the Species of *Melody,* and bring in fomething of a different Character from the true *Diatonick,* and for that Purpofe have Ufe for a *Scale* of *Semitones,* I fhall have Occafion to fpeak of afterwards : But let us now proceed to fhew how thefe Notes are proportioned to the *natural* ones, *i. e.* to fhew the Quantity of the *Semitones* occafioned by thefe *accidental* Notes, and then fee how far the *Syftem* is perfected by them.

---

§ 2. *Of the true Proportions of the* Semitonick Scale, *and how far the Syftem is perfected by it.*

THERE is great Variety, or I may rather call it Confufion, in the Accounts that Writers upon *Mufick* give of this Matter ; they make different Divifions without explaining the Reafons of them. But fince I have fo clearly explained the Nature and Defign of this Improvement, it will be eafy to examine any Divifion, and prove its Fitnefs, by comparing it with the End : And from the Things above faid, we have this *general Rule* for judging of them, *viz.* That, the Divifion which makes a Series, from whofe every Note we can find any *diatonick Interval,* upward or downward, with leaft and feweft Errors, is moft perfect.

THERE are Two Divifions that I propofe to explain here ; and after thefe I fhall explain the
ordi-

ordinary and moſt approven Way of bringing
Spinets and ſuch kind of Inſtruments to Tune;
and ſhew the true Proportion that ſuch Tuning
makes among the ſeveral Notes.

THE *firſt Diviſion* is this : Every *Tone* of
the *diatonick* Series is divided into Two Parts
or *Semitones*, whereof the one is the *natural
Semitone* 15 : 16, and the other is the Remainder of that from the *Tone, viz.* 128 : 135
in the *t g.* and 24 : 25 in the *t l.* and the *Semitone*
15 : 16 is put in the loweſt Place in each, except
the *t g.* betwixt *f* and *g*, where 'tis put in the
upper Place ; and the whole *Octave* ſtands as
in the following Scheme, where I have written
the *Ratios* of each Term to the next in a Fraction ſet betwixt them below.

SCALE of *SEMITONES*.

c . c✳ . d . d✳ . e . f . f✳ . g . g✳ . a . ♭ . b . cc•

$$\frac{15}{16} \quad \frac{128}{135} \quad \frac{15}{16} \quad \frac{24}{25} \quad \frac{15}{16} \quad \frac{128}{135} \quad \frac{15}{16} \quad \frac{15}{16} \quad \frac{24}{25} \quad \frac{15}{16} \quad \frac{128}{135} \quad \frac{15}{16}$$

IT was very natural to think of dividing each.
Tone of the *diatonick Scale*, ſo as the *Semitone* 15 : 16 ſhould be one Part of each Diviſion ;
becauſe this being an unavoidable and neceſſary
Part of the *natural Scale*, would moſt readily
occur as a fit Degree in the Diviſion of the
Tones thereof ; eſpecially after conſidering that
this Degree 15 : 16 is not very far from the
exact Half of a *Tone*. *Again* there muſt be
ſome Reaſon for placing theſe *Semitones* in one
Order rather than another, *i. e.* placing 15 : 16
uppermoſt in the *Tone f : g*, and undermoſt in

all

all the reft ; which Reafon is this, that hereby there are fewer Errors or Defects in the
Scale; particularly, the 15 : 16 is fet in the upper Place of the *Tone f : g,* becaufe by this
the greateft Error in the *diatonick Scale* is
perfectly corrected, *viz.* the falfe *4th* betwixt
f and *b* upward, which exceeds the true *harmonical 4th* by the *Semitone* 128 : 135, and this
Semitone being placed betwixt *f* and *f✳*, makes
from *f✳* to *b* a true *4th ;* and corrects alfo
an equal Defect in the *Interval b-f* taken upward, which inftead of a true *5th* wants 128 :
135, and is now juft, by taking *f✳* for *f, that
is,* from *♭* up to *f✳* is a juft *5th.* There were
the fame grofs Errors in the *natural 8ve* proceeding from *f,* which are now corrected by the
altered *b viz. ♭,* which is a true *4th* above *f,*
whereas *b* (natural) is to the *f* below as 32 : 45
exceeding a true *4th* by 128 : 135 ; alfo from *b*
(natural) up to *f* is a falfe *5th,* as 45 : 64, but from
♭ to *f* is a juft *5th* 2 : 3 ; and therefore refpecting thefe Corrections of fo very grofs Errors, we fee a plain Reafon why the greater
Semitone 15 : 16 is placed betwixt *f✳* and *g,*
and betwixt *a* and *♭* : For the Place of it in the
other *Tones,* I fhall only fay, in general, that
there are fewer Errors as I have placed them
than if placed otherwife ; and I fhall add this
Particular, that we have now from the Key *c*
both the *diatonick Series* with the *3d l.* and *3d
g.* and their Accompanyments all in their juft
Proportions, only we have 9 : 16, *viz.* from *c*
to *♭* for the leffer *7th,* which tho' it make not

fo

fo many *harmonious* Relations to the other *diatonick* Notes as 5 : 9 would do, yet confidering
a *7th* is ftill but a *Difcord,*and for what Reafon
♭·was made a greater *Semitone* 15 : 16 above *a*.
This *7th* ought to be accounted the beft here ;
yet the other 5 : 9 has Place in other Parts of
the *Scale* ; I fhall prefently fhew you other
Reafons why 9 : 16 is the beft in the Place
where I have put it, *viz.* betwixt *c* and ♭.

CONCERNING this *Scale* of *Semitones,* Ob-
ferve 1*mo,* From any Letter to the fame again
comprehending Thirteen Notes is always a true
8*ve,* as from *c* to *c,* or from *c*✳ to *c*✳. 2*do.*
We have Three different *Semitones* 15 : 16 the
greateft, 128 : 135 the *middle,* and 24 : 25 the
leaft, which, when I have Occafion to fpeak of,
I fhall mark thus, *fg. fm. fl.* The firft is
the Difference of a 3*d g.*and 4*th;* the fecond the
Difference of *t g.* and *fg.* and the Third the
Difference of *t l.* and *fg.* (or of 3*d g.* and 3*d l.*
or 6*th g.* and 6*th l.*) 3*tio.* We have by this
Divifion alfo Three different *Tones,* *viz.* 8 : 9
compofed of *fg.* and *fm.* as *c : d ;* then 9 : 10
compofed of *fg.* and *fl.* as *d ; e ;* and 225 :
256 compofed of Two *fg.* as *f*✳ *: g*✳, which
occurs alfo betwixt *b* and *c*✳,and no where elfe,
all the reft being of the other Two Kinds which
are the true *Tones* of the *natural Scale.* And
tho' we might fuppofe other Combinations of
thefe *Semitones* to make new *Tones,* yet their
Order in this *Scale* affording no other, we are
concerned no farther with them. Now *obferve,*
this laft *Tone* 225 : 256 being equal to 2 *fg.*
must

muſt be alſo the greateſt of theſe Three *Tones*;
ſo that what is the greateſt of the Two *natural Tones*, is now the Middle of theſe Three,
and therefore when you meet with *t g.* underſtand always the *natural Tone* 8 : 9, unleſs it be
otherwiſe ſaid.

4to. L E T us now conſider how the *Intervals*
of this *Scale* ſhall be denominated; we have already heard the Reaſon of theſe Names 3*d*,
4*th*, 5*th*, &c. given to the *Intervals* of the *Scale*
of *Muſick*; they are taken from the Number of
Notes comprehended betwixt the Extremes
(*incluſive*) of any *Interval*, and expreſs in their
principal Deſign, the Number of Notes from the
Fundamental of an 8*ve concinnouſly* divided to
any *acute* Term of the Series, tho' to make
them of more univerſal Uſe they are alſo applied
to the *accidental Intervals.* See *Chap.* 8. So
that whatever *Interval* contains the ſame Number of Degrees is called by the ſame Name;
and hence we have ſome *Concords* ſome *Diſcords* of the ſame Name; ſo in the *diatonick
Scale*, from *c* to *e* is a 3*d g. Concord*, and from
e to *g* a 3*d l.* and from *d* to *f* is alſo called a
3*d*, becauſe *f* is the 3*d* Note *incluſive* from *d*,
yet it is *Diſcord.* See *Chap.* 8. If we conſider
next, that the Notes added to the *Scale* are
not deſigned to alter the Species of *Melody*, but
leave it ſtill *diatonick*, only they correct the
Defects ariſing from ſomething foreign to the
Nature and Uſe of the *Scale* of *Muſick*, *viz.*
the limiting and fixing of the Sounds; then we
ſee the Reaſon why the ſame Names are ſtill
con-

continued : And tho' there are now more Notes
iu an*Octave*, and fo a greater Number of different
Intervals, yet the *diatonick* Names comprehend
the whole, by giving to every *Interval* of an e-
qual Number of Degrees the fame Name, and
making a Diftinction of each into greater and leffer. Thus an *Interval* of 1 *Semitone* is called
a leffer Second or 2*d l.* of 2 *Semitones* is a 2*d g.*
of 3 *Semitones* a 3*d l.* of 4, a 3*d g.* and fo on
as in this *Table.*

Denominations. 2dl. 2dg. 3dl. 3dg. 4thl. 4thg. 5th. 6thl. 6thg. 7thl. 7thg. 8ve.
Num. of Sem. 1 - 2 - 3 - 4 - 5 - 6 - 7 - 8 - 9 - 10 - 11 - 12.

In which we have no other Names, than thefe
already known in the *diatonick Scale*, except
the 4*th* greater, which for equal Reafon might
be called a 5*th* leffer, becaufe 'tis a Middle betwixt 4*th* and 5*th*, i.e. betwixt 5 and 7 *Semitones* ;
and therefore we may call all *Intervals* of 6 *Semitones Tritones* (for 6 *Semitones* make 3 *Tones*)
and thefe of 5 *Semitones* call them fimply 4*ths*;
and fo all the Names of the *diatonick Scale* remain unaltered, and we have only the Name
of *Tritone* added, which yet is not new, for I
have before obferved, that it is ufed in the *diatonick Scale*, and thus all is kept very diftinct;
and if we proceed above an *Octave*, we compound the Names with an *Octave* and thefe below. Again take Notice, that as in the pure
diatonick Scale, the Names of 3*d*, 4*th*, &c. anfwer to the Number of Letters which are betwixt the Extremes (inclufive) of any *Interval*, whereby the Denomination of the *Interval* is known, by knowing the Letters by which
the

the Extremes of it are expreſt, ſo in this new
Scale the ſame will hold, by taking any Letter
with or without the *Sharp* or *Flat* for the ſame
Letter, and applying to the *accidental* Notes, in
ſome Caſes the Letter of the Note below with
a *Sharp*, and in others that of the Note above
with a *Flat* : For *Example.* $d\sharp$–g is a 3d, and
includes 4 Letters ; but if for $d\sharp$ we take $e♭$,
then $e♭$–g, which is the ſame individual *Interval*, contains but 3 Letters; alſo if for $♭$ we
take $a\sharp$, then $a\sharp$–$c\sharp$, which is a true 3d l.
includes 3 Letters, whereas $♭$–$c\sharp$ has but Two.
There is only one Exception, for the *Interval*
b-f, which is a 4$th$$g$. contains 5 Letters, and
cannot be otherwiſe expreſt, unleſs you take $c\sharp$
which is equal to f *natural*; or take $c♭$, which
is equal to b *natural*; but this is not ſo regular,
and indeed makes too great a Confuſion; tho' I
have ſeen it ſo done in the Compoſitions of the
beſt Maſters, which yet will not make it reaſonable, unleſs in the particular Caſe where 'tis
uſed, it could not have been ſo conveniently ordered otherwiſe : But if we call the ſame *Interval* a 5th leſſer, then the *Rule* is good; yet
if we call every *Tritone* a 5th, we ſhall ſtill have
an Exception, for then f–b contains only 4 Letters ; and therefore 'tis beſt to call all *Intervals*
of 6 *Semitones*, *Tritones*, and then they are not
ſubject to this *Rule*. In this therefore we ſee a
Reaſon, why 'tis better that the *accidental* Note
ſhould be named by the Letter of the *natural
Note*, than to make Twelve Letters in an O-
ctave; beſides, the *Melody* being ſtill *diatonick*,
theſe

thefe *accidental* Notes are only in place of the others; and by keeping the fame Names, we preferve the Simplicity of the *Syftem* better.

5to. Having thus fettled the Denominations of the *Intervals* of this *femitonick Scale*, we muft next *obferve*, that of each Denomination there are Differences in the Quantity, arifing from the Differences of the *Semitones* of which they are compofed, as is very obvious in the *Scale*: And thefe again may be diftinguifhed into *true* and *falfe*, i. e. fuch as are either *harmonical* or *concinnous Intervals* of the *natural Scale*, and fuch as are not; and in each Denomination we find there is one that is *true*, and all the reft are *falfe*, except the *Tritones* which are all *falfe*, tho' they are ufed in fome very particular Cafes.

6to. Let us next enquire into all the Variety and the precife Quantity of every *Interval* within this new *Scale*, that we may thereby know what Defects ftill remain. We have already obferved, that there are Three different *Semitones* and as many *Tones*; hence it is plain, there are neither more nor lefs than Three different *7ths* of each Species, *i. e.* lefler and greater, which are the Complements of thefe *Semitones* and *Tones* to *Octave*, as here.

Semit.	7th g.		7th l.	Tone.
15 - 16 - 30	128 - 225 - 256
128 - 135 - 256	9 - 16 - 18
24 - 25 - 48	5 - 9 - 10

And

And to know where each of thefe *7ths* lies, and all the *Examples* of each in the *Scale*, 'tis but taking all the *Examples* of thefe *Semitones* and *Tones*, which are to be found at Sight in the *Scale* marked with the *Semitones*, as you fee in Page 294. and you have the correfpondent *7ths* betwixt the one Extreme of that *Semitone* or *Tone*, and the *Octave* to the other Extreme. Then for the other *Intervals*, viz. 3*ds*, 6*ths*, 4*ths*, 5*ths*, which are *harmonical*, I have in the *Table-plate*, *Fig.* fet all the *Examples* of fuch of them as are *falfe*, with their refpective *Ratios* ; and with the *Ratios* of the 6*th* and 5*th* I have fet an *e* or *d*, to fignify an exceffive, or a deficient *Interval* from the true *Concord* ; and confequently their correfpondent 3*ds* and 4*ths* will be as much on the contrary deficient or exceffive. All the reft of the *Intervals* of thefe feveral Denominations, containing 3 , 4 , 5 , 7 , 8 or 9 *Semitones*, are true of their feveral Kinds, whofe *Ratios* we have frequently feen, and fo they needed not be placed here. Then for the *Tritones*, you have in the laft Part of the *Table* all their Variety and *Examples* ; by the Nature of this *Interval* it exceeds a *true* 4*th*, and wants of a *true* 5*th* ; you'll eafily find the Difference by the *Ratio*.

N o w we have feen all the Variety of *Intervals* in this new *Scale* ; and by what's explain'd we know where all the Extremes of each ly: and it will be eafy to find the true *Ratio* of any *Interval*, the Letters or Names of whofe Extremes in the *Scale* are given, *viz.* by finding in
the

the *Scale* how many *Semitones* it contains, and thereby the Denomination of it, by which you'll fnd its *Ratio* in the preceeding *Table*, unlefs it be a true *Concord*, and then it is not in the *Table*, which is a Sign of its being *true*. And as to this *Table*, obferve, that I have no Refpect to the different Characters of Letters, and you muft fuppofe every *Example* to be taken upward in the *Scale*, from the firft Letter of the *Example* to the fecond, counting in the natural Order of the Letters.

7mo. W E are now come to confider how far the *Scale* is perfected; and firft *obferve*, that there are no greater or leffer, and precifely no other Errors in it, than the Differences of the Three *Semitones*, which are thefe following;

of which the up-permoft is the leaft,

$$\text{Diff. of} \begin{cases} \int g. \text{ and } \int m. = 2025 : 2048 \\ \int m. \text{ and } \int l. = 80 : 81 \\ \int g. \text{ and } \int l. = 125 : 128 \end{cases}$$

and the lower the greateft Error. In the *diatonick Scale* fome *Intervals* erred a whole *Semitone*, and all the reft only by a *Comma* 80 ∶ 81; here we have one Error a very little greater, and another leffer: All the *5ths* and *4ths* except Three, are *juft* and *true*; of the *3d l.* and *6th g.* there are as many *true* as *falfe*; and of the *3d g.* and *6th l.* we have Five *falfe* and Seven *true*. Thefe Errors are fo fmall, that in a fingle Cafe the Ear will bear it, efpecially in the *imperfect Concords* of 3d and 6th; but when many of thefe Errors happen in a Song, and efpecially in the

prin-

principal *Intervals* that belong to the *Key*, it
will interrupt the *Melody*, and the Inftrument
will appear out of Tune (as it really is with
refpect to that Song :)   But then we muft *obferve*, that as the Order of thefe *Semitones* is
different in every *Octave*, proceeding from each
of the Twelve different *Keys* or Letters of the
Scale ; fo we find that fome Songs will proceed
better, if begun at fome Notes, than at others.
If we compare one *Key* with another, then we
muft prefer them according to the Perfection of
their principal *Intervals*, viz. the 3*d*, 5*th* and
6*th*, which are Effentials in the *Harmony* of
every *Key* : And let any Two Notes be propofed to be made *Keys* of the fame *Species*, viz.
both with the 3*d l*, &c. or 3*dg*, &c. We can
eafily find in the preceeding *Table* what *Intervals* in the *Scale* are *true* or *falfe* to each of
them; and accordingly prefer the one or the
other: But I fhall proceed to

T H E *fecond Divifion* of the 8*ve* into *Semitones* which I promifed to explain, and it is
this: Betwixt the Extremes of the *t g.* and *t l.*
of the *natural Scale* is taken an *harmonical Mean*
which divides it into Two *Semitones* nearly
equal, thus, the *t g.* 8 : 9 is divided into Two
Semitones which are 16 : 17 and 17 : 18, as
here 16 : 17 : 18, which is an *arithmetical* Divifion, the Numbers reprefenting the Lengths
of Chords; but if they reprefent the Vibrations,
the Lengths of the Chords are reciprocal,*viz.* as
$1 : \frac{16}{17} : \frac{8}{9}$ which puts the greater *Semitone* $\frac{16}{17}$ next
the lower Part of the *Tone*, and the lefler $\frac{17}{18}$ next

the

the upper, which is the Property of the *harmonical* Divifion : The fame Way the *t l,* 9 : 10 is divided into thefe Two Semit. 18 : 19, and 19 : 20, and the whole 8*ve* ftands thus.

$$c . c✲ . d . d✲ . e . f . f✲ . g . g✲ . a . ♭ . b . c$$

$$\frac{16}{17} \quad \frac{17}{18} \, \frac{18}{19} \quad \frac{19}{20} \, \frac{15}{16} \, \frac{16}{17} \quad \frac{17}{18} \, \frac{18}{19} \quad \frac{19}{20} \, \frac{16}{17} \, \frac{17}{18} \, \frac{15}{16}$$

IN this Scale we have thefe Things to obferve, 1 *mo.* That every *Tone* is divided into Two, *Semit.* whereof I have fet the greater in the loweft Place. 2*do.* We have hereby Five different *Semitones* ; out of which as they ftand in the Scale we have Seven different *Tones*, as here.

Sem.		Tones.
$\frac{16}{17} ✠ \frac{17}{18}$	=	$\frac{8}{9}$
$\frac{17}{18} ✠ \frac{18}{19}$	=	$\frac{17}{19}$
$\frac{18}{19} ✠ \frac{19}{20}$	=	$\frac{9}{10}$
$\frac{19}{20} ✠ \frac{15}{16}$	=	$\frac{57}{64}$
$\frac{15}{16} ✠ \frac{16}{17}$	=	$\frac{15}{17}$
$\frac{19}{20} ✠ \frac{16}{17}$	=	$\frac{76}{85}$
$\frac{17}{18} ✠ \frac{15}{16}$	=	$\frac{85}{96}$

CONSIDERING how, by a *harmonical Mean,* the 8*th,* 5*th,* and 3*dg.* were divided into their *harmonical* or *concinnous* Parts; it could not but readily occur to divide the *Tones* the fame Way, when a Divifion was found necef- fary ; but we are to confider what Effect this Divifion has for perfecting of Inftruments. It would be more troublefom than difficult to calculate a *Table* of all the Variety of *Ratios* contain'd in this *Scale;* I fhall leave you to this Exer- cife for your Diverfion, and only tell you here, that ha- ving

ving calculate all the 5*ths* and 4*ths*, I find
there are only Seven true 5*ths*, and as many
4*ths*, whereas in the former *Scale* there were
Nine ; and then for the Errors, there are none
of them above a *Comma* 80 : 81 ; in short, there
is one false 5*th* and 4*th* whose Error is a *Comma*, and the rest are all very much less ; and, tho'
there are fewer true 5*ths* and 4*ths* here, yet the
Errors being far less and more various, compen-
sate the other Loss: As to the 3*ds* and 6*ths*,
there are also here more of them false than in
the preceeding *Scale*, for of each there are but
Four true *Intervals*, but the Errors are generally much less, the greatest being far less than
the greatest in the other *Scale*.

I shall say no more upon this, only let you
know, That Mr. *Salmon* in the *Philosophical
Transactions* tells us, That he made an Experiment of this *Scale* upon Chords exactly in these
Proportions, which yielded a perfect Consort
with other Instruments touched by the best
Hands : But observe, that he places the lesser
Semit. lowest, which I place uppermost ; and
when I had examined what Difference this
would produce, I found the Advantage would
rather be in the Way I have chosen. And this
brings to mind a Question which Mr. *Simpson*
makes in his *Compend* of *Musick, viz.* Whether
the greater or lesser *Semitone* lies from *a* to ♭;
he says 'tis more rational to his Understanding,
that the lesser *Semitone* ♭ next *a* ; but he does
not explain his Reason ; he speaks only of the
arithmetical Division of a Chord into equal
Parts,

Parts, but has not minded the *harmonical* Division of an *Interval*, by which we have feen the *diatonick Scale* fo naturally conftituted, whereby the greater Part is always laid next the graveft Extreme : But in fhort, when we fpeak of the Reafon of this, we muft confider the Defign of thefe *Semitones*, and which one in fuch a Place anfwers the End beft, and then I believe there will be no Reafon found why it fhould be as Mr. *Simpfon* fays, rather than the other Way.

§ 3. *Of the common Method of Tuning* Spinets, *demonftrating the Proportions that occur in it ; and of the Pretence of a nicer Method confidered.*

THE laft Thing I propofed to do upon this Subject, was to explain the ordinary Way of tuning Spinets and that Kind of Inftruments ; for whether it be, that the tuning them in accurate Proportions in the Manner mentioned is not eafily done, or that thefe Proportions do not fufficiently correct the Defects of the Inftrument, there is another Way which is generally followed by *practical Muficians* ; and that is Tuning by the Ear, which is founded upon this Suppofition, that the Ear is perfectly Judge of an 8*ve* and 5*th*. The *general Rule* is, to begin at a certain Note as *c*, taken toward the Middle of
the

the Inſtrument, and tuning all the 8*ves* up and down, and alſo the 5*ths*, reckoning Seven *Semitones* to every 5*th*, whereby the whole will be tuned ; but there are Differences even in the Way of doing this, which I ſhall explain.

Some and even the Generality who deal with this Kind of Inſtrument, tune not only their *Octaves*, but alſo their 5*ths* as perfectly *Concord* as their Ear can judge, and conſequently make the 4*ths* perfect, which indeed makes a great many Errors in the other *Intervals* of 3*d* and 6*th* (for the *diſcord Intervals*, they are not ſo conſiderable;) others that affect a greater Nicety pretend to diminiſh all the 5*ths*, and make them deficient about a Quarter of a *Comma*, in order to make the Errors in the reſt ſmaller and leſs ſenſible : But to be a little more particular, I ſhall ſhew you the Progreſs that's made from Note to Note; and then conſider the Effect of both theſe Methods. In order to this, let us view again the *Scale* with its 12 *Semitones* in an *Octave*; but we have Uſe for Two *Octaves* to this Purpoſe. Then 1*mo*. Beginning at *c* take it at a certain Pitch, and tune all its *Octaves* above and below ; then 2*do*. Tune *g* a 5*th* above *c*, and next tune all the *Octaves* of *g* ; 3*tio*. Take *d* a 5*th* above *g*, and then tune all the *Octaves* of *d*. 4*to*. Take *a* a 5*th* above *d*, then tune all the *Octaves* of *a*. 5*to*. Take *e* a 5*th* above *a*, and tune all the *Octaves* of *e*: Then, 6*to*. Take *b* (natural) a 5*th* above *e*, and tune all the *Octaves* of *b*. 7*mo*. Take *f♯* a 5*th* above *b*,

then

then tune all the *Octaves* of *f*※. 8*vo*. *c*※ a
5*th* above *f*※, and then all the *Octaves* of *c*※.
9*no*. Take *g*※ a 5*th* above *c*※, then all its
Octaves; and having proceeded so far, we have
all the *Keys* tuned except *f*, *d*※, and *ƭ* ; for
which, 1*omo*. Begin again at *c*, and take *f* a
5*th* downward, then tune all the *f*s. 11*mo*.
Take *ƭ* a 5*th* downward to *f*, and tune all the
*ƭ*s. *Lastly*. Take *d* ※a 5*th* below *ƭ*, and then
tune all the *Octaves* of *d*※ ; and so the whole
Instrument is in Tune. And *observe*, That having tuned all the *Octaves* of any *Key*, the next
Step being to take a 5*th* to it, you may take
that from any of the Keys of that Name.

Now supposing all these *Octaves* and 5*ths*
to be in perfect Tune, we shall examine the
Effects it will have upon the rest of the *Intervals* ; and in order to it, I have exprest this
Tuning in *Plate* 1. *Fig. 6.* by drawing Lines
betwixt every Note, and another, according to
the Method of Procedure; but I have only
marked the 5*ths*, supposing the *Octaves* to be
tuned all along as you proceed; then I have
marked the Progress from 5*th* to 5*th* by Numbers set upon them to signify the 1*st*, 2*d*, &c.
Step; and in the Method there taken you see
all the Notes tuned from *c* to *f*※ above its
Octave : We suppose all the other Notes above
and below in the Instrument to have been tuned by *Octaves* to these, but for the Thing in
Hand we have Use for no more of the *Scale*.
Observe next, That I have marked the *Semitones* betwixt every Note by the Letters *g*, *l*.
viz.

viz. greater and leffer; for there are only Two Kinds in this *Scale*, as we fhall prefently fee, and alfo what they are, for the natural *Sem.* 15 : 16 is not to be found here ; and while I fpeak of this *Scale* and of *Semitones* greater and leffer, I mean always thefe Two, unlefs it be faid otherwife.

I f we find the Degrees of this *Scale* in the *Tones* or *Semitones*, we fhall by thefe eafily find the Quantity of every other *Interval* ; and in the following Calculations I take all the *Examples* upward from the firft Letter named, and therefore I have made no Diftinction in the Character of the Letters : To begin, from *c* to *g* is a 5*th* 2 : 3, and from *g* to *d* a 5*th*, therefore from *c* to *d* is Two 5*ths* 4 : 9; out of this take an *Octave*, the Remainder is 8 : 9 a *t g.* and confequently *c-d* is a *t g.* 8 : 9 ; by this Method you'll prove that each of thefe *Intervals* marked in the following *Table* is a *t g.* 8 : 9. In the next Place, confider, from *a* to *e* is a 5*th*, therefore from *e* to *a* is a 4*th* : But from *f* to *a* there are Two *t g.* as in the preceeding *Table*, whofe Sum is 64 : 81, which taken from a 4*th* 3 : 4, leaves this *Semitone* 243 : 256 for *e* : *f* (which is lefs than 15 : 16 by a *Comma*) then if we fubftract this from a *Tone* 8 : 9, it leaves 2048 : 2187, a greater *Semitone* than the former, and if we mark the one *l.* and the other *g.* all the

c	-	*d*
d	-	*e*
d✕	-	*f*
e	-	*f✕*
f	-	*g*
f✕	-	*g✕*
g	-	*a*
a	-	*b*
l	-	*c*

All greater Tones 8:9

Semi-

Semitones from *d* to *a*, will be as I have marked them in the *Fig.* referred to; for fince *e* : *f*✳ is a *t g.* and *e* . *f* is a *f l.* therefore *f* . *f*✳ is a *f g.* and fo of the reft, every Two Semitones from *d* to *a* being a *t g.* Again fince *f* - *c* is a *5th*, and alfo *e* - *b*, taking away what's common to both, *viz. f* - *b*, there remains on each Hand thefe equal Parts *e* . *f* and *b* . *c*, fo that *b* . *c* is alfo a *f l.* and fince *ƚ* : *c* is a *t g.* and *b* . *c* a *f l.* *ƚ* . *b* muft be a *f g.* and alfo *a* . *ƚ* a *f l.* becaufe *a* : *b* is a *t g.* *Next*, from *c*✳ to *g*✳ is a *5th*, alfo from *d*✳ to *ƚ*, and taking away *d*✳-*g*✳ out of both, there remains *c*✳ : *d*✳ equal to *g*✳-*ƚ*, which contains Two *f l.* but *d* . *d*✳ is already found to be a *f l.* therefore *c*✳ . *d* is *f l.* and *c* : *d* being a *t g.* *c* . *c*✳ muft be a *f g.*

THUS we have difcovered all the *Semitones* within the *Octave*; of which as they ftand in the Scale, we have only Two different *Tones*, *viz.* the *t g.* 8 : 9 and another which is lefier 59049 : 65536 compofed of Two of the lefier *Semitones*, as you fee betwixt *c*✳ : *d*✳, and alfo betwixt *g*✳ : *ƚ* ; in every other Place of the Scale it is a *t g.*

LET us next confider the other *Intervals*, and *firft*, We have all the *Octaves* and *5ths* perfect except the *5th* *g*✳ - *d*✳ which is 531441 : 786432, wanting of a true *5th* more than a *Comma*, *viz.* the Difference of the *f g.* and *f l.* as is evident in the Scheme, for *g* - *d* is a true *5th* but the *Interval* *g*✳ - *d* is common to *g* - *d*, and *g*✳ - *d*✳, and being taken from both,

leaves

leaves in the firſt the *ſg. g . g✳*, and in laſt the
ſl. d . d✳; then all the *4ths* are of conſequence perfect, except *d✳ - g✳*, which exceeds as much as its correſpondent *5th* is deficient. But *Laſtly*, For the *3ds* and *6ths* they
are all falſe, plainly for this Reaſon, that in the
whole Series there is no leſſer *Tone 9 : 10*,
which with the *t g. 8 : 9* makes a true *3d g.*
nor any of the greater *Semitone 15 : 16*, which
with *t g* makes a *3d l.* And for the Errors they
are eaſily diſcovered, in the *3d g.* (and the Correſpondent *6 l.*) the Error is either an Exceſs
of a Comma 80 : 81 the Difference of *t g.* and
t l. of the *natural Scale*; which happens in
theſe Places where Two *t g.* ſtand together, as
in the *3d g.* from *c* to *e*; or it is a Deficiency
equal to the Difference of the leſſer *Tone 9 :
10*, and the *Tone* above mentioned 59049 :
65536, which *Tone* is leſs than 9 : 10 by this
Difference 32768, 32805 (as in the *3d g. c✳ :
f*) which is greater than a Comma; and for
the *3d l.* (and its *6th g.*) it has the ſame Errors, and is either deficient a Comma, *viz.* the
Difference of the *ſg.* 15 : 16 and the *ſl.* 243 :
256, as in the *3d l. c : d✳*, or exceeds by the
Difference of the new *ſg.* 2048 : 2187 and the
ſg. 15 : 16 which is leſs than the other by this
Difference 32768 : 32805 which is greater than
a Comma.

Now the *5ths* and *4ths* are all perfect but
one, yet the *3ds* and *6ths* being all falſe,
there is no Note in all the *Scale* from which
we have a true *diatonick* Series; and the Errors

rors being equal to a Comma in some and
greater in others, makes this *Scale* less perfect
than any yet described ; at least than the first
Division explained, in which there were only
3 false 5*ths*, whereof Two err by a Comma, and the other by a lesser Difference; and
having many true 3*ds* and 6*ths*, seems plainly a
more perfect Scale. These Errors may still be
made less by multiplying the *artificial Keys*,
and placing them betwixt such Notes of the
preceeding *Scale* as may correct the greatest
Errors of the most usual *Keys* of the *diatonick*
Series, aud of such Divisions you have Accounts
in *Mersennus* and *Kircher*; but a greater Number
than 13 Keys in an *Octave* is so great a Difficulty for
Practice,that they are very rare,and our best Compositions are performed on Instruments with 13
Notes in the *Octave*, and as to the tuning of these,

L E T us now consider the Pretences of
the nicer Kind of *Musicians*; they tell us,
'That in tuning by *Octaves* and 5*ths*, they
diminish all the 5*ths* by a Quarter of a
Comma, or near it (for the *Ratio* 80 : 81 cannot be divided into 4 equal Parts, and exprest in
rational Numbers) in order to make the Errors through the whole Instrument very small
and insensible. I shall not here trouble you
with Calculations made upon this Supposition,
because they can be easily done by those who
understand what has been hitherto explained
upon this Subject ; therefore I say no more but
this, That it must be an extraordinary Ear that
can judge exactly of a Quarter *Comma,* and I
shall

shall add, That some Practisers upon *Harpsi-chords* have told me they always tune their 5*ths* perfect, and find their Instrument answer very well. 'Tis true they cannot deny that the same Song will not go equally well from every *Key*, which argues still the Imperfection of the Instrument ; but there is no Song but they can find some *Key* that will answer. If a very just and accurate Ear can diminish the Errors, so as to make them yet smaller and more equal thro' the whole Instrument, I will not say but they may make more of the *Octaves* like other, and consequently make it an indifferent Thing which of these *Keys*, that are brought to such a Likeness, you begin your Song at ; but even these cannot deny that a Song will do better from one *Key* than another ; so that the Defects are not quite removed even as to Sense.

Dr. *Wallis* has a Discourse in the *Philoso-phical Transactions* concerning the Imperfecti-on of Organs, and the Remedy applied to it ; the Imperfection he observes is the same I have already spoken of, *viz.* That from every Note you cannot find any *Interval* in its just Proportion. 'Tis true indeed the Doctor only considers the Imperfection of a *Scale* of *Semitones*, and parti-cularly one constituted in the *Ratio* of the 2*d* Kind of Division abovementioned ; he does not say directly for what Reasons a *Scale* of *Semi-tones* was necessary ; but, as if he supposed that plain enough, he says there are still some Defects ; and therefore, says he, *Instead of these Propor-tions (of the* Semitones*) it is so ordered, if I mi, stake* *miſtake not the Practice, that the* 13 *Pipes within an* Octave, *as to their Sounds, with reſpect to* acute *and* grave, *ſhall be in continual Proportion, whereby it comes to paſs that each Pipe doth not expreſs its proper Sound, but ſomething varying from it, which is called* Bearing ; *and this,* ſays he, *is an Imperfection in this noble Inſtrument.* Again, he ſays, That the *Semitones* being all made equal, they do indifferently anſwer all Poſitions of *mi* (*i.e.* of the Two *natural Semitones* in an *Octave* ; of the Uſe of this Word *mi*, we ſhall hear again) and tho' not exactly to any, yet nearer to ſome than to others ; whence it is that the ſame Song ſtands better in one Key than another. I have ſhewn above, that a *Scale* of *Degrees* accurately equal, which will coincide with the Terms of the *natural Scale* is not poſſible ; and now let me ſay, That tho' the *Octave* may be divided into 12 equal *Semitones* by *geometrical* Methods, *that is,* 13 Lines may be conſtructed, which ſhall be in continued *geometrical Proportion,* and the greateſt to the leaſt be as 2 to 1, yet none of theſe Terms can be expreſt by rational Numbers, and ſo 'tis impoſſible that ſuch a *Scale* could expreſs any true *Muſick,* and hence I conclude, that this *Bearing* does not make the *Semitones* exactly equal, tho' they may be ſenſibly ſo in a ſingle Compariſon of one with another ; and ſuppoſing them equal, the Doctor ſays the ſame Song will ſtand better at one *Key* than another ; which may be very true, becauſe none of the Terms of ſuch a *Scale* can

poſſibly

possibly fall in with thefe of the *natural Scale*, which are all expreft by rational Numbers, and the other are all Surds; whereas had we a Scale of equal Degrees, coinciding with the *natural Scale*, every *Key* would neceffarily be alike for] every Song. Thefe Imperfections, fays the Doctor, might be further remedied by multiplying the Notes within an *Octave*, yet not without fomething of bearing, unlefs to every *Key* (he means of the Seven *natural* ones) be fitted a diftinct Scale or Set of Pipes rifing in the true Proportions, which would render the Inftrument impracticable: But even this I think would not do; for let us fuppofe that from any one *Key* as *c*, we have a Series of true *diatonick* Notes, in both the Species of *fharp* and *flat Key*, let a Song be begun there as the *principal Key*, and fuppofe it to change into any or all of the *confonant Keys* within that *Octave*, then 'tis plain that if a Series is fitted to all thefe *natural* Notes of the *Key c*, the Inftrument is fo perfected for *c*, that any Piece of true *diatonick Mufick* may begin there; but fuppofe, for the Accommodation of one Inftrument to another, we would begin the Piece in *g*, 'tis plain this cannot be done with the fame Accuracy as from *c* perfected as we have fuppofed, unlefs to thefe Notes that proceed *concinnoufly* from *g*, and are now confidered as the *natural* Notes of that Key, be alfo fitted other Scales for anfwering the Modulations of the Song from the *principal Key* (which is now *g*) to the other *confonant Keys*. And if we fhould but perfect Two Keys

of

of the whole Inftrument in this Manner, what a Multitude of Notes muft there be ? But I have done with this.

---

§ 4. *A brief Recapitulation of the preceeding Sections.*

THE *Amount* of all that has been faid upon this Subject of the *Syftem* of *Mufick*, with refpect to Inftruments having fixt Sounds, is in fhort this. 1*mo.* Becaufe the Degrees of the true *natural diatonick Scale* are unequal ; fo that from every Note to its *Octave* contains a different Order of *Degrees* ; therefore from any Note we cannot find any *Interval*, in a Series of fixt Sounds conftituted in thefe *Ratios* ; which yet is neceffary, that all the Notes of a Piece of *Mufick* which is carried thro' feveral Keys, may be found in their juft Tune ; or that the fame Song may be begun indifferently at any Note, as will be neceffary or at leaft very convenient for accommodating fome Inftruments to others, or thefe to the human Voice, when it is required that they accompany each other in *Unifon.* 2*do.* 'Tis impoffible that fuch a *Scale* can be found ; yet Inftruments are brought to a tolerable Perfection, by dividing every *Tone* into Two *Semitones*, making of the whole *Octave* 12 *Semitones*, which in a fingle Cafe are fenfibly e-
qual

qual. 3*tio.* These *Semitones* may be made in exact
Proportions, according to the Methods above explained; or the Instrument tun'd by the Ear, as is also explained, which reduces all to the particular
Kinds of Degrees and Order also shown above.
4*to.* The *diatonick* Series, beginning at the lowest Note, being first settled upon any Instrument,
and distinguished by their Names *a . b . c . d .*
e . f . g. the other Notes are called *fictitious*
Notes, taking the Name or Letter of the Note
below with a ✳ as *c*✳, signifying that 'tis a
Semitone higher than the Sound of *c* in the *natural* Series, or this Mark ♭ with the Name of
the Note above signifying a *Semitone* lower, as
d♭ ; which are necessary Notes in a *Scale* of
fixt Sounds, for the Purposes mentioned in the
last Article ; what Reasons make them to be
named sometimes the one, sometimes the other
Way shall be shewn afterwards ; and *observe,*
that since there is no Note betwixt *e* and *f,*
which is the *natural Semitone,* therefore *f* cannot be marked ♭, for with that Mark it would
be *e* ; nor can *e* be marked ✳, which would
raise it to *f* ; but *e* is capable of a ♭, as *f* is of a
✳. So *b . c* being the other *natural Semitone,*
b is incapable of a ✳, which would make it
coincide with *c,* but it properly takes a ♭, and
when this Mark is set alone it expresses *flat b* ;
again *c* receives not a ♭, for *e*♭ is equal to *b*
natural, but it takes a ✳. All the rest of the
Notes *d . g . a* are made either ♭ or ✳ because
they have a *Tone* on either Hand above and below. Hence it is, that *b* and *e* are said to be
naturally

naturaly ſharp, as *c* and *f* naturally *flat* ; and
yet in ſome Caſes I have ſeen *c* and *f* marked ♭,
and *b* and *e* marked ✳, which makes theſe
Letters ſo marked coincide with the natural
Notes next below and above. *3tio*. Becauſe the
Semitones are very near equal, therefore in *Practice* (upon ſuch Inſtruments at leaſt) they are
all accounted equal, ſo that no Diſtinction is
made of *Tones* into greater and leſſer ; and for
the other *Intervals* they are alſo conſidered here
without any Differences, every Number of *Semitones* having a diſtinct Name, according to the
Rule already laid down ; and therefore when a
true 3*d* or 4*th*, &c. is required from any Note,
we muſt take ſo many *Semitones* as make an
Interval of that Denomination in general, which
will in ſome Caſes be true, and in others a falſe
Interval, and cannot be otherwiſe in ſuch Inſtruments.   *4to*. The Differences among the *Semitones*, in the beſt tuned Inſtruments, is the
Reaſon that a Song will go better from one
Note or *Key* of the Inſtrument than another ;
becauſe the Errors occur more frequently in
ſome Combinations and Succeſſions of Notes
than in others ; and happen alſo in the more
principal Parts of one *Key* than another.

AND becauſe the Deſign of theſe new Notes
is not to alter the Species of the true *diatonick*
Melody, but to correct the Defects ariſing not
from the Nature of the Syſtem of *Muſick* it ſelf,
but the Accident of limiting it to fixt Sounds;
therefore beginning at any Note, if we take
an 8*ve concinnouſly* divided by *Tones* and *Semitones*

tones in the *diatonick* Order (which will be found more exact from fome Notes than others becaufe of the fmall Errors that ftill remain) that may be juftly called a *natural Series*, and all thefe Notes *natural Notes* with refpect to the Firft or *Fundamental* from which they proceed ; and yet in the common Way of fpeaking about thefe Things, no 8*ve* is called a *natural Key* that takes in any of thefe Notes marked ✳ or ♭, in order to make it a concinnous Series. And, as I have obferved in another Place, there is no *Key* called *natural* in the whole Scale but *C* and *A*. I have alfo explained that there are properly but Two Kinds of *Keys* or *Modes*, the *greater* with the 3*d g*, &c. as in the 8*ve C*, and the *leffer* with the 3*d l*, &c. as in *A* ; but whenever in any Syftem of fixt Sounds we can find a Series that is a true Key (or fo near that we take it for one)there is no other Reafon of calling that an *artificial Key*, than the arbitrary Will of thofe who explain thefe Things to us, unlefs they make the Word *artificial* include the Imperfections of thefe *Keys*, which I believe they don't mean, becaufe they fuppofe the Errors are inconfiderable ; for with refpect to the Tune or Voice, 'tis equally a natural Key, begin at what Pitch you will ; and we can fuppofe one Inftrument fo tuned as to play along *Unifon* with the Voice, and be in a *natural Key*, and in another fo tuned as that, to go *unifon* with the fame Voice, it muft take an artificial Key : But I fhall have Occafion to confider this again in the next *Chapter*, where

I

I shall also shew you what Letters or Notes must be taken in to make a true *diatonick Scale* of either Species proceeding from any one of the Twelve different Letters in this new *Scale.*

THE *diatonick* Series upon all Instruments, being kept distinct by the Seven distinct Letters, is always first learned; and because in every 8*ve* of the *diatonick Scale*, there are Two *Semitones* distant one from another by 2 Tones or 3, therefore if the first 8*ve* of the *diatonick* Series upon any Instrument is learned, by the Place of the Two *Semitones*, we shall easily know how we ought to name the first and lowest Note; for if the 3*d* and 7*th* Degrees are *Semitones*, then the first Note is *c*, if the 2*d* and 6*th* then it is *d*, and so of the rest, which are easily found by Inspection into a *Scale* carried to Two 8*ves*. And different Instruments begin at [*i. e.* their lowest Note is named by] different Letters; in some Cases because the *natural Series*, which is always most considerable, is more easily found if we begin with one particular Order of the Degrees; and in other Cases the Reason may be the making one Instrument *concord* to another. So *Flutes* begin in *f*, *Hautboys*, *Violins*, and some *Harpsichords* begin in *g*, tho' the last may be made to begin in any Letter. As to the *Violin*, let me here observe, that it is a Kind of mixt Instrument, having its Sounds partly fixed and partly unfixed: It has only Four fixt Sounds, which are the Sounds of the Four Strings untouched by the Finger, and are called *g - d - a - e.* and can with very small

Trouble

Trouble be altered to a higher or lower Pitch, which is one Conveniency ; all the reft of the Notes being made by fhortning the String with one's Finger, are thereby unfixed Sounds, and a good Ear learns to take them in perfect Tune with refpect to the preceeding Note ; fo that from any Note up or down may be found any *Interval* propofed ; and therefore we may begin a Song at any Note, with this Provifion that it be moft eafy and convenient for the Hand ; yet a Habit of Practice in every *Key* may make this Condition unneceffary. There is only this one Variation to be obferved, that by making the Four open Strings true 5*ths*, all continuous, *d-a* is here a true 5*th*, which in the *diatonick* Series wants a *Comma* ; from this follow other Variations from the Order of the *diatonick Scale* ; as here, from *g* (the firft Note of the 4*th* String) to *a* is made a greater *Tone*, that it may be a true 8*ve* below *a* the firft Note of the 2*d* String, which is occafioned by making *d-a* a true 5*th*, whereas in the *Scale g-a* is a leffer *Tone* : And fo from *a* to *b* will be made a leffer *Tone*, tho' 'tis *t g.* in the *Scale*, that *g - b* may be made a true 3*d g.* which are Advantages when we begin in *g.* The fame happens in the 3*d* String, whofe firft Note is *d,* from which to the next Note *e* will be made a *t g.* that it may be an 8*ve* to the firft Note of the firft String, yet *d : e* in the *Scale* is a *t l. Again,* if having made *d-f* on the 3*d* String a true 3*d l.* we would rife to a true 5*th* above *d,* 'tis plain *f : g* muft be a *t l.* to make *g.* a true 4*th* to *d,* and then *g : a* will

be

be a *t g*, becaufe *d-a* is a 5*th* in this Tuning;
which is plainly inverting the Order of the *Scale*,
for there *f* : *g* is *t g*. and *g* : *a* a *t l.* but ftill
this is an Advantage, that we can exprefs any
Order of Degrees from any Note; fo that fometimes we can make that a *t g.* which at other
times the *Melody* requires to be a *t l.* Yet let
me obferve in the *laft* Place, that if all thefe in-
termedia e Notes betwixt the open Sounds of
the Four Strings, be conftantly made in the
fame Tune, they become thereby fixt Sounds;
and this Inftrument will then have as great Imperfections as any other; and indeed confidering
that the ftopping of the String to take thefe
Notes in Tune is a very mechanical Thing, at
leaft the doing of it right in a quick Succeffion
of Notes muft proceed altogether from Habit,
'tis probable we take them always in the fame
Tune; nor do I believe that any Practifer on
this Inftrument dare be very pofitive on the contrary; yet I don't fay 'tis impoffible to do otherwife, for I know a Habit of playing the fame
Piece in feveral *Keys* might make one fenfible
of the contrary, if obferved with great Attention; and upon the larger Inftruments of this
Kind, that have Frets upon the Neck for directing to the right Note, it would be very fenfible; and even upon the *Violin,* we find that fome
Songs go better from one Key than another;
which proves that thofe at leaft to whom this
happens, take thefe Notes always in the fame
Tune.

HAV-

HAVING done what I propoſed for explaining the *Theory* of *Sounds* with reſpect to *Tune*, the Order ſeems to require, that I ſhould next conſider that of *Time* ; but tho' this be very conſiderable in Practice, yet there is much leſs to be ſaid about it in *Theory*; and therefore I chuſe to explain next the *Art* of *writing Muſick,* where I ſhall have Occaſion to ſay what is needful with reſpect to the TIME.

CHAP. XI.

The Method *and* Art *of* Writing Muſick, *particularly how the Differences of* Tune *are repreſented.*

---

§ 1. *A general Account of the* Method.

WHAT this Title imports has been explained in *Chap.* 1. § 2. And to come to the Thing it ſelf, let us conſider.

IT was not enough to have diſcovered ſo much of the Nature of Sound, as to make it ſerviceable to our Pleaſure, by the various Combinations

binations of the Degrees of *Tune*, and Meafures
of *Time*; it was neceffary alfo, for enlarging
the Application, to find a Method how to reprefent thefe fleeting and tranfient Objects, by
fenfible and permanent Signs; whereby they are
as it were arrefted; and what would otherwife
be loft even to the *Compofer*, he preferves for
his own Ufe, and can communicate it to others
at any Diftance; I mean he can direct them
how to raife the like Ideas to themfelves, fuppofing they know how to take Sounds in any
Relation of *Tune* and *Time* directed; for the
Bufinefs of this Art properly is, to reprefent the
various Degrees and Meafures of *Tune* and
Time in fuch a Manner, that the Connection
and Succeffion of the Notes may be eafily and
readily difcovered, and the skilful Practifer may
at Sight find his Notes, or, as they fpeak, read
any Song.

A s the Two principal Parts of *Mufick* are
the *Tune* and *Time* of Sounds, fo the Art of
writing it is very naturally reduced to Two
Parts correfponding to thefe. The firft, or the
Method of reprefenting the Degrees of *Tune*, I
fhall explain in this Chapter; which will lead me
to fay fomething in general of the other, a more
full and particular Account whereof you fhall
have in the next Chapter.

W e have already feen how the Degrees of *Tune*
or the *Scale* of *Mufick* may be expreft by 7 Letters
repeated as oft as we pleafe in a different Character; but thefe, without fome other Signs, do not
exprefs the Meafures of *Time*, unlefs we fuppofe all
the

the Notes of a Song to be of equal Length. Now, fuppofing the Thing to be made not much more difficult by thefe additional Signs of *Time*, yet the Whole is more happily accomplifhed in the following Manner.

I f we draw any Number of parallel Lines, as in *Plate* 1. *Fig.* 7. Then, from every Line to the next Space, and from every Space to the next Line up and down, reprefents a Degree of the *diatonick Scale* ; and confequently from every Line or Space to every other at greater Diftance reprefents fome other Degree of the Scale, according as the immediate Degrees from Line to Space, and from Space to Line are determined. Now to determine thefe we make Ufe of the Scale expreft by 7 Letters, as already explained, *viz.* $c:d; e.f:g;a:b.$ c-- where the Tone greater is reprefented by a Colon (:) the Tone leffer by a Semicolon (;) and the Semitone greater by a Point (.). If the Lines and Spaces are marked and named by thefe Letters, as you fee in the Figure, then according to the Relations affigned to thefe Letters (*i. e.* to the Sounds expreft by them) the Degrees and Intervals of Sound expreft by the Diftances of Lines and Spaces are determined.

As to the Extent of the *Scale* of *Mufick*, it is infinite if we confider what is fimply poffible, but for Practice, it is limited ; and in the prefent Practice 4 *Octaves*, or at moft 4 *Octaves* with a *6th*, comprehending 34 *diatonick* Notes, is the greateft Extent. There is fcarcely any

one

one Voice to be found that reaches near fo far,
tho' feveral different Voices may; nor any one
fingle Piece of *Melody*, that comprehends fo
great an Interval betwixt its higheft and loweft
Note : Yet we muft confider not only what
Melody requires, but what the Extent of feveral Voices and Inftruments is capable of, and
what the *Harmony* of feverals of them requires;
and in this refpect the whole Scale is neceffary,
which you have reprefented in the Figure directed to; I fhall therefore call it the *univerfal
Syftem*, becaufe it comprehends the whole Extent of modern Practice.

But the Queftion ftill remains, How any
particular Order and Succeffion of Sounds is reprefented ? And this is done by fetting certain
Signs and Characters one after another, up and
down on the Lines and Spaces, according to
the Intervals and Relations of *Tune* to be expreft ; *that is*, any one Letter of the Scale, or
the Line or Space to which it belongs, being
chofen to fet the firft Note on, all the reft are
fet up and down according to the Mind of the
Compofer, upon fuch Lines and Spaces as are
at the defigned Diftances, *i. e.* which exprefs
the defigned Interval according to the Number
and Kind of the intermediate Degrees; and
mind that the firft Note is taken at any convenient Pitch of *Tune*; for the Scale, or the
Lines and Spaces, ferve only to determine the
Tune of the reft with relation to the firft, leaving us to take that as we pleafe: For *Example*,
if the firft Note is placed on the Line *c*, and
the

the next defigned a *Tone* or 2*d g.* above, it if
fet on the next Space above, which is *d*; or i
it is defigned a 3*d g.* it is fet on the Line above
which is *e*; or on the fecond Line above, if it
was defigned 5*th*, as you fee reprefented in the
2*d* Column of the Scale in the preceeding Figure, where I have ufed this Character O for a
Note. And here let me obferve in general, that
thefe Characters ferve not only to direct how
to take the Notes in their true *Tune*, by the
Diftance of the Lines and Spaces on which
they are fet ; but by a fit Number and Variety
of them, (to be explained in the next Chapter)
they exprefs the *Time* and Meafure of Duration of the Notes ; whereby 'tis plain that thefe
Two Things are no way confounded ; the relative Meafures of *Tune* being properly determined by the Diftances of Lines and Spaces,
and the *Time* by the Figure of the Note or
Character.

'T is eafy to *obferve* what an Advantage
there is in this Method of Lines and Spaces,
even for fuch *Mufick* as has all its Notes of
equal Length, and therefore needs no other
Thing but the Letters of the Scale to exprefs
it ; the Memory and Imagination are here
greatly affifted, for the Notes ftanding upward
and downward from each other on the Lines
and Spaces, exprefs the rifing and falling of the
Voice more readily than different Characters of
Letters ; and the Intervals are alfo more readily
perceived.

O b-

OBSERVE in the next Place, That with
respect to Instruments of Musick, I suppose their
Notes are all named by the Letters of the Scale,
having the same Distances as already stated in
the Relations of Sounds exprest by these Letters; so that knowing how to raise a Series of
Sounds from the lowest Note of any Instrument
by *diatonick* Degrees (which is always first
learned) and naming them by the Letters of
the Scale, 'tis easily conceived how we are directed to play on any Instrument, by Notes set
upon Lines and Spaces that are named by the
same Letters. It is the Business of the Masters
and Professors of several Instruments to teach the
Application more expresly. And as to the
human Voice, observe, the Notes thereof, being confined to no Order, are called *c* or *d*, &c.
only with respect to the Direction it receives
from this Method; and that Direction is also
very plain; for having taken the first Note at
any convenient Pitch, we are taught by the
Places of the rest upon the Lines and Spaces
how to tune them in relation to the first, and
to one another.

Again, as the *artificial* Notes which divide
the *Tones* of the *natural* Series, are exprest by
the same Letters, with these Marks, ✳, ♭, already explained, so they are also plac'd on the
same Lines and Spaces, on which the *natural*
Note named by that Letter stands; thus *c*✳ and
c belong to the same Line or Space, as also
d✳ and *d*. And when the Note on any Line or
Space ought to be the *artificial* one, it is marked

ked ✖ or ♭ ; and where there is no fuch Mark
it is always the *natural* Note. Thus, if from
a (*natural*) we would fet a 3*d g.* upward, it
is *c*✖ ; or a 3*d l.* above *g*, it is *b flat* or ♭, as
you fee in the 2*d* Column of the preceeding
Figure. Thefe artificial Notes are all determined on Inftruments to certain Places or Pofitions,
with refpect to the Parts of the Inftrument and
the Hand; and for the Voice they are taken
according to the Diftance from the laft Note,
reckoned by the Number of *Tones* and *Semitones* that every greater *Interval* contains.

T H E laft general *Obferve* I make here is, that
as there are Twelve different Notes in the *femitonick Scale*, the Writing might be fo ordered, that from every Line a Space to the next
Space or Line fhould exprefs a *Semitone*; but it
is much better contrived, that thefe fhould exprefs the *Degrees* of the *diatonick Scale* (i. e.
fome *Tones* fome *Semitones*) for hereby we
can much eafier difcover what is the true *Interval* betwixt any Two Notes, becaufe there
are fewer Lines and Spaces interpofed, and the
Number of them fuch as anfwers to the Denomination of the *Intervals*; fo an *Octave* comprehends Four Lines and Four Spaces; a 5*th*
comprehends Three Lines and Two Spaces, or
Three Spaces and Two Lines ; and fo of o-
thers. I have already fhewn, how it is better
that there fhould be but Seven different Letters,
to name the Twelve Degrees of the *femitonick
Scale*; but fuppofing there were Twelve Letters, it is plain we fhould need no more Lines

to

to comprehend an *Octave*, becaufe we might
affign Two Letters to one Line or Space, as
well as to make it, for *Example*, both *c✳* and
c, whereof the one belonging to the *diatonick
Series*, fhould mark it for ordinary, and upon
Occafions the other be brought in the fame
Way we now do the Signs ✳ and ♭.

---

§ 2. *A more particular Account of the Method; where, of the* Nature *and* Ufe *of* Clefs.

THO' the *Scale* extends to Thirty Four
diatonick Notes, which require Seventeen
Lines with their Spaces, yet becaufe no one
fingle Piece of *Melody* comprehends near fo many Notes, whatever feveral Pieces joyned in one
Harmony comprehend among them ; and becaufe every Piece or fingle Song is directed or
written diftinctly by it felf ; therefore we never
draw more than Five Lines, which comprehend
the greateft Number of the Notes of any fingle
Piece ; and for thofe Cafes which require more,
we draw fhort Lines occafionally, above or below the 5, to ferve the Notes that go higher or
lower. See an *Example* in *Plate* 1. *Fig.* 8.
    AGAIN, tho' every Line and Space may be
marked at the Beginning with its Letter, as has
been done in former Times ; yet, fince the Art
has been improven, only one Line is marked,
by which all the reft are eafily known, if we
reckon up or down in the Order of the Letters ;
                                                    the

the Letter marked is called the *Clef* or *Key*, becaufe by it we know the Names of all the other Lines and Spaces, and confequently the true Quantity of every *Degree* and *Interval*. But becaufe every Note in the *Octave* is called a *Key*, tho' in another Senfe, this Letter marked is called in a particular Manner the *figned Clef*, becaufe being written on any Line, it not only *figns* or marks that one, but explains all the reft. And to prevent Ambiguity in what follows, by the Word *Clef*, I fhall always mean that Letter, which, being marked on any Line, explains all the reft; and by the Word *Key* the principal Note of any Song, in which the Melody clofes, in the Senfe explained in the laft *Chapter*. Of thefe *figned Clefs* there are Three, *viz.* *c*, *f*, *g*; and that we may know the Improvement in having but one *figned Clef* in one particular Piece, alfo how and for what Purpofe Three different *Clefs* are ufed in different Pieces, confider the following Definition.

A *Song* is either *fimple* or *compound*. It is a *fimple Song*, where only one Voice performs; or, tho' there be more, if they are all *Unifon* or *Octave*, or any other *Concord* in every Note, 'tis ftill but the fame Piece of *Melody*, performed by different Voices in the fame or different Pitches of *Tune*, for the *Intervals* of the Notes are the fame in them all. A *compound Song* is where Two or more Voices go together, with a Variety of *Concords* and *Harmony*; fo that the *Melody* each of them makes, is a diftinct and different *fimple Song*, and all together
ther

ther make the *compound*. The *Melody* that
each of them produces is therefore called a
PART of the *Compofition*; and all fuch *Compo-
fitions* are very properly called *fymphonetick
Mufick*, or *Mufick* in *Parts*; taking the Word
Mufick here for the *Compofition* or *Song* it felf.

Now, becaufe in this *Compofition* the *Parts*
muft be fome of them higher and fome lower,
(which are generally fo ordered that the fame
Part is always higheft or loweft, tho' in modern *Compofitions* they do frequently change,)
and all written diftinctly by themfelves, as is
very neceffary for the Performance; therefore
the Staff of Five Lines upon which each *Part*
is written, is to be confidered as a *Part* of the
univerfal Syftem or *Scale*, and is therefore called
a *particular Syftem*; and becaufe there are but
Five Lines ordinarily, we are to fuppofe as many above and below, as may be required for a-
ny fingle *Part*; which are actually drawn in
the particular Places where they are neceffary.

THE higheft *Part* is called the TREBLE,
or ALT whofe *Clef* is g, fet on the 2d Line of
the *particular Syftem*, counting upward: The
loweft is called the BASS, *i. e. Bafis*, becaufe
it is the Foundation of the *Harmony*, and formerly in their *plain Compofitions* the *Bafs* was
firft made, tho' 'tis otherwife now; the *Bafs-
clef* is f on the 4th Line upward: All the other
Parts, whofe particular Names you'll learn from
Practice, I fhall call MEAN PARTS, whofe
Clef is c, fometimes on one, fometimes on another Line; and fome that are really *mean*
Parts

Parts are set with the g *Clef.* See *Plate* 1.
Fig. 8. where you'll observe that the *c* and *f*
Clefs are marked with Signs no way resembling
these Letters; I think it were as well if we u-
sed the Letters themselves, but Custom has carried it otherwise; yet that it may not seem
altogether a Whim, *Kepler* in *Chap.   Book*
3*d* of his *Harmony*, has taken a critical Pains
to prove, that these Signs are only Corruptions
of the Letters they represent; the curious may
consult him.

We are next to consider the Relations of
these *Clefs* to one another, that we may know
where each *Part* lies in the *Scale* or *general System*, and the natural Relation of the *Parts* a-
mong themselves, which is the true Design and
Office of the *Clefs.* Now they are taken 5*ths*
to one another, *that is,* the *Clef f* is lowest, *c*
is a 5*th* above it, and *g* a 5*th* above *c.* See
them represented in *Plate* 1. *Fig.* 7. the last
Column of the *Scale*; and *observe,* that tho' in
the *particular Systems*, the *Treble* or *g Clef* is
ordinarily set on the 2*d* Line, the *Bass* or *f*
Clef on the 4*th* Line, and the *mean* or *c Clef*
on the 3*d* Line (especially when there are but
Three *Parts*) yet they are to be found on o-
ther Lines; as particularly the *mean Clef*, which
most frequently changes Place, because there
are many *mean Parts*, is sometimes on the 1*st*,
the 2*d*, the 3*d* or 4*th* Line; but on whatever
Line in the separate *particular System* any *Clef*
is signed, it must be understood to belong to the
same Place of the *general System*, and to be the
same

fame individual Note or Sound on the Inftrument which is directed by that *Clef*, as I have
diftinguifh'd them in the *Scale* upon the Margin
of the 3*d* Column ; fo that to know what Part
of the *Scale* any particular *Syftem* is, we muft
take its *Clef* where it ftands figned in the *Scale*
(*i. e.* the laft mentioned *Fig.*) and take as
many Lines above and below it, as there are
in the particular *Syftem*; or thus, we muft apply
the *particular Syftem* to the *Scale*, fo as the *Clef*
Lines coincide, and then we fhall fee with what
Lines of the *Scale* the other Lines of the particular *Syftem* coincide : For *Example*, if we find
the *Clef* on the 3*d* Line upward, in a *particular Syftem* ; to find the coincident Five Lines
to which it refers in the *Scale*, we take with
the *f Clef* Line, Two Lines above and Two
below. Again, if we have the *c Clef* on the
4*th* Line, we are to take in the *Scale* with the
Clef Line, One Line above and Three below,
and fo of others; fo that according to the different Places of the *Clef* in a particular *Syftem*,
the Lines in the *Scale* correfpondent to that
Syftem may be all different, except the *Clef*
Line which is invariable : And that you may
with Eafe find in the *Scale* the Five Lines coincident with every particular *Syftem*, upon
whatever Line of the Five the *Clef* may be fet,
I have drawn Nine Lines acrofs, which include
each Five Lines of the *Scale*, in fuch a Manner, that you have the *particular Syftems* diftinguifhed for every relative Pofition of any of
the Three figned *Clefs*.

A s

As to the Reaſon of changing the relative Place of the *Clef*, *i. e.* its Place in the *particular* Syſtem, 'tis only to make this comprehend as many Notes of the Song as poſſible, and by that Means to have fewer Lines above or below it ; ſo if there are many Notes above the *Clef* Note and few below it, this Purpoſe is anſwered by placing the *Clef* in the firſt or ſecond Line ; but if the Song goes more below the *Clef*, then it is beſt placed higher in the Syſtem : *In ſhort*, according to the Relation of the ot er Notes to the *Clef* Note, the *particular Syſtem* is taken differently in the *Scale*, the *Clef* Line making one in all the Variety, which conſiſts only in this, *viz.* taking any Five Lines immediately next other, whereof the *Clef* Line muſt always be one.

By this conſtant and invariable Relation of the *Clefs*, we learn eaſily how to compare the particular Syſtems of ſeveral *Parts*, and know how they communicate in the *Scale*, *i. e.* which Lines are *uniſon*, and which are different, and how far, and conſequently what Notes of the ſeveral Parts are *uniſon*, and what not : For you are not to ſuppoſe that each *Part* has a certain Bounds within which another muſt never come; no, ſome Notes of the *Treble*, for *Example*, may be lower than ſome of the *mean Parts*, or even of the *Baſs* ; and that not only when we compare ſuch Notes as are not heard together, but even ſuch as are. And if we would put together in one Syſtem, all the *Parts* of any Compoſition that are written ſeparately. The Rule

is

is plainly this, *viz.* Place the Notes of each
Part at the fame Diſtances above and below the
proper *Clef*, as they ſtand in the ſeparate Syſtem.
And becauſe all the Notes that are conſonant
(or heard together) ought to ſtand, in this Deſign, perpendicularly over each other, therefore
that the Notes belonging to each *Part* may be
diſtinctly known, they may be made with ſuch
Differences as ſhall not confuſe or alter their Significations with reſpect to Time, and only ſignify that they belong to ſuch a *Part* ; by this
Means we ſhall ſee how all the *Parts* change
and paſs thro' one another, *i. e.* which of them,
in every Note, is higheſt or loweſt or *uniſon* ;
for they do ſometimes change, tho' more generally the *Treble* is higheſt and the *Baſs* loweſt,
the Change happening more ordinarily betwixt
the *mean Parts* among themſelves, or theſe
with the *Treble* or *Baſs* : The *Treble* and *Baſs*
Clefs are diſtant an *Octave* and *Tone*, and their
Parts do ſeldom interfere, the *Treble* moving
more above the *Clef* Note, and the *Baſs* below.

WE ſee plainly then, that the Uſe of particular ſign'd *Clefs* is an Improvement with reſpect to the *Parts* of any *Compoſition* ; for unleſs ſome one Key in the particular Syſtems were
diſtinguiſhed from the reſt, and referred invariably and conſtantly to one Place in the *Scale*,
the Relations of the *Parts* could not be diſtinctly marked ; and that more than one is neceſſary, is plain from the Diſtance there muſt be a-
mong the Parts : Or if one Letter is choſen for
all,

all, there muſt be ſome other Sign to ſhew
what *Part* it belongs to, and the Relation of
the Parts. Experience having approven the Number and Relations of the ſigned *Clefs* which are
explained, I ſhall add no more as to that, but
there are other Things to be here obſerved.

Tʜᴇ chooſing theſe Letters *f . c . g* for ſigned *Clefs*, is a Thing altogether arbitrary; for
any other Letter within the Syſtem, will explain
the reſt as well; yet 'tis fit there be a conſtant
Rule, that the ſeveral *Parts* may be right diſtinguiſhed; and concerning this *obſerve* again,
that for the Performance of any ſingle Piece the
Clef ſerves only for explaining the *Invervals* a-
mong the Lines and Spaces, ſo that we need
not mind what Part of any greater Syſtem it is,
and we may take the firſt Note as high or low
as we pleaſe: For as the proper Uſe of the *Scale*
is not to limit the abſolute Degree of *Tone*, ſo
the proper Uſe of the ſigned *Clef* is not to limit
the Pitch, at which the firſt Note of any *Part*
is to be taken, but to determine the *Tune* of
the reſt with relation to the firſt, and, conſidering all the *Parts* together, to determine the
Relations of their ſeveral Notes, by the Relations
of their *Clefs* in the *Scale* : And ſo the Pitch of
Tune being determined in a certain Note of one
Part, the other Notes of that *Part* are determined, by the conſtant Relations of the Letters
of the *Scale*; and alſo the Notes of the other
Parts, by the Relations of their *Clefs*. To
ſpeak particularly of the Way of tuning the Inſtruments that are employed in executing the
ſeveral

feveral *Parts*, is out of my Way ; I fhall only fay this, that they are to be fo tuned as the *Clef* Notes, wherever they ly on the Inftruments which ferve each *Part*, be in the forementioned Relations to one another.

As the *Harpfichord* or *Organ* (or any other of the Kind) is the moft extenfive Inftrument, we may be helped by it to form a clearer *Idea* of thefe Things : For confider, a *Harpfichord* contains in itfelf all the *Parts* of *Mufick*, I mean the whole *Scale* or *Syftem* of the modern Practice ; the foremoft Range of Keys contains the *diatonick* Series beginning, in the largeft Kind, in *g*, and extending to *c* above the Fourth *8ve*; which therefore we may well fuppofe reprefented by the preceeding *Scale*. In Practice, upon that Inftrument, the *Clef* Notes are taken in the Places reprefented in the Scheme ; and other Inftruments are fo tuned, that, confidering the *Parts* they perform, all their Notes of the fame Name are *unifon* to thofe of the *Harpfichord* that belong to the fame *Part*. I have faid, the *Harpfichord* contains all the *Parts* of Mufick ; and indeed any Two diftinct *Parts* may be performed upon it at the fame Time and no more; yet upon Two or more *Harpfichords* tuned *unifons*, whereby they are in Effect but one, any Number of *Parts* may be executed : And in this Cafe we fhould fee the feveral *Parts* taken in their proper Places of the Inftrument, according to the Relations of their *Clefs* explained : And as to the tuning the Inftrument, I fhall only add, that there is a certain Pitch to which

it

it is brought, that it may be neither too *high* nor too *low*, for the Accompaniment of other Inftruments, and efpecially for the human Voice, whether in *Unifon* or taking a different *Part* ; and this is called the CONSORT PITCH. To have done, you muft confider, that for performing any one fingle *Part*, we may take the *Clef* Note in any 8*ve*, *i. e.* at any Note of the fame Name, providing we go not too high or too low for finding the reft of the Notes of the Song: But in a *Confort* of feveral *Parts*, all the *Clefs* muft be taken, not only in the Relations, but alfo in the Places of the Syftem already mentioned, that every Part may be comprehended in it : Yet ftill you are to mind, That the *Tune* of the Whole, or the abfolute Pitch, is in it felf an arbitrary Thing, quite foreign to the Ufe of the *Scale* ; tho' there is a certain Pitch generally agreed upon, that differs not very much in the Practice of any one Nation or Set of Muficians from another. And therefore,

WHEN I fpeak of the Place of the *Clefs* in the *Scale* or *general Syftem*, you muft underftand it with refpect to a *Scale* of a certain determined Extent; for this being undetermined, fo muft the Places of the *Clefs* be : And for any *Scale* of a certain Extent, the *Rule* is, that the *mean Clef c* be taken as near the Middle of the *Scale* as poffible, and then the *Clef g* a 5*th* above, and *f* a 5*th* below, as it is in the prefent *general Syftem* of Four 8*ves* and a 6*th*, reprefented in the preceeding Scheme, and actually determined upon *Harpfichords.*

IN

IN the *laſt Place* conſider, that ſince the
Lines and Spaces of the *Scale*, with the Degrees
ſtated among them by the Letters, ſufficiently
determine how far any Note is diſtant from a-
nother, therefore there is no Need of different
Characters of Letters, as would be if the Scale
were only expreſt by theſe Letters : And when
we ſpeak of any Note of the *Scale*, naming it
by *a* or *b*, &c. we may explain what Part of
the *Scale* it is in, either by numbring the *8ves*
from the loweſt Note, and calling the Note ſpoken of (for *Example*) *c* in the loweſt *8ve* or in
the *2d 8ve*, and ſo on : Or, we may determine
its Place by a Reference to the Seat of any of
the Three *ſigned Clefs* ; and ſo we may ſay of
any Note, as *f* or *g*, that it is ſuch a *Clef* Note,
or the firſt or ſecond, *&c. f* or *g* above ſuch a
Clef. Take this Application, ſuppoſe you ask
me what is the higheſt Note of my Voice, if
I ſay *d*, you are not the wiſer by this Anſwer,
till I determine it by ſaying it is *d* in the fourth
Octave, or the firſt *d* above the *Treble Clef*. But
again, neither this Queſtion nor the Anſwer is
ſufficiently determined, unleſs it have a Reference to ſome ſuppoſed Pitch of *Tune* in a certain fixt Inſtrument, as the ordinary *Conſort
Pitch* of a *Harpſichord*, becauſe, as I have frequently ſaid, the *Scale* of *Muſick* is concerned
only with the Relation of Notes and the Order
of Degrees, which are ſtill the ſame in all Differences of *Tune*, in the whole Series.

§. 3.

§ 3. *Of the* Reafon, Ufe, *and* Variety *of the* Signatures *of* CLEFS.

I Have already faid, that the *natural* and *arti-ficial* Note expreffed by the fame Letter, as *c* and *c✳*, are both fet on the fame Line or Space. When there is no ✳ or ♭ marked on any Line or Space, at the Beginning with the *Clef*, then all the Notes are natural; and if in any particular Place of the Song, the artificial Note is required, 'tis fignified by the Sign ✳ or ♭, fet upon the Line a Space before that Note; but if a ✳ or ♭ is fet at the Beginning in any Line or Space with the *Clef*, then all the Notes on that Line or Space are the artificial ones, *that is*, are to be taken a *Semitone* higher or lower than they would be without fuch a Sign; the fame affects all their 8*ves* above or below, tho' they are not marked fo. And in the Courfe of the Song, if the natural Note is fometimes required, it is fignified by this Mark ♮. And the marking the *Syftem* at the Beginning with Sharps or Flats, I call the *Signature* of the *Clef*.

IN what's faid, you have the plain *Rule* for Application; but that we may better conceive the Reafon and Ufe of thefe Signatures, it will be neceffary to recollect, and alfo make a little clearer, what has been explained of the Nature of *Keys* or *Modes*, and of the Original and Ufe of the *fharp* and *flat* Notes in the *Scale*. I have

in

in *Chap.* 9. explained what a *Key* and *Mode*
in *Mufick* is ; I have diftinguifhed betwixt thefe
Two, and fhewn that there are and can be but
Two different *Modes*, the *greater* and the *leffer*,
according to the Two *concinnous* Divifions of the
8*ve*,*viz.* by the 3*d g.* or the 3*d l.* and their proper
Accompanyments; and whatever Difference you
may make in the abfolute Pitch of the whole
Notes, or of the firft Note which limites all the
reft, the fame individual Song muft ftill be in
the fame *Mode* ; and by the *Key* I underftand
only that Pitch or Degree of *Tune* at which
the *fundamental* or clofe Note of the *Melody*,
and confequently the whole 8*ve* is taken ; and
becaufe the *Fundamental* is the principal Note
of the 8*ve* which regulates the reft, it is peculiarly called the *Key*. Now as to the Variety
of *Keys*, if we take the Thing in fo large a
Senfe as to fignify the abfolute Pitch of *Tune*
at which any fundamental Note may be taken,
the Number is at leaft indefinite; but in Practice
it is limited, and particularly with refpect to
the Denominations of *Keys*, which are only
Twelve, *viz.* the Twelve different Names or
Letters of the *femitonick Scale* ; fo we fay the
Key of a Song is *c* or *d*, &c. which fignifies
that the *Cadence* or *Clofe* of the *Melody* is upon
the Note of that Name when we fpeak of any
Inftrument ; and with refpect to the human
Voice, that the clofe Note is *Unifon* to fuch a Note
on an Inftrument ; and generally, with refpect
both to Inftruments and Voice, the Denomination of the *Key* is taken from the Place of the
                                                 clofe

cloſe Note upon the written *Muſick, i. e.* the
Name of the Line or Space where it ſtands :
Hence we ſee, that tho' the Difference of *Keys*
refers to the Degree of *Tune*, at which the *Fundamental*, and conſequently the whole 8*ve* is
taken, in Diſtinction from the *Mode* or Conſtitution of an *Octave*, yet theſe Denominations determine the Differences only relative y, with
reſpect to one certain Series of fixt Sounds, as a
Scale of Notes upon a particular Inſtrument, in
which all the Notes of different Names are different *Keys*, according to the general Definition,
becauſe of their different Degrees of *Tune*; but
as the tuning of the whole may be in a different
Pitch, and the Notes taken in the ſame Part of
the Inſtrument, are, without reſpect to the tuning of the Whole, ſtill called by the ſame Names
c or *d*, &c. becauſe they ſerve only to mark
the Relation of *Tune* betwixt the Notes, therefore 'tis plain, that in Practice a Song will be ſaid
to be in the ſame *Key* as to the Denomination,
tho' the abſolute *Tune* be different, and to be in
different *Keys* when the abſolute *Tune* is the
ſame; as if the Note *a* is made the *Key* in one
Tuning, and in another the Note *d uniſon*
to *a* of the former. Now, this is a Kind of Limitation of the general Definition, yet it ſerves
the Deſign beſt for Practice, and indeed cannot be otherwiſe without infinite Confuſion. I
ſhall a little below make ſome more particular
Remarks upon the Denominations of Sounds or
Notes raiſed from Inſtruments or the human
Voice: But from what has been explained, you'll
easily

eafily underftand what Difference I put betwixt
a *Mode* and a *Key*; of *Modes* there are only
Two, and they refpect what I would call the
Internal Conftitution of the 8*ve*, but *Keys* are
indefinite in the more general and abftract Senfe,
and with regard to their Denominations in
Practice they are reduced to Twelve, and have
refpect to a Circumftance that's *external* and
accidental to the *Mode*;and therefore a *Key* may
be changed under the fame *Mode*, as when the
fame Song,which is always in the fame *Mode*, is
taken up at different Notes or Degrees of *Tune*,
and from the fame *Fundamental* or *Key* a Series
may proceed in a different *Mode*, as when different Songs begin in the fame Note. But then
becaufe common Ufe applies the Word *Key* in
both Senfes, *i. e.* both to what I call a *Key* and
a *Mode*, to prevent Ambiguity the Word *fharp*
or *flat* ought to be added when we would exprefs the *Mode*; fo that a *fharp Key* is the fame
as a greater *Mode*, and a *flat Key* a leffer *Mode*;
and when we would exprefs both *Mode* and
Key, we joyn the Name of the *Key* Note, thus,
we may fay fuch a Song is for *Example* in the
fharp or *flat Key c*, to fignifie that the fundamental Note in which the Clofe is made is
the Note called *c* on the Inftrument, or *unifon* to it in the Voice ; or generally, that
it is fet on the Line or Space of that Name
in Writing ; and that the 3*d g.* or 3*d l.* is ufed
in the *Melody*, while the Song keeps within that
Key; for I have alfo obferved, that the fame
Song may be carried thro' different *Keys*, or
make

make fucceffive *Cadences* in different Notes,
which is commonly ordered by bringing in fome
Note that is none of the natural Notes of the
former *Key*, of which more immediately : But
when we hear of any *Key* denominated *c* or *d*
without the Word *fharp* or *flat*, then we can
underftand nothing but what I have called the
Key in Diftinction from the *Mode*, *i. e.* that the
Cadence is made in fuch a Note.

AGAIN, I have in *Chap.* 10. explained the
Ufe of the Notes we call *fharp* and *flat*, or *artificial* Notes, and the Diftinction of *Keys* in that
refpect into *natural* and *artificial*; I have fhewn
that they are neceffary for correcting the Defects of Inftruments having fixt Sounds, that beginning at any Note we may have a true concinnous *diatonick* Series from that Note, which
in a *Scale* of fixt Degrees in the 8*ve* we cannot
have, all the Orders of Degrees proceeding from
each of the Seven *natural* Notes being different,
of which only Two are concinnous, *viz.* from
c which makes a *fharp Key*, and from *a* which
makes a *flat Key* ; and to apply this more particularly, you muft underftand the Ufe of thefe
fharp or *flat* Notes to be this, that a Song,
which, being fet in a *natural Key* or without *Sharps* and *Flats*, is either too high
or too low, may be tranfpofed or fet in another more convenient *Key* ; which neceffarily
brings in fome of the artificial Notes, in order to make a *diatonick* Series from this
new *Key*, like that from the other ; and when
the Song changes the *Key* before it come to the
                                                    final

final Clofe, tho' the principal *Key* be natural,
yet fome of thefe into which it changes may
require artificial Notes, which are the effential
and natural Notes of this new *Key*; for tho'
this be called an artificial Key, 'its only fo with
refpect to the Names of the Notes in the fixt
Syftem, which are ftill natural with refpect to
their proper *Fundamental*, viz. the *Key* into
which the Piece is tranfpofed, or into which it
changes where the principal *Key* is natural.

AND even with refpect to the human Voice,
which is under no Limitation, I have fhewn the
Neceffity of thefe Names, for the fake of a regular, diftinct and eafy Reprefentation of Sounds,
for directing the Voice in Performance. I fhall next
more particularly explain by fome Examples, the
Bufinefs of keeping in and going out of *Keys*. *Example.* Suppofe a Song begins in *c*, or at leaft
makes the firft Clofe in it; if all the Notes
preceeding that Clofe are in true mufical Relation to *c* as a *Fundamental* in one Species, fuppofe as a *fharp Key*, *i. e.* with a 3*d g.* the Melody has been ftill in that *Key* (See *Example* 5.
Plate 3.) But if proceeding, the Compofer brings
in the Note *f*✳ he leads the *Melody* out of the
former *Key*, becaufe *f*✳ is none of the natural
Notes of the 8*ve c*, being a falfe 4*th* to *c*. A-
gain, he may lead it out of the *Key* without
any falfe Note, by bringing in one that belongs
not to the Species in which the Melody was
begun: Suppofe after beginning in the *fharp
Key c*, he introduces the Note *g*✳, which is a
6*th l.* to *c*, and therefore harmonious, yet it belongs

longs to it as a *flat Key*, and confequently is
out of the *Key* as a *fharp* one: And becaufe the
fame Song cannot with any good Effeā be made
to clofe twice in the fame Note in a different
Species, therefore after introducing the Note *g*✳,
the next Clofe muft be in fome other Note as *a*,
and then the *Key* in both Senfes will be changed, becaufe *a* has naturally a 3*d l* ; and therefore when any Note is faid to be out of a *Key*,
'tis underftood to be out of it either as making
a falfe *Interval*, or as belonging to it in another
Species than a fuppofed one, *i. e.* if it belong to
it as a *fharp Key*, 'tis out of it as a *flat* one ; fo in
Example 3. *Plate* 3. the firft Clofe is in *a* as a
fharp Key, all the preceeding Notes being natural to it as fuch ; then proceeding in the fame
Key, you fee *g* (*natural*) introduced, which
belongs not to *a* as a *fharp Key*, and alfo *a*✳, which is quite out of the former
Key : By thefe Notes a Clofe is brought on
in *b*, and the *Melody* is faid to be out of the
firft *Key*, and is fo in both Senfes of the Word
Key, for *b* here has a 3*d l* ; then the *Melody* is
carried on to a Clofe in *d*, which is a Third
Key, and with refpeā to that Piece is indeed
the *principal Key*, in which alfo the Piece begins ; but I fhall confider this again ; it was e-
nough to my Purpofe here, that all the Notes
from the Beginning to the firft Clofe in *a* were
natural to the *Oāave* from *a* with a 3*d g* ; and
tho' the 3*d g.* above the Clofe is not ufed in the
Example, yet the 6*th l.* below it is ufed, which
is the fame Thing in determining the Species.

I

I have explained already, that with the 3*d l.*
the *6th l.* and *7th l,*or *6th g.* and *7th g.* are ufed
in different Circumftances ; and therefore you
are to mind that the *6th g.*or *7th g.* being introduced upon a *flat Key*, does not make any
Change of it ; fo that tho' the *6th l.* and *7th l.*
is a certain Sign of a *flat Key*, yet the *6th g.*
and *7th g.* belong to either Species ; therefore
the Species is only certainly determined by the
3*d* in both Cafes; and fo in the preceeding *Example*, where I fuppofe *g*✳ is introduced upon
the *fharp Key c*, the next Clofe cannot be in
c, becaufe *g*✳ being a *6th l*, to *c*, requires a 3*d
l.* which would altogether deftroy that Unity of
Melody which ought to be kept up in every
Song; therefore when I fay the fame Song cannot clofe twice in one Note in different Species,
the Determination of that Difference depends on
the 3*d*, which being the *greater*, muft always have
the *6th g.* and *7th g.* but the 3*d l.* takes fometimes
the *6th l.* and *7th l.* fometime the *6th g.* and
7th g. See *Ex.* 6. *Plate* 3. where the whole keeps
within the *flat Key a*, and clofes twice in it; the
firft Clofe is brought on with the *6th l.*and *7th l.*
the next Clofe in the *Octave* above is made
with the *6th g.* and 8*th g.* but a Clofe in *a*, u-
fing the 3*d g.* would quite ruine the Unity of
the *Melody;* yet the fame Song may be carried
into different *Keys*, of which fome are *fharp*,
fome *flat*, without any Prejudice ; but of all
thefe there muft be one *principal Key*, in
which the Song fets out, and makes moft frequent *Cadences*, and at leaft the *final Cadence*.

                                    THE

THE laſt Thing I ſhall *obſerve* upon this Subject of *Keys* is, that ſometimes the *Key* is changed, without bringing the *Melody* to a *Cadence* in the *Key* to which it is transferred, *that is,* a Note is introduced, which belongs properly to another *Key* than that in which the *Melody* exiſted before, yet no *Cadenc* made in that *Key*; as if after a *Cadence* in the *ſharp Key c,* the Note *g✳* is brought in, which ſhould naturally lead to a Cloſe in *a,* yet the *Melody* may be turned off without any formal and perfect *Cloſe* in *a,* and brought to its next Cloſe in another *Key.*

I return now to explain the Reaſon and Uſe of the *Signatures* of *Clefs.* And *firſt,* Let us ſuppoſe any Piece of *Melody* confined ſtrictly to one *Mode* or *Key,* and let that be the natural *ſharp Key c,* from which as the Relation of the Letters are determined in the *Scale,* there is a true *muſical* Series and Gradation of Notes, and therefore it requires no ✳ or ♭, conſequently the Signature of the *Clef* muſt be plain: But let the Piece be tranſpoſed to the *Key d,* it muſt neceſſarily take *f✳* inſtead of *f,* and *c✳* for *c,* becauſe *f✳* is the true 3*dg.* and *c✳* the true 7*th g.* to *d.* See an *Example* in *Plate* 3. *Fig.* 5. Now if the *Clef* be not ſigned with a ✳ on the Seat of *f* and *c,* we muſt ſupply it wherever theſe Notes occur thro' the Piece, but 'tis plainly better that they be marked once for all at the Beginning.

AGAIN, ſuppoſe a Piece of *Melody,* in which there is a Change of the *Key* or *Mode*; if the
same

fame *Signature* anfwer all thefe *Keys*, there is
no more Queftion about it ; but if that cannot
be, then the *Signature* ought to be adjufted to
the *principal Key*, rather than to any other,
as in *Example* 3. *Plate* 3. in which the *princi-*
pal Key is *d* with a 3*dg.* and becaufe this demands *f✱* and *c✱* for its 3*d* and 7*th*, therefore
the Signature expreffeth them. 'The Piece aftual-
ly begins in the *principal Key*, tho' the firft
Clofe is made in the 5*th* above, *viz.* in *a*, by
bringing in *g✱* ; which is very naturally managed, becaufe all the Notes from the Beginning
to that Clofe belong to both the *fharp Keys d*
and *a*, except that *g✱* which is the only Note
in which they can differ; then you fee the *Me-*
lody proceeds for fome time in Notes that are
common to both thefe *Keys*, tho' indeed the
Impreffion of the laft *Cadence* will be ftrongeft ;
and then by bringing *g* (natural) and *a✱*, it
leaves both the former *Keys* to clofe in *b*; and
here again there is as great a Coincidence with
the *principal Key* as poffible, for the *flat Key*
b has every one of its effential Notes common
with fome one of thefe of the *fharp Key d*, except *a✱* and *g✱* the 6*thg.* and 7*th g.* which that
flat Key may occafionally make ufe of; but as
it is managed here, the 6*th l.* is ufed, fo that it
differs from the *principal Key* only in one Note
a✱ ; then the *Melody* is after this Clofe immediately transferred to the *principal Key*, making there the *final Cadence.* In what Notes every
Key differs from or coincides with any other,
you may learn from the *Scale* of *Semitones* ;
                                          but

but you shall see this more easily in a following *Table*.

To proceed with our *Signatures*, you have, in what's said, the true Use and Reason of the *Signatures* of *Clefs*; in respect of which they are distinguished into *natural*, and *artificial* or *transposed Clefs*; the first is when no ✳ or ♭ is set at the Beginning; and when there are, it is said to be *transposed*. We shall next consider the *Variety* of *Signatures* of *Clefs*, which in all are but 12. and the most reasonable Way of making the artificial Notes, either in the general Signature, or where they occur upon the Change of the *Key*.

In the *semitonick Scale* there are 12 different Notes in an *Octave* (for the 13*th* is the same with the 1*st*) each of which may be made the *Fundamental* or *Key* of a Song, *i. e.* from each of them we can take a Series of Notes, that shall proceed *concinnously* by Seven *diatonick Degrees* of *Tones* and *Semitones* to an *Octave*, in the Species either of a *sharp* or *flat Key*, or of a *greater* or *lesser Mode* (the small Errors of this *Scale* as it is fixt upon Instruments, being in all this Matter neglected.) Now, making each of these 12 Letters or Notes a *Fundamental* or *Key*-note, there must be in the Compass of an *Octave* from each, more or fewer, or different *Sharps* and *Flats* necessarily taken in to make a *concinnous* Series of the same Species, *i. e.* proceeding by the greater or lesser 3*d* (for these specify the *Mode*, and determine the other Differences, as has been explained); and since from every one of the 12 *Keys* we may proceed *con-*
cinnous-

cinnoufly, either with a greater or leffer 3*d*, and
their Accompanyments, it appears at firft Sight,
that there muft be 24 different *Signatures* of
Clefs, but you'll eafily underftand that there are
but 12. For the fame *Signature* ferves Two
different *Keys*, whereof the one is a *fharp* and
the other a *flat Key*, as you fee plainly in the
Nature of the *diatonick Scale*, in which the O-
Elave from *c* proceeds *concinnoufly* by a 3*dg.*
and that from *a* (which is a 6*thg.* abcve, or a
3*dl.* below *c*) by a 3*dl.* with the 6*th l.* and 7*th
l.* for its Accompanyments, which I fuppofe here
effential to all *flat Keys* ; confequently, if we
begin at any other Letter, and by the Ufe of ✳
or ♭ make a *concinnous diatonick Series* of either Kind, we fhall have in the fame Series,
continued from the 6*th* above or 3*d* below, an
Elave of the other Species; therefore there can be
but 12 different *Signatures* of *Clefs*, whereof 1 is
plain or *natural*, and 11 *tranfpofed* or *artificial*.

WHAT the proper Notes of thefe *tranfpofed
Clefs* are, you may find thus ; let the *Scale* of
Semitones be continned to Two *Oltaves*, then
begin at every Letter, and, reckoning Two *Semitones* to every *Tone*, take Two *Tones* and
one *Semitone*, then Three *Tones* and one *Semitone*, which is the Order of a *fharp Key* or
of the natural *Oltave* from *c*, the Letters which
terminate thefe *Tones* and *Semitones*, are the
effential or natural Notes of the *Key* or *Oltave*,
whofe *Fundamental* is the Letter or Note you
begin at: By this you'll find the Notes beong-
ing to every *fharp Key* ; and thefe being continued,

nued, you'll have alfo the Notes belonging to e-
very *flat Key*, by taking the *6th* above the
fharp Key for the *Fundamental* of the *flat* : But
to fave you the Trouble, I have collected them
in one *Table*. See *Plate* 2. *Fig.* 1. The *Table*
has Two Parts, and the upper Part contains 16
Columns : From the 3 to the 14 inclufive, you have
expreft in each an *Octave*, proceeding from fome
the 12 Notes of different Names within the
femitonick Scale, the *Fundamental* whereof you
take in the lower End of the Column, and reading it upward, you have all the Letters or
Names belonging to that *Octave* in a diatonick
Scale, in the Species of a *fharp Key* : In the
1ft Column on the left Hand you have the Degrees marked in *Tones* and *Semitones*, without
any Diftinction of greater and leffer *Tone* : In
the Fifth Column, you have the Denominations of the *Intervals* from the *Fundamental*.
Then for the 12 *flat Keys* take, as I faid before, the *6ths* above the other, and they are
the *Fundamentals* of the *flat Keys*, whofe
Notes are all found by continuing the Scale
upward : But as to finding the Note where
any *Interval* ends, 'tis as well done by counting
downward; for fince 'tis always an *Octave* from
any Letter to the fame again, and alfo fince a
7th upward falls in the fame Letter with a *2d*
downward, a *6th* upward in the fame with a *3d*
downward, and a *3d* upward in the fame with
a *6th* downward, alfo a *4th* or *5th* upward
in the fame with a *5th* or *4th* downward;
therefore in the 16th Column, you fee *Key flat*
written

written againſt the Line in which the *6ths* of
the 12 *ſharp Keys* ſtand ; and the Denomination of the *Intervals* are written againſt theſe
Notes where they terminate ; and becauſe the
Scale in that Table is carried but to one
Octave, ſo that we have only a 3*d l.* above the
Fundamental of the *flat Key,* therefore the reſt
of the *Intervals* are marked at the Letters below, which will be eaſier underſtood if you'll
ſuppoſe the Key to ſtand below, and theſe *Intervals* to be reckoned upwards. In the 2*d*
Part of the *Table* you have a Syſtem of 5 Lines
marked with the *Treble* or *g Clef,* in 13 Diviſions
each anſwering to a Column of the upper Part;
and theſe expreſs all the various *Signatures* of
the *Clef, that is,* all the *accidental* or *ſharp*
and *flat* Notes that belong to any of the 12 *Keys*
of the *Scale.*

WITH Reſpect to the Names and Signatures in
the Table, there remain ſome Things to be explained : I told you in the laſt *Chapter* that
upon the main it was an indifferent Thing whether the artificial Notes in the Scale were named from the Note below with a ✻, or from that
above with a ♭ : Here you have each of them
marked, in ſome Signatures ✻ and in others ♭ ;
but in every particular Signature the Marks are
all of one Kind ✻ or ♭, tho' one Signature is ✻,
and another ♭ ; and theſe are not ſo ordered at random; the Reaſon I ſhall explain to
you : In the firſt Place there is a greater Harmony with reſpect to the Eye ; but this is a
ſmall Matter, a better Reaſon follows ; *conſi-*
der,

der, every Letter has two Powers, *i. e.* is capable of reprefenting Two Notes, according as you take it *natural* or plain, as *c*, *d*, &c. or *tranfpofed* as *c✳* or *d♭* ; again, every Line and Space is the Seat of one particular Letter : Now if we take Two Powers of one Letter in the fame *Octave* or *Key*, the Line or Space to which it belongs muft have Two different Signs ; and then when a Note is fet upon that Line or Space, how fhall it be known whether it is to be taken *natural* or *tranfpofed?* This can only be done by fetting the proper Signs at every fuch Note ; which is not only troublefom, but renders the general Signature ufelefs as to that Line or Space : This is the Reafon why fome Signatures are made ✳ rather than ♭, and contrarily ; for *Example*, take for the *Fundamental c✳*, the reft of the Notes to make a *fharp Key* are *d✳* . *f* : *f✳* : *g✳* : *a✳* : *c*. where you fee *f* and *c* are taken both *natural* and *tranfpofed*, which we avoid by making all the artificial Note ♭, as in the Table, thus *d♭* : *e♭* . *f* : *g♭* : *a♭* : ♭ : *c* . *d♭*. 'Tis true that this might be helped another Way, *viz.* by taking all the Notes ✳ *i. e.* taking *e✳* for *f*, and *b✳* for *c* ; but the Inconveniency of this is vifible, for hereby we force Two natural Notes out of their Places, whereby the Difficulty of performing by fuch Direction is increafed : In the other Cafes where I have marked all ♭ rather than ✳, the fame Reafons obtain : And in fome Cafes, fome Ways of figning with ✳ would have both thefe Inconveniencies. The fame Reafons make it
necefary

neceſſary to have ſome Signature ✳ rather than
♭; but the *Octave* beginning in g♭ is ſingular
in this Reſpect, that it is equal which Way it
is ſigned, for in both there will be one natural
Note diſplaced unavoidably; as I have it in
the Table *b* natural is ſigned c♭, and if you
make all the Signs ✳, you muſt either take in
Two Powers of one Letter, or take e✳ for *f*.
Now neither in this, nor any of the other
Caſes will the mixing of the Signs remove the
Inconveniencies; and ſuppoſe it could, another
follows upon the Mixture, which leads me to
ſhew why the ſame Clef is either all ✳ or all ♭,
the Reaſon follows.

THE Quantity of an *Interval* expreſt by
Notes ſet upon Lines and Spaces marked ſome
✳, ſome ♭, will not be ſo eaſily diſcovered, as
when they are all marked one Way, becauſe
the Number of intermediate Degrees from Line
to Space, and from Space to Line, anſwers not
to the Denomination of the *Interval*; for *Example*, if it is a 5*th*, I ſhall more readily diſcover it when there are 5 intermediate Degrees
from Line to Space, than if there were but 4;
thus, from g✳ to d✳ is a 5*th*, and will appear
as ſuch by the Degrees, among the Lines and
Spaces; but if we mark it g✳, e♭, it will have
the Appearance of a 4*th*; alſo from f✳ to a✳
is a 3*d*, and appears ſo, whereas from f✳ to ♭
looks like a 4*th*; and for that Reaſon Mr.
Simpſon in his *Compend of Muſick* calls it a leſſer 4*th*, which I think he had better called an
apparent 4*th*; and ſo by making the Signs of the

Clef

Clef all of one Kind, this Inconveniency is faved with refpect to all *Intervals* whofe both Extremes have a tranfpofed Letter; and as to fuch *Intervals* which have one Extreme a *natural* Note, or expreft by a plain Letter, and the other *tranfpofed*, the Inconveniency is prevented by the Choice of the ✸ in fome *Keys*, and of the ♭ in others; for *Example*, from *d* to *f*✸ is a 3*dg*. equal to that from *d* to *g*♭, but the firft only appears like a 3*d*, and fo of other *Intervals* from *d*, which therefore you fee in the Table are all figned ✸. *Again* from *f* to ♭ or *f* to *a*✸ is a 4*th*, but the firft is the beft Way of marking it; there are no more tranfpofed Notes in that *Octave*, nor any other *Octave*, whofe *Fundamental* is a natural Note, that is marked with ♭.

It muft be owned, after all, That whatever Way we chufe the Signs of tranfpofed Notes, the Sounds or Notes themfelves on an Inftrument are individually the fame; and marking them one Way rather than another, refpects only the Conveniencies of reprefenting them to the Eye, which ought not to be neglected; efpecially for the Direction of the human Voice, becaufe that having no fixt Sounds (as an Inftrument has,whofe Notes may be found by a local Memory of their Seat on the Inftrument) we have not another Way of finding the true Note but computing the *Interval* by the intermediate *diatonick Degrees*, and the more readily this can be done, it is certainly the better.

Now

Now you are to *obferve*, that, as the *Sig-nature* of the *Clef* is defigned for, and can ferve but one *Key*, which ought rather to be the *principal Key* or *Octave* of the Piece than any other, fhewing what tranfpofed Notes belong to it, fo the Inconveniency laft mentioned is re-medied, by having the Signs all of one Kind, on-ly for thefe *Intervals* one of whofe Extremes is the *Key*-note, or Letter : But a Song may modulate or change from the *principal* into other *Keys*, which may require other Notes than the *Signature* of the *Clef* affords ; fo we find ✳ and ♭ upon fome particular Notes con-trary to the *Clef*, which fhews that the *Melo-dy* is out of the *principal Key*, fuch Notes be-ing natural to fome other *fubprincipal Key* into which it is carried ; and thefe Signs are, or ought always to be chofen in the moft conve-nient Manner for expreffing the *Interval*; for *Example*, the *principal Key* being *C* with a 3*d* g. which is a *natural Octave* (*i. e.* expreffed all with plain Letters) fuppofe a Change into its 4*thf* ; and here let a 4*th* upward be required, we muft take it in ♭ or *a*✳ ; the firft is the beft Way, but either of them contradicts the *Clef* which is *natural*; and we no fooner find this than we judge the Key is changed. But again, a Change may be where this Sign of it cannot appear, *viz.* when we modulate into the 6*th* of a *fharp principal Key*, or into the 3*d* of a *flat principal Keys*; becaufe thefe have the fame Signature, as has been already fhown, and have

fuch

such a Connection that, unless by a Cadence, the Melody can never be said to be out of the *principal Key*. And with respect to a *flat principal Key*, *observe*, That if the *6th g.* and *7th g.* are used, as in some Circumstances they may, especially towards a Cadence, then there will be necessarily required upon that *6th* and *7th*, another Sign than that with which its Seat is marked in the general Signature of the Clef, which marks all flat Keys with the lesser *6ths* and *7ths*; and therefore in such Case (*i. e.* where the principal *Key is flat*) this Difference from the *Clef* is not a Sign that the Melody leaves the *Key*, because each of these belong to it in different Circumstances; yet they cannot be both marked in the *Clef*, therefore that which is of more general Use is put there and the other marked occasionally.

FROM what has been explained, you learn another very remarkable Thing, *viz.* to know what the *principal Key* of any Piece is, without seeing one Note of it; and this is done by knowing the Signature of the *Clef* : There are but Two Kinds of *Keys* (or *Modes* of *Melody*) distinguished into *sharp* and *flat*, as already explained; each of which may have any of the 12 different Notes or Letters of the *semitonick Scale* for its *Fundamental*; in the 1st and 6th Line of the upper Part of the preceeding Table you have all these *Fundamentals* or *Key*-notes, and under them respectively stand the Signatures proper to each, in which, as has been

the

often faid, the flat Keys have their *6th* and *7th*
marked of the *leffer* Kind; and therefore as by
the *Key*, or *fundamental* Note, we know the
Signature, fo reciprocally by the Signature we
can know the *Key*; but 'tis under this one Limitation that, becaufe one Signature ferves Two
Keys, a *fharp* one, and a *flat*, which is the *6th*
above or *3d* below the *fharp* one, therefore we
only learn by this, that it is one of them, but
not which ; for *Example*, if the *Clef* has no
tranfpofed Note but *f*✻, then the Key is *g* with
a *3d g.* or *e* with a *3d l.* If the *Clef* has |̷
and *e*|̷, the Key is |̷ with a *3d g.* or *g.* with a
3d l. as fo of others, as in the Table: I know
indeed, for I have found it fo in the Writing
of the beft Mafters, that they are not ftrict and
conftant in obferving this Rule concerning the
Signature of the C ef, efpecially when the principal Key is a *flat* one ; in which Cafe you'll
find frequently, that when the *6th l.* or *7th l.*
to the Key, or both, are tranfpofed Notes, they
don't fign them fo in the *Clef*,but leave them to
be marked as the Courfe of the Melody requires ;
which is convenient enough when the Piece is
fo conducted as to ufe the *leffer 6th* and *7th*
feldomer than the *greater.*

§ 4. *Of*

§ 4. *Of Tranſpoſition.*

THERE are Two Kinds of *Tranſpoſition,* the one is, the changing the Places or Seats of the Notes or Letters among the Lines and Spaces, but ſo as.every Note be ſet at the ſame Letter; which is done by a Change with reſpect to the *Clef :* The other is the changing of the Key, or ſetting all the Notes of the Song at different Letters, and performing it conſequently in different Notes upon an *Inſtrument :* Of theſe in Order.

1. *Of Tranſpoſition with reſpect to the Clef.*

THIS is done either by removing the ſame *Clef* to another Line; or by uſing another *Clef;* but ſtill with the ſame Signature, becauſe the Piece is ſtill in the ſame Key : How to ſet the Notes in either Caſe is very eaſy : For the 1ſt, You take the firſt Note at the ſame Diſtance above or below the *Clef*-note in its new Poſition, as it was in the former Poſition, and then all the reſt of the Notes in the ſame Relations or Diſtances one from another; ſo that the Notes are all ſet on Lines and Spaces of the ſame Name. For the 2d, or ſetting the *Muſick* with

with a different *Clef*, you muſt mind that the
Places of the Three *Clef*-notes are invariaɒle in
the *Scale*, and are to one another in theſe Relations, *viz.* the *Mean* a 5*th* above the Baſs ;
and the *Treble* a 5*th* above the *Mean*, and
conſequently Two 5*ths* above the Baſs :   Now
when we would tranſpoſe to a new *Clef*,ſuppoſe
from the *Treble* to the *Mean*, whereveer we
ſet that new *Clef*, we ſuppoſe it to be the ſame
individual Note, in the ſame Place of the *Scale*,
as if the Piece were that *Part* in a *Compoſition* to which this new *Clef* is generally appropriated, that ſo it may direct us to the ſame
individual Notes we had before Tranſpoſition :
Now from the fixt Relations of the Three
Clefs in the Scale, it will be eaſy to find the
Seat of the firſt tranſpoſed Note, and then all
the reſt are to be ſet at the ſame mutual Diſtances they were at before ; for *Example*, ſuppoſe the firſt Note of a Song is *d*, a 6*th* above
the *Baſs-clef*, the Piece being ſet with that *Clef*,
if it is tranſpoſed and ſet with the *Mean-clef*,
then wherever that *Clef* is placed, the firſt Note
muſt be the 2*d g.* above it, becauſe a 2*d g.* a-
bove the *Mean* is a 6*th g.* above the *Baſs-clef*,
the Relation of theſe Two being a 5*th* ; and
ſo that firſt Note will ſtill be the ſame individual *d:* Again, let a Piece be ſet with
the *Treble-clef*, and the firſt Note be *e*, a
3*d l.* below the *Clef*, if we tranſpoſe this
to the *Mean-clef*, the firſt Note muſt be a
3*d g.* above it, which is the ſame individual
Note *e* in that Scale, for a 3*d l.* and 3*d g.*
make

make a 5th the Diftance of the *treble* and *mean Clefs.*

THE Ufe and Defign of this *Tranfpofition* is, That if a Song being fet with a certain *Clef* in a certain Pofition, the Notes fhall go far a-bove or below the *Syftem* of Five Lines, they may, by the Change of the Place of the fame *Clef* in the particular *Syftem*, or taking a new *Clef*, be brought more within the Compafs of the Five Lines : That this may be effected by fuch a Change is very plain ; for *Example*, Let any Piece be fet with the *Treble Clef* on the firft Line, (counting upward) if the Notes lie much below the *Clef* Note, they are without the *Sy-ftem*, and 'tis plain they will be reduced more within it, by placing the *Clef* on any other Line above; and fo in general the fetting any *Clef* lower in a particular *Syftem* reduces the Notes that run much above it ; and fetting it higher reduces the Notes that run far below. The fame is effected by changing the *Clef* it felf in fome Cafes, tho' not in all, *Thus*, if the *Treble Part*, or a Piece fet with the *Treble Clef*, runs high a-bove the *Syftem*, it can only be reduced by changing the Place of the fame *Clef* ; but If it run without the *Syftem* below, it can be redu-ced by changing to the *Mean* or *Bafs Clef*. If the *mean Part* run above its particular Syftem, it will be reduced by changing to the *Treble Clef* ; or if it run below, by changing to the *Bafs Clef*. *Laftly.* If the *Bafs Part* run with-out its Syftem below, it can only be reduced by changing the Place of the fame *Clef*, but running

above

above, it may be changed into the *mean* or *treble Clef.* Now as to the Position of the new *Clef,* you must choose it so that the Design be best answered ; and in every Change of the *Clef* the Notes will be on Lines and Spaces of the same Name, or denominated by the same Letter, they refer also to the same individual Place of the *Scale* or *general System,* differing only with respect to their Places in the particular *System* which depend on the Difference of the *Clefs* and their Positions, and therefore will always be the same individual Notes upon the same Instrument.

A s to both these *Transpositions* I must *observe,* that they increase the Difficulty of Practice, because the Relations of the Lines and Spaces change under all these *Transpositions,* and therefore one must be equally familiar with all the Three *Clefs,* and every Position of them, so that under any Change we may be able with the same Readiness to find the Notes in their true Relations and Distances : And as this is not acquired without great Application, I think it is too cruel a Remedy for the Inconveniency to which it is applied : It is better, I should think, to keep always the same *Clef* for the same *Part,* and the same Position of the *Clef* ; but if one will be Master of several Instruments, and be able to perform any *Part,* then he must be equally well acquainted with all their proper *Clefs,* but still the Position of the *Clef* in the particular *System* may be fixt and invariable.

2. *Of*

2. *Of* Transposition *from one* Key *to another.*

THE Design of this *Transposition* is, That
a *Song*, which being begun in one Note is too
high or low, or any other way inconvenient,
as may be in some Cases for certain Instruments,
may be begun in another Note, and from that
carried on in all its just *Degrees* and *Intervals.*
The *Clef* and its Position are the same, and the
Change now is of the Notes themselves from one
Letter and its Line or Space to another. In
the former *Transposition* the Notes were expressed by the same Letters, but both removed to
different Lines and Spaces ; here the Letters
are unmoved, and the Notes of the Song are
transferred to or expressed by other Letters, and
consequently set also upon different Lines and
Spaces, which it is plain will require a different *Signature* of the *Clef.* Now we are easily
directed in this Kind of *Transposition*, by the
preceeding *Table*, *Plate* 2. *Fig.* 1. For there
we see the *Signature* and Progress of Notes in
either *sharp* or *flat Keys* beginning at every
Letter : The lower Line of the upper Part of
the *Table* contains the *fundamental Notes* of
the Twelve *sharp Keys* ; and under them are
their *Signatures*, shewing what *artificial* Notes
are necessary to make a *concinnous diatonick*
Series from these several *Fundamentals :* In
the *6th* Line above are the same Twelve Letters, considered as *Fundamentals* of the Twelve
flat Keys, which have the same Signatures with
the

the *sharp Keys* standing in the under Line, and in the same Column : So that 'tis equal to make any of these Twelve Notes the *Key* Note, changing the *Signature* according to the *Table*: And *observe*, tho' the *Fundamentals* of the Twelve *flat Keys* stand in the Table as *6ths* to the Twelve *sharp Keys*, yet that is not to be understood as if the *flat Keys* must all be a *6th* above (or in their *8ves* a *3d* below) the *sharp Keys* ; it happens so there only in the Order and Relation of the Degrees of the *Scale* : But as the Fundamentals of the Twelve *flat Keys* are the same Letters with those of the *sharp Keys*, they shew us that the same Key may either be the *sharp* or *flat*, with a different Signature.

But to make this Matter as plain as possible, I shall consider the Application of it in Two distinct Questions. 1*mo*. Let the *Fundamental* or *Key* Note to which you would *transpose* a Song be given, to find the proper Signature. *Rule*. In the first or *6th* Line of the upper Part, according as the Key is *sharp* or *flat*, find the given *Key* to which you would transpose, and under it you have the proper Signature. For *Example*, Suppose a Song in the *sharp Key c*, which is natural, if you would transpose it to *g*, the *Clef* must be signed with *f✕*, or to *d* and it must have *f✕* and *c✕*. *Again*, suppose a Song in a *flat Key* as *d* whose Signature has *b flat*, if you transpose it to *e* the *Signature* has *f✕*, or to *g* and it has *♭* and *e♭*. 2*do*. Let any *Signature* be assigned to find the *Key* to which we must

transf-

transpose. *Rule.* In the upper Part of the Table in
the same Column with the given *Signature* you'll
find the *Key* sought, either in the 1*st* or 6*th*
Line according as the Key is *sharp* or *flat*. But
without considering the *Key*, or whether the
Signature be regular or not, we may know
how to *transpose* by considering the Signature as
it is and the first Note, *thus,* find the *Signature* with which it is already set, and in the
same Column in the upper Part find the Letter
of the first Note; in that same Line (betwixt
Right and Left) find the Letter where you desire to begin, and under it is the proper *Signature* to be now used: Or having chosen a certain *Signature* you'll find the Note to begin at,
in the same Column, and in the same Line with
the Note it began in formerly. Having thus
your *Signature*, and the Seat of the first Note,
the rest are easily set up and down at the same
mutual Distances they were in formerly; and
where any ✳, ♭ or ♮ is occasionally upon any
Note, mark it so in the correspondent Note in
the Transposition;but mind that if a Note with
a ✳ or ♭ is transposed to a Letter which in the
new *Signature* is contrarily ♭ or ✳, then mark
that Note ♮; and reciprocally if a Note marked
♮ is transposed to a Letter, which is natural in
the new Signature, mark it ✳ or ♭ according
as the ♮ was the removing of a ♭ or ✳ in the
former *Signature*. In all other Cases mark the
transposed Note the same Way it was before.
For *Examples* of this Kind of *Transposition,* see
Plate 3. *Examples* 3 and 5.

§ 5. Of

§ 5. *Of Sol-fa-ing, with some other particular Remarks about the Names of Notes.*

IN the second Column of the preceeding *Table*, you have these Syllables written a-gainst the several Letters of the *Scale, viz. fa, sol, la, fa, sol, la, mi, fa,* &c. Formerly these Six were in use, *viz. ut, re, mi, fa, sol, la* ; from the Application whereof the Notes of the *Scale* were called *G sol re ut, A la mi re,* &c. and afterwards a 6*th* was added, *viz. si* ; but these Four *fa, sol, la, mi* being only in Use a - mong us at present, I shall explain their Use here, and speak of the rest, which are still in Use with some Nations, in *Chap.*14. where you shall learn their Original. As to their Use, it is this in general ; they relate chiefly to *Singing* or the human Voice, that by applying them to every Note of the *Scale* it might not only be pronounced more easily, but principally that by them the *Tones* and *Semitones* of the *natural Scale* may be better marked out and distingui-shed.

THIS Design is obtain'd by the Four Syllables *fa, sol, la, mi,* in this Manner ; from *fa* to *sol* is a *Tone,* also from *sol* to *la,* and from *la* to *mi,* without distinguishing the greater and lesser

Tone ;

Tone ; but from *la* to *fa*, alſo from *mi* to *fa* is a *Semitone :* Now if theſe are applied in this Order, *fa, ſol, la, fa, ſol, la, mi, fa,* &c. they expreſs the natural Series from *c,* as in the Table ; and if it is repeated to another *8ve,* we ſee how by them to expreſs all the Seven different Orders of *Tones* and *Semitones* within the *diatonick Scale.* If the *Scale* is extended to Two *8ves,* you'll perceive that by this Rule 'tis always true, tho' it were further extended *in infinitum,* that above *mi* ſtands *fa, ſol, la,* and below it the ſame reverſed *la, ſol, fa ;* and that one *mi* is always diſtant from another by an *Octave,* (which no other Syllable is) becauſe after *mi* aſcending comes always *fa, ſol, la, fa, ſol, la,* which are taken reverſe deſcending. But now you'll ask a more particular Account of the Application of this ; and that you may underſtand it, conſider, the firſt Thing in teaching to ſing is, to make one raiſe a *Scale* of Notes by *Tones* and *Semitones* to an *Octave,* and deſcend again by the ſame Notes, and then to riſe and fall by greater *Intervals* at a Leap, as a 3*d,* 4*th* and 5*th,* &c. And to do all this by beginning at Notes of different Pitch ; then theſe Notes are repreſented by Lines and Spaces, as above explained, to which theſe Syllables are applied ; 'tis ordinary therefore, to learn a Scholar to name every Line and Space by theſe Syllables: But ſtill you'll ask, to what Purpoſe ? The Anſwer is, That while they are learning to *tune* the *Degrees* and *Intervals* of Sound expreſt by Notes ſet upon Lines and Spaces, or

learn-

learning a Song to which no Words are applied, they may do it better by an articulate Sound; and chiefly that by knowing the *Degrees* and *Intervals* expreſt by theſe Syllables, they may more readily know the true Diſtance of their Notes. I ſhall firſt make an End of what is to be ſaid about the Application, and then ſhew what an uſeleſs Invention this is.

THE only Syllable that is but once applied in Seven Letters is *mi*, and by applying this to different Letters, the Seat of the Two *natural Semitones* in the 8*ve*, expreſſed by *la-fa* and *mi-fa*, will be placed betwixt different Letters (which is all we are to notice where the Difference of the greater and leſſer *Tone* is neglected, as in all this) But becauſe the Relation of the Notes ex-preſt by the ſeven plain Letters, *c, d, e, f, g, a, b*, which we call the *natural Scale*, are ſup-poſed to be fixt and unalterable, and the De-grees expreſt by theſe Syllables are alſo fixt, therefore the natural Seat of *mi* is ſaid to be *b*, becauſe then *mi-fa* and *la-fa* areapplied to the *natural Semitones b.c* and *e.f*, as you ſee in the Table : But if *mi* is applied to any other of the Seven *natural* Notes, then ſome of the *artifi-cial* Notes will be neceſſary, to make a Series anſwering to the *Degrees* which we ſuppoſe are invariably expreſt by theſe Syllables ; but *mi* may be applied not only to any of the Seven *na-tural* Notes, it may alſo be applied to any of the Five *artificial* Ones : And now to know in any Caſe (*i. e.* when *mi* is applied to any of the Twelve Letters of the *ſemitonick Scale*)to what

Notes

Notes the other Syllables are applied, you need
but look into the preceeding Table, where if
you suppose *mi* applied to any Letter of that
Line where it stands, the Notes to which *fa,
sol, la* are applied are found in the same Column with that Letter, and in the same Line
with these Syllables. By this Means I hope you
have an easy Rule for *sol-fa-ing*, or naming the
Notes by *sol, fa,* &c. in any *Clef* and with any
Signature.

 B υ τ now let us consider of what great Importance this is, either to the understanding or
practising of *Musick.* In the *first* Place, the
Difficulty to the Learner is increased by the
Addition of these Names, which for every different Signature of the *Clef* are differently applied ; so that the same Line or Space is in one
Signature called *fa,* in another *sol,* and so on :
And if a Song modulates into a new *Key,* then
for every such Change different Applications
of these Names may be required to the same
Note, which will beget much Confusion and
Difficulty : And if you would conceive the
whole Difficulty, consider, as there are 12 different Seats of *mi* in the *Octave,* therefore the
naming of the Lines and Spaces of any particular *System* and *Clef* has the same Variety ; and
if one must learn to name Notes in every *Clef*
and every Position of the *Clef,* then as there is
one ordinary Position for the *Treble-clef,* one
for the *Bass,* and Four for the *mean,* if we apply to each of these the 12 different *Signatures,*
and consequent Ways of *sol-fa-ing,* we have

in all 72 various Ways of applying the Names
of *fol, fa,* &c. to the Lines and Spaces of a particular *Syftem;* not that the fame Line can have
72 different Names, but in the Order of the
Whole there is fo great a Variety : And if we
fuppofe yet more Pofitions of the *Clefs,* the Variety will ftill be increafed, to which you muft
add what Variety happens upon changing the
Key in the Middle of any Song. Let us next
fee what the Learner has by this troublefom
Acquifition : After confidering it well, we find
nothing at all; for as to naming the Notes,
pray what want we more than the Seven Letters already applied, which are conftant and certain Names to every Line and Space under all
different *Signatures,*the *Clef* being the fame and
in the fame Pofition; and how much more fimple
and eafy this is any Body can judge. If it be
complained that the Sounds of thefe Letters are
harfh when ufed in rafiing a Series of Notes,
then, becaufe this feems to make the Ufe of
thefe Names only for the fofter Pronounciation
of a Note, let Seven Syllables as foft as poffible
be chofen and joyned invariably to the Letters
or alphabetical Names of the *Scale* ; fo that as
the fame Line or Space is, in the fame *Clef* and
Pofition, always called by the fame Letter,
whether 'tis a *natural* or *artificial* Note, fo let
it be conftantly named by the fame Syllable ;
and thus we leave the true Diftance or *Interval*
to be found by the *Degrees* among the Lines
and Spaces, as they are determined by the Letters applied to them ; or rather, fince the *In-*
tervals

tervals are sufficiently determined by the alphabetical Names applied to the Lines and Spaces,
there is no Matter whether the syllabical Names
be conftant or not, or what Number there be
of them, *that is*, we may apply to any Note at
random any Syllable that will make the Pronounciation foft and eafy, if this be the chief
End of them, as I think it can only be, becaufe
the *Degrees* and *Intervals* are better and more
regularly expreft by the *Clef* and *Signature* :
Nay, 'tis plain, that there is no Certainty of a-
ny *Interval* expreft fimply by thefe Syllables,
without confidering the Lines and Spaces with
their Relations determined by the Letters ; for
Example, If you ask what Diftance there is
betwixt *fol* and *la*, the Queftion has different Anfwers, for 'tis either a *Tone* or a 5*th*, or one of thefe
compounded with 8*ve*, and fo of other *Examples*,
as are eafily feen in the preceeding Scheme : But
if you ask what is betwixt *fol* in fuch a Line or
Space, and *la* in fuch a one above or below,
then indeed the Queftion is determined ; yet 'tis
plain, that we don't find the Anfwer by thefe
Names *fa*, *fol*, but by the Diftances of the Lines
and Spaces, according to the Relations fettled
among them by the Letters with which they
are marked.

I know this Method has been in Credit, and
I doubt will continue fo with fome People, who,
if they don't care to have Things difficult to
themfelves, may perhaps think it an Honour
both to them and their Art, that it appear *my-
fterious*; and fome fhrewd Gueffers may poffibly
alledge

alledge fomethiug elfe ; but I fhall only fay that, for the Reafons advanced, I think this an impertinent Burden upon *Mufick*,

Further Reflections upon the Names of Notes.

As there is a Neceffity, that the Progreffion of the *Scale* of *Mufick*, and all its *Intervals*, with their feveral Relations, fhould be diftinctly marked, as is done by means of Letters reprefenting Sounds; fo it is neceffary for Practice, that the Notes and *Intervals* of Sound upon Inftruments fhould be named by the fame Letters, by which we have feen a clear and eafy Method of expreffing any Piece of *Melody*, for directing us how to produce the fame upon a mufical Inftrument: But then obferve, that as the *Scale* of *Mufick* puts no Limitations upon the abfolute *Degree* of *Tune*, only regulating the relative Meafures of one Note to another, fo the Notes of Inftruments are called *c*, *d*, &c. not with refpect to any certain Pitch of *Tune*, but to mark diftinctly the Relations of one Note to another; and, without refpect to the Pitch of the Whole, the fame Notes, *i. e.* the Sounds taken in the fame Part of the Inftrument, are always named by the fame Letters, becaufe the Whole makes a Series, which is conftantly in the fame Order and Relation of *Degrees*. For *Example*, Let the Four Strings of a Violin be tuned as high or low as you pleafe, being always *5ths* to one another, the Names of the Four open Notes are ftill called *g*,*d*,*a*,*e*, and fo of the

the other Notes; and therefore, if upon hearing
any Note of an Inftrument we ask the Name of
it, as whether it is *c* or *d*, &c. the Meaning
can only be, what Part of the Inftrument is it
taken in, and with what Application of the
Hand? For with refpect to the abfolute *Tune*
it cannot be called by one Letter rather than a-
nother, for the Note which is called *c*, according to the forefaid general Rule, may in one
Pitch of *Tuning* be equal to the Note called
d, in another Pitch.

But for the human Voice, confider there is
no fixt or limited Order of its *Degrees*, but an
Octave may be raifed in any Order; therefore
the Notes of the Voice cannot be called *c* or *d*,
&c. in any other Senfe than as being *unifon* to
the Note of that Name upon a fixt Inftrument:
Or if a whole *Octave* is raifed in any Order of
Tones and *Semitones*, contained within the *diatonick Scale*, fuppofe that from *c*, each of thefe
Notes may be called *c*, *d*, &c. in fo far as they
exprefs the Relations of thefe Notes one to a-
nother. And *laftly*, With refpect to this Method of writing *Mufick*, when the Voice takes
Direction from it, the Notes muft at that Time
be called by the Letters and Names that direct it in taking the *Degrees* and *Intervals* that
compofe the *Melody*; yet the Voice may begin ftill in the fame Pitch of *Tune*, whatever
Name or Letter in the Writing the firft Note
is fet at, becaufe thefe Letters ferve only to
mark the Relations of the Notes: But in Inftruments, tho' the *Tune* of the Whole may be
higher

higher or lower, the fame Notes in the Writing
direct always to the fame individual Notes with
refpect to the Name and the Place of the Inftrument, which has nothing parallel to it in the
human Voice. Again, tho' the Voice and Inftruments are both directed by the fame Method of Writing *Mufick*, yet there is one very
remarkable Difference betwixt the Voice and
fuch Inftruments as have fixt Sounds ; for the
Voice being limited to no Order of *Degrees*,
has none of the Imperfections of an Inftrument,
and can therefore begin in *Unifon* with any
Note of an Inftrument, or at any other convenient Pitch, and take any *Interval* upward or
downward in juft *Tune :* And tho' the unequal
Ratios or *Degrees* of the *Scale*, when the Sounds
are fixt, make many fmall Errors on Inftruments, yet the Voice is not fubjected to thefe :
But it will be objected, that the Voice is directed
by the fame *Scale*, whofe Notes or Letters have
been all along fuppofed under a certain determinate Relation to one another, which feems
to lay the Voice under the fame Limitations
with Inftruments having fixt Sounds, it it follow
the precife Proportions of thefe Notes as they
ftand in the *Scale :* The Anfwer to this is, That
the Voice will not, and I dare fay cannot poffibly follow thefe erroneous Proportions ; becaufe the true harmonious Diftances are much eafier taken, to which a good Ear will naturally lead:
Confider again, that becaufe the Errors are fmall
in a fingle Cafe, and the Difference of *Tones*
or of *Semitones* fcarce fenfible, therefore they
are

are confidered as all equal upon Inftruments;
and the fame Number of *Tones* or *Semitones* is,
every where thro' the *Scale*, reckoned the fame
or an equal *Interval*, and fo it muft pafs with fome
fmall unavoidable Errors. Now that the Voice
may be directed by the fame *Scale* or *Syftem* of
Notes, the Singer will alfo confider them as e-
qual, and in like manner take the fame Number for the fame *Interval*; yet, by the Direction
of a well tuned Ear, will take every *Interval* in
its due Proportion, according to the Exigences
of the *Melody*; fo if the *Key* is *d*, and the Three
firft Notes of a Song were fet in *d, e, f*, the
Voice will take *d-e* a *t g*. and *e-f* a *f g*. in order
to make *d-f* a true 3*d l*. which is defective a
Comma in the *Scale*, becaufe *d-e* is a *t l*. In a-
nother Cafe the Voice would take thefe very
Notes according to the *Scale*, as here, fuppofe
the *Key c*, and the firft Three Notes *c, d, f*, the
Voice will take *c-d* a *t g*. becaufe that is a more
perfect Degree than *t l*. and then will take *f* not
a true 3*d l* to *d*, but a true 4*th* to the *Key c*,
which the *Melody* requires rather than the other,
whereby *d-f* is made a deficient 3*d l*; and if
we fuppofe *e* is the third Note, and *f* the Fourth,
the Voice will take *e* a *t l* above *d*, in order to
make *c-e* a true 3*d g*. I don't pretend that thefe
fmall Differences are very fenfible in a fingle
Cafe, yet 'tis more rational to think that a good
Ear left to itfelf will take the Notes in the beft
Proportions, where there is nothing to determine it another Way, as the Accompanyment
of an Inftrument; and then it is demonftrated
by

by this, that in the beſt tuned Inſtruments having fixt Sounds, the ſame Song will not go
equally well from every Note; but let a Voice
directed by a juſt Ear begin *uniſon* to any Note
of an Inſtrument, there ſhall be no Difference :
I own, that by a Habit of ſinging and uſing the
Voice to one Pitch of *Tune*, it may become
difficult to ſing out of it, but this is accidental
to the Voice which is naturally capable of ſinging alike well in every Pitch within its Extent
of Notes, being equally uſed to them all.

APPENDIX.

Concerning Mr. Salmon's *Propoſal for reducing
all* Muſick *to one* Clef.

'TIS certainly the Uſe of Things that makes
    them valuable; and the more univerſal the
Application of any Good is, it is the more to
their Honour who communicate it : For this
Reaſon, no doubt, it would very well become
the Profeſſors of ſo generous an Art as *Muſick*,
and I believe in every reſpect would be their
Intereſt, to ſtudy how the Practice of it might
be made as eaſy and univerſal as poſſible ; and
to encourage any Thing that might contribute
towards this End.

  IT will be eaſily granted that the Difficulty
of Practice is much increaſed by the Difference
of *Clefs* in particular Syſtems, whereby the ſame
Line or Space, *i. e.* the firſt or ſecond Line, *&c.*

is

is fometimes called *c*, fometimes *g* : With refpect to *Inftruments* 'tis plain ; for if every Line
and Space keeps not conftantly the fame Name,
the Note fet upon it muft be fought in a different Place of the Inftrument ; And with refpect
to the Voice, which takes all its Notes according to their Intervals betwixt the Lines and
Spaces, if the Names of thefe are not conftant
neither are the Intervals conftantly the fame in
every Place ; therefore for every Difference
either in the Clef or Pofition of it, we have a new
Study to know our Notes, which makes difficult
Practice, efpecially if the *Clef* fhould be changed in the very middle of a Piece, as is frequently done in the modern Way of writing Mufick.
Mr. *Salmon* reflecting on thefe Inconveniencies,
and alfo how ufeful it would be that all fhould
be reduced to one conftant *Clef*, whereby the
fame Writing of any Piece of Mufick would e-
qually ferve to direct the Voice and all Inftruments, a Thing one fhould think to be of very
great Ufe, he propofes in his *Effay to the Ad-
vancement of Mufick*, what he calls an univerfal Character, which I fhall explain in a few
Words. In the 1*ft* Place, he would have the
loweft Line of every particular Syftem conftantly called *g*, and the other Lines and Spaces to
be named according to the Order of the 7 Letters ; and becaufe thefe Pofitions of the Letters are fuppofed invariable, therefore he thinks
there's no Need to mark any of them ; but
then, 2*do.* That the Relations of feveral *Parts*
of a Compofition may be diftinctly known ; he

marks

marks the *Treble* with the Letter T at the Beginning of the System ; the *Mean* with M. and the Bass with B. And the *g*s that are on the lowest Line of each of these Systems, he supposes to be *Octaves* to each other in Order. And then for referring these *Systems* to their corresponding Places in the general *System*, the *Treble g*, which determines all the rest, must be supposed in the same Place as the *Treble* Clef of the common Method ; but this Difference is remarkable, That tho' the *g* of the *Treble* and *Bass* Systems are both on Lines in the general *System*, yet the *Mean g*, which is on a Line of the particular System, is on a Space in the general one, because in the Progression of the Scale, the same Letter, as *g*, is alternately upon a Line and a Space; therefore the *Mean* System is not a Continuation of any of the other Two, so as you could proceed in Order out of the one into the other by Degrees from Line to Space, because the *g* of the *Mean* is here on a Line, which is necessarily upon a Space in the Scale; and therefore in referring the mean *System* to its proper relative Place in the *Scale*, all its Lines correspond to Spaces, of the other and contrarily ; but there is no Matter of that if the *Parts* be so written separately as their Relations be distinctly known, and the Practice made more easy ; and when we would reduce them all to one general *System*, it is enough we know that the Lines of the mean Part must be changed into Spaces, and its Spaces into Lines. 3*tio.* If the Notes of any

Part

Part go above or below its *Syftem*, we may
fet them as formerly on fhort Lines drawn on
Purpofe : But if there are many Notes together
above or below, Mr. *Salmon* propofes to reduce
them within the *Syftem* by placing them on the
Lines and Spaces of the fame Name, and pro-
fixing the Name of the *Octave* to which they
belong. To underftand this better, confider, he
has chofen three diftinct *Octaves* following one
another ; and becaufe one *Octave* needs but
4 Lines therefore he would have no more in
the particular Syftem ; and then each of the
three particular Syftems expreffing a diftinct
Octave of the Scale, which he calls the proper
Octaves of thefe feveral *Parts*, if the Song run
into another *Octave* above or below, 'tis plain,
the Notes that are out of the *Octave* peculiar
to the *Syftem*, as it ftands by a general Rule
marked *T* or *M* or *B*, may be fet on the fame
Lines and Spaces ; and if the *Octave* they belong to be diftinctly marked, the Notes may be
very eafily found by taking them an *Octave*
higher or lower than the Notes of the fame
Name in the proper *Octave* of the *Syftem*. For
Example, If the Treble *Part* runs into the
middle or Bafs *Octave*, we prefix to thefe Notes
the Letter *M* or *B*, and fet them on the fame
Lines and Spaces, for all the Three Syftems,
have in this Hypothefis the Notes of the fame
Name in the fame correfpondent Places ; if the
Mean run into the *Treble* or *Bafs Octaves*,
prefix the Signs *T* or *M*. And *laftly*, Becaufe
the *Parts* may comprehend more than 3 O-
*   ctaves*

Etaves, therefore the Treble may run higher than an *Octave,* and the *Bass* lower; in such Cases, the higher *Octave* for the *Treble* may be marked *T't.* and the lower for the *Bass* *Bb.* But if any Body thinks there be any considerable Difficulty in this Method, which yet I'm of Opinion would be far less than the changing of *Clefs* in the common Way, the Notes may be continued upward and downward upon new Lines and Spaces, occasionally drawn in the ordinary Manner, and tho' there may be many Notes far out of the *System* above or below, yet what's the Inconveniency of this ? Is the reducing the Notes within 5 Lines, and saving a little Paper an adequate Reward for the Trouble and Time spent in learning to perform readily from different Clefs ?

As to the *Treble* and *Bass,* the Alteration by this new Method is very small ; for in the common Position of the *Bass-clef,* the lowest Line is already *g* ; and for the Treble it is but removing the *g* from the *2d* Line, its ordinary Position, to the first Line; the greatest Innovation is in the *Parts* that are set with the *c Clef.*

AND now will any Body deny that it is a great Advantage to have an universal Character in *Musick,* whereby the same Song or *Part* of any Composition may, with equal Ease and Readiness be performed by the Voice or any Instrument; and different *Parts* with alike Ease by the same Instrument? 'tis true that each *Part* is marked with its own *Octave,* but the Design of this is only to mark the Relation of
the

the *Parts*, that feveral Voices or Inftruments performing thefe in a Concert may be directed to take their firft Notes in the true Relations which the Compofer defigned ; but if we fpeak of any one fingle Part to be fung or performed alone by any Inftrument, the Performer in this cafe will not mind the Diftinction of the *Part*, but take the Notes upon his Inftrument, according to a general Rule, which teaches him that a Note in fuch a Line or Space is to be taken in fuch a certain Place of the Inftrument. You may fee the Propofal and the Applications the Author makes of it at large in his Effay, where he has confidered and anfwered the Objections he thought might be raifed ; and to give you a fhort Account of them, confider, that befides the Ignorance and Superftition that haunts little Minds, who make a Kind of Religion of never departing from received Cuftoms, whatever Reafon there may be for changing ; or perhaps the Pride and Vanity of the greateft Part of Profeffors of this Art, joyned to a falfe Notion of their Intereft in making it appear difficult, for the rational Part of any Set and Order of Men is always the leaft ; befides thefe, I fay, the greateft Difficulty feems to be, the rendring what is already printed ufelefs in part to them that fhall be taught this new Method, unlefs they are to learn both, which is rather enlarging than leffening their Task : But this new Method is fo eafy, and differs fo little in the *Bafs* and *Treble Parts*, from what obtains already, that I think it would
add

add very little to their Task, who by the common Method, muft learn to fing and play from all *Clefs* and Variety of Pofitions ; and then *Time* would wear it out, when new *Mufick* were printed, and the former reprinted in the Manner propofed.   Mr. *Salmon* has been a Prophet in guefling what Fate it was like to have ; for it has lain Fifty Years neglected : Nor do I revive it with any better Hope.   I thought of nothing but confidering it as a Piece of Theory, to explain what might be done, and inform you of what has been propofed.   I cannot however hinder my felf to complain of the Hardfhips of learning to read cleverly from all *Clefs* and Pofitions of them : If one would be fo univerfally capable in *Mufick* as to fing or play all *Parts*, let him undergo the Drudgery of being Mafter of the Three *Clefs*; but why may not the Pofitions be fixt and unalterable ? And why may not the fame *Part* be conftantly fet with the fame *Clef*, without the Perplexity of changing, that thofe who confine themfelves to one Inftrument, or the Performance of one *Part*, may have no more to learn than what is neceffary ? This would fave a great deal of Trouble that's but forrily recompenfed by bringing the Notes within or near the Compafs of Five Lines, which is all can be alledged, and a very filly Purpofe confidering the Confequence.

CHAP.

꧁꧂꧁꧂꧁꧂꧁꧂꧁꧂꧁꧂꧁꧂꧁꧂꧁꧂

C H A P. XII.

Of the Time *or* Duration *of Sounds in* Mufick.

---

§ 1. *Of the* Time *in general, and its Subdivifion into* abfolute *and* relative ; *and particularly of the* Names, Signs, *and* Proportions, *or relative* Meafures *of Notes, as to* Time.

WE are now come to the fecond general Branch of the *Theory* of *Mufick,* which is to confider the *Time* or *Duration* of Sounds in the fame Degree of *Tune.*

TUNE and *TIME* are the Affections or Properties of Sound, upon whofe Difference or Proportions *Mufick* depends. In each of thefe fingly there are very powerful Charms : Where the *Duration* of the Notes is equal, the Differences of *Tune* are capable to entertain us with an endlefs Variety of Pleafure, either in an art-
full

ful and well ordered Succeffion of fimple Sounds,
which is *Melody*, or the beautiful *Harmony* of
Parts in Confonance: And of the Power of *Time*
alone, *i. e.* of the Pleafure arifing from the various Meafures of *long* and *fhort*, or *fwift* and
flow in the Succeffion of Sounds differing only in
Duration, we have Experience in a *Drum*,
which has no Difference of Notes as to *Tune*.
But how is the Power of *Mufick* heightned,
when the Differences of *Tune* and *Time* are artfully joined: 'Tis this Compofition that can
work fo irrefiftibly on the Paffions, to make
one heavy or cheerful; it can be fuited to Occafions of Mirth or Sadnefs; by it we can raife,
and at leaft indulge, the folemn compofed
Frame of our Spirits, or fink them into a trifling
Levity: But enough for Introduction.

I N explaining this Part there is much lefs to
do than was in the former; the Caufes and Meafures of the Degrees of *Tune*, with the *Inter-*
vals depending thereon: And all their various
Connections and Relations, were not fo eafily
difcovered and explained, as we can do what relates to this, which is a far more fimple Subject.

T H E *Reafon* or *Caufe* of a long or fhort
Sound is obvious in every Cafe; and I may fay,
in general, it is owing to the continued Impulfe
of the efficient Caufe, for a longer or fhorter
Time upon the fonorous Body; for I fpeak here
of the artful Duration of Sound. See *Page* 17.
where I have explained the Diftinction betwixt
natural and artificial Duration, to which I fhall
here

here add the Confideration of thofe Inftruments
that are ftruck with a Kind of inftantaneous Motion, as *Harpfichords* and *Bells*, where the
Sounds cannot be made longer or fhorter by
Art; for the Stroke cannot be repeated fo oft
as to make the Sound appear as one continued
Note; and therefore this is fupplied by the
Paufe and Diftance of *Time* betwixt the ftriking one Note and another, *i. e.* by the Quicknefs or Slownefs of their Succeffion; fo that *long*
and *fhort*, *quick* and *flow* are the fame Things
in *Mufick*; therefore under this Title of the
Duration of Sounds, muft be comprehended
that of the Quicknefs or Slownefs of their Succeffion, as well as the proper Notion of *Length*
and *Shortnefs*: And fo the Time of a Note is
not computed only by the uninterrupted Length
of the Sound, but alfo by the Diftance betwixt
the Beginning of one Sound and that of the next.
And mind that when the Notes are in the ftrict
Senfe long and fhort Sounds, yet fpeaking of
their Succeffion we fay alfo, that it is quick or
flow, according as the Notes are fhort or long;
which Notion we have by confidering the Time
from the Beginning of one Note to that of another.

NEXT, as to the Meafure of the *Duration*
of a Note, if we chufe any fenfibly equal Motion, as the Pulfes of a well adjufted Clock or
Watch, the *Duration* of any Note may be meafured by this, and we may juftly fay, that it
is equal to 2, 3 or 4, *&c.* Pulfes; and if any o-
ther Note is compared to the fame Motion,
we

we shall have the exact Proportion of the *Times*
of the Two, expreft by the different Number of
Pulses. Now, I need give no Reaſon to prove,
that the *Time* of a Note is juftly meaſured by
the fucceſſive Parts of an equable Motion ; for
tis felf-evident, that it cannot be better done ;
and indeed we know no other Way of meaſuring *Time*, but by the Succeſſion of Ideas in
our own Minds.

W E come now to examine the particular
Meaſures and Proportions of *Time* that belong
to *Muſick* ; for as in the Matter of *Tune*, every Proportion is not fit for obtaining the Ends
of *Muſick*, ſo neither is every Proportion of
Time ; and to come cloſe to our Purpoſe, obſerve,

T I M E in *Muſick* is to be conſidered either
with reſpect to the *abſolute Duration* of the
Notes, *i. e.* the Duration conſidered in every
Note by it ſelf, and meaſured by ſome external
Motion foreign to the *Muſick*; in reſpect of
which the Succeſſion of the whole is ſaid to be
quick or ſlow : Or, it is to be conſidered with
reſpect to the *relative* Quantity or Proportion
of the Notes, compared one with another.

N o w, to explain theſe Things, we muſt firſt
know what are the *Signs* by which the *Time*
of Notes is repreſented. The Marks and Characters in the modern Practice are theſe Six,
whoſe Figures and Names you ſee in *Plate* 2.
Fig. 3. And *obſerve*, when Two or more
Quavers or *Semiquavers* come together, they
are made with one or Two Strokes acroſs their
Tails

Tails, and then they are called *tied Notes.*
These Signs express no *absolute Time,* and are
in different Cases of different Lengths, but their
Measures and how they are determined, we
shall learn again, after we have considered,

The relative Quantity or Proportions of Time.

This Proportion I have signified by Numbers written over the Notes or *Signs* of *Time;*
whereby you may see a *Semibreve* is equal to
Two *Minims,* a *Minim* equal to Two *Crotch-*
ets, a *Crotchet* equal to Two *Quavers,* a *Qua-*
ver equal to Two *Semiquavers,* a *Semiquaver*
equal to Two *Demi-semiquavers.* The Proportions of Length of each of these to each o-
ther are therefore manifest: I have set over each
of them Numbers which express all their mutual Proportions; so a *Minim* is to a *Quaver* as
16 to 4, or 4 to 1, *i. e.* a *Minim* is equal to
Four *Quavers,* and so of the rest. Now
these Proportions are double, (*i. e.* as 2 : 1) or
compounded of several Doubles, so 4 : 1 contains
2 : 1 twice ; but there is also the Proportion of
3 : 1 used in *Musick :* Yet that this Part may be
as simple and easy as possible, these Proportions
already stated among the Notes, are fixt and invariable ; and to express a Proportion of 3 to 1
we add a Point (.) on the right Side of any
Note, which is equal to a Half of it, where
by a pointed *Semibreve* is equal to Three *Mi-*
nims, and so of the rest, as you see in the
Figure. From these arise other Proportions, as
of 2 to 3, which is betwixt any Note (as a
Crotchet)

Crotchet) plain, and the fame pointed ; for the plain *Crotchet* is Two *Quavers*, and the pointed is Three. Alfo we have the Proportion of 3 to 4, betwixt any Note pointed, and the Note of the next greater Value plain, as betwixt a pointed *Crotchet* and a plain *Minim*. And of thefe arife other Proportions, but we need not trouble our felves with them, fince they are not directly ufeful; and that we may know what are fo, fuffer me to repeat a little of what I have faid elfewhere, *viz.* that

THINGS that are defigned to affect our Senfes muft bear a due Proportion with them ; and fo where the Parts of any Object are numerous, and their Relations perplext, and not eafily perceived, they can raife no agreeable Ideas ; nor can we eafily judge of the Difference of Parts where it is great ; therefore, that the Proportion of the *Time* of Notes may afford us Pleafure, they muft be fuch as are not difficultly perceived : For this Reafon the only *Ratios* fit for *Mufick*, befides that of Equality, are the double and triple, or the *Ratios* of 2 to 1 and 3 to 1 ; of greater Differences we could not judge, without a painful Attention ; and as for any other *Ratios* than the multiple Kind (*i. e.* which are as 1 to fome other Number) they are ftill more perplext. 'Tis true, that in the Proportions of *Tune* the *Ratios* of 2 : 3, of 3 : 4, &c. produce *Concord*; and tho' we conclude thefe to be the Proportions, from very good Reafons, yet the Ear judges of them after a more fubtil Manner; or rather indeed we are confcious of no fuch

Thing

Thing as the Proportions of the different Numbers of Vibrations that constitute the *Intervals* of Sound, tho' the Agreeableness or Disagreeableness of our Sensations seem to depend upon it, by some secret Conformity of the Organs of Sense with the Impulse made upon them in these Proportions ; but in the Business of *Time*, the good Effect depends entirely upon a distinct Perception of the Proportions.

Now, the Length of Notes is a Thing merely accidental to the Sound, and depends altogether upon our Will in producing them: And to make the Proportions distinct and perceivable, so that we may be pleased with them, there is no other Way but to divide the Two Notes compared into equal Parts ; and as this is easier done in multiple Proportions, because the shorter Note needs not be divided, being the Divisor or Measure of the imaginary Parts of the other   so 'tis still easier in the first and more simple Kind as 2 to 1, and 3 to 1 ; and the Necessity of such simple Proportions in the *Time* is the more, that we have also the *Intervals* of *Tune* to mind along with it.   But observe, that when I say the *Ratio* of Equality, and those of 2 to 3 and 3 to 1, are the only *Ratios* of *Time* fit for *Musick*, I do not mean that there must not be, in the same Song, Two Notes in any other Proportion ; but you must take it this Way, *viz.* that of Two Notes immediately next other, these ought to be the *Ratios*, because only the Notes in immediate Succession are or can be directly minded, in propor-

portioning the Time, whereof one being taken
at any Length, the other is meafured with relation to it, and fo on: And the Proportions of
other Notes at Diftances I call accidental Proportions. Again *obferve*, that even betwixt Two
Notes next to other, there may be other Proportions of greater Inequality, but then it is betwixt Notes which the Ear does not directly
compare, which are feparate by fome Paufe, as
the one being the End of one Period of the
Song, and the other the Beginning of another ;
or even when they are feparate by a lefs Paufe,
as a *Bar* (which you'll have explained prefently.) Sometimes alfo a Note is kept out very
long, by connecting feveral Notes of the fame
Value, and directing them to be taken all as one,
but this is always fo ordered that it can be eafily
fubdivided in the Imagination, and efpecially by
the Movement of fome other *Part* going along,
which is the ordinary Cafe where thefe long
Notes happen, and then the *Melody* is in the
moving *Part*, the long Note being defigned only for *Harmony* to it ; fo that this Cafe is no
proper Exception to the Rule, which relates to
the *Melody* of fucceffive Sounds, but here the
Melody is transferred from the one *Part* to another. And *laftly*, confider that it is chiefly in
brisk Movements, where neither of the Two
Notes is long, that no other Proportions betwixt
them than the fimple ones mentioned are admitted,

§ 2. *Of*

§ 2. *Of the* abfolute Time ; *and the various* Modes, *or* Conftitution *of Parts of a Piece of* Melody, *on which the different Airs in* Mufick *depend, and particularly of the Diftinction of* common *and* triple Time, *and the Defcription of the* Chronometer *for meafuring it.*

FROM the Principles mentioned in the laft Article, we conclude that there are certain Limits beyond which we muft not go, either in Swiftnefs or Slownefs of *Time*, i. e. Length or Shortnefs of Notes ; and therefore let us come to Particulars, and explain the various Quantities, and the Way of meafuring them.

IN order to this we muft here confider another Application of the preceeding Principles, which is, that a Piece of *Melody* being a Compofition of many Notes fucceffively ranged, and heard one after another, is divifible into feveral Parts ; and ought to be contrived fo as the feveral Members may be eafily diftinguifhed, that the Mind, perceiving this Connection of Parts conftituting one Whole, may be delighted with it ; for 'tis plain where we perceive there are Parts, the Mind will endeavour to diftinguifh them, and when that cannot be eafily done, we muft be fo far difappointed of our Pleafure. Now a Divifion into equal Parts is, of all others, the moft fimple and eafily perceived; and in the prefent Cafe, where fo many other Things require our Attention, as the various
Com-

Combinations of *Tune* and *Time*, no other Division can be admitted: Therefore,

EVERY *Song* is actually divided into a certain Number of equal Parts, which we call *Bars* (from a Line that feparates them, drawn ftraight acrofs the Staff, as you fee in *Plate* 2.) or *Meafures*, becaufe the Meafure of the *Time* is laid upon them, or at leaft by means of their Subdivifions we are affifted in meafuring it; and therefore you have this Word *Meafure* ufed fometime for a *Bar*, and fometime for the *abfolute* Quantity of *Time*; and to prevent Ambiguity, I fhall afterwards write it in *Italick* when I mean a *Bar*.

BY faying the *Bars* are all equal I mean that, in the fame Piece of *Melody*, they contain each the fame Number of the fame Kind of Notes, as *Minims* or *Crotchets*, &c. or that the Sum of the Notes in each (for they are varioufly fubdivided) reckoned according to their *Ratios* one to another already fixt, is equal; and every Note of the fame Name, as *Crotchet*, &c. muft be made of the fame *Time* through the whole Piece, confequently the *Times* in which the feveral *Bars* are performed are all equal; fee the *Examples* of *Plate* 3. But what that *Time* is, we don't yet know; and indeed I muft fay it is a various and undetermined Thing. Different Purpofes, and the Variety which we require in our Pleafures, make it neceffary that the Meafures of a *Bar*, or the Movement with refpect to quick and flow, be in fome Pieces greater, and in others lefler;

leſſer ; and this might be done by having the
Quantity of the Notes of *Time* fixt to a certain
Meaſure, ſo that wherever any Note occurred
it ſhould always be of the ſame *Time*; and then
when a quick Movement were deſigned, the
Notes of ſhorter *Time* would ſerve, and the
longer for a ſlow *Time* ; and for determining
theſe Notes we might uſe a Pendulum of a certain Length, whoſe Vibration being the fixt
Meaſure of any one Note, that would determine
the reſt ; and it would be beſt if a *Crotchet*
were the determined Note, by the Subdiviſion
or Multiplication whereof, we could eaſily meaſure the other Notes; and by Practice we might
eaſily become familiar with that Meaſure ; but
as this is not the Method agreed upon, tho'
it ſeems to be a very rational and eaſy one, I
ſhall not inſiſt upon it here.

I n the preſent Practice, tho' the ſame Notes
of *Time* are of the ſame Meaſure in any one
Piece, yet in different Pieces they differ very
much, and the Differences are in general marked by the Words *ſlow, brisk, ſwift,* &c. written at the Beginning ; but ſtill theſe are uncertain Meaſures, ſince there are different Degrees
of *ſlow* and *ſwift* ; and indeed the true Determination of them muſt be learnt by Experience
from the Practice of Muſicians ; yet there are
ſome Kind of general Rules commonly delivered
to us in this Matter, which I ſhall ſhew you,
and at the ſame Time the Method uſed for
aſſiſting us to give each Note its true Proportion, according to the Meaſure or determined
Quantit.

Quantity of *Time*, and for keeping this equal thro' the Whole. But in order to this, there is another very confiderable Thing to be learnt, concerning the *Mode* or *Conftitution* of the *Meafure* ; and firft *obferve*, That I call this Difference in the abfolute Time the different *Movements* of a Piece, a Thing very diftinct from the different *Meafure* or *Conftitution* of the *Bar*, for feveral Pieces may have the fame *Meafure*, and a different *Movement*. Now by this *Conftitution* is meant the Difference with refpect to the Quantity of the *Meafure*, and the particular Subdivifion and Combination of its Parts ; and by the total Quantity, I underftand that the Sum of all the Notes in the *Meafure* reckoned according to their fixt Relation, is equal to fome one or more determined Notes, as to one *Semibreve* or to Three *Minims* or *Crotchets*, &c. which yet without fome other Determination is but relative : And in the Subdivifion of the *Meafure* the Thing chiefly confidered is, That it is divifible into a certain Number of equal Parts, fo that, counting from the Beginning of the *Meafure*, each Part fhall end with a Note, and not in the Middle of one (tho' this is alfo admitted for Variety;) for *Example*, if the Meafure contain 3 *Minims*, and ought to be divided into Three equal Parts, then the Subdivifion and Combination of its leffer Parts ought to be fuch, that each Part, counting from the Beginning, fhall be compofed of a precife Number of whole Notes, without breaking in upon any Note ; fo if the firft Note were

were a *Crotchet*, and the fecond a *Minim*, we could not take the firft 3*d* Part another Way than by dividing that *Minim*.

We confidered already how neceffary it is that the *Ratios* of the *Time* of fucceffive Notes be fimple, which for ordinary are only as 2 to 1, or 3 to 1, and in any other Cafes are only the Compounds of thefe *Ratios*, as 4 to 1 ; fo in the *Conftitution* of the *Meafure*, we are limited to the fame *Ratios*, i. e. the Meafures are only fubdivided into 2 or 3 equal Parts ; and if there are more, they muft be Multiples of thefe Numbers as 4 to 6, is compoffed of 2 and 3 ; again *obferve*, the *Meafures* of feveral Songs may agree in the total Quantity, yet differ in the Subdivifion and Combination of the leffer Notes that fill up the *Meafure* ; alfo thofe that agree in a fimilar or like Combination or Subdivifion of the *Meafure*, may yet differ in the total Quantity. But to come to Particulars.

Of common *and* triple Time.

These *Modes* are divided into Two general Kinds, which I fhall call the *common* and *triple Mode*, called ordinarily *common* and *triple Time*.

1. *COMMON TIME* is of Two Species ; the 1*ft* where every *Meafure* is equal to a *Semibreve*, or its Value in any Combination of Notes of a leffer relative Quantity ; the 2*d*, where every *Meafure* is equal to a *Minim*, or its Value in leffer Notes. The *Movements* of this Kind of *Meafure* are very various ; but there are Three common Diftinctions, the firft is *flow*, fignified

at

at the Beginning by this Mark C, the 2*d* is *brisk*, fignified by this ₵, the 3*d* is very *quick* fignified by this 𝕯; but what that *flow*, *brisk*, and *quick* is, is very uncertain, and, as I have faid already, muft be learned by Practice : The neareft Meafure I know, is to make a *Quaver* the Length of the Pulfe of a good Watch, and fo the *Crotchet* will be equal to 2 Pulfes, a *Minim* equal to 4, and the whole *Meafure* or *Semibreve* equal to 8 Pulfes; and this is very near the Meafure of the brisk *common Time*, the flow *Time* being near as long again, as the quick is about half as long. Some propofe to meafure it thus, *viz.* to imagine the *Bar* as actually divided into 4 *Crotchets* in the firft Species, and to make the whole as long as one may diftinctly pronounce thefe Four Words, *One*, *two*, *three*, *four*, all of equal Length ; fo that the firft *Crotchet* may be applied to One, the 2*d* to Two, *&c.* and for other Notes proportionally; and this they make the brisk Movement of *common Time*; and where the *Bar* has but Two *Crotchets*, then 'tis meafured by *one*, *two* : But this is ftill far from being a certain Meafure. I fhall propofe fome other Method prefently, mean while

LET us fuppofe the Meafure or Quantity fixt, that we may explain the ordinary Method practifed as a Help for perferving it equal thro' the whole Piece.

THE total *Meafure* of *common Time* is equal to a *Semibreve* or *Minim*, as already faid; but thefe are varioufly fubdivided into Notes of
lefler

leſſer Value. Now to keep the *Time* equal, we make uſe of a Motion of the Hand, or Foot (if the other is employed,) thus; knowing the true *Time* of a *Crotchet*, we ſhall ſuppoſe the *Meaſure* actually ſubdivided into 4 *Crotchets* for the firſt Species, and the half *Meaſure* will be 2 *Crotchets*,therefore the Hand or Foot being up, if we put it down with the very Beginning of the firſt Note or *Crotchet*, and then raiſe it with the Third, and then down with the Beginning of the next *Meaſure*, this is called *Beating* the *Time* ; and by Practice we acquire a Habit of making this Motion very equal, and conſequently of dividing the *Meaſure* in Two equal Parts : Now whatever other Subdiviſion the *Meaſure* conſiſts of, we muſt calculate, by the Relation of the Notes, where the firſt Half ends, and then applying this equable Motion of the Hand or Foot,we make the firſt as long as the Motion down (or as the Time betwixt its being down and raiſed again,for the Motion is frequently made in an Inſtant ; and the Hand continues down for ſome Time,) and the other Half as long as the Motion up (or as the Hand remains up,) and having the half *Meaſure* thus determined, Practice very ſoon learns us to take all the Notes that compoſe it in their true Proportion one to another, and ſo as to begin and end them preciſely with the *beating*. In the *Meaſure* of Two *Crotchets*, we beat down the firſt and the ſecond up.

OBSERVE, That ſome call each Half of the *Meaſure*, in *common Time*, A TIME ; and

and fo they call this the *Mode* or *Meafure* of
Two *Times*, or the *Dupla-meafure*. Again
you'll find fome mark the *Meafure* of Two
Crotchets with a 2 or $\frac{2}{4}$, fignifying that 'tis e-
qual to Two Notes, whereof 4 make a *Semi-
breve*; and fome alfo marked $\frac{4}{8}$ which is the
very fame Thing, *i. e.* 4 Quavers.

2. *TRIPLE TIME* confifts of many different Species, whereof there are in general 4,
each of which have their Varieties under it ;
and the common Name of *Triple* is taken
from this, that the Whole or Half *Meafure*
is divifible into 3 equal Parts, and fo beat.

THE 1*ft* *Species* is called the *fimple Triple*,
whofe *Meafure* is equal either to 3 *Semibreves*,
to 3 *Minims*, or to 3 *Crotchets*, or to 3 *Quavers*,
or laftly to 3 *Semiquavers* ; which are mark-
ed thus, *viz.* $\frac{3}{1}$ or $\frac{3}{2}$ or $\frac{3}{4}$ $\frac{3}{8}$ $\frac{3}{16}$, but the laft is not
much ufed, nor the firft, except in Church-mu-
fick. The *Meafure* in all thefe, is divided into
3 equal Parts or *Times*, called from that properly *Triple-time*, or the *Meafure* of 3 *Times*,
whereof 2 are beat down, and the 3*d* up.

THE 2*d* *Species* is the *mixt Triple*: its
Meafure is equal to 6 *Crotchets* or 6 *Quavers*
or 6 *Semiquavers*, and accordingly marked $\frac{6}{4}$ or
$\frac{6}{8}$ or $\frac{6}{16}$, but the laft is feldom ufed. Some Authors add other Two, *viz.* 6 *Semibreves* and
6 *Minims*, marked $\frac{6}{1}$ or $\frac{6}{2}$ but thefe are not in
ufe. The *Meafure* here is ordinarily divided
into Two equal Parts or *Times*, whereof one is
beat down, and one up ; but it may alfo be divided into 6 *Times*, whereof the firft Two are
beat

beat down, and the 3*d* up, then the next Two
down and the laſt up, *that is,* beat each Half
of the Meaſure like the *ſimple Triple* (upon
which Account it may alſo be called a *compound
Triple,*) and becauſe it may be thus divided
either into Two or 6 *Times* (*i. e.* Two *Triples*)
'tis called *mixt,* and by ſome called the Meaſure of 6 *Times.*

THE 3*d Species* is the *compound Triple,* con-
ſiſting of 9 *Crotchets,* or *Quavers* or *Semiqua-
vers* marked thus $\frac{9}{4}, \frac{9}{8}, \frac{9}{16}$; the firſt and the
laſt are little uſed, and ſome add $\frac{9}{1} \frac{9}{2}$ which are
never uſed. This *Meaſure* is divided either in-
to 3 equal Parts or *Times,* whereof Two are
beat down and one up; or each Third Part
of it may be divided into 3 *Times,* and beat
like the *ſimple Triple,* and for this 'tis called the
Meaſure of 9 *Times.*

THE 4*th Species* is a *Compound* of the 2*d
Species,* containing 12 *Crotchets* or *Quavers* or
Semiquavers marked $\frac{12}{4} \frac{12}{8} \frac{12}{16}$, to which ſome
add $\frac{12}{1}$ and $\frac{12}{2}$ that are not uſed; nor are the
1ſt and 3*d* much in Uſe, eſpecially the 3*d.*
The *Meaſure* here may be divided into Two
Times, and beat one down and one up; or each
Half may be divided and beat at the 2*d* Species,
either by Two or Three, in which Caſe it will
make in all 12 *Times,* hence called the Meaſure
of 12 *Times.* See Examples of the moſt ordinary Species in *Plate* 3*d.*

NOW as to the Movement of theſe ſeveral
Kinds of *Meaſures* both *duple* and *triple,* 'tis
various and as I have ſaid, it muſt be learned
by

by Practice ; yet ere I leave this Part, I shall make these general *Observations*, *First*. That the *Movement* in every Piece is ordinarily marked by such Words as *slow*, *swift*, &c. But because the *Italian* Compositions are the Standard and Model of the better Kind of modern *Musick*, I shall explain the Words by which they mark their Movements, and which are generally used by all others in Imitation of them : They have 6 common Distinctions of *Time*, expressed by these Words, *grave*, *adagio*, *largo*, *vivace*, *allegro*, *presto*, and sometimes *prestissimo*. The first expresses the slowest Movement, and the rest gradually quicker; but indeed they leave it altogether to Practice to determine the precise Quantity. *2do.* The Kind of *Measure* influences the *Time* exprest by these Words, in respect of which we find this generally true, that the Movements of the same Name, as *adagio* or *allegro*, &c. are swifter in *triple* than in *common Time*. *3tio.* We find *common Time* of all these different Movements; but in the *triple*, there are some Species that are more ordinarily of one Kind of Movement than another: Thus the triple $\frac{3}{2}$ is ordinarily *adagio*, sometimes *vivace* ; the $\frac{3}{4}$ is of any Kind from *adagio* to *allegro* ; the $\frac{3}{8}$ is *allegro*, or *vivace* ; the $\frac{6}{4}$ $\frac{6}{8}$ $\frac{9}{8}$ are more frequently *allegro* ; the $\frac{12}{8}$ is sometimes *adagio* but oftner *allegro*. Yet after al , the *allegro* of one Species of *triple* is a quicker Movement than that of another, so very uncertain these Things are.

THERE is another very considerable Thing to be minded here, *viz.* that the Air or Humour

mour

mour of a *Song* depends very much upon thefe different *Modes* of *Time*, or *Conftitutions* of the *Meafure*, which joined with the Variety of Movements that each *Mode* is capable of, makes this Part of *Mufick* wonderfully entertaining; but we muft be acquainted with *practical Mufick* to underftand this perfectly; yet the following general Things concerning the Species of *Triple*, may be of fome Ufe to remark.

1*mo*. As to the Differences in each Species, fuch as $\frac{3}{2}$; $\frac{3}{4}$ · $\frac{3}{8}$ in the *fimple triple*, there is more Caprice than Reafon; for the fame Piece of *Melody* may be fet in any of thefe Ways without lofing any Thing of its true Air, fince the *Relation* of the Notes are invariable, and there is no certain Quantity of the *abfolute Time*, which is left to the arbitrary Direction of thefe Words, *adagio*, *allegro*, &c.

2*do*. Of the feveral Species of *triple*, there are fome that are of the fame *relative Meafure*, as $\frac{3}{2}$ · $\frac{6}{4}$ · $\frac{12}{8}$; and $\frac{3}{4}$ · $\frac{6}{8}$; thefe are fo far of the fame *Mode* as the Meafure of each contains the fame total Quantity; for Three *Minims* and Six *Crotchets* and Twelve *Quavers* are equal, and fo are Three *Crotchets* equal to Six *Quavers*; but the different *Conftitutions* of the *Meafure*, with refpect to the Subdivifions and Connections of the Notes, make a moft remarkable Difference in the Air: For *Example*, The Time of $\frac{3}{2}$ confifts generally of *Minims*, and thefe fometimes mixt with *Semibreves* or with *Crotchets*, and fome *Bars* will be all *Crotchets*; but is contrived fo that the Air requires the

Meafure

Meaſure to be divided and beat by Three *Times*,
and will not do another Way without mani-
feſtly changing and ſpoiling the Humour of the
Song: Suppoſe we would beat it by Two *Times*,
the firſt Half will always (except when the
Meaſure is actually divided into Six *Crotchets*,
which is very ſeldom) end in the Middle, or
within the *Time* of ſome Note; and tho' this is
admitted ſometimes for Variety (whereof afterwards) yet it is rare compared with the general
Rule, which is, to contrive the Diviſion of the
Meaſure ſo that every Down and Up of the
Beating ſhall end with a particular Note; for
upon this depends very much the Diſtinctneſs
and, as it were, the Senſe of the *Melody*; and
therefore the Beginning of every *Time*, or *Beating* in the *Meaſure*, is reckoned the *accented*
Part thereof. For the Time $\frac{6}{4}$ it conſiſts of
Crotchets ſometimes mixt with *Quavers*, and
even with *Minims*, but ſo ordered that 'tis either *dupla* or *tripla*, as above explained, which
makes a great Difference in the Air. The
Time $\frac{12}{8}$ is alſo mixt of *dupla* and *tripla*, and
conſiſts generally of *Quavers*, and ſometimes of
Crotchets, but theſe are tied always by Three;
and we have the *Bar* frequently compoſed of
Twelve *Quavers* tied Three and Three;
which, if we ſhould ty Two and Two, would
quite alter the Air: The Reaſon is, That in
this *Mode* there are in each *Bar* Four remarkably accented Parts, which are diſtant from each
other by Three *Quavers*; and the true Reaſon
of tying the *Quavers* in that manner, ſeems to
me

me to be, the marking out thefe diftinct Parts of the *Meafure*; but when the *Quavers* are tied in even Numbers by Two or Four, or by Six, it fuppofes the Accent upon the 1*ft*, 3*d*, and 5*th Quaver*; which gives another Air to the *Melody*, and always a wrong one, when the skilful Compofer defigned it otherwife. The fame Reafons take place in the Difference of thefe Times $\frac{3}{4}$. $\frac{6}{8}$; the firft confifts more ordinarily of *Crotchets*, and *Quavers* tied in even Numbers, becaufe 'tis divided into Three Parts or *Times*; but the other is mixt of *dupla* and *tripla*, and therefore 'tis tied in Threes, unlefs it be fubdivided into *Semiquavers*, and then thefe are tied in even Numbers, becaufe Two *Semiquavers* make a *Quaver*.

AGAIN, there is another Queftion to be confidered here, *viz.* What is the real Difference betwixt $\frac{3}{4}$ and $\frac{6}{4}$, and betwixt $\frac{3}{8}$, $\frac{6}{8}$ and $\frac{12}{8}$? The Lengths of the feveral Strains, or more general Periods of the Song, depend upon thefe, which make a confiderable Difference; but their principal Difference lies in the proper Movements of each, and a certain Choice of the fucceffive Notes that agree only with that Movement; fo $\frac{6}{4}$ is always *allegro*, and would have no agreeable Air if it were performed *adagio* or *largo*: Another Thing is, that the Beginning of each *Bar* is a more diftinct and accented Part than the Beginning of any *Time* in the Middle of a *Bar*, and therefore if we fhould take a Piece fet $\frac{6}{4}$, and fubdivide its *Bars* to make it $\frac{3}{4}$, there would be Hazard of feparat-
ing

ing Things that ought to ftand in a clofer Connection; and if we put Two *Bars* in one of a
Piece fet $\frac{3}{4}$, to make it $\frac{6}{4}$, then we fhould joyn
Things that ought to be diftinct: But I doubt I
have already faid more than can be well underftood withcut fome Acquaintance with the
Practice; yet there is one Thing I cannot omit
here, *viz.* that in *common Time* we have in fome
Cafes *Quavers* tied by Threes, and the Number 3 written over them, to fignify that thefe
Three are only the Time of other Two *Quavers* of that Meafure.

OBSERVE, in explaining what a *Bar* or
Meafure is, I have faid that all the *Meafures*
of the fame Piece of *Melody* or *Song*, are of
equal *relative* Value; and the Differences in this
refpect are brought under the Diftinction of different *Modes* and *Species*; but that is taking the
Unity of the Piece in the ftricteft Senfe. We have
alfo a Variety of fuch Pieces united in one principal *Key*, and fuch an Agreement of Air as is
confiftent with the different *Modes* of *Time*; and
fuch a Compofition of different Airs is called, in
a large Senfe, one Piece of *Melody*, under the
general Name of *Sonata* if 'tis defigned only for
Inftruments, or *Cantata* if for the Voice; and
thefe feveral leffer Pieces have alfo different
Names, fuch as *Allemanda, Gavotta,*&c. (which
are always *common Time*) *Minuet, Sarabanda,
Giga, Corrante, Siciliana,*&c. which are *triple
Time.*

Of

Of the CHRONOMETER.

I have fpoken a little already of the meafuring the *abfolute Time*, or determining the *Movement* of a Piece by means of a *Pendulum*, a Vibration of which being applied to any one Note, as a *Crotchet*, the reft might be eafily determined by that. Monfieur *Loulie* in his *Elemens, ou Principes de Mufique*, propofes for this Purpofe a very fimple and eafy Machine of a *Pendulum*, which he calls a CHRONOMETER; it confifts of one large Ruler or Piece of Board, Six Foot or Seventy Two Inches long, to be fet on End; it is divided into its Inches, and the Numbers fet fo as to count upward; and at every Divifion there is a fmall round Hole, thro' whofe Center the Line of Divifion runs. At Top of this Ruler, about an Inch above the Divifion 72, and perpendicular to the Ruler is inferted a fmall Piece of Wood, in the upper Side of which there is a Groove, hollowed along from the End that ftands out to that which is fixt in the Ruler, and near each End of it a Hole is made: Thro' thefe Holes a *Pendulum* Chord is drawn, which runs in the Groove; at that End of the Chord that comes thro' the Hole furtheft from the Ruler the Ball is hung, and at the other End there is a fmall wooden Pin which can be put in any of the Holes of the Ruler; when the Pin is in the upmoft Hole at 72, then the *Pendulum* from the Top to the Center of
the

the Ball, muſt be exactly Seventy Two Inches ; and therefore whatever Hole of the Ruler it is put in, the *Pendulum* will be juſt ſo many Inches as that Figure at the Hole denotes. The Uſe of this Machine is ; the Compoſer lengthens or ſhortens his *Pendulum* till one Vibration · be equal to the deſigned Length of his *Bar*, and then the *Pin* ſtands at a certain Diviſion, which marks the Length of the *Pendulum* ; and this Number being ſet with the *Clef*, at the Beginning of the Song, is a Direction to others how to uſe the *Chronometer* in meaſuring the Time according to the Compoſer's Deſign ; for, with the Number is ſet the Note (*Crotchet* or *Minim*) whoſe Value he would have the Vibration to be ; which in brisk *common Time* is beſt a *Minim* or half *Bar*, or even a whole *Bar* when that is but a *Minim*, and in ſlow *Time* a *Crotchet* : In *triple Time* it will do well to be the 3*d* Part, or Half or 4*th* Part of a *Bar* ; and in the *ſimple Triples* that are *allegro*, let it be a whole *Bar*. And if in every *Time* that is *allegro*, the Vibration is applied to a whole or half *Bar*, Practice will teach us to ſubdivide it juſtly and equally. And mind, to make this Machine of univerſal Uſe, ſome canonical Meaſure of the Diviſions muſt be agreed upon, that the Figure may give a certain Direction for the Length of the *Pendulum*.

§ 3. Con-

§ 3. *Concerning* Refts *or* Paufes *of* Time ; *and
fome other neceffary Marks in writing* Mufick.

AS Silence has very powerful Effects in *Oratory*, when it is rightly managed, and
brought in agreeable to Circumftances, fo in
Mufick, which is but another Way of expreffing
and exciting Paffions, Silence is fometimes ufed
to good Purpofe : And tho it may be neceffary
in a fingle Piece of *Melody* for expreffing fome
Paffion, and even for the Pleafure depending on
Variety, where no Paffion is directly minded,
yet it is ufed more generally in *fymphonetick*
Compofitions ; for the fake of that Beauty and
Pleafure we find in hearing one Part move on
while another refts, and this interchangeably;
which being artfully contrived, has very good
Effects. But my Bufinefs in this Place is only to
let you know the Signs or Marks by which this
Silence is expreffed.

THESE *Refts* are either for a whole *Bar*,
or more than one *Bar*, or but the Part of
a *Bar* : When it is for a Part of a *Bar*,
then it is expreffed by certain Signs correfponding to the Quantity of certain Notes of
Time, as *Minim, Crotchet*, &c. and are accordingly called *Minim-refts, Crotchet-refts*, &c.
See their Figure in *Plate* 2. *Fig.* 3. where the
Note and correfponding Reft are put together ;
and

and when any of thefe occur either on Line or
Space, for 'tis no Matter where they are fet,
that Part is always filent for the *Time* of a *Minim* or *Crotchet*, &c. according to the Nature of
the *Reft*. A *Reft* will be fometimes for a
Crotchet and *Quaver*, or for other Quantities of
Time, for which there is no particular Note;
in this Cafe the Signs of Silence are not multiplied or made more difficult than thofe of Sound,
but fuch a Silence is marked by placing together as many *Refts* of different *Time* as make
up the whole defigned *Reft*; which makes the
Practice more eafy, for by this we can more readily divide the Meafure, and give the juft Al-
lowance of *Time* to the *Refts* : But let Practice
fatisfie you of thefe Things.

W H E N the *Reft* is for a whole *Bar*, then the
Semibreve Reft is always ufed, both in *common*
and *triple Time*. If the Reft is for Two *Meafures*, then it is marked by a Line drawn crofs
a whole Space, and crofs a Space and an Half
for Three *Meafures*, and crofs Two Spaces for
Four *Meafures*, and fo on as you fee marked in
the Place above directed. But to prevent all
Ambiguity, and that we may at Sight know the
Length of the *Reft*, the Number of *Bars* is
ordinarily written over the Place where thefe
Signs ftand.

I know fome Writers fpeak differently about
thefe *Refts*, and make fome of them of different
Values in different Species of *triple Time* : For
Example, they fay, that the Figure of what is
the *Minim-reft* in *common Time*, expreffes the
Reft

Reſt of Three *Crotchets* ; and that in the *Triples* $\frac{6}{8}$ $\frac{6}{16}$ $\frac{12}{8}$ $\frac{12}{16}$ it marks always an half *Meaſure*, however different theſe are among themſelves : Again, that the *Reſt* of a *Crotchet* in *common Time* is a *Reſt* of Three *Quavers* in the *Triple* $\frac{9}{8}$, and that the *Quaver-reſt* of *common Time* is equal to Three *Semiquavers* in the *triple* $\frac{9}{16}$. But this Variety in the Uſe of the ſame Signs is now generally laid aſide, if ever it was much in Faſhion ; at leaſt there is a good Reaſon why it ought to be out, for we can obtain our End eaſier by one conſtant Value of theſe Marks of Silence, as they are above explained.

THERE are ſome other Marks uſed in writing of *Muſick*, which I ſhall explain, all of which you'll find in *Plate* 2. A *ſingle Bar* is a Line acroſs the Staff, that ſeparates one *Meaſure* from another. A *double Bar* is Two parallel Lines acroſs the Staff, which ſeparates the greater Periods or Strains of any particular or *ſimple Piece*. A *Repeat* is a Mark which ſignifies the Repetition of a Part of the Piece; which is either of a whole Strain, and then the double *Bar*, at the End of that Strain, which is repeated, is marked with Points on each Side of it ; and ſome make this the Rule, that if there are Points on both Sides, they direct to a Repetition both of the preceeding and following Strain, *i. e.* that each of them are to be play'd or ſung twice on End ; but if only one of theſe Strains ought to be repeated, then there muſt be Points only on that Side, *i. e.* on the left, if

it

it is the preceeding, or the Right if the following Strain: When only a Part of a Strain is to be repeated, there is a Mark set over the Place where that Repetition begins, which continues to the End of the Strain.

A *Direct* is a Mark set at the End of a Staff, especially at the Foot of a Page, upon that Line or Space where the first Note of the next Staff is set.

You'll find a Mark, like the Arch of a Circle drawn from one Note to another, comprehending Two or more Notes in the same or different Degrees ; if the Notes are in different Degrees, it signifies that they are all to be sung to one Syllable, for Wind-instruments that they are to be made in one continued Breath, and for stringed Instruments that are struck with a Bow, as Violin, that they are made with one Stroke. If the Notes are in the same Degree, it signifies that 'tis all one Note, to be made as long as the whole Notes so connected ; and this happens most frequently betwixt the last Note of one *Bar* and the first of the next, which is particularly called *Syncopation*, a Word also applied in other Cases : Generally, when any *Time* of a *Measure* ends in the Middle of a Note, *that is*, in *common Time*, if the Half or any of the 4*th* Parts of the *Bar*, counting from Beginning, ends in the Middle of a Note, in the *simple Treble* if any 3*d* Part of the *Measure* ends within a Note, in the *compound Treble* if any 9*th* Part, and in the Two *mixt Triples*, if any 6*th* or 12*th* Part ends in the Middle of

any

any Note, 'tis called *Syncopation*, which properly fignifies a ftriking or breaking of the *Time*, becaufe the Diftinctnefs of the feveral *Times* or Parts of the *Meafure* is as it were hurt or interrupted hereby, which yet is of good Ufe in *Mufick* as Experience will teach.

Yo u'll find over fome fingle Notes a Mark like an Arch, with a Point in the Middle of it which has been ufed to fignifie that that Note is to be made longer than ordinary, and hence called a *Hold*; but more commonly now it fignifies that the *Song* ends there, which is only ufed when the *Song* ends with a Repetition of the firft Strain or a Part of it; and this Repetition is alfo directed by the Words, *Da capo*, *i. e.* from the Beginning.

Over the Notes of the *Bafs-part* you'll find Numbers written, as 3 . 5, *&c.* thefe direct to the *Concords* or *Difcords*, that the Compofer would have taken with the Note over which they are fet, which are as it were the Subftance of the *Bafs*, thefe others being as Ornaments, for the greater Variety and Pleafure of the *Harmony*.

CHAP.

❀❀❀❀❀❀❀❀❀❀❀❀❀❀

C H A P. XIII.

Containing the general Principles and Rules
of HARMONICK COMPOSITION.

---

§ 1. *D E F I N I T I O N S.*

1. *Of* Melody *and* Harmony *and their* Ingredients.

THO' thefe, and alfo the next *Definition* concerning the *Key,* have been already largely explained; yet 'tis neceſſary they be here repeated with a particular View to the Subject of this Chapter.

MELODT is the agreeable Effect of different *muſical* Sounds, fucceſſively ranged and difpofed; fo that *Melody* is the Effect only of one fingle Part; and tho' it is a Term chiefly applicable to the *Treble,* as the *Treble* is moſtly to be diſtinguiſhed by its *Air,* yet in fo far as the *Baſs* may be made airy, and to fing well, it may be alfo properly faid to be *melodious.*

HAR-

HARMONY is the agreeable Refult of the Union of Two or more *mufical* Sounds heard at one and the fame Time ; fo that *Harmony* is the Effect of Two Parts at leaft : As therefore a continued Succeffion of *mufical* Sounds produces *Melody*, fo does a continued Combination of thefe produce *Harmony*.

O f the Twelve *Intervals* of *mufical* Sounds, known by the Names of *Second leffer*, *Second greater, Third leffer, Third greater, Fourth, falfe Fifth*, (which is called *Tritone* or *Semidiapente* in *Chap.* 8. § 4.) *Fifth, Sixth leffer, Sixth greater, Seventh leffer, Seventh greater* and *Octave*, all *Melody* and *Harmony* is compofed ; for the *Octaves* of each of thefe are but Replications of the fame Sounds ; and whatever therefore is or fhall be faid of any or of all of thefe Sounds, is to be underftood and meant as faid alfo of their *Octaves*.

T h e s e *Intervals*, as they are expreffed by Notes, ftand, as in *Example* 1. *C* being the *fundamental* Note from which the reft receive their Denominations : Or they may ftand as in the Second *Example*, where *g* is the *fundamental* Note ; for whatever be the *Fundamental*, the Diftances of Sound are to it, and reciprocally to each other the fame.

O f thefe *Intervals* Two, *viz.* the *Octave* and *Fifth*, are called *perfect Concords* ; Four, *viz.* the Two 3*ds* and Two 6*ths*, are called *imperfect Concords* ; Five *viz.* the falfe *Fifth*, the Two *Seconds* and Two *Sevenths*, are *Difcords*. The *Fourth* is in its own Nature a *perfect Concord*

cord; but becaufe of its Situation, lying betwixt
the 3*d* and the 5*th*, it can never be made ufe
of as a *Concord*, but when joined with the 6*th*
with which it ftands reciprocally in the Relation of a 3*d*; it is therefore commonly claffed
among the *Difcords*, not on account of the Nature of the *Interval*, but becaufe of its little
Ufe in the *Harmony* of *Concords*.

2. *Of the principal* Tone *or* Key.

THE *Key* in every Piece and in every Part
of each Piece of *mufical* Compofition is that
Tone or Sound which is predominant and
to which all the reft do refer (See above
Chap. 9.)
EVERY Piece of *Mufick*, as a *Concerto, So-*
nata or *Cantata* is framed with due regard to
one particular Sound called the *Key*, and in
which the Piece is made to begin and end; but
in the Courfe of the *Harmony* of any fuch
Piece, the Variety which in *Mufick* is fo neceffary to pleafe and entertain, requires the introducing of feveral other *Keys.*
IT is enough here to confider, that every
the leaft Portion of any Piece of *Mufick* has its
Key; which rightly to comprehend we are to
take Notice, that a well tuned Voice, tho' un-
accuftomed to *Mufick*, afcending by Degrees
from any Sound affigned, will naturally proceed
from fuch Sound to the 2*d g.* from thence to
the

the 3*d l.* or to the 3*d g.* indifferently from either of thefe to the 4*th,* from thence to the 5*th,* from thence to the 6*th l.* or 6*th g.* accordingly as it has before either touched at the 3*d l.* or 3*d g.* from either of thefe to the 7*th g.* and from thence into the *Octave* : From which it is inferred, that of the 12 *Intervals* within the Compafs of the *Octave* of any Sound affigned, feven are only *natural* and *melodious* to that Sound, *viz.* the 2*d g.* 3*d g.* 4*th,* 5*th,* 6*th g.* 7*th g.* and 8*ve,* if the proceeding be by the 3*d g.* but if it is by the 3*d l.* the Seven natural Sounds are the 2*d g.* 3*d l.* 4*th,* 5*th,* 6*th l.* 7*th g.* and 8*ve,* as they are exprefs'd in the *Examples,* 3*d* and 4*th.*

As therefore the 3*d* and 6*th* may be either greater or leffer, from thence it is that the *Key* is denominated *fharp* or *flat ;* the *fharp Key* being diftinguifhed by the 3*d g.* and the *Flat* by the 3*d l.*

In fuch a Progreffion of Sounds, the *fundamental* one to which the others do refer, is the *principal Tone* or *Key;* and as here *C* is the *Key,* fo may any other Note be the *Key,* by being made the *fundamental* Note to fuch like Progreffion of Notes, as is already exemplified.

Whatever be the *Key,* none but the Seven *natural* Notes can enter into the Compofition of its *Harmony:* The Five other Notes that are within the Compafs of the *Octave* of the *Key, viz.* the 2*d l.* 3*d l.* falfe 5*th,* 6*th l.* 7*th l.*

7th l. in a *sharp Key*; and the *2d l.* *3d g. false 5th,* *6th g.* and *7th l.* in a *flat* one, are always extraneous to the *Key.*

WHEN these Seven Notes shall happen to be mentioned in the *Bass* as Notes, I shall for Distinction's sake express them by the Names of *2d Fundamental* or *2d f. 3d f. 4th f. 5th f. 6th f. 7th f.* the *Octave* being a Replication of the *Key,* will need no other Name than the *Key f.* But when any of the *Octaves* of these Seven Notes shall happen to be mentioned as Ingredients of the *Treble,* I shall describe them by the simple Names of *2d, 3d, 4th, 5th,* &c. Thus, when the *3d f.* or its *Octave,* which is the same Thing, shall happen to be considered as a *Treble* Note, it is to be marked simply thus (*3d*) as being a *Third* to the *Key Fund.* Thus the *5th f.* or its *Octave,* when considered as a Note in the *Treble,* is to be simply marked thus (*5th*) as being a *5th* to the *Key f:* Or thus (*3d*) as being a *3d* to the *3d f:* Or thus (*6th*) as being a *6th* to the *7th f.* and so of the rest.

EACH of the Seven *natural* Notes therefore in each *Key,* considered as *fundamental,* or as Notes of the *Bass,* have their respective *3ds 5ths, 6ths,* &c. which respective *3ds, 5ths, 6ths,* &c. must be some one, or *Octaves* to some one or other of the 7 *fundamental* Notes that are *natural* to the Key; because, as was said before, nothing can enter into the *Harmony* of any *Key,* but its Seven *natural* Notes and their Octaves.

2. *Of*

3. *Of Compofition.*

UNDER this Title of *Compofition* are juftly comprehended the *practical Rules*. 1mo. Of *Melody*, or the Art of making a fingle *Part*, i. e. contriving and difpofing the fingle Sounds, fo that their Succeffion and Progrefs may be agreeable ; and 2do. Of *Harmony*, or the *Art* of difpofing and conferting feveral fingle *Parts* fo together, that they may make one agreeable Whole. And here *obferve*, the Word *Harmony* is taken fomewhat larger than above in *Chap.* 7. for *Difcords* are ufed with *Concords* in the *Compofition* of *Parts*, which is here expreft in general by the Word *Harmony* ; which therefore is diftinguifhed into the *Harmony* of *Concords* in which no *Difcords* are ufed, and that of *Difcords* which are always mixt with *Concords*. *Obferve* alfo that this Art of *Harmony* has been long known by the Name of *Counterpoint* ; which arofe from this, That in the Times when *Parts* were firft introduced, their *Mufick* being fo fimple that they ufed no Notes of different Time, that Difference depending upon the Quantity of Syllables of the Words of a Song, they marked their *Concords* by Points fet againft one another. And as there were no different Notes of Time, fo the *Parts* were in every Note made *Concord* : And this afterwards was called *fimple* or *plain Counterpoint*, to diftinguifh it from another Kind, wherein Notes of different Value were ufed, and *Difcords* brought
in

in betwixt the *Parts*, which was called *figurate Counterpoint*.

OBSERVE again, *Melody* is chiefly the Bufinefs of the Imagination ; fo that the Rules of *Melody* ferve only to prefcribe certain Limits to it, beyond which the Imagination, in fearching out the Variety and Beauty of Air, ought not to carry us : But *Harmony* is the Work of Judgment; fo that its Rules are more certain, extenfive, and in Practice more difficult. In the Variety and Elegancy of the *Melody*, the Invention labours a great deal more than the Judgment ; but in *Harmony* the Invention has nothing to do, for by an exact Obfervation of the Rules of *Harmony* it may be produced without that Affiftance from the Imagination.

IT may not be impertinent here to obferve, that it is the great Bufinefs of a Compofer not to be fo much attach'd to the Beauty of *Air*, as to neglect the folid Charms of *Harmony* ; nor fo fervilly fubjected to the more minute Niceties of *Harmony*, as to detract from the *Melody* ; but, by a juft Medium, to make his Piece confpicuous, by preferving the united Beauty both of *Air* and *Harmony*.

---

§ 2. *Rules of* Melody.

I. ANY Note being chofen for the *Key*, and its Quality of *fharp* or *flat* determined, no Notes muft be ufed in any *Part* but the *natural*

tural and *eſſential* Notes of the *Key*, as theſe
are already ſhewn : And for changing or *modulating* from one *Key* to another, which may
alſo be done, you'll find Rules below in
§. 5.

II. Concerning the Succeſſion of *Intervals* in
the ſeveral *Parts*, you have theſe general
Rules.

1. THE *Treble* ought to proceed by as little
Intervals, as is poſſibly conſiſtent with that Variety of *Air*, which is its diſtinguiſhing Character.

2. THE *Baſs* may proceed either gradually
or by larger *Intervals*, at the Will of the Compoſer.

3. THE aſcending by the Diſtance of a *falſe*
5*th* is forbid, as being harſh and diſagreeable;
but deſcending by ſuch a Diſtance is often
practiſed eſpecially in the *Baſs*.

4. To proceed by the Diſtance of a ſpurious
2*d, that is,* from any Note that is ✻, to the Note
immediately above or below it that is ♭; or from
any Note ♭ to the Note immediately above or
below it ✻, is very offenſive. As we are in greateſt Danger of tranſgreſſing this Rule in a *flat
Key*, becauſe of the 6*th l.* and 7*th g.* which
are Two of the *natural* Notes of the *Harmony*, we are therefore to take Care, that deſcending from the *Key* we may proceed by the 7*th
l.* to the 6*th l.* and aſcending to it we may proceed by the 6*th g.* to the 7*th g.* For altho' the
6*th g.* and 7*th l.* are not of the Seven Notes of

a *flat Key*, yet they may be thus made Ufe of as Tranfitions, without any Offence.

5. THE proceeding by the Diftance of a 7*th l.* in any of the Parts, is very harfh.

THUS far may Rules be given to correct the Irregularities of Invention in point of *Air* ; but to acquire or improve it, nothing lefs is neceffary than to be acquainted with the *Melody* of the more celebrated Compofers, fo as to have the more ordinary, and, as it were, common Places of their *Melody,*familiar to the Ear ; and what is further neceffary will, in due Time, naturally follow a Genius turned that Way.

§ 3. *Of the Harmony of* Concords, *or fimple* Counterpoint.

THE *Harmony* of *Concords* is compofed of the *imperfect,* as well as of the *perfect Concords* ; and therefore may be faid to be *perfect* and *imperfect,* according as the *Concords* are of which it is compofed ; thus the *Harmony* that arifes from a Conjunction of any Note with its 5*th* and *Octave* is *perfect,* but with its 3*d* and 6*th* is *imperfect.*

IT has been already fhewn what may enter into the *Harmony* of any *Key,* and what may not. I proceed to fhew how the Seven natural Notes, and their *Octaves* in any *Key,* may ftand together in a *Harmony* of *Concord* ; and how

how the feveral *Concords* may fucceed other;
and then make fome particular Application,
which will finifh what is defig d on this
Branch.

I. *How the* Concords *may ftand together.*

1. To apply, *firft,* the preceeding Diftinction of *perfect* and *imperfect* Harmony; take
this *general Rule, viz.* to the *Key f.* to the *4th f.*
and to the *5th f.* a *perfect Harmony* muft be
joyned. To the *2d f.* to the *3d f.* and to the
7th f. an *imperfect Harmony* is in all Cafes in-
difpenfably required. To the *6th f.* a perfect or
imperfect Harmony is arbitrary.

OBSERVE, In the Compofition of Two
Parts, tho' a *3d* appears only in the *Treble*
upon the *Key f.* the *4th f.* and the *5th f.* yet
the perfect *Harmony* of the *5th* is always fuppofed, and muft be fupplied in the Accompanyments of the *thorough Bafs* to thefe fundamental Notes.

2. But more particularly in the *Compofition*
of Two Parts.

The Rules *are,*
1. The *Key f.* may have either its *Octave,*
its *3d* or its *5th.*

2. The *4th f.* and *5th f.* may have either
their refpective *3ds* or *5ths*; and the firft may
have its *6th*; as, to favour a contrary Motion,
the laft may have its *Octave.*

3. The

3. THE *6th f.* may have either its 3*d*, its 5*th* or its *6th*.

4. THE 2*d f.* 3*d f.* and 7*th f.* may have either their respective 3*ds* or *6ths* ; and the last may, on many Occasions, have its *false* 5*th.*

THESE Rules are still the same whether the the *Key* is *sharp* or *flat*, as they are exemplified in *Example* 5, 6, 7, 8, 9, 10, 11.

AFTER having considered what are the several *Concords,*that may be *harmoniously* applied to the seven *fundamental* Notes; it is next to be learned, how these several *Concords* may succeed each other, for therein lies the greatest Difficulty of *musical Composition.*

II. *The general* Rules *of* Harmony, *respecting the Succession of* Concords.

1. THAT as much as can be in *Parts* may proceed by a contrary Movement,*that is*, when the *Bass* ascends, the *Treble* may at the same Time *descend, & vice versa* ; but as it is impossible this can always be done, the Rule only prescribes the doing so as frequently as can be, *Exam.* 12.

2. The *Parts* moving the same Way either upwards or downwards, Two *Octaves* or Two 5*ths* must never follow one another immediately, *Exam.* 13.

3. TWO *6ths l.* must never succeed each other immediately ; the Danger of transgressing which lies chiefly in a *sharp Key,*where the *6th* to the *6th f.* and to the 7*th f.* are both *lesser.* *Exam.* 14.

4. WHENEVER

4. WHENEVER the *Octave* or 5*th* is to be made ufe of, the *Parts* muft proceed by a contrary Movement to each other; except the *Treble* move into fuch *Octave* or 5*th* gradually;which Rule muft be carefully obferved, becaufe the Occafions of tranfgreffing it do moft frequently occur,*Ex.* 15.

5. If in a *fharp Key*, the *Bafs* defcends gradually from the 5*th f.* to the 4*th f* ; the laft muft never in that Cafe have its proper *Harmony* applied to it, but the Notes that were *Harmony* to the preceeding 5*th f.*muft be continued upon the 4*th f. Exam.* 16.

6. *THIRDS* and 6*ths* may follow one another immediately,as often as one has a Mind. *Exam.* 17.

HERE then are the *Rules* of *Harmony* plainly exhibited, which tho' few in Number, yet the Beginner will find the Obfervance of them a little difficult, becaufe Occafions of tranfgreffing do moft frequently offer themfelves.

IN the former *Article* it is fhewn what *Concords* may be applied to each *Fundamental* or *Bafs*-note ; and here is taught how the *Parts* may proceed joyntly, the *Section* 2*d* fhewing how they may proceed fingly, and what in either Cafe is to be avoided. It remains therefore now to make the Application.

III. *A particular Application of the preceeding* Rules, *to two* Parts.

WHEREAS it is natural to Beginners, firft to imagine the *Treble*, and then to make a *Bafs*

to

to it, the *Treble* being the fhining Part, in which
the Beauty of *Melody* is chiefly to appear ; in
Compliance therewith, I fhall, by inverting as
it were the Rules in the foregoing Section, fet
forth, in the following Rules, which of the Seven
fundamental Notes, in the *fharp* and *flat Keys*,
can properly be made ufe of to each of theSeven
natural Notes that may enter into the *Treble* ;
of which an exact Remembrance will very
much facilitate the attaining a Readinefs in the
Practice of *fingle Counterpoint*.

RULES *for making a* Bafs *to a* Treble, *in
the* fharp *as well as* flat Key.

1. T HE *Key* may have for its *Bafs*, either
the *Key f*. the 4*th f*. to which it is a
5*th*, the 3*d f*. to which it is a 6*th*, or the 6*th
f*. to which it is a 3*d*.

2. T HE 2*d* may have for its *Bafs*, either the
7*th f*. to which it is a 3*d*, or the 5*th f*. to which
is is a 5*th*, and fometimes the 4*th f*. to which
it is a 6*th*.

3. T HE 3*d* can rarely have any other *Bafs*
but the *Key f*. tho' fometimes it may have the
6*th f*. to which it is a 5*th*.

4. T HE 4*th* may have for its *Bafs* either
the 2*d f*. to which it is a 3*d*, or the 6*th f*. to
which it is a 6*th*, and fometimes, to favour a
contrary Movement of the *Parts*, it may have
the 7*th f*. to which it is a falfe 5*th*, which
ought to refolve in the 3*d*, the *Bafs* afcending
to

to the *Key*, and the *Treble* defcending to the 3*d*.

5. T H E 5*th* may have for its *Bafs*, either the 3*d f.* to which it is a 3*d*, the *Key* to which it is a 5*th*, the 7*th f.* to which it is a 6*th* ; or, fometimes, to favour a contrary Movement of the *Parts*, it may have the 5*th f.* to which it is an *Octave*.

6. T H E 6*th* may only have for its *Bafs* the 4*th f.* to which it is a 3*d*.

7. T H E 7*th* may have for its *Bafs*, either the 5*th f.* to which it is a 3*d*, or the 2*d f.* to which it is a 6*th*.

I have carefully avoided the mentioning the 3*ds* and 6*ths*, particularly as they are *greater* or *leffer*, which would inevitably puzzle a Beginner : According to the Plan I have followed, there is no need to be fo particular, becaufe when a 3*d* and 6*th* are mentioned here in general, one is always to underftand fuch a 3*d* and fuch a 6*th* as makes one of the Seven *natural* Notes of the *Key*; thus when I fay that in a *fharp* K*ey* the 5*th* is a 3*d*, to the 3*d f.* I muft neceffarily mean that it is a 3*d l.* to it, becaufe the 3*d g.* to the 3*d f.* is one of the Five extraneous Notes; juft fo when I fay that in a *flat* K*ey* the 5*th* is a 3*d* to the 3*d f.* I muft needs mean that it is a 3*dg.* to it, becaufe the 3*d l.* to it is one of the Five extraneous Notes : Thus when I fay that the 3*d f.* in either *Key* may have a 3*d* or a 6*th* for its *Treble* Note, it muft be underftood as if I faid that fuch 3*d* and 6*th* in

a

a *sharp Key* must be both lesser, and in a *flat Key*, they must be both greater, because in the first or *sharp Key* the 3*d g.* and 6*th g.* of the 3*d f.* are extraneous, and so are the 3*d l.* and the 6*th l.* of the 3*d f.* in a *flat Key:* But considering how much it would embarass and multiply the Rules, to have characterized the 3*ds* and 6*ths* so particularly, I have therefore contrived the Plan I proceed upon, so as to avoid both these Inconveniencies, and by being general make the same Rules rightly understood, serve both for a *sharp* and a *flat Key.*

BUT now that the Contents of the foregoing Rules may be the more easily committed to the Memory, I shall therefore convert them into this Scheme, where the *Asterism* is intended to denote what is but used sometimes.

Scheme *drawn from the preceeding Rules.*

The Octaves of the		may stand in the Treble either as a		to the
	Key		3d,5th,6th,or 8ve.	6f.4f.3f.Kf.
	2d		3d, 5th, 6th*	7f.5f.4f.
	3d		3d,5th*	Kf. 6f.
	4th		3d, 5th l.* 6th.	2f.7f.6f.
	5th		3d,5th,6th,8ve.	3f.Kf.7f.5f.
	6th		3d,	4f.
	7th		3d, 6th.	5f.2f.

See this exemplified, *Example* 18.

These Rules being well understood, and exactly committed to the Memory, the *Treble* in *Ex.* 19. is supposed to be assign'd, and the *Bass* composed to it according to these and the former Rules.

THE

THE firft Thing I am to obferve in the *Treble* is, that its *Key* is *c natural, i. e.* with the 3*d g.* becaufe it begins and ends in *c* without touching any Note but the Seven that belong to the *Harmony* of that *Key.*

THE fecond Note in the *Treble* is the *fecond* in the *Harmony* of the *Key*; which, according to the Rules, might have ftood as a 3*d* to the *Bafs,* as well as a 5*th*; to which therefore the *Bafs* might have been *b,* as well as *g.* but I rather chufed the latter, becaufe having begun pretty high with the *Bafs,* I forefaw I fhould want to get down to *c* below, for a *Bafs* to the 3*d* Note in the *Treble*; and therefore I chufed *g* here rather than *b,* being a more natural and melodious Tranfition to *c* below.

THE third Note in the *Treble,* and 3*d* in the *Harmony* of the *Key,* has *c* the *Key f.* for its *Bafs,* becaufe it is almoft the only *Bafs* it can have: And I chufed to take the *Key* below for the Reafon I juft now mentioned.

THE fourth Note in the *Treble* and 4*th* in the *Harmony* of the *Key,* has the 2*d f.* for its *Bafs,* which here is *d*; it is capable of having for its *Bafs* the 6*th f.* but confidering what behoved to follow, it would not have been fo natural.

THE fifth Note in the *Treble* and 5*th* in the *Harmony* of the *Key,* has for its *Bafs* the 3*d f.* which is here *e.* it might have had *c* the *Key* for its *Bafs,* and the going to *f* afterwards would have fung as well; but I chufed to afcend gradually

gradually with the *Bafs*, to preferve an Imitation that happens to be between the Parts, by the *Bafs* afcending gradually to the 5th *f*. from the Beginning of the fecond *Bar*, as the *Treble* does from the Beginning of the firft *Bar*.

THE fixth Note in the *Treble*, and *Key* in the *Harmony*, ftands as a 5th ; and has for its *Bafs* the 4th *f*. rather than any other it might have had, for the Reafon juft now mentioned.

THE feventh Note in the *Treble*, and 7th in the *Harmony* of the *Key*, has the 5th *f*. rather than the 2d *f*. for its *Bafs*, not only on account of the Imitation I took Notice of, but to favour the contrary Movement of the *Parts* ; and befides, confidering what behoved to follow in the *Bafs*, the 2d *f*. would not have done fo well here ; and the Tranfition from it to the *Bafs* Note that muft neceffarily follow, would not have been fo natural. As to the following Notes of the *Bafs* I need fay nothing ; for the Choice of them will appear to be from one of thefe Two Confiderations, either that they are the only proper *Bafs* Notes that the *Treble* could admit of, or that one is chofen rather than another to favour the contrary Movement of the *Parts*.

I chufed rather to be particular in fetting forth one *Example* than to perplex the Beginner with a Multitude of them; I have therefore only added a fecond, which I refer to the Student's own Examination ; both which are fo contrived, as to be capable of being tranfpofed
into

into a *flat* Key, with the Alteration of the 3*d* and 6*th.*

WHEN thefe *Examples* are thoroughly examined, the next Step I would advife the Beginner to make, would be to tranfpofe thefe *Trebles* into other *Keys*; and then endeavour to make a *Bafs* to them in thefe other *Keys:* For to him, the fame *Treble* in different *Keys* will be in fome Meafure like fo many different *Trebles,* and will be equally conducive to his Improvement. And when he has finifhed the *Bafs* in thefe other *Keys*, let him caft his Eyes on the *Example*, and tranfpofe the *Bafs* here into the fame *Keys*, that he may obferve wherein they differ, and in what they agree; by which Comparifon he will be able to difcover his Faults, and become a Mafter to himfelf. And by the Time that he can with Facility write a *Bafs* to thefe Two *Trebles,* in all the ufual *Keys*, which upon Examination he fhall find to coincide with the *Examples*, I may venture to affure him that he has conquered the greateft Difficulty.

NOTWITHSTANDING the infinite Variety of *Air* there may be in *Mufick*, I take it for granted, that there are a great many common Places in point of *Air*, equally familiar to all Compofers, which neceffarily produce correfpondent common Places in *Harmony*; thus it moft frequently happens that the *Treble* defcends from the 3*d* to the *Key*, as at the *Example* 20, as often will the *Treble* defcend from

the

the *7th* to the *5th*. *Examples* 21, 22, and in
this Cafe the *Bafs* is always the 5 *f.* as in that
the *Bafs* is always the *Key f.* Thus frequently
in the *Treble*, after a Series of Notes the *Air*
will terminate and come to a Kind of *Reft* or
Clofe upon the *2d* or *7th* ; in both which the
Bafs muft always be the *5th f.* as in *Examples*
23, 24. Some other common Places will appear fufficiently in the *Examples*, and others, for
the Beginner's Inftruction, he will beft gather
himfelf from the Works of Authors, particularly
of *Corelli*.

As a thorough Acquaintance with fuch common Places, will be a great Affiftance to the Beginner, I would firft recommend to him the
Practice of thofe here fet forth, in all the *ufual*
Keys fharp as well as *flat*, till they are become
very familiar to. him : But in tranfpofing them
to *flat Keys*, the Variation of the *3d* and *6th* is
to be carefully adverted to.

AFTER *fimple Counterpoint*, wherein nothing
but *Concords* have Place, the next Step is to
that *Counterpoint* wherein there is a Mixture of
Difcord ; of which there are Two Kinds, that
wherein the *Difcords* are introduced occafionally to ferve only as Tranfitions from *Concord* to
Concord, or that wherein the *Difcord* bears a
chief Part in the *Harmony*.

§ 4. *Of*

§ 4. *Of the Use of* Difcords, *or* **Figurate Coun-**terpoint.

1. *Of the* tranfient Difcords *that are fubfervi-ent to the* Air, *but make no Part of the* Har-mony.

EVERY *Bar* or *Meafure* has its accented and unaccented Parts: The Beginning and Middle, or the Beginning of the firft Half of the *Bar,* and Beginning of the latter Half thereof in *common Time;*and the Beginning,or the firft of the Three Notes in *triple Time,* are always the accented Parts of the *Meafure.* So that in *com-mon Time* the firft and third *Crotchet* of the *Bar,* or if the Time be very flow, the 1*ft,* 3*d,* 5*th* and 7*th Quavers* are on the accented Parts of the *Meafure,* the reft are upon the unaccen-ted Parts of it.   In the various Kinds of *Triple* whether $\frac{3}{2}\frac{3}{4}\frac{3}{8}$ or $\frac{6}{8}\frac{12}{8}$ the Notes go always Three and Three, and that which is in the Middle of every Three is always unaccented, the firft and laft accented ; but the Accent on the firft is fo much ftronger, that, in feveral Cafes, the laft is accounted as if it had no Accent ;   fo that a *Difcord* duly prepared never ought to come up-on it.

THE *Harmony* muft always be full upon the accented Parts of the *Meafure,* but upon the unaccented Parts that is not fo requifite: Where-fore *Difcords* may tranfiently pafs there with-out

out any Offence to the Ear : This the *French*
call *Suppofition*, becaufe the tranfient *Difcord*
fuppofes a *Concord* immediately to follow it,
which is of infinite Service in *Mufick*, as con-
tributing mightily to that infinite Variety of
Air of which *Mufick* is capable.

O f SUPPOSITION there are feveral
Kinds. The firft Kind is when the Parts proceed gradually from *Concord* to *Difcord*, and
from *Difcord* to *Concord* as in the *Examples*
25 and 26. where the intervening *Difcord*
ferves only as a Tranfition to the following *Concord.*

B y imagining all the *Crotchets* in the *Treble*
to be *Minims,*and all the *Semibreves* in the *Bafs*
of the *Example* 25. to be pointed, 'it will ferve
as an *Example* of this Kind of *Suppofition* in
triple Time.

T h e r e is another Kind, when the Parts do
not proceed gradually from the *Difcord* to the
Concord, but defcend to it by the Diftance of a
3*d.* as in the *Examples* 27 and 28. where the
Difcord is efteem'd as a Part of the preceeding
Concord.

T h e r e is a third Kind refembling the fecond, when the rifing to the *Difcord* is gradual, but the defcending from it to the following
Concord is by the Diftance of a 4*th*, as in *Example* 29. in which the *Difcord* is alfo confidered as a Part, or Breaking of the preceeding
Concord.

T h e r e

THERE is a fourth Kind very different from the Three former, when the *Difcord* falls upon the accented Parts of the *Meafure*, and when the rifing to it is by the Diftance of a *4th* ; but then it is abfolutely neceffary to follow it immediately by a gradual Defcent into a *Concord* that has juft been heard before the *Harmony*;by which the *Difcord* that preceeds gives no Offence to the Ear,ferving only as a Tranfition into the *Concord*, as in *Example* 30.

THUS far was neceffary to be taught by way of *Inftitution* upon the Subject of SUPPOSITION; what further Liberties may be taken that Way in making Divifions upon holding Notes, as in *Example* 31. may be eafily gathered from what has been faid ; obferving this as a Principle never to be departed from, that the lefs one deviates from the Rules, for the fake of *Air*, the better.

2. *Of the* HARMONY *of* DISCORDS.

THE *Harmony* of *Difcords* is, that wherein the *Difcords* are made ufe of as a folid and fubftantial Part of the *Harmony* ; for by a proper Interpofition of a *Difcord* the fucceeding *Concords* receive an additional Luftre. Thus the *Difcords* are in *Mufick* what the ftrong Shades are in Painting; for as the Lights there, fo the *Concords* here, appear infinitely more beautiful by the Oppofition.

THE DISCORDS are 1*mo*. the 5*th* when joyn'd with the 6*th*, to which it ftands in relation as

a

a *Difcord*, and is therefore treated as a *Dif-cord* in that Place ; not as it is a 5*th* to the *Bafs* in which View it is a perfect *Concord*, but as being joyn'd with the Note immediately above it, there arifes from thence a Senfation of *Dif-cord*.

2*do*. THE 4*th*, tho' in its own Nature it is a *Concord* to the *Bafs*, yet being joyn'd with the 5*th*, which is immediately above it, is alfo ufed as a *Difcord* in that Cafe.

3*tio*. THE *Ninth* which is in effect the 2*d*, and is only called the *Ninth* to diftinguifh it from the 2*d*, which under that Denominati-on is ufed in a different Manner, is in its own Nature a *Difcord*.

4*to*. THE 7*th* is in its own Nature a *Dif-cord*.

5*to*. THE 2*d* and 4*th* is made ufe of when the *Bafs* fyncopates, in a very different Man-ner from that of ufing thofe above mentioned, as will appear in the *Examples*.

As I treat only of Compofition in Two Parts, there is no Occafion to name the *Concords* with which, in Compofition of Three or more *Parts*, the *Difcords* are accompanied ; thefe, I take for granted, are known to the Performer of the *thorough Bafs* ; and tho' in Compofition of Two *Parts* they cannot appear, yet they are always fuppofed and fupplied by the Accom-panyments of the *Bafs*.

Of

Of Preparation *and* Resolution *of* Discords.

The *Discords* here treated of are introduced into the *Harmony* with due Preparation; and they must be succeeded by *Concords,* commonly called the *Resolution* of the *Discord.*

The *Discord* is *prepared,* by subsisting first in the *Harmony* in the Quality of a *Concord, that is,* the same Note which becomes the *Discord* is first a *Concord* to the *Bass* Note immediately preceeding that to which it is a *Discord;* the *Discord* is *resolved,* by being immediately succeeded by a *Concord* descending from it by the Distance only of 2d *g.* or 2d *l.*

As the *Discord* makes a substantial Part of the *Harmony,* so it must always possess an accented Part of the *Measure :* So that in *common Time* it must fall upon the 1st and 3d *Crotchet* ; or, if the Time be extremely slow, upon the 1st, 3d, 5th or 7th *Quaver* of the *Bar* ; and in *triple Time* it must fall on the first of every Three *Crotchets,* or of every Three *Minims,* or of every Three *Quavers,* according as the *triple Time* is, there being various Kinds of it.

In order then to know how the *Discords* may be properly introduced into the *Harmony,* I shall examine what *Concords* may serve for their *Preparation* and *Resolution ; that is,* Whether the *Concords* going before and following such and such a *Discord* may be a 5th, 6th, 3d or *Octave.*

The

THE *5th* may be *prepared*, by being either an *8ve, 6th* or *3d*; it may be *resolved* either into the *6th* or *3d*, but moſt commonly into the *3d. Example* 32.

THE *4th* may be *prepared* in all the *Concords*; and may be *resolved* into the *6th*, *3d* or *8ve*, but moſt commonly into the *3d. Example* 33.

THE *9th* may be *prepared* in all the *Concords* except the *8ve*, and may be *resolved* into the *6th*, *3d* or *8ve*, but moſt commonly into the *8ve. Example* 34.

THE *7th* may be *prepared* in all the *Concords;* and may be *resolved* into the *3d, 6th* or *5th*, but moſt commonly into the *6th* or *3d. Example* 35.

THE *2d* and *4th* are made uſe of after a quite different Manner from the other *Diſcords*, being *prepared* and *resolved* in the *Baſs. Thus*, when the *Baſs* deſcends by the Diſtance of a *2d*, and the firſt Half of the Note falls upon an unaccented Part of the *Meaſure*, then either the *4th* or the *2d* may be applied to the laſt or accented Half of the Note ; if the *2d*, it is continued upon the following Note in the *Baſs*, and becomes the *3d* to it ; if the *4th* is applied, the *Treble* riſes a Note, and becomes a *6th* to the *Baſs. Example* 36.

FROM all which I muſt obſerve, that the *5th* and *7th* are *Diſcords* of great Uſe, becauſe, even in Two Parts, they may be made uſe of ſucceſſively for a pretty long Series of Notes without Interruption, eſpecially the *7th*, as producing

ducing a moſt beautiful *Harmony*. The *4th* is not uſeful in Two Parts in this ſucceſſive Way, but is otherwiſe very uſeful. The *9th* in the ſame Manner is only uſeful as the *4th* is.

HAVING once diſtinctly underſtood how the *Diſcords* are introduced and made a Part of the *Harmony*, by the *Examples* that I have exhibited in plain Notes, it may not be amiſs to take a View, in the *Examples* here ſet forth, how theſe plain Notes may be broke into Notes of leſs Value ; and being ſo divided, how they may be diſpoſed to produce a Variety of *Air* : Which *Examples* may ſuffice to give the Beginner an *Idea* how the *Diſcords* may be divided into Notes of ſmall Value, for the ſake of *Air*. Of the Manner of doing it there is an infinite Variety, and therefore to have ſhewn all the poſſible Ways how it may be done, would have required an infinite Number of *Examples* : I ſhall therefore only give one Caution, that in all ſuch Breakings the firſt Part of the diſcarding Note muſt diſtinctly appear, and after the remaining Part of it has been broke into a Diviſion of Notes of leſs Value, according to the Fancy of the Compoſer, ſuch Diviſion ought to lead naturally into the *reſolving Concord* that it may be alſo diſtinctly heard. See *Example* 37.

HAVING now conſidered the Matter of *Harmony* as particularly as is neceſſary to do by way of *Inſtitution*, to qualify the Student for reading and receiving Inſtruction from the
Works

Works of the more celebrated Compofers, which is the utmoft that any *Treatife* in my Opinion ought to aim at, I proceed to defcribe the Nature of *Modulation,* and to give the Rules for guiding the Beginner in the Practice of it.

§ 5. *Of* MODULATION; *and*

1mo. *What it is.*

ALTHO' every Piece of *Mufick* has one particular *Key* wherein it not only begins and ends, but which prevails more through the whole Piece; yet the Variety that is fo neceffary to the Beauty of *Mufick* requires the frequent changing of the *Harmony* into feveral other *Keys*; on Condition always that it return again into the *Key* appropriated to the Piece, and terminate often there by middle as well as final *Cadences,* efpecially if the Piece be of any Length, elfe the middle *Cadences* in the Key are not fo neceffary.

THESE other *Keys,* whether *fharp* or *flat* into which the *Harmony* may be changed, muft be fuch whofe *Harmonies* are not remote to the *Harmony* of the *principnl Key* of the Piece ; becaufe otherwife the Tranfitions from the *principal Key* to thofe other intermediate ones, would be unnatural and inconfiftent with that

Analo-

Analogy which ought to be preserved between all the Members of the same Piece. Under the 'Term of *Modulation* may be comprehended the regular Progression of the several Parts thro' the Sounds that are in the *Harmony* of any particular *Key* as well as the proceeding naturally and regularly with the *Harmony* from one *Key* to another : The Rules of *Modulation* therefore in that Sense are the Rules of *Melody* and *Harmony*, of which I have already treated; so that the Rules of *Modulation* only in this last Sense is my present Business.

SINCE every Piece must have one *principal Key*, and since the Variety that is so necessary in *Musick* to please and entertain, forbids the being confin'd to one *Key*, and that therefore it is not only allowable but requisite to *modulate* into and make *Cadences* upon several other *Keys*, having a Relation and Connection with the *principal Key*, I am first to consider what it is that constitutes a Connection between the *Harmony* of one *Key* and that of another, that from thence it may appear into what *Key's* the *Harmony* may be led with Propriety : And in order to comprehend the better wherein this Connection between the *Harmony* of different *Keys* may consist, I shall first shew what it is that occasions an Inconsistency between the *Harmony* of one *Key* and that of another.

2. *Of the* Relation *and* Connection *of* Keys.

IT has been already set forth, that each *Key* has Seven Notes belonging to it and no more.

In

In a *ſharp Key* theſe are fix'd and unalterable ;
but in a *flat Key* there is one that varies, *viz.*
the 7*th.* Hitherto I have accounted the 7*th g.*
one of the Seven natural Notes in a *flat Key,*
and I behoved to do ſo in the Matter of *Har-*
mony, becauſe the 7*th g.* is the 3*d g.* to the 5*th,*
without the Help of which there would be no
Cadence on the *Key;* and beſides, it is alone by
the Help of it that one can aſcend into the *Key.*
But here when I conſider not the particular Exi-
gencies of the *Harmony* in a *flat Key,* but the
general Analogy there is between the *Harmony*
of one *Key* and that of another, I muſt reckon
that the 7*th* which is eſſential in a *flat Key* is
the 7*th l.* becauſe both the 3*d* and 6*th* in a
flat Key are leſſer, therefore as to our preſent
Enquiry the 7*th g.* in a *flat Key* muſt be hence-
forth accounted extraneous.

THE diſtinguiſhing Note in each *Key,* next
to the *Key*-note it ſelf, is the 3*d;* any *Key*
therefore that has for its 3*d* any one of the Five
extraneous Notes of another *Key,* under what
Denomination ſoever of ♯ or ♭ is diſcrepant with
that other *Key* to which ſuch 3*d* is extraneous.
Thus the extraneous Notes of the *ſharp Key c*
being *c*♯, *d*♯, *f*♯, *g*♯, *a*♯, or as the ſame Notes
may happen to be differently denominated *d*♭,
e♭, *g*♭, *a*♭, ♭ : The *ſharp Key a* therefore having *c*♯ for its 3*d,* the *ſharp Key b* having *d*♯
for its 3*d,* the *ſharp Key e* having *g*♯ for its 3*d,*
the *ſharp Key f*♯ having *a*♯ for its 3*d,* or the
flat Key ♭ having *d*♭ for its 3*d,* the *flat Key c*
having *e*♭ for its 3*d,* the *flat Key e*♭ having *g*♭
for

for its 3d, the *flat Key* f having a♭ for its 3d, and the *flat Key* g having ♭ for its 3d, are all, I fay, difcrepant with the *fharp Key* c, becaufe the 3ds which are the diftinguifhing Notes of thefe other *Keys* are all extraneous Notes to c, with a 3dg. and fince any *Key* which has for its 3d any one of the Five extraneous Notes of another *Key*, is difcrepant with that other *Key*, *a fortiori* therefore any one of the Five extraneous Notes of a *Key* being a *Key* it felf, is utrerly difcrepant with a *Key*, to which fuch *Key*-note it felf is extraneous; thus therefore c✕, d✕, f✕, g✕, a✕, or, d♭, e♭, g♭, a♭, ♭ being confidered as *Keys*, whether with 3dg. or 3dl. are utterly difcrepant to c with a 3dg. becaufe they are all extraneous to it.

A *Key* then being affign'd as a *principal Key*, as none of its five extraneous Notes can either be *Keys* themfelves, or 3ds to *Keys* that can have any Connexion with it, fo it will from thence follow, that the Seven *natural* Notes of the *Key* affigned, being conftituted *Keys* with fuch 3ds as are one or other of the Seven *natural* Notes of the faid *Key* affign'd, may be accounted confonant to it ; provided they do not effentially introduce the *principal Key* or its 3d under a new Denomination, *that is*, the *Key* affign'd being for *Example* the *fharp Key* c, no *Key* can be confonant to it, that introduces necelfarily and effentially c✕, which is the *Key* under a new Denomination, or e✕, which is its 3d under a new Denomination, and different from what they were in the *Key* affign'd; therefore

fore to the *sharp Key* c, which I shall take for
the *principal Key* assign'd, the *flat Keys d, e* and
a, also the *sharp Keys f* and g are consonant ;
but the *flat Key b,* altho' both it self and its
3*d* are Two of the Seven *natural* Notes of the
Key assigned, is not consonant to it, because it
would essentially introduce *c*♯ for its 2*d,* which
being the *Key* assign'd under a new Denomination, would produce a very great Inconsistency
with it.   And here, lest from thence the Beginner may form this Objection against the *flat Key
d,* being reckoned consonant to the *sharp Key c,*
as I have done, because that *Key d* does introduce *c*♯ for its 7*th g.*   I must inform him, as I
have before observed, that the 7*th g.* to a *flat
Key* is only occasionally made Use of; and that
the 7*th l.* is the 7*th* that is essential in a *flat
Key.*

T H E *flat Key* c being the *principal flat Key*
assigned, the *flat Keys f* and g, also the *sharp
Keys e♭, a♭* and *♭* are consonant to it, but the
flat Key d, tho' both it self and its 3*d* are of the
natural Notes of the *Key* assigned, yet as this
flat Key d being constituted a *Key,* behoved to
have *e* for its Second, which is the 3*d* of the
Key assigned, under a different Denomination,
therefore it cannot be admitted as a consonant
Key to it.

T o the *Harmony* therefore of a *flat principal Key,* as well as of a *sharp one,* there are
Five *Keys* that are consonant, that, with all
the Elegancy and Property imaginable, may be
introduced in the Course of the Modulation of
    any

any one Piece of *Mufick.* To all *ſharp princi-pal Keys* the Five conſonant *Keys* are the 2*d*, 3*d*, 4*th*, 5*th* and 6*th* to the *principal Key*, with their reſpective 3*ds*, viz. with the 2*d*, the 3*dl*. 3*d*, 3*dl*. 4*th*, 3*dg*. 5*th*, 3*dg*. 6*th*, 3*dl*. To all *flat principal Keys* the Five conſonant *Keys* are the 3*d*, 4*th*, 5*th*, 6*th* and 7*th* to the *principal Key*, with their reſpective 3*ds*, viz. with the 3*d*, the 3*dg*. 4*th*, 3*dl*. 5*th*, 3*dl*. 6*th*, 3*dg*. 7*th*, 3*dg*. each of which conſonant *Keys*, tho' reckoned dependent upon their *principal Key* with regard to the Structure of the whole Piece, yet with reſpect to the particular Places where they pre-vail, they are each of them *principal* ſo long as the *Modulation* continues in them, and the Rules of *Melody* and *Harmony* are the ſame way to be obſerved in them as in the *principal Key*; for all *Keys* of the ſame Kind are the ſame, and this Subordination here diſcourſed of is only *accidental*; for no *Key* in its own Nature is more to be accounted *principal* than another.

T H E ſeveral *Keys* then that may enter into the Compoſition of the ſame Piece being known, it is material next to learn in what Order they may be introduc'd; and herein one muſt have Recourſe to the current Practice of the Maſters of *Compoſition*; from which, tho' indeed no certain Rules can be gathered, becauſe the Or-der of introducing the conſonant *Keys* is very much at the Diſcretion of the Compoſer, and in the Work of the ſame Author is often vari-ous, yet generally the Order is thus.

I N

IN a *ſharp principal Key*, the firſt *Cadence* is upon the *principal Key* it ſelf often; then follow in Order *Cadences* on the 5*th*, 3*d*, 6*th*, 2*d*, 4*th*, concluding at laſt with a *Cadence* on the *principal Key*. In a *flat principal Key* the intermediate *Cadences* are on the 3*d*, 5*th*, 7*th*, 4*th* and 6*th*. Now, whatever Liberty may be taken in varying from this Order, yet the beginning and ending with the *principal Key* is a Principle never to be departed from; and as far as I have obſerved, it ought to be a Rule alſo, that in a *ſharp principal Key*, the 5*th*, and in a *flat* one the 3*d*, ought to have the next Place to the *principal Key*.

3*tio*. How the *Modulation* is to be performed.

IT now remains to ſhew, how to *modulate* from one *Key* to another, ſo that the Tranſitions may be eaſy and natural; but how to teach this Kind of *Modulation* by Rules is the Difficulty; for altho' it is chiefly performed by the Help of the 7*th g*. of the *Key* into which we are reſolved to change the *Harmony*, whether it be *ſharp* or *flat*; yet the Manner of doing it is ſo various and extenſive, as no Rules can circumſcribe: Wherefore in this Matter, as well as in other Branches of my Subject, I muſt think it enough to explain the Nature of the Thing ſo, and to give the Beginner ſuch general Notions of it, as he may be able to gather by his own Obſervation, in the Courſe of his Studies of this Kind, what no Rules can teach.

THE

THE 7*th g.* in either *ſharp* or *flat* K*ey* is the 3*dg.* to the 5*thf.* of the *Key*, by which the *Cadence* in the *Key* is chiefly perform'd; and by being only a *Semitone* under the *Key*, is therefore the moſt proper Note to lead into it, which it does in the moſt natural Manner that can be imagin'd; inſomuch that the 7*th g.* is never heard in any of the *Parts*, but the Ear expects the *Key* ſhould ſucceed it; for whether it be uſed as a 3*d* or as a 6*th*, it doth always affect us with ſuch an imperfect Senſation, that we naturally expect ſomething more perfect to follow, which cannot be more eaſily and ſmoothly accompliſhed, than by the ſmall *Interval* of a *Semitone*, to paſs into the perfect *Harmony* of the *Key*; from hence it is that the Tranſition into any *Key* is beſt effected, by introducing its 7*th g.* which ſo naturally leads to it; and how this 7*th g.* may be introduced, will beſt appear in the *Examples*.

IN *Ex.* 38. the *Key* is firſt the *ſharp Key* *c*, but *f✳*, which is the 7*thg.* to *g*, introduces and leads the *Harmony* into the firſt conſonant *Key* of *c* with a 3*d g.* In this *Example f✳* ſtands in the *Treble* a 6*th*; but it may alſo ſtand a 3*dg.* as in *Ex.* 39. or it may be introduced into the *Baſs* with its proper *Harmony* of a 3*d* or 6*th*, as in *Examples* 40 and 42. or it may, as a 6*thg.* or 3*dg.* in the *Treble*, be the reſolving *Concord* of a preceeding *Diſcord*, as in *Examples* 41 and 44. or it may ſtand in the *Treble* as a 4*thg.* accompanied alſo in that Caſe with a 2*d*, or ſuppoſed to be ſo as in *Ex.* 46.

46. or otherwife ufed as in *Examples* 45 and 47. The *Modulation* changes from the *fharp Key c* into the *flat Key a*, one of its confonant *Keys*, whofe 7*th g.* is introduced in the Quality of a *6th g.* and 3*d g.* ferving as the *Refolutions* of preceeding *Difcords*. In *Examples* 48 and 51. the *6th* is applied to the *Key,* which is always a good Preparation to lead the *Harmony* out of it; for a *Key* can be no longer a *Key* when a *6th* is applied. The remaining *Examples* fhew how the *Harmony* may pafs through feveral *Keys* in the Compafs of a few Notes.

F R O M thefe *Examples* I fhall deduce fome few Obfervations, that may ferve as fo many Rules to guide the Beginner in this firft Attempt.

1*ft.* T H E 7*th g.* of the *Key* into which we intend to lead the *Harmony,* is introduced into the *Treble* either as a 3*d g.* or *6th g.* or as a 4*th g.* with its fuppofed Accompanyments of 4*th* and *6th*; and as 3*d g.* or *6th g.* it is commonly the *Refolution* of a preceeding *Difcord.*

2*d.* W H E N this 7*th g.* comes into the *Treble* in what Quality foever, as 3*d g.* *6th g.* &c. it is either fucceeded immediately by that Note which is the *Key* whereto it immediately leads, or immediately preceeded by it, and moft commonly the laft; in which Cafe the *Treble* muft of confequence defcend to it by the Diftance of a *Semitone.* Thus, when we are to change the *Harmony* from the *fharp Key c* to the *flat Key a,* that is, from a *fharp principal Key* into its

6*th,*

6th, we ufe it in the *Treble* as the *6th* to the *principal Key c,* or as the *5th* to *d,* or as the *3d* to *f;* and being once upon the Note which we defign to be the *Key,* the falling half a Note to its *7th g.* for fixing the *Harmony* fairly in the *Key,* is moft eafily perform'd; thus were we to go from a *principal Key* into the *3d,* we fhould ufe a *6th* on the *5 f.;* or were we to go into the *2d,* we fhould ufe a *6th* on the *4 f.* and the rather, becaufe in the *Key* whereto we defign to go, a *6th* is the proper *Harmony,* for that *5th f.* of the *principal Key* becomes the *3d f.* of the *3d,* when it is conftitute a *Key;* and fo does the *4th f.* of the *principal Key* become the *3d f.* of the *2d,* when conftitute a *Key.*

3tio. WHEN the *7th g.* of the *Key,* into which we defign to change the *Harmony,* is introduced in the *Bafs,* it is always immediately fucceeded by the *Key;* and then the Tranfition to the *7th g.* is moft part gradual, by the *Interval* of a *Tone* or *Semitone,* or by the *Interval* of a *3d l.* But moft commonly it is introduced into the *Bafs,* by proceeding to it from the *natural* Note of the fame Name, *that is,* from a Note that is *natural* in the *Key,* as from *f* to *f✕* in the *fharp Key c,* or from ♭ to *b* in the *flat Key d.*

4to. WHEN the *7th g.* of the *Key* to which we defign to lead the *Harmony,* is one of the Seven *natural* Notes of the *Key* wherein the *Harmony* already is, the introducing it into the *Bafs* is moft *natural,* as being of courfe ; this happens when we would *modulate* from a *fharp Key* into its *4th,* or from a *flat Key* into its *3d.*

3d. In which Cafes the *7th g.* is introduced into the *Bafs,* and in the *Treble* the *falfe* *5th* is applied to it, which refolves into the *3dg.*

5to. W H E N this *7th g.* comes into the *Bafs,* it muft of neceffity have either a *3d l. 6th l.* or *falfe* *5th* in the *Treble* ; if a *3d l.* it refolves into the *8ve,* if a *6th l.* it commonly paffes into the *falfe* *5th,* and from thence refolves into the *3d* of the *Key.*

6to. B Y applying the *6th* to any Note of the *Key,* to which the *5th* is a more *natural Harmony,* as for *Example,* to the *Key* it felf, to the *4th f.* or *5th f.* a Preparation is thereby made for going into another *Key,* viz. into that Note which is fo made Ufe of, as a *6th* to any of thefe *fundamental* Notes, as in the *Examples.*

H A V I N G thus explained the Nature of *Modulation* from one *Key* to another, it may feem natural to treat now of *Cadences;* but of thefe I cannot fuppofe a Performer of the *Thorough-bafs* ignorant, they being fo frequent in *Mufick;* all I fhall therefore fay of them is, that they muft always be finifhed with an accented Part of the *Meafure.* As to what concerns *Fugues* and *I-mitations* I am to fay nothing, becaufe thefe are to be learnt more by a Courfe of Obfervation than by Rule. What I propofed was, to fet forth the *Principles* of *Compofition* in Two Parts, by way of *Inftitution* only, not daring to proceed any further than the fmall Knowledge I have of *Mufick* would lead me with Safety.

C H A P.

≈≈≈≈≈≈≈≈≈≈≈≈≈≈≈≈≈≈≈≈≈≈≈≈≈≈≈

CHAP. XIV.

Of the ANCIENT MUSICK.

---

§ 1. *Of the* Name, *with the various* Definitions *and* Divisions *of the* Science.

THE Word M u s i c k comes to us from the Latin Word *Mufica,* if not immediately from a Greek Word of the fame Sound, from whence the *Romans* probably took theirs; for they got much of their Learning from the *Greeks.* Our Criticks teach us, that it comes from the Word *Mufa,* and this from a Greek Word which fignifies to fearch or find out, becaufe the *Mufes* were feigned to be Inventreffes of the *Sciences,* and particularly of *Poetry* and thefe *Modulations* of Sound that conftitute *Mufick.* But others go higher, and tell us, the Word *Mufa* comes from a Hebrew Word, which fignifies *Art* or *Difcipline;* hence *Mufa* and *Mufica* anciently fignified

Learn-

Learning in general, or any Kind of *Science*; in which Sense you'll find it frequently in the Works of the ancient Philofophers.　But *Kircher* will have it from an *Egyptian* Word; becaufe the Reftoration of it after the Flood was probably there, by reafon of the many Reeds to be found in their Fens, and upon the Banks of the *Nile*. *Hefychius* tells us, that the *Athenians* gave the Name of *Mufick* to every *Art*. From this it was that the *Poets* and *Mythologifts* feigned the nine *Mufes* Daughters of *Jupiter*, who invented the Sciences, and prefide over them, to affift and infpire thefe who apply to ftudy them, each having her particular Province. In this geneal Senfe we have it defin'd to be, the orderly Arangement and right Difpofition of Things; in fhort, the Agreement and *Harmony* of the Whole with its Parts, and of the Parts among themfelves. *Hermes Trifmegiftus* fays, *That* Mufick *is nothing but the Knowledge of the Order of all Things*; which was alfo the Doctrine of the *Pythagorean* School, and of the *Platonicks*, who teach that every Thing in the Univerfe is *Mufick*. Agreeable to this wide Senfe, fome have diftinguifhed Mufick into *Divine* and *Mundane*; the firft refpects the Order and Harmony that obtains among the Celeftial Minds; the other refpects the Relations and Order of every other Thing elfe in the Univerfe. But *Plato* by the *divine Mufick* underftands, that which exifts in the *divine* Mind, *viz.* thefe archetypal Ideas of Order and Symmetry, according to which GOD formed all Things; and as this Order

exifts

exifts in the Creatures, it is called *Mundane Mufick* : Which is again fubdivided, the remarkable Denominations of which are, *Firft, Elementary* or the Harmony of the firft Elements of Things ; and thefe according to the Philofophers, are Fire, Air, Water, and Earth, which tho' feemingly contrary to one another, are, by the Wifdom of the Creator, united and compounded in all the beautiful and regular Forms of Things that fall under our Senfes. 2*d. Celeftial*, comprehending the Order and Proportions in the Magnitudes, Diftances, and Motions of the heavenly Bodies, and the Harmony of the Sounds proceeding from thefe Motions : For the *Pythagoreans* affirmed that they produce the moft perfect *Confort* ; the Argument, as *Macrobius* in his Commentary on *Cicero's Somnium Scipionis* has it, is to this Purpofe, *viz.* Sound is the Effect of Motion, and fince the heavenly Bodies muft be under certain regular and ftated Laws of Motion, they muft produce fomething mufical and concordant; for from random and fortuitous Motions, governed by no certain Meafure, can only proceed a grating and unpleafant Noife : And the Reafon, fays he, why we are not fenfible of that Sound, is the Vaftnefs of it, which exceeds our Senfe of Hearing ; in the fame Manner as the Inhabitants near the Cataracts of the *Nile*, are infenfible of their prodigious Noife. But fome of the Hiftorians, if I remember right, tell us that by the Exceffivenefs of the Sounds, thefe People are rendred quite deaf, which makes that

De.non-

Demonſtration ſomewhat doubtful, ſince we hear every other Sound that reaches to us. Others alledge that the Sounds of the Spheres, being the firſt we hear when we come into the World, and being habituated to them for a long Time, when we could ſcarcely think or make Reflection on any Thing, we become incapable of perceiving them afterwards. But *Pythagoras* ſaid he perceived and underſtood the Celeſtial Harmony by a peculiar Favour of that Spirit to whom he owed his Life, as *Jamblichus* reports of him, who ſays, That tho' he never ſung or played on any Inſtrument himſelf, yet by an inconceivable Sort of Divinity, he taught others to imitate the Celeſtial Muſick of the Spheres, by Inſtruments and Voice : For according to him, all the Harmony of Sounds here below, is but an Imitation, and that imperfect too, of the other. This Species is by ſome called particularly the *Mundane Muſick*. 3d. *Human*, which conſiſts chiefly in the Harmony of the Faculties of the human Soul, and its various Paſſions; and is alſo conſidered in the Proportion and Temperament, mutual Dependence and Connection, of all the Parts of this wonderful Machine of our Bodies. 4th. Is what in a more limited and peculiar Senſe of the Word was called *Muſick*; which has for its Object *Motion*, conſidered as under certain regular Meaſures and Proportions, by which it affects the Senſes in an agreeable Manner. All Motion belongs to Bodies, and Sound is the Effect of Motion, and cannot be without it; but all Motion does

not

not produce Sound, therefore this was again
fubdivided. Where the Motion is without
Sound, or as it is only the Object of Seeing, it
was called *Mufica Orcheftria* or *Saltatoria,*
which contains the Rules for the regular Motions of *Dancing* ; alfo *Hypocritica,* which
refpects the Motions and Geftures of the *Pantomimes.* When Motion is perceived only by
the Ear, *i. e.* when Sound is the Object of *Mufick,* there are Three Species; HARMONICA,
which confiders the Differences and Proportion
of Sounds, with refpect to *acute* and *grave ;*
RYTHMICA, which refpects the Proportion of
Sounds as to Time, òr the Swiftnefs and Slownefs of their Succeffions ; and METRICA,
which belongs properly to the *Poets,* and refpects the verfifying Art : But in common Accep-
tation 'tis now more limited, and we call nothing *Mufick* but what is heard ; and even then
we make a Variety of *Tones* neceffary to the
Being of *Mufick.*

ARISTIDES QUINTILIANUS, who writes
a profeft Treatife upon *Mufick,* calls it the
Knowledge of finging, and of the Things that
are joyned with finging (*ἐπιστήμη μέλɛς καὶ τῶν
περὶ μελος συμβαινόντων,* which *Meibomius* tranflates, *Scientia cantus, eorumq; quæ circa cantum
contingunt*) and thefe he calls the Motions of
the Voice and Body, as if the *Cantus* it felf
confifted only in the different Tones of the
Voice. *Bacchius* who writes a fhort Introduction to Mufick in Queftion and Anfwer, gives
the fame Definition. Afterwards; *Ariftides* confiders

fiders *Mufick* in the largeft Senfe of the Word, and divides it into *Contemplative* and *Active.* The firft, he fays, is either *natural* or *artificial*; the *natural* is *arithmetical*, becaufe it confiders the Proportion of Numbers, or *phyfical* which difputes of every Thing in Nature; the *Artificial* is divided into *Harmonica*, *Rythmica* (comprehending the dumb Motions) and *Metrica*: The *active*, which is the Application of the *artificial*, is cither *enunciative* (as in Oratory,) *Organical* (or Inftrumental Performance,) *Odical* (for Voice and finging of Poems,) *Hypocritical* (in the Motions of the *Pantomimes.*) To what Purpofe fome add *Hydraulical* I do not underftand, for this is but a Species of the *Organical*, in which Water is fome way ufed for producing or modifying the Sound. The mufical Faculties, as they call them, are, *Melopæia* which gives Rules for the *Tones* of the Voice or Inftrument, *Rythmopæia* for Motions, and *Poefis* for making of Verfe. Again, explaining the Difference of *Rythmus* and *Metrum*, he tells us, That *Rythmus* is applied Thee Ways; either to immoveable Bodies, which are called *Eurythmoi*, when their Parts are right proportioned to one another, as a well made Statue; or to every Thing that moves, fo we fay a Man walks handfomly (*compofite*,) and under this *Dancing* will come, and the Bufinefs of the *Pantomimes*; or particularly to the Motion of Sound or the Voice, in which the *Rythmus* confifts of long and fhort Syllables or Notes, (which he calls *Times*) joyned together (in

Suc-

Succeſſion) in ſome kind of Order, ſo that their Cadence upon the Ear may be agreeable; which conſtitutes in *Oratory* what is called a numerous Stile, and when the *Tones* of the Voice are well choſen 'tis an *harmonious* Stile. RYTHMUS is perceived either by the Eye or the Ear, and is ſomething general, which may be without *Metrum*; but this is perceived only by the Ear, and is but a Species of the other, and cannot exiſt without it : The firſt is perceived without Sound in Dancing; and when it exiſts with Sounds it may either be without any Difference of *acute* and *grave*, as in a *Drum*, or with a Varitey of theſe, as in a Song, and then the *Harmonica* and *Rythmica* are joyned ; and if any *Poem* is ſet to *Muſick*, and ſung with a Variety of *Tones*, we have all the Three Parts of *Muſick* at once. *Porphyrius* in his Commentaries on *Ptolemey's Harmonicks*, inſtitutes the Diviſion of *Muſick* another Way; he takes it in the limited Senſe, as having *Motion* both dumb and ſonorous for its Object; and, without diſtinguiſhing the *ſpeculative* and *practical*, he makes its Parts theſe Six, *viz. Harmonica, Rythmica, Metrica, Organica, Poetica, Hypocritica* ; he applies the *Rythmica* to Dancing, *Metrica* to the Enunciative, and *Poetica* to Verſes.

ALL the other ancient Authors agree in the ſame threefold Diviſion of *Muſick* into *Harmonica, Rythmica* and *Metrica:* Some add the *Organica*, others omit it, as indeed it is but an accidental Thing to *Muſick*, in what Species of
Sounds

Sounds it is expreſt. Upon this Diviſion of *Muſick*, the more ancient Writers are very careful in the Inſcription or Titles of their Books, and call them only *Harmonica*, when they con-fine themſelves to that Part, as *Ariſtoxenus*, *Euclid*, *Nicomachus*, *Gaudentius*, *Ptolomey*, *Bryennius*; but *Ariſtides* and *Bacchius* call theirs *Muſica*, becauſe they profeſs to treat of all the Parts. The *Latines* are not always ſo accurate, for they inſcribe all theirs *Muſica*, as *Boethius*, tho' he only explains the *Harmonica* ; and St. *Auguſtin*, tho' his Six Books *de Muſica* ſpeak only of the *Rythmus* and *Metrum*; *Mar-tianus Capella* has a better Right to the Title, for he makes a Kind of Compend and Tranſla-tion of *Ariſtides Quintil.* tho' a very obſcure one of as obſcure an Original. *Aurelius Caſſiodorus* needs ſcarcely be named, for tho' he writes a Book *de Muſica*, 'tis but barely ſome general Definitions and Diviſions of the Science.

The *Harmonica* is the Part the Ancients have left us any tolerable Account of, which are at leaſt but very general and *Theorical* ; ſuch as it is I purpoſe to explain it to you as diſtinctly as I can; but having thus far ſettled the Defi-nition and Diviſion of *Muſick* as delivered by the Ancients, I chuſe next to conſider hiſto rically.

§ 2. *The*

§ 2. *The Invention and Antiquity of* Musick, *with the Excellency of the Art in the various Ends and Uses of it.*

OF all human Arts *Musick* has justest Pretences to the Honour of *Antiquity*: We scarce need any Authority for this Assertion; the Reason of the Thing demonstrates it, for the Conditions and Circumstances of human Life required some powerful Charm, to bear up the Mind under the Anxiety and Cares that Mankind soon after his Creation became subject to; and the Goodness of our blessed *Creator* soon discovered it self in the wonderful Relief that *Musick* affords against the unavoidable Hardships which are annexed to our State of being in this Life; so that *Musick* must have been as early in the World as the most necessary and indispensable Arts. For

If we consider how natural to the Mind of Man this kind of Pleasure is, as constant and universal Experience sufficiently proves, we cannot think he was long a Stranger to it. Other Arts were revealed as bare Necessity gave Occasion, and some were afterwards owing to Luxury; but neither Necessity nor Luxury are the Parents of this heavenly Art; to be pleased with it seems to be a Part of our Constitution; but 'tis made so, not as absolutely necessary to our Being, 'tis a Gift of God to us for our more happy and comfortable Being; and therefore we can make no doubt that this Art was among the very first that were known to Men. It is

reason-

reasonable to believe, that as all other Arts, so this was rude and simple in its Beginning, and by the Industry of Man, prompted by his natural Love of Pleasure, improven by Degrees. If we consider, again, how obvious a Thing Sound is, and how manifold Occasions it gives for Invention, we are not only further confirmed in the Antiquity of this Art, but we can make very shrewd Guesses about the first Discoveries of it. *Vocal Musick* was certainly the first Kind ; Man had not only the various *Tones* of his own Voice to make his Observations upon, before any other Arts or Instruments were found, but being daily entertained by the various natural Strains of the winged Choirs, how could he not observe them, and from hence take Occasion to improve his own Voice, and the Modulations of Sound, of which it is capable ? 'Tis certain that whatever these Singers were capable of, they possess it actually from the Beginning of the World ; we are surprised indeed with their sagacious Imitations of human Art in Singing, but we know no Improvements the Species is capable of; and if we suppose that in these Parts where Mankind first appeared, and especially in these first Days, when Things were probably in their greatest Beauty and Perfection, the Singing of Birds was a more remarkable Thing, we shall have less Reason to doubt that they led the Way to Mankind in this charming Art : But this is no new Opinion; of many ancient Authors, who agree in this very just Conjecture, I shall only let you hear *Lucretius Lib.* 5.

At

At liquidas avium voces imitarier ore
Ante fuit multo, quam lævia carmina cantu
Concelebrare homines poſſent, aureiſque juvare.

T H E firſt Invention of Wind-inſtruments he
aſcribes to the Obſervation of the Whiſtling of
the Winds among the hollow Reeds.

Et Zephyri cava per calamorum ſibila primum
Agreſteis docuere cavas inflare cicutas,
Inde minutatim dulceis didicere querelas,
Tibia quas fundit digitis pulſata canentum.

or they might alſo take that Hint from ſome
Thing that might happen accidentally to them
in their handling of Corn-ſtalks or the hollow
Stems of other Plants. And other Kinds of Inſtruments were probably formed by ſuch like Acci-
dents : There were ſo many Uſes for Chords
or Strings, that Men could not but very ſoon
obſerve their various Sounds, which might give
Riſe to ſtringed Inſtruments : And for the pulſatile Inſtruments, as Drums and Cymbals, they
might ariſe from the Obſervation of the hollow
Noiſe of concave Bodies. To make this Account of the Invention of Inſtruments more probable, *Kircher* bids us conſider, That the firſt
Mortals living a paſtoral Life, and being conſtantly in the Fields, near Rivers and among
Woods, could not be perpetually idle ; 'tis probable therefore, ſays he, That the Invention of
Pipes and Whiſtles was owing to their Diverſions
and

and Exercifes on thefe Occafions ; and becaufe
Men could not be long without having Ufe for
Chords of various Kinds, and varioufly bent,
thefe, either by being expofed to the Wind, or
neceffarily touched by the Hand, might give
the firft Hint of ftringed Inftruments; and becaufe, even in the firft fimple Way of Living,
they could not be long without fome *fabrile*
Arts, this would give Occafion to obferve various
Sounds of hard and hollow Bodies, which might
raife the firft Thought of the *pulfatile* Inftruments; hence he concludes that *Mufick* was a-
mong the firft Arts.

IF we confider *next*, the Opinion of thofe
that are Ancients to us, who yet were too far
from the Beginning of Things to know them
any other way than by Tradition and probable
Conjecture ; we find an univerfal Agreement in
this Truth, That *Mufick* is as ancient as the
World it felf, for this very Reafon, that it is
natural to Mankind. It will be needlefs to
bring many Authorities, one or Two fhall ferve:
Plutarch in his *Treatife of Mufick*, which is
nothing but a Converfation among Friends, a-
bout the Invention, Antiquity and Power of
Mufick, makes one afcribe the Invention to
Amphion the Son of *Jupiter* and *Antiopa*, who
was taught by his Father; but in the Name of
another he makes *Apollo* the Author, and to
prove it, alledges all the ancient Statues of this
God, in whofe Hand a mufical Inftrument was
always put. He adduces many Examples to
prove the natural Influence *Mufick* has upon
the

the Mind of Man, and fince he makes no lefs than a *God* the Inventor of it, and the *Gods* exifted before Men, 'tis certain he means to prove, both by Tradition and the Nature of the Thing, that it is the moft ancient as well as the moft noble Science. *Quintilian* (*Lib.* 1. *Cap.* 11.) alledges the Authority of *Timagenes* to prove that *Mufick* is of all the moft ancient Science; and he thinks the Tradition of its Antiquity is fufficiently proven by the ancient *Poets*, who reprefent *Muficians* at the Table of *Kings*, finging the Praifes of the Gods and Heroes. *Homer* fhews us how far *Mufick* was advanced in his Days, and the Tradition of its yet greater Antiquity, while he fays it was a Part of his Hero's Education. The Opinion of the divine Original and Antiquity of Mufick, is alfo proven by the Fable of the Mufes, fo univerfal among the Poets; and by the Difputes among the Greek Writers concerning the firft Authors, fome for *Orpheus*, fome for *Amphion*, fome for *Apollo*, &c. As the beft of the Philofophers own'd the Providence of the Gods, and their particular Love and Benevolence to Mankind, fo they alfo believed that *Mufick* was from the Beginning a peculiar Gift and Favour of Heaven; and no Wonder, when they looked upon it as neceffary to affift the Mind to a raifed and exalted Way of praifing the Gods and good Men.

I fhall add but one Teftimony more, which is that of the *facred Writings*; where *Jubal* the Sixth from *Adam*, is called *the Father*

ther of such as handle the Harp and Organ ;
whether this signifies that he was the Inventor,
or one who brought thefe Inftruments to a good
Perfection,or only one who was eminently skilled in the Performance, we have fufficient Reafon to believe that *Mufick* was an Art long before his Time ; fince it is rational to think that
vocal Mufick was known long before *Inftrumen-*
tal, and that there was a gradual Improvement
in the Art of modulating the Voice ; unlefs *A-*
dam and his Sons were infpired with this Knowledge, which Suppofition would prove the Point
at once. And if we could believe that this Art
was loft by the Flood, yet the fame Nature remaining in Man, it would foon have been re-
vered ; and we find a notable Inftance of it in
the Song of Praife which the *Ifraelites* raifed
with their Voices and Timbrels to G O D,
for their Deliverance at the *Red Sea* ; from
which we may reafonably conjecture it was an
Art well known, and of eftablifhed Honour long
before that Time.

I t may be expected I fhould, in this Place,
give a more particular Hiftory of the *Inventors*
of *Mufick* and *mufical Inftruments,* and other
famous *Muficians* fince the Flood. As to the
Invention, I think there is enough faid already
to fhow that *Mufick* is natural to Mankind ;
and therefore inftead of *Inventors,* the Enquiry
ought properly to be about the *Improvers* of it;
and I own it would come in very naturally here:
But the Truth is, we have fcarce any Thing
                                                      left

left us we can depend upon in this Matter; or at leaft we have but very general Hints, and many of them contrary to each other, from Authors that fpeak of thefe Things in a tranfient Manner: And as we have no Writings of the Age in which *Mufick* was firft reftored after the Flood, fo the Accounts we have are fuch uncertain Traditions, that no Two Authors agree in every Thing. *Greece* was the Country in *Europe* where Learning firft flourifhed; and tho' we believe they drew from other Fountains, as *Egypt* and the more Eaftern Parts, yet they are the Fountains to us, and to all the Weftern World: Other Antiquities we neither know fo well, nor fo much of, at leaft of fuch as have any Pretence to a greater Antiquity; except the *Jewifh*; and tho' we are fure they had *Mufick*, yet we have no Account of the Inventors among them, for 'tis probable they learned it in *Egypt*; and therefore this Enquiry about the *Inventors* of *Mufick* fince the Flood, muft be limited to *Greece*. PLUTARCH, JULIUS POLLUX, ATHENEUS, and a few more, are the Authorities we have principally to truft to, who take what they fay from other more ancient Authors of their Tradition. I hope to be forgiven if I am very fhort in the Account of Things of fuch Uncertainty.

AMPHION, the *Theban,* is by fome reckoned the moft ancient *Mufician* in *Greece*, and the Inventor of it, as alfo of the *Lyra*. Some fay *Mercury* taught him, and gave him a *Lyre* of Seven Strings. He is faid to be the firft who

taught

taught to play and fing together. The Time he lived in is not agreed upon.

CHIRON the *Pelithronian,* reckoned a *Demigod,* the Son of *Saturn* and *Phyllira,* is the next great Mafter ; the Inventor of Medicine ; a famous *Philofopher* and *Mufician,* who had for his Scholars *Æfculapius, Jafon, Hercules, Thefeus, Achilles,* and other Heroes.

DEMODOCUS is another celebrated *Mufician,* of whom already.

HERMES, or MERCURY TRISMEGISTUS, another *Demigod,* is alfo reckoned amongft the Inventors or Improvers of *Mufick* and of the *Lyra.*

LINUS was a famous *Poet* and *Mufician.* Some fay he taught *Hercules, Thamyris* and *Orpheus,* and even *Amphion.* To him fome afcribe the Invention of the *Lyra.*

OLYMPUS the *Myfian* is another Benefactor to *Mufick* ; he was the Difciple of *Marfyas* the Son of *Hyagnis* the *Phrygian* ; this *Hyagnis* is reckoned the Inventor of the *Tibiæ,* which others afcribe to the Mufe *Euterpe,* as *Horace* infinuates, -- *Si neque tibias* Euterpe *cohibet.*

ORPHEUS the *Thracian* is alfo reckoned the Author, or at leaft the Introducer of various Arts into *Greece,* among which is *Mufick* ; he pactifed the *Lyra* he got from *Mercury.* Some fay he was Mafter to *Thamyris* and *Linus.*

PHEMIUS of *Ithaca. Ovid* ufes his Name for any excellent Mufician ; *Homer* alfo names him honourably.

TER-

TERPANDER the *Lesbian*, liv'd in the Time of *Lycurgus*, and set his Laws to *Musick*. He was the first who among the *Spartans* applied *Melody* to *Poems*, or taught them to be sung in regular Measures. This is the famous *Musician* who quelled a Sedition at *Sparta* by his *Musick*. He and his Followers are said to have first instituted the *musical Modes*, used in singing Hymns to the *Gods*; and some attribute the Invention of the *Lyre* to him.

THALES the *Cretan* was another great Master, honourably entertain'd by the *Lacedemonians*, for instructing their Youth. Of the Wonders he wrought by his Musick, we shall hear again.

THAMYRIS the *Thracian* was so famous, that he is feigned to have contended with the *Muses*, upon Condition he should possess all their Power if he overcame, but if they were Victors he consented to lose what they pleased; and being defeat, they put out his Eyes, spoiled his Voice, and struck him with Madness. He was the first who used *instrumental Musick* without Singing.

THESE are the remarkable Names of *Musicians* before *Homer*'s Time, who himself was a *Musician*; as was the famous Poet *Pindar*. You may find the Characters of these mentioned at more large, in the first Book of *Fabritius*'s *Bibliotheca Græca*.

WE find others of a later Date, who were famous in *Musick*, as *Lasus Hermionensis, Melanippides, Philoxenus, Timotheus, Phrynnis,*
Epi-

Epigonius, Lyfander, Simmicus, Diodorus the *Theban;* who were Authors of a great Variety and luxurious Improvements in *Mufick.* *Lafus,* who lived in the Time of *Darius Hyftafpes,* is reckoned the firft who ever wrote a Treatife upon *Mufick.* *Epigonius* was the Author of an Inftrument called *Epigonium,* of 40 Strings; he introduced Playing on the *Lyre* with the Hand without a *Plectrum* ; and was the firft who joyned the *Cithara* and *Tibia* in one Concert, altering the Simplicity of the more ancient *Mufick;* as *Lyfander* did by adding a great many Strings to the *Cithara.* *Simmicus* alfo invented an Inftrument called *Simmicium* of 35 Strings. *Diodorus* improved the *Tibia,* which at firft had but Four Holes, by contriving more Holes and Notes.

TIMOTHEUS, for adding a String to his *Lyre* was fined by the *Lacedemonians,* and the String ordered to be taken away. Of him and *Phrynnis,* the Comic Poet *Pherecrates* makes bitter Complaints in the Name of *Mufick,* for corrupting and abufing her, as *Plutarch* reports: For, among others, they chiefly had completed the Ruin of the ancient fimple *Mufick,* which, fays *Plutarch,* was nobly ufeful in the Education and forming of Youth, and the Service of the *Temples,* and ufed principally to thefe Purpofes, in the ancient Times of greateft Wifdom and Virtue ; but was ruined after theatrical Shews came to be fo much in Fafhion, fo that fcarcely the Memory of thefe ancient Modes remained in his Time. You fhall have fome

Account

Account afterwards of the ancient Writers of *Muſick*.

As we have but uncertain Accounts of the Inventors of *muſical Inſtruments* among the Ancients, ſo we have as imperfect an Account of what theſe Inſtruments were, ſcarce knowing them any more than by Name. The general Diviſion of Inſtruments is into *ſtringed* Inſtruments, *Wind* Inſtruments and the *pulſatile* Kind; of this laſt we hear of the *Tympanum* or *Cymbalum*, of the Nature of our Drum; the *Greeks* gave it the laſt Name from its Figure, reſembling a Boat.

There were alſo the *Crepitaculum, Tintinabulum, Crotalum, Siſtrum*; but, by any Accounts we have, they look rather like Childrens Rattles and Play Things than *muſical Inſtruments*.

Of *Wind*-inſtruments we hear of the *Tibia*, ſo called from the Shank-bone of ſome Animals, as Cranes, of which they were firſt made. And *Fiſtula* made alſo of Reeds. But theſe were afterwards made of Wood and alſo of Mettal. How they were blown, whether as *Flutes* or *Hautboys* or otherwiſe, and which the one Way, and which the other, is not ſufficiently manifeſt. 'Tis plain, ſome had Holes, which at firſt were but few, and afterwards increaſed to a greater Number; ſome had none. Some were ſingle Pipes, and ſome a Combination of ſeverals, particularly Pan's *Syringa*, which conſiſted of Seven Reeds joyned together
ſide-

fideways; they had no Holes, each giving but
one Note, in all Seven diftinct Notes; but at
what mutual Diftances is not very certain, tho'
perhaps they were the Notes of the natural or
diatonick Scale ; but by this Means they would
want an 8*ve*, and therefore probably otherwife
conftituted.   Sometimes they played on a fingle
Pipe, fometimes on Two together, one in each
Hand.   And left we fhould think there could
little *Mufick* be expreft by one Hand, *If. Voffius*
alledges, they had a Contrivance by which they
made one Hole exprefs feveral Notes, and cites
a Paffage of *Arcadius* the Grammarian to
prove it : That Author fays, indeed, that there
were Contrivances to fhut and open the Holes,
when they had a Mind, by Pieces of Horn he
calls *Bombyces* and *Opholmioi* (which *Julius
Pollux* alfo mentions as Parts of fome Kind of
Tibiæ) turning them upwards or downwards,
inwards or outwards: But the Ufe of this is not
clearly taught us, and whether it was that the
fame Pipe might have more Notes than Holes,
which might be managed by one Hand : Perhaps it was no more than a like Contrivance in
our common Bagpipes, for tuning the Drones
to the *Key* of the Song.   We are alfo told that
Hyagnis contrived the joyning of Two Pipes,
fo that one Canal conveyed Wind to both,
which therefore were always founded together.

    WE hear alfo of *Organs*, blown at firft by a
Kind of Air-pump, where alfo Water was fome
way ufed, and hence called *Organum Hydraulicum*; but afterwards they ufed Bellows. *Vitruvius*

vius has an obscure Description of it, which *If. Vossius* and *Kircher* both endeavour to clear.

THERE were *Tubæ*, and *Cornua*, and *Litui*, of the Trumpet Kind, of which there were different Species invented by different People. They talk of some Kind of *Tubæ*, that without any Art in the *Modulation*, had such a prodigious Sound, that was enough to terrify one.

OF *stringed Instruments* the first is the *Lyra* or *Cithara* (which some distinguish:) *Mercury* is said to be Inventor of it, in this Manner; after an Inundation of the *Nile* he found a dead Shell-fish, which the *Greeks* call *Chelone*, and the *Latins Testudo*; of this Shell he made his *Lyre*, mounting it with Seven Strings, as *Lucian* says; and added a Kind of *jugum* to it, to lengthen the Strings, but not such as our Violins have, whereby one String contains several Notes; by the common Form this *jugum* seems no more than Two distinct Pieces of Wood, set parallel, and at some Distance, but joyn'd at the farther End, where there is a Head to receive Pins for stretching the Strings. *Boethius* reports the Opinion of some that say, the *Lyra Mercurii* had but Four Strings, in Imitation of the mundane *Musick* of the Four Elements: But *Diodorus Siculus* says, it had only Three Strings, in Imitation of the Three Seasons of the Year, which were all the ancient *Greeks* counted, *viz.* Spring, Summer and Winter. *Nicomachus, Horace, Lucian* and others say, it had Seven Strings, in Imitation of the Seven Planets. Some reconcile *Diodorus*

odorus, with the laft, thus, they fay the more ancient *Lyre* had but Three or Four Strings, and *Mercury* added other Three, which made up Seven. *Mercury* gave this Seven-ftringed *Lyre* to *Orpheus,* who being torn to Pieces by the *Bacchanals,* the *Lyre* was hung up in *Apollo's* Temple by the *Lesbians:* But others fay, *Pythagoras* found it in fome Temple of *Egypt,* and added an eighth String. *Nicomachus* fays, *Orpheus* being killed by the *Thracian* Women, for contemning their Religion in the *Bacchanalian* Rites, his *Lyre* was caft into the Sea, and thrown up at *Antiſſa* a City of *Leſbos;* the Fiſhers finding it gave it to *Terpander,* who carrying it to *Egypt,* gave it to the Priefts, and call'd himfelf the Inventor. Thofe who call it Four-ftring'd, make the Proportions thus, betwixt the 1ſt and 2d, the *Interval* of a 4th, 3 : 4, betwixt the 2d and 3d, a *Tone* 8 : 9, and betwixt the 3d and 4th String another 4th: The Seven Strings were *diatonically* difpofed by *Tones* and *Semitones,* and *Pythagoras's* eighth String made up the *Octave.*

THE Occafion of afcribing the Invention of this Inftrument to fo many Authors, is probably, that they have each in different Places invented Inftruments much refembling other. However fimple it was at firft, it grew to a great Number of Strings; but 'tis to no Purpofe to repete the Names of thefe who are fuppofed to have added new Strings to it.

FROM this Inftrument, which all agree to be firft of the ftringed Kind in *Greece,* arofe a Multitude

titude of others, differing in their Shape and Number of Strings, of which we have but indistinct Accounts. We hear of the *Pfalterium, Trigon, Sambuca, Pectis, Magadis, Barbiton, Teftudo* (the Two laft ufed by *Horace* promifcuoufly with the *Lyra* and *Cithara*) *Epigonium, Simmicium, Pandura*, which were all ftruck with the Hand or a *Plectrum* ; but it does not appear that they ufed any Thing like the Bows of Hair we have now for Violins, which is a moft noble Contrivance for making long and fhort Sounds, and giving them a thoufand Modifications 'its impoffible to produce by a *Plectrum.*

Kircher alfo obferves, that in all the ancient Monuments, where Inftruments are put in the Hands of *Apollo* and the Mufes, as there are many of them at *Rome* fays he, there is none to be found with fuch a *jugum* as our Violins have, whereby each String has feveral Notes, but every String has only one Note : And this he makes an Argument of the Simplicity and Imperfection of their Inftruments. Befides feveral Forms of the *Lyra* Kind, and fome *Fiftulæ*, he is pofitive they had no Inftruments worth naming. He confiders how careful they were to tranfmit, by Writing and other Monuments, their moft trifling Inventions, that they might not lofe the Glory of them; and concludes, if they had any Thing more perfect, we fhould certainly have heard of it, and had it preferved, when they were at Pains to give us the Fi-

gure

gure of their trifling Reed-pipes, which the Shepherds commonly ufed. But indeed I find fome Paffages, that cannot be well underftood, without fuppofing they had Inftruments in which one String had more than one Note: Where *Pherecrates* (already mention'd) makes *Mufick* complain of her Abufes from *Timotheus*'s Innovations; fhe fays, he had deftroyed her who had Twelve *Harmonies* in Five Strings; whether thefe *Harmonies* fignify fingle Notes or Confonances, 'tis plain each String muft have afforded more than one Note. And *Plutarch* afcribes to *Terpander* a *Lyre* of Three Chords, yet he fays it had Seven Sounds, *i. e.* Notes.

I have now done as much as my Purpofe required. If you are curious to hear more of this, and fee the Figures of Inftruments both ancient and modern, go to *Merfennus* and *Kircher*.

§ 3. *Of the* Excellency *and various* Ufes *of* Mufick.

THo' the Reafons alledged for the Antiquity of *Mufick*, fhew us the Dignity of it, yet I believe it will be agreeable, to enter into a more particular Hiftory of the Honour *Mufick* was in among the Ancients, and of its various Ends and Ufes, and the pretended Virtues and Powers of it.

THE

THE Reputation this Art was in with the *Jewish* Nation, is I suppose well known by the *sacred History.* Can any Thing shew the Excellency of an Art more, than that it was reckoned useful and necessary in the Worship of GOD; and as such, diligently practised and cultivated by a People, separated from the rest of Mankind, to be Witnesses for the Almighty, and preserve the true Knowledge of GOD upon the Earth? I have already mentioned the Instance of the *Israelites* Song, upon their Delivery at the Red Sea, which seems to prove that *Musick* both *vocal* and *instrumental,* was an approven and stated Manner of worshipping GOD: And we cannot doubt that it was according to his Will, for *Moses* the Man of GOD, and *Miriam* the Prophetess, were the Chiefs of this sacred Choir: And that from this Time to that of the Royal Prophet *David,* the Art was honoured and encouraged by them both publickly and privately, we can make no Doubt; for when *Saul* was troubled with an evil Spirit from the LORD, he is advised to call for a cunning Player on the *Harp,* which supposes it was a well known Art in that Time; and behold, *David,* yet an obscure and private Person, being famous for his Skill in *Musick,* was called; and upon his playing, Saul *was refreshed and was well, and the evil Spirit departed from him.* Nor when *David* was advanced to the Kingdom thought he this Exercise below him, especially the religious Use of it. When the *Ark* was brought from *Kirjath-jearim,* David *and*

all

all Israel *played before* G O D *with all their Might, and with Singing, and with Harps, and with Pfalteries, and with Timbrels, and with Cymbals, and with Trumpets,* 1 Chron. 13. 8. And the Ark being fet up in the City of *David,* what a folemn Service was inftituted for the publick Worfhip and Praife of G O D; Singers and Players on all Manner of Inftruments, *to minifter before the Ark of the* L O R D *continually, to record, and to thank, and praife the Lord* G O D *of* I S R A E L. Thefe feem to have beeen divided into Three *Choirs,* and over them appointed Three *Choragi* or Mafters, *Afaph, Heman* and *Jeduthun,* both to inftruct them, and to prefide in the Service: But *David* himfelf was the chief *Mufician* and *Poet* of *Ifrael.* And when *Solomon* had finifhed the *Temple,* behold, at the Dedication of it, *the* Levites *which were the Singers, all of them of* Afaph, *of* Heman, *of* Jeduthun, *having Cymbals, and Pfalteries, and Harps, ftood at the Eaft-end of the Altar, praifing and thanking the* L O R D. And this Service, as *David* had appointed before the *Ark,* continued in the *Temple;* for we are told, that the King and all the People having dedicated the Houfe to G O D,—*The Priefts waited on their Offices: the Levites alfo with Inftruments of* Mufick *of the* L O R D, *which* David *the King had made to praife the* L O R D.

THE Prophet *Elifha* knew the Virtue of *Mufick,* when he called for a Minftrel to compofe his Mind (as is reafonably fuppofed) before *the Hand of the* L O R D *came upon him.*

To

To this I shall add the Opinion and Testimony of St. *Chrysostom*, in his Commentary on the 40*th* *Psalm.* He says to this Purpose, ' That God knowing Men to be slothful and ' backward in spiritual Things, and impatient ' of the Labour and Pains which they require, ' willing to make the Task more agreeable, ' and prevent our Weariness, he joyn'd *Melody* ' or *Musick* with his Worship; that as we are ' all naturally delighted with *harmonious* Num- ' bers, we might with Readiness and Cheerful- ' ness of Mind express his Praise in sacred ' Hymns. For, says he, nothing can raise the ' Mind, and, as it were, give Wings to it, free ' it from Earthliness, and the Confinement 'tis ' under by Union with the Body, inspire it with ' the Love of Wisdom, and make every thing ' pertaining to this Life agreeable, as well mo- ' dulated Verse and divine Songs *harmoniously* ' composed. Our Natures are so delighted with ' *Musick*, and we have so great and necessary ' Inclination and Tendency to this Kind of Plea- ' sure, that even Infants upon the Breast are ' soothed and lulled to Rest by this means. A- gain he says, ' Because this Pleasure is so fami- ' liar and connate with our Minds, that we ' might have both Profit and Pleasure, God ' appointed Psalms, that the Devil might not ' ruine us with prophane and wicked Songs. And tho' there be now some Difference of Opi- nion about its Use in sacred Things, yet all Christians keep up the Practice of singing Hymns and Psalms, which is enough to confirm the ge-

neral

neral Principle of *Mufick*'s Suitableneſs to the Worſhip of GOD.

IN St. *John*'s Viſion, the Elders are repreſented with *Harps* in their Hands; and tho' this be only repreſenting Things in Heaven, in a Way eaſieſt for our Conception, yet we muſt ſuppoſe it to be a Compariſon to the beſt Manner of worſhipping GOD among Men, with reſpect at leaſt to the Means of compoſing and raiſing our Minds, or keeping out other Ideas, and thereby fitting us for entertaining religious Thoughts.

LET us next conſider the Eſteem and Uſe of it among the ancient *Greeks* and *Romans*. The Glory of this Art among them, eſpecially the *Greeks*, appears firſt, according to the Obſervation of *Quintilian*, by the Names given to the *Poets* and *Muſicians*, which at the Begining were generally the ſame Perſon, and their Characters thought to be ſo connected, that the Names were reciprocal; they were called *Sages* or *Wiſemen*, and the *inſpired*. *Salmuth* on *Pancirollus* cites *Ariſtophanes* to prove, that by *cithare callens*, or one that was skilled in playing on the *Cithara*, the Ancients meant a Wiſeman, who was adorned with all the Graces; as they reckoned one who had no Ear or Genius to *Muſick*, ſtupid, or whoſe Frame was diſordered, and the Elements of his Compoſition at War among themſelves. And ſo high an Opinion they had of it, that they thought no Induſtry of Man could attain to ſuch an excellent Art ; and hence they believed this Faculty

to

to be an Inspiration from the Gods; which also
appears particularly by their making *Apollo* the
Author of it, and then making their most ancient *Musicians*, as *Orpheus*, *Linus*, and *Amphion*, of divine Offspring. *Homer*, who was himself both *Poet* and *Musician*, could have supposed nothing more to the Honour of his Profes-
sion, than making the Gods themselves delighted with it; after the fierce Contest that happened among them about the *Grecian* and *Trojan* Affairs, he feigns them recreating themselves with *Apollo*'s Musick ; and after this,
'tis no Wonder he thought it not below his
Hero to have been instructed in, and a diligent
Practiser of this Godlike Art. And do not the
Poets universally testify this Opinion of the Excellency of *Musick*, when they make it a Part
of the Entertainment at the Tables of Kings ;
where to the Sound of the *Lyre* they sung the
Praises of the Gods and Heroes, and other useful Things: As *Homer* in the *Odyssea* introduces
Demodocus at the Table of *Alcinous*, King of
Phæacea, singing the *Trojan* War and the Praises of the Heroes : And *Virgil* brings in *Jopas*
at the Table of *Dido*, singing to the Sound of
his golden *Harp*, what he had learned in natural Philosophy, and particularly in Astronomy
from *Atlas*; upon which *Quintilian* makes this
Reflection, that hereby the *Poet* intends to
shew the Connection there is betwixt *Musick*
and heavenly Things; and *Horace* teaches us
the same Doctrine, when addressing his *Lyre*, he

cries

cries out, *O decus Phœbi, & dapibus supremi, grata testudo, Jovis.*

AT the Beginning, *Musick* was perhaps sought only for the sake of innocent Pleasure and Recreation; in which View *Aristotle* calls it the Medicine of that Heaviness that proceeds from Labour; and *Horace* calls his Lyre *laborum dulce lenimen*: And as this is the first and most simple, so it is certainly no despicable Use of it; our Circumstances require such a Help to make us undergo the necessary Toils of Life more cheerfully. *Wine and Musick cheer the Heart,* said the wise Man; and that the same Power still remains, does plainly appear by universal Experience. Men naturally seek Pleasure, and the wiser Sort studying how to turn this Desire into the greatest Advantage, and mix the *utile dulci,* happily contrived, by bribing the Ear, to make Way into the Heart. The severest of the Philosophers approved of *Musick,* because they found it a necessary Means of Access to the Minds of Men, and of engaging their Passions on the Side of Virtue and the Laws; and so *Musick* was made an Handmaid to Virtue and Religion.

JAMBLICHUS in the Life of *Pythagoras* tells us, That Musick was a Part of the Discipline by which he formed the Minds of his Scholars. To this Purpose he made, and taught them to make and sing, Verses calculated against the Passions and Diseases of their Minds; which were also sung by a Chorus, standing round one that plaid upon the Lyre, the Modulations
whereof

whereof were perfectly adapted to the Design and Subject of the Verses. He used also to make them sing some choice Verses out of *Homer* and *Hesiod*. Musick was the first Exercise of his Scholars in the Morning; as necessary to fit them for the Duties of the Day, by bringing their Minds to a right Temper; particularly he designed it as a Kind of Medicine against the Pains of the Head, which might be contracted in Sleep: And at Night, before they went to rest, he taught them to compose their Minds after the Perturbations of the Day, by the same Exercise.

Whatever Virtue the *Pythagoreans* ascribed to *Musick*, they believed the Reason of it to be, That the Soul it self consisted of Harmony; and therefore they pretended by it to revive the primitive Harmony of the Faculties of the Soul. By this primitive Harmony they meant that which, according to their Doctrine, was in the Soul in its pre-existent State in Heaven. *Macrobius*, who is plainly *Pythagorean* in this Point, affirms, That every Soul is delighted with *musical* Sounds; not the polite only but the most barbarous Nations practise *Musick*, whereby they are excited to the Love of Vertue, or dissolved in Softness and Pleasure: The Reason is, says he, That the Soul brings into the Body with it the Memory of the *Musick* which it was entertained with in Heaven: And there are certain Nations, says he, that attend the Dead to their Burial with Singing; because they believe the Soul returns to Heaven the Fountain

or

or Original of *Mufick*, *Lib.* 2. in *Somnium Scipionis*. And becaufe this Sect believed the *Gods* themfelves to have celeftial Bodies of a moft perfect harmonious Compofition, therefore they thought the *Gods* were delighted with it; and that by our Ufe of it in facred Things, we not only compofe our Minds, and fit them better for the Contemplation of the *Gods*, but imitate their Happinefs, and thereby are acceptable to them, and open for our felves a Return into *Heaven*.

ATHENAEUS reports of one *Clinias* a *Pythagorean*, who, being a very cholerick and wrathful Man, as foon as he found his Paffion begin to rife, took up his Lyre and fung, and by this means allayed it. But this Difcipline was older than *Pythagoras*; for *Homer* tells us, That *Achilles* was educated in the fame manner by *Chiron*, and feigns him, after the hot Difpute he had with *Agamemnon*, calming his Mind with his Song and Lyre : And tho' *Homer* fhould be the Author of this Story, it fhews however that fuch an Ufe was made of *Mufick* in his Days ; for 'tis reafonable to think he had learned this from Experience.

THE virtuous and wife *Socrates* was no lefs a Friend to this admirable Art; for even in the Decline of his Age he applied himfelf to the Lyre, and carefully recommended it to others. Nor did the divine *Plato* differ from his great Mafter in this Point; he allows it in his *Common-wealth*; and in many Places of his Works fpeaks with the greateft Refpect of it, as a moft ufeful Thing in Society ;
he

he fays it has as great Influence over the Mind,
as the Air has over the Body; and therefore he
thought it was worthy of the Law to take Care
of it : He underftood the Principles of the Art
fo well that, as *Quintilian* juftly obferves, there
are many Paffages in his Writings not to be underftood without a good Knowledge of it.
Ariftotle in his *Politicks* agrees with *Plato* in
his Sentiments of *Mufick*.

ARISTIDES the Philofopher and Mufician,
in the Introduction to his Treatife on this Subject, fays, 'tis not fo confined either as to the
Subject Matter or Time as other Arts and
Sciences, but adds Ornament to all the Parts
and Actions of human Life :   Painting, fays he,
attains that Good which regards the Eye, Medicine and Gymnaftick are good for the Body,
Dialectick and that Kind helps to acquire Pru-
dence, if the Mind be firft purged and prepared
by *Mufick* :   Again, it beautifies the Mind
with the Ornaments of Harmony,   and forms
the Body with decent Motions :   'Tis fit for
young ones, becaufe of the Advantages got by
Singing ; for Perfons of more Age, by teaching
them the Ornaments of modulate Diction, and
of all Kinds of Eloquence; to others more advanced it teaches the Nature of Number, with
the Variety of Proportions, and the Harmony
that thereby exifts in all Bodies, but chiefly the
Reafons and Nature of the Soul. He fays, as
wife Husband-men firft caft out Weeds and
noxious Plants, then fow the good Seed, fo Mufick is ufed to compofe the Mind, and fit it for
receiving

receiving Inftruction : For Pleafure, fays he, is not the proper End of Mufick, which affords Recreation to the Mind only by accident, the propofed End being the inftilling of Virtue. Again, he fays, if every City, and almoft every Nation loves Decency and Humanity, Mufick cannot poffibly be ufelefs.

I T was ufed at the Feafts of Princes and Heroes, fays *Athenæus*, not out of Levity and vain Mirth; but rather as a Kind of Medicine, that by making their Minds cheerful, it might help their Digeftion : There, fays he, they fung the Praifes of the Gods and Heroes and other ufeful and inftructive Compofures, that their Minds might not be neglected while they took Care of their Bodies; and that from a Reverence of the Gods, and by the Example of good Men, they might be kept within the Bounds of Sobriety and Moderation.

B u t we are not confined to the Authority and Opinion of Philofophers or any particular Perfons ; we have the Teftimony of whole Nations where it had publick Encouragement, and was made neceffary by the Law; as in the moft Part of the *Grecian* Common-wealths.

A T H E N A E U S affures us, That anciently all their Laws divine and civil, Exhortations to Vertue, the Knowledge of divine and human Things, the Lives and Actions of illuftrious Men, and even Hiftories and mentions *Herodotus*, were written in Verfe and publickly fung by a *Chorus*, to the Sound of Inftruments ; they found this by Experience an effectual means to

im-

imprefs Morality, and a right Senfe of Duty :
Men were attentive to Things that were propofed to them in fuch a fweet and agreeable
Manner, and attracted by the Charms of harmonious Numbers, and well modulated Sounds,
they took Pleafure in repeating thefe Examples
and Inftructions, and found them eafier retain-
ed in their Memories. *Ariftotle* alfo in his
Problems tells us, That before the Ufe of Letters, their Laws were fung *mufically*, for the
better retaining them in Memory. In the
Story of ORPHEUS and AMPHION, both of
them *Poets* and *Muficians*, who made a wonderful Impreffion upon a rude and uncultivated
Age, by their virtuous and wife Inftructions,
inforced by the Charms of *Poetry* and *Mufick* :
The fucceeding Poets, who turned all Things
into Myftery and Fable, feign the one to have
drawn after him, and tamed the moft favage
Beafts, and the other to have animated the
very Trees and Stones, by the Power of *Mufick.*
Horace had received the fame Traditions of
all the Things I have now narrated, and with
thefe mentions other Ufes of *Mufick* : The
Paffage is in his Book *de arte Poetica,* and is
worth repeating.

Silveftres homines, facer interprefq; deorum,
Cædibus & victu fædo, deterruit Orpheus :
Dictus ob hoc lenire tigres, rabidofq; leones :
Dictus & Amphion, Thebanæ conditor arcis,
Saxa movere fono teftudinis, & prece blanda
Ducere quo vellet. Fuit hæc fapientia quondam,

Publica privatis fecernere, facra profanis :
Concubitu prohibere vago : dare facra maritis :
Oppida moliri : leges incidere ligno :
Sic honor, & nomen divinis vatibus, atque
Carminibus venit.   Poft hos infignis Homerus,
Tyrtæufq; *mares animos in martia bella*
Verfibus exacuit. Dictæ per carmina fortes :
Et vitæ monftrata via eft : & gratia regum
Pieriis tentata modis : ludufq; repertus,
Et longorum operum finis : ne forte pudori,
Sit tibi mufa lyræ folers, & cantor Apollo.

F R O M thefe Experiences I fay, the Art was
publickly honour'd by the Governments of *Greece.*
It was by the Law made a neceffary Part of the
Education of Youth. *Plato* affures us it was
thus at *Athens ;* in his firft *Alcibiades,* he mentions to that great Man, in *Socrates*'s Name,
how he was taught *to read and write, to play
on the Harp, and wreftle.* And in his *Crito,* he
fays, did not the *Laws* moft reafonably appoint
that your Father fhould educate you in *Mufick*
and *Gymnaftick?* And we find thefe Three
Grammar, Mufick and *Gymnaftick* generally
named together, as the known and neceffary
Parts of the Education of Youth, efpecially of
the better Sort : *Plutarch* and *Athenæus* give
abundant Teftimony to this ; and *Terence* having laid the Scene of his Plays in *Greece,* or
rather only tranflated, and at moft but imitated
Menander, gives us another Proof, in the *Act*
3. *Scene* 2. of his *Eunuch. Fac periculum in*
literis, fac in palæftra, in muficis. Quæ liberum
fcire æquum eft adolefcentem folertem dabo.

T H E

THE Use of *Musick* in the Temples and solemn Service of their *Gods* is past all question. *Plato* in his *Dialogues* concerning the Laws, gives this Account of the sacred Musick. 1*mo*. That every Song consist of pious Words. 2*do*. That we pray to God to whom we sacrifice. 3*tio*. That the Poets, who know that Prayers are Petitions or Requests to the Gods, take good Heed they don't ask Ill instead of Good, and do nothing but what's just, honest, good and agreeable to the Laws of the Society; and that they shew not their Compositions to any private Person, before those have seen and approven them who are appointed Judges of these Things, and Keepers of the Laws: Then, Hymns to the Praises of the Gods are to be sung, which are very well connected with Prayer; and after the Gods, Prayers and Praises are to be offered to the *Dæmons* and *Heroes.*

As they had poetical Compositions upon various Subjects for their publick Solemnities, so they had certain determinate *Modes* both in the *Harmonia* and *Rythmus,* which it was unlawful to alter; and which were hence called *Nomi* or *Laws,* and *Musica Canonica.* They were jealous of any Innovations in this Matter, fearing that a Liberty being allowed, it might be abused to Luxury; for they believed there was a natural Connection betwixt the publick Manners and *Musick*: *Plato* denied that the *musical Modes* or Laws could be changed without a Change of the publick Laws; he meant, the

In-

Influence of *Muſick* was ſo great, that the Changes in it would neceſſarily produce a proportional Change of Manners and the publick Conſtitution.

The Uſe of it in *War* will eaſily be allowed to have been by publick Authority ; and the Thing we ought to remark is, that it was not uſed as a mere Signal, but for inſpiring Courage, raiſing their Minds to the Ambition of great Actions, and freeing them from baſe and cowardly Fear; and this was not done without great Art, as *Virgil* ſhews when he ſpeaks of *Miſenus*,

　　　　— *Quo non præſtantior alter,*
Ære ciere viros, martemque accendere cantu.

From *Athens* let us come to *Lacedemon,* and here we find it in equal Honour. Their Opinion of its natural Influence was the ſame with that of their Neighbours : And to ſhew what Care was taken by the Law, to prevent the Abuſe of it to Luxury, the Hiſtorians tell us that *Timotheus* was fined for having more than Seven Strings on his *Lyre,* and what were added ordered to be taken away. The *Spartans* were a warlike People, yet very ſenſible of the Advantage of fighting with a cool and deliberate Courage ; therefore as *Gellius* out of *Thucydides* reports, they uſed not in their Armies, Inſtruments of a more vehement Sound, that might inflame their Temper and make them more furious, as the *Tuba, Cornu* and *Lituus,*
　　　　　　　　　　　　　　　　but

but the more gentle and moderate Sounds and Modulations of the *Tibia*, that their Minds being more compoſed, they might engage with a rational Courage. And *Gellius* tells us, the *Cretans* uſed the *Cithara* to the ſame Purpoſe in their Armies. We have already heard how this People entertain'd at great Expence the famous *Thales* to inſtruct their Youth in *Muſick* ; and after their Muſick had been thrice corrupted, thrice they reſtored it.

Iꜰ we go to *Thebes*, *Epaminondas* will be a Witneſs of the Eſteem it was in, as *Corn. Nepos* informs us.

Aᴛʜᴇɴᴀᴜꜱ reports, upon the Authority of *Theopompus*, that the *Getan* Ambaſſadors, being ſent upon an Embaſſy of Peace, made their Entry with *Lyres* in their Hands, ſinging and playing to compoſe their Minds, and make themſelves Maſters of their Temper. We need not then doubt of its publick Encouragement among this People.

Bᴜᴛ the moſt famous Inſtance in all *Greece*, is that of the *Arcadians*, a People, ſays *Polybius*,in Reputation for Virtue among the *Greeks*; eſpecially for their Devotion to the Gods. *Muſick*, ſays he, is eſteem'd every where, but to the *Arcadians* it is neceſſary, and allowed a Part in the Eſtabliſhment of their State, and an indiſpenſable Part of the Education of their Children. And tho' they might be ignorant of other Arts and Sciences without Reproach, yet none might preſume to want Knowledge in Muſick,

fick, the Law of the Land making it neceffary;
and Infufficiency in it was reckoned infamous
among that People. It was not thus eftablifhed,
fays he, fo much for Luxury and Delight, as
from a wife Confideration of their toilfom and
induftrious Life, owing to the cold and melancholy Air of their Climate; which made them
attempt every Thing for foftning and fweetning
thofe Aufterities they were condemned to. And
the Negleſt of this Difcipline he gives as the
Reafon of the Barbarity of the *Cynæthians* a
People of *Arcadia*.

We fhall next confider the State of Mufick
among the ancient *Romans*. Till Luxury and
Pride ruin'd the Manners of this brave Nation,
they were famous for a fevere and exaſt Virtue.
And tho' they were convinced of the native
Charms and Force of *Mufick*, yet we don't find
they cherifhed it to the fame Degree as the
Greeks; from which one would be tempted to
think they were only afraid of its Power, and
the ill Ufe it was capable of; a Caution that
very well became thofe who valued themfelves
fo much, and juftly, upon their Piety and good
Manners.

CORN. NEPOS, in his Preface, takes Notice of the
Differences betwixt the *Greek* and *Roman Cuftoms*,
particularly with refpeſt to *Mufick*; and in the
Life of *Epaminondas*, he has thefe Words, *Sci-
mus enim muficum noftris moribus abeffe a prin-
cipis perfona; faltare etiam in vitiis poni, quæ
omnia apud* Græcos *& gratia & laude digna du-
cuntur.*

CICE-

CICERO in the Beginning of the first Book of his *Tusculan* Questions, tells us, that the old *Romans* did not study the more soft and polite Arts so much as the *Greeks*; being more addicted to the Study of Morality and Government: Hence Musick had a Fate somewhat different at *Rome*.

BUT the same *Cicero* shews us plainly his own Opinion of it. *Lib.* 2. *de Legibus* ; *Assentior enim* Platoni, *nihil tam facile in animos teneros atque molles influere quam varios canendi sonos. Quorum dici vix potest quanta sit vis in utramque partem, namque & incitat languentes, & languefacit incitatos, & tum remittit animos, tum contrahit.* Certainly he had been a Witness to this Power of Sound, before he could speak so; and I shall not believe he had met with the Experiment only at *Athens.* A Man so famous for his Eloquence, must have known the Force of harmonious Numbers, and well proportioned *Tones* of the Voice.

QUINTILIAN speaks honourably of *Musick.* He says, *Lib.* 1. *Chap.* 11. Nature seems to have given us this Gift for mitigating the Pains of Life, as the common Practice of all labouring Men testifies. He makes it necessary to his Orator, because, says he, *Lib.* 8. *Chap.* 4. it is impossible that a Thing should reach the Heart which begins with choking the Ear ; and because we are naturally pleased with Harmony, otherwise Instruments of Musick that cannot express Words would not make such surprising
                                and

and various Effects upon us. And in another Place, where he is proving *Art* to be only Nature perfected, he says, *Musick* would not otherwise be an *Art*, for there is no Nation which has not its *Songs* and *Dances*.

SOME of the first Rank at *Rome* practised it. *Athenæus* says of one *Masurius* a Lawyer, whom he calls one of the best and wisest of Men, and inferior to none in the Law, that he applied himself to Musick diligently. And *Plutarch* places *Musick, viz.* singing and playing on the *Lyre*, among the Qualifications of *Metella* the Daughter of *Scipio Metellus*.

MACROBIUS in the 10 *Chap. Lib.* 2. of his *Saturnalia* shews us, that neither Singing nor Dancing were reckoned dishonourable Exercises even for the Quality among the ancient *Romans*; particularly in the Times betwixt the Two *Punick* Wars, when their Virtue and Manners were at the best; providing they were not studied with too much Curiosity, and too much Time spent about them; and observes that it is this, and not simply the Use of these that *Salust* complains of in *Sempronia*, when he says she knew *psallere & saltare elegantius quam necesse erat probæ*. What an Opinion *Macrobius* himself had of *Musick* we have in part shewn already; to which let us add here this remarkable Passage in the Place formerly cited. *Ita denique omnis habitus animæ cantibus gubernatur, ut & ad bellum progressui & etiam receptui canatur, cantu & excitante & rursus sedante virtutem; dat somnos adimitque,*

nec-

necnon curas & immittit & retrahit, iram
fuggerit, clementiam fuadet, corporum quoque
morbis medetur. Hinc eſt quod ægris remedia
præftantes præcinere dicuntur. The Abuſe of
it, which 'tis probable lay chiefly in their idle,
ridiculous and laſcivious Dancing, or perhaps
their ſpending too much Time even in the moſt
innocent Part of it, and not applying it to the
true Ends, made the wiſer Sort cry out, and
brought the Character of a *Muſician* into ſome
Diſcredit. But we find that the true and proper *Muſick* was ſtill in Honour and Practice a-
mong them: Had *Rome* ever ſuch Poets, or
were they ever ſo honoured as in *Auguſtus's*
Reign ? *Horace,* tho' he complains of the Abuſe
of the Theatre and the *Muſick* of it, yet in many Places he ſhews us, that it was then the
Practice to ſing Verſes or *Odes* to the Sound of
the *Lyre,*or of *Pipes,*or of both together; *Lib.*
4. *Ode 9. Verba loquor focianda chordis. Lib.* 2.
Ep. 2. *Hic ego verba lyræ motura ſonum con-*
nectere digner ? In the firſt *Ode, Lib.* 1. he gives
us his own Character as a Poet and *Muſician,*
Si neque tibias Euterpe *cohibet, &c.* He ſhews
us that it was in his Time uſed both publickly
in the Praiſe of the *Gods* and Men, and privately for Recreation, and at the Tables of the
Great, as we find clearly in theſe Paſſages. *Lib.*
4. *Ode* 11. *Condiſce modos amanda voce quos*
reddas, minuentur atræ carmine curæ. Lib. 3.
Ode 28. *Nos cantabimus invicem* Neptunum,
tu curva recines lyra Latonam,*&c.* Lib. 4. Ode
15. *Noſque & profeſtis lucibus & facris - Rite*
                                                Deos

Deos prius adprecati, virtute functos more patrum duces, Lydis *remisto carmine tibiis* Trojamque, *&c. canemus.* Epode 9. *Quando repostum cacubum ad festas dapes tecum. — Beate* Mecænas *bibam ? Sonante mistis tibiis carmen lyra.* Lib. 3. Ode 11. *Tuque testudo — Nunc & divitum mensis & amica templis.*

F O R all the Abuses of it, there were still some, even of the best Characters, that knew how to make an innocent Use of it : *Sueton* in *Titus*'s Life, whom he calls *Amor ac deliciæ generis humani,* among his other Accomplishments adds, *Sed ne* Musicæ *quidem rudis, ut qui cantaret & psalleret jucunde scienterque.*

T H E R E is enough said to shew the real Value and Use of *Musick* among the Ancients. I believe it will be needless to insist much upon our own Experience ; I shall only say, these Powers of *Musick* remain to this Day, and are as universal as ever. We use it still in *War* and in *sacred Things,* with Advantages that they only know who have the Experience. But in common Life almost every Body is a Witness of its sweet Influences.

W H A T a powerful Impression musical Sounds make even upon the *Brute* Animals, especially the feathered Kind, we are not without some Instances. But how surprising are the Accounts we meet with among the old Writers ? I have reserved no Place for them here. You may see a Variety of Stories in *Ælian*'s History of Animals;

mals, *Strabo*, *Pliny*, *Marcianus Capella*, and others.

BEFORE I leave this, I muſt take Notice of ſome of the extraordinary Effects a cribed to *Muſick*. *Pythagoras* is ſaid to have had an abſolute Command of the human Paſſions, to turn them as he pleaſed by *Muſick :* They tell us, that meeting a young Man who in great Fury was running to burn his Rival's Houſe, *Pythagoras* allayed his Temper, and diverted the Deſign, by the ſole Power of *Muſick*. The Story is famous how *Timotheus*, by a certain Strain or Modulation, fired *Alexander*'s Temper to that Degree, that forgetting himſelf, in a warlike Rage he killed one of the Company; and by a Change of the *Muſick* was ſoftned again, even to a bitter Repentance of what he had done. But *Plutarch* ſpeaks of one *Antigenides* a *Tibicen* or Piper, who by ſome warlike Strain had tranſported that *Hero*, ſo far that he fell upon ſome of the Company. *Terpander* quelled a Sedition at *Sparta* by means of *Muſick*. *Thales* being called from *Crete*, by Advice of the Oracle, to *Sparta*, cured a raging Peſtilence by the ſame Means. The Cure of Diſeaſes by *Muſick* is talked of with enough of Confidence. *Aulus Gellius Lib.* 4. *Chap.* 13. tells us it was a common Tradition, that thoſe who were troubled with the *Sciatica* (he calls them *Iſchiaci*) when their Pain was moſt exquiſite, were eaſed by certain gentle Modulations of *Muſick* performed upon the *Tibia;* and ſays, he had read in *Theophraſtus* that, by certain artful

Modu-

Modulations of the same Kind of Inftrument, the Bites of Serpents or Vipers had been cured. *Clytemneftra* had her vicious Inclinations to Unchaftity corrected by the Applications of *Muficians*. And a virtuous Woman is faid to have diverted the wicked Defign of two Rakes that affaulted her, by ordering a Piece of *Mufick* to be performed in the *Spondean* Mode. The Truth and Reality of thefe Effects fhall be confidered afterwards.

§ 4. *Explaining the* HARMONICK *Principles of the* Ancients; *and their* Scale *of* Mufick.

Indroduction. *Of the ancient Writers on* Mufick.

THESE Principles are certainly to be found no where, but among thofe who have written profeffedly upon the Subject ; I fhall therefore introduce what I'm to deliver, with a fhort Account of the ancient Writers upon *Mufick.*

I have already obferved, that the firft Writer upon *Mufick* was *Lafus Hermionenfis* ; but his Work is loft, as are the Works of very many more, both *Greek* and *Latin*, of which you'll find a large Catalogue in the 3*d* Book of *Fabritius's Bibliotheca graeca* ; where you'll alfo find an Account of fome others, that are pretended to be ftill in Manufcript in fome Libraries.

ries. Here I shall only say a few Words concerning these Authors that are still extant and already made publick.

ARISTOXENUS the Disciple of *Aristotle*, is the eldest Writer extant on this Subject; he calls his Book *Elements* of *Harmonicks*; and tho' in his *Division* he speaks of the rest of the Parts, yet he explains there only the *Harmonica*. He wrote a Treatise upon the other Parts, which is lost.

EUCLID, the Author of the *Elements* of *Geometry*, is next to *Aristoxenus*, he writes an *Introduction* to *Harmonicks*.

ARISTIDES QUINTILIANUS wrote after *Cicero's* Time ; he calls his Book, *Of Musick*, because he treats of both the *Harmonica* and *Rythmica*.

ALYPIUS stands next, who writes only an Account of the Greek *Semeiotica*, or of the Signs by which the various Degrees of *Tune* were noted in any Song.

GAUDENTIUS the Philosopher makes a Kind of short Compend of *Aristoxenus*, which he calls an *Introduction* to *Harmonicks*.

NICOMACHUS the *Pythagorean* writes a Compend. of *Harmonicks*, which he says was done at the Request of some great Woman, and promises a more complete Treatise of *Musick*: 'tis supposed that *Boethius* had seen and made Use of it, from several Passages he cites, which are not in this Compend; but 'tis lost since.

BACCHIUS a Follower of *Aristoxenus*, writes a very short *Introduction* to the *Art* of *Musick* in Dialogue.

OF

O F thefe Seven *Greek* Authors, we have a fair Copy, with Tranflation and Notes, by *Mei-bomius.*

CLAUDIUS PTOLOMAEUS the famous Mathematician, about the Time of the Emperor *Antoninus Pius,* writes in *Greek* Three Books of *Harmonicks.* He ftrikes a Medium betwixt the *Pythagoreans* and *Ariftoxenians,* in explaining the *harmonick* Principles. Of this Author, with his prolix Commentator *Porphyrius,* we have a fair Copy with Tranflations and Notes, by the learned Doctor *Wallis.* Vol. III. of his mathematical Works. And from the fame Hand we have alfo, with Tranflation and Notes.

MANUEL BRYENNIUS, long after any of the former, who writes of *Harmonicks.* In his firft Book he follows *Euclid,* and in his 2*d* and 3*d Ptolomy.*

I have fpoken of *Plutarch*'s Book de *Mufica,* in the § 1.

O F the *Latins* we have

BOETHIUS, in the Time of *Theodorick* the *Goth,* he writes *de mufica,* but explains only the *harmonick* Principles ; 'tis with his other Works.

MARTIANUS CAPELLA in the 9*th* Book of his Treatife *de nuptiis Philologiæ & Veneris,* writes *de mufica,* in which he is but a forry Copier from *Ariftides.* We have this Work with *Meibomius*'s Collection of the *Greek* Writers.

St.

St. A U G U S T I N writes *de musica,* but he treats only of the *Rythmi* and *pedes metrici ;* 'tis among his Works.

A U R E L I U S C A S S I O D O R U S, in the Time of *Theodorick,* among his other Works, and particularly *de artibus ac disciplinis liberalium literarum,* treats *de musica ;* 'tis a very short Sketch, amounting to no more than some general Definitions and Divisions.

T H E R E are one or Two more Authors, which I have not seen : But these mentioned contain the whole Doctrine that's left us by the Ancients; and perhaps we might spare severals of these without great Loss, Two or Three of them containing the Whole ; so true it is what *Gerhard Vossius* remarks of them, *nempe alii alios illaudato more exscripserunt.*

T H E S E then are the Authorities and Originals, from which I have taken the following Account of the ancient *System* of *Musick.* It will be needless therefore, after I have told you this, to make a troublesom and tedious Citation for every Thing I mention.

Of the ancient H A R M O N I C A.

H o w the ancient Writers *defined* and *divided* M U S I C K has been explained in § 1. of this *Ch.* and needs not be repeted. My Business here is with the Part they called *Harmonica,* which treats of Sounds and their Differences, with respect to *acute* and *grave. Ptolomy* calls it *a Power or Faculty perceptive of the Difference*

of

of Sounds, with respect to Acuteness *and* Gravity; *and* Bryennius *calls it a speculative and practical Science, of the Nature of the *harmonick* Agreement in Sounds.

T H E Y reduce the Doctrine of *Harmonicks* into Seven Parts, *viz.* 1*st*. Of *Sounds*. 2*d*. Of *Intervals*. 3*d*. Of *Systems*. 4*th*. Of the *Genera* or different Kinds, with respect to the Constitution and Division of the *Scale*. 5*th*. Of the *Tones* or *Modes*. 6*th*. Of *Mutations* or *Changes*. 7*th*. Of the *Melopœia* or Art of making *Melody* or Songs. Of these in Order.

I. O f S o u n d. This *Ptolomy* considers in a large Sense, comprehending the whole Object of Hearing, and calls it by a general Name ψοφος, *i. e. Strepitus*, or any Kind of Sound. As it is capable of a Difference in *Acuteness* and *Gravity*, *Aristoxenus* calls it Φονὴ, *i. e. Vox*, or Voice. As to the Nature and Cause of Sound, they agree that it is the Effect of the Percussion of the Air, whose Motion is propagated to the Ear, and there raises a Perception. The principal Difference they consider in Sounds is of *Acuteness* and *Gravity*, which is produced by a quicker or flower Motion in the Vibrations of the Air. A Sound considered in a certain determinate Degree of *Acuteness* or *Gravity*, they call Φθόϙγος, *i. e. Sonus*; and they define it thus, *Aristox.* Φωνῆς πῖωσις ἐπὶ μίαν τάϛιν, ὁ Φθόϙγος, *i. e. Sonus est vocis casus in unam tensionem. Aristides* considers it with regard to its Use, and calls it τάϛιν μελωδικὴν, *tensionem melodicam. Nicomachus* defines it,
                                                      Φωνῆς

φωνῆς ἐμμελῶς ἀπλατῆ τάσιν, *vocis ad cantum
aptæ tensionem, latitudinis expertem.* Thus they
diſtinguiſhed Sounds, according as their Degree
of *Acuteneſs* or *Gravity* was fit or not for
Song ; ſuch as were fit were alſo called *concinnous* Sounds, and others *inconcinnous.* Theſe
Words *wanting Latitude*, were added to con-
tradict a Notion of *Laſus* and the *Epigonians*,
that a Voice could not poſſibly remain for any
determinate Time in one Degree, but made
continually ſome little Variations up and down,
tho' not very ſenſible.

T H E N they conſider a Voice as changing
from *acute* to *grave*, or from this to that ; and
hereby form the Notion of a Motion of the
Voice, which they ſay is Twofold ; the one *concinnous*, by which we change the Voice in common Speaking, the other *diſcrete*, as in Singing.
See above *Ch.* 2. And ſome added a Third and
middle Kind, whereby, ſay they, we read a Poem.

I N Sounds (φθόγγοι) they conſider Three
Things, *Tenſion*, which is the Reſt or Standing
of the Voice in any Degree, *Intenſion* and *Re-
miſſion* are the Motions of the Voice upward
and downward, whereby it acquires *Acuteneſs*
or *Gravity :* And when it moves, all the Diſtance or Difference betwixt the firſt and laſt
Degree or *Tenſion*, they called the *Place* thro'
which it moved. Then there is *Diſtenſion* or
Difference of *acute* and *grave*, in which the
Quantity that is the mathematical Object conſiſts ; this they ſaid is naturally infinite, but with
reſpect either to our Senſes, or what Sounds we
can

can poffibly raife by any Means, it is limited ;
and this brings us to the Second Head.

II. OF INTERVALS. An *Interval* is the
Difference of Two Sounds, in refpect of *acute*
and *grave*; or, that imaginary Space which is
terminated by Two Sounds differing in *Acutenefs* or *Gravity*. *Intervals* were confidered as
differing, 1*mo*. in Magnitude. 2*do*. As the Extremes were *Concord* or *Difcord*. 3*tio*. As compofite or incompofite, *that is*, fimple or compound. 4*to*. As belonging to the different *genera* (of which again.) 5*to*. As rational or
irrational, *i. e.* fuch as we can difcern and meafure, and which neither exceed our Capacities
in Greatnefs or Littlenefs.

As to the meafuring of *Intervals*, and, as
Ptolomy calls it, the *Criterions* in *Harmonicks*,
there was a notable Difference among the *Philofophers*, which divided them into Two Sects,
the *Pythagoreans* and *Ariftoxenians* ; betwixt
whom *Ptolomy* ftriking a Midft, made a Third
Sect.

PYTHAGORAS and his Followers meafured
all the Differences of *Acutenefs* and *Gravity*,
by the *Ratios* of Numbers. They fuppofed
thefe Differences to depend upon the different
Velocities of the Motions that caufe Sound; and
thought therefore, that they could only be accurately meafured by the *Ratios* of thefe Velocities. Which *Ratios* were firft inveftigate by *Pythagoras*, as *Nicomachus* and others inform us,
in this Manner, *viz.* Paffing by a Smith's Shop,
he perceived a Concord or Agreement betwixt
the

the Sounds of Hammers ſtriking the Anvil: He went in, and made ſeveral Experiments, to find upon what the Difference really depended; and at laſt making Experiments upon Strings, which he ſtretched by various Weights, he found, ſay they, that if Four Chords, in every Thing elſe equal and alike, are ſtretched by Four Weights, as 6 . 8 . 9 . 12. they yield the *Concord* of *Octave* betwixt the firſt and laſt, a 4*th* betwixt the firſt and Second, as alſo betwixt the Third and laſt, a 5*th* betwixt the firſt and Third, and alſo betwixt the Second and laſt; and that betwixt the Second and Third was exactly the Difference of 4*th* and 5*th*; being all proven by the Judgment of a well tuned Ear: Hence he determined theſe to be the true *Ratios* that accurately expreſs theſe *Intervals.*

BUT we have found an Error in this Account, which *Vincenzo Galileo,* in his Dialogues of the ancient and modern *Muſick,* is, for what I know, the firſt who obſerves; and from him *Meibomius* repetes it in his Notes upon *Nicomachus.* We know, that if Four Strings are in Length, as theſe Numbers 6 . 8 . 9 . 12. (*cæteris paribus*) their Sounds make the *Intervals* mentioned. But whatever *Ratio* of Length makes any *Interval,* to make the ſame by Two Chords, in every other Thing equal, but ſtretcht by different Weights, theſe Weights muſt be as the Squares of the unequal Lengths, *i. e.* for an *Octave* 1 : 4, for a 5*th* 4 : 9, and for a 4*th* 9 : 16. (See above *Ch.* 2.) Hence by the *Ratios* of the Lengths of Chords, which are reciprocally as the

the Numbers of Vibrations, all the Differences of *acute* and *grave* are measured. The *Pythagoreans* justly reckoned that the minute Differences could by no means be trusted to the Ear, and therefore judged and measured all by *Ratios*.

ARISTOXENUS on the contrary, thought Reason had nothing to do in the Case; that Sense was the only Judge; and that the other was too subtil, to be of any good Use: He therefore took the 8*ve*, 5*th* and 4*th*, which are the first and most simple *Concords* by the Ear. By the Difference of the 4*th* and 5*th* he found the *Tonus*: And this being once settled as an *Interval* the Ear could judge of, he pretended to measure every *Interval* by various Additions and Subductions made of these mentioned, one with another. Particularly, he calls *Diatessaron* equal to Two *Tones* and a Half; and taking Two *Tones*, or *Ditonum*, out of *Diatessaron*, the Remainder is the *Hemitonium*; then the Sum of *Tonus* and *Hemitonium* is the *Triemitonium*. To get an Idea of the Method of bringing out these *Intervals*, suppose Six Sounds $a:b:c:d:e:f$. If *a* is the lowest, we can by the Ear take *d* a 4*th* and *e* a 5*th* upward; then from *e* downward we can take *b* a 4*th*, so that $a:b$ and $d:e$ are each the *Tonus* or Difference of 4*th* and 5*th*; also from *b* we can take upward *f* a 5*th*, and downward from *f* a 4*th* at *c*; hence we have other Two *Tones* $b:c$ and $e:f$, also a *Hemitonium* $c.d$, a *Ditonum* $a\mathbin{\underline{\ }}c$ or $d\mathbin{-}f$, a *Triemitonium* $b\mathbin{\underline{\ }}d$ or $c\mathbin{-}e$.

But

But the Inaccuracy of this Method of determining *Intervals* is very great.

P T O L O M E Y argues ftrongly againft the laft Sect, that while they own thefe different Ideas of *acute* and *grave*, which arife from the Relations of the Sounds among themfelves; and that the Differences in the Lengths of Chords which yield thefe Sounds, are the fame; yet they neither know nor enquire into the Relation: But as if the *Interval* were the real Thing, and the Sound the imaginary, they only compare the Differences of the *Intervals*, making by this Means a Shew of doing fomething in *Mufick* by Number and Proportion; which yet, fays he, they act contrary to; for they don't determine what every Species is in it felf; as we define a *Tone* to be the Difference of Two Sounds which are to one another as 8 : 9; but they fend us to another Thing as indeterminate, when they call it the Difference of a 4*th* and 5*th*. Whereas if we would raife a *Tone* exactly, we need neither 4*th* nor 5*th*. And if we ask how great that Difference is, they cannot tell us; if perhaps they don't fay, 'tis equal to Two fuch Intervals, whereof *Diateffaron* contains 5, or *Diapafon* 12, and fo of the reft; but what that is they determine not. Again, by confidering the mere Interval, they do nothing at all; for the mere Diftance is neither Concord nor concinnous, nor any Thing real; whereas by comparing Two Sounds together we determine the *Ratio* or Relation, and the Quality of their Difference, *i.e.* whether it conftitutes Concord

or

or Difcord, by the Form of that *Ratio*. Next, he fhews the Fallacy of *Ariftoxenus*'s Demonftration, whereby he pretended to prove that a *4th* was equal to Two *Tones* and a Half. I need not trouble you with it here; for we have learnt already that a *Tone* 8 : 9 is not divifible into Two equal Parts. But then he alfo finds fault with the *Pythagoreans* for fome falfe Speculations about the Proportions; and having too little Regard to the Judgment of the Ear, while they refufe fome *Concords* that the Ear approves, only becaufe the *Ratio* does not agree with their arbitrary Rule; as we fhall hear immediately.

THEREFORE he would have Senfe and Reafon always taken together in all our Judgments, about Sounds, that they may mutually help and confirm one another. And of all the Methods to prove and find the *Ratios* of Sounds, he recommends as the moft accurate, this, *viz.* to ftretch over a plain Table an evenly well made String, fixt and raifed equally at both Ends, over Two immoveable Bridges of Wood, fet perpendicularly to the Table, and parallel to each other; betwixt them a Line is to be drawn on the Table, and divided into as many equal Parts as you need, for trying all Manner of *Ratios*; then a moveable Bridge runs betwixt the other Two, which juft touches the String, and being fet at the feveral Divifions of the Line, it divides the Chord into any *Ratio* of Parts; whofe Sounds are to be compared together, or with

with the Sound of the Whole. This he calls *Canon Harmonicus*. And thofe who determined the *Intervals* this Way, were particularly called *Canonici*, and the others by the general Name of *Mufici*.

Of Concords. They defined this, An Agreement of Two Sounds that makes them, either fucceffively or jointly heard, pleafant to the Ear. They owned only thefe Three fimple ones, *viz.* the *Fourth* 3 : 4, and *Fifth* 2 : 3 called *Dia-teffaron* and *Dia-pente*, and the *Octave* 1 : 2, which they called *Dia-pafon* ; the Reafon of thefe Names we fhall hear again. Of *compound Concords*, the *Pythagoreans* owned only the Sum of the 5*th* and 8*ve* 1 : 3, and the double 8*ve* 1 : 4 or *Dif-dia-pafon*, but others owned alfo the Sum of 4*th* and 8*ve*, 3 : 8. The Reafon why the *Pythagoreans* rejected the compound 4*th*, 3 : 8 was, That they admitted nothing for *Concord* but the *Intervals* whofe *Ratios* were *multiple* or *fuperparticular*, i. e. where the greater Term contained the other a precife Number of Times, as 3 : 1, or where the greater exceeded the leffer only by 1, as 3 : 2 or 4 : 3. becaufe thefe are the moft fimple and perfect Forms of Proportion : But *Ptolomy* argues againft them from the Perfection of the *Dia-pafon*, whereby 'tis impoffible that any Sound fhould be *Concord* to its one Extreme, and Difcord to the other. The Extremes *Dia-pafon* and *Difdia-pafon*, *Ptolomy* calls *Omophoni* or *Unifons*, becaufe they agree as one Sound. The 4*th* and 5*th* and their
Com-

Compounds he calls *Synphoni* or *confonant*; the o-
ther *Intervals* belonging to *Mufick* he calls *Emme-.
li* or *concinnous*. Others call thofe of equal Degree
Omophoni, the 8*ves Antiphoni*, the 4*ths* and 5*ths
Paraphoni*; others call the 5*ths* only *Paraphoni*,
and the 4*ths Synphoni*, but all agree to call the
Difcords *Diaphoni*.

THE abftract Reafonings of the *Pythagoreans* about the *Ratios* of the *Concords*, you
have in *Ptolomy* ; but more particularly in
Euclid's Sectio Canonis. The *fundamental Principle* is, That every *Concord* arifes either from
a *Multiple* or *fuperparticular Ratio*. The
other neceffary Premiffes are. 1*mo*. That a *multiple Ratio* twice compounded, (*i. e.* multiplied
by 2,) makes the Total a *multiple Ratio*. *Euclid* proves it his own Way; but to our Purpofe
it is fhorter done thus $a : ra$, and $ra : rra$, are
both *Multiples*, and in the fame *Ratio* ; then
$a : rra$ is the Compound of thefe Two, and is
alfo *multiple*. 2*do*. The Converfe is true, that
if any *Ratio* twice compounded makes the total *Multiple*, that *Ratio* is it felf multiple. 3*tio*.
A *fuperparticular Ratio*, admits neither of one
or more geometrical mean Proportionals : Which
I thus demonftrate, *viz.* the Difference of the
Terms being 1, 'tis plain there can be no middle
Term in whole Numbers ; but the firft of any
Number (n) of *geometrical* Means betwixt a
and $a+1$, (which reprefents any *fuperparticular
Ratio*) is the $n+1$ Root of this Quantity $\overline{a}^n \times \overline{a+1}$
which being a whole Number, if it have
no Root in whole Numbers, cannot have one in

a

a mixt Number, *that is,* can have no Root at all ; and confequently there can be no Mean betwixt *a* and *a*+1. Nor can the Matter be mended by multiplying the Terms of the *Ratio,* as if for *a* : *a*+1 we take *ra* : *ra* + *r*; becaufe if we have not here a *Mean* in whole Numbers, we cannot have it at all; and if we have it in whole Numbers, then all the Series as well as the Extremes, will reduce to radical Terms contrary to the laft *Demonftr. 4to.* From the 2*d* and 3*d* follows, that a *Ratio* not multiple being twice compounded, the Total is a *Ratio,* neither *multiple* nor *fuperparticular.* Again, from the 2*d* follows, that if any *Ratio* twice compofed make not a *multiple Ratio,* it felf is not *multiple.* 5*to,* The *multiple Ratio* 2 : 1 (which is the leaft and moft fimple of the Kind) is compofed of the Two greateft *fuperparticular Ratios* 3 : 2 and 4 : 3, and cannot be compofed of any other Two that are *fuperparticular.* From thefe Premiffes the Concords are deduced thus : *Diateffaron* and *Diapente* are *Concords;* and they muft be *fuperparticular Ratios,* for neither of them twice compofed makes a *Concord;* the Sum therefore not being *multiple,* the fimple *Ratio* is not *multiple;* yet this *Ratio* being *Concord,* muft be *fuperparticular.* *Diapafon* and *Difdiapafon* are both *Concords,* and they are alfo *multiple :* The *Difdiapafon* cannot be *fuperparticular,* becaufe it has a *Mean* (which is the *Diapafon,*) therefore 'tis *multiple;* and *diapafon* is *multiple,* becaufe being twice compofed, it makes a *Multiple, viz.* the *Difdiapafon*

pafon ; then he proves that *Diapafon* is duple
2 : 1. Thus, it cannot be any greater *Multiple*
as 1 : 3 ; for it is compofed of Two *fuperparti-*
culars, viz. Diateffaron and *Diapente* : But 2 : 1
is compofed of the Two greateft *fuperparti-*
culars 3 : 2 and 4 : 3. Now if the Two greateft *fuperparticulars* make the leaft Multiple
2 : 1, no other Two are equal to it, and far
lefs to a greater ; and the *8ve* being multiple,
and compofed of Two *fuperparticulars*, muft
therefore be 2 : 1. From this 'tis alfo concluded that *Diateffaron* is 4 : 3, *Diapente* 3 : 2,
and *Difdiapafon* 1 : 4; and the reft are deduced from thefe.

DISCORDS are either (*Emmeli*) *concinnous*,
i. e. fit for *Mufick*, which is by fome alfo applied to *Concords*, or (*Ecmeli*) *inconcinnous*. Of
the *Concinnous* they numbred thefe, *viz. Diefis,*
Hemitonium, Tonus, Triemitonium, Ditonum.
There are different Species of each; and of their
Quantities we fhall hear again.

THE *fimple Intervals* are called *Diaftems,*
which are different according to the *Genera,*
of which below; the *Compound* are called
Syftems, of which next.

III. OF SYSTEMS. A *Syftem* is an *Interval*
compofed, or conceived as compofed, of feveral
leffer. As there is no leaft *Interval* in the Nature of the Thing, fo we can conceive any
given *Interval* as compofed of, or equal to the
Sum of others ; but here a *Syftem* is an *Inter-*
val which is actually divided in Practice ; and
where

where along with the Extremes we conceive
always some intermediate Terms. As *Syftems*
are only a Species of *Intervals*, so they have
all the same Diftinctions, except that of *Compofite* and *Incompofite*. They were also diftinguifhed feveral other Ways not worth Pains to
repeat. But there are Two we cannot pafs over,
which are thefe, *viz.* into *concinnous* and *inconcinnous*; the firft compofed of fuch Parts, and in
fuch Order as is fit for *Melody* ; the other is of
an oppofite Nature. Then into *perfect* and *imperfect* : Any *Syftem* lefs than *Difdiapafon* was
reckoned *imperfect*; and that only called *Perfect*, becaufe within its Extremes are contained
Examples of the fimple and original *Concords*,
and in all the Variety of Order, in which their
concinnous Part ought to be taken; which Differences conftitute what they call'd the *Species*
or *Figuræ confonantiarum*; which were alfo
different according to the *Genera:* It was alfo
called the *Syftema maximum*, or *immutatum*, becaufe they thought it was the greateft Extent,
or Difference of *Tune*, that we can go in making good *Melody*; tho' fome added a *5th* to the
Difdiapafon for the greateft Syftem ; and fome
fuppofe Three *8ves*; but they all owned the
Diapafon to be the moft *perfect*, with refpect to
the Agreement of its Extremes; and that however many *8ves* we put in the *Syftema maximum*, they muft all be conftituted or fubdivided
the fame Way as the firft : And therefore when
we know how *8ve* was divided, we know the
Nature of their *Diagramma*, which we now
call

call the *Scale of Musick* ; the Variety of which
constitutes what they called the *Genera melodiæ*,
which were also subdivided into *Species* ; and
these must next be explained.

IV. OF the GENERA. By this Title is meant
the various Ways of subdividing the consonant
Intervals (which are the chief Principles of *Melody*) into their *concinnous* Parts. As the *Octave*
is the most perfect Interval, and all other *Concords* depend upon it ; so according to the modern *Theory* we consider the Division of this
Interval, as containing the true Division of the
whole Scale : (See above *Chap.* 8.) But the Ancients went to work with this somewhat differently : The *Diatessaron* or 4th was the least
Interval they admitted as *Concord*; and therefore they sought first how that might be most
concinnously divided; from which they constituted the *Diapente* or 5th, and *Diapason* or 8ve :
Thus, the Sum of 4th and 5th is an *Octave*,
and their Difference is a *Tonus* ; if therefore to
the same Fundamental, suppose *a*, we take a
4th *b*, 5th *c*, and 8ve *d*, then also *b-d* is a 5th,
and *c - d* a 4th, and *b* : *c* is the *Tonus* ; which
they called particularly the *Tonus diazeucticus*,
because it separates or stands in the Middle
betwixt Two *4ths*, one on either Hand, *a - b*,
and *c - d*. This *Tonus* they reckoned indispensable in rising to a 5th : And therefore, the
Division of the 4th being made, the Addition
of this *Tone* made the 5th ; and adding another
4th, the same Way divided as the first, completed the 8ve. Now the *Diatessaron* being

as

as it were the Root or Foundation of their Scale, what they call'd the *Genera* arofe from its various Divifions : Hence they defined the GENUS (*modulandi*) *the manner of dividing the* TETRACHORD, *and difpofing its four Sounds* (as to their Succeffion :) And this Definition fhews us in general, That the 4*th* was divided into 3 *Intervals* by two middle Terms, fo as to contain 4 Sounds betwixt the Extremes: Hence we have the Reafon of the Name *Dia-teffaron,* (i. e. *per quatuor ;*) and becaufe from the 4*th* to the 5*th* was always the *Tone,* the 5*th* contained 5 Notes, and hence called *Dia-pente* (i. e, *per quinque:*) And with refpect to the *Lyra* and its Strings, thefe Intervals were called *Tetrachordum* and *Pentechordum.* But the 8*ve* was called *Diapafon,* (as it were *per omnes*) becaufe it contains in a manner all the different Notes of Mufick ; for after one *Octave* all the reft of the Notes of the Scale were reckoned but as it were Repetitions of it : Yet with refpect to the Lyre, it was alfo called *Octochordum.* The *Difdiapafon* and all other Names of this Kind being now plain enough, need not be infifted on: And we fhall proceed.

BY univerfal Confent the *Genera* were Three, *viz.* the *Enharmonick, Chromatick* and *Dia-tonick.* The Reafons of thefe Names we fhall have prefently ; but the two laft were varioufly fubdivided into different *Species* ; and even the firft, tho' 'tis commonly reckoned to be without any Species, yet different Authors propofed different

ferent Divifions, under that Name, tho' without diftinguifhing Names of Species, as were added to the other Two.

ARISTOXENUS who meafured all by the Ear, expreffed his Conftitutions of the *Genera* in this Manner : He fuppofes the *Tonus* (*dia-zeucticus*) or Difference of the 4*th* and 5*th*, to be divided into 12 equal Parts; which, to prevent Fractions, *Ptolomy*, when he explains them, doubles, and makes 24; fo that the whole 4*th* muft contain 60 of them. A certain Number of thefe *imaginary* Intervals he affign-ed to each of the Three Parts into which the 4*th* is to be divided; and all together made up thefe Six following Divifions, which I take with the common Latin Names.

$$
\overbrace{}^{4th}
$$

$$a - b - c - d.$$

Enharmonium	$6 + 6 + 48 = 60$	

Chroma.
- *Molle* . . . . $\quad 8 + 8 + 44 = 60$
- *Hemiolion* . . . . $\quad 9 + 9 + 42 = 60$
- *Tonicum* . . . . . . $12 + 12 + 36 = 60$

Diatonum
- *Molle* . . . . $\quad 12 + 18 + 30 = 60$
- *Intenfum* . . . . . $\quad 12 + 24 + 24 = 60$

IN the *Enharmonium*, fuppofe *a*, (mark-ed at the Top of the Table) the firft and low-eft Note of the *Tetrachord*, from that to the 2*d b*, is 6 of the Parts mentioned; to the 3*d c*, is other 6, and from the 3*d* to the acuteft Note *d*, is an Interval equal to 48 of thefe Parts : In this Manner you can explain all the reft. Six of them he called a *Diefis Enharmonica* ; 8 a
                                                    Diefis

Diesis trientalis, 9 a *Diesis quadrantalis*,, 12 a *Hemitonium*, 24 a *Tonus*, 36 a *Triemitonium*, and 48 a *Ditonum*; but to measure all these accurately by the Ear was an extravagant Pretence. Let us consider the Divisions that were made by *Ratios*.

BESIDES some particular *Ratios* of *Archytas*, *Eratosthenes* and *Didymus*, (who were all Musicians) which I pass by, *Ptolomy* gives us an Account of the following 8 Divisions of the *Tetrachord*; where the Fractions express the *Ratio* betwixt each Sound (marked by the Letters standing above) and the next, in order from *a* the lowest, *i. e.* suppose any of the lower Notes *a, b* or *c* to be 1. the Fraction betwixt that and the next expresses the Proportion of that next to it.

Diatessaron.

$$a - b -- c - d.$$

Enharmonium . . . . . . $\frac{45}{46} \times \frac{23}{24} \times \frac{4}{5} = \frac{3}{4}$

Chroma $\begin{cases} \textit{Molle} \\ \textit{or} \\ \textit{Antiquum} \\ \textit{Intensum} \end{cases}$

$\cdot \frac{27}{28} \times \frac{14}{15} \times \frac{5}{6} = \frac{3}{4}$

. . $\frac{21}{22} \times \frac{11}{12} \times \frac{6}{7} = \frac{3}{4}$

Diatonum $\begin{cases} \textit{Molle} \\ \textit{Tonicum} \\ \textit{Ditonicum} \\ \textit{or} \\ \textit{Pythagor.} \end{cases}$

Molle . . . $\frac{20}{21} \times \frac{9}{10} \times \frac{7}{8} = \frac{3}{4}$

Tonicum . . . $\frac{27}{28} \times \frac{7}{8} \times \frac{8}{9} = \frac{3}{4}$

$\frac{243}{256} \times \frac{8}{9} \times \frac{8}{9} = \frac{3}{4}$

K k 2   *The Table continued*

$$
Diatonum \begin{cases} Intenfum \\ \text{or} \\ Syntonum \\ \mathcal{E}quabile. \end{cases} \quad \frac{15}{16} \times \frac{8}{9} \times \frac{9}{10} = \frac{3}{4} \\ \frac{11}{12} \times \frac{10}{11} \times \frac{9}{10} = \frac{3}{4}
$$

THESE different *Species* were alfo called the *Colores* (*Chroai*) *generum* : *Molle* expreffes a Progreffion by fmall Intervals, as *Intenfum* by greater ; the other Names are plain enough. The Two firft Intervals of the *Enharmonium*, are called each a *Diefis* ; the Third is a *Ditonum*, and particularly the 3*d g.* already explained. The Two firft of the *Chromatick* are called *Hemitones*, and the Third is *Triemitonium* ; and in the *Antiquum* it is the 3*d l.* above explained. The firft in the *diatonick* is called *Hemitonium*, and the other Two are *Tones*; particularly the $\frac{243}{256}$ is called *Limma* (*Pythagoricum*;) $\frac{7}{8}$ is the greateft of the *Tones*, and $\frac{10}{11}$ the leaft ; but the $\frac{8}{9}$ and $\frac{9}{10}$ are the *Tonus major* and *minor* above explained.

As to the Names of the *Genera* themfelves, the *Enharm.* was fo called as by a general Name ; or fome fay for its Excellence (tho' where that lies we don't well know.) The *Diatonum*, becaufe the *Tones* prevail in it. The *Chromatick* was fo called, fay fome, from χρόα *color*, becaufe as Colour is. fomething betwixt Black and White, fo the *Chrom.* is a *medium* betwixt the other Two.

BUT

But now to what Purpose all thefe Divifions were contrived, we cannot well learn by
any Thing that they have told us. The *Enharm.* was by all acknowledged to be fo difficult,
that few could practife it, if indeed any ever
could do it accuratcly; and they own much the
fame of the *Chromatick.* Such Inequalities in
the Degrees of the *Scale,* might be ufed for
attacking the Fancy, and humouring fome dif-
orderly Motions : But what true Melody could
be made of them, we cannot conceive. All
acknowledged, that the *Diatonick* was the true
Melody which Nature had formed all Mens Ears
to receive and be fatisfied with ; and therefore
it was the general Practice; tho' in their Speculations of the Proportions they had the Differences you fee in the *Table.* And tho' *Diatonick*
was the prevailing Kind, yet ftill a Queftion remained among them, Whether it fhould be
Ariftoxenus's Diatonum intenfum, or the *Pytha-
gorick,* which *Eratofthenes* contended for: (But
here obferve, the *Pythagoreans* departed from
their Principles, by admitting the *Limma,* which
is neither multiple nor fuperparticular ;) or what
Ptolomy calls the *Syntonum* or *intenfum,* which
Didymus maintain'd. The *Ariftox.* could give no
Proof of theirs, becaufe it was impoffible for the
Ear to determine the Difference accurately: The o-
ther Two might be tried and proven by the *Canon
harmonicus*; but if they tuned by the Ear, they
might difpute on without any Certainty of the
Kind they followed. As to the Species we now
make

make Ufe of, the fame may be faid ; but I fhall confider it afterwards.

Now, thefe Parts of the *Diateffaron* are what they called the *Diaftems* of the feveral *Genera*, upon which their Differences depend : Which are called in the *Enharm.* the *Diefis* and *Dito-num* ; in the *Chromatick*, the *Hemitonium* and *Triemitonium*; in the *Diaton.* the *Hemitonium* (or *Limma*) and the *Tonus* ; but under thefe general Names, which diftinguifh the *Genera*, there are feveral different *Intervals* or *Ratios*, which conftitute the *colores generum*, or Species of *Enharm. Chrom.* and *Diatonick*, as we have feen : And we are alfo to *obferve*, that what is a *Diaftem* in one *genus* is a *Syftem* in another : But the *Tonus diazeuɑ̆icus* 8 : 9 is effential in all the *Kinds*, not as a neceffary Part of every Tetrachord, but neceffary in every Syftem of 8*ve*, to feparate the 4*th* and 5*th*, or disjoin the feveral *Tetrachords* one from another.

Of the DIAGRAMMA *or* Scale.

WE have already feen the effential Prin-ciples, of which the ancient *Scale* or *Diagramma*, which they called their *Syftema perfeɑ̆um*, was compofed, in all its different Kinds. Let us now confider the Conftruɑ̆ion of it; in order to which I fhall take the *Tetrachords dia-tonically.* I have already faid, that the Extent of it is a *Difdiapafon*, or Two 8*ves* in the *Ra-tio*

tio 1 : 4.: But in that Space they make Eighteen Chords, tho' they are not all different Sounds. And, to explain it, they reprefent to us Eighteen Chords or Strings of an Inftrument, as the *Lyre,* fuppofed to be tuned according to the Proportions explained in any one *Genus.* To each of thefe Chords (or Sounds) they gave a particular Name, taken from its Situation in the *Diagramma,* or alfo in the *Lyre;* which Names are commonly ufed by the *Latins* without any Change. They are thefe, *Proflambanomenos, Hypate-hypaton, parhypate-hypaton, Lichanos-hypaton, Hypate-mefon, parhypate-mefon, Lichanos-mefon, Mefe, Trite-fynemmenon, Paranete-fynemmenon, Nete-fynemmenon, Paramefe, Trite-diezeugmenon, Paranete-diezeugmenon, Nete-diezeugmenon, Trite-hyperbolæon, Paranete-hyperbolæon, Nete-hyperbolæon.*

THAT you may underftand the Order and Conftitution of their *Scale* and the Senfe of thefe Names, take this fhort Hiftory of it. While the *Lyre* was *Tetra.* (or had but Four Strings) thefe were called in order from the *graveft* Sound *Hypate, Parhypate, Paranete, Nete;* which Names are taken from their Place in the *Diagram,* in which anciently they fet the *graveft* uppermoft, or their Situation in the *Lyre,* hence called *Hypate, i. e. fuprema,* (*Chorda, fcil.*) the next is *parhypate, i. e. fubfuprema* or *juxta upremam;* then *Paranete, i. e. penultima* or *juxta ultimam,* and then *Nete, i.e. ultima,* as here.

THIS

Hypate	⎫	T HIS refpects the ancient
ʃ:		*Lyra,* whofe Chords were de-
Parhypate		dicate to, or made fymbolical
t:	⎬	of the Four Elements: Which according to fome contained
Paranete		an 8*ve,* but fome fay only a
t:		*Diateſſaron* 3 : 4, and the De-
Nete	⎭	grees I have marked by *ʃ* for *Semitone,* and *t* for a *Tone,*

without Diftinction.

Hypate	⎫	N EXT to this fucceeded the
ʃ·		*Septichord Lyre* of *Mercury,*
Parhypate		which ftands thus. *Meſe* is *me-*
t:		*dia. Lichanos,* fo called from
Lichanos		the *digitus index* with which
t:		the Chord was ftruck, as fome
Meſe	⎬	fay, or from its being the *In-*
ʃ:		*dex* of the *Genus,* according to
Trite		its Diftance from *Hypate;* it was
t:		alfo called *Hypermeſe, i. e. ſu-*
Paranete		*pra mediam. Trite* fo called
t:		as the Third from *Nete* ; and
Note	⎭	it is alfo called *Parameſe, i. e.*

juxta mediam. This contains
Two Tetrachords conjunct in *Meſe,* which is
common to both, and are particularly called the Tetrachords *Hypaton,* and *Neton ;* fo that
thefe which were formerly Names of fingle
Chords, are now Names of whole Tetrachords;
but as yet there was no great Neceffity for the
Diftinction, as we fhall fee afterwards.

Hy-

Hypate
f :
    Parhypate
t :
    Lichanos
t :
    Mese
t :
    Paramese
f :
    Trite
t :
    Paranete
t :
    Nete

BUT *Pythagoras* finding the Imperfection of this *Syftem*, added an 8*th* Chord to complete an 8*ve*: And this he did by separating the Two Tetrachords by the *Tonus diazeuEticus* ; fo the Whole ftood thus. Where we have Two Tetrachords, one from *Hypate* to *Mese*, and the other from *Paramese* to *Nete*; the *Tonus diazeuEticus* coming betwixt them, *i. e.* betwixt *Mese* and *Paramese.* So here *Paramese* and *Trite* are different Chords, which were the fame before.

BUT there was another *oEtichord Lyre* attributed to *Terpander*; where inftead of disjoining the Two Tetrachords of the *feptichord Lyre*, he added another Chord a *Tone* lower than *Hypate*, called *Hyper-hypate*, *i. e. fuper fupremam*, becaufe it ftood above in the *Diagram* ; or *Proflambanomenos*, *i. e. affumptus*, becaufe it belonged to none of the Two Tetrachords : The reft of the Names were unchanged.

OBSERVE, the *feptichord Lyre* was made fymbolical of the Seven Planets. *Hypate* reprefented *Saturn*, with refpeEt to his periodical Revolution, which is flower than that of any of the reft, as the graveft Sounds are always produced by floweft Vibrations, and fo of the
reft

reft gradually. But others make *Nete* reprefent *Saturn* with refpect to his diurnal Motion round the Earth (in the old Aftronomy) which is the fwifteft, as the acuteft Sounds are alfo produced by quickeft Vibrations, and fo of the reft. When the 8*th* Chord was added, it reprefented the *Cælum ftelliferum.*

AFTERWARDS a third Tetrachord was added to the *feptichord Lyre;* which was either conjunct with it, making Ten Chords, or difjunct, making Eleven. The Conjunct was particularly diftinguifhed by the Name *Synemmenon, i. e. Tetrachordum conjunctarum;* and the other by the Name of *Diezeugmenon, i. e. disjunctarum.* And now the middle Tetrachord was called *Mefon (mediarum;)* and to the Words *Hypate, Parhypate, Lichanos, Trite, Paranete, Nete,* are now added the Name of the Tetrachord, which is neceffary for Diftinction ; and the Whole ftands thus,

Tetra. { *Hypate, hypaton.*
{ *Parhypate, hyp.*
Hyp. { *Lichanos, hyp.*
{ *Hypate, mefon,*
{ *Parh, Mef.*
Mef. { *Lich. Mef.*
{ *Mefe* - - - *Mefe.* } *Tonus*
{ *Trite Synem.* } { *Paramefe* } *diezeuct.*
Syn. { *Paranete, Syn.* } *Diezeug.* { *Trite Diezeug.*
{ *Nete, Syn.* } { *Paranete Diezeug.*
{ *Nete Diezeug.*

Ar

A t length another Tetrachord was added, called *Hyperbolæon* (*i. e. excellentium* or *excedentium*) the acuteſt of all ; which being conjunct with the *Diezeugmenon*, the *Nete Diezeugmenon* was its graveſt Chord, the other Three being called *Trite, Paranete,* and *Nete Hyperbolæon* ; and now the Four Tetrachords *Hypaton, Meſon, Diezeugmenon, Hyperbolæon,* made in all Fourteen Chords, to which, to complete the *Diſdiapaſon,* a *Proſlambanomenos* was added ; all which with the *Trite Paranete,* and *Nete Synemmenon* make up the Eighteen Chords mentioned ; which yet are but Sixteen different Sounds, for the *Paranete Syn.* coincides in the *Trite Diez.* as the *Nete Syn.* with the *Paranete Diez.* So that theſe Two differ only in the *Trite Syn.* and *Parameſe* betwixt which there is a *Semitone.* And now ſee the whole *Diagram* together in the following Page ; where to favour the Imagination more, inſtead of marking the *Tone* and *Semitone* by ſ and *t.* the Chords that have a *Tone* betwixt them are ſet further aſunder than thoſe that have a *Semitone.* At the ſame Time I have annexed the Letters by which the *modern Scale* is above explained, that you may ſee to what Part of that this ancient *Scale* correſponds. And becauſe we place the graveſt Notes in the lower Part of our *Diagram* (as the ancient *Latins* came at laſt to do, tho' they ſtill applied *Hypate* to the *graveſt,* and *Nete* to the *acuteſt,* to prevent Confuſion) I ſhall do it ſo here.

DIA-

DIAGRAMMA VETERUM.

	aa Nete, *Hyperbol.*	*Tetrachor.*
	g Paranete, *Hyperbol.*	*Hyperbolæon.*
	f Trite, *Hyberbol.*	
	e Nete, *Diezeug.*	
Nete, Syncm.	*d* Paranete *Diezeug.*	*Diezeugmenon.*
Paranete, Syn.	*c* Trite, *Diezeug.*	
	b Paramefe.	
Trite, Synem.	♭	
Mefe.	*a* Mefe.	
	G Lichanos, *Mefon,*	*Mefon.*
	F Parhypate, *Mefon,*	
	E Hypate, *Mefon.*	
	D Lichanos, *hypaton.*	*Hypaton.*
	C Parhypate, *hypaton.*	
	B Hypate, *hypaton.*	
	A Proflambanomenos.	

Synenmenon.

You fee, that by twice applying *Hypate,*
Parhypate and *Lichanos* ; alfo *Trite, Parane-*
te and *Nete* Three Times; the Difficulty of too
many Names is avoided: And by the Diftinction of *Tetrachords* with thefe particular Names
for the refpective Chords, 'tis eafily imagined in
what Place of the *Diagram* any Chord ftands.
But if we confider every *Tetrachord* by it felf,
then we may apply thefe common Names to its
Chords, *viz. Hypate, Parhypate* (or *Trite*)
Licha-

Lichanos (or *Paranete*) and *Nete:* And then
when Two *Tetrachords* are conjunct, the *Hypate* of the one is the *Nete* of the other, as *Hypate meſon·* is equivalent to *Nete hypaton;* and
in the *Diagram, Meſe* is the *Nete meſon* and
the *Hypate ſynem.* and *Parameſe* is the *Hypate
diezeug.* And laſtly, *Nete diezeug.* is equal to
Hypate hyperbolæon. We ſhall know the Uſe
of the *Tetrachord ſynemmenon*, when we come
to explain the Buſineſs of their *Mutations.* The
Reſt of the *Diagram* from *Proſlamban.* is a
concinnous Series, anſwering to the *flat Series*
of the *diatonick Genus*, explained in the *Ch.* 8.
and the Order from *Parhypate hypaton* contains the *ſharp Series* above explained. Obſerve,
tho' there are certain *Syſtems*, particularly diſtinguiſhed as *Tetrachords*, yet we have *Tetrachords* (*i. e. Intervals* of Four Sounds) in o-
ther Parts of the *Scale*, that are true 4*ths* 3 : 4.
Again, if to any true 4*th* a *Tonus diazeug.* is
added, we have the *Diapente*, as from *Proſlamb.* to *Hypate meſon.*

I have explained the *Diagram* in the *diatonick genus;* but the ſame Names are applied
to all the Three *Genera;* and according to the
Differences of theſe, ſo are the Relations of the
ſeveral Chords to one another. But ſince the
Conſtitution of the *Scale* by *Tetrachords* is the
ſame in all, and that the *Genera* differ only in
the *Ratios* which the Two middle Chords of the
Tetrachord bear to the Extremes; therefore
theſe Extremes were called *ſtanding* or *immoveable Sounds* (ἑςῶτες ſoni ſtantes) and all the middle
ones

ones were called *moveable* (κινητοὶ *ſoni mobiles*) for
to raiſe a Series from a given *Fundamental* or *Proſlambanomenos*, the firſt and laſt Chord of each
Tetrachord is invariably the ſame, or common
to every *Genus*; but the middle Chords vary
according to the *Genus*. So the *Parhypate* or
Trite, Lichanos or *Paranete* of each *Tetrachord* is variable, and all the reſt of the Chords
of the *Diagram* are invariable.

T H E next Thing to be conſidered is, what
they called the *Figures* or *Species* of the *conſonant Syſtems*, viz. of the 4*th*, 5*th* and 8*ve* (for
they extended this Speculation no further than
the *ſimple Concords.*) The *colores generum*
differed according to the Difference of the conſtituent Parts of the *Diateſſaron*; but the *figuræ* or *ſpecies conſonantiarum* differ only according to the Order and Poſition of the *concinnous*
Parts of the *Syſtem:* So that in the ſame *Diagram* (or Series) and under every Difference of
Genus and *Color*, there are Differences of the
Figuræ. Now, tho' of a certain Number of
different conſtituent Parts, there will be a certain Number of different Poſitions or Combinations of the Whole; yet in every *Genus* there
is a certain *Diaſtem* agreed upon to be the *Charaĉteriſtick*; and according to the Poſition of
this in the *Syſtem*, ſo are the different *Figuræ*
reckoned; the Combinations proceeding from
the Differences of the other *Diaſtems* being ne-
glećted in this Matter. *Ptolomy* makes the
Charaĉteriſtick of the *Diateſſaron*, the *Ratio* of
the Two *acuteſt* Chords in every **Genus**; and
　　　　　　　　　　　　　　　　　　　　　　of

of the *Diapafon*, the *Tonus diezeucticus* But
Euclid reckons them otherwife, and applies
the fame Mark to 4*th*, and 5*th* and 8*ve*; thus
in the *Enharmonick* the *Ditonum* is the Characteriftick; in the *Chromatick* it is the *Triemitonium* ; and in the *Diatonick* the *Semitone.*
If we take Two conjunct *Tetrachords*, as from
Hypate-hypaton to *Mefe*, we fhall find in that
all the Figures of the *Diateffaron*, which are
only Three ; for there are but Three Places of
the *Diateffaron* in which the Characteriftick can
exift; there are Four Figures of the *Diapente*
which are to be found in Two disjunct *Tetrachords*, betwixt *Hypate-mefon* and *Nete-diezeugmenon.* The 8*ve* is compofed of the 4*th*
and 5*th*, and the Three Species of 4*th* joined to
each of the Four Species of 5*th*, make in all 12
Species of 8*ves*; but we confider here only thofe
Connections of 4*th* and 5*th*, that are actually in
the *Syftem*, which are only Seven, to be found
from *Proflambanomenos* to *Nete-hyperbolæon*,
i. e. in the Compafs of a *Difdiapafon. Proflambanomenos* being the loweft Chord of the
firft 8*ve*, and *Lichanos-mefon* of the laft 8*ve* ;
for *Mefe* begins another Revolution of the *Diapafon*, proceeding the fame Way as from *Proflambanomenos* : And becaufe this *Syftem* of *Difdiapafon* contains all the Species of the *Concords*
it was called *perfect.* And obferve, that in every 8*ve Euclid's Characteriftick* occurs twice, and
they are always afunder by Two and Three *Diefes*, or *Hemitones*, or *Tones* (according to the
Genus) alternatively. What was the Order they
thought

thought moſt *concinnous* and *harmonious*, we
ſhall ſee preſently.

V. OF TONES or MODES. They took
the Word *Tone* in four different Senſes. 1. For
a ſingle Sound, as when they ſaid the *Lyra* has
Seven *Tones*, i. e. Notes. 2. For a certain *Interval*, as the Difference of the 4th and 5th.
3. For the *Tenſion* of the Voice, as when we
ſay, One ſings with an *acute* or a *grave* Voice.
4. For a certain *Syſtem*, as when they ſaid, The
Dorick or *Lydian Mode*, or *Tone;* which is
the Senſe to be particularly conſidered in this
Place.

THIS is the Part of the ancient *Harmonica*
which we wiſh they had explained more clearly to
us; for it muſt be owned there is an unaccountable
Difference among the Writers, in their Definitions, Diviſions and Names of the *Modes*. As
to the Definition, I find an Agreement in this,
that a *Mode*, or *Tone* in this Senſe, is a certain
Syſtem or *Conſtitution* of Sounds; and they a-
gree too, that an *Octave* with all its intermediate Sounds is ſuch a Conſtitution: But the ſpecifick Differences of them ſome place in the
Manner of Diviſion or Order of its *concinnous*
Parts; and others place merely in the *Tenſion* of
the Whole, *i. e.* as the whole Notes are *acuter*
or *graver*, or ſtand higher and lower in the *Scale*
of *Muſick*, as *Bryennius* ſays very expreſly. *Boethius* has a very ambiguous Definition, he firſt
tells us, that the *Modes* depend on the Seven
different Species of the *Diapaſon*, which are alſo called *Tropi;* and theſe, ſays he, are *Con-
ſtitu-*

*ſtitutiones in totis vocum ordinibus, vel gravi-
tate vel acumine differentes.* Again he ſays,
*Conſtitutio eſt plenum veluti modulationis cor-
pus, ex conſonantiarum conjunctione conſiſtens,
quale eſt* Diapaſon, &c. *Has igitur conſtitutio-
nes, ſi quis totas faciat acutiores, vel in gra-
vius totas remittat ſecundum ſupradictas* Diapaſon *conſonantiæ ſpecies, efficiet modos ſeptem.*
This is indeed a very ambiguous Determination,
for if they depend on the Species of 8*ves*, to
what Purpoſe is the laſt Clauſe; and if they
differ only by the Tenor or Place of the whole
8*ve*, i. e. as 'tis taken at a higher or lower
Pitch, what Need the Species of 8*ves* be at all
brought in: His Meaning perhaps is only to ſignify, that the different Orders or Species of 8*ves*
ly in different Places, *i. e.* higher and lower in
the *Scale*. *Ptolomy* makes them the ſame with
the Species of *Diapaſon*; but at the ſame Time
he ſpeaks of their being at certain Diſtances
from one another. Some contended for Thirteen, ſome for Fifteen *Modes*, which they placed at a *Semitone's* Diſtance from each other;
but 'tis plain, theſe underſtood the Differences
to be only in their Place or Diſtances one from
another; and that there is one certain *harmonious* Species of *Octave* applied to all, *viz.* that
Order which proceeds from *Proſlamb.* of the *Syſtema immutatum*, or the *A* of the modern *Syſtem*. *Ptolomy* argues, that if this be all, they
may be infinite, tho' they muſt be limited for
Uſe and Practice; but indeed the Generality define them by the *Species diapaſon*, and therefore

fore make only Seven Modes; but to what they tend, and the true Ufe, is fcarcely well explained, and we are left to guefs and reafon about it; I fhall confider them upon both the Suppofitions, and firft as they are the Species of *Octaves*, and here I fhall follow *Ptolomy*.

The *Tones* have no different Denominations from the *Genera*; and what's faid of them in one *Genus* is applicable to all; and I fhall here take the *diatonick*. The *Syftem* of *Difdiapafon* already explained in the *Diagram* (coinciding with the Series from *A* of the modern *Scale*) is the *Syftema immutatum*; which I fhall, in what follows here, call the *Syftem* without Diftinction. The Seven Species of *Octaves*, as they proceed in Order from *A . B . C . D . E . F . G*, are the Seven *Tones*, which differ in their Modulations, *i. e.* in the Diftances of the fucceffive Sounds, according to the fixt *Ratios* in the *Syftem*. Thefe Seven *Ptolomy* calls, The 1*ft*, *Dorick*, the fame with the *Syftem*, or beginning in *A* or *Proflamb*. 2d, *Hypo-lydian*, beginning in and following the Order from *B* or *Hyp-hyp*. 3d, *Hypophrygian*, beginning at *C* or *Parh-hy*. 4th, *Hypodorian* at *D*. 5th, *Mixolydian* in *E*. 6th, *Lydian* in *F*. 7th, *Phrygian* in *G*. The laft Three he takes in the *Octaves* above, for a Reafon will prefently appear. Now, every *Mode* being confidered by it felf as a diftinct *Syftem*, may have the Names *Proflamb. hyp-hyp*. &c. applied to it; for thefe fignify only in general the Pofitions of the Chords in any particular *Syftem*; if they are fo applied, he calls them the *Pofitions*; for

Ex-

Example, the firſt Chord, or graveſt Note of any *Mode* is called its *Proſlamb. poſitione*, and ſo of the reſt in Order. But again theſe are conſidered as coinciding, or being uniſon, with certain Chords of the *Syſtem*; and theſe Chords are called the *poteſtates*, with reſpect to that *Mode*; for *Example*, the *Hypodorian* begins in *D*, or *Lichanos hypaton* of the *Syſtem*, which therefore is the *poteſtas* of its *Proſlamb.* as *Hyp-meſon* is the *poteſtas* of its *hyp-hyp.* and ſo of others, *that is*, theſe Two Chords coincide and differ only in Name ; and we alſo ſay, that ſuch a numerical Chord as *Proſl. poſitione* of any Mode is ſuch a Chord, as *hyp-hyp. poteſtate*, which is equivalent to ſaying, that *hyp-hyp.* of the *Syſtem* is the *Poteſtas* of the *Proſlamb. poſitione* of that Mode.

You'll eaſily find what Chord of the *Syſtem* or *Dorick Mode* is the 2*d*, 3*d*, &c. Chord of any other Mode, by counting up from the Chord of the *Syſtem* in which that Mode begins. Or contrarily, to know what numerical Chord of any Mode correſponds to any Chord of the *Syſtem*, count from this Chord to that in which the Mode begins, and you have the Number of the Chord; to which you may apply the Names *Proſlamb.* &c. or *a, b,* &c. And the Chords of any Mode being thus named to you, you'll ſolve the preceeding *Problems* eaſieſt, by finding what numerical Chord of the *Mode*, that is the Name of; for *Example*, to find what Chord of the *Mode Hypodorian* coincides with the *Parhypate-meſon* of the *Syſtem* (or *Dorick Mode*)

The

The *Hypo-dor, Mode* begins, or has its *Pro-slamb. pofitione,* in *D* or *Lichanos-hyp.* of the *Syftem,* betwixt which and *Parhy-mef.* are Three Chords (inclufive) therefore the Thing fought is the Third Chord, or *Parhyp-hyp. pofitione* of the *hyperdorian Mode.* Again, to find what Chord of the *Syftem* is the *poteftas* of the *Lych-hyp* or 4th Chord of the *Hypo-phr. Mode.* This begins in *C* or *Parhyp-hyp.* of the *Syftem,* and the 4th above is *Parhy-mefon* or F the Thing fought. But more univerfally, to find what Chord of any Mode correfponds to any Chord of any other Mode; you may eafily folve this by the *Table Plate* 2. *Fig.* 1. explained above in *Chap.* 11. § 3. Thus, find in the Column of plain Letters, the Letters at which the Modes propofed begin, againft which in the fame Lines you muft find the Letter *a,* which is the *Pro-slamb. pofitione,* or firft Chord of thefe Modes; and then thefe refpective Columns compared, fhew what Chord of the one correfponds to any of the other. *Obferve* alfo, that were it propo-fed to begin in any Chord of any *Mode* (*i. e.* at any Chord of the *Syftem,* or Letter of the *plain Scale*) and make a Series proceeding from that, in the Order of any other *Mode*; we eafily know by this *Table* what Chords of the *Syftem* muft be altered to effect this; for *Example,* to begin in *e,*(which is *Hyp-mefon* of the *Syftem* or *dorick Mode, Proflamb.* of the *Phrygian Mode,* &c.) if we would proceed from this in the Order of the *Hypo-lydian,*which begins at *b* of the *Syftem,* we muft find *e* in the Column of plain Letters,

and

and in the fame Line find *b*; the Signature of
the Letters of that Column where *b* ftands,
fhews what Chords are to be changed : And by
this *Table* you folve all thefe *Problems*, with a
great deal more Eafe, than by the long and perplext Schemes which fome of the Ancients give
us : But let us return.

PTOLOMY in *Chap.* 10. *Lib.* 2. propofes to
have his *Modes* at thefe Diftances, *viz. tone,
tone, limma, tone, tone, limma.* The *Hypodorian* being fet loweft, then *Hypo-phr. Hypo-
lyd. Dorick, Phrygian* and *Mixolydian,* yet according to the Syftem they won't ftand at thefe
Diftances, nor in that Order. But in the next
Chap. it appears that he means only to take
them fo as their *Mefe - poteftate* (or thefe Chords
of each which is the firft of a Series fimilar to
the *Syftema immutatum,*) fhall ftand in that Order ; and to this Purpofe he makes the *Dorick*
the *Syftema immut.* and the *Profl.* of the reft
in order as already mentioned ; only he takes
Mixolyd. Lyd. and *Phryg.* in the 8*ve* above,
i. e. at *Nete diez. Trite hyperbol. Param-
hyperbol.* whereby their *Mefes poteftate* ftand
in the Order mentioned ; otherwife they had
ftood in an Order juft reverfe of their *proflamb.
pofitione.* And now, if we would know at what
Diftances the *Mefes poteftate* of thefe *Modes* are
let us find what numerical Chord of each *Mode*
is its *Mefe poteftate,* and let it be expreft by the
Letters applied *pofitione,* as already explained :
Then we muft fuppofe that from *a* of the *Syftem*
(or *Dorick Mode*) a Series proceeds in each of
the

the Seven different Orders; and by the Table laſt mentioned, we ſhall know, in the Manner alſo explained, what Chords are to be altered for each; therefore taking theſe Chords that are the *Meſes poteſtate* of each Mode, we ſhall ſee their mutual Diſtances. As *Ptolomy* has placed the *Proſlambanomenos*, or *a, poſitione* of each Mode, their *Meſes poteſtate* are in the Chords *e : f✳. g : a : b : c✳. d.* in order from *Hypo-dor.* as above mentioned, *that is*, when all the Orders are transferred to the *Proſlamb.* of the *Dorick Mode*, the neceſſary Variety of Signatures cauſes the *f* and *c* to be marked ✳ for the *Hypo-phr.* and *Lydian* Modes, and theſe *f✳* and *c✳* are the *Meſes poteſtate* of theſe Modes; all the reſt are plain; therefore the *mutual* Diſtances of theſe *Meſes poteſtate* are expreſſed in the Scheme by (:) which ſignifies a *Tone*, (.) a *Semitone* or *limma*, which are different from what he had formerly propoſed.

DOCTOR *Wallis* in explaining theſe by the modern *Syſtem*, chuſes the Signature for the *Lydian* Mode, ſo that *a* (its *Proſlamb.*) has a *flat* Sign, and the *Meſe-poteſtate* of it is *c plain* : But ſince this explained is the only Senſe according to which the Diſtances of theſe *Meſes-poteſtate* can be found, and ſince 'tis more rational, that when any *Mode* is to be transferred to the *Proſl-poſitione* of another, that *Proſl.* ſhould not be altered; for otherwiſe it is transferred to another Note; therefore I was obliged to differ from the Doctor in that Particular: But neither does his Method ſet the *Meſes poteſtate* at the

Diſtances

Diſtances which *Ptolomy* mentions, and which by Examination I find cannot poſſibly be done without changing the *Proſl.* of the *Syſtema immutatum.*

ANCIENTLY there were but Three *Modes,* the *Dorick, Lydian* and *Phrygian,* ſo called from the Countries that uſed them, and particularly called *Tones* becauſe they were at a *Tone's* Diſtance from each other; and afterwards the reſt were added and named from their Relations to the former, particularly the *Hypodorian,* as being below the *Dorian,* and ſo of the reſt; for which Reaſon 'tis by ſome placed firſt, and they make its *Proſlambanomenos* the loweſt Sound that can be diſtinctly heard. But we ſhould be eaſy about their Names or Order, if we underſtood the true Nature and Uſe of them.

IF the *Modes* are indeed nothing elſe but the Seven Species of *Octaves,* the Uſe of them we can only conceive to be this, *viz.* That the *Proſl.* of any Mode being made the principal Note of any Song, there may be different Species of Melody anſwering to theſe different Conſtitutions; but then we are not to conceive that the *Proſl.* or Fundamental of any Mode is fixt to one particular Chord of the *Syſtem,* for *Ex.* the *Phrygian* to *g*; ſo that we muſt always begin there, when we would have a Piece of Melody of that Species: When we ſay in general that ſuch a *Mode* begins in *g.* 'tis no more than to ſignifie the Species of 8*ve,* according as they
appear

appear in a certain fixt *Syſtem* ; but we may begin in any Chord of the *Syſtem*, and make it
the *Proſ!.* of any *Mode*, by adding new Chords,
or altering the Tuning of the old (in the Manner already mentioned:) If the Deſign is no more,
but that a Song may be begun higher or lower,
that may be done by beginning at the ſame
Chord, which is the *Proſ.* of any Mode in the
Syſtem, and altering the *Tune* of the Whole,
keeping ſtill the fixt Order (which as I have already ſaid, is that in our modern natural Scale,
from *a*) but it will be eaſier to begin in a Chord
which is already higher or lower, and transfer
the *Mode* in which the Song is, to that Chord.
If every Song kept in one *Mode*, there was
Need for no more than one *diatonick* Series, and
by occaſional changing the Tune of certain
Chords, theſe Tranſpoſitions of every Mode to
every Chord may be eaſily performed ; and I
have ſpoken already of the Way to find what
Chords are to be altered in their tuning to effect
this, by the various Signatures of ♯ and ♭ : But if
we ſuppoſe that in the Courſe of any Song a new
Species is brought in, this can only be effected
by having more Chords than in the fixt *Syſtem*,
ſo as from any Chord of that, any Order or Species of 8*ve* may be found.

I f this be the true Nature and Uſe of the
Tones, I ſhall only obſerve here, that according
to the Notions we have at preſent of the Principles and Rules of *Melody*, as they have been
explained in ſome of the preceeding *Chapters*,
moſt of theſe Modes are imperfect, and incapable

pable of good Melody; becaufe they want fome of thofe we reckon the effential and natural Notes of a true *Mode* (or *Key*) of which we reckon only Two Species, *viz.* that from *c* and *a*, or the *Parhypate-hypaton* and *Proflambano-menos* of the ancient fixt Syftem.

Again, if the effential Difference of the *Modes* confifts only in the *Gravity* or *Acutenefs* of the whole 8*ve*; then we muft fuppofe there is one Spe-cies or concinnous Divifion of the 8*ve*, which being applied to all the Chords of the *Syftem*, makes them true *Fundamentals* for a certain Series of fucceffive Notes. Thefe Applications may be made in the Manner already mentioned ; by changing the *Tune* of certain Chords in fome Cafes ; but more univerfally, by adding new Chords to the *Syftem*, as the artificial or *fharp* and *flat* Notes of the modern Scale above ex-plained. But in this Cafe, again, where we fuppofe they admitted only one *concinnous* Spe-cies, we muft fuppofe it to be correfponding to the 8*ve a*, of what we call the *natural* Scale; becaufe they all ftate the Order of the *Syftema immutatum* in the *Diagram*, fo as it anfwers to that 8*ve*.

B u t what a fimple *Melody* muft have been produced by admitting only one concinnous Se-ries, and that too wanting fome ufeful and ne-ceffary Chords? We have above explained, that the *flat* Series, fuch as that beginning in *a*, has Two of its Chords that are variable, *viz.* the 6*th* and 7*th*, whereof fometimes the greater, fometimes the leffer is ufed ; and therefore a

Syftem

Syftem that wants this Variety muft be fo far imperfect : And what has been explained in *Chap.* 13. fhews how impoffible it is to make any good Modulation or Change from one *Key* to another, unlefs both the Species of *fharp* and *flat Key* be admitted in the *Syftem*; which Experience and all the Reafonings in the preceeding *Chapters* demonftrate to be neceffary.

PTOLOMY has a Paffage relating to the *Modes*, with which I fhall end this Head, *Lib.* 2. *Chap.* 7. of the *Mutations with refpect to what they call* Tones. He fays, thefe Mutations with refpect to *Tones* was not introduced for the fake of *acuter* or *graver* Sounds, which might be produced by raifing or lowering the whole Inftrument or Voice, without any Change in the Song ; but upon this Account, that the fame Voice beginning the fame Song now in a higher Note then in a lower, may make a Kind of Change of the *Mode.* This, to make any Senfe, muft fignify that the fame Song might be contrived fo, as feveral Notes higher or lower might be ufed as *Fundamentals* to a certain Number of fucceffive Notes ; and all together make one Song ; like what I explained of our modern Songs making Cadences in different Notes, fo as the Song may be faid to begin there again. If this is not the Senfe, then what he fays is plainly a Contradiction. But this may be the true Ufe of the *Tones*, in either of the Hypothefes concerning their effential Differences. He fays in the Beginning of that *Chap.* " The *Mutations* which are made
" by

" by whole *Syſtems,* which we properly call
" *Tones,* becauſe theſe Differences conſiſt in
" *Tenſion,* are infinite with reſpect to Poſſibility,
" as Sounds are, but actually and with reſpect
" to Senſe they are finite." All this ſeems plainly to put the Difference of the *Tones* only in the
Acuteneſs or *Gravity* of the Whole, elſe how
do their Differences conſiſt in *Tenſion,* which
ſignifies a certain Tenor or Degree of *Tune ;*
and how can they be called *infinite,* if they
depend on the different Conſtitutions of the 8*ve.*
Yet elſewhere he argues, that they are no o-
ther than the Species of 8*ves,* and as ſuch makes
their Number Seven ; and accordingly, in all
his Schemes, ſets down their different Modulations : But in *Chap.* 6. he ſeems more plainly
to take in both theſe Differences, for he ſays,
there are Two principal Differences with reſpect
to the Change of the *Tone,* one whereby the
whole Song is ſung higher or lower, the other
wherein there is a Change of the *Melody* to a-
nother Species than it was begun in ; but this
he thinks is rather a Change of the Song or
Melos than of the *Tone,* as if again he would
have us think this depended only on the *Acuteneſs* and *Gravity* of the Whole; ſo obſcurely
has the beſt of all the ancient Writers delivered
himſelf on this Article that deſerved to have
been moſt clearly handled. But that I may
have done with it, I ſhall only ſay, it muſt be
taken in one of the Senſes mentioned, if not in
both, for another I think cannot be found. Let
me

me alſo add, that the Moderns who have en-
deavoured to explain the ancient Muſick take
theſe *Modes* for the Species of 8*ves*. If you'll
except *Meibomius*, who, in his Notes upon *A-
riſtides*, affirms that the Differences of the
Modes upon which all the different Effects depended, were only in the Tenſion or Acuteneſs
and Gravity of the whole *Syſtem*. But there
are *Modes* I call the *Antiquo-modern Modes*,
which ſhall be conſidered afterwards.

OBSERVE. The *Tetrachord Synemmenon*,
which makes what they called the *Syſtema con-
junctum*, was added for joyning the upper and
lower *Diapaſon* of the *Syſtema immutatum* ;
that when the Song having modulated thro'
Two conjunct Tetrachords, and being come to
Meſe, might for Variety paſs either into the
disjunct Tetrachord *Diezeugmenon* or the conjunct *Synemmenon*. 'Tis made in our *Syſtem* by
b flat, *i. e.* putting only a *Semitone* betwixt *a*
and *b* ; ſo that from *b* to *d* (in 8*ve*,) makes
Three conjunct Tetrachords ; and the Uſe of
that new Chord *♭* with us is properly for perfecting ſome 8*ve* from whoſe Fundamental in
the fixt *Scale* there is not a right concinnous
Series.

VI. OF MUTATIONS. This ſignifies the
Changes or Alterations that happen in the Order of the Sounds that compoſe the *Melody*.
Ariſtox. ſays, 'tis as it were a certain *Paſſion* in
the Order of the *Melody*. It properly belongs
to the *Melopœia* to explain this, but is always
put by it ſelf as a diſtinct Part of the *Harmonica.*

nica. Thefe Changes are Four. 1. In the *Ge-nus*; when the Song begins in one as the *Chro-matick*, and paffes into another as the *Diato-nick.* 2. In the *Syftem*, as when the Song paffes out of one Tetrachord, as *Mefon*, into another, as *Diezeugmenon*; or more generally, when it paffes from a high Place of the *Scale* to a low, or contrarily, *that is*, the Whole is fung fome-times high, fometimes low ; or rather, a Part of it is high, and a Part of it low. 3. In the *Mode* or *Tone*, as when the Song begins in one, as the *Dorick*, and paffes into another, as the *Lydian* : What this Change of the *Mode* figni-fies according to the modern Theory has been explained already. 4. In the *Melopœia*, that is, when the Song changes the very *Air*, fo as from gay and fprightly to become foft and lan-guifhing, or from a *Manner* that expreffes one Paffion or Subject to the Expreffion of fome other ; and therefore fome of them call this a Change in the *Manner* (*fecundum morem*) : But to exprefs Paffion, or to have what they called *Pathetick Mufick*, the various *Rythmus* is abfolutely neceffary to be join'd ; and there-fore among the *Mutations* fome place this of the *Rythmus*, as from *Jambick* to *Choraick* ; but this belongs properly to the *Rythmica.* Now thefe are at beft but mere Definitions, the Rules when and how to ufe thefe Changes, ought to be found in the *Melopœia*.

VII. Of the Melopoeia, or Art of ma-king *Melody* or Songs. After the End and Prin-ciples of any Art are fuppofed to be diftinctly
enough

enough fhewn, the Thing to be expected is, that
the *Rules* of Application be clearly fet forth. But
in this, I muft fay it, the Ancients have left us
little elfe than a Parcel of Words and Names ;
fuch a Thing they call fuch a Name ; but the
Ufe of that Thing they leave you to find.   The
Subftance of their Doctrine according to *Euclid*
is this.   After he has faid that the *Melopœia* is
the Ufe of the Parts (or Principles) already explained.   He tells us, it confifts of Four Parts,
firft αγογη, which the *Latins* called *ductus,*
that is, when the Sounds or Notes proceed by
continuous Degrees of the *Scale,* as *a. b. c.*
2d. πλοκη, *nexus,* which is, when the Sounds
either afcending or defcending are taken alternately, or not immediately next in the *Scale,* as
a, c, b, d. or *a, d, b, e, c, f,* or thefe reverfely
d, b, c, a.   3d. πετ]εία, *Petteia,* (for the *La-*
tins made this *Greek* Name their own) when
the fame Note was frequently repeated together, as *a, a, a.*   4th, τονη, *Extenfio,* when
any one Note was held out or founded remarkably longer than the reft.   This is all *Euclid*
teaches us about it.   But *Ariftides Quintilia-*
nus, who writes more fully than any of them,
explains the *Melopœia* otherwife.   He calls it
the *Faculty* or *Art* of making *Songs,* which has
Three Parts, *viz.* ληψις, μιξις, χρῆσις, which
the *Latins* call *fumtio, miftio, ufus.*

N o t to trouble our felves with long *Greek*
Paffages, I fhall give you the Definitions of thefe
in *Meibomius*'s Words, 1. S u m t i o *eft per*
quam mufico datur a quali vocis loco Syftema fit
faci-

faciendum, utrum ab Hypatoide *an reliquorum aliquo.* 2. Mistio, *per quam aut fonos inter fe aut vocis locos coagmentamus, aut modulationis genera, aut modorum Syftema.* 3. Usus, *certa quædam modulationis confectio, cujus fpecies tres,* viz. Du&tus, Petteia, Nexus. As to the Definitions of the Three principal Parts, the Author of the *Dictionaire de Mufique* puts this Senfe upon them, *viz. Sumtio* teaches the Compofer in what Syftem he ought to place his Song, whether high or low, and confequently in what *Mode* or *Tone,* and at what Note to begin and end. *Miftio,* fays he, is properly what we call the Art of *Modulating* well, *i. e.* after having begun in a convenient Place, to profecute or conduct the Song, fo as the Voice be always in a convenient *Tenfion;* and that the effential Chords of the *Mode* be right placed and ufed, and that the Song be carried out of it, and return again agreeably. *Ufus* teaches the Compofer how the Sounds ought to follow one another, and in what Situations each may and ought to be in, to make an agreeable *Melody,* or a good *Modulation.* For the Species of the *Ufus : Ariftides* defines the *du&tus* and *nexus* the fame Way as *Euclid* does; and adds, that the *du&tus* may be performed Three Ways, or is threefold, viz. *du&tus re&tus,* when the Notes afcend, as *a, b, c ; revertens,* when they defcend *c, b, a ;* or *circumcurrens,* when having afcended by the *fyftema disjun&tum,* they immediately defcend by the *fyftema conjun&tum,* or move downwards betwixt the fame Extremes,

in

in a different Order of the intermediate Degrees, as having afcended thus, *a : b : c : d*, the Defcent is *d : c : ♭ : a*, or *c : d : e : f*, and *f : e♭ . d : c*. But the *Petteia* he defines, *Qua cognofcimus quinam fonorum omittendi, & qui funt adfumendi, tum quoties illorum finguli : porro a quonam incipiendum, & in quem definiendum: atque hæc quoque morem exhibet*. In fhort, according to this Definition the *Petteia* is the whole Art.

THERE were alfo what they called, The *modi melopœiæ*, of which *Ariftides* names thefe, *Dithyrambick, Nomick*, and *Tragick* ; called *Modes* for their expreffing the feveral Motions and Affections of the Mind. The beft Notion we can form of this is, to fuppofe them fomething like what we call the different Stiles in *Mufick*, as the *Ecclefiaftick*, the *Choraick*, the *Recitative*, &c. But I think the *Rythmus* muft have a confiderable or the greateft Share in thefe Differences.

BUT now if you'll ask where are the particular practical Rules, that teach when and how all thefe Things are to be done and ufed, I muft own, I have found nothing of this Kind particular enough to give me a diftinct *Idea* of their Practice in *Melody*. It is true, that *Ariftoxenus* employs his whole 3*d* Book very near, in fomething that feems defigned for Rules, in the right Conduct of Sounds for making *Melody*. But Truth is, all the tedious and perplext Work he makes of it, amounts to no more than fhewing.

ing, what general Limitations we are under,
with refpect to the placing of *Intervals* in Succeffion, according to the feveral *Genera,* and
the Conftitution of the *Syftema immutatum,* or
what we call the naturally *concinnous* Series.
You'll underftand it by One or Two *Examples*:
Firft, in the *Diatonick* Kind, he fays, That Two
Semitones never follow other immediately, and
that a *Hemitone* is not to be placed immediately above and below one *Tone,* but may be
placed above and below Two or Three *Tones;*
and that Two or Three *Tones* may be placed
together but no more. Then as to the Two
other *Genera,* to underftand what he fays, *obferve,* that the lower Part of the *Tetrachord* containing Two *Diefes* in the One, and Two *Hemitones* in the other *Genus* (whofe Sums are
always lefs than the remaining *Ditone* or *Triemitone* that makes up the *Diateffaron*) is called
πυκνὸν *fpiffum,* becaufe the *Intervals* being fmall,
the Sounds are as it were fet thick and near
other; oppofite to which is ἀπυκνὸν *non fpiffum*
or *rarum :* Notice too, that the Chords that
belonged to the *fpiffum* were called πυκνοὶ, and
particularly the loweft or *graveft* of the Three
in every *Tetrachord* were called βαρύπυκνοι,(from
βάρυς *gravis,*) the middle μεσόπυκνοι (from με-
σος *medius*) the acuteft ὀξύπυκνοι (from ὀξὺς
acutus). Thofe that belonged not to the πυκνὸν were called ἀπυκνοὶ, *extra fpiffum.* Now
then, with refpect to the *Enharmonick* and
Chromatick we are told, that Two *Spiffa,* or
Two

Two *Ditones, Triemitones,* or *Tones* cannot
be put together ; but that a *Ditone* may ftand
betwixt Two *fpiffa* ; that a *Tone* (it muft be
the *diazeucticus* betwixt Two *Tetrachords*)
may be placed immediately above the *Ditone*
or *Triem.* but not below, and below the *Spif-
fum* but not above.   There is a World more of
this kind, that one fees at Sight almoft in the
Diagram, without long tedious Explications ;
and at beft they are but very general Rules.
There is a Heap of other Words and Names
mentioned by feveral Authors, but not worth
mentioning.

B U T at laft I muft obferve and own, That
any Rules that can poffibly be given about this
Practice, are far too general, either to teach
one to compofe different Species of *Melody*, or
to give a diftinct Idea of the Practice of others ;
and that 'tis abfolutely neceffary for thefe Purpofes that we have a Plenty of *Examples* in
actual Compofitions, which we have not of the
Ancients. There is a natural Genius, without
which no Rules are fufficient : And indeed
what Rules can be given, when a very few general Principles are capable of fuch an infinite
Application; therefore Practice and Experience
muft be the Rule ; and for this Reafon we find
both among the Ancients and Moderns, fo very
few, and thefe very general Rules for the Compofition of Melody. Befides the Knowledge of
the *Syftem*, and what we call Modulation or
keeping in and changing the *Mode* or *Key* ;
there are other general Principles that Nature
                                     teacheth

teacheth us, and which muſt be attended to, if we
would produce good Effects, either for the Entertainment of the Fancy with the Variety we
find ſo indiſpenſable in our Pleaſures, or for imi-
tating Nature, and moving the Affections.
Theſe are, *firſt*, the different Species of Sounds
abſtract from the Acuteneſs, as Drums, Trumpets, Violins, Flutes, Voice, &c. which as they
give different Senſations, ſo they are fit for expreſſing different Things, and raiſing or humouring different Paſſions; to which we may add the
Differences of ſtrong and weak, or loud and low
Sounds. 2*do*. Tho' a Piece of Melody is ſtrictly the ſame, whether it is performed by an a-
cute or grave Voice; yet 'tis certain, That a-
cute Sounds and grave, have different Effects ;
ſo that the one is more applicable to ſome Subjects
than the other ; and we know that, in general,
acute Sounds (which are owing to quicker Vibrations) have ſomething more brisk and
ſprightly than the graver, which are better applied to the more calm Affections, or to ſad
and melancholy Subjects ; but there is a great
Variety betwixt the Extremes; and different
Cuſtoms and Manners may alſo make a Difference : We find by Experience a lively Motion in our Blood and Nerves, under ſome
Affections of Mind, as Joy and Gladneſs ; and
in the more boiſterous Paſſions, as Anger, that
Motion is ſtill greater ; but others are accompanied with more calm and ſlow Motions ; and
ſince Bodies communicate their Motion, and the
Effect is proportional to the Cauſe, we ſee a
natural

natural Reafon of thefe different Effects of acute and grave Sounds.   *3tio.* The Effects of Melody have a great Dependence on the alternate Paffage or Movement of the Sounds up and down, *i. e.* from acute to grave, and contrarily; or its continuing for lefs or more Time in one Place; but the Variety here is infinite ; yet Experience teaches fome general Leffons; for *Example*, if a Man in the Middle of a Difcourfe turns angry, 'tis natural to raife his Voice; this therefore ought to be expreft by raifing the Melody from grave to acute ; and contrarily a finking of the Mind to Melancholy muft be imitated by the falling of the Sounds; a more evenly State by a like Conduct of the Melody. Again, the taking of the Sounds by immediate Degrees, or alternatively, or repeating the fame Note, and the moving by greater or leffer Intervals, have all their proper and different Effects : Thefe, and their various Combinations, muft all be under the Compofer's Confideration ; but who can poffibly give Rules for the infinite Variety in the State and Temper of human Minds, and the proper Application of Sounds for expreffing or exciting thefe ? And when Compofitions are defigned only for Pleafure in general, what an infinite Number of Ways may this be produced ?

AGAIN it muft be minded, That the *Ryth-mus* is a very principal Thing in *Mufick*, efpecially of the *pathetick* Kind ; for 'tis this Variety of Movements in the quick or flow Succeffions, or Length and Shortnefs of Notes, that's
the

the confpicuous Part of the *Air*, without which
the other can produce but very weak Effects ;
and therefore moft of the Ancients ufed to call
the *Rythmus* the *Male*, and the *Harmonica*
the *Female*. And as to this I muft take Notice
here, That the Ancients feem to have ufed
none but the long and fhort Syllables of the
Words and Verfes which were fung, and always
made a Part of their *Mufick* ; therefore the
Rythmica was nothing with them but the Explication of the *metrical Feer*, and the various
Kinds of Verfes which were made of them : And
for the *Rythmopœia*, or the Art of applying thefe,
I am confident no Body will affirm they have
left us any more than very general Hints, that
can fcarce be called *Rules :* The reading of
Ariftides and St. *Auguftin* will, I believe, con-
vince you of this ; and all the reft put together
have not faid as much about it. I fuppofe the
ancient Writers, who in their Divifions of *Mufick*, make the *Rythmica* one Part, and in their
Explications of this fpeak of no other than that
which belongs to the Words and Verfes of their
Songs, I fay thefe will be a fufficient Proof that
they had no other. But you'll fee it further
confirmed immediately, when we confider the
ancient Notes or Writing of *Mufick*. As to the
modern Rythmus, I need fay littie about it ;
that it is a Thing very different from the ancient, is manifeft to any Body who. confiders
what I have faid of theirs, and has but the
fmalleft Acquaintance with our Mufick. That
the *Meafures* and *Modes* of TIME explained
in

in *Ch.* 12. and all the poffible Subdivifions and Conftitutions of them, are capable to afford an endlefs
Variety of *Rythmus*, and exprefs any Thing that
the Motion of Sound is capable of, is equally certain to the experienced; and therefore I fhall fay
no more of it here : Only *obferve*, That as I
faid about the *Harmonica*, fo of this 'tis certainly true, That the Rules are very general :
We know that quick and flow Movements fuit
different Objects; when we are gay and cheerful we love airy Motions; and to different Subjects and Paffions different Movements muft be
applied, for which Nature is our beft Guide :
Therefore the *practical Writers* leave us to our
own Obfervations and Experience, to learn how
to apply thefe Meafures of Time, which they
can only defcribe in general, as I have done,
and refer us to Examples for perfecting our Idea
of them, and what they are capable of.

Of the ancient Notes, *and* Writing *of* Mufick.

We learn from *Alipius* (*vid. Meibom. Edi-*
tion.) how the *Greeks* marked their Sounds.
They made ufe of the Letters of their Alphabet : And becaufe they needed more Signs than
there were Letters, they fupplied that out of
the fame Alphabet; by making the fame Letter exprefs different Notes, as it was placed up-
right or reverfed, or otherwife put out of the
common Pofition ; and alfo making them imperfect, by cutting off fomething, or by doubling
fome Strokes. For *Example*, the Letter *Pi*
expreffes

expreſſes different Notes in all theſe Poſitions and
Forms, *viz.* Π . ɪɪ . ⊏ . ⊐ Γ . ꓶ, *&c.* But that
we may know the whole Task a Scholar had to
learn, conſider, that for every *Mode* there were
18 Signs (becauſe they conſidered the *Tetrachordum ſynemmenon,* as if all its Chords had
been really different from the *Diezeugmenon*) and
for every one of the Three *Genera* they were alſo
different; again the Signs that expreſſed the ſame
Note were different for the Voice and for the Inſtruments. *Alipius* gives us the Signs for 15 different Modes, which with the Differences of the
3 *Genera,* and the Diſtinction betwixt Voice and
Inſtrument, makes in all 1620; not that theſe
are all different Characters, for the ſame Character is uſed ſeveral Times, but then it has
differerent Significations; for *Example,* in the
diatonick Genus Φ is *Lichanos hypaton* of
the *Lydian* Mode, and *Hypate meſon* of the
Phrygian, both for the Voice; ſo that they are
in effect as different Characters to a Learner.
What a happy Contrivance this was for making
the Practice of *Muſick* eaſy, every Body will
judge who conſiders, that 15 Letters with ſome
ſmall Variation for the *Chordæ mobiles,* in order to diſtinguiſh the *Genera,* was ſufficient for
all. In *Boethius*'s Time the ·*Romans* were
wiſe enough to eaſe themſelves of this unneceſ-
ſary Difficulty ; and therefore they made uſe
only of the firſt 15 Letters of their Alphabet:
But afterwards Pope *Gregory* the Great, conſidering that the 8*ve* was the ſame in effect with
the firſt, and that the Order of Degrees was the
ſame

same in the upper and lower 8*ve* of the *Dia-gram*, he introduced the Use of 7 Letters, which were repeated in a different Character. But hitherto there was no such Thing as any Mark of *Time*; these Characters, expressing only the Degrees of *Tune*, which therefore were always placed in a Line, and the Words of the Song under them, so that over every Syllable stood a Note to mark the Accent of the Voice: And for the *Time*, that was according to the long and short Syllable of the Verse ; tho' in some very extraordinary Cases we hear of some particular Marks for altering the natural or ordinary Quantity.

I shall end this Part with observing that among all the ancient Writers on *Musick*, there is not one Word to be found relating to *Composition* in *Parts*, or joining several different *Melodies* in one *Harmony*, as what we call *Treble, Tenor, Bass,* &c. But this shall be more particularly examined in the next *Section*.

---

§ 5. *A short* HISTORY *of the Improvements in* MUSICK.

FOR what Reasons the *Greek* Musicians made such a difficult Matter of their Notes and Signs we cannot guess, unless they did it designedly to make their Art mysterious, which is an odious Supposition; but one can scarcely think it was otherwise, who considers how obvious

vious

vious it was to find a more eafy Method.
This was therefore the firft Thing the *Latins*
correcded in the *Greek Mufick,* as we have already heard was done by *Boethius,* and further
improved by *Gregory* the Great.

T H E next Step in this Improvement is commonly afcribed to *Guido Aretinus* a *Benediḉin*
Monk, of *Aretium* in *Tufcany,* who, about the
Year 1024, (tho' there are fome Differences a-
bout the Year) contrived the Ufe of a Staff of
5 Lines, upon which, with its Spaces he marked his Notes, by fetting Points (.) up and down
upon them, to denote the Rife and Fall of the
Voice, (but as yet there were no different
Marks of *Time*;) he marked each Line and
Space at the Beginning of the Staff, with *Gregory's* 7 Letters, and when he fpake of the
Notes, he named them by thefe inftead of the
long *Greek* Names of *Proflambanomenos,*&c. The
Correfpondence of thefe Letters to the Names
of the Chords in the *Greek Syftem* being fettled,
fuch as I have already reprefented in their *Diagram,* the Degrees and Intervals betwixt any
Line or Space, and any other were hereby underftood. But this Artifice of Points and Lines
was ufed before his Time, by whom invented
is not known ; and this we learn from *Kircher,*
who fays he found in the *Jefuites* Library at
Meffina a Greek manufcript Book of Hymns,
more than 700 Years old; in which fome Hymns
were written on a Staff of 8 Lines, marked at
the Beginning with 8 Greek Letters; the Notes
or Points were fet upon the Lines, but no Ufe
made

made of the Spaces: *Vincenzo Galileo* confirms
us alfo in this.   But whether *Guido* knew this,
is a Queftion ; and tho' he did, yet it was well
contrived to ufe the Spaces and Lines both, by
which the Notes ly nearer other, fewer Lines
are needful for any Interval, and the Diftances
of Notes are eafier reckoned.

Bu т there is yet more of *Guido's* Contrivance, which deferves to be confidered ; *Firft.*
He contrived the 6 mufical Syllables, *ut, re, mi,
fa, fol, la,* which he took out of this Latin
Hymn.

*UT queant laxis RE fonare fibris
MI ra geftorum FAmuli tuorum,
SO Lve polluti LAbii reatum,
            O pater alme.*

In repeating this it came into his Mind, by a
Kind of divine Inftinct fays *Kircher*, to apply
thefe Syllables to his Notes of *Mufick :* A wonderful Contrivance certainly for a *divine Inftinct !*
But let us fee where the Excellency of it lies :
Kircher fays, by them alone he unfolded all
the Nature of *Mufick*, diftinguifhed the *Tones*
(or *Modes*) and the Seats of the Semitones :
Elfewhere he fays, That by the Application of
thefe Syllables he cultivated *Mufick*, and made
it fitter for Singing.   In order to know how he
applied them, there is another Piece of the
Hiftory we muft take along, *viz.* That finding
the *Greek Diagram* of too fmall Extent, he added 5 more Chords or Notes in this Manner ;
                                    having

having applied the Letter A to the *Pro,lamba-nomenos*, and the reft in Order to *Nete Hyper-bolæon,* he added a Chord, a *Tonus* below *Proflam.* and called it *Hypo-proflambanomenos,* and after the Latins *g.* but commonly marked with the Greek *Gamma* Γ; to fhew by this, fay fome, that the Greeks were the Inventors of *Mufick*; but others fay he meant to record him-felf (that Letter being the firft in his Name) as the Improver of *Mufick*; hence the *Scale* came to be called the *Gamm.* Above *Nete Hyperbolæon* he added other 4 Chords, which made a new disjunct *Tetrachord,* he called *Hyper-hyper-bolæon*; fo that his whole *Scale* contained 20 *diatonick Notes,* (for this was the only *Genus* now ufed) befides the *b* flat, which correfponded to the *Trite Synemmenon* of the Ancients, and made what was afterwards called the Series of *b molle,* as we fhall hear.

Now the Application of thefe Syllables to the *Scale* was made thus: Betwixt *mi* and *fa* is a *Semitone*; *ut : re, re : mi, fa : fol,* and *fol : la* are Tones (without diftinguifhing greater and leffer;) then becaufe there are but 6 Syllables, and 7 different Notes or Letters in the 8*ve*; therefore, to make *mi* and *fa* fall upon the true Places of the natural Semitones, *ut* was applied to different Letters, and the reft of the 6 in order to the others above; the Letters to which *ut* was applied are *g . c . f.* according to which he diftinguifhed three Series, *viz.* that which begun with *ut* in *g,* and he called it the Series of *b durum,* becaufe *b* was a whole Tone above

a,

a; that which begun with *ut* in *c* was the Series of *b* natural, the same as the former; and when *ut* was in *f,* it was called *b molle,* wherein *b.* was only a *Semitone* above *a.* See the whole Scale in the following Scheme, where observe, the Series of *b* natural stands betwixt the other two, and communicates with both; so that to name the Chords of the Scale by these Syllables, if we would have the Semitones in their natural Places, *viz. b . c,* and *e . f,* then we apply *ut* to *g,* and after *la,* we go into the Series of *b* natural at *fa,* and after *la* of this, we return to the former at *mi,* and so on ; or we may begin at *ut* in *c,* and pass into the first Series at *mi,* and then back to the other at *fa :* By which Means the one Transition is a Semitone, *viz. la . fa,* and the other a Tone *la : mi.* To follow the Order of *b molle*

GUIDO's SCALE.

	B dur.	nat.	molle
e e	la	mi	
d d	sol	re	la
c c	fa	ut	sol
b b	mi		
♭♭			fa
a a	re	la	mi
g	ut	sol	re
f		fa	ut
e	la	mi	
d	sol	re	la
c	fa	ut	sol
b	mi		
♭			fa
a	re	la	mi
G	ut	sol	re
F		fa	ut
E	la	mi	
D	sol	re	
C	fa	ut	
B	mi		
A	re		
Γamm	ut		

b molle, we may begin with *ut* in *c* or *f*, and make Tranfitions the fame Way as formerly : Hence came the barbarous Names of *Gammut*, *Are*, *Bmi*, &c. with which the Memories of Learners ufed to be oppreffed. But now what a perplext Work is here, with fo many different Syllables applied to every Chord, and all for no other Purpofe but marking the Places of the Semitones, which the fimple Letters, *a . b . c*, &c. do as well and with infinite more Eafe. Afterwards fome contrived better, by making Seven Syllables, adding *Si* in the Blanks you fee in the Series betwixt *la* and *ut*, fo that *mi-fa* and *fi-ut* are the two natural Semitones : Thefe 7 completing the 8*ve*, they took away the middle Series as of no Ufe, and fo *ut* being in *g* or *f*, made the Series of *B durum* (or natural, which is all one) and *B molle*. But the *Englifh* throw out both *ut* and *fi*, and make the other 5 ferve for all in the Manner explained in *Chap.* 11. where I have alfo fhewn, the Unneceffarinefs of the Difficulty that the beft of thefe Methods occafions, and therefore fhall not repete it here. This wonderful Contrivance of *Guido*'s 6 Syllables, is what a very ingenious Man thought fit to call *Crux tenellorum ingeniorum* ; but he might have faid it of any of the Methods ; for which Reafon, I believe, they are laid afide with very many, and, I am fure, ought to be fo with every Body.

BUT to go one with *Guido* ; the Letters he applied to his Lines and Spaces, were called *Keys*, and at firft he marked every Line and

and Space at the Beginning of a Staff with its
Letter ; afterwards marked only the Lines, as
some old Examples shew ; and at last marked
only one, which was therefore called the *signed
Clef* ; of which he distinguished Three different
ones, *g* , *c* , *f* ; (the three Letters he had placed his *ut* in) and the Reason of this leads us to
another Article of the History, *viz.* That *Guido*
was the Inventor of *Symphonetick Composition,*
(for if the Ancients had it, it was lost ; but this
shall be considered again) the first who joyned
in one *Harmony* several distinct *Melodies,* and
brought it even the length of 4 *Parts, viz.
Bass, Tenor, Counter, Treble* ; and therefore
to determine the Places of the several *Parts*
in the general *System,* and their Relations to
one another, it was necessary to have 3 different
signed Clefs (*vid. Chap.* 11.)

H E is also said to be the Contriver of those
Instruments they call *Polyplectra,* as *Spinets*
and *Harpsichords* : However they may now differ in Shape,   he contrived what is called the
Abacus and the *Palmulæ,* that is, the *Machi-
nery* by which the String is struck with a Plectrum made of Quills. Thus far go the Improvements of *Guido Aretinus,* and what is called the
Guidonian System ; to explain   which he wrote
a Book he calls his *Micrologum.*

T H E next considerable Improvement was
about 300 Years after *Guido,* relating to the
Rythmus, and the Marks by which the Duration of every Note was known ; for hitherto they
had but imitated the Simplicity of the Ancients,
                                                and

and barely followed the Quantity of the Syllables, or perhaps not fo accurate in that, made all their Notes of equal Duration, as fome of the old *Ecclefiaftick Mufick* is an Inftance of. To produce all the Effects *Mufick* is capable of, the Neceffity of Notes of different Quantity was very obvious; for the *Rythmus* is the Soul of *Mufick*; and becaufe the natural Quantity of the Syllables was not thought fufficient for all the Variety of Movements, which we know to be fo agreeable in *Mufick*, therefore about the Year 1330 or 1333, fays *Kircher*, the famous *Joannes de Muris*, Doctor at *Paris*, invented the different Figures of Notes, which exprefs the *Time*, or Length of every Note, at leaft their true relative Proportions to one another; you fee their Names and Figures in *Plate*, 2 *Fig.* 3. as we commonly call them. But anciently they were called, *Maxima, Longa, Brevis, Semibrevis, Minima, Semiminima, Chroma*, (or *Fufa*) *Semichroma*. What we call the *Demifemiquaver* is of modern Addition. But whether all thefe were invented at once is not certain, nor is it probable they were; at firft 'tis like they ufed only the *Longa* and *Brevis*, and the reft were added by Degrees. Now alfo was invented the Divifion of every Song in feparate and diftinct *Bars* or *Meafures*. Then for the Proportion of thefe *Notes* one to another it was not always the fame; fo a *Long* was in fome Cafes equal to Two *Breves*, fometimes to Three, and fo of others; and this Difference was marked generally at the Beginning; and fometimes by the

Pofition

Poſition or Way of joyning them together in the Middle of the Song; but this Variety happened only to the firſt Four. *Again,* reſpecting the mutual Proportions of the Notes, they had what they called *Modes, Prolations* and *Times:* The Two laſt were diſtinguiſhed into *Perfeƈt* and *Imperfeƈt*; and the firſt into *greater* and *leſſer,* and each of theſe into *perfeƈt* and *imperfeƈt :* But afterwards they reduced all into 4 *Modes* including the *Prolations* and *Times.* I could not think it worth Pains to make a tedious Deſcription of all theſe, with their Marks or Signs, which you may ſee in the already mentioned *Diƈtionaire de Muſique:* I ſhall only obſerve here, That as we now make little Uſe of any Note above the *Semibreve,* becauſe indeed the remaining 6 are ſufficient for all Purpoſes, ſo we have caſt off that Difficulty of various and changeable Proportions betwixt the ſame Notes : The Proportions of 3 to 1 and 2 to 1 was all they wanted, and how much more eaſy and ſimple is it to have one Proportion fixt, *viz.* 2 : 1 (*i. e.* a *Large* equal to Two *Longs,* and ſo on in Order) and if the Proportion of 3 : 1 betwixt Two ſucceſſive Notes is required, this is, without any Manner of Confuſion or Difficulty, expreſſed by annexing a Point (.) on the Right Hand of the greateſt of the Two Notes, as has been above explained; ſo that 'tis almoſt a Wonder how the Elements of *Muſick* were ſo long involved in theſe Perplexities, when a far eaſier Way of coming to the ſame End was not very hard to find.

W E

We shall observe here too, That till these *Notes* of various *Time* were invented, instrumental Performances without Song must have been very imperfect if they had any; and what a wonderful Variety of Entertainments we have by this Kind of Composition, I need not tell you.

There remain Two other very considerable Steps, before we come to the present State of the Scale of Musick. *Guido* first contrived the joyning different *Parts* in one *Concert,* as has been said, yet he carried his *System* no further than 20 *diatonick* Notes: Now for the more simple and plain Compositions of the Ecclesiastick Stile, which is probable was the most considerable Application he made of Musick, this Extent would afford no little Variety : But Experience has since found it necessary to enlarge the *System* even to 34 diatonick Notes, which are represented in the foremost Range of Keys on the Breast of a *Harpsichord* ; for so many are required to produce all that admirable Variety of Harmony, which the Parts in modern Compositions consist of, according to the many different Stiles practised: But a more considerable Defect of his System is, That except the Tone betwixt *a* and *b,* which is divided into Two Semitones by ♭ (flat) there was not another Tone in all the Scale divided; and without this the System is very imperfect, with respect to fixt Sounds, because without these there can be no right Modulation or Change from

Key

Key to *Key*, taking Mode or *Key* in the Sense
which I have explained in *Chap*. 9. Therefore
the *modern System* has in every *8ve* 5 artificial
Chords or Notes which we mark by the Letters of the *natural* Chords, with the Distinction
of ✳ or ♭, the Necessity and true Use of which
has been largely explained in *Chap*. 8. and therefore not to be insisted on here ; I shall only *observe*, That by these additional Chords, we
have the *diatonick* and *chromatick Genera* of
the Ancients mixed ; so that Compositions may
be made in either Kind, tho' we reckon the
diatonick the true natural Species ; and if at
any Time, Two *Semitones* are placed immediately in Succession ; for *Example*, if we sing
c . *c*✳. *d*, which is done for Variety, tho' sel-
dom, so far this is a Mixture of the *Chromatick*; but then to make it pure *Chromatick*, no
smaller Interval can be sung after Two *Semitones* ascending than a *Triemitone*, nor descending less than a *Tone*; because in the pure *chromatick* Scale the *Spissum* has always above it a
Triemitone, and below it either a *Triemitone* or
a *Tone*.

T H E last Thing I shall consider here is, how
the *Modes* were defined in these Days of Improvement ; and I find they were generally characterized by the Species of *8ve* after *Ptolomy*'s
Manner, and therefore reckoned in all 7. But
afterwards they considered the *harmonical* and
arithmetical Divisions of the *8ve*, whereby it
resolves into a 4*th* above a 5*th*, or a 5*th* above

a 4*th*

a 4*th*. And from this they conftituted 12 *Modes*, making of each 8*ve* two different Modes according to this different Divifion ; but becaufe there are Two of them that cannot be divided both Ways, therefore there are but 12 Modes. To be more particular, confider, in the natural Syftem there are 7 different *Octaves* proceeding from thefe 7 Letters, *a, b, c, d, e, f, g ;* each of which has Two middle Chords, which divide it *harmonically* and *arithmetically*, except *f*, which has not a true 4*th*, (becaufe *b* is Three Tones above it, and a 4*th* is but Two *Tones* and a *Semitone*) and *b*, which confequently wants the true 5*th* (becaufe *f* is only Two *Tones* and Two *Semitones* above it, and a true 5*th* contains 3 *Tones* and a *Semitone*) therefore we have only 5 *Octaves* that are divided both Ways, *viz. a, c, d, e, g,* which make 10 Modes according to thefe different Divifions, and the other Two *f* and *b* make up the 12. Thefe that are divided harmonically, *i. e.* with the 5*ths* loweft were called *authentick*, and the other *plagal* Modes. See the following Scheme.

To thefe Modes they gave the Names of the ancient *Greek Tones*, as *Dorian, Phrygian :* But feveral Authors differ in the Application of thefe Names, as they do about the Order, as, which they fhall call the firft and fecond, *&c.* which being arbitrary Things, as far as I can underftand, it were as idle to pretend to recon-

cile

MODES.

Plagal.   *Authentick.*
8*ve.*   8*ve.*

4*th.*   5*th.*   4*th.*

g — c --- g — c
a — d — a — d
b — e — b — e
c — f --- c — f
d --- g --- d — g
e — a — e --- a

cile them, as it was in them to differ about it. The material Point is, if we can find it, to know what they meant by thefe Diftinctions, and what was the real Ufe of them in *Mufick*; but even here where they ought to have agreed, we find they differed. The beft Account I am able to give you of it is this: They confidered that an 8*ve* which wants a 4*th* or 5*th*, is imperfect; thefe being the *Concords* next to 8*ve*, the Song ought to touch thefe Chords moft frequently and remarkably; and becaufe their *Concord* is different, which makes the Melody different, they eftablifhed by this Two Modes in every natural *Octave*, that had a true 4*th* and 5*th*: Then if the Song was carried as far as the *Octave* above, it was called a *perfect Mode*; if lefs, as to the 4*th* or 5*th*, it was *imperfect*; if it moved both above and below, it was called a *mixt Mode*: Thus fome Authors fpeak about thefe *Modes*. Others confidering how indifpenfable a Chord the 5*th* is in every *Mode*, they took for the *final* or *Key*-note in the arithmetically divided *Octaves*, not the loweft Chord of that *Octave*, but that very 4*th*; for *Example*, the *Octave* g is arithmetically divided thus, g - c - g, c is a 4*th* above the lower g, and a 5*th* below the upper

per

per *g*, this *c* therefore they made the *final* Chord of the Mode, which therefore properly speaking is *c* and not *g* ; the only Difference then in this Method, betwixt the *authentick* and *plagal Modes* is, that the *Authentick* goes above its Final to the *Octave*, the other afcends a *5th*, and defcends a *4th*, which will indeed be attended with different Effects, but the Mode is effentially the fame, having the fame Final to which all the Notes refer. We muft next confider wherein the Modes of one Species, as *Authentick* or *Plagal*, differ among themfelves: This is either by their ftanding higher or lower in the Scale, *i. e.* the different Tenfion of the whole *Octave*; or rather the different Subdivifion of the *Octave* into its concinnous Degrees ; there is not another. Let us confider then whether thefe Differences are fufficient to produce fo very different Effects, as have been afcribed to them, for *Example*, one is faid to be proper for Mirth, another for Sadnefs, a Third proper to Religion, another for tender and amorous Subjects, and fo on : Whether we are to afcribe fuch Effects merely to the Conftitution of the *Octave*, without Regard to other Differences and Ingredients in the Compofition of Melody, I doubt any Body now a Days will be abfurd enough to affirm ; thefe have their proper Differences, 'tis true, but which have fo little Influence, that by the various Combinations of other Caufes, one of thefe Modes may be ufed to different Purpofes. The greateft and moft influencing Difference is that of
thefe

thefe *Octaves*, which have the 3*d l.* or 3*d g.* making what is above called the *sharp* and *flat Key* But we are to notice, that of all the 8*ves*, except *c* and *a*, none of them have all their effential Chords in juft Proportion, unlefs we neglect the Difference of Tone greater and leffer, and alfo allow the *Semitone* to ftand next the Fundamental in fome flat Keys (which may be ufeful, and is fometimes ufed;) and when that is done, the *Octaves* that have a flat 3*d* will want the 6*th g.* and 7*th g.* which are very neceffary on fome Occafions ; and therefore the artificial Notes ✕ and ♭ are of abfolute Ufe to perfect the *Syftem.* *Again*, if the Modes depend upon the Species of 8*ves*, how can they be more than 7 ? And as to this Diftinction of *authentick* and *plagal*, I have fhewn that it is imaginary, with refpect to any effential Difference conftituted hereby in the Kind of the Melody; for tho' the carrying the Song above or below the *Final*, may have a different Effect, yet this is to be numbred among the other Caufes, and not afcribed to the Conftitution of the *Octaves.* But 'tis particularly to be remarked, that thefe Authors who give us *Examples* in actual Compofition of their 12 Modes, frequently take in the artificial Notes ✕ and ♭ to perfect the *Melody* of their *Key*; and by this Means depart from the Conftitution of the 8*ve*, as it ftands in the fixt natural Syftem. So we can find little certain and confiftent in their Way of fpeaking about thefe Things; and their Modes are all reducible to Two, *viz.* the *sharp* and *flat* ; o-
ther

ther Differences refpecting only the Place of the
Scale where the Fundamental is taken : I conclude therefore that the true Theory of *Modes*
is that explained in *Chap.* 9. where they are
diftinguifhed into Two Species, *fharp* and *flat*,
whofe Effects I own are different ; but other
Caufes (*vid. Pag.* 547, &c.) muft concur to any
remarkable Effect ; and therefore 'tis unreafon-
able to talk as if all were owing to any one
Thing. Before I have done there is another
Thing you are to be informed of, *viz.* That
what they called the Series of *b molle*, was no
more than this, That becaufe the 8*ve f* had
a 4*th* above at *b, exceffive* by a *Semitone*, and
confequently the 8*ve b* had a 5*th* above as
much deficient, therefore this artificial Note *b
flat* or ♭, ferved them to tranfpofe their *Modes*
to the Diftance of a 4*th* or 5*th*, above or below; for taking ♭ a Semitone above *a*, the
reft keeping their *Ratios* already fixt, the Series proceeding from *c* with *b* natural (*i. e.* a
Tone above *a*) is in the fame Order of. Degrees, as that from *f* with *b flat* (i. e, ♭ a Semitone above *a*;) but *f* is a 4*th* above *c*, or a
5*th* below ; therefore to tranfpofe from the
Series of *b* natural to *b molle* we afcend a
4*th* or defcend a 5*th*; and contrarily from
b molle to the other :   This is the whole Myftery ; but they never fpeak of the other Tranfpofitions that may be made by other artificial
Notes.

   Y o u may alfo *obferve*, that what they called
the *Ecclefiaftick Tones*, are no other than cer-
                                                       tain

tain Notes in the *Organ* which are made the
Final or *Fundamental* of the Hymns; and as
Modes they differ, some by their Place in the
Scale, others by the *sharp* and *flat* 3d; but even
here every Author speaks not the same Way:
'Tis enough we know they can differ no other
Way, or at least all their Differences can be reduced to these. At first they were Four in Number, whose *Finals* were *d, e, f, g* constituted *au-
thentically* : This Choice, we are told, was first
made by St. *Ambrose* Bishop of *Milan*; and for
being thus chosen and approven, they pretend the
Name *Authentick* was added: Afterwards *Gregory* the *Great* added Four *Plagals a, b, c, d,*
whose Finals are the very same with the first
Four, and in effect are only a Continuation of
these to the *4th* below; and for this Connection
with them were called *plagal,* tho' the Deri-
vation of the Word is not so plain.

BUT 'tis Time to have done; for I think I
have shewn you the principal Steps of the Improvement of the *System* of *Musick,* to the present State of it, as that is more largely explained in the preceeding *Chapters.* I have only one
Word to add, that in *Guido*'s Time and long
after, they supposed the Division of the *Tetrachord* to be *Ptolomy*'s *Diatonum diatonicum, i.
e.* Two *Tones* 8 : 9, and *a limma* $\frac{243}{256}$; till
Zarlinus explained and demonstrated, that it
ought to be the *intensum,* containing the Tone
greater 8 : 9, lesser 9 : 10, and *Semitone* 15 : 16;
which *Kepler* strongly argues for ; as he also
shews

shews how inconsistently they spake about the *Modes,* where he reduces all to the Two Species of *sharp* and *flat.* 'Tis true, *Galileo* approves the other, as common Practice shewed that the Difference was insensible ; yet it must be meant only with respect to common Practice. I have already explained, how this Difference in fixt Instruments is the very Reason of their Imperfection after the greatest Pains to correct them ; and how the natural Voice will, without any Direction, and even without perceiving it, choose sometimes a greater, sometimes a lesser *Tone* : Therefore I think Nature guides us to the Choice of this Species : If the commensurate *Ratios* of Vibrations are the Cause of *Concord* then certainly 4 : 5 is better than 64 : 81. The first arises from the Application of a simple general Rule upon which the more perfect *Concords* depend; the other comes in as it were arbitrarily. How the Proportions happen upon Instruments depends upon the Method of tuning them ; of which enough has been already said.

---

§ 6. *The* ancient *and* modern Musick *compared.*

THE last Age was famous for the War that was raised, and eagerly maintain'd by two different Parties, concerning the ancient and modern *Genius* and *Learning.* Among the disputed Points *Musick* was one, I know of nothing

thing new to be advanced on either Side; so that I might refer you to those who have examined the Question already : But that nothing in my Power may be wanting to make this Work more acceptable, I shall put the Substance of that Controversy into the best Form I can, and shall endeavour to be at the same Time short and distinct.

THE Question in general is, Whether the *Ancients* or the *Moderns* best understood and practised *Musick?* Some affirm that the *ancient* Art of *Musick* is quite lost, among other valuable Things of Antiquity, *vid. Pancirollus, de Musica.* Others pretend, That the true Science of *Harmony* is arrived to much greater Perfection than what was known or practised among the Ancients. The Fault with many of the Contenders on this Point is, that they fight at long Weapons; I mean they keep the Argument in *generals,* by which they make little more of it than some innocent Harangues and Flourishes of Rhetorick, or at most make bold Assertions upon the Authority of some misapplied Expressions and incredible Stories of ancient Writers, for I'm now speaking chiefly of the Patrons of the ancient Musick.

IF Sir *William Temple* was indeed serious, and had any Thing else in his View, but to shew how he could declaim, he is a notable Instance of this. *Says he,* " What are become " of the Charms of Musick, by which " Men and Beasts were so frequently inchanted,
" and

" and their very Natures changed, by which
" the Paffions of Men were raifed to the greateft
" Height and Violence, and then as fuddenly
" appeafed, fo as they might be *juftly* faid, to
" be turned into Lions or Lambs, into Wolves
" or into Harts, by the Power and Charms of
" this admirable Art?" And he might have added too, by which the Trees and Stones were animated; in Spite of the Senfe which *Horace* puts
upon the Stories of *Orpheus* and *Amphion.* But
this Queftion fhall be confidered prefently. Again
he fays, " 'Tis agreed by the Learned, that
" the Science of Mufick, fo admired of the
" Ancients, is wholly loft in the World, and
" and that what we have now, is made up out
" of certain Notes that fell into the Fancy or
" Obfervation of a poor Friar, in chanting his
" Mattins. So that thofe Two divine Excel-
" lencies of *Mufick* and *Poetry,* are grown in a
" Manner, but the one *Fiddling* and the other
" *Rhyming,* and are indeed very worthy the Ig-
" norance of the *Friar,* and the Barbaroufnefs
" of the *Goths* that introduced them among us."
Some learned Men indeed have faid fo ; but as
learned have faid otherwife : And for the Defcription Sir *William* gives of the modern *Mu-*
fick, it is the pooreft Thing ever was faid, and
demonftrates the Author's utter Ignorance of
Mufick : Did he know what Ufe *Guido* made
of thefe Notes? He means the Syllables, *ut,*
re, mi, &c. for thefe are the Notes he invented.
If the modern *Mufick* falls fhort of the ancient,

it

it muſt be in the Uſe and Application ; for the
Materials and Principles of *Harmony* are the
ſame Thing, or rather they are improven ; for
Guido's Scale to which he applied theſe Syllables, is the ancient *Greek* Scale only carried to
a greater Extent ; and which is much improven
ſince.

As I have ſtated the Queſtion, we arc firſt to
compare the *Principles* and then the *Practice*.
As to the *Principles* I have already explained
them pretty largely, at leaſt as far as they have
come to our Knowledge, by the Writings on this
Subject that have eſcaped the Wrack of Time.
Nor is there any great Reaſon to ſuſpect that
the beſt are loſt, or that what we have are but
Sketches of their Writings : For we have not a
few Authors of them, and theſe written at different Times; and ſome of them at good Length;
and by their Introductions they propoſe to handle
the Subject in all its Parts and Extent, and
have actually treated of them all.

MEIBOMIUS, no Enemy to the ancient
Cauſe, ſpeaking of *Ariſtides*, calls him, *Incom-
parabilis antiquæ muſicæ Auctor, & vere exem-
plar unicum,* who, he ſays, has taught and
explained all that was ever known or taught
before him, in all the Parts' We have *Ariſtoxenus* ; and for what was written before him,
he affirms to have been very deficient : Nor do
the later Writers ever complain of the Loſs of
any valuable Author that was before them.

Now I ſuppoſe it will be manifeſt to the
unprejudiced, who conſider what has been explained

plained both of the ancient and modern Principles and Theory of *Harmonicks,* that they
have not known more of it than we do, plainly
becaufe we know all theirs ; and that we have
improven upon their Foundation, will be as plain
from the Accounts I have given of both, and
the Comparifon I have drawn all along in explaining the *ancient Theory* ; therefore I need
infift no more upon this Part. The great Difpute is about the Practice.

To underftand the ancient *Practice* of *Mufick,* we are firft to confider what the Name
fignified with them. I have already explained
its various Significations ; and fhewn, that in the
moft particular Senfe, *Mufick* included thefe
Three Things, *Harmony, Rythmus* and *Verfe :*
If there needs any Thing to be added, take thefe
few Authorities. In *Plato*'s firft *Alcibiades, Socrates* asks what he calls that Art which teaches
to *fing, play* on the *Harp,* and *dance?* and
makes him Anfwer, *Mufick :* But finging among
them was never without Verfe. This is again
confirmed by *Plutarch,* who fays, " That in
" judging of the Parts of *Mufick,* Reafon and
" Senfe muft be employed ; for thefe three
" muft always meet in our Hearing, *viz. Sound,*
" whereby we perceive *Harmony ; Time,*
" whereby we perceive *Rythmus ;* and *Letters*
" or *Syllables,* by which we underftand what
" is faid." Therefore we reafonably conclude,
that their Mufick confifted of Verfes fung by one
or more Voices, alternately, or in Choirs; fometimes

times with the Sound of Inſtruments, and ſometimes by Voices only ; and whether they had
any *Muſick* without Singing, ſhall be again conſidered.

LET us now conſider what *Idea* their Writers
give us of the *practical Muſick :* I don't ſpeak
of the Effects, which ſhall be examined again,
but of the *practical Art.* This we may expect,
if 'tis to be found at all, from the Authors who
write *ex profeſſo* upon Muſick, and pretend to
explain it in all its Parts. I have already ſhewn,
that they make the *muſical Faculties* (as they
call them) theſe, *viz. Melopœia, Rythmopœia,*
and *Poeſis.* For the *Firſt,* to make the Compariſon right, I ſhall conſider it under theſe
Two Heads, *Melody* and *Symphony,* and begin
with the laſt. I have obſerved, in explaining
the Principles of the ancient *Melopœia,* that it
contains nothing but what relates to the Conduct of a ſingle Voice, or making what we call
Melody: There is not the leaſt Word of the *Concert* or *Harmony* of Parts ; from which there
is very great Reaſon to conclude, that this was
no Part of the ancient Practice, and is altogether a modern Invention, and a noble one too;
the firſt Rudiments of which I have already
ſaid we ow to that ſame poor Friar (as Sir
William Temple calls him) *Guido Aretinus.*
But that there be no Difference about mere
Words, obſerve, that the Queſtion is not, Whether the Ancients ever joyned more Voices or
Inſtruments together in one *Symphony* ; but,
whether ſeveral Voices were joyned, ſo as each
                                                    had

had a diftinct and proper *Melody*, which made
among them a Succeffion of various *Concords* ;
and were not in every Note *Unifons*, or at the
fame Diftance from each other, as 8*ves* ? which
laft will agree to the general Signification of the
Word *Symphonia*; yet 'tis plain, that in fuch Cafes
there is but one Song, and all the Voices perform
the fame individual *Melody* ; but when the *Parts*
differ, not by the Tenfion of the Whole, but by
the different Relations of the fucceffive Notes,
This is the modern Art that requires fo peculiar
a Genius, and good Judgment, in which therefore 'tis fo difficult to fucceed well. The
ancient *Harmonick* Writers, in their Rules and
Explications of the *Melopœia*, fpeak nothing of
this Art : They tell us, that the *Melopœia* is
the Art of making Songs ; or more generally,
that it is the Ufe of all the Parts and Principles
that are the Subjects of *harmonical Contempla-*
tion. Now is it at all probable, that fo confiderable an Ufe of thefe Principles was known
among the Ancients, and yet never once mentioned by thofe who profeffed to write of *Mu-*
fick in all its Parts ? Shall we think thefe con-
cealed it, becaufe they envied Pofterity fo valuable an Art? Or, was it the Difficulty of explaining it that made them filent ? They might at
leaft have faid there was fuch an Art; the Definition of it is eafy enough : Is it like the reft
of 'their Conduct to neglect any Thing that
might redound in any Degree to their own Praife
and Glory ? Since we find no Notice of this
Art

Art under the *Melopœia,* I think we cannot expect it in any other Part. If any Body should
think to find it in the Part that treats of *Sy-*
stems, because that expresses a Composition of
several Things, they'll be disappointed : For these
Authors have considered Systems only as greater
Intervals betwixt whose Extremes other Notes
are placed, dividing them into lesser *Intervals,*
in such Manner as a single Voice may pass a-
greeably from the one Extreme to the other.
But in distinguishing *Systems* they tell us, some
are σύμφωνα some διάφωνα, *i. e.* some *consonant*
some *dissonant :* Which Names expressed the
Quality of these *Systems, viz.* that of the first,
the Extremes are fit to be heard together,
and the other not ; and if they were not used in
Consonance, may some say, these Names are
wrong applied : But tho' they signified that
Quality, it will not prove they were used in Consonance, at least in the modern Way : Besides,
when they speak plainly and expresly of their
Use in Succession or *Melody,* they use the
same Names, to signify their Agreement : And
if they were used in Consonance in the Manner
described, why have we not at least some general Rules to guide us in the Practice ? Or rather,
does not their Silence in this demonstrate there
was no such Practice ? But tho' there is nothing
to be found in those who have written more
fully and expresly on Musick, yet the Advocates
for the ancient Musick find Demonstration
enough, they think, in some Passages of Authors
that have given transient Descriptions of Musick:
But

But if thefe Paffages are capable of any other
good Senfe than they put upon them, I think the
Silence of the profeffed Writers on *Mufick* will
undoubtedly caft the Balance on that Side. To
do all Juftice to the Argument, I fhall produce
the principal and fulleft of thefe Kind of Paffages in their Authors Words. *Ariftotle* in his
Treatife concerning the World, περι κοσμε, *Lib.*
5. anfwers that Queftion, If the World is made
of contrary Principles, how comes it that it is
not long ago diffolved? He fhews that the Beauty and Perfection of it confifts in the admirable
Mixture and Temperament of different Things,
and among his Illuftrations brings in *Mufick* thus,
Μεσικὴ δε ὀξεῖς ἄμα και βαρεῖς, μακρύς τε και
βραχεῖς Φθόγγες μίξασα, ἐν διαφόραις Φωναῖς,
μίαν ἀπετέλεσεν ἁρμονίαν, which the Tranflators
juftly render thus, *Mufica acutis & gravibus
fonis, longifque & brevibus una permixtis in
diverfis vocibus, unum ex illis concentum red-
dit, i. e. Mufick,* by a Mixture of acute and
grave, alfo of long and fhort Sounds of different
Voices, yields one abfolute or perfect *Concert.*
Again, in *Lib.* 6. explaining the Harmony of
the celeftial Motions, where each Orb, fays
he, has its own proper Motion, yet all tend to
one harmonious End, as they alfo proceed from
one Principle, making a *Choir* in the Heavens
by their Concord, and he carries on the Comparifon with Mufick thus: Καθάπερ δε ἐν χορῷ χο-
ρυφαίε καταρξαντες, συνεπηχεῖ πᾶς ὁ χορὸς ἀν-
δρων ἔ9 ὅτε και γυναικων εν διαφόραις Φωναῖς ὀξυ-
τέραις και βαρυτέραις μιαν ἁρμονίαν ἐμμελῆ κεραν-
νύντων.

νύντων. *Quemadmodum fit in* Choro, *ut auſpi-*
cianti præſuli aut præcentori, accinat omnis
chorus, e viris interdum fœminiſque compoſitus,
qui diverſis ipſis vocibus, gravibus ſcilicet &
acutis concentum attemperant. i. e. As in a
Choir, after the *Præcentor* the whole *Choir* ſings,
compoſed ſometimes of Men and Women, who
by the different Acuteneſs and Gravity of their
Voices, make one *concinnous* Harmony.

Let *Seneca* appear next, *Epiſtle* 84. *Non*
vides quam multorum vocibus Chorus conſtet ?
Unus tamen ex omnibus ſonus redditur, aliqua illic
acuta eſt, aliqua gravis, aliqua media. Acce-
dunt viris fœminæ, interponuntur tibiæ, ſingu-
lorum latent voces, omnium apparent. i. e. Don't
you ſee of how many Voices the *Chorus* conſiſts? yet they make but one Sound: In it ſome
are acute, ſome grave, and ſome middle: Women are joyned with Men, and Whiſtles alſo
put in among them: Each ſingle Voice is con-
cealed, yet the Whole is manifeſt.

Cassiodorus ſays, *Symphonia eſt tempera-*
mentum ſonitus gravis ad acutum, vel acuti
ad gravem, modulamen efficiens, ſive in voce ſive
in percuſſione, ſive in flatu. i. e. Symphony is
an Adjuſtment of a grave Sound to an acute, or
an acute to a grave, making *Melody.*

Now the moſt that can be made of theſe
Paſſages is, That the Ancients uſed *Choirs* of
ſeveral Voices differing in Acuteneſs and Gravity; which was never denied : But the Whole
of theſe Definitions will be fully anſwered, ſuppoſing

poſing they ſung all the ſame *Part* or *Song* only in different Tenſions, as 8*ve* in every Note. And from what was premiſed I think there is Reaſon to believe this to be the only true Meaning.

But there are other conſiderable Things to be ſaid that will put this Queſtion beyond all reaſonable Doubt. The Word *Harmonia* ſignifies more generally the Agreement of ſeveral Things that make up one Whole ; but ſo do ſeveral Sounds in Succeſſion make up one *Song*, which is in a very proper Senſe a Compoſition. And in this Senſe we have in *Plato* and others ſeveral Compariſons to the *Harmony* of Sounds in *Muſick*. But 'tis alſo uſed in the ſtrict Senſe for *Conſonance*, and ſo is equivalent to the Word *Symphonia*. Now we ſhall make *Ariſtotle* clear his own Meaning in the Paſſages adduced : He uſes *Symphonia* to expreſs Two Kinds of *Conſonance* ; the one, which he calls by the general Name *Symphonia*, is the Conſonance of Two Voices that are in every Note *uniſon*, and the other, which he calls *Antiphonia*, of Two Voices that are in every Note 8*ve*: In his *Problems*, § 19. *Prob.* 16. He asks why *Symphonia* is not as agreeable as *Antiphonia* ; and anſwers, becauſe in *Symphonia* the one Voice being altogether like or as *One* with the other, they eclipſe one another. The *Symphoni* here plainly muſt ſignify *Uniſons*, and he explains it elſewhere by calling them *Omophoni*: And that the 8*ve* is the *Antiphoni* is plain, for it was a common Name to 8*ve* ; and *Ariſtotle* himſelf
explains

explains the *Antiphoni* by the Voice of a Boy
and a Man that are as *Nete* and *Hypate*, which
were 8*ve* in *Pythagoras*'s Lyre. *Again,* I own
he is not speaking here of *Unison* and 8*ve* simply
considered, but as used in *Song* : And tho' in
modern *Symphonies* it is also true, that *Unison*
cannot be so frequently used with as good Effect as
8*ve*, yet his Meaning is plainly this, *viz.* that when
Two Voices sing together one Song, 'tis more
agreeable that they be 8*ve* than *unison* with one
another, in every Note : This I prove from
the 17*th Probl.* in which he asks why *Diapente* and *Diatessaron* are never sung as the
Antiphoni ? He answers, because the *Antiphoni*, or Sounds of 8*ve*, are in a Manner both the
same and different Voices ; and by this Likeness,
where at the same Time each keeps its own
distinct Character, we are better pleased : Therefore he affirms, that the 8*ve* only can be sung in
Symphony (διὰ πασῶν συμφωνία μόνη ᾄδεται.)
Now that by this he means such a *Symphony* as
I have explained, is certain, because in modern *Counterpoint* the 4*th*, and especially
the 5*th* are indispensable ; and indeed the
5*th* with its Two 3*ds*, are the Life of the
Whole. *Again,* in *Probl.* 18. he asks why
why the *Diapason* only is *magadised* ? And answers, because its Terms are the only *Antiphoni :* Now that this signifies a Manner of Singing,
where the Sounds are in every Note 8*ve* to one
another, is plain from this Word *magadised,*
taken from the Name of an Instrument μαγά-
διος, in which Two Strings were always struck
toge-

together for one Note. *Athenæus* makes the
Magadis the same with the *Barbiton* and
Pectis; and *Horace* makes the Muse *Polyhymnia* the Inventor of the *Barbiton.* — *Nec Polyhymnia* Lesboum *refugit tendere* Barbiton.—
And from the Nature of this Instument, that it
had Two Strings to every Note, some think it
probable the Name *Polyhymnia* was deduced.
Athenæus reports from *Anacreon*, that the *Magadis* had Twenty Chords ; which is a Number sufficient to make us allow they were doubled ; so that it had in all Ten Notes : Now
anciently they had but Three *Tones* or *Modes*,
and each extended only to an 8*ve.* and being a
Tone asunder, required precisely Ten Chords ;
therefore *Athenæus* corrects *Possidonius* for saying the Twenty Chords were all distinct Notes,
and necessary for the Three *Modes.* But he
further confirms this Point by a Citation from
the Comick Poet *Alexandrides*, who takes a
Comparison from the *Magadis*, and says, *I am,
like the* Magadis, *about to make you understand
a Thing that is at the same Time both sublime
and low* ; which proves that Two Strings were
struck together, and that they were not *unison.*
He reports also the Opinion of the Poet *Jon*,
that the *Magadis* consisted of Two Flutes,
which were both sounded together. From all
this 'tis plain, That by *magadised, Aristotle*
means such a Consonance of Sounds as to be in
every Note at the same Distance, and consequently to be without *Symphony* and Parts according
to the modern Practice. *Athenæus* reports also.
of

of *Pindar*, that he called the Mufick fung by a Boy and a Man *Magadis* ; becaufe they fung together the fame Song in Two *Modes*.   Mr. *Perault* concludes from this, that the Strings of the *Magadis* were fometimes 3*ds*, becaufe *Ariftotle* fays, the 4th and 5th are never *magadifed* : But why may not *Pindar* mean that they were at an 8*ve*'s Diftance ; for certainly *Ariftotle* ufed that Comparifon of a Boy and a Man to exprefs an 8*ve* : Mr. *Perault* thinks it muft be a 3*d* becaufe of the Word *Mode*, whereof anciently there were but Three ; and confirms it by a Paffage out of *Horace*, Epod. 9. *Sonante miftum tibiis carmen lyra* ; *hac* Dorium *illis* Barbarum : By the *Barbarum*, fays he, is to be underftood the *Lydian*, which was a *Ditone* above the *Dorian* : But the Difficulty is, that the Ancients reckoned the *Ditone* at beft a *concinnous Difcord* ; and therefore 'tis not probable they would ufe it in fo remarkable a Manner : But we have enough of this.   The Author laft named obferves, that the Ancients probably had a Kind of fimple Harmony, in which Two or Three Notes were tuned to the principal Chords of the *Key*, and accompanied the Song.   This he thinks probable from the Name of an Inftrument *Pandora* that *Athenæus* mentions ; which is likely the fame with the *Mandora*, an Inftrument not very long ago ufed, fays he, in which there were Four Strings, whereof one ferved for the Song, and was ftruck by a *Plectrum* or Quill tied to the Forefinger : The other Three were tuned

fo

fo as Two of them were an 8*ve*, and the other
a Middle dividing the 8*ve* into a 4*th* and 5*th*:
They were ftruck by the Thumb, and this regulated by the *Rythmus* or Meafure of the Song,
i. e. Four Strokes for every Meafure of common
Time, and Three for Triple. He thinks *Horace*
points out the Manner of this Inftrument in *Ode*
6. Lesbium *fervate pedem, meique pollicis
ictum,* which he thus tranflates. *Take Notice, you who would joyn your Voice to the
Sound of my Lyre, that the Meafure of my Song
is* Sapphick, *which the ftriking of my Thumb
marks out to you.* This Inftrument is parallel
to our common Bagpipe.

THE Paffages of *Ariftotle* being thus cleared, I
think *Seneca* and *Caffiodorus* may be eafily given
up. *Seneca* fpeaks of *vox media*, as well as *acuta*
and *gravis*; but this can fignify nothing, but
that there might be Two 8*ves*, one betwixt the
Men and Women and the fhrill *Tibiæ* might be
8*ve* above the Women : But then the latter
Part of what he fays deftroys their Caufe ; for
fingulorum voces latent can very well be faid
of fuch as fing the fame Melody *Unifon* or *Octave*,
but would by no Means be true of feveral
Voices performing a modern *Symphony*, where
every Part is confpicuous, with a perfect Harmony in the Whole. For *Caffiodorus*, I think
what he fays has no Relation to *Confonance*,
and therefore I have tranflated it, *An Adjuftment of a grave Sound to an acute, or an acute
to a grave making Melody* : If it be alledged
that *temperamentum* may fignifie a Mixture, I fhall
yield

yield it ; but then he ought to have said, *Temperamentum sonitus gravis & acuti* ; for what means *sonitus gravis ad acutum*, and again *acuti ad gravem* ? But in the other Case this is well enough, for he means, That Melody may confist either in a Progress from acute to grave, or contrarily : And then the Word *Modulamen* was never applied any other way than to succeffive Sounds.　There is another Paffage which *If. Voffius* cites from *Ælian* the *Platonick*, Συμφωνία δε ἐςι δυοῖν ἤ πλειόνων φθόγ[ω]ν ὀξύτη[τι] καὶ βαρύτητι διαφερόν[ω]ν κατα τὸ αὐτὸ π[]ῶσις καὶ κρᾶσις, i. e. Symphony confifts of Two or more Sounds differing in Acutenefs and Gravity, with the fame Cadence and Temperament: But this rather adds another Proof that what Symphonies they had were only of feveral Voices finging the fame *Melody* only in a different Tone.

After fuch evident Demonftrations, I think there needs no more to be faid to prove that *Symphonies* of different *Parts* are a modern Improvement. From their rejecting the 3*ds* and 6*ths* out of the Number of *Concords*, the fmall Extent of their Syftem being only Two *Octaves*, and having no Tone divided but that betwixt *Mefe* and *Paramefe*, we might argue that they had no different *Parts :* For tho fome fimple Compofitions of Parts might be contrived with thefe Principles, yet 'tis hard to think they would lay the Foundations of that Practice, and carry it no further ; and much harder to believe they would never fpeak one Word of fuch an Art and Practice, where they profefs to explain all

the

the Parts of Mufick. But for the *Symphonies* which we allow them to have had, you'll ask why thefe Writers don't fpeak of them, and why it feems fo incredible that they fhould have had the other Kind without being ever mentioned, when they don't mention thefe we allow? The Reafon is plain, becaufe the Mufician's Bufinefs was only to compofe the *Melody*, and therefore they wanted only Rules about that; but there was no Rule required to teach how feveral Voices might joyn in the fame Song, for there is no Art in it: Experience taught them that this might be done in *Unifon* or *Octave*; and pray what had the Writers more to fay about it? But the modern *Symphony* is a quite different Thing, and needs much to be explained both by Rules and Examples. But tis Time to make an End of this Point: I fhall only add, That if plain *Reafon* needs any Authority to fupport it, I can adduce many Moderns of Character, who make no Doubt to fay, That after all their Pains to know the true State of the ancient *Mufick*, they could not find the leaft Ground to believe there was any fuch Thing in thefe Days as *Mufick* in *Parts*. I have named *Perrault*, and fhall only add to him *Kircher* and Doctor *Wallis*, Authors of great Capacity and infinite Induftry.

Our next Comparifon fhall be of the *Melody* of the Ancients and Moderns; and here comes in what's neceffary to be faid on the other Parts of *Mufick*, *viz.* the *Rythmus* and *Verfe*. In order to this Comparifon, I fhall diftinguifh

Melody

Melody into *vocal* and *inftrumental*. By the firft I mean *Mufick* fet to Words, efpecially Verfes; and by the other *Mufick* compofed only for Inftruments without Singing. For the *vocal* you fee by the Definition that *Poetry* makes a neceffary Part of it : This was not only of ancient Practice, but the chief, if not their only Practice, as appears from their Definitions of *Mufick* already explain'd. 'Tis not to be expected that I fhould make any Comparifon of the ancient and modern Poetry ; 'tis enough for my Purpofe to obferve, That there are admirable Performances in both; and if we come fhort of them, I believe 'tis not for want either of Genius or Application : But perhaps we fhall be obliged to own that the *Greek* and *Latin* Languages were better contrived for pleafing the Ear. We are next to confider, that the *Rythmus* of their *vocal Mufick* was only that of the Poetry, depending altogether on the Verfe, and had no other Forms or Variety than what the metrical Art afforded : This has been already fhewn, particularly in explaining their mufical Notes; to which add, That under the Head of *Mutations,* thofe who confider the *Rythmus* make the Changes of it no other than from one Kind of *metrum* or *Verfe* to another, as from *Jambick* to *Choraick :* And we may notice too, That in the more general Senfe, the *Rythmus* includes alfo their Dancings, and all the theatrical Action. I conclude therefore that their vocal *Mufick* confifted of Verfes, fet **to** *mufical Tones,* and fung by one or more

Voices

Voices in Choirs or alternately; fometimes with
and alfo without the Accompanyment of Inftruments: To which we may add, from the
laft Article, That their Symphonies confifted
only of feveral Voices performing the fame Song
in different Tones as *Unifon* and *Octave*. For
inftrumental Mufick (as I have defined it) 'tis not
fo very plain that they ufed any: And if
they did, 'tis more than probable the *Rythmus*
was only an Imitation of the poetical Numbers,
and confifted of no other Meafures than
what were taken from the Variety and Kinds of
their Verfes; of which they pretended a fufficient Variety for exprefling any Subject according to its Nature and Property: And fince the
chief Defign of their *Mufick* feems to have been
to move the Heart and Paffions, they needed
no other *Rythmus*. I cannot indeed deny that
there are many Paffages which fairly infinuate
their Practice upon Inftruments without Singing;
fo *Athenæus* fays, *The* Synaulia *was a Conteft
of Pipes performing alternately without finging.*
And *Quintilian* hath this Expreffion, *If the
Numbers and Airs of* Mufick *have fuch a Vertue, how much more ought eloquent Words to
have?* That is to fay, the other has Virtue
or Power to move us, without Refpect to the
Words. But if they had any *Rythmus* for inftrumental Performances, which was different
from that of their *poetical Meafures,* how
comes it to pafs that thofe Authors who have
been fo full in explaining the Signs by which
their Notes of *Mufick* were reprefented, fpeak
not

not a Word of the Signs of Time for Inftruments? Whatever be in this, it muft be owned that Singing with Words was the moft ancient Practice of *Mufick*, and the Practice of their more folemn and perfect Entertainments, as appears from all the Inftances above adduc ed, to prove the ancient Ufe and Efteem of *Mufick*: And that it was the univerfal and common Practice, even with the Vulgar, appears by the paftoral Dialogues of the Poets, where the Conteft is ordinarily about their Skill in *Mufick*, and chiefly in Singing.

LET us next confider what the prefent Practice (among *Europeans* at leaft) confifts of. We have, *firft*, vocal *Mufick* ; and this differs from the ancient in thefe Refpects, *viz.* That the Conftitution of the *Rythmus* is different from that of the Verfe, fo far, that in fetting Mufick to Words, the Thing principally minded is, to accommodate the long and fhort Notes to the Syllables in fuch Manner as the Words may be well feparated, and the accented Syllable of every Word fo confpicuous, that what is fung may be diftinctly underftood : The Movement and Meafure is alfo fuited to the different Subjects, for which the Variety of Notes, and the Conftitutions or Modes of Time explained in *Chap.* 12. afford fufficient means. Then we differ from the Ancients in our inftrumental Accompanyments, which compofe Symphonies with the Voice, fome in *Unifon*, others making a diftinct *Melody* ; which produces a ravifhing Entertainment they were not bleft with, or at leaft

with

without which we fhould think ours imperfect.
Then there is a delightful Mixture of pure inftrumental Symphonies, performed alternately
with the Song. *Laftly,* We have Compofitions
fitted altogether for Inftruments : The Defign
whereof is not fo much to move the Paffions, as
to entertain the Mind and pleafe the Fancy
with a Variety of Harmony and *Rythmus*; the
principal Effect of which is to raife Delight and
Admiration.   This is the plain State of the ancient and modern *Mufick*, in refpect of Practice:
But to determine which of them is moft perfect,
will not perhaps be fo eafily done to fatisfie
every Body.   Tho' we believe theirs to have
been excellent in its Kind, and to have had noble Effects ; this will not pleafe fome, unlefs we
acknowledge ours to be barbarous, and altogether ineffectual.   The Effects are indeed the
true Arguments ; but how fhall we compare
thefe, when there remain no Examples of ancient Compofition to judge by ? fo that the Defenders of the ancient *Mufick* admire a Thing
they don't know ; and in all Probability judge
not of the modern by their perfonal Acquaintance with it, but by their Fondnefs for their
own Notions.   Thofe who ftudy our *Mufick*,
and have well tuned Ears, can bear Witnefs
to its noble Effects: Yet perhaps it will be replied, *That this proceeds from a bad Tafte, and
fomething natural, in applauding the beft Thing
we know of any Kind.*   But let any Body produce a better, and we fhall heartily applaud it.
They bid us bring back the ancient *Muficians,*
and

and then they'll effectually shew us the Difference; and we bid them learn to understand the
modern Musick, and believe their own Senses:
In short we think we have better Reason to determine in our own Favours, from the Effects
we actually feel, than any Body can have from
a Thing they have no Experience of, and can
pretend to know no other Way than by Report:
But we shall consider the Pretences of each Par-
ty a little nearer. I have already observed, that
the principal End the Ancients proposed in
their *Musick,* was to move the Passions; and to
this purpose Poetry was a necessary Ingredient.
We have no Dispute about the Power of poetical Compositions to affect the Heart, and move
the Passions, by such a strong and lively Representation of their proper Objects, as that noble
Art is capable of : The Poetry of the Ancients
we own is admirable ; and their Verses being
sung with harmonious Cadences and Modulations, by a clear and sweet Voice, supported by
the agreeable Sound of some Instrument, in such
Manner that the Hearer understood every Word
that was said, which was all delivered with a
proper Action, *that is,* Pronunciation and Ges-
tures suitable to, or expressive of the Subject, as
we also suppose the Kind of Verse, and the
Modulation applied to it was; taking their vocal
Musick in this View, we make no Doubt that
it had admirable Effects in exciting Love, Pity,
Anger, Grief, or any Thing else the Poet had
a Mind to : But then they must be allowed to
affirm, who pretend to have the Experience of
it,

it, That the modern *Musick* taking it in the same Senſe, has all theſe Effects. *Whatever Truth* may be in it, I ſhall paſs what Doctor *Wallis* alledges, *viz. That theſe ancient Effects were moſt remarkably produced upon Ruſticks, and at a Time when* Muſick *was new, or a very rare Thing* : But I cannot however miſs to obſerve with him, That the Paſſions are eaſily wrought upon. The deliberate Reading of a Romance well written will produce Tears, Joy, or Indignation, if one gives his Imaginations a Looſe; but much more powerfully when attended with the Things mentioned : So that it can't be thought ſo very myſterious and wonderful an Art to excite Paſſion, as that it ſhould be quite loſt. Our Poets are capable to expreſs any moving Story in a very pathetick Manner: Our *Muſicians* too know how to apply a ſuitable Modulation and *Rythmus* : And we have thoſe who can put the Whole in Execution ; ſo that a Heart capable of being moved will be forced to own the wonderful Power of *modern Muſick* . The *Italian* and *Engliſh* Theatres afford ſufficient Proof of this ; ſo that I believe, were we to collect Examples of the Effects that the *acting of modern Tragedies* and *Operas* have produced, there would be no Reaſon to ſay we had loſt the Art of exciting Paſſion. But 'tis needleſs to inſiſt on a Thing which ſo many know by their own Experience. If ſome are obſtinate to affirm, *That we are ſtill behind the Ancients in this Art, becauſe they have never felt ſuch Effects of it;* I ſhall ask them if
they

they think every Temper and Mind among the Ancients was equally difposed to relifh, and be moved by the fame Things? If Tempers differed then, why may they not now, and yet the Art be at leaft as powerful as ever? Again have we not as good Reafon to believe thofe who affirm they feel this Influence, as you who fay you have never experienced it? And if you put the Matter altogether upon the Authority of others, pray, is not the Teftimony of the Living for the one, as good as that of the Dead for the other?

BUT ftill there are Wonders pretended to have been performed by the ancient *Mufick*, which we can produce nothing like; fuch as thofe amazing Tranfports of Mind, and hurrying of Men from one Paffion to another, all on a fudden, like the moving of a Machine, of which we have fo many Examples in Hiftory, *See Page* 495. For thefe I fhall anfwer, That what we reckon incredible in them may juftly be laid upon the Hiftorians, who frequently aggravate Things beyond what's ftriĉtly true, or even their Credulity in receiving them upon weak Grounds; and moft of thefe Stories are delivered to us by Writers who were not themfelves Witneffes of them, and had them only by Tradition and common Report. If nothing like this had ever been juftly objeĉted to the ancient Hiftorians, I fhould think my felf obliged to find another Anfwer: But fince 'tis fo, we may be allowed to doubt of thefe Faĉts, or fufpeĉt at leaft that they are in a great Degree *hyperbolical.* Confider but

the

Circumſtances of ſome of them as they are told,
and if they are literally true, and can be accounted for no other Way but by the Power of
Sound, I muſt own they had an Art which is
loſt: For *Example*, the quelling of a Sedition ;
let us repreſent to our ſelves a furious Rabble,
envenomed with Diſcontent, and enraged with
Oppreſſion ; or let the Grounds of their Rebel-
lion be as imaginary as you pleaſe, ſtill we muſt
conſider them as all in a Flame; ſuppoſe next
they are attacked by a skilful Muſician, who
addreſſes them with his Pipe or Lyre; how likely is it that he ſhall perſwade them by a Song
to return to their Obedience, and lay down their
Arms? Or rather how probable is it that he
may be torn to Pieces, as a ſolemn Mocker of
their juſt Reſentment? But that I may allow ſome
Foundation for ſuch a Story, I ſhall ſuppoſe
a Man of great Authority for Virtue, Wiſdom
and the Love of Mankind, comes to offer his
humble and affectionate Advice to ſuch a Company ; I ſuppoſe too, he delivers it in Verſe,
and perhaps ſings it to the Sound of his Lyre,
(which ſeems to have been a common Way of
delivering publick Exhortations in more ancient
Times, the *Muſick* being uſed as a Means to
gain their Attention.) I don't think it impoſſible that this Man may perſwade them to
Peace, by repreſenting the Danger they run,
aggravating the Miſchief they are like to bring
upon themſelves and the Society, or alſo correcting the falſe Views they may have had of
Things. But then will any Body ſay, all this
is

is the proper Effect of *Musick*, unless Reasoning be also a Part of it ? And must this be an *Example* of the Perfection of the ancient Art, and its Preference to ours ? In the same Manner may other Instances alledged be accounted for, such as *Pythagoras*'s diverting a young Man from the Execution of a wicked Design, the Reconcilement of Two inveterate Enemies, the curing of *Clytemnestra*'s vicious Inclinations, &c. *Horace*'s Explication of the Stories of *Orpheus* and *Amphion*, makes it probable we ought to explain all the rest the same Way. For the Story of *Timotheus* and *Alexander*, as commonly represented, it is indeed a very wonderful one, but I doubt we must here allow something to the Boldness or Credulity of the Historian : That *Timotheus*, by singing to his Lyre, with moving Gesture and Pronunciation, a well composed Poem of the Atchievements of some renowned Hero, as *Achilles*, might awaken *Alexander*'s natural Passion for warlike Glory, and make him express his Satisfaction with the Entertainment in a remarkable Manner, is nowise incredible : We are to consider too the Fondness he had for the *Iliad*, which would dispose him to be moved with any particular Story out of that : But how he should forget himself so far, as to commit Violence on his best Friend, is not so easily accounted for, unless we suppose him at that Time as much under the Power of *Bacchus* as of the *Muses* : And that a softer Theme sung with equal Art, should please a Hero who was

not

not infenfible of *Venus*'s Influences is no Myftery, efpecially when his Miftrefs was in Company: But there is nothing here above the Power
of modern *Poetry* and *Mufick,* where it meets
with a Subject the fame Way difpofed, to be
wrought upon. To make an End of this, I
muft obferve, that the Hiftorians, by faying too
much, have given us Ground to believe very
little. What do you think of curing a raging
Peftilence by *Mufick?* For curing the Bites of
Serpents, we cannot fo much doubt it, fince that
of the *Tarantula* has been cured in *Italy.* But
then they have no Advantage in this Inftance :
And wemuft mind too that this Cure is not performed by exquifite Art and Skill in *Mufick* ; it
does not require a *Correlli* or *Valentini,* but is
performed by Strains difcovered by random
Trials without any Rule : And this will ferve
for an Anfwer to all that's alledged of the Cure
of Difeafes by the ancient *Mufick.*

'T i s Time to bring this Comparifon to an
End ; and after what's explained I fhall make
no Difficulty to own, that I think the State of
Mufick is much more perfect now than it was
among the ancient *Greeks* and *Romans.* The
Art of *Mufick,* and the true Science of *Harmony* in Sounds is greatly improven. I have allowed their *Mufick* (including Poetry and the theatrical Action) to have been very moving ; but
at the fame Time I muft fay, their *Melody* has
been a very fimple Thing, as their *Syftem* or
Scale plainly fhews, whofe Difference from the
modern I have already explained.

And

And the confining all their *Rythmus* to the poetical Numbers, is to me another Proof of it,
and shews that there has been little Air in their
Musick; which by this appears to have been only
of the recitative Kind, *that is*, only a more
musical Speaking, or *modulated* Elocution; the
Character of which is to come near Nature, and
be only an Improvement of the natural Accents
of Words by more pathetick or emphatical *Tones*;
the Subject whereof may be either Verse or
Prose. And as to their Instruments of *Musick*, for any Thing that appears certain
and plain to us, they have been very simple.
Indeed the publick Laws in *Greece* gave
Check to the Improvement of the Art of *Harmony*, because they forbade all Innovations in
the primitive simple Musick; of which there are
abundance of Testimonies, some whereof have
been mentioned in this *Chapter*, and I shall add
what *Plato* says in his Treatise of the Laws,
viz. That they entertain'd not in the City the
Makers of such Instruments as have many Strings,
as the *Trigonus* and *Pectis*; but the *Lyra* and
Cithara they used, and allowed also some simple
Fistulæ in the Country. But 'tis certain, that
primitive Simplicity was altered; so that from
a very few Strings, they used a greater Number:
But there is much Uncertainty about the Use of
them, as whether it was for mixing their *Modes*,
and the *Genera*, or for striking Two Chords
together as in the *Magadis*. Since I have mentioned *Instruments*, I must observe Two Things,
First, That they pretend to have had *Tibiæ* of
di ffe-

different Kinds, whofe fpecifick Sounds were
excellently chofen for expreffing different Subjects. *Then,* there is a Defcription of the *Or-*
ganum hydraulicum in *Tertullian,* which fome
adduce to prove how perfect their *Inftruments*
were. — *Specta portentofam* Archimedis *muni-*
ficentiam ; organum hydraulicum dico, tot mem-
bra, tot partes, tot compagines, tot itinera
vocum, tot compendia fonorum, tot commercia
modorum, tot acies tibiarum, & una moles erunt
omnia ; where he had learnt this pompous Defcription of it I know not ; for one can get but
a very obfcure *Idea* of it from *Vitruvius,* even
after *Kircher* and *Voffius*'s Explications. But I
hope it will not be pretended to have been more
perfect than our modern Organs: And what have
they to compare of the ftringed Kind, with our
Harpfichords; and all the Inftruments that are
ftruck with a Bow ?

AFTER all, if our *Melody* or Songs are only e-
qual to the Ancients, I hope the Art of *Mufick* is
not loft as fome pretend. But then, what an Improvement in the Knowledge of pure *Harmony*
has been made, fince the Introduction of the modern *Symphonies?* Here it is, that the Mind is ra-
vifhed with the Agreement of Things feemingly
contrary to one another. We have here a Kind
of Imitation of the Works of Nature, where different Things are wonderfully joyned in one
harmonious Unity : And as fome Things appear
at firft View the fartheft removed from Symmetry and Order, which from the Courfe of Things
we learn to be abfolutely neceffary for the Perfection

on and Beauty of the Whole ; fo *Difcords* being artfully mixed with *Concords*, make a more perfect Compofition, which furprifes us with Delight. If the Mind is naturally pleafed with perceiving of Order and Proportion, with comparing feveral Things together, and difcerning in the midft of a feeming Confufion, the moft perfect and exact Difpofition and united Agreement; then the modern *Concerts* muft undoubtedly be allowed to be Entertainments worthy of our Natures : And with the Harmony of the Whole we muft confider the furprifing Variety of Air, which the modern *Conftitutions* and *Modes* of *Time* or *Rythmus* afford; by which, in our inftrumental Performances, the Senfe and Imagination are fo mightily charmed. Now, this is an Application of Mufick to a quite different Purpofe from that of moving Paffion : But is it reafonable upon that Account, to call it idle and infignificant, as fome do, who I therefore fufpect are ignorant of it ? It was certainly a noble Ufe of *Mufick* to make it fubfervient to Morality and Virtue ; and if we apply it lefs that Way, I believe 'tis becaufe we have lefs Need of fuch Allurements to our Duty : But whatever be the Reafon of this, 'tis enough to the prefent Argument, that our *Mufick* is at leaft not inferior to the ancient in the pathetick Kind : And if it be not a low and unworthy Thing for us to be pleafed with Proportion and Harmony, in which there is properly an intellectual Beauty, then it muft be confeffed, that the modern *Mufick* is more perfect than the ancient. But why
muft

muft the moving of particular Paffions be the
only Ufe of *Mufick ?* If we look upon a noble
Building, or a curious Painting, we are allowed
to admire the Defign, and view all its Proportions and Relation of Parts with Pleafure to
our Underftandings, without any refpect to the
Paffions. We muft obferve again, that there is
fcarce any Piece of *Melody* that has not fome
general Influence upon the Heart ; and by being
more fprightly or heavy in its Movements, will
have different Effects; tho' it is not defigned to
excite any particular Paffion, and can only be faid
in general to give Pleafure, and recreate the
Mind. But whyfhould we difpute about a Thing
which only Strangers to *Mufick* can fpeak ill of?
And for the *Harmony* of different Parts, the Defenders of the ancient *Mufick* own it to be a valuable Art, by their contending for its beingan-
cient : Let me therefore again affirm, that the
Moderns have wonderfully improven the Art of
Mufick. It muft be acknowledged indeed, that
to judge well, and have a true Relifh of our
more elaborate and complex *Mufick,* or to be
fenfible of its Beauty, and taken with it, requires
a peculiar Genius, and much Experience, without which it will feem only a confufed Noife ;
but I hope this is no Fault in the Thing. If
one altogether ignorant of Painting looks
upon the moft curious Piece, wherein he finds
nothing extraordinary moving to him, becaufe
the Excellency of it may ly in the Defign and
admirable Proportion and Situation of the Parts
which he takes no Notice of : Muft we therefore

fore fay, it has nothing valuable in it, and capable to give Pleafure to a better Judge ? What, in *Mufick* or *Painting*, would feem intricate and confufed, and fo give no Satisfaction to the unskilled, will ravifh with Admiration and Delight, one who is able to unravel all the Parts, obferve their Relations and the united *Concord* of the Whole. But now, if this be fuch a real and valuable Improvement in *Mufick*, you'll ask, How it can be thought the Ancients could be ignorant of it, and fatisfy themfelves with fuch a fimple *Mufick*, when we confider their great Perfection in the Sifter Arts of Poetry and Painting, and all other Sciences. I fhall anfwer this by asking again, How it comes that the Ancients left us any thing to invent or improve ? And how comes it that different Ages and Nations have Genius and Fondnefs for different Things. The Ancients ftudied only how to move the Heart, to which a great many Things neceffarily concurred, as *Words*, *Tune* and *Action*; and by thefe we can ftill produce the fame Effects ; but we have alfo a new Art, whofe End is rather to entertain the Underftanding, than to move particular Paffions. What Connection there is betwixt their improving other Sciences and this, is not fo plain as to make any certain Conclufion from it. And as to their *Painting*, there have been very good Reafons alledged to prove, That they followed the fame Tafte there as in the *Mufick*, *i. e.* the fimple obvious Beauties, of which every Body might judge and be fenfible. Their End was to pleafe and move the People, which is
bet-

better done by the Senses and the Heart than by the Understanding ; and when they found sufficient Means to accomplish this, why should we wonder that they proceeded no further, especially when to have gone much beyond, would likely have losed their Design. But, say you, this looks as if they had been sensible there were Improvements of another Kind to be made : Suppose it was so, yet they might stop when, their principal End was obtained. And *Plutarch* says as much, for he tells us it was not Ignorance that made the ancient Musick so simple, but it was so out of Politick : Yet he complains, that in his own Time, the very Memory of the ancient Modes that had been so useful in the Education of Youth, and moving the Passions was lost thro' the Innovations and luxurious Variety introduced by later Musicians ; and now, when a full Liberty seems to have been taken, may we not wonder that so little Improvement was made, or at least so little of it explained and recorded to us by these who wrote of Musick, after such Innovations were so far advanced.

I shall end this Dispute, which is perhaps too tedious already, with a short Consideration of what the boldest Accuser of the modern *Musick,* *Isaac Vossius,* says against it, in his Book *de poematum cantu & viribus Rythmi.* He observes, what a wonderful Power Motion has upon the Mind, by Communication with the Body; how we are pleased with *rythmical* or *regular Motion* ; then he observes, that the ancient *Greeks* and *Latins* perceiving this, took an infinite

Paius

Pains to cultivate their Language, and make it as harmonious, especially in what related to the *Rythmus*, or Number, and Combination of long and short Syllables, as possible ; to this End particularly were the *pedes metrici* invented, which are the Foundations of their Versification; and this he owns was the only *Rythmus* of their *Musick*, and so powerful, that the whole Effect of *Musick* was ascribed to it, as appears, says he, by this Saying of theirs, τὸ πᾶν παρὰ μουσι-κοῖς ὁ ρυθμὸς : And to prove the Power attributed to the *Rythmus*, he cites several other Passages. That it gives Life to *Musick*, especially the *pathetick*, will not be denied; and we see the Power of it even in plain Prose and Oratory : But to make it the *Whole*, is perhaps attributing more than is due : I rather reckon the Words and Sense of what's sung, the principal Ingredient; and the other a noble Servant to them, for raising and keeping up the Attention, because of the natural Pleasure annexed to these Sensations. 'Tis very true, that there is a Connection betwixt certain Passions, which we call Motions of the Mind, and certain Motions in our Bodies; and when by any external Motion these can be imitated and excited, no doubt we shall be much moved; and the Mind, by that Influence, becomes either gay, soft, brisk or drowsy : But how any particular Passion can be excited without such a lively Representation of its proper Object, as only Words afford, is not very intelligible ; at least this appears to me the most just and effectual Way. But let us

the

hear what Notion others had of this Matter, *Quintilian* fays, *If the Numbers of Mufick have fuch Influence, how much more ought eloquent Words to have ?* And in all the ancient *Mufick* the greateft Care was taken, that not a Syllable of the Words fhould be loft, for fpoiling the Senfe, which *Voffius* himfelf obferves and owns. *Pancirollus,* who thinks the Art loft, afcribes the chief Virtue of it to the Words. — *Siquidem una cum melodia integra percipiebantur verba :* And the very Reafon he gives, that the modern *Mufick* is lefs perfect, is, that we hear Sounds without Words, by which fays he, the ear is a little pleafed, without any Entertainment to the Underftanding: But all this has been confidered already. *Voffius* alledges the *mimick* Art, to prove, that the Power of Motion was equal to the moft eloquent Words ; but we fhall be as much ftraitned to believe this, as the reft of their Wonders.   Let them believe it who will, that a *Pantomime* had Art to make himfelf eafily underftood without Words, by People of all Languages: And that *Rofcius* the Comedian, could exprefs any Sentence by his Geftures, as fignificantly and varioufly, as *Cicero* with all his Oratory.   Whatever this Art was, 'tis loft, and perhaps it was fomething very furprifing ; but 'tis hard to believe thefe Stories literally.   However to the Thing in Hand, we are concerned only to confider the *mufical* or *poetical Rythmus.*

Voffius fays, that *Rythmus* which does not contain and exprefs the very Forms and Figures of

of Things, can have no Effect ; and that the
ancient poetical Numbers alone are juftly contrived for this End.   And therefore the modern
Languages and Verfe are altogether unfit for
Mufick; and we fhall never have, fays he, any
right *vocal Mufick*, till our Poets learn to make
Verfes that are capable to be fung, *that is*, as
he explains it, till we new model our Languages, reftore the ancient metrical Feet, and ba-
nifh our barbarous Rhimes.   Our Verfes, fays
he, run all as it were on one Foot, without Diftinction of Members and Parts, in which the
Beauty of Proportion is to be found ; therefore
he reckons, that we have no *Rythmus* at all in
our Poetry; and affirms, that we mind nothing
but to have fuch a certain Number of Syllables
in a Verfe, of whatever Nature, and in whatever Order.   Now, what a rafh and unjuft Cri-
ticifm is this! if it was fo in his Mother Tongue, the *Dutch*, I know not; but I'm certain it
is otherwife in *Englifh*. 'Tis true, we don't follow the metricalCompofition of the Ancients ;yet
we have fuch a Mixture of ftrong and foft, long
and fhort Syllables, as makes our Verfes flow,
rapid, fmooth, or rumbling, agreeable to the
Subject.   Take any good *Englifh* Verfe, and by
a very fmall Change in the Tranfpofition of a
Word or Syllable, any Body who has an Ear
will find, that we make a very great Matter of
the *Nature* and *Order* of the Syllables.   But
why muft the ancient be the only proper *Metre*
for *Poetry* and *Mufick*? He fays, their *Odes* were
fung, as to the *Rythmus*, in the fame Manner

as

as we scan them, every *pes* being a distinct Bar
or Measure, separate by a distinct Pause ; but in
the bare Reading, that Distinction was not accurately observed, the Verse being read in a
more continuous Manner. Again he notices,
that after the Change of the ancient Pronunciation, and the Corruption of their Language,
the *Musick* decayed till it became a poor and in-
significant Art. Their *Odes* had a regular Return of the same Kind of Verse ; and the same
Quantity of Syllables in the same Place of every
similar Verse : But there's nothing, says he, but
Confusion of Quantities in the modern *Odes*; so
that to follow the natural Quantity of our Syllables, every Stanza will be a different Song, o-
therwise than in the ancient Verses : (He
should have minded, that every Kind of *Ode* was
not of this Nature; and how heroick Verses
were sung, if this was necessary, I cannot see,
because in them the *Dactylus* and *Spondeus* are
sometimes in one Place of the Verse, and sometimes in another.) But instead of this, he says,
the *Moderns* have no Regard to the natural
Quantity of the Syllables, and have introduced
an unnatural and barbarous Variety of long and
short Notes, which they apply without any Regard to the Subject and Sense of the Verse, or
the natural Pronunciation : So that nothing
can be understood that's sung, unless one knows
it before; and therefore, no wonder, says he, that
our *vocal Musick* has no Effects. Now here is indeed a heavy Charge, but Experience gives me
Authority to affirm it to be absolutely false. We
have

have *vocal Mufick* as pathetick as ever the ancient was. If any Singer don't pronounce intelligibly, that is not the Fault of the *Mufick,* which is always fo contrived, as the Senfe of the Words may be diftinctly perceived. But this is impoffible, fays he, if we don't follow the natural Pronunciation and Quantity; which is I think, precarioufly faid; for was the Singing of the ancient *Odes* by feparate and diftinct Meafures of metrical Feet, in which there muft frequently be a Stop in the very Middle of a Word, Was this I fay the natural Pronunciation, and the Way to make what was fung beft underftood? Himfelf tells us, they read their Poems otherwife. And if Practice would make that diftinct enough to them, will it not be as fufficient in the other Cafe. Again, to argue from what's ftrictly natural, will perhaps be no Advantage to their Caufe; for don't we know, that the Ancients admitted the moft unnatural Pofitions of Words, for the fake of a numerous Stile, even in plain Profe; and took ftill greater Liberties in Poetry, to depart from the natural Order in which Ideas ly in our Mind; far otherwife than it is in the modern Languages, which will therefore be moe eafily and readily underftood in Singing, if pronounced diftinctly, than the ancient Verfe could be, wherein the Conftruction of the Words was more difficult to find, becaufe of the Tranfpofitions. Again the Difference of long and fhort Syllables in common Speaking, is not accurately obferved; not even in the ancient Languages; for *Example,* in common Speaking,

who

who can diftinguifh the long and fhort Syllables
in thef e Words, *fatis, nivis, mifit.* The Senfe
of a Word generally depends upon the right Pronunciation of one Syllable, or Two at moft in
very long Words; and if thefe are made confpicuous, and the Words well feparated by a
right Application of the long and fhort Notes,
as we certainly know to be done, then we follow the natural Pronunciation more this Way
than the other. If 'tis replied, that fince we
pretend to a poetical *Rythmus,* fuitable to different Subjects, why don't we follow it in our
Mufick ? I fhall anfwer, that tho' that *Rythmus* is more diftinguifhed in the Recitation of
Poems, yet our *mufical Rythmus* is accommo-
dated alfo to it; but with fuch Liberty as is neceffary to make good *Melody ;* and even to
produce ftronger Effects than a fimple Reciting
can do; and I would ask, for what other Rea-
fonthe Ancients fung their Poems in a Manner
different from the bare reading of them? Still
he tells us, that we want the true *Rythmus,* which
can only make pathetick *Mufick;* and if there
is any Thing moving in our Songs, he fays,
'tis only owing to the Words ; fo that Profe
may be fung as well as Verfe: That the Words
ought naturally to have the greateft Influence,
has been already confidered; and I have feen
no Reafon why the ancient poetical *Rythmus*
fhould have the only Claim to be pathetick;
as if they had exhaufted all the Combinations
of long and fhort Sounds, that can be moving
or agreeable : But indeed the Queftion is a-
bout

about Matter of Fact, therefore I shall appeal to Experience, and leave it; after I have minded you, that by this Defence of the *modern Musick*, I don't say it is all alike good, or that there can be no just Objection laid against any of our Compositions, especially in the setting of *Musick* to Words; I only say, we have admirable Compositions, and that the Art of *Musick*, taken in all that it is capable of, is more perfect than it was among the old *Greeks* and *Romans*, at least for what can possibly be made appear.

F I N I S.

Plate.1

Fig.7 / Scale with Examples of Notes and Clefs

Treble. Mean. Bass.

e.d.
c.b
a.g
f.e
d.c.
b.c
g.f
e.d.
a.b
f.e.
d.c.
b.a
g.a.
e.d.
c.b
a.g

Sign'd Clefs

Treble. Mean. Bass.

Fig.8

f.e.c
b.c
d.e.f
d

Fig.6

C.g.c*:d:d*.e:f.f*.g.g*.a:a*.b:c.c*:d:d*. e:f.f*

Fig.5 / Table of All ye Simple Manual ratios in the Diatonick Scale

						1/2
15th	a	1/4				8/15
14th	B	4/15			1/2	3/5
13th	A	3/10		1/2	9/16	5/8
12th	G	1/3		5/9	5/8	2/3
11th	F	3/8	1/2	9/16	5/8	3/4
10th	E	2/5	8/15	3/5	2/3	4/5
9th	D	4/9	1/2	9/16	20/27	5/6
8th	C	1/2	9/16	5/8	3/4	5/6
7th	b	8/15	3/5	2/3	3/4	8/9
6th	a	3/5	27/40	3/4	9/10	J
5th	g	2/3	3/4	5/6	9/10	J
4th	f	3/4	27/32	15/16	J	
3d	e	4/5	9/10	J		
2d	d	8/9	J			
fund	C	J				

Fig.1

A — — B
D
a.

Fig.2

Tensions
9
4
4

Lengths
C 3
A 3
B 2

Fig.3

diameter 2
(A) 3
(B) 3
(C) 2
Tension 9
9
4

Fig.4

360:300:288:270:240:225:216:180

4th 3+ 3+ 4th
3+ 4th 5th 6th 6th 8+
4+ 4+ 5th 6th 64

Plate 2   Fig. 1.

Universal Table of the Signatures of Clefs; Shewing how to transpose from any key to any other; And how to Sol-fa Any Song.

Sem:	fa	c	d♭	d	e♭	e	f	g♭	g	a♭	a♭	b	8ve	3ᵈ L
tone	mi	b	c	c♯	d	d♯	e	f	f♯	g	g♯	a a♯	7ᵗʰ g	2ᵈ g
tone	la	a♭	b	c	c♯	d	e♭	e	f	f♯	g	g♯	6ᵗʰ g	Fund
tone	Sol	g	a♭	a♭	b	c	d♭	d	e♭	e	f	f♯	5ᵗʰ	7ᵗʰ L
Sem.	fa	f	g♭	g	a♭	a♭	b	c♭	c	d♭	d	e♭ e	4ᵗʰ	6ᵗʰ L
tone	la	e	f	f♯	g	g♯	a♭	b	c	c♯	d	d♯	3ᵈ g	5ᵗʰ
tone	Sol	d	e♭	e	f	f♯	g	a♭	a♭	b	c	c♯	2ᵈ g	4ᵗʰ
	fa	c	d♭	d e♭	e	e	f	g♭	g	a♭	a♭	b	Fund	3ᵈ L

Sharp key   Flat key

fig. 2 / **Table of False Intervals in the Hemitonick Scale**

Ratios $\overbrace{3^d : \; 6^{th}}^{8ve}$ *Ratios*

64:75 = $\overbrace{c* - e - c*}$ = 75:128 . e

id = d* – f* – d* = idem .

id = g* – b – g* = id

27:32 = d – f – d = 16 : 27 . e

id = f* – a – f* = id .

id . = g – b – g = id .

_____

$\overbrace{3^d g \quad 6^{th} \int}$

25:32 = $\overbrace{e – g* – e}$ = 16 : 25 . d

id = a – c* – a = id .

id = b – d – b = id .

405:512 = f* – b – f* = 256 : 405 . d

64:81 = b – d – b = 81 : 128 . d

_____

$\overbrace{4^{th} : 5^{th}}$

512:675 = $\overbrace{c* – f* – c*}$ = 675 : 1024 . e

20:27 = a – d – a = 27 : 40 . d

id = b – d* – b = id

_____

$\overbrace{Tritone \quad Tritone}$

32:45 = $\overbrace{c – f* – c}$ = 45 : 64

id = c* – g – c* = ia

id = f – b – f = id

id = g* d – g* = id

id = a* – e – a* = id

25 36 = a – d* – a = 18 : 25

fig 3/ Names, Figures and proportions of Notes.

Ex.a 1
Adagio
Ex.a 2
Allegro
Ex. 3d
Allegro
Ex. 3d transposd
Allegro
Ex. 4th
Allegro
Ex. 5th
Adagio
Ex. 5th. transposd.
Adagio
Ex. 6th.
Largo
Ex.a 7th.
Vivace
Ex. 8th.
Allegro
Ex. 9th.
Allegro
Ex. 10
Allegro
Ex. 11.
Allegro

Plate 4th.
Exe 1.
Ex. 2.
Ex. 3.
Ex. 4.
Ex. 5 th
Ex. 6.
Ex. 7
Ex. 8
8 5 3 maj. 3 Min 3 6 3 6 3 6 5 3 3
Key. f
2d f
3d f
4th. f
Ex 9
Ex. 10
Ex. 11
Ex. 12
5 3 5 6 3 5 6 3 3 6 5♭
5th f
6th f
7th f
Ex. 13.
Ex. 14.
Ex. 15.
Ex. 16
bad bad bad bad good bad good good
Ex. 17
Ex. 18.
Ex. 19. first Lesson.

(Exe.19) 1st Lesson, transported to a flat-key.   Plate 5.

Ex. 19. 2d. Lesson.

2d. Lesson, transported to a flat-key.

Ex. 20   21

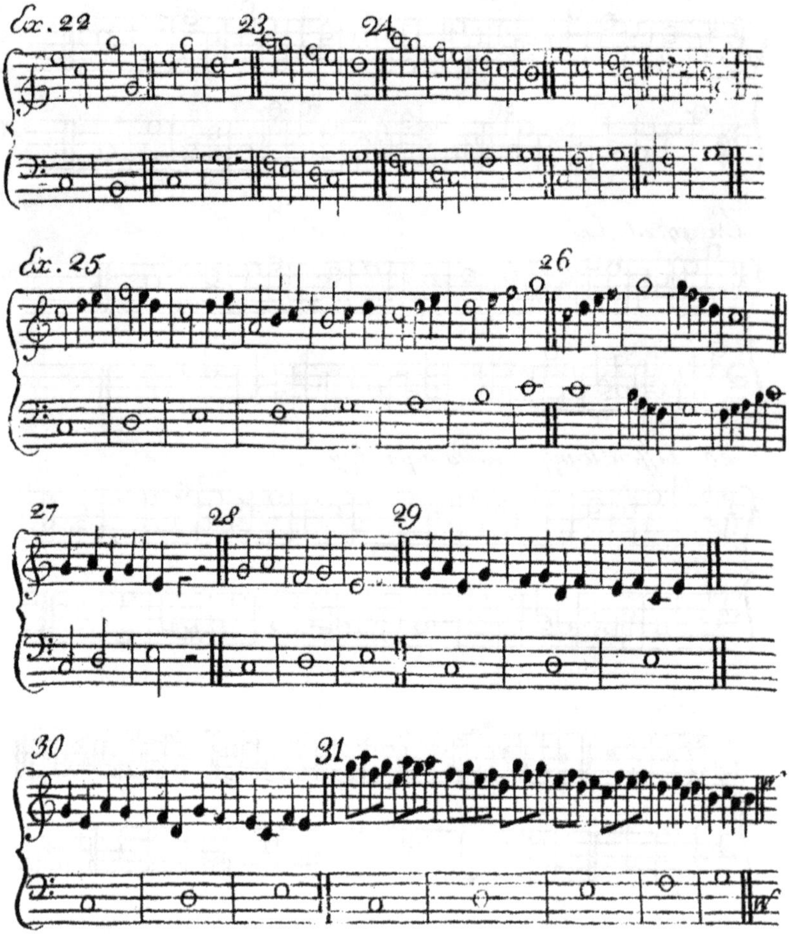
Ex. 22
23
24
Ex. 25
26
27
28
29
30
31

Plate 6.th

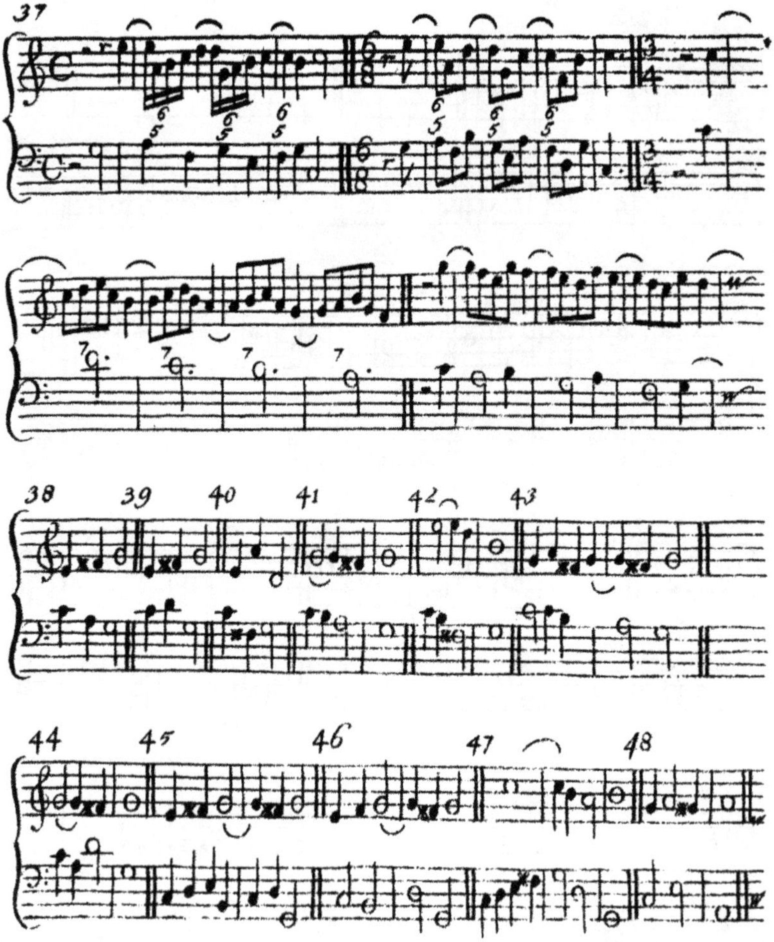
37
38
39
40
41
42
43
44
45
46
47
48

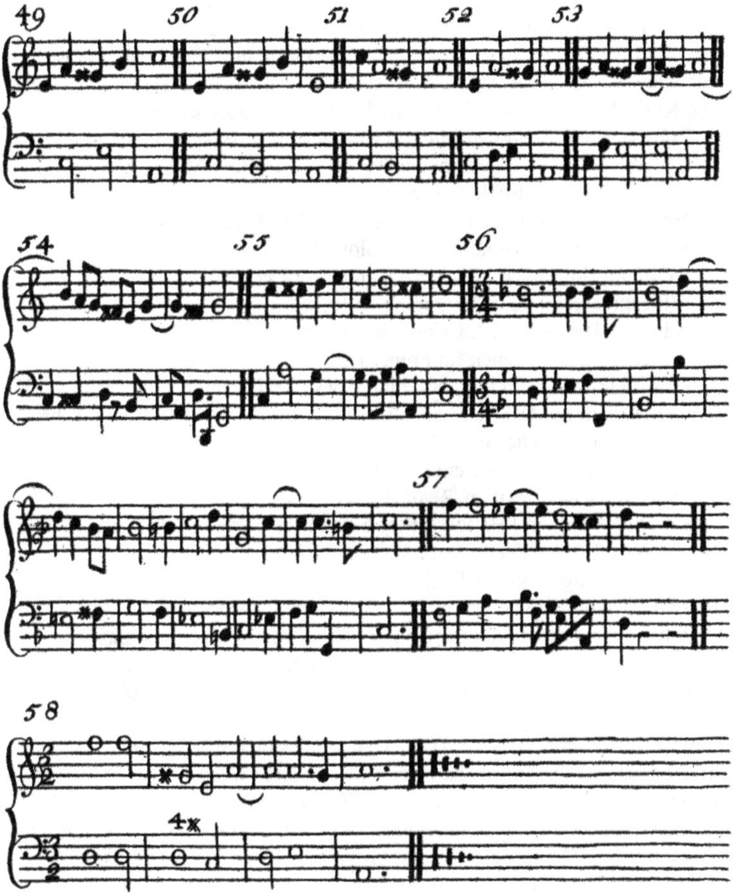
49
50
51
52
53
54
55
56
57
58
4♯

Music and Books published by Travis & Emery Music Bookshop:

Anon.: Hymnarium Sarisburiense, cum Rubricis et Notis Musicis.
Anon.: Säcularfeier des Geburtstages von Ludwig van Beethoven
Agricola, Johann Friedrich from Tosi: Anleitung zur Singkunst.
Bach, C.P.E.: edited W. Emery: Nekrolog or Obituary Notice of J.S. Bach.
Bateson, Naomi Judith: Alcock of Salisbury
Bathe, William: A Briefe Introduction to the Skill of Song
Bax, Arnold: Symphony #5, Arranged for Piano Four Hands by Walter Emery
Burney, Charles: The Present State of Music in France and Italy
Burney, Charles: The Present State of Music in Germany, The Netherlands …
Burney, Charles: An Account of the Musical Performances ... Handel
Burney, Karl: Nachricht von Georg Friedrich Handel's Lebensumstanden.
Burns, Robert: The Caledonian Musical Museum ..The Best Scotch Songs. (1810)
Cobbett, W.W.: Cobbett's Cyclopedic Survey of Chamber Music. (2 vols.)
Corrette, Michel: Le Maitre de Clavecin
Crimp, Bryan: Dear Mr. Rosenthal … Dear Mr. Gaisberg …
Crimp, Bryan: Solo: The Biography of Solomon
Crotch, William: Substance of Several Courses of Lectures on Music
d'Indy, Vincent: Beethoven: Biographie Critique
d'Indy, Vincent: Beethoven: A Critical Biography
d'Indy, Vincent: César Franck (in French)
Fischhof, Joseph: Versuch einer Geschichte des Clavierbaues. (Faksimile 1853).
Frescobaldi, Girolamo: D'Arie Musicali per Cantarsi. Primo & Secondo Libro.
Geminiani, Francesco: The Art of Playing the Violin.
Handel; Purcell; Boyce; Geene et al: Calliope or English Harmony: Volume First.
Häuser: Musikalisches Lexikon. 2 vols in one.
Hawkins, John: A General History of the Science and Practice of Music (5 vols.)
Herbert-Caesari, Edgar: The Science and Sensations of Vocal Tone
Herbert-Caesari, Edgar: Vocal Truth
Hopkins and Rimboult: The Organ. Its History and Construction.
Hunt, John: - see separate list of discographies at the end of these titles
Isaacs, Lewis: Hänsel and Gretel. A Guide to Humperdinck's Opera.
Isaacs, Lewis: Königskinder (Royal Children) A Guide to Humperdinck's Opera.
Kastner: Manuel Général de Musique Militaire
Lacassagne, M. l'Abbé Joseph : Traité Général des élémens du Chant.
Lascelles (née Catley), Anne: The Life of Miss Anne Catley.
Mainwaring, John: Memoirs of the Life of the Late George Frederic Handel
Malcolm, Alexander: A Treaty of Music: Speculative, Practical and Historical
Marx, Adolph Bernhard: Die Kunst des Gesanges, Theoretisch-Practisch
May, Florence: The Life of Brahms
May, Florence: The Girlhood Of Clara Schumann: Clara Wieck And Her Time.
Mellers, Wilfrid: Angels of the Night: Popular Female Singers of Our Time
Mellers, Wilfrid: Bach and the Dance of God
Mellers, Wilfrid: Beethoven and the Voice of God
Mellers, Wilfrid: Caliban Reborn - Renewal in Twentieth Century Music
Mellers, Wilfrid: Darker Shade of Pale, A Backdrop to Bob Dylan

Music and Books published by Travis & Emery Music Bookshop:

Mellers, Wilfrid: François Couperin and the French Classical Tradition

Mellers, Wilfrid: Harmonious Meeting

Mellers, Wilfrid: Le Jardin Retrouvé, The Music of Frederic Mompou

Mellers, Wilfrid: Music and Society, England and the European Tradition

Mellers, Wilfrid: Music in a New Found Land: ... ... American Music

Mellers, Wilfrid: Romanticism and the Twentieth Century (from 1800)

Mellers, Wilfrid: The Masks of Orpheus: ...... the Story of European Music.

Mellers, Wilfrid: The Sonata Principle (from c. 1750)

Mellers, Wilfrid: Vaughan Williams and the Vision of Albion

Panchianio, Cattuffio: Rutzvanscad Il Giovine

Pearce, Charles: Sims Reeves, Fifty Years of Music in England.

Playford, John: An Introduction to the Skill of Musick.

Purcell, Henry et al: Harmonia Sacra ... The First Book, (1726)

Purcell, Henry et al: Harmonia Sacra ... Book II (1726)

Quantz, Johann: Versuch einer Anweisung die Flöte trave rsiere zu spielen.

Rameau, Jean-Philippe: Code de Musique Pratique, ou Methodes.

Rameau, Jean-Philippe: Erreurs sur La Musique dans l'Encyclopédie

Rastall, Richard: The Notation of Western Music.

Rimbault, Edward: The Pianoforte, Its Origins, Progress, and Construction.

Rousseau, Jean Jacques: Dictionnaire de Musique

Rubinstein, Anton : Guide to the proper use of the Pianoforte Pedals.

Sainsbury, John S.: Dictionary of Musicians. (1825). 2 vols.

Serré de Rieux, Jean de : Les dons des Enfans de Latone

Simpson, Christopher: A Compendium of Practical Musick in Five Parts

Spohr, Louis: Autobiography

Spohr, Louis: Grand Violin School

Tans'ur, William: A New Musical Grammar; or The Harmonical Spectator

Terry, Charles Sanford: Bach's Chorals – Parts 1, 2 and 3.

Terry, Charles Sanford: John Christian Bach

Terry, Charles Sanford: J.S. Bach's Original Hymn-Tunes for Congregational Use.

Terry, Charles Sanford: Four-Part Chorals of J.S. Bach. (German & English)

Terry, Charles Sanford: Joh. Seb. Bach, Cantata Texts, Sacred and Secular.

Terry, Charles Sanford: The Origins of the Family of Bach Musicians.

Tosi, Pierfrancesco: Opinioni de' Cantori Antichi, e Moderni

Tosi, Pierfrancesco: Observations on the Florid Song.

Van der Straeten, Edmund: History of the Violoncello, The Viol da Gamba ...

Van der Straeten, Edmund: History of the Violin, Its Ancestors... (2 vols.)

Walther, J. G. [Waltern]: Musicalisches Lexikon [Musikalisches Lexicon]

Wagner, Richard: Beethoven (Leipzig 1870)

Wagner, Richard: Lebens-Bericht (Leipzig 1884)

Wagner, Richard: The Musaic of the Future (Translated by E. Dannreuther).

Zwirn, Gerald: Stranded Stories From The Operas

Travis & Emery Music Bookshop

17 Cecil Court, London, WC2N 4EZ, United Kingdom.
Tel. (+44) 20 7240 2129

© Travis & Emery 2010

Discographies by Travis & Emery:

Discographies by John Hunt.

1987: 978-1-906857-14-1: From Adam to Webern: the Recordings of von Karajan.

1991: 978-0-951026-83-0: 3 Italian Conductors and 7 Viennese Sopranos: 10 Discographies: Arturo Toscanini, Guido Cantelli, Carlo Maria Giulini, Elisabeth Schwarzkopf, Irmgard Seefried, Elisabeth Gruemmer, Sena Jurinac, Hilde Gueden, Lisa Della Casa, Rita Streich.

1992: 978-0-951026-85-4: Mid-Century Conductors and More Viennese Singers: 10 Discographies: Karl Boehm, Victor De Sabata, Hans Knappertsbusch, Tullio Serafin, Clemens Krauss, Anton Dermota, Leonie Rysanek, Eberhard Waechter, Maria Reining, Erich Kunz.

1993: 978-0-951026-87-8: More 20th Century Conductors: 7 Discographies: Eugen Jochum, Ferenc Fricsay, Carl Schuricht, Felix Weingartner, Josef Krips, Otto Klemperer, Erich Kleiber.

1994: 978-0-951026-88-5: Giants of the Keyboard: 6 Discographies: Wilhelm Kempff, Walter Gieseking, Edwin Fischer, Clara Haskil, Wilhelm Backhaus, Artur Schnabel.

1994: 978-0-951026-89-2: Six Wagnerian Sopranos: 6 Discographies: Frieda Leider, Kirsten Flagstad, Astrid Varnay, Martha Moedl, Birgit Nilsson, Gwyneth Jones.

1995: 978-0-952582-70-0: Musical Knights: 6 Discographies: Henry Wood, Thomas Beecham, Adrian Boult, John Barbirolli, Reginald Goodall, Malcolm Sargent.

1995: 978-0-952582-71-7: A Notable Quartet: 4 Discographies: Gundula Janowitz, Christa Ludwig, Nicolai Gedda, Dietrich Fischer-Dieskau.

1996: 978-0-952582-75-5: Leopold Stokowski (1882-1977): Discography and Concert Register

1996: 978-0-952582-76-2: Makers of the Philharmonia: 11 Discographies: Alceo Galliera, Walter Susskind, Paul Kletzki, Nicolai Malko, Issay Dobrowen, Lovro Von Matacic, Efrem Kurtz, Otto Ackermann, Anatole Fistoulari, George Weldon, Robert Irving.

1996: 978-0-952582-72-4: The Post-War German Tradition: 5 Discographies: Rudolf Kempe, Joseph Keilberth, Wolfgang Sawallisch, Rafael Kubelik, Andre Cluytens.

1996: 978-0-952582-73-1: Teachers and Pupils: 7 Discographies: Elisabeth Schwarzkopf, Maria Ivoguen, Maria Cebotari, Meta Seinemeyer, Ljuba Welitsch, Rita Streich, Erna Berger.

1996: 978-0-952582-75-5: Leopold Stokowski: Discography and Concert Listing.

1996: 978-0-952582-76-2: Makers of the Philharmonia: 11 Discographies Alceo Galliera, Walter Susskind, Paul Kletzki, Nicolai Malko, Issay Dobrowen, Lovro Von Matacic, Efrem Kurtz, Otto Ackermann, Anatole Fistoulari, George Weldon, Robert Irving.

1996: 978-0-952582-77-9: Tenors in a Lyric Tradition: 3 Discographies: Peter Anders, Walther Ludwig, Fritz Wunderlich.

1997: 978-0-952582-78-6: The Lyric Baritone: 5 Discographies: Hans Reinmar, Gerhard Huesch, Josef Metternich, Hermann Uhde, Eberhard Waechter.

1997: 978-0-952582-79-3: Hungarians in Exile: 3 Discographies: Fritz Reiner, Antal Dorati, George Szell.

1997: 978-1-901395-00-6: The Art of the Diva: 3 Discographies: Claudia Muzio, Maria Callas, Magda Olivero.

1997: 978-1-901395-01-3: Metropolitan Sopranos: 4 Discographies: Rosa Ponselle, Eleanor Steber, Zinka Milanov, Leontyne Price.

1997: 978-1-901395-02-0: Back From The Shadows: 4 Discographies: Willem Mengelberg, Dimitri Mitropoulos, Hermann Abendroth, Eduard Van Beinum.

1997: 978-1-901395-03-7: More Musical Knights: 4 Discographies: Hamilton Harty, Charles Mackerras, Simon Rattle, John Pritchard.

1998: 978-1-901395-95-2: More Giants of the Keyboard: 5 Discographies: Claudio Arrau, Gyorgy Cziffra, Vladimir Horowitz, Dinu Lipatti, Artur Rubinstein.

1998: 978-1-901395-94-5: Conductors On The Yellow Label: 8 Discographies: Fritz Lehmann, Ferdinand Leitner, Ferenc Fricsay, Eugen Jochum, Leopold Ludwig, Artur Rother, Franz Konwitschny, Igor Markevitch.

1998: 978-1-901395-96-9: Mezzo and Contraltos: 5 Discographies: Janet Baker, Margarete Klose, Kathleen Ferrier, Giulietta Simionato, Elisabeth Hoengen.

1999: 978-1-901395-97-6: The Furtwaengler Sound Sixth Edition: Discography and Concert Listing.

1999: 978-1-901395-98-3: The Great Dictators: 3 Discographies: Evgeny Mravinsky, Artur Rodzinski, Sergiu Celibidache.

1999: 978-1-901395-99-0: Sviatoslav Richter: Pianist of the Century: Discography.

2000: 978-1-901395-04-4: Philharmonic Autocrat 1: Discography of: Herbert Von Karajan [Third Edition].

2000: 978-1-901395-05-1: Wiener Philharmoniker 1 - Vienna Philharmonic and Vienna State Opera Orchestras: Discography Part 1 1905-1954.

2000: 978-1-901395-06-8: Wiener Philharmoniker 2 - Vienna Philharmonic and Vienna State Opera Orchestras: Discography Part 2 1954-1989.

2001: 978-1-901395-07-5: Gramophone Stalwarts: 3 Separate Discographies: Bruno Walter, Erich Leinsdorf, Georg Solti.

2001: 978-1-901395-08-2: Singers of the Third Reich: 5 Discographies: Helge Roswaenge, Tiana Lemnitz, Franz Voelker, Maria Mueller, Max Lorenz.

2001: 978-1-901395-09-9: Philharmonic Autocrat 2: Concert Register of Herbert Von Karajan Second Edition.

2002: 978-1-901395-10-5: Sächsische Staatskapelle Dresden: Complete Discography.

2002: 978-1-901395-11-2: Carlo Maria Giulini: Discography and Concert Register.

2002: 978-1-901395-12-9: Pianists For The Connoisseur: 6 Discographies: Arturo Benedetti Michelangeli, Alfred Cortot, Alexis Weissenberg, Clifford Curzon, Solomon, Elly Ney.

2003: 978-1-901395-14-3: Singers on the Yellow Label: 7 Discographies: Maria Stader, Elfriede Troetschel, Annelies Kupper, Wolfgang Windgassen, Ernst Haefliger, Josef Greindl, Kim Borg.

2003: 978-1-901395-15-0: A Gallic Trio: 3 Discographies: Charles Muench, Paul Paray, Pierre Monteux.

2004: 978-1-901395-16-7: Antal Dorati 1906-1988: Discography and Concert Register.

2004: 978-1-901395-17-4: Columbia 33CX Label Discography.

2004: 978-1-901395-18-1: Great Violinists: 3 Discographies: David Oistrakh, Wolfgang Schneiderhan, Arthur Grumiaux.

2006: 978-1-901395-19-8: Leopold Stokowski: Second Edition of the Discography.

2006: 978-1-901395-20-4: Wagner Im Festspielhaus: Discography of the Bayreuth Festival.

2006: 978-1-901395-21-1: Her Master's Voice: Concert Register and Discography of Dame Elisabeth Schwarzkopf [Third Edition].

2007: 978-1-901395-22-8: Hans Knappertsbusch: Kna: Concert Register and Discography of Hans Knappertsbusch, 1888-1965. Second Edition.

2008: 978-1-901395-23-5: Philips Minigroove: Second Extended Version of the European Discography.

2009: 978-1-901395-24-2: American Classics: The Discographies of Leonard Bernstein and Eugene Ormandy.

2010: 978-1-901395-25-9: Dirigenten der DDR: Conductors of the German Democratic Republic

Discography by Stephen J. Pettitt, edited by John Hunt:
1987: 978-1-906857-16-5: Philharmonia Orchestra: Complete Discography 1945-1987

Available from: Travis & Emery at 17 Cecil Court, London, UK.
(+44) 20 7 240 2129. email on sales@travis-and-emery.com .

www.ingramcontent.com/pod-product-compliance
Lightning Source LLC
Chambersburg PA
CBHW070942150426
42812CB00063B/2724